# OXFORD READINGS IN CLASSICAL STUDIES

The series provides students and scholars with a representative selection of the best and most influential articles on a particular author, work, or subject. No single school or style of approach is privileged: the aim is to over a broad overview of scholarship, to cover a wide variety of topics, and to illustrate a diversity of critical methods. The collections are particularly valuable for their inclusion of many important essays which are normally difficult to obtain and for the first-ever translations of some of the pieces. Many articles are thoroughly revised and updated by their authors or are provided with addenda taking account of recent work. Each volume includes an authoritative and wide-ranging introduction by the editor surveying the scholarly tradition and considering alternative approaches. This pulls the individual articles together, setting all the pieces included in their historical and cultural contexts and exploring significant connections between them from the perspective of contemporary scholarship. All foreign languages (including Greek and Latin) are translated to make the texts easily accessible to those without detailed linguistic knowledge.

OXFORD READINGS IN CLASSICAL STUDIES

**Homer's** *Iliad*
Edited by Douglas L. Cairns

**Menander, Plautus, and Terence**
Edited by Erich Segal

**The Greek Novel**
Edited by Simon Swain

**Ancient Literary Criticism**
Edited by Andrew Laird

**Aeschylus**
Edited by Michael Lloyd

**Ovid**
Edited by Peter E. Knox

**The Attic Orators**
Edited by Edwin Carawan

**Lucretius**
Edited by Monica R. Gale

**Catullus**
Edited by Julia Haig Gaisser

**Seneca**
Edited by John G. Fitch

**Vergil's** *Eclogues*
Edited by Katharina Volk

**Vergil's** *Georgics*
Edited by Katharina Volk

*All available in paperback*

*Oxford Readings in Classical Studies*

# Livy

Edited by
JANE D. CHAPLIN AND
CHRISTINA S. KRAUS

OXFORD
UNIVERSITY PRESS

# OXFORD
## UNIVERSITY PRESS

Great Clarendon Street, Oxford OX2 6DP

Oxford University Press is a department of the University of Oxford.
It furthers the University's objective of excellence in research, scholarship,
and education by publishing worldwide in

Oxford New York

Auckland Cape Town Dar es Salaam Hong Kong Karachi
Kuala Lumpur Madrid Melbourne Mexico City Nairobi
New Delhi Shanghai Taipei Toronto

With offices in

Argentina Austria Brazil Chile Czech Republic France Greece
Guatemala Hungary Italy Japan Poland Portugal Singapore
South Korea Switzerland Thailand Turkey Ukraine Vietnam

Oxford is a registered trade mark of Oxford University Press
in the UK and in certain other countries

Published in the United States
by Oxford University Press Inc., New York

© Oxford University Press 2009

The moral rights of the author have been asserted
Database right Oxford University Press (maker)

First published 2009

British Library Cataloguing in Publication Data

Data available

Library of Congress Cataloging in Publication Data

Library of Congress Control Number: 2009924643

Typeset by SPI Publisher Services, Pondicherry, India
Printed in Great Britain
on acid-free paper by
CPI Antony Rowe, Chippenham, Wiltshire

ISBN 978–0–19–928633–1 (Hbk.)
978–0–19–928634–8 (Pbk.)

1 3 5 7 9 10 8 6 4 2

'even Livy…'


W. W. Capes, *Livy* (1880) 98
G. W. Botsford, *The Roman Assemblies* (1909) 302
E. G. Staveley, '*The Significance of the Consular Tribunate*',
   *JRS* 43 (1953) 33
A. Momigliano, *on Pagans, Jews, and Christians* (1987) 277
P. Zanker, *The Power of Images in the Age of Augustus*
   (1988) 101
G. Forsythe, *A Critical History of Early Rome* (2005) 323
S. A. Takâcs, *Vestal Virgins, Sibyls, and Matrons* (2008) 11

http://www.robertchristgau.com/xg/music/dion ysus-emp.php
   (R. Christgau, Dean of American Rock Critics; 02–01–2009)
etc.

# *Preface*

This is the first volume in the series Oxford Readings in Classical Studies devoted to a historian, and one of only a very few to feature a prose author. Written history is, as Quintilian said, a very close relative of the poets: Livy not only begins his Preface with a partial hexameter, but ends it by saying that if historians had the habit, like poets, of beginning 'with good omens, and with vows and prayers to the gods and goddesses that they may grant us success', he would do so. The statement, however, is in the contrary-to-fact form: such is *not* the habit of historians, even ancient ones. Nonetheless, the Livy who emerges from the articles collected in this volume is very much a historian conscious of the poetics of prose: a writer of historiographical representations of the Roman past, devoted to using the explanatory and descriptive resources of narrative as a means of understanding both the past and the present.

The editors, for our part, are conscious that there are other things to do with Livy. We have not, for example, included articles treating his text as historical information for particular events; nor, for reasons primarily of space, have we chosen to follow the 'post-mortem adventures of Livy' (Ullman (1955)). With one exception, we have not included articles whose aim is to demonstrate Livy's (now discredited) affiliation with the 'precepts' of Cicero. Finally, we have included no article with the title, or even subtitle, 'Livy and Augustus'. The Introduction explains our approach to Livy, which we acknowledge to be partial; we hope, however, that by choosing and arranging the selections as we have, we have produced a coherent portrait of a talented historiographer working within a particular set of ancient literary and cultural expectations. We hope, above all, that these selections will inspire readers to find out what else Livy, and the rich scholarship on him, has to offer.

Most of the articles are minimally revised versions of the original publications. We have trimmed some of the quoted foreign languages. English translations have been substituted for Latin and Greek or given alongside, except in the case of technical terms and passages quoted to illustrate lexical and stylistic points. Several of the authors provided vii

their own translations. The opening lines of the *Odyssey* in John Moles's article are from Robert Fagles' Penguin translation; the quotations from Sallust in the same article are by Tony Woodman (also published by Penguin). The editors supplied the others, from Oxford World's Classics editions where possible and with consultation of the Loeb and/ or Penguin elsewhere. We invited all of the living authors included here to write an Addendum to their essays; a few took us up on the invitation, and Professor Liebeschuetz updated his footnotes as well. (The selections of Oakley and Rich were both rewritten for this volume, and therefore lack such an epilogue.) Those Addenda without initials following were written collaboratively by the editors, as was the Introduction. We have aimed, in the Addenda, to situate each article in the larger context of Livian scholarship, and have made suggestions for further readings, along the lines of, 'people who liked this article also read ...'. In the Introduction and Addenda we refer to articles included in the volume by the author's name only (e.g. 'see Stadter').

Many friends, colleagues, and family have been pulled into the vortex of this project. We would especially like to thank David Levene, Robert Parker, and Tony Woodman for advice, criticism, and encouragement; Andrew Feldherr, Mary Jaeger, and Stephen Oakley for help in choosing the articles to include; and our very patient authors for allowing their work to be reprinted, and for helping us bring the articles up to date. For the editing, we had the invaluable and patient services of Rebecca Scholtz, without whom this book would never have seen the light of day; she also acted as a one-woman focus group to help us to assess the usefulness and comprehensibility of the articles included here. Her work was made possible by the Faculty Research Assistant Fund of Middlebury College. We want also to thank Christopher van den Berg, Leofranc Holford-Strevens, David Levene, and Irene Peirano for help with translating. Middlebury College provided digitizing services (our thanks to Duncan Sanford and Shel Sax in particular), while the printer and photocopier in the Department of Classics at Yale University worked overtime in the July heat to bring this all together. Finally, we owe a debt of gratitude to Hilary O'Shea, Dorothy McCarthy, and the team at Oxford University Press, both for suggesting the project and for putting up with the wait.

*JDC and CSK*

*Middlebury Vt and New Haven Ct, July 2008*

# Contents

# Abbreviations

| | |
|---|---|
| *CAH* X² | A. K. Bowman, E. Champlin, and A. Lintott (eds.) (1996), *Cambridge Ancient History*. Vol. X. *The Augustan Empire 43 B.C.–A.D. 69*. 2nd edn. (Cambridge). |
| *CIL* | (1893– ), *Corpus Inscriptionum Latinarum* (Berlin). |
| *HRR* | H. Peter (1906–14), *Historicorum Romanorum Reliquiae*. Vol. I. 2nd edn. and Vol. II (Leipzig). Reprinted with addenda 1993. |
| *ILS* | H. Dessau (ed.) (1892), *Inscriptiones Latinae Selectae*. 3 vols. (Berlin). |
| *MRR* | T. R. S. Broughton (1951–86), *The Magistrates of the Roman Republic*. 3 vols. (New York). |
| *OCD²* | M. Cary *et al.* (eds.) (1949), *The Oxford Classical Dictionary*. 2nd edn. Oxford. |
| *OLD* | P. G. W. Glare (1968–82), *Oxford Latin Dictionary* (Oxford). |
| *RE* | A. F. von Pauly *et al.* (1894–1963), *Pauly's Real-encyclopädie der classischen Altertumswissenschaft* (Stuttgart). |
| *TLL* | (1900– ), *Thesaurus Linguae Latinae* (Leipzig). |
| W–M | W. Weissenborn, H. J. Müller, and O. Rossbach (eds.) (1880–1924), *Titi Livi ab urbe condita libri*. (Berlin). Later reprinted. |

We have not regularized our contributors' references to ancient authors, which therefore follow different conventions (e.g. Cic. *Leg.*, Cic. *de leg.*, Cic. *De Leg.*)

# Introduction

*J. D. CHAPLIN and C. S. KRAUS*

Consult most general introductions to Livy, and you will quickly learn which criteria he and his History fail to meet. Livy held no public office; Livy did not travel; Livy did not work from primary sources; Livy was not analytical; Livy had an inadequate knowledge of Greek; Livy did not regard accuracy as his chief aim or responsibility. Equally, most scholarly treatments from the second half of the nineteenth century to the second half of the twentieth are quick to point out deficiencies. Livy mindlessly copied his sources; Livy did not strive for coherence but focused on giving literary polish to individual episodes; Livy had at best an imperfect grasp of politics, geography, or warfare; Livy was interested in psychology rather than in sociological or economic questions.

These criticisms arise from a particular view of how historians should work and what they should tell us. In the past thirty years, however, a new school of thought about ancient historical narrative has developed. Individual appraisals have accorded Livy increasing respect, and his status among scholars has risen. The purpose of this volume is to make both the nature of that shift and the value of these current views clear and accessible to undergraduates (for whom this series is intended), as well as to anyone curious about Livy's status early in the twenty-first century. The introduction that follows traces the general trajectory of Livian scholarship over the past 150 years, situates Livy temporally, and then, drawing on the context provided by that information, gives an overview of the articles included in this volume.

## LIVIAN SCHOLARSHIP[1]

The modern study of Livy rests on two German publications: H. Nissen's 1863 *Kritische Untersuchungen über die Quellen der vierten und fünften Dekade des Livius* ('Critical Inquiries into the Sources for the Fourth and Fifth Decades of Livy') and K. Witte's 1910 'Über die Form der Darstellung in Livius' Geschichtswerk' ('Concerning the Shape of the Narrative in Livy's History'). Nissen divided the material in Livy's Books 31–45 according to its sources, either Polybius (a second-century BCE Greek historian) or various Roman authors of the second and first centuries BCE. This approach was influential, not least because a very particular way in which ancient historians differ from modern is that they regularly started from, and often closely followed, the narratives composed by their predecessors. Though we no longer believe that this is the way ancient historians always worked, it is the case that narratives—rather than documents or archival research—served as the basis for much ancient historiography. Earlier writers, then, are often the source for the content and general emplotment of much of Livy's narrative. Broadly speaking, Nissen regarded the Polybian sections as more historically reliable than the Roman ones. Nissen's research stands at the forefront of a school of Livian criticism called 'Quellenforschung' or 'source-criticism'. Practitioners attempted to attribute definitively each historical detail in Livy to one of his predecessors. Active 'Quellenforschung' in its most unimaginative form had exhausted itself by the middle of the twentieth century, but it continued to influence the underlying conception of Livy as a transcriber, rather than an original thinker.

Witte's work was equally influential and in many ways more flattering to the historian. Again using Polybius as a starting point, he showed how Livy surpassed his Greek source by polishing individual narratives ('Einzelerzählungen', or 'episodes') into highly effective

---

[1] The following account is highly schematic, omitting both exceptions and different types of scholarship (e.g. commentaries, textual criticism) altogether. It also—for simplicity's sake—disregards scholars working before Nissen and Witte. It does, however, give a broad sense of how Livian studies have evolved over the past century and a half.

passages of literary art. At the same time, however, Witte argued that Livy was not interested in producing a coherent narrative on a broader scale. As with Nissen, Witte had many followers interested in applying his technique throughout Livy's text. The most important was the German scholar E. Burck, a shrewd and sympathetic reader of Livy, who produced both a study of the first pentad (Books 1–5) and one of the third decade (Books 21–30). Like Nissen and Witte, Burck concentrated on parts of Livy where there are surviving texts against which we can compare his own history (either a contemporary writer, as Dionysius of Halicarnassus, or a source, as Polybius). Burck not only demonstrated Livy's ability to construct narratives on a larger scale than the 'Einzelerzahlung', he also made clear his literary and historiographical intelligence.

The paradoxical legacy of the 'Quellenforschung' and 'Einzerzählerungen' models was an author regarded simultaneously as a mindless conduit to earlier sources and a literary genius. Though one can understand how the two might coexist in one writer, it is an uncomfortable position, especially when dealing with a writer whom many—including Tacitus and Macchiavelli—have regarded as a master of the historiographical art. The key word here is historiographical: that is, the art and study of the *representation* of the historical past, rather than that past itself. The gap between history and literature, which formerly coincided with modern academic categories (themselves equally the products of nineteenth-century German scholarship), is a wholly regrettable distortion of the ancient understanding of history as a form of literature. Neither Greeks nor Romans thought of history and literature as separable. History in the sense of a written account of the past was a branch of high literature, a prose genre with its own conventions and audience expectations, and strong formal affiliations with both oratory and epic poetry. It dealt with what we might call facts or data, and writers of history routinely charged their predecessors with lying; yet their understanding of truth is not coterminous with ours. All ancient historians, for example, included speeches that they could not have heard and for which they had no written record; all included the thoughts and feelings of their human subjects—again, often things for which they could have no record, written or oral. Though it can be argued that ancient historians were interested in creating an explanatory account that would model the past 'as it really was', in Leopold von Ranke's famous description of what a historian should aim for ('wie es eigentlich gewesen'[2]), it is also clear that there is a mismatch between ancient and contemporary understandings of such inherently difficult concepts as 'truth' and 'reality'. The view of Livy that has predominated until relatively recently tends to conflate ancient and modern understandings, and expects from Livy (and other ancient historians) the same positivist approaches and values held by many modern historians.

Scholars investigating historiography rather than history, however, after having seriously taken on board the implications of these fundamental differences between modern and ancient thinking, have endeavoured to define and explain exactly what the principles and practices of classical historical writing were. Two influential Romanists who have spearheaded this movement are T. P. Wiseman (especially *Clio's Cosmetics*, 1979 and 'Practice and Theory in Roman Historiography', 1981) and A. J. Woodman (beginning with his work on Velleius Paterculus, but especially in his *Rhetoric in Classical Historiography*, 1988). Interest in the ancient practices of historiography has been highly beneficial to Livy. Coupled with the increasingly refined application of the methodologies of Nissen and Witte, the historiographical approach has made Livy a vastly more interesting and complex author and helps to account for the tectonic shift in Livian studies in the past few decades. It also—by putting more attention on Livy's own creative and intellectual contribution to his text—must make us more sceptical about his value for making a transparent reconstruction of Roman history.

The shift in the way many scholars view Roman historiography runs parallel to the problems and possibilities brought to the philosophy and practice of history by what is known as 'the linguistic turn', that is, the proposition that our perception of the world, present and past, is mediated through language, which is not a transparent medium through which we perceive reality, but is constitutive of reality itself. In other words—to shift to an epistemological

---

[2] Ranke's phrase occurs in the preface to his *Geschichten der Romanischen und Germanischen Volker von 1494 bis 1535* (1824); for an entertaining discussion of the phrase, its historical context, and its influence see Grafton (1997) 69–71.

formulation—the sole access we have to events is through description. This is not necessarily to claim (though some theorists would)
that there are not differences between fact-based and fictional narratives; but it does mean that one cannot peel away parts of a text to
get to the 'reality' it describes. Rather one has to study the surviving
representations of that past, seeking to understand the depiction
of past events, and what that depiction can tell us about the individuals and cultural communities that produced them.[3] Whether or
not one accepts this view of reality, it must be acknowledged that
written accounts of events always refract them in some way; as
a consequence, the distinction between 'history' and 'literature'
must now be far more problematic than heretofore. The study of
all ancient historians has benefited immensely from this shift in
perspective.[4]

## LIVY'S LIFE AND WORK

We know very little about Livy the man, and almost every piece of
information we have has been used to argue about his ideological
approach to his History. He was a native of Patavium (modern
Padua), lived in Rome, attended declamations, came to know Augustus
and his family, and may have returned to Patavium before he died
(for the evidence see Kraus (1994a) 1–4). His birthplace has led
numerous scholars to associate him with the 'traditional morality'
and 'fervid patriotism' of Roman 'provincials', and—from a very early
point—with an unsophisticated outlook ('Patavinitas': see below,
258, 412–13). His modest *persona* within the text has implied that he

[3] The journal *History and Theory*, founded in 1960, is dedicated to these and other
issues involving the philosophy and practice of history. For ancient history, Clark
(2004) is especially valuable.
[4] The 'linguistic turn' has been accompanied by a shift in literary studies, sometimes called the 'cultural turn', represented primarily by New Historicism. This looks
at literary artefacts as documents of the cultural production of a society, incompre-
hensible without their historical and cultural context. Again, this brings 'history' and
'literature' closer together. For an introduction, see Veeser (1994) and Gallagher and
Greenblatt (2000).

has an uncritical viewpoint, and the general belief that he had no military or political experience has seemed to confirm this. And finally, his reported interactions with Augustus have produced a picture of Livy meekly following the Leader. Though we cannot address all of these areas here, we do want to focus on the problem of Livy's relationship, not with Augustus the man, but with the Augustan age and its sensibility.

Though there is still some uncertainty about his dates, it is now generally accepted that Livy lived from 64 BCE to CE 12 (possibly 17). On any reckoning, he is an almost exact contemporary of Augustus (63 BCE–CE 14) and thus lived through almost exactly the same events. For many years, therefore, Livy was regarded unproblematically—and without need for further definition—as an 'Augustan'. Chronologically, this is obviously true, and in that sense of 'Augustan' there is no question but that the historian shares many characteristics with his contemporaries. And indeed, the Augustan aesthetic sensibility, as seen in other contemporary writers (as well as in the monuments built in the last decades BCE) is for many critics a gauge by which to evaluate Livy's writing.

But not only aesthetics are at issue here. More pressing for many scholars are the political and historical questions that are seen— rightly or wrongly—as intimately connected with the date when Livy began writing. When scholars look at Livy, they have seen very different men, ranging from a conservative, nostalgic hankerer after 'the Republic' to a fervent supporter of the Augustan programme(s). At 1.19.3 Livy refers to 'Caesar Augustus', nomenclature that must postdate Octavian's assumption of the *cognomen* 'Augustus' in January of 27 BCE. This encouraged people to see him as a post-27 author, plain and simple; hence the only question worth asking about his views seemed to be whether he was pro- or anti-Augustus. A different approach was suggested by Luce, however (following a suggestion by Bayet), who argued forcefully that the version of Book 1 that we now have is a second edition. In turn, Woodman (1988) argued equally forcefully for what has now become the general consensus, that Livy started to write in the mid-30s, before Octavian defeated Antony at Actium (31 BCE), before he took the name Augustus, and before Augustus' version of one-man rule became the workable solution to the civil wars of the first century.

Similar issues arise when dealing with Livy's endpoint (on this see Henderson (1989)). The last dated event he mentions is the death of Drusus the Elder in 9 BCE. This seems in hindsight a rather unclimactic event. Some scholars, therefore, have thought that Livy did not live to complete his original plan, and might have continued to write. Others have argued that he originally intended to end his History with the death of Cicero in 43 BCE. This finale is attractive to scholars who see Livy as a Republican sympathizer, who would (naturally) have venerated Cicero. If such was his original plan, however, he must have changed his mind, since he manifestly continued to write the history of another thirty-four years. The books that continue the History into the Augustan period have, in turn, been variously understood: on the one hand, as a supplement comprising Livy's endorsement of the new regime (Roman history did not, in fact, end with the Republic!); on the other, as a reluctant continuation until the point when Drusus, famous as the last true republican sympathizer, died in the forests of Germany. None of these interpretations receives much support from the surviving text of Livy, but speculation about his attitude toward the Principate has seemed irresistible.

In any case, scholars are now taking a far more nuanced approach to 'Augustanism', which is a polyvalent and complex phenomenon, and can accomodate multiple attitudes even in a single work of a single author.[5] Livy's work, which spanned a fifty-year writing career, is no more monolithic than that of Horace (another near-exact contemporary) or Virgil—or, indeed, than that of Augustus himself, whose aims and attitudes constantly evolved over his equally lengthy public career.

The incomplete state of Livy's oeuvre contributes to the debate about his Augustanism. Though other Livian works are mentioned by ancient sources, the only one of which we can say anything certain is the *Ab urbe condita (AUC)*. Livy's history originally had 142 'books' (= papyrus rolls). Of these, thirty-five (1–10 and 21–45) survive more or less complete (Books 41, 43, and 44 have significant gaps). We are thus missing all of his treatment of contemporary

[5] See especially Kennedy (1992) and Galinsky (1996), and for the Romans' constructions of history and use of periodization see Feeney (2007).

history—precisely the Books that might have solved the 'Augustus' question, or at least given us some idea of how Livy represented the Principate. There does also survive a set of summaries of all the original books (except for 136–7), known as the Periochae, which were probably composed in the fourth century CE (on them see Begbie (1967)). They vary in length from a few pages to a paragraph or even a few sentences per book. Where it is possible to compare the summaries with the surviving books, it is evident that they do not correspond in any consistent or reliable way with what Livy wrote. Since neither the extant text nor the Periochae offers solid evidence for the impact of current events on Livy's interpretation of the past, or for his treatment of those events, this is an area where scholars can and do disagree.

Because the narrative proceeds year by year (apart from Book 1, which treats the regal period by reign), Livy is generally classified as an 'annalistic' historian rather than a writer of (e.g.) monographs (such as Sallust's *Bellum Catilinae*) or biographical history (such as Curtius Rufus' *History of Alexander the Great of Macedon*). Annalistic history is more than just a chronological record. Roman public life followed the cycle of the annual magistracies, together with the assigning of duties, disposition of troops, reporting of noteworthy extra-natural happenings, and so forth. This structure provided a highly functional organizational principle for a historiographical narrative. Livy was not the first to use this structure, but his annalistic history is the only one before Tacitus' to survive in quantity.

It is clear that Livy both followed and schematized 'real time': in particular, he manipulates the position of many details to fit his interpretative framework, rather than following a chronology reflecting that of the events he represents. So, for instance, people tend to die at the end of the textual year, regardless of when they might actually have perished. It is also clear that, as a literary form, annalistic history was built on the skeleton of the cycle of republican magistracies (and not the temporally undifferentiated stream of one-man rule): Livy's choice of form, then, has political consequences, and his choice of method may be correlated with his political understanding. This approach has long been commonplace among scholars reading Tacitus; but it still needs to be emphasized for his greatest model, Livy.

## READING LIVY

The articles collected in this volume both reflect intellectual trends since the mid-nineteenth century and explore the relationship between Livy and his political and cultural milieu. Two episodes in his History—the 'rape of Lucretia' and the 'Conference of Nicaea'—give a sense of the different ways scholars have looked at Livy's narrative. To begin with the latter, in Book 33 Livy describes a meeting between T. Quinctius Flamininus, a Roman general, and Philip V, ruler of the Macedonians. This event is known as the Conference of Nicaea and occurred in 197 BCE. In the article included in this volume Walsh discusses the episode in a section devoted to 'Conferences' as typical scenes. He notes the way Livy inserts into the leaders' exchange a silence that is not found in Polybius' account of the same episode. Tränkle also notes a difference between the two historians' respective handling of the conversation, pointing out that, while willing to criticize Philip's levity, Livy streamlines the portrayal of Flamininus, omitting the banter and humour he engaged in and making him sublimely dignified and virtuous. Catin, itemizing Livy's own display of wit, ignores the passage; presumably it does not fit his case to draw attention to Livy's scolding of Philip: 'By nature he [Philip] was more inclined to jokes than is seemly for a king, and not even in serious business could he sufficiently control his laughter' (32.34.3).

In writing about the rape and suicide of Lucretia, both Joshel and Feldherr dwell on the way her body becomes an increasingly public spectacle; both of them, further, want to interpret Livy's choreography in the context of his Augustan present; both also use Cicero as a reference point for views on the relationship of state and individual. Yet Joshel reads Lucretia's story, along with that of Verginia in Book 3, as an expression of male anxiety about violation and loss of order and control: the assaulted women must die in order for their men to assert control and establish order (or, more broadly, empire). For Feldherr, Lucretia's death becomes a 'paradigm of sacrifice' that models what Livy and his contemporaries give up to participate in the new Rome emerging under Augustus. At the conclusion of her article, Scafuro compares Hispala (the 'prostitute of repute' whose information leads to magistrates' taking control of the worship of Bacchus in Italy) to Lucretia and Verginia, noting Livy's practice of focusing on female figures at moments of public crisis.

As this range of interpretations shows, there is no one necessary or even correct way to read Livy. Whether the material of his text appears to fit neatly into our idea of history (an important diplomatic conference between men representing Rome and Macedonia) or our notion of fiction (the mythologized rape and suicide of a woman that brought down 250 years of monarchic rule), different readers will find different things to do with his remarkably rich narrative. If the articles in this volume are read in order, they illustrate one possible approach. The first two pieces ('Outlook') set the stage, much as Livy does in his *Preface*. Luce's 1965 article remains fundamental reading for the relationship between Livy's narrative and the Augustan principate. By making the case for a 'second edition' of Books 1–5, Luce untethers Livy from the necessity of a post-Actian, even post-27 interpretation that requires Livy to be in some way responding to Augustus the *princeps*. The greater chronological freedom then permits us to see Livy as having conceived his historiography independently from, even if harmoniously with, Augustus' reforms. Moles's reading of the *Preface* assumes that Livy is an independent thinker, offering his own judgements on the fallout from the civil wars and triumviral period.

In the *Preface*, Livy foregrounds not his sources and methodology (as modern historians regularly do) but his view of the past, from the origins of Rome to his present day. The second set of articles ('Structure') deals with his translation of that view into a highly structured narrative. Stadter's article offers the broadest possible coverage, addressing the distribution of material throughout the original 142 books. Rich demonstrates how Livy organizes time: in Books 2–10 the year-narratives conform to no particular pattern; in Books 21–45 they alternate between external and internal events. In the late Republic, Rich suggests, the breakdown of order will have required an altogether different organization. Both scholars read Livy's structural devices as corresponding to political structures. Finally, Luce looks at the organization of material within Book 5, revealing the architecture of the career of Camillus and the sack of Rome by the Gauls and discussing the relevance of that structure to Livy's historiographical project.

The third section ('Language and Style') gathers together articles exploring Livy's Latinity. Catin was highly attuned to its nuances, and in this selection from his book, he itemizes the places where Livy's sense of humour is detectable, in everything from broad comedy to irony and the driest of wit. The piece is extremely useful for readers wanting to develop an ear for the tone of the narrative. Walsh's article laid the groundwork for his later, highly influential book *Livy: His Historical Aims and Methods* (1961). The article is an economical guide to an important feature of Livy's style, and one which has come increasingly to the fore in studies of Roman historiography: that is, the use of type-scenes (such as sieges, naval battles, conferences, conversations, speeches). McDonald's article has long been a standard exposition of Livy's 'style, syntax, and diction' and thus a good place to start for anyone interested in close study of Livy's Latinity. Finally, Phillips goes systematically through the 'triumph notices', noting different linguistic registers, patterns, and deviations, and generally showing how even in the supposedly bare-bones annalistic sections, Livy wrote with extreme care and to great effect. This third section has one major and truly regrettable omission: it lacks a good, up-to-date treatment of Livy's speeches. Speeches—both direct and indirect—feature prominently in Livy's text. As well as containing some of his finest prose, they offer a key locus for investigating Livy's use of oratorical, rather than narrative, technique. Though they have been an obvious and worthy object of scholarly attention, we were unable to choose an appropriate, article-length discussion of them. (See, for some suggestions for further reading on speeches, the Addenda to Walsh and Burck.)

The analytical techniques developed in the pieces in this third group are all deployed by the scholars in the next section (Section IV: 'Narrative'), as they interpret different parts of Livy's History. The selection from Burck's book on the third decade is representative of his overall approach to Livy. In both his book-length studies of the *AUC* narrative he uses running commentary to highlight, through comparison with other sources, what is distinctive about Livy's depiction of the Roman past. In Books 29 and 30 the focus is on Scipio Africanus, the invasion of North Africa, and the defeat of Hannibal and Carthage. The articles of Solodow and Scafuro typify much of the literature on Livy that has been published in academic journals. Each uses the analysis of a single episode to make a larger point about the way Livy relates history. Focusing on the Roman hero Horatius, Solodow explores the complex ways in which Livy draws his audience into the story, positioning readers to see people and actions from multiple perspectives and leaving them to puzzle out messages and meanings for themselves. Livy's use of the repertoire of New Comedy underpins Scafuro's reading of the Bacchanalian Conspiracy as narrated in Book 39. Much of the scholarly discussion around this episode has centred on the historicity of Livy's account. Scafuro, by contrast, examines how the historian emplots the events as a comedy, only to subvert them to show the necessity of subordinating personal concerns to the public good.[6]

Ancient historiography dealt with public concerns (Section V: 'Cultural History'). For the Romans these included religion, which was less about faith, belief, or theology (as today's Christians understand them) than about the correct observance of ritual and the maintenance of good relations with the gods, which were then manifested in the thriving of the state. Livy incorporates a great deal of religious material in his treatment of Roman history; Liebeschuetz's article is a classic treatment of how and why he does so. Joshel's article tackles Livy's representation of Rome's patriarchal structure, arguing that he reveals a need to police the boundaries between public and private in order to ensure that private weakness not emasculate the state and debilitate its capacity to construct an empire. Citizenship and 'Romanness' are the subject of Feldherr's article. He shows how Livy's handling of the transition from monarchy to Republic in Books 1 and 2 establishes models for political change in his own day.

After these explorations of individual topics and episodes, this volume ends where many would begin, with Livy's use of sources (VI: 'Sources and Working Methods'). The prioritizing of sources is usually predicated on the belief that as a writer of history Livy must clear first the hurdle of reliability. The Livy of this volume, however, is an interpreter of the past: no matter where his material comes

---

[6] White (1973) remains essential for the understanding of how style, especially the plot of a narrative, affects historical representation; see also Gay (1974) and Woodman (1988). Momigliano (1981) offers a hostile assessment of White's project.

from, to understand his project, we have to understand his treatment of it. Only then can we fairly evaluate his selection and judgement of the 'hard core' that makes up the historical content of his work. This hard core is the primary concern in the selections from the commentaries of Oakley and Briscoe. Oakley catalogues the places where Livy refers to sources and discusses his use of them in Books 6–10; Briscoe reviews the standard categories of annalistic and Polybian material, listing the Polybian passages from which Livy worked. Finally, Tränkle offers one way of using this kind of information, examining Livy's reading of Polybius to show how the Roman rewrote his predecessor's drier account into one calculated to make the audience identify with those participating in the course of events.

## CONCLUSION

Reading Livy, then, is no simple matter; and there is yet one more challenge. Truly great authors leave a lasting impression on their readers. Just as Thucydides has succeeded in making the Peloponnesian War uniquely consequential by writing about it, and just as every account of the early Principate takes on some of Tacitus' cynical colouring, so too has Livy left centuries of readers imprinted with his particular interpretation of regal and Republican Roman history. Our focus on warfare and politics, our notions of the periodization of these centuries, our weighting of the importance of the Gallic sack, the Punic wars, Hellenistic monarchs and their relationships with Rome—all are formed in accordance with or in reaction to Livy. It is almost impossible to think outside his narrative.

There is thus all the more need to accept that ancient historical writing had generic expectations that were fundamentally different from those associated with modern historiography; to appreciate the ways Livy positions himself in his text and in his own historical context; to take into account his tendency to interpret history through the expansion and compression of material over textual space; to be alert to his tactics as a narrator; to recognize the Romanness of his text; and to discern as much as possible how and where he deviates from earlier written accounts. The reward is, that if we read Livy carefully, as an author who wrote about the past in full awareness of its complexity and with the aim of creating some kind of order in our understanding of it, we may adopt some of his nuanced outlook and be better readers of any kind of text.

# I

# Outlook

# 1

## The Dating of Livy's First Decade

### T. J. Luce

Evidence which would help to determine when the extant parts of Livy's huge history of Rome were written and published is meager and often of slight value. The historian was reluctant to refer directly to contemporary personalities, events, and issues; and the passages in which scholars have ventured to see indirect references and allusions are neither many nor easy of interpretation. Only the first book can be dated with apparent certainty; the narrow limits are both surprising and gratifying: surprising because of uncertainty and latitude elsewhere, gratifying because an almost exact date is available for the commencement of Livy's historical writing. The passage in question is at 1.19.2–3 and concerns the closing of the gates of Janus:

He [Numa] made the temple of Janus at the foot of the Argiletum an indicator of peace and war: when open, it signified that the state was in arms; when closed, that surrounding peoples were at peace. Twice since the reign of Numa it has been closed, once in the consulship of Titus Manlius after the end of the First Punic War, and a second time, which the gods granted our age to see, after the war at Actium when the emperor Caesar Augustus established peace over land and sea.

The passage must date after January 16, 27 BCE, when the title Augustus was given to Octavian, and before 25 BCE when Augustus closed the gates for a second time, following his subjugation of Spain in the years 27–25 BCE.[1] Other passages in the *Ab Urbe Condita* which

---

[1] Paratore (1950: 441) believes that to expect Livy to distinguish between Augustus' two closings 'would seem an ironic pedantry', and would bring the date for the

can be used for dating purposes are few and not very helpful. At 4.20.7 (437 BCE) Livy mentions that Augustus, 'founder or restorer of all temples', discovered the linen corselet which Aulus Cornelius Cossus had dedicated in the temple of Juppiter Feretrius as part of the *spolia opima*, or spoils of honor. At 28.12.12 he refers in passing to the final subjugation of Spain 'under the leadership and auspices of Augustus Caesar', but whether this refers to Augustus' own campaign in 27–25 BCE only, or to Agrippa's Cantabrian campaign in 20–19 BCE as well, is uncertain. Periocha 59 mentions that Augustus, when speaking in the senate on behalf of his law 'On the Obligation to Marry for Members of the Orders of Society' of 18 BCE, quoted from a speech of Quintus Metellus, censor in 131 BCE. These represent the sum total of direct references to contemporary persons and events in Livy; that all concern the person of Augustus is worthy of note and is perhaps of some significance. Except for the passage at 1.19.3, none are of any real value in dating, since the historian must have written on the average of slightly more than three books a year in order to reach the last, Book 142, by CE 17, the year of his death. The dating of 27–25 BCE for the publication of the first book, possibly of the first pentad,[2] went unquestioned until Professor Jean Bayet suggested that the sections concerning Augustus in Books One and Four were later additions which formed part of a second edition of the first pentad.[3] His theory has been rejected by subsequent scholars, save for Professor Ronald Syme, who considers the proposal possible but by no means certain.[4] Hypotheses of second editions are generally distasteful, for they smack of the drastic

beginning of composition down. But the phrase 'after the war at Actium' is intended to give not a *terminus post quem*, but the occasion for the closing, and is parallel to 'after the end of the First Punic War'.

[2] I follow Bornecque (1933: 16–17) in believing that Livy planned and published the early books (at least through Book 45) in groups of five, or multiples thereof (cf. 6.1.1–3; 31.1.1–5) and that the prefaces, or preambles, to Books 1, 2, 6, 21, and 31 indicate the particular groupings. To these should be added Book 16, which introduced the pentad on the First Punic War, and which began with a preface concerning 'the origin of the Carthaginians and the beginnings of their city' (Per. 16). Since Book Two has its own preface, it is probable that Book One was published separately.

[3] Bayet (1940: xvi–xxii). Soltau (1894b: 611–17) believed that Livy made numerous later insertions throughout the *Ab Urbe Condita*, the Augustus references among them.

[4] Syme (1959: 27–87, esp. 42–50).

and desperate; this is particularly true when, as in Bayet's argumentation, no single passage cited as a later addition seems particularly compelling or necessary. But the question of later additions and of a second edition is neither idle nor academic; in particular, if it can be shown that the passages concerning Augustus in Books One and Four, dating soon after 27 BCE, are later additions, the composition of the first pentad must be pushed back, possibly before the Battle of Actium. A sizeable body of literature, predicated on the assumption that the composition of the first pentad is 'Augustan', whether in tone, attitudes, themes, or allusions, would thus be called into question. Yet in the absence of any direct statement or testimony, the evidence for later additions will necessarily be oblique and indirect: authors who wish to add or amend will try to integrate the new material as best they can. But argumentation resting wholly on the oblique and the indirect will not persuade fully, if at all; what is needed is at least one example of later addition which is clear and compelling.

The passage which betrays convincing signs of later insertion is that appended to the account of how Aulus Cornelius Cossus won the *spolia opima* in 437 BCE, the second after Romulus to do so. Livy first describes the events which led to the battle outside the walls of Fidenae between the Romans and the combined forces of Fidenae, Veii, and the Faliscans (4.17.6–18.8); the description climaxes with the famous story of how Cossus killed Tolumnius, the king of Veii, and claimed the right to dedicate the *spolia opima* in the temple of Juppiter Feretrius (19.1–20.4). Livy introduces the episode by stating that Cossus was a military tribune at the time ('There was at that time among the cavalrymen a tribune of the soldiers named Aulus Cornelius Cossus', 19.1).[5] The description of the encounter itself (19.1–8) is followed by the return of the army to Rome; Livy closes out the year (20.1–4) with a brief account of the triumph of the dictator, the laying of the *spolia opima* in the temple, and the award to Cossus of a golden crown, which the dictator placed in the temple of Juppiter on the Capitoline. The passage which is suspected of later addition follows (4.20.5–11). Livy begins by changing his mind about what he has just written: Cossus could not have been a military tribune when he

---

[5]  On the formulaic nature of this introduction see Ogilvie (1965: 18 and 2.33.5 n.).

claimed the *spolia opima*, for only a *dux* (military leader) who killed
the leader of the enemy while fighting under his own auspices was
eligible to make the claim. Cossus must have been consul during the
year in question, and the inscription which Augustus Caesar saw when
rebuilding and restoring the temple confirms the fact: 'The inscription written on Cossus' spoils shows that both earlier historians and
I are wrong about which office he held, and that Cossus won them
in his capacity as consul' (4.20.6). Livy then discusses the difficulties
which result from this conclusion: none of the ancient sources,
neither the earlier historians nor the Libri Lintei, put the consulship
of Cossus in this year; nor could the winning of the *spolia opima* in
this year have been confused with Cossus' later consulship, for that
was part of a three-year period without any wars, when disease and
famine were so great that some annals reported nothing but the
names of the consuls. Livy then mentions that three years after this
consulship Cossus was first consular tribune and then *magister equitum* (master of the horse), in the latter capacity distinguishing himself
in a cavalry battle.[6] But the historian dismisses conjecture and reiterates his belief that Cossus was consul when he won the *spolia opima*:
'Conjecture is open to everyone, but it is pointless. For despite all the
opinions that might be advanced, the fact remains that the winner of
the fight wrote that he was Aulus Cornelius Cossus, consul.'[7] Several
features of this section are suggestive of later addition, but the decisive
passage comes twelve chapters later (32.4):

[The dictator] declared . . . that his master of the horse, Aulus Cornelius, would
show the same prowess in battle as he had in the earlier war, when as tribune of
the soldiers he killed Lars Tolumnius, the King of Veii, in sight of the two
armies and brought the spoils of honor to the temple of Juppiter Feretrius.

That Livy should first designate Cossus military tribune, and then, on
the basis of a communication from Augustus, decide instead that Cossus
was consul, but not correct the previous narrative, is peculiar; that he
should designate Cossus military tribune in a passage twelve chapters
later, however, can be satisfactorily explained only by supposing that

---

[6] Two other traditions existed: one that Cossus won the *spolia opima* as consular
tribune (Servius *ad Aen.* 6.841), the other, as *magister equitum* (Val. Max. 3.2.4).
[7] In the translation I have given Ogilvie's repunctuation of the OCT text (1965:
4.20.11 n.).

4.20.5–11 is a later addition. The attempts to explain the contradiction in some other way are not convincing.

One explanation is that since Livy's history is full of contradictions and errors, this particular one should not be used to suggest anything so drastic as a second edition.[8] At first sight this is satisfying; errors and contradictions in the *Ab Urbe Condita* are frequent and occasionally flagrant. But when we are invited to compare this error with the kinds characteristic of Livy—mistranslation, reproduction of errors in sources, confusion in reconciling sources—the comparison breaks down. Such errors result either from rather mechanical reproduction of source material, from a lack of real interest in a particular problem or fact, or from inability to resolve the discrepancies in the sources. Yet none of these explanations is relevant here. There is no mechanical reproduction, but a page of discussion in the first person; no lack of interest in this extraordinary and flattering communication from the emperor;[9] no inability in making a decision, for Livy twice states his personal belief that Cossus was consul. It is wrong to suggest that because he was generally uninterested in this type of historical problem, he was therefore uninterested in this particular case.[10] Young historians did not receive a communication from the emperor every day, and it is unlikely that they would soon forget it. It is most improbable that the communication, his full page discussion, and his own stated judgment should have slipped his mind twelve chapters later, either when in the act of composition or when reading over his manuscript prior to publication.

A second attempt to explain the contradiction is to suppose that Livy was sceptical of the discovery by Augustus of the linen corselet: 'There may...be more than absent-mindedness (and more than inadequate revision) in the subsequent statement that when Cossus

---

[8] See Walsh (1961*b*: 30); for the types of errors in Livy he refers to his book (1961*a*: 143 ff.).

[9] Livy's words do not make clear exactly under what circumstances the information reached him (4.20.7); but since it will be shown that the information was a later addition to a completed text, the communication was certainly deliberate and probably direct.

[10] See Syme (1959: 47): 'He probably regarded the whole business as a vexatious perturbation in a smooth and satisfactory narrative.' The remark at 8.18.2 is typical: 'I find that the cognomen of the consul is reported in various histories as Flaccus and Potitus; but it matters little what the truth is.'

won the distinction he was a military tribune.'[11] Livy's failure to
conceal the fact that the literary sources put Cossus' consulship
some years later is cited in support of this notion: the historian
wishes the reader to realize that the sources are opposed to the
'evidence' of Augustus. The argument is not persuasive. Livy cannot
avoid discussing the problem; not only the literary sources, but his
own narrative from 4.17.7 on, demand some sort of acknowledge-
ment of the difficulties. Moreover, the historian accepts without
question that Cossus was consul when he won the *spolia opima*;
only a *dux* could do that, and it is confirmed by the inscription on
the corselet. Livy's only concern is *when* the incident took place, and
it is on this point that decision is difficult (4.20.11): 'Conjecture is
open to all, but in my opinion it is pointless. You may subject the
matter to every opinion, although the man who engaged in the
combat...wrote that he was Aulus Cornelius Cossus, consul.' To
suppose that Livy deliberately designated Cossus military tribune
twelve chapters later in order to give vent to his spleen and skepti-
cism is untenable.

A third attempt to explain the contradiction has been made by R. M.
Ogilvie,[12] who admits that 4.20.5–11 must have been added after 4.32.4
was written; but it is unnecessary, in his view, to suppose that the whole
of Books 1–5 had been already composed, or that the addition is proof
of a second edition. This solution seems at first sight attractive, but a
closer examination reveals several difficulties. If Livy had not yet
completed and published the first pentad before adding 4.20.5–11,
what would have prompted Augustus to communicate this piece of
information to a relatively young man from Padua who had not yet
published anything of his history? Several explanations are possible.
Perhaps the first book had been published separately, had revealed the
young man's talent, and now Augustus, in anticipation of what was to
come—after 4.32.4 had been written, but before Books 2–5 had been
published—communicated his discovery to Livy. The timetable is
tight, but possible. A second solution might be that Augustus directly
or indirectly heard of Livy's account of Cossus through a public recital,
and communicated his discovery before the historian had actually

---

[11] Walsh (1961*b*: 30).
[12] See Ogilvie (1958: 41, cf. 46) and (1965: 4.20.5–11 n.). He also notes that Livy's
narrative presupposes a knowledge of 4.29.7–30.16. But see below, n. 23.

published anything. Again, the timetable is tight, but possible. But on either showing we must suppose that Livy never reread what he had written; if he had, 4.32.4 would certainly have been altered. It is reasonable to assume that authors reread what they have written before publishing; it is also reasonable to assume that young writers would not forget the chief point of an imperial communication, particularly when reminded of it (and of their own twice-stated belief) twelve chapters earlier. The only solution which will avoid these objections is that 4.20.5–11 was inserted after the pentad had been finished, when Augustus, noticing Livy's mistake, informed him of his own discovery in the temple of Juppiter Feretrius.

The reason for Augustus' interest in the matter and for his desire that the new information be included in Livy's account is not far to seek. In 29 BCE Marcus Licinius Crassus, proconsul of Macedonia, claimed the right to dedicate the *spolia opima* for having defeated the Bastarnae in battle and having killed their chief, Deldo. Octavian refused to allow Crassus' claim, alleging that Crassus was not a holder of the full *imperium* fighting under his own auspices.[13] Octavian did not wish to be eclipsed, even temporarily, and was concerned with the one precedent which Crassus could cite in support of his claim— that of A. Cornelius Cossus. The inscription on the corselet was almost certainly manufactured for the occasion: linen could hardly have survived intact for over four hundred years, particularly in a temple whose roof had fallen in and whose interior was exposed to the elements at the time when Atticus suggested to Octavian that he restore the temple.[14] Moreover, Cossus would have been designated praetor, not consul, at this early period, and his cognomen in the form of COS or COSO could not, as has been suggested, have been misinterpreted for consul, since cognomina do not occur on early inscriptions.[15] The attempt to claim the inscription as genuine by postulating a later restoration at the time when M. Marcellus

---

[13] See Dessau (1906: 142–51). Dio 51.24.3–7 says that Crassus was not a commander with independent *imperium*.

[14] Nepos, *Atticus* 20.3. The suggestion was made before March 31, 32 BCE, the date of Atticus' death, probably not long before. When the actual restoration was begun and completed is not known. See Ogilvie (1965: 4.20.7 n.).

[15] On the misinterpretation of COS see Rutgers (1618), cited by Ogilvie (1965: 4.20.5–11 n.); Hirschfeld (1913: 398–9).

dedicated the *spolia opima* and when COS was added in the light of
Cossus' later consulship[16] would invite belief were it not for the
providential coincidence that Augustus found exactly what he
needed to combat the claim of Crassus at exactly the moment he
needed it. Many scholars have been disposed to assume that Augustus would be trustworthy and scrupulous in such matters, but this is
'an assumption that would have startled most contemporaries of that
young man, whatever their political allegiance'.[17]

The passage at 4.32.4 thus shows that the earlier section at 4.20.5–11
was added after the completion of Books 1–5;[18] further traces of
addition are also evident in the manner of its incorporation into the
text. At first sight 4.20.5–11 appears to conform to Livy's practice of
adding variations and doubts at the end of narrative units;[19] but the
similarity is deceiving, for here the historian is not appending a variant
or doubt, but is correcting a mistake. For this procedure there is no
parallel elsewhere in the *Ab Urbe Condita*;[20] it at once raises the
question why, if the historian wrote 4.20.5–11 before publication, he
did not rewrite the entire episode in the light of Augustus' communication. The answer is clear: such rewriting would involve the historian
in several serious difficulties. By making Cossus consul from the beginning of the account of 437 BCE he would have to eliminate altogether
a pair of consuls (4.17.7), a dictator and his *magister equitum* (4.17.8–
9), and would be obliged to manufacture a colleague for Cossus or to
omit the colleague's name. But it is not Livy's habit wilfully to make
such alterations or to suppress the testimony of his written sources,

[16] Bishop (1948: 187–91).

[17] Syme (1959: 44–5).

[18] Bayet (Budé, 1940: n. 3), curiously, never cites this passage in support of his
theory of a second edition. Syme (1959: 47–50) has rightly rejected certain arguments
adduced by Bayet: Livy's failure to mention Augustus when Romulus' foundation of
the temple of Juppiter Feretrius is first mentioned (1.10.6–7), and Livy's supposedly
skeptical treatment of the traditions of the Julian *gens*.

[19] e.g. 7.6.5–6; 10.5.13; 21.15.3–6; 33.10.7–10; 38.55–7. See Ogilvie's remarks
(1965: 4.20.5–11 n.).

[20] A possible exception occurs at 38.56.8–57.8. But this section, concerning the
trials of the Scipios, exhibits such monumental confusion both in the sources and in
the historian's own thinking that it is not a significant parallel (cf. 39.52.1–6). At
21.15.3–6 he realizes that a mistake has been made; but since he is unable to
distinguish between the true and the false elements in the narrative, he cannot recast
what he has written or pinpoint in advance for the reader's benefit the areas of doubt.

particularly in the early part of his history, where he frequently confesses the doubtful and conflicting nature of the evidence.[21] What is peculiar, therefore, about the inclusion of 4.20.5–11 is not so much that he failed to rewrite the previous section as that he failed to note the disagreement either at the beginning of the year, when the new consuls enter office (4.17.7), or when Cossus himself is introduced (4.19.1). When the *identity* of magistrates is in doubt, Livy's habit is to note discrepancies when the magistrates are first mentioned; when their *activities* are in question, he appends variants at the end of the narrative unit.[22] This fixed technique is not only absent here, but has been reversed, and is a further sign of later addition. The sentence which introduces the digression is also peculiar: it recapitulates in a strangely formal and unnecessarily detailed manner what has just been said: 'I have followed all earlier authorities in stating that Aulus Cornelius Cossus was military tribune when he dedicated the spoils of honor in the temple of Juppiter Feretrius'. The sentence is unlike the clipped, abbreviated style which he customarily employs when appending variant versions, and reads as if it were written not in immediate continuation, but as the introductory sentence of a passage written and inserted at a later date.[23]

---

[21] e.g. his remarks at Pref. 6–9; 2.18.4–7; 2.21; 4.7.10–12; 6.1.1–3; 8.40. Even when a version is particularly repugnant to his moral sensibilities (and one not attested by all the sources), he feels he must include it (8.18.3): 'I must nevertheless report what has been handed down, lest I deprive any writer of his credit.'

[22] On the identity of magistrates see 2.18.4–7, 54.3; 4.23.1–3; 7.18.10; 10.3.3–4, 9.10–14. On variant activities see 8.40, 9.28.5. The account of the year 302 BCE illustrates both techniques: at 10.3.3–4 the confusion in the names of dictator and two possible *magistri equitum* is recorded, but notation of the discrepancy concerning their activities is reserved until 10.5.13.

[23] Certain other peculiarities may be due to a hasty and careless insertion of 4.20.5-11 into the completed text. Livy says concerning Cossus' consulship in 428 BCE that it was part of a three year period of pestilence and crop shortages; yet *four* years are really involved: Lucius Papirius Crassus and Lucius Iulius (4.30.1), Lucius Sergius Fidenas and Hostius Lucretius Tricipitinus (4.30.4), Aulus Cornelius Cossus and Titus Quinctius Poenus (4.30.4: see Ogilvie 1965: 4.20.8 n.), Gaius Servilius Ahala and Lucius Papirius Mugillanus (4.30.12). Similarly, Livy's statement that this consulship came in the *seventh* year after the killing of Tolumnius in 437 BCE may be due to his own careless counting and not to discrepancies among his sources. It is also odd that, after using a source *other* than Licinius Macer for 4.17–20 (see Ogilvie 1958: 40–6), Licinius' use of the Libri Lintei should be the only source specifically cited in the ensuing discussion (4.20.8); this may reflect an inaccurate memory of which source was used for the preceding section. Livy is alternating Licinius with another source (Valerius Antias?) throughout the book; he uses Licinius for 4.21–30.

The section at 4.20.5–11 was thus inserted after the completion of
the first pentad. Were other passages involved as well? It is not
unreasonable to suppose that there were. A few scholars claim to
have found a large number of later additions.[24] But a caveat must be
given. The one passage (4.32.4) which shows that 4.20.5–11 was
added later also reveals something about the circumstances under
which the addition was made: the failure to correct 4.32.4 is clear
evidence that no general revision—not even a fairly superficial
rereading—was given the text; we are therefore concerned not with
a second edition, but with 'additions and corrections', probably few
in number (possibly this is the only one) and involving little or no
rewriting (certainly nothing before or after 4.20.5–11 appears to have
been changed).

Augustus was the cause for the addition of 4.20.5–11 to the completed narrative; this suggests the possibility that the other passage in
the first decade which concerns him (1.19.3) may also have been added
at the same time. The evidence, however, is not quite so clear. Certainly
the context reveals no contradictions or striking irregularities of style;
yet a number of peculiarities are sufficient at least to bring the passage
into question. First, as Bayet noted,[25] the sentence can be removed
without doing violence to the train of thought; if it were removed, the
text would betray no sign that anything was missing. But we can go
further and argue that its removal would improve the sequence of
thought and the manner of expression. At 19.2 Livy says that Numa
decided to make the temple of Janus 'an indicator of peace and war',
next states that it had twice been closed since his reign (19.3), then
declares that Numa closed it, and continues in a lengthy sentence to
describe the effects on the people. It is odd that he should describe the
subsequent closings before stating the fact of its initial closing (19.2
only recounts Numa's intentions); and the ablative absolute, *clauso eo*
('After the closing...'), used to describe Numa's act, is not immediately clear, coming as it does after the statement concerning Augustus;
it would be more natural after 19.2. It should also be noted that if, as at
4.20.5–11, Livy had wanted to insert 1.19.3 but not be forced to alter

---

[24] Bayet (Budé, 1946: 125 [cf. 118–21]), and Soltau (1894*b*: 611–17).
[25] Bayet (Budé, 1940: xvii). W–M also had raised the possibility of later insertion,
*Einl.* 10.

the original text, the present location is the only place he could have done so.

These considerations are suggestive of later addition, but no more. In order to strengthen the hypothesis that 1.19.3 is a later addition, it is necessary to examine the one other passage in the first decade which can be used for dating purposes: the excursus on Alexander the Great in Book Nine (17–19). A close and detailed investigation into the nature and purpose of the digression is required in order to establish a date of writing and to provide evidence for Livy's rate of composition.

All scholars and commentators, even the historian himself, have admitted that the excursus is peculiar. But there has been much disagreement about precisely wherein the peculiarity lies. Livy confesses that digressions are foreign to his method and plan of composition,[26] but most scholars have felt that not only is the presence of this lengthy digression unusual, but its particular substance and expression are so extraordinary that they, too, require explanation. Two principal theories have been advanced, each of which has attracted numerous and distinguished supporters. The first is that Livy is replying to an attack on Rome made by the historian Timagenes; the phrase, 'the most feckless of the Greeks, who exalt the glory of even the Parthians against Rome's renown' (9.18.6), has prompted the hypothesis; it is a theory of long standing, and has been most recently (and most attractively) argued by Piero Treves.[27] Timagenes of Alexandria, brought to Rome in 55 BCE, rose from a lowly position to establish a well-known rhetorical school and to become a friend of Augustus; but his sharp tongue and disparaging remarks about the fortune of the Princeps estranged the two men. Augustus forbade Timagenes access to his home thereafter, and the historian in revenge burned those books of his history which concerned the emperor. Timagenes found refuge with Asinius Pollio and became an outspoken critic of

---

[26] 9.17.1.

[27] Schwab (1834) first proposed the theory. Treves (1953: 25, n. 2) gives the bibliography on the subject. Recent advocates of the theory are Ogilvie (1965: 4); Bowersock (1965: 108–10, 125–6). The latter points out (109, n. 2) that 'the most feckless of the Greeks' need not refer to Timagenes alone, but could include writers such as Metrodorus of Scepsis (cf. Plin. *NH* 34.16.34; Plut. *Luc.* 22; DH *A.R.* 1.4). This is possible, although Metrodorus himself had been long dead by the mid-twenties BCE.

Augustus and of Rome: 'Timagenes, who begrudged our city's good
fortune, used to say that fires at Rome saddened him for only one
reason: he knew that what was built up was bound to be better than
what had burned down.'[28] No ancient source specifically connects
Timagenes with the kind of remarks on Alexander or the Parthians
which are found in Livy, but his general hostility to Rome and to the
imperial house has been sufficient cause for theorizing that it is he to
whom Livy is replying: certainly no other person of whom we know is
a better candidate for 'the most feckless of the Greeks'.

A second theory has been put forward by W. B. Anderson and has
found favor with a number of scholars.[29] Anderson has emphasized
the extremely rhetorical nature of the excursus, from which he
inferred that it was originally written as a declamation. What he
regarded as blatant rhetoric, absurd exaggerations, careless statements, and weak argumentation led him to postulate that the excursus was 'a youthful dissertation, an exercise composed by Livy about
the age of eighteen, when he was a pupil in the school of a *rhetor* at
Patavium'.[30] The excursus, he believed, was inserted rather clumsily
and was not later revised, 'probably from what Boswell calls "pro-
crastination continued from day to day"'.[31]

Certain aspects of each of these theories are attractive; others are
not. Perhaps it is best to discuss the latter first. All attempts to show
that the excursus is 'out of place' or is an insertion fail, chiefly
because the historian himself admits that what he is about to write
is contrary to his usual practice. The excursus is introduced gradually
and in a logically connected sequence: Livy follows his character
sketch of Papirius Cursor (9.16.12–18) by asserting that 'no one of
that time contributed more to the welfare of Rome'.[32] This brings to

---

[28] Sen. *Ep.* 91.13. The chief testimonia, some conflicting and none without
difficulties, are: Suidas, s.v. Τιμαγένης and Πωλίων; Sen. *Contr.* 10.5.21–22; Sen. *De
ira* 3.23.4–8; Quint. 10.1.75. Jacoby (*FGrH* ii.88) has collected the fragments.

[29] Anderson (1908: 94–9), summarized in Anderson (1928: 255–8). Anderson's
thesis is followed by Walters-Conway (1919); Laistner (1947: 68); Bonner (1949: 157).

[30] Anderson (1908: 94).

[31] Anderson (1908: 99).

[32] Anderson (1908: 91) suggests that this is a reminiscence of Ennius' line 'The
Roman state is founded on the morality and men of old'. Possibly, but the correspondence is not very remarkable, and similar phrases occur elsewhere: e.g. 8.7.16; 4.40.9.

mind the belief of some that Cursor would have been a match for
Alexander, had the latter invaded Italy. The general subject of the
digression, 'what the outcome would have been had Rome gone to
war with Alexander' (17.2), is thus naturally introduced. The digression closes with a solemn declaration and prayer (19.17), and is
followed by the words: 'Marcus Folius Flaccina and Lucius Plautius
Venox were then (*inde*) elected the next consuls' (20.1). Some have
seen in this abrupt transition and in the use of *inde* further signs of
insertion.[33] But such brief announcements at the start of a new year,
especially with *inde* or *deinde*, are frequent in Livy and do not prove
that the previous section was inserted.[34] Besides, it is difficult to
know how the historian could have made a smooth transition between two such dissimilar subjects. Treves, on the other hand, has
attempted to prove that the excursus is out of place.[35] He maintains
that synchronization requires it come either when Livy mentions
Alexander at 8.3.7, or when he records the founding of Alexandria at
8.24.1. Treves postulates that Book Eight had already been published
and the writing of Book Nine was under way when Timagenes' attack
on Rome's greatness prompted Livy to immediate and vigorous
rebuttal. Accurate chronology, however, is not one of the historian's
strong points, much less strict synchronization.[36] Of the two passages
which Treves cites in Book Eight, Livy describes the first (340 BCE) as
'the same period in which Alexander the Great flourished', while in
the second (326 BCE) he postdates the founding of Alexandria five
years. There is, moreover, no evidence to show that Livy planned or
published in single books rather than in pentads or groups of pentads
at this early stage in his writing, and much which suggests the
contrary. Finally, Andersen's notion that the excursus is 'youthful'
must be rejected. The rhetoric is admittedly plentiful and heady, but
this is true of most of Livy's speeches. The frequent use of the first
and second persons is also unremarkable; the Preface, for example, is
replete with it. Exaggeration and inaccuracy of statement, as well as
elementary blunders in military matters, are also poor evidence for

[33] So Anderson (1908: 94); Soltau (1894*b*: 613–15).
[34] See e.g. 2.28.1, 43.1, 49.9, 54.1.
[35] Treves (1953: 14 ff.).
[36] For some striking examples see Walsh (1961*a*: 145–51).

youthfulness: all occur regularly throughout the extant corpus.[37] But even if these could be accepted as proofs of youth, it is difficult to understand why the mature man, many years later, would insert unchanged in his history a school declamation which is supposedly so flamboyant, inept, and puerile.

Perhaps the most significant aspect of the excursus, as Treves and others have seen, is that it is a direct rejoinder to some person or persons who had attacked the majesty of Rome; it is not merely a declamation on a general and familiar theme, popular in the schools or as a subject for public recital. The attackers are 'the most feckless of the Greeks', who extolled Alexander and the Parthians at the expense of Rome (9.18.6):

As if there were any danger–which the most feckless of the Greeks, who exalt the glory of even the Parthians against Rome's renown, are fond of repeating over and over–that the Roman people could not have withstood the majesty of Alexander's name–a man whom I doubt they had ever even heard of!

The frequent sarcasm and references to opposing arguments all presuppose the existence of a specific polemic or polemics,[38] the chief points of which emerge clearly from the historian's remarks. First, Alexander was a great general, a point which Livy must admit, but which he severely qualifies: 'Indeed I do not deny that Alexander was a great military leader, but...' (17.5); and no Roman could have equalled him, which Livy stoutly denies. Second, Alexander was a great soldier and tactician, 'for they make him no less famous for these qualities as well', but Livy heaps scorn upon those who believe that no Roman was his equal (17.12):

In fighting on the battlefield—for they make him no less famous in this endeavor—Manlius Torquatus or Valerius Corvus would of course have shrunk from meeting Alexander face to face—men who had distinguished

---

[37] Walsh (1961a: 138–72) gives numerous examples of carelessness and inaccuracy. In military matters Livy reveals that he is ignorant (as well as disinterested) in the most basic elements, even when he has Polybius to guide him. See Walsh's instructive and amusing article (1958b: 83–8).

[38] Treves (1953: 20, 24, 45) urges this point vigorously and repeatedly. Note, for instance, that the opposing arguments are not fictitious or anticipated: there are no expressions such as 'someone may say', only third person plurals, present in tense and indicative in mood.

themselves as regular soldiers before becoming commanders! The Decii would have shrunk back, who hurled themselves into the enemy's midst, having vowed to perish in the attempt! Papirius Cursor would have shrunk back—he who possessed such strength of body and spirit!

Third, the mere majesty of Alexander's name, declare 'the most feckless of the Greeks' (9.18.6–7), would have frightened the Romans into capitulation, just as the fame of the Parthians does at the present. Livy ignores for the moment the thrust concerning Parthia, but replies that if the Athenians could speak out against Alexander even though practically within sight of the smoldering ruins of Thebes, to deny that the Romans would at least do as much is ludicrous. Livy's estimate of the Athenians was not high.[39] Fourth, 'there are people who extol Alexander's greatness because, while the Romans lost many battles but never a war, Alexander never lost a battle; but they do not realize that they are comparing the deeds of a single individual (and a youth, at that) with those of a people who had been waging war for eight hundred years'.[40]

These arguments illustrate the nature of the Greek attack: malicious, insidious, and designed to irritate Roman sentiment and sensibilities. It is no wonder that Livy, who firmly believed in Rome's superiority, should be goaded into making a vigorous rebuttal—particularly against the Greeks for whom he had little esteem: 'a people more energetic in speech than in action' (8.22.8). The attack, moreover, was cleverly aimed at subverting two Roman boasts, immortalized by the poets, enshrined in tradition, and whose exaggerated chauvinism made them particularly vulnerable to attack. The first formed the chief subject of the Greek polemic and of Livy's defense: Rome would easily have conquered Alexander if he had invaded Italy. This was a boast of long standing; Plutarch relates that Appius Claudius Caecus, in his famous speech to the Senate against the acceptance of Pyrrhus' overtures of peace, referred to the claim as 'those words of yours that you are forever telling the world'.[41] Whether or not this sentiment comes from Claudius' actual speech is problematic; Cicero, for instance, appears to have derived his knowledge of the speech not from the original, but from Ennius'

---

[39] Cf. 31.44.9.     [40] 9.18.9.     [41] Plut. *Pyrrhus* 19.2.

famous version.[42] The sentiment probably goes back at least to the poet,[43] but whatever its origin, it enjoyed wide currency. The second boast was equally venerable and well known: Rome had lost many battles, but had never lost a war. Lucilius had immortalized it in the famous lines (Marx: 613–14):

The Roman people have often been overcome and defeated in many a battle, but never in a war, which is all that matters.

'The most feckless of the Greeks' were quick to point out that Alexander had never lost a battle. The thrust was clever, irritating, and difficult to parry. At first Livy says that it is unfair to compare the brief career of an individual youth to the eight-hundred-year-old history of a whole people (18.8–9). But his most telling retort is reserved for later (19.9), when, instead of attempting to undercut the idea, he gives it a further twist: 'If Alexander had lost one battle, he would have lost the war. In Rome's case, if the defeats at Caudium or Cannae could not break her, what conflict could?' He then refers to the remark of Alexander's uncle, Alexander of Epirus, that in going to Asia the young man was proceeding to the women's quarters, while he in Italy was facing the men.[44]

Indeed, far from being inept and puerile, the historian's answer to 'the most feckless of the Greeks' is frequently clever and pointed. References to the Roman tradition are sweeping, impassioned, and often exaggerated: vehicles hardly suited to wit, sarcasm, and irony. Livy therefore draws freely on the Greek tradition, both in general and in reference to Alexander in particular. An unexpected facet of the historian's personality is thereby revealed, one almost totally suppressed in his grave and preternaturally solemn account of Rome's heroic past. 'The most feckless of the Greeks' were fortunate to have a conqueror as famous and romantic as Alexander for the protagonist of their attack. Unfortunately the hostile Peripatetic tradition existed. Livy adopted it. He pretends mock shame at what he must relate about 'so great a king' (18.4); but, alas, the facts were stubborn and undeniable (18.5). As for Alexander's conquest, Darius

[42] Malcovati (1955: 1). Some scholars, e.g. Bardon (1952–6: i. 22–3), believe that Appius' speech was extant in its original form.
[43] This is the attractive suggestion of Alfonsi (1962: 505–6).
[44] Aulus Gellius reports the remark more fully (17.21.33).

was so sunk in effeminate luxury that he was 'more truly the booty than the enemy'. If Alexander had come to Italy (17.16),

he would have said it was no Darius he was facing, whom he defeated in a bloodless rout as the king was dragging his line of women and eunuchs along, weighed down with purple, gold and other trappings of his station, more truly the booty than the enemy, defeated for no other reason than Alexander's scorn of such an impotent display.

After his bloodless victory Alexander's plunge into luxury and degeneracy was swift and total (18.1–5): Livy mentions his adoption of Persian dress, the demand that all prostrate themselves before him, his cruelty, the murder of his friends, his drunkenness, his anger, his false claim of divine descent. Such carryings-on, of course, sadden and tend to lessen confidence (18.5): 'We don't reckon such defects in a commander among his strengths, do we?' And if Alexander had continued to live, what, wonders Livy, would he have been like by the time he had reached Italy? The historian makes a few suggestions (18.3, 5). He also adopts a number of ideas and anecdotes, either Greek in origin or involving Greeks, in order to embellish his reply to 'the most feckless of the Greeks'. The favorite Greek idea that those who experience great good fortune almost invariably suffer eclipse is exploited fully. Alexander died very young (17.5): 'a youth in the full tide of success, not yet having experienced a reverse'; but as all know, a long life is enough to ensure a fall from good fortune: Cyrus the Great is cited as an example, 'whom the Greeks praise especially' (17.6), and, in Roman affairs, Pompey the Great.[45] And Alexander's behavior in the face of success was an extreme example of what could happen (18.1). Indeed, Livy implies that Alexander's plunge into vice and degeneracy after success presaged a descent to ruin so precipitous and total as to be particularly exemplary. Had he continued to live, Rome's victory would have been neither surprising nor

---

[45] The passage must therefore date after 48 BCE. In the phrase 'just as Pompey the Great recently', the *modo* is not evidence for early dating (cf. Anderson 1928: 258): at 22.14.13 *modo* is used after a lapse of 24 years, and at 6.40.17 after 22 years; cf. 5.52.9 (all from speeches); but the earlier the passage is dated, the less exceptional the use of *modo* becomes. Livy's view that Pompey's downfall was caused by his long life, which allowed bad luck ultimately to befall him, is in line with his Pompeian sympathies reported in Tacitus (*Ann.* 4.34.3). The epithet Magnus, however, is probably the chief reason Pompey was chosen as an example.

wonderful (17.4, 18.3, 19.10–11, 19.17). Livy also uses the judgment of Rome and of Italy which the Greeks themselves had given: Cineas, who said that the Roman Senate was a council of kings (17.14); or Alexander's own uncle, who made the disparaging comparison between his own and his nephew's lot in war (19.10–11). Livy's words at 17.17 suggest that 'the most feckless of the Greeks' had also described how Alexander had overcome the strangeness and difficulties of far-off India; it was doubtless stated or implied that Italy would have been an easy conquest by comparison. Livy obliges them by depicting the sight which would have met the conqueror's eyes after crossing: the passes of Apulia, the mountains of Lucania, and the slaughtered remnants of his uncle, Alexander of Epirus, and of his army.

The excursus is thus a vigorous, chauvinistic rebuttal to a Greek polemic against Rome. A second striking feature, which Anderson stressed, is its highly rhetorical nature.[46] The same style and devices, of course, are characteristic of the historian's speeches. What is remarkable, therefore, is not so much that the excursus is rhetorical, as that it is oratorical: the style is unsuited to expository prose. The incongruity is strange, especially when we consider that Livy was a careful stylist to whom the appropriate marriage of content with style was a major concern.[47] Perhaps it is best to base any interpretation on what appears most obvious: the excursus is oratorical because Livy delivered it orally. A remark of the elder Seneca suggests that the historian frequented the halls of declamation; we know that he gave readings from his history to small but appreciative audiences.[48] The excursus may therefore have been delivered separately and incorporated into

---

[46] Anderson (1908: 94–5): 'Balanced structure, antithetic or chiastic, with or without Asyndeton, meets the eye everywhere. The First Person Singular occurs ten times, the Second Person Singular twice. Rhetorical repetition is there in abundance; there are many rhetorical questions and exclamations, and rhetorical elaboration is evident throughout. To these points may be added the free use of rhetorical adverbs and particles, the ironical *videlicet* (17.12), and *vero* (17.15, 18.6), *at hercule* (18.6), and *ne* (19.10); also expressions which remind us of many similar turns found in Cicero's speeches when the orator wishes to pass persons or things in rapid review,— *ut omittam* (17.6); *recenseam*...? (17.7); *referre piget* (18.4); *quot...nominem?* (18.12).'

[47] See the excellent article by McDonald (1957: 155–72); also Walsh (1961*a*: 219–70).

[48] Cf. Sen. *Contr.* 9.2.26 and Bonner (1949: esp. 40, 133, 156–7). For his recitations see Suidas s.v. Κορνοῦτος, and Cichorius (1922: 261–9). Bornecque (1933: 9–10) maintains, unnecessarily, that Livy himself was a professional rhetor.

the history soon after. It is more likely, however, that it was written as a part of the history which Livy intended to deliver orally. Since it was a vigorous and immediate reply to a Greek polemic (itself doubtless delivered orally[49]), Livy wrote it in oratorical form and delivered it in an oratorical manner. The style was left unchanged when Books 6–10, or more probably 6–15 (see below), were published, probably because, far from hoping to conceal the occasion and nature of the excursus, Livy wished his readers to be reminded of them.[50]

In this highly-colored verbal rejoinder to Rome's detractors, patriotic sentiments are, of course, given free rein; all that redounds to Rome's glory is fully exploited and often exaggerated. The peroration is particularly vainglorious: in all the wars with Antiochus, Philip, and Perseus, says Livy, Rome experienced neither reverses nor danger (19.14). As a matter of fact, Rome has never suffered a defeat in an infantry battle, never in a pitched battle, never on even ground, and certainly never on a site of her own choosing (19.15). To such sweeping assertions and fervid patriotism, however, there is one startling exception. The charge of 'the most feckless of the Greeks who also side against the Romans by lauding the fame of the Parthians' (18.6), that the Romans were afraid of the Parthians, far from being refuted, is lamely admitted (19.16). The admission comes at the end of the excursus and in the midst of the most exaggerated claims: the whole remarkable section deserves attention:

May no evil attend my words and may civil wars be silent! We have never suffered a reverse in an infantry battle, never in a pitched battle, never on even ground, and certainly never on a site of our own choosing: a heavy-armed soldier has reason to fear cavalry, arrows, untrod mountain passes, and trackless wastes where no supplies can come. But he has repulsed and will repulse a thousand armies more formidable than those of Macedon and

---

[49] It should be noted that Timagenes ran his own school of rhetoric at Rome: Suidas, s.v. Τιμαγένης and Πωλίων.

[50] Livy attempts to soften the immediate topicality of the excursus in the context of his historical narrative by claiming that such digressions are 'pleasant bypaths' and furnish 'refreshment for my mind', and that the theme has long been a subject of quiet reflection (cf. Cic. *De Inv.* 1.1). But the theme is presented in a far from reflective or quiet manner. Some of the peculiarities of the excursus may be due to mockery or parody of his opponent's speech: e.g. the overly formal and formulaic treatment of the statement of theme and of 'topic headings' (17.3–5, 19.1).

of Alexander, if only our love of peace and our concern for civil harmony may continue unbroken![51]

The reference to the Parthian cavalry and archers, and particularly to the debacles of Crassus in the desert and of Antony in the mountains is unmistakable. The charge must have played such a featured role in the Greek attack that to ignore it would have been tantamount to humiliating admission. Livy can only point to the irregular and cowardly nature of Parthian warfare, by saying that any infantry soldier of a regular army *would* fear sneak attacks, carried on from a distance and mounted in difficult terrain. But this is lame; he knows it, and attempts to conceal it by sandwiching the subject in among proud boasts and fervent prayers. It is clear that he has no really effective weapon at hand with which to rebut his opponents. Scholars have recognized that the passage must date before 20 BCE, when the lost standards were recovered; it was a much publicized and much lauded accomplishment.[52] Livy would surely have made full use of it, had he known of it. A few scholars have also rightly seen that the passage must date even before 23 BCE, for in that year negotiations were initiated which were to lead to the recovery of the standards.[53] The Parthian king asked for the return of his young son, who had come into Roman hands by the treachery of Tiridates, pretender to the Parthian throne, and for the surrender of Tiridates himself. Augustus refused to surrender the pretender, but released the young prince; Dio Cassius says that this was the occasion which initiated negotiations for the return of the standards.[54] Had Livy known of these proceedings, he certainly would have exploited them

---

[51] I follow the necessary deletion after *sileant* of *nunquam ab equite hoste* of the mss., as suggested by Dobree and Madvig. The passage makes sense only if the contrast is kept throughout: between infantry and cavalry, pitched battle and guerilla warfare, even or favorable ground and mountainous or unfavorable terrain. See Treves (1953: 11 n. 3, 27 n. 6); cf. Anderson (1908: 100–1).

[52] *Res Gestae* 29: 'I forced the Parthians to hand over to me the spoils and standards of three Roman armies and to seek as suppliants the friendship of the Roman people. I placed the standards in the inner shrine of the temple of Mars Ultor.'

[53] W–M Einl. 10 and 9.18.6 n.; Treves (1953: 20–1); cf. Anderson (1928: 258).

[54] Dio 53.33.1–2, Justinus 42.5. For a recent discussion of these negotiations see Ziegler (1964: 45 ff.), who doubts that any formal agreement was reached in 23 BCE (cf. Dio 54.8.1).

with pleasure. The situation invited exploitation for partisan purposes, particularly in such a chauvinistic tract as the excursus: the Parthian king reduced to begging for his son and for the return of a dangerous pretender, Augustus' gracious release of the young prince, and the king willing to countenance giving up the standards without a fight. But as it is, Livy has little to say which would mitigate the charge that the Romans feared the Parthians. Book Nine must therefore date before 23 BCE.

The ninth book, of course, was composed as part of a larger thematic unit. The grouping, however, can scarcely be the second pentad alone; Book Ten breaks off at a critical stage in the Samnite Wars: the final campaigns and the double triumph of Manius Curius Dentatus are three years away and were not recounted until Book Eleven. The three following books concerned the war with Pyrrhus, while the fifteenth brought the account down to the eve of the First Punic War. Livy thus planned, and doubtless published, Books 6–15 as a unit: the Conquest of Italy. It possessed its own introduction (6.1.1–3), devoting five books to the Samnite Wars and three to the Pyrrhic War, with Book Six introducing the preliminaries and Book Fifteen relating the aftermath.[55] Since the ninth book was composed before 23 BCE, it is likely that most, if not all, of the decade of which it forms a part was also composed by then. It follows that if the passage at 1.19.3 concerning Augustus' closing of the gates of Janus, dating between 27 and 25 BCE, was not a later insertion, Livy must have written the first fifteen books at a remarkable rate of speed. Between January 16, 27 BCE, and sometime in 23 BCE, he would have to write and publish Book One, write and publish Books 2–5, add at Augustus' suggestion the

[55] At 10.31.10 Livy says that this is his fourth book on the Samnite Wars (i.e. Books 7–10). If he had wished, the Samnite Wars could have been concluded by the tenth book; the books of the second pentad are considerably shorter than those of the first. His desire to carry the reader over to the new pentad as smoothly as possible is also shown by the introduction of the new consuls for 292 BCE at the end of the tenth book (47.5). This same 'carry-over' technique has been noticed elsewhere by Walsh (1961a: 6): 'In many cases he postpones the treatment of a major event to have an arresting topic for the beginning of a new section. Thus the capture and destruction of Carthage are described in LI, the capture of Jugurtha in LXVI, and the murder of Julius Caesar in CXVI.' The detached nature of the introductory and the concluding books is also characteristic of Books One and Five in the first pentad: see Burck (1934: 8–9). Numerous scholars have agreed that Books 6–15 were designed as a unit: e.g. Bornecque (1933: 14); Bayet (Budé, 1940: xii); Syme (1959: 30); Klotz (1926: 819).

passage at 4.20.5–11, and write and publish Books 6–15. It is true that the historian, in order to reach Book 142 by the time of his death in CE 17, must have written continuously and on an average of three books a year. Such rapid composition for the early books is admittedly not impossible; but it is not very likely either. The length of the early books is one indication: the first pentad is considerably longer than any of the others: Book Three, for example, is more than twice the length of Book Thirty-two.[56] The historical problems were also more difficult for the early period, and the five centuries covered by Books 1–5 created additional problems by virtue of their very length, diversity, and complexity. The early books also reveal that greater care in structure and composition was brought to them than to the later books, particularly those from Book Thirty-one on. Erich Burck's illuminating analysis of the first pentad reveals that much reading and planning must have preceded the actual writing, while the techniques of detailed narration are carefully and artfully employed.[57] The later books have not received such high, or such consistent, praise; the material was more detailed, more prosaic, and less congenial to Livy's moral, romantic, and literary predilections. Where we can check his adaptation from Polybius, 'a clear and somewhat damning picture emerges of a mind rapidly and mechanically transposing the Greek, and coming to full consciousness only when grappling with the more congenial problems of literary presentation'.[58] Finally, it is reasonable to suppose that the historian composed more slowly at the start, before he had found his method and style, and while the problems of dealing with the sources were still strange.

There are two further points which, while not proving an early date for the first decade, are better suited to early dating. The first concerns Livy's fervent prayer at the end of the excursus that the civil wars may not break out again and that the present love of peace may

---

[56] Birt (1882: 310 ff.) gives the figures.

[57] Burck (1934: 8–9).

[58] Walsh (1961*a*: 144). Even the care and effort which Livy customarily employed in composing speeches decline noticeably in the fourth and fifth decades: see Walsh (1961*a*: 221). Witte (1910: 270–305, 359–419), who did pioneer work on Livy's narrative techniques and artistry in the later books, admitted that the historian's efforts were sporadic and confined to 'individual episodes': see esp. 418–19. Cf. Syme (1959: 41): 'It would be a bold man who argued that Livy needed more than two or three weeks to produce Book 31.'

continue, which suggests that the civil wars were recent and that Augustus' rule was still quite new (9.19.15, 17). The later the passage is dated, the more peculiar the passionate vehemence becomes: unflattering to the government and to the emperor, impolitic for the writer, and most out of place in the highly patriotic and defensive reply to 'the most feckless of the Greeks', where weaknesses are either ignored or mitigated as much as possible. The same considerations apply to Livy's pessimistic references to his own time which he expresses elsewhere in the history, particularly in the Preface.[59] Most are confined to the first decade; thereafter they become rare.[60] A second consideration is the dating of Livy's birth, which recent scholars are inclined to put in 64 BCE, rather than in 59 BCE, the traditional year.[61] Of the two dates, 64 BCE is by far the more likely. The historian would thus have been in his late thirties when he began the first of his 142 books. Again, there is nothing impossible in this; many Roman historians, such as Sallust and Tacitus, came to their tasks in middle age. But Livy's historical output was huge, his other

[59] Pref. 4–5, 9–12; 7.25.9, 40.2; cf. Bayet (Budé, 1940: xx). Syme (1959: 49–50) dismisses these references: 'they prove nothing', which is true, but they are suggestive, particularly in the light of the tendentious nature of the excursus. The conspiracy of Varro Murena in 23 BCE, however, hardly seems adequate to account either for the sweeping condemnation in the Preface or for the remarks in the excursus. Syme finds that 'perhaps the strongest plea is the tone of the Preface, encouraging an early date, before the years of peace'.

[60] Sentiments such as that at 26.22 are infrequent. This is not to say that Livy was the mouthpiece for official optimism (silence is seldom golden in matters of propaganda), but only that as the disturbances of the civil wars receded into the past, Livy's pessimism lost some of its immediate sharpness. The remarks at 43.13 make it clear that his preference for the past and distaste for the present (cf. Pref. 4–5) may have changed in degree, but not in substance. On Livy's relations with Augustus, I follow Walsh's sensible and conservative estimate (1961*a*: 10–19) and (1961*b*: 26–37).

[61] Jerome, *ad Euseb. Chron. ad ann. Abr. 1958*: 'The orator Messalla Corvinus is born, as well as Titus Livius, the historian, from Patavium.' It has long been recognized that Messalla's birth is too late, and the suggestion that *Caesare et Bibulo* of 59 BCE have been confused with *Caesare et Figulo* of 64 BCE is reasonable and attractive: see Schulz (1886: 1–8). Hirst (1926: 138–9) was the first to see that, since Livy and Messalla are bracketed together and since the latter's birth has been postdated some five years, the same should hold true for the historian. The earlier date has been accepted as the more likely by Syme (1959: 40–2); Walsh (1961*a*: 1–2); Ogilvie (1965: 1). But whether Livy's death should be moved from CE 17 to CE 12 is questionable. Messalla's death is postdated by five years and his age is given by Jerome (*ad ann. Abr.*

known writings were few,[62] and evidence for any other activity in early life is lacking. In view of the earlier date of birth, an earlier date for the commencement of his historical writing is attractive.

The passage at 4.20.5–11 was certainly a later addition, and it is probable that 1.19.3 was also. When and under what circumstances were the additions made? The section concerning Cossus must have been added when Augustus' refusal to allow Licinius Crassus to dedicate the *spolia opima* was still topical, and when a statement of precedent in a work such as Livy's seemed desirable. Crassus killed the chieftain, Deldo, while proconsul of Macedonia in 29 BCE and was voted a triumph; he campaigned again in 28 BCE and returned to the city late that year. He did not celebrate his triumph until July, 27 BCE. When Crassus made the actual claim is not known: possibly not until his return to Rome. Livy's addition was made after January 16, 27 BCE, since he terms the Princeps Augustus, and undoubtedly no more than one to two years after Crassus' triumph. Thereafter the situation would have lost much of its urgency, and justification long postponed might be interpreted more as a confession of weakness than delivered from a position of strength. In other words, 4.20.5–11 was written within the same period as 1.19.3: between 27 and 25 BCE; 4.20.5–11 was an addition to a completed text—another consideration which suggests that the passage four books earlier was also an addition.

---

2029): 'The orator Messalla Corvinus... killed himself in the seventy-second year of life', indicating that the year of death was calculated from birth by years of age. But no age is given for Livy (*ad ann. Abr.* 2033): 'Livy, the historian, dies at Patavium', which suggests that Jerome was not counting by years of life, but was dating by consuls once more. The superscription of the Periocha of Book 121 states that Books 121–141 were published after the death of Augustus. It has been argued recently (Syme 1959: 38–9, 71–2); Ogilvie (1965: 1, 3) that this does not preclude an earlier date for Livy's death: his heirs may have suppressed the books, which concerned Augustus' reign itself, because of the embarrassing, possibly incriminating, contents. Possibly; but the most likely source of information for the writer of this attenuated Periocha was the book itself, doubtless its preface; Klotz (1926: 819) understands 'by Livy in his preface' with 'is said'. Livy would thus have survived the emperor; politic postponement may have been the historian's own doing.

[62] Sen. *Ep.* 100.9 says that Livy wrote 'both dialogues, which you might reckon as much philosophical as historical, and books that are overtly philosophical', which were perhaps early works: see Walsh (1961a: 4). He also wrote an essay on style, in the form of a letter to his son (Quint. 10.1.39).

How much time elapsed between the completion of the first pentad and the additions? The answer must be that it was not long. If Livy's work had been available to the public for a number of years, the text would have been well known, frequently copied, and impossible to recall.[63] It would not have been suitable for Augustus' purposes. Perhaps Livy had completed the text and had allowed a number of friends to read it and suggest improvements. The practice was common, and corrections could easily be made.[64] Such a period must have been at least a few months in duration, and was probably somewhat longer.[65] The historian may also have given recitations from the early books before allowing a wider circle of acquaintances (possibly professional booksellers as well) to make copies; corrections and additions could easily be made at this juncture also. Even if some copies had gone out whose whereabouts were still known, alterations were possible. Cicero, for instance, requested Atticus to change 'through your copyists' the name of Eupolis in his *Orator* to that of Aristophanes 'not only in your own books, but also in those of others'. The change was made.[66] Authors could even contemplate making changes when so many copies had been distributed that alteration was possible only in some, but not in all. Cicero, for example, asked Atticus to delete the name of L. Corfidius from his speech *Pro Ligario* even though 'it has received wide distribution'; the mistake still remains in our manuscripts.[67] Changes of a more drastic nature were also possible. Cicero had given his *De Gloria* to Atticus for copying and distribution, but while on a southern voyage discovered that he had used the same preface for the *De Gloria* as he had for the third book of the *Academics*. 'It happened,' he explained,

---

[63] On the general question of publishing and correcting see Birt (1882: esp. 342–70) and Sommer (1926: 389–422).

[64] For instance, at *Ad Att.* 13.21.3, Cicero, who at first liked Atticus' suggested change of a verb to *inhibere*, now finds that it is unsuitable. He asks Atticus to change it back as before, and to pass the information on to Varro, who also had a copy.

[65] 'Young historians seeking to establish a reputation do not sit on their manuscripts for years': Walsh (1961*b*: 29). Probably, although Horace (*A.P.* 388) advises young writers to wait nine years, and Quintilian (10.4.2) recommends a lengthy interval; yet these recommendations doubtless reflect ideals more than practice.

[66] *Ad Att.* 12.6.3. See *Orator* 29. Cf. Sommer's remarks (1926: 412–15).

[67] *Ad Att.* 13.44.3. See *Pro Lig.* 33. He had declined earlier to add a remark concerning Tubero's wife and stepdaughter, 'for it has been widely disseminated' (*Ad Att.* 13.20.2).

'because I keep a volume of prefaces, from which I usually select one
when I have begun a treatise.' Cicero composed a new preface and
sent it on to Atticus: 'Cut off the old one,' are his instructions, 'and
glue this new one on.'[68] Even complete rewriting and recasting could
be done after copies of the initial version had been made. Cicero
originally wrote his *Academics* in two books, using Catulus and
Lucullus as principal speakers. Atticus had made complete copies
of this version when Cicero decided to dedicate the treatise to Varro,
to redivide the work into four books, and to eliminate Catulus and
Lucullus in favor of Varro himself as an interlocutor. 'Please don't fret
at your loss in having had the version of the *Academics* you now
possess copied out in vain. The new version, after all, is far more
brilliant, concise, and better.'[69] Hence Livy's additions could have
been made at any time up to and beyond the copying and distribution of his manuscript. If not too many copies had been made and
were still accessible, corrections could be made in all; otherwise,
alterations were possible only in some. A passage in Fronto suggests
that once copying and distribution had increased beyond a certain
point, attempts at correction were futile.[70]

One further passage deserves attention: the opening words of the
Preface. The passage is not offered as additional evidence for later
insertions in the first pentad; but because it raises a difficult problem
which has hitherto been ignored or glossed over, it deserves discussion, and because one solution of the problem might be that it,
too, was involved in the later changes, it merits consideration
here. The opening words, as Quintilian noted (9.4.74), form the
beginning of a dactylic line: *facturusne operae pretium sim* ('Whether
it will be worthwhile'). This is the reading in all our modern texts, but
not in any extant manuscripts: Quintilian alone preserves the true
reading:

The ends of verses suit the opening of a speech: 'although I fear, judges...'
and 'It has been my observation, judges...' But beginnings do not suit
beginnings, as Livy did in opening with an hexameter line, 'Whether it will

---

[68]  *Ad Att.* 16.6.4.
[69]  *Ad Att.* 13.13.1. Cf. *Ad Att.* 13.12.3.
[70]  Fronto, *Ad Verum Imp.* 2.9, p. 137 Nabor; cf. *Ad Antonium Imp.* 2.8, p. 111
Nabor.

be worthwhile...'—for so he published it, and it is better than how it is emended.

Scholars have assumed, probably rightly, that the reading of the manuscripts, *facturusne sim operae pretium*,[71] is the alternate reading to which Quintilian refers; the change certainly eliminates the dactylic rhythm. But there is disagreement concerning its origin. Some have supposed that it is the result of an early corruption of the text,[72] others that it was a deliberate attempt to correct a stylistic fault: one scholar has imagined that the ancients were so surprised by the dactylic rhythm that they independently and spontaneously made the same correction.[73]

The difficulty in resolving the problem is chiefly caused by our not knowing what Quintilian's sources of information were. He clearly did not think that the second reading was a corruption; it was, rather, a deliberate correction of a stylistic fault. The correction, moreover, involved only a single reading; Quintilian is referring not to a number of possible rearrangements, but to one specific rewording which was familiar to many people. It had not become well known merely by word of mouth or as part of manuscript marginalia, but was the only reading of many texts; otherwise, there would have been no reason for him to inform his readers what the original line was. Finally, the alteration must have been of long standing, since the rhetor's words indicate that the correction by his day had become widespread and familiar to many.

How could such a 'correction' have been made? To postulate a spontaneous emendation by many manuscript owners, all independently agreeing on the new word order, is untenable. And to suppose that some individual made the correction at an early date, possibly

---

[71] Except for O, which inserts the clause *si a primordio... perscripserim* between *facturusne sim* and *operae pretium*.

[72] So Walters-Conway, *app. crit.*, but their explanation of the corruption on the basis of the variant in O is unclear to me; that O's readings, however, are particularly archetypal has recently been disputed: see Ogilvie (1957: 68–81, esp. 79–80). Ogilvie (1965: Pref. 1 n.) states that Quintilian speaks of 'the corrupt order', which 'had already gained currency by his own day'. But Quintilian is clearly speaking of a deliberate correction of a stylistic fault.

[73] Bayet (Budé, 1940: 2, n. 1): 'The abrupt familiarity of this opening is countered in the text by a dactylic rhythm, which would have surprised the ancients, to the point of making them correct the order of the first words in their manuscripts.'

within the historian's lifetime, and that the corrector's influence was
so great that it supplanted the author's original text seems equally
untenable. Private persons might alter their manuscripts in error or
in ignorance,[74] but there is no evidence to suggest that a critic's
'improvement' (worse than the original, in Quintilian's view) of a
famous writer's exact words could ever achieve such wide currency.

The explanation that the alternate version was caused by an early
textual corruption is much more plausible, but is not without difficulties. It is odd that a scribe's attention-span should have been so
brief that by the second word an error had been committed, and still
odder that the corruption should have been so swiftly reproduced
and so widely accepted, particularly when the opening rhythm was
striking and memorable, the author distinguished, and the work
monumental and celebrated.[75] We would also have to suppose that
Quintilian had mistaken a corruption for a correction of a stylistic
defect. But this is unlikely. Since he possessed primary evidence
concerning the original reading,[76] his interpretation of the alternate
version was probably based on some positive information as well.

Another explanation is possible. Perhaps the 'corrector' was not
the ancients en masse, some unknown critic, or a careless copyist, but
the historian himself; the alternate reading could have formed part
of the 'additions and corrections' to the first pentad. The theory is
attractive in a number of ways, but, like the other hypotheses, is not
without its difficulties. First, Quintilian's words make it clear that he
did not think Livy himself was responsible for the rewording. Second,
although to begin a prose sentence with the opening rhythm of a
poetic line was considered a stylistic fault, much can be said in
defense of this particular usage. Those who believe that Livy's hexameter opening, as well as that of Tacitus in the *Annales*, was written
unconsciously are surely mistaken.[77] P. G. Walsh has shown that the
attention which the ancients paid to style, particularly in *exordia*,

---

[74] Cf. Quint. 9.4.39; Aul. Gell. 20.6.14.

[75] But the copyists admittedly were often careless, as Cicero's complaint to his
brother testifies, *Ad Quint. fr.* 3.5.6.

[76] Possibly from the autograph itself, or from an early copy: for parallels see Aul.
Gell. 9.14.7, 1.21; Plin. *NH* 13.83.

[77] So W–M *ad loc.*; Gries (1949: 40); Syme (1958: 357); cf. Koestermann (1963–8:
i. 1.1.1 n.).

precludes mere accident, and has convincingly argued that the dactylic rhythm (not necessarily the wording or substance) is a deliberate echo of Rome's first writers of *Annales*—the poets who wrote in hexameter verse—and of Quintus Ennius in particular.[78] Livy's concern to emphasize the ancient and illustrious descent of this traditional form of historical writing overcame any qualms he may have felt about beginning a prose sentence with a hexameter verse. Third, while the dactylic rhythm may have brought censure from some quarters, the historian's definite opinions on style in general and his outspoken criticism of fellow writers suggest that he was not the kind of man who would waver or retreat from a position already taken, particularly one which has much to be said in its defense.[79]

On the other hand, the hypothesis has its attractions. Livy was a comparatively young man who was just beginning his history; the ideas on style which he expressed in later life were not likely to have been so set or so definite at this early period. He had just published the first pentad when the emperor's communication concerning Cossus, as well as the recent closing of the gates of Janus, necessitated a few additions. It could well be that several critics had taken sharp and immediate exception to the dactylic opening, allusions to early *Annales* in hexameter verse notwithstanding.[80] Pollio's celebrated jeer at Livy's *patavinitas* ('Patavinity') is evidence that contemporary critics of the historian's style were not lacking.[81] Livy had an excellent opportunity for rearranging the opening words when he made the other additions to the first pentad. Quintilian's critical remarks supply him with a motive, the later additions supply him with an opportunity; it may be more than accident that all extant manuscripts

[78] Walsh (1961*a*: 253–4). Cf. Ullmann (1932: 72–6) and (1933: 57–69).

[79] Livy wrote a treatise on style in the form of a letter to his son, in which he counseled the youth to read Demosthenes and Cicero, and then those who are most like them (Quint. 10.1.39). Livy vigorously condemned the style of Sallust: Sen. *Contr.* 9.1.13. For his views on the use of recondite words see Sen. *Contr.* 9.2.26. On the general subject see Walsh (1961*a*: 43–5, 245–70).

[80] Possibly the allusion to the early poets escaped them; Quintilian, at least, does not seem aware of it.

[81] Reported by Quintilian at 1.5.56. Whatever wider meaning Pollio may have intended (cf. Syme 1939: 485), at least part of the censure was directed at Livy's style and Latinity: this is how Quintilian unhesitatingly interpreted it. For a recent discussion of the vexed question see Walsh (1961*a*: 267–70).

contain the section on Cossus, the sentence concerning Augustus' closing of the gates of Janus, and the alternate version of the opening line.

The following conclusions result. The first pentad was complete by 27 BCE. Soon after, the emperor's communication concerning Cossus, and the closing of the gates of Janus,[82] prompted additions; possibly on this occasion Livy himself altered the dactylic opening of the Preface. His rate of composition continued steadily, for by 23 BCE Book Nine, and most probably the whole of Books 6–15, had been completed. The writing of the first pentad would require two to three years, and possibly longer; problems of composition were new, historical cruces numerous and difficult, opportunities for literary embellishment and moral instruction especially inviting. It was a period in which the historian took particular delight, as he admits (Pref. 4–5), and it is likely to have claimed more of his energies and time than did many later sections. Since he must have begun composition about the time of the Battle of Actium (possibly earlier), his decision to write the history of the Roman people 'from the beginning of the City' must have been taken before that date. Much background reading and large-scale planning also preceded regular composition.[83]

The first pentad, therefore, can scarcely be termed 'Augustan' either in inspiration or in execution; it was written in the years before the title was given to Octavian and before most of his policies and programs had been enacted. In truth, all the passages in which scholars have ventured to discern allusions to the emperor and his reign are tenuous at best; some interpretations are fanciful in the extreme.[84] Many are as suited to the period before c.30 BCE as after,[85]

[82] If Livy wrote Book One after the initial closing of the gates of Janus by Octavian in 29 BCE, the passage at 1.19.3 may have required only the addition of 'Augustus' to 'by the emperor Caesar' after January 16, 27 BCE. But the book was probably written earlier, and all of 1.19.3 added subsequently.

[83] Burck's analysis of the complex and carefully-wrought design of the first pentad presupposes that extensive reading and careful structuring of the larger events and themes preceded actual composition; *op. cit.* (1934).

[84] Ogilvie (1965: 2) gives a convenient list of passages, together with reference to his notes; to these add Pref. 9.

[85] Such as at 1.32.5, 53.1, 56.2, 57.9, 59.12; 3.58.4, 68.7; 4.3.7; consult Ogilvie's notes (1965: 2).

and, in some, broad generalization has been unnecessarily inter-preted as a mask for specific reference.[86] Yet the search for 'Augustan' influence has been as persistent as its individual conclusions have been ephemeral. Livy has been viewed both as a fervent propagandist for the Augustan regime and as an independent critic, subtly warning the Princeps against the excesses of authoritarianism.[87] One theory maintains that the historian strove to use the adjective *augustus* in significant contexts flattering to the emperor, while another study has shown that he neglected so many opportunities to use the word in this way that the hypothesis is untenable.[88] Similar theories have met with similar refutations. It is true, however, that in many significant ways Livy's views in the first pentad coincide with Augustus' program of religious, social, and moral reform. Yet many of these reforms came years after the first pentad had appeared, whatever theory of dating be invoked. The tendency to assume in these matters that the historian adopted, reflected, or was reacting to, the ideas of the central government and of its leader has been almost automatic and nearly ubiquitous. The tendency should be resisted, and the assumption questioned. Instead of searching for Augustan allusions in Livian history, it might be more profitable to investigate to what extent Augustan policy was influenced by the Livian concept of the Roman past.

---

[86] e.g. at Pref. 9: 'we can endure neither our vices nor the remedies needed to cure them,' has been interpreted as referring to Augustus' abortive social legislation of 28 BCE (Prop. 2.7.1). The theory, first proposed by Dessau (1903: 461–6), has found favor with some scholars (e.g. Ogilvie 1965: *ad loc*.; Williams 1962: 28 ff.) But Syme (1959: 42–3), and Walsh (1961*a*: 11) have rightly rejected the suggestion. At 1.56.2 Ogilvie (1965) has interpreted *haec nova magnificentia* ('this new magnificence') as referring to Agrippa's cleaning and presumed repairing of the Cloaca Maxima in 33 BCE, and to the restoration of the *pulvinar* (a deity's cushioned couch) by Augustus (*Res Gestae* 19) at the Circus Maximus, destroyed by fire in 31 BCE (Dio 50.10). This is possible, but not necessary; even if one or both references are accepted, they do not necessitate composition as late as 28–27 BCE.

[87] For an example of the first view see Cochrane (1940: esp. 103–113). For the latter view, see Petersen (1961: 440–52).

[88] On the flattering use of *augustus* see Taylor (1918: 158–61); Scott (1925: 82–105); Stübler (1941: 10–17). For the opposing evidence see Erkell (1952: 19–25). For the improbability of theories which connect Augustus with the portraits of Romulus, Numa, Camillus, Decius, and Scipio Africanus, see Walsh's remarks (1961*a*: 16–1).

## ADDENDUM

This, the first of Luce's major contributions to Livian studies, repositioned the terms of the debate by opening anew the complex issue of how and when the first pentad was disseminated. On the question of detecting references in Livy's narrative to contemporary events, see Haehling (1989); readers without German should consult the very thorough review by Briscoe (1990). On what it means to be an 'Augustan' writer, see Galinsky (1996) 226–9, discussing the distinctions between the different generations encompassed by Augustus' forty-five years of political dominance. Kennedy (1992) is an important and influential discussion of the terms 'Augustan' and 'anti-Augustan'.

The relationship between Livy and Augustus has featured in almost every extended discussion of the historian for the past half century. Syme's (1959) article, 'Livy and Augustus', argued forcefully for Livy's role as propagandist for the Augustan regime. That debate is summarized by Deininger (1985); in this volume see also the articles by Moles and Feldherr. Arguments for direct influence include Luce's own (1990) discussion of Livy's response to Augustus' political aims in the sculpture program and the *elogia* in his forum; Miles (1995) sees ways in which Livy wrote around the authoritative presence of the emperor (see especially chapter 1).

The Cossus episode is particularly well-treated: for a start, see Sailor (2006) with further bibliography. On the specific issue of the date of composition and its relationship to the interpretation of the text, see Moles, Woodman (1988), and Henderson (1989). For the Alexander digression, see most recently Morello (2002), with bibliography in note 7; she discusses the episode as an example of counterfactual history. The digression is also treated by Spencer (2002), in a study of Roman responses to Alexander the Great.

For the stylistic issues raised by Luce's discussion of the opening line, see Moles and Addendum. On book production, authors, and readers, see van Sickle (1980), Kenney (1982), and Starr (1987).

# 2

# Livy's Preface[1]

## J. L. Moles

Whether in writing the history of the Roman people from the foundation of the city the result will be worth the effort invested, I do not really know (nor, if I did, would I presume to say so), [2]for I realize that this is a time-honoured task that many have undertaken, each succeeding writer thinking he will either bring greater accuracy to the facts or surpass his unpolished predecessors in artistry and style. [3]However that may be, it will still be a source of satisfaction to celebrate to the best of my ability the history of the greatest nation on earth; and if in this throng of writers my own fame should be eclipsed, I will console myself with the thought of the nobility and greatness of those who overshadow my own.

[4]What is more, the task is immense, since Rome's history stretches back over seven hundred years and since the state has now grown so large from small beginnings that it struggles under the incubus of its own great size. Moreover, I do not doubt that Rome's foundation and early years will bring less pleasure to the majority of my readers, who will want to press on to recent times, in the course of which the strength of a mighty people has long been bent on its own undoing. [5]I on the other hand shall regard as an additional reward of my labour the opportunity to turn away from the sight of the evils that our age has witnessed for so many years and, for the bit of time my full attention is fixed on those early days, to be wholly free from the anxiety that may assail a writer's mind, though it cannot deflect it from the truth.

[1] This is a revised version of a paper given to the Cambridge Philological Society in October 1992 and to a seminar in All Souls, Oxford, in November 1992. I thank all those who made helpful comments on those occasions and Chris Kraus, Ruth Morello, an anonymous referee, and (as always) Tony Woodman for valuable criticisms of written versions. The translation of Livy's Preface is from T. J. Luce, *Livy: The Rise of Rome*, Oxford World's Classics (Oxford, 1998), 3–4, and is reproduced by permission of Oxford University Press.

[6]Events before the city was founded or planned, which have been handed down more as pleasing poetic fictions than as reliable records of historical events, I intend neither to affirm nor to refute. [7]To antiquity we grant the indulgence of making the origins of cities more impressive by commingling the human with the divine, and if any people should be permitted to sanctify its inception and reckon the gods as its founders, surely the glory of the Roman people in war is such that, when it boasts Mars in particular as its parent and the parent of its founder, the nations of the world would as easily acquiesce in this claim as they do in our rule.

[8]Yet I attach no great importance to how these and similar traditions will be criticized or valued. [9]My wish is that each reader will pay the closest attention to the following: how men lived, what their moral principles were, under what leaders and by what measures at home and abroad our empire was won and extended; then let him follow in his mind how, as discipline broke down bit by bit, morality at first foundered; how it next subsided in even greater collapse and then began to topple headlong in ruin—until the advent of our own age, in which we can endure neither our vices nor the remedies needed to cure them.

[10]The special and salutary benefit of the study of history is to behold evidence of every sort of behavior set forth as on a splendid memorial; from it you may select for yourself and for your country what to emulate, from it what to avoid, whether basely begun or basely concluded. [11]Yet either the love of the task I have set myself deceives me or there has never been any state grander, purer, or richer in good examples, or one into which greed and luxury gained entrance so late, or where great respect was accorded for so long to small means and frugality—[12]so much so that the less men possessed, the less they coveted. Recently wealth has brought greed in its train, manifold amusements have led to people's obsession with ruining themselves and with consuming all else through excess and self-indulgence.

But complaints, which will not be pleasing even at a later time when they will perhaps be necessary, should at least be banished from the commencement of such a great undertaking. [13]Rather, if we were to adopt the practice of poets, we would more gladly begin with good omens, and with vows and prayers to the gods and goddesses that they may grant us success as we embark upon this vast enterprise.

Few of the many treatments of this famous preface[2] seem to recognize the need for close reading of the text. The present paper sets out

[2] e.g. Dessau (1903); Ferrero (1949); Leggewie (1953); Vretska (1954); Oppermann (1955), reprinted in Burck (1967); Walsh (1955), reprinted in Burck (1967: 181–99); Leeman (1961), reprinted in Burck (1967: 200–14); Janson (1964: 64–74); Ogilvie (1965: 23–9); W–M (1965: 75–82); Mazza (1966); Ruch (1967); Heurgon (1970:

to remedy this deficiency in the hope of achieving three main aims: (1) to demonstrate the coherence and power of Livy's argument, as well as the subtlety of its exposition and the richness of its language; (2) to resolve certain specific problems; (3) to further the continuing debate on important general questions in ancient historiography.

Facturusne operae pretium sim si a primordio urbis res populi Romani perscripserim nec satis scio nec, si sciam, dicere ausim, (2) quippe qui cum veterem tum volgatam esse rem videam, dum novi semper scriptores aut in rebus certius aliquid allaturos se aut scribendi arte rudem vetustatem superaturos credunt.

The dactylic rhythm of the first words *facturusne . . . sim* poses an immediate challenge: why does Livy begin by writing poetry? Indeed, as is well known, ancient readers found the challenge so overwhelming that they emended the text to remove the rhythm, and only Quintilian (9.4.74) preserved the original reading.[3]

What of the general sentiment? If he writes a history of the Roman people from the first beginnings of the city,[4] Livy is not sure whether he will make/achieve *operae pretium*, nor, if he were sure, would he dare say so. Most ancient historians, even those (like Livy) who emphasize the difficulty of their task, make great claims for themselves and their work. Livy's apparent diffidence is strikingly at variance with the historiographical norm,[5] and he himself makes

21–6); Paschalis (1982); Korpanty (1983); Coppola (1983–4); Woodman (1988: 128–40); Wheeldon (1989: 33–63, esp. 56–9); Henderson (1989: 64–85); Cizek (1992); there is a bibliography for the years 1933–1978 by Kissel in *ANRW* 2.30.2 (1982: 931–2), and a brief overview by J. E. Phillips, ibid. 1001–2. The normally valuable Herkommer (1968) is unhelpful on Livy's preface.

[3] The suggestion of Luce (1965: 234–7) that the emendation is Livy's own response to criticism seems to me untenable: as Luce admits, (1) it runs counter to Quintilian's testimony and (2) hardly accords with Livy's known opinionatedness; more important (3), the hexameter opening forcefully introduces a debate about the relationship between poetry and historiography which is integral to the preface.

[4] *a primordio urbis* begins the story before the foundation of the city (cf. 7 *primordia urbium*).

[5] e.g. Hdt. *praef.*; Thuc. 1.1.1–2, 1.22.4; Polyb. 1.1.4, 1.2.8; Sall. *BC* 3.1–2, 4.3; *BJ* 4.1–4, 5.1; Diod. 1.1.1. Despite imprecise formulations, Ogilvie (1965: 24) is essentially right on Livy's deviation from the norm, *pace* Henderson (1989: 69), even though the emphasis on the task's magnitude is itself a commonplace (e.g. Thuc. 1.22.3; Sall. *BC* 3.2; Ogilvie 1970: *addenda*). In fact the closest parallels for Livy's sentiment are in various works of Cicero, especially the preface to the *Orator* (1.1–3), which conceivably influenced Livy directly (Janson 1964: 70).

this point explicit, by contrasting his own unassertiveness (*nec satis scio nec, si sciam, dicere ausim*) with the confidence (*credunt*) and competitiveness (*superaturos*) of the *novi semper scriptores*. Livy's diffidence is further emphasised by his disavowal of the *audacia/ τόλμα* normally regarded as indispensable to high literary endeavour.[6] The effect, then, of the general sentiment is in its way as surprising as that of the poetic opening rhythm. Immediately we are faced with a paradox: a modesty which forms part of a *captatio benevolentiae* designed to disarm the reader, but which is yet striking and even assertive: 'by contrast with both Tacitus and Sallust, Livy draws attention to himself straightaway: of the fourteen instances of the first-person verb, six come in the first sentence'.[7]

The familiar phrase *operae pretium est* literally means 'there is a return on the work' or 'there is a reward for trouble', but reference varies according to speaker and addressee. In the case of 'I find it worthwhile', it is my while; in 'it is worth your while', it is your while. Whose *opera* and whose *pretium*, then, are envisaged here?

On one level, the answer seems to be Livy's. Sections 1–4 make play with a standard 'work'–'pleasure' or *utile–dulce* contrast and so Livy's 'pleasure' (3 *iuvabit*) compensates for the uncertainty of his *operae pretium* (1). There are also clear verbal parallels between lines 1–2 (*facturusne... perscripserim*) and the start of section 4, and, even more so, between lines 1–2 and the start of section 5.

In the first case, *operae* in 1 parallels *operis* in 4; in lines 1–2 Livy's project consists of writing up the *res* of the Roman people from the very beginnings of the city and in section 4 the *res* is *immensi operis*, and though in this latter case the *res* is in the first instance the historian's subject, it soon 'slides' into being the thing itself—the Roman empire, so that it has similar reference to *res* in line 1. Thus the *opus/opera* seems to be Livy's.[8]

In the case of the verbal parallels between lines 1–2 and the start of section 5, *operae pretium* and *laboris praemium* look very similar, and analysis seems to substantiate the similarity. In section 5 Livy's additional (cf. *quoque*) *praemium* for his *labor* will be escape from

6  *TLL* 2.1243.8 ff., 1248.3 ff., 1256.22 ff.; Brink (1971: 92); Macleod (1977: 362 n. 14).
7  Wheeldon (1989: 56).
8  As also in 5.21.9 (quoted p. 64).

the miseries of the present; his first *praemium* is the sheer joy he will get from the task—*iuvabit* in section 3. The certainty of this joy compensates for the uncertainty of his prospects of success in section 1. So *operae pretium* in 1 must also refer to the question of what recompense Livy will get for his *opera*: a concern that he makes explicit in section 3—will he win *fama* or not?

On another level, however, the answer seems to be the reader's *opera* and *pretium*: the general context is one of appeal for the favour of the reader, and later (4) Livy considers the question of the reader's pleasure. So the 'work'–'pleasure' contrast cuts both ways: there is Livy's pleasure in section 3, but also the reader's pleasure in section 4. And this pleasure itself contrasts with the *immensum opus* of the subject matter. Both parties seem to be involved in 'work' (*opera/opus/labor*), just as both may obtain 'pleasure'. Further support for this interpretation is provided, if we accept, as we should, that in this highly poetic opening passage Livy's use of *operae pretium* evokes Ennius, one of whose fragments from the Annals reads *audire est operae pretium procedure recte | qui rem Romanam Latiumque augescere voltis* (494(465)**xlvi in Skutsch's edition), where it is the audience's *opera* and *pretium*.[9] In 1 *operae pretium* we may also hear, at any rate retrospectively, yet another voice: that of Sall. *BC* 12.3 (*operae pretium est, quom domos atque villas cognoveris in urbium modum exaedificatas, visere templa deorum, quae nostri maiores, religiosissimi mortales, fecere* ['When you contemplate houses and villas built on the model of cities, it is worthwhile to view the temples of the gods which our ancestors, the most pious of mortals, made.']),[10] where again it is the reader's *operae pretium*.

Hence *facturus... operae pretium* conveys two distinct meanings: (1) Will Livy get a worthwhile return (in glory) on all the work he will have put into writing his vast *History*? (2) Will his readers get a worthwhile return on the work they will have to put into reading it? While distinct, these meanings are complementary: a writer is rewarded when his readers feel rewarded: if they like his work, they reward him with glory.

---

[9] For Livy's opening words as a quotation from Ennius see Lundström (1915: 1–24); cf. also Liv. 3.26.7 *operae pretium est audire qui omnia prae divitiis humana spernunt* ('For those who despise all things human apart from wealth it is worthwhile to hear...').

[10] See n. 60.

This ambiguous phraseology suggests the ideal relationship between the historian and his readers, when they are, as it were, at one.
Having at the start of the preface suggested this ideal union of
historian and readers, Livy will go on to emphasize the current gulf
between the two parties and then progressively narrow that gulf.
Thus the relationship of historian and readers is a vital element in
the overall argument of the preface and it is signposted from the very
start in accordance with a common technique in classical literature,
variously called 'suspension of thought', 'putting down a marker', or
even 'anticipating a solution'.[11]

Livy explains his uncertainty abut his prospects of success by the
fact that he 'sees' that the *res*, here clearly 'the subject', is both *vetus* and
*volgata*. The general implications are clear enough. The *res* is *volgata*
because many people have treated it (a notion reinforced by 3 *turba*);
it is *vetus* because it is an 'old theme', and it largely concerns what is
literally 'ancient' history. With such material it is hard to do anything
fresh[12] or worthwhile. Here again, Livy's situation seems to be the
reverse of the norm (usually indicated by a prefatory boast of primacy
or novelty: cf. e.g. Vitruv. 5 *praef.* 1 on the novelty of historiography).

The following *dum*-clause, however, has been taken in three distinct ways: (a) as a gloss on the description *veterem... volgatam* (the
usual interpretation);[13] (b) as a further point: Livy's difficulties
(*quippe... videam*) are compounded by the fact that there will be
competition in the future from *novi scriptores* in *AUC* history
(Woodman's interpretation);[14] (c) as a further point: Livy's difficulties are compounded by the continuing competition from *novi
scriptores* in *any* historiographical field.[15]

---

[11] 'Suspension of thought': e.g. the scholars cited by Woodman (1988: 147 n. 13);
'putting down a marker' / 'anticipating a solution': Moles (1986: 37–8, 56 n. 29) and
(1990: 373 n. 125).
[12] Note that literary *audacia* (which Livy claims to lack) characteristically concerns
originality (n. 6).
[13] e.g. W–M (1965: 76): '*dum* is here not a simple temporal particle, but builds up
the explanatory force... of the indefinite *vulgatam rem*'.
[14] Woodman (1988: 130 and 151 n. 56).
[15] This interpretation is entailed by the suggestions that *novi... scriptores* alludes
to Nepos and Cicero (Budé, Bayet and Baillet 1947: 1 n. 1), or Pollio (Mazza 1966: 72;
Heurgon 1970: 22), or Sallust (Mazza 1966: 72; Girod in Chevallier 1980: 69, cf. Cizek
1992: 359). In fact, as we shall see, the idea that *novi scriptores* makes any specific
references is excluded by *semper*.

Interpretation (c) has many advocates but can be dismissed out of hand: *rebus* echoes *rem* and *res, vetustatem* echoes *veterem*. The *novi scriptores* are engaged with the same *res* as Livy himself, i.e. *AUC* history.

Interpretation (b) seems to gain support from the temporal shift from *veterem* to *novi*, but there are numerous considerations against it: (i) the link between *veterem rem* and *vetustatem*; (ii) the very reference to *rudem vetustatem* (Livy would have to be looking far into the future before that description could be applied, even pejoratively, to himself); (iii) the use of *et* in *iuvabit tamen rerum gestarum memoriae principis terrarum populi pro virili parte et ipsum consuluisse* (3), which seems to imply 'I myself also', i.e. besides the mass of *novi semper scriptores*; (iv) the phrase *in tanta scriptorum turba* (3), which obviously picks up *novi semper scriptores*, and seems to refer to a *turba* which already to some extent exists and which in some sense includes Livy; (v) the reference to the *nobilitate ac magnitudine* of those who may overshadow Livy, which reads like an allusion to the social distinction of Livy's predecessors among historians;[16] (vi) the clause *utcumque erit* at the start of 3, which is naturally taken as 'whether or not I achieve *operae pretium*', the two future tenses *facturus . . . sim* and *erit* going together. This reading is also supported by the seemingly parallel use of *utcumque* in section 8.[17] On interpretation (b), however, it would have to mean 'whether or not my suspicions of future rivalry are justified' (Woodman), which seems very forced.

What, then, of the temporal shift from *veterem* to *novi*? The key is Livy's use of *semper*. As its arresting position suggests, *semper* here functions like the Greek ἀεί or ἐξῆς sandwiched between definite article and noun. An excellent parallel is Livy 5.42.6 *nec ullum erat tempus quod a novae semper cladis alicuius spectaculo cessaret* (cited by W–M). At any point in time there are always 'new writers' of Roman history from the very beginnings. They are 'new' in relation both to the *res* itself ('ancient history') and to their predecessors. We can thus define the implications of the *dum*-clause more precisely. The *res* is *volgata* because 'new writers' in a perpetual sequence attempt to tackle it; for the same reason it is 'old hat'. Because it is

---

[16] Ogilvie (1965: 25–6); cf. in general Badian (1966: 1–38).
[17] Cf. n. 42.

*vetus* in the sense of being ancient history, one of the things the *novi* can try to do is to establish the facts more securely; because it is pretty hoary, the other thing they can do is to try to give it some modern polish.

This analysis raises another point. *vetustatem* must cover both 'old history' in the sense of ancient history—that meaning is validated by the link with *veterem*—and 'old history' in the sense of what earlier historians have written—that meaning is validated by the contrast with *novi scriptores*. Thus *vetustatem* has a double aspect: it implies the union of theme and writer, just as *operae pretium* implied the union of writer and reader. This slippage or doubleness of reference is an important aspect of the language, and hence of the thought, of the whole preface.

Livy, then, envisages three diverse ways in which historians attempt to improve on previous histories of Rome from the beginning: (1) adducing more accurate facts. This is widely recognized in ancient historiography as a standard method whereby a historian may surpass his predecessors;[18] (2) writing about old things in modern style; (3) improving upon the literary style of older historians.

An important question, however, arises: to what extent does Livy identify himself with the attitudes and techniques of the *novi semper scriptores*? In a literal sense Livy is a *novus scriptor* and obviously (as the reader will soon discover) his *History* does do the three things which the *novi semper scriptores* try to do. The very project of writing a history of Rome from the beginning implicates Livy in a tradition where his work comes into comparison with all the other treatments, past, present and future, of this hackneyed theme, and where it must justify itself to its potential readership (hence the *et* of section 3 and Livy's presence *in tanta scriptorum turba*).

Yet at the same time Livy contrives some distance between himself and the *novi semper scriptores*. He is something of an outsider looking in upon the historiographical rat-race (*videam*); as we have seen, his stated diffidence and modesty contrast sharply with the historiographical norm; and his motivation (3 *rerum gestarum memoriae ... consuluisse*)

---

[18] e.g. Hecataeus, *FGH* 1 F 1; Thuc. 1.20.3, 22.2–3; Sall. *BJ* 94.2; Tac. *Hist.* 1.1.2–3, *Ann.* 1.1.2–3. Note that Livy assumes that this is a central purpose of *some* historians, *pace* the general argument of Woodman (1988).

is public-spirited rather than competitive and individualistic (*super-aturos*). Moreover, later in the preface Livy will register alienation from the sheer idea of *novitas*, and the frenetic endeavours of the *novi semper scriptores* will find their counterpart in the perverse taste of the majority of Livy's readers for *haec nova* (4) and indeed in the accelerating collapse of the Roman state itself (9). Inevitably himself a *novus scriptor* and hence needing to impress his readers, Livy is nevertheless outside and above the general run of historians: his motivation is loftier and he will give his readers something different and something better. This is the implication beneath the surface modesty and diffidence. The argument proceeds (3):

Utcumque erit, iuvabit tamen rerum gestarum memoriae principis terrarum populi pro virili parte et ipsum consuluisse; et si in tanta scriptorum turba mea fama obscuro sit, nobilitate ac magnitudine eorum me qui nomini officient meo consoler.

Whether or not Livy will achieve *operae pretium*, he will still derive joy from having made his own personal effort to the best of his ability to foster the *memoria* of the *res gestae* of the pre-eminent nation of the world; that in itself will be a *pretium* in the absence of a more tangible *pretium* of *fama* (which is assumed to be the ancient historian's usual goal).[19] This thought is neatly pointed by ring-structure, 3 *officient* picking up 1 *facturusne*: if Livy does not 'make a return on his work' (by achieving *fama*), it will be because 'more successful historians 'make against' his *nomen*. This is the first of several verbal plays whereby *facio*-compounds articulate various factors 'making against' Livy's prospects of 'making a return on his work'. And if he does not get his *fama*, he can also console himself with the thought of the *nobilitas* and *magnitudo* of his successful rivals.

As with the description of the *novi semper scriptores*, it is difficult to resist the feeling that Livy is here being somewhat ironic, even sarcastic, about other *AUC* historians. For while on one level *in tanta scriptorum turba* echoes a phrase in Sallust's preface to the *Histories* (*Hist.* 1, fr. 3M *nos in tanta doctissumorum hominum copia* ['In so

[19] Cf. e.g. (besides the present passage) Hdt. *Praef.*; Thuc. 1.22.4; Sall. *BC* 1.1–4, 3.1–2; *BJ* 1.3, 2.4, 4.1; Plin. *Ep.* 5.8.1–2; Lucn. *Hist. Conscr.* 5. Ultimately, of course, Livy got that *fama* and freely admitted that *gloria* was part of his motivation: Plin. *NH Praef.* 16.

great a body of most learned men, we...']) and while *turba* is not *necessarily* a pejorative term, Livy's wording lacks the positively respectful tone of Sallust's and also picks up, and takes colour from, the somewhat ironic *novi semper scriptores*. Moreover, *magnitudine*, as it were within the light imagery, creates the slightly bizarre notion that these writers' sheer size will put him in the shade, and outside the light imagery it must, because of the link with *tanta turba*, suggest volume or bulk, as well as greatness. And the associations of *magnitudo* seem further undermined by the following sentence (4 *magnitudine laboret sua*).[20] There is, further, an agreeable tension in the mere idea of *nobiles* and *magni viri* comprising a *turba*. Finally, the whole sentiment *nobilitate ac magnitudine eorum me qui nomini officient meo consoler* evokes the topic of epic poetry whereby dying warriors console themselves with the thought of the greatness of their vanquishers.[21] While this evocation serves to reinforce both the analogy between Livy's *History* and epic poetry and the analogy (already suggested by *vetustatem*) between the writer of history and his theme (because Livy as historian is like the warriors about whom he is writing), it also makes another contrast with traditional historiographical claims and one not devoid of wry humour: instead of achieving immortality through his immortal work Livy runs the risk of achieving complete annihilation through failure.[22]

Yet at the same time this sentence also implies positive claims. Quite apart from the general analogies between Livy's *History* and epic and between historian and theme, the fact that, if Livy's rivals overshadow him, they will do so *nobilitate ac magnitudine* helps to give more colour to the parallel phrase *pro virili parte*, of Livy's own efforts: he has played not just his own individual part but a positively manly one (this is quite a common ambiguity of *virilis*). There is, then, much more of an analogy between the heroic quality of the

---

[20] I disagree therefore with Phillips (1982: 1002) and with Wheeldon (1989: 58), who sees in *magnitudine* the implication 'greatness of value'. See also p. 76 on 11 *maior*.

[21] For the epic topic see Harrison (1991: 268) on *Aen.* 10.829–31 and Bömer (1969–86) on Ov. *Met.* 5.191 and 10.80–1.

[22] 1 *novi semper scriptores* and 3 *nobilitate...consoler* themselves suffice to disprove Ogilvie's celebrated contention (1965: 4) that 'no touches of humour are to be found in the history'.

subject matter and the qualities of Livy the historian than his modest protestations at first sight convey. This analogy will be further strengthened by Livy's exhortation to his readers in section 9. There the reader must pay his own individual attention (*pro se quisque*) to great Roman *viri*. Livy's historical project is itself exemplary of 'virile' individual public service and, moreover, *unites* the normally opposed *utile (rerum gestarum memoriae principis terrarum populi . . . consuluisse)* and *dulce (iuvabit)*, though as yet the 'pleasure' is felt only by Livy the writer.

The first reason for Livy's uncertainty about his success was the view that the *res* is *vetus* and *volgata*; the second (*praeterea*) is the immense size of the *res*, which obviously poses severe practical difficulties for him as historian. In section 4 the *res* is in the first instance the historian's subject-matter but it then 'slides' into being the Roman state itself, which from small beginnings has now grown to the point that *magnitudine laboret sua*,[23] an unenthusiastic description that foreshadows the explicitly critical remarks at the end of this section (*se ipsae conficiunt*). Then comes a third reason for Livy's uncertainty: the majority of his readers will get less pleasure from the first origins[24] than from contemporary history, their taste for the latter clearly in Livy's opinion being altogether perverse. In the light of the Sallustian echoes and allusions throughout the preface, of the stress in the immediate context on Rome's self-destruction and of the use of

---

[23] On the slide see W–M (1965: 77) and cf. 7.29.2 'What a great series of events! How often the most extreme point of danger was reached so that our empire could extend to its current greatness, which can barely be sustained!' Note also that *iam magnitudine laboret sua*, with reference to the Roman state, subverts Sall. *BC* 53.5 *res publica magnitudine sui imperatorum atque magistratuum vitia sustentabat* ('The commonwealth by its own greatness sustained the faults of its commanders and magistrates'). Some scholars seem to see in *quae ab exigui . . . laboret sua* an allusion to the physical text (e.g. Wheeldon 1989: 58; Henderson 1989: 69); because of *iam laboret* such a reading seems to me impossible at the time when Livy was at the beginning of his vast project (even though 4 *festinantibus ad haec nova* has a (looser) proleptic function in relation to Livy's *History*), but perfectly plausible once Livy had produced several decades and indeed inevitable by the time Livy's *History* had reached the period described in *magnitudine laboret sua*. On the interpretative point see p. 67. On the general theme of Rome's organic growth see Ruch (1968: 123–31).

[24] In *primae origines proximaque originibus* one might detect a sly allusion to an already-existing treatment, Cato's *Origines*, whose aesthetic merits were disparaged by Cicero (*Leg.* 1.6, *De or.* 2.53).

*festinare* (below), there may well be an implicit allusion here to Sallust's *Histories*,[25] though this does not exclude the general contrast between ancient and contemporary history.

The use of *festinare* requires careful consideration. There are two main implications: first, that Livy's readers are readers 'in a hurry', hence the size of the *res* poses difficulties for readers as well as historian; second, that they greatly prefer to read about *haec nova*. The word also has interesting associations. It is a favourite of Sallust in the sense of speedy military or political activity and it can also imply *excessive* speed.[26] Hence the whole phrase *festinantibus ad haec nova* has almost Gadarene swine-like implications, as if of the actual participants in the civil wars, i.e. here again there is an implied slide, this time between the historical theme (specifically the real-life agents in the contemporary political drama) and its readers.

Another possible resonance stems from Cicero's use of *festinatio* in reference to his own importunate desire that his achievements of the years 63 to 58 be commemorated by the historian Lucceius (*Fam.* 5.12.1, 9).[27] Livy's acquaintance with the letter to Lucceius seems plausible, given his general interest in Cicero and in historiographical theory and given that the expression *tota mente* (5) is paralleled not only in Cic. *Clu.* 190 and *Phil.* 10.23 but also in *Fam.* 5.12.2 (*mens tota*),[28] i.e. in a context shortly after Cicero's allusion to his *festinatio*. Indeed, *tota mente* could be read as a 'flag' for a Ciceronian context.

There would then be an analogy between Cicero's 'hasty desire' for the commemoration of his own recent achievements (as opposed to Lucceius' treatment of the more remote period of the Italian and Civil wars of 90–81) and that of the majority of Livy's readers for *haec nova* (as opposed to *primae origines* etc.; note also Cicero's criticism of the tedium of *annales* [*Fam.* 5.12.6]). This analogy would suggest a

---

[25] Oppermann (1967: 171). Cf. also n. 23.
[26] Sallust: e.g. *BC* 6.5, 27.2; *BJ* 39.2, 55.3, 66.1, 76.4, 102.9; *Hist.* frr. 2.46, 4.34M; excessive speech: *TLL* 6.1.617 ff.
[27] I owe this suggestion to Ruth Morello.
[28] As noted by Woodman (1988: 151 n. 55). The availability of Cicero's correspondence in Livy's time and later is an old problem, but (a) Shackleton Bailey's case for Neronian publication of *Ad Atticum* (1965–70: i. 59–73) seems (to me) over-dismissive of earlier evidence; (b) Velleius certainly used Cicero's correspondence directly (Woodman 1983: 115); (c) even Shackleton Bailey finds the availability of *Ad fam.* much less problematic (1977: i. 24).

series of contrasts with Livy's position, which in turn would bear on fundamental questions about historiography and its purpose that are highly germane to the whole argument of the preface. Thus Cicero, like the *festinantes* and like most of the *novi semper scriptores*, seeks the *gloria* of self-commemoration in, and by, history; Livy affects not to care if his personal *fama* is overshadowed, and he proclaims history's value to be the provision of *exempla* which will make his readers better men and save the state (10). Cicero, like the *festinantes*, has an unhealthy preoccupation with the present or recent past; Livy upholds the value of the past from the very beginning. Cicero, like the *festinantes*, is a reader in a hurry, obsessed with hot news, and wants a relatively brief, self-contained, work, rather than a long one; Livy will advocate (9) critical and slow reading commensurate with the size of his subject-matter—the past from the very beginning all the way down to the present. Cicero, like the *festinantes*, derives perverse pleasure from the contemplation of *mala*, both present and past; Livy will avert his gaze from present horrors for as long as possible and will actually try to rectify them, and his pleasure will be of a loftier kind. One might even see Livy as playing the serious 'Lucceian' role as opposed to the self-interested and frivolous role of Cicero, for Livy's stress on the difficulty of his task (3 *res est... immensi operis*) has its counterpart in Cicero's description of Lucceius' project (*Fam.* 5.12.2 *neque... eram nescius quantis oneribus premerere susceptarum rerum et iam institutarum* ['I am not unaware how great a burden from projects you have undertaken and in fact started weighs on you']), a description which may well reflect Lucceius' own wording (cf. Horace's Pollio ode).

The cumulative case for allusion to Cicero's letter to Lucceius thus seems attractive and its consequences for the definition of Livy's own historical project considerable.[29] The allusion could also be given

---

[29] The letter to Lucceius raises questions about the nature of ancient historiography too large for proper consideration here. Nevertheless, whether or not Livy is responding to the letter, enough has been said to show that a major ancient historian could entertain conceptions of historiography altogether more serious and profound, alike on an intellectual, moral and emotional plane, than anything there suggested by Cicero. This analysis also suggests that the conventional picture of Livy 'the Ciceronian' requires considerable modification.

value in the context of Livy's implicit debate throughout the preface
with Sallust.[30]

The description of *haec nova* contains another *facio*-compound:
*haec nova quibus iam pridem praevalentis populi vires se ipsae con-
ficiunt.* This element of Livy's subject-matter 'makes against' his
prospects of success. This is not because it will offend his readers,
who actually like the disastrous *haec nova*, but because it pains Livy
himself, a thought which the sequel makes explicit.

Livy is absolutely confident of this unfortunate prejudice for
contemporary history on the part of the majority of his potential
readers, and his confidence on this point contrasts sharply with his
hesitations about his history's prospects of success in section 1. It
seems now as if a great gulf has opened up between historian and
readers, in contrast to the ideal union adumbrated in *operae pretium*.
His readers' perverse pleasure in contemporary history also seems
diametrically opposed to the disinterested 'joy' which Livy feels in his
task. Livy emphasizes this gulf with a further forthright pronouncement (5 *ego contra*) on a further point of difference between him and
the majority of his readers: his additional reward for his task, with the
latter's undoubtedly unpleasant aspects (*laboris* is coloured by *laboret*
in 4, cf. *conficiunt* [above]), is a temporary escape from the present to
'those old things' (*prisca illa*). The fact that the *res* is *vetus*, which in
section 2 seemed a disadvantage to be overcome, has now turned into
a positive blessing. The imagery of section 5, which is imagery of
sight (*a conspectu... vidit*), also finds its counterpart in section 3: the
public glory, the limelight, that Livy might win if his *History* proves a
success means much less to him emotionally than this immersion in
the past, temporary though it must be.

Indeed, at this point the two parties to the historical enterprise are,
as it were, travelling in precisely opposite directions, Livy towards the
very beginning of the Roman past (*prisca illa... repeto*, cf. 3 *res...
quae supra septingentesimum annum repetatur*) and his readers towards the present (*ad haec nova*), and at very different speeds, his
readers 'rushing', he lingering 'a wee while'.[31] It is another bonus that
(unlike contemporary history) early history will not be politically

---

[30] See p. 85.
[31] Ogilvie's folksy rendering (1965: 26) of the colloquial *tantisper*.

dangerous for him as writer—a consideration that obviously does
not apply to his readers, so again historian and readers seem poles
apart.[32] It is true that the phrase used of Livy's readers, *legentium
plerisque*, allows for the possibility of a select minority which does
share Livy's tastes, but this implication is relatively trivial: Livy is not
proclaiming a Callimachean elitism: he is concerned to achieve a
large readership (9). We note also here that Livy the historian
proposes to record the truth[33] and that his qualification of Sallust's
proud boast (*Hist.* 1, fr. 6M *neque me diversa pars in civilibus armis
movit a vero* ['Nor has a different side in the civil wars shifted me
from the truth']) has the effect of re-emphasising his 'modesty'.[34]
In this section, too, the use of *efficere* suggests another factor 'making
against' Livy's prospects of success: the danger attendant upon writing contemporary history. Finally, *scribentis* rings with 1 *perscripserim*, marking the end of that part of the preface which is devoted to
Livy's project in general before he moves on to enumerate the
contents of the *History* (6),[35] beginning with the pre-*AUC* material.

[32] Wheeldon (1989: 56) interprets this section rather differently: Livy creates 'in
the authorial persona itself a model of the kind of reader he would wish his audience
to imitate'; while there is something in this formulation (since Livy certainly represents his attitude here as superior to that of the majority of his readers and since his
whole 'virile' historical project has itself exemplary value (pp. 58–9, it neglects (a) the
illusory quality of the escapism here envisaged, and (b) the fact that Livy's own
'definition' of 'the past' is modified as the preface progresses.

[33] On the face of it *omnis expers curae quae scribentis animum, etsi non flectere a
vero, sollicitum tamen efficere posset* supports the thesis that truth in ancient historiography consisted largely in impartiality (Woodman 1988: 71–4, 79–80, 82–3, 86, 93,
101–2, 105–6, 111, 194, cf. also Cizek 1988: 18–20), but (a) the impartiality requirement does not exclude other requirements such as accuracy, judicious assessment of
sources etc.; (b) it is itself largely invoked in connection with contemporary or near-
contemporary history (Luce 1989: 16–31), as by Livy here, and therefore does not
apply to remoter periods. A different attempt to play down Livy's emphasis on truth
is that of Wheeldon (1989: 56 n. 63): 'Livy's claim to veracity arises almost *en passant*,
perhaps indicating a desire to seem not to protest the claim too much.' But, as will
become clear, Livy's truth claim is given ever more weight as the preface proceeds.

[34] In the event Livy may have been deterred by *sollicitudo* to the extent of
postponing publication of Books 121–42 until after Augustus' death, but I cannot
go into that insoluble question. What matters in this context is that the preface does
commit Livy to going down to 'the present' at the time of writing.

[35] While section 6 begins the enumeration of contents, it is linked thematically in a
number of ways with 4–5. The discussion of pre-*AUC* material arises naturally from
the allusion in 4 to the distaste of the majority of his readers for *primae origines* (if not
pleasurable, such material has at least the positive quality of making *augustiora* the

Livy intends neither to affirm nor to refute traditions about the pre-foundation period, which are more *decora* to *poeticae fabulae* than to history. *decora* is used of what is generically appropriate, though connotations of beauty are also relevant. The contrast here between poetry and historiography seems to reactivate the problem posed by Livy's opening words, with their dactylic rhythm and apparent allusion to Ennius.

There is a fundamental implication here: the history, as opposed to the *fabulae*, will be true, and true in the most basic sense: factually true.[36] This implication is confirmed by 5.21.9, where Livy introduces a *fabula* into the narrative in words that echo the present section of the preface: *sed in rebus tam antiquis si quae similia veris sint pro veris accipiantur, satis habeam; haec ad ostentationem scenae gaudentis miraculis aptiora quam ad fidem neque adfirmare neque refellere est operae pretium* ('But this story has more of the miracle-working one sees on the stage than credibility and is not worth my taking the trouble to affirm or refute').

The basic distinction between *poeticae fabulae* and *incorrupta rerum gestarum monumenta* has been acclaimed by some scholars as novel and original.[37] It is certainly different from the robust dismissiveness of Sempronius Asellio (fr. 2 *HRR*: *id fabulas pueris narrare, non historias scribere* ['that is to tell stories to boys, not to write history']). But Livy's stance is recognisably part-Thucydidean—in the distinction between 'myth'/poetry and history (Thuc. 1.21.2, 1.22.4)—and part-Herodotean—in the refusal to pass judgement on 'what is said' / *fabulae* (Hdt. 1.5.3, 7.152.3). This invocation of the two greatest historians among Livy's predecessors in the whole field of historiography already implies great claims for his own history.

Livy's description of historical works—6 *incorruptis rerum gestarum monumentis*—also has important implications. Though the description is general, clearly Livy's own *History* belongs in this category, and in so far as *incorruptis* suggests both imperishable and truthful, Livy approaches the Herodotean claim of an immortal ἀπόδεξις and the

*primordia urbium*), from the allusion to *prisca illa* in 5, and from the implication, in his allusion to contemporary history (5), that he is concerned to record the truth (so is the pre-*AUC* material true and does its truth matter?).

[36] Cf. also n. 33.
[37] e.g. Ferrero (1949: 19 n. 1); Mazza (1966: 91 n. 18).

Thucydidean claim of a κτῆμα ἐς ἀεί: his initial modesty is further undermined. And in so far as *incorruptis . . . monumentis* also suggests 'uncontaminated' in a medical sense, it anticipates both the medical imagery and the crucial historical and historiographical claims of sections 9–10.

As for the *fabulae*, they should be viewed with indulgence (7), an indulgence which allows two licences, the second a particularization of the first: (1) ancient history[38] has the right to make foundings of cities more august[39] by mingling human and divine. Within the economy of Livy's use of *facio* and *facio*-compounds in this preface, *faciat* here has real force. Granted the relative insignificance of such material in truly historical terms, it remains a plus if a historical work can include the mingling of human and divine.[40] (2) If any people has the right to trace its origins back to divine authors, all-conquering Rome has the right to trace its origin back to Mars, so that the nations of the world may as well bear (*patiantur*) this, just as they bear (*patiuntur*) the Roman *imperium* itself. The second of these licences may seem curiously emphatic, but it foregrounds the 'martial' element of the Roman character and it sets up a hierarchy: humans in general; the rest of the human race; the Roman imperial race; the gods; and it also provides a thumb-nail sketch of the history of Rome from its divine origins to the foundation, its expansion and present position as mistress of the world apparently under divine protection. (So in one sense it is a spelling-out of the implications of the phrase *principis terrarum populi* in section 3.)

A problem remains with this section: what is the relationship between Livy's principle for dealing with pre-*AUC*[41] *fabulae* (*nec adfirmare nec refellere*) and the belief of some of the *novi semper scriptores* (*in rebus certius aliquid allaturos*)? That Livy himself is

[38] *antiquitati* has the same double reference as 3 *vetustatem*, = both 'ancient history' and 'ancient historians'.

[39] The thesis of Coppola (1983–4: 67–70), that 7 *augustiora . . . auctores* and 9 *auctum* allude to Augustus must be rejected, not only because an honorific allusion to Augustus in the preface would sit ill with the emphasis on contemporary crisis, but also because of the explicit reference to *Augustus* in 1.19.3, especially if that reference is a later insertion (p. 69), which would entail a pre-27 date for the preface.

[40] Cic. *De inv.* 1.23 recommends this mingling as a way of securing the favourable attention of readers (Ogilvie 1965: 27).

[41] And sometimes post-*AUC fabulae*: 5.21.9 (quoted p. 64).

generally committed to the recording of *certiora* is explicit in the second preface at the beginning of Book 6 (6.1.3 *certiora . . . exponentur*) and consistent with the various truth claims made in this preface (5, 6, 10). But this passage makes it clear that the attainment of *certius aliquid* is impossible with pre-*AUC* material and Livy re-emphasises the point in 1.3.2, in connection with the question of the relationship between Ascanius/Iulus and the *gens Iulia*, in words that recall section 2 of the preface: *haud ambigam—quis enim rem tam veterem pro certo adfirmet?–hicine fuerit Ascanius an maior quam hic* ('I will not debate–for who could establish the truth of a matter so ancient?–whether the boy in question was this Ascanius or an older brother'). Of course to say that *certius aliquid* is unattainable in pre-*AUC* history is not to deny the validity of the whole process. Nevertheless, one of the rhetorical effects of this section must be to suggest that the quest for *certius aliquid* is a secondary consideration. In this respect also Livy contrives to present himself as different from some of the conventional *novi scriptores*.

Livy then (8), in one of the many ring structures of the preface, reaffirms his relative indifference to the truth question about these pre-foundation traditions and others like them.[42] The heavy stress in this section on the truth question about pre-*AUC fabulae* and Livy's elaborate profession of non-judgement on it combine to create another rhetorical effect: that is, to make readers forget that they simply dislike all this old stuff (4). They will thus pay greater heed to Livy's exhortation to ignore the truth question and to turn their individual attention[43] to *illa . . . quae vita, qui mores fuerint* etc. (another Ennian allusion).[44] In so doing, the reader will be behaving

---

[42] 8 *utcumque* corresponds structurally to 3 *utcumque* and fulfils the same function: to characterize the preceding material as relatively unimportant by comparison with what follows.

[43] 9 *intendat animum* and *sequatur animo* contrast with 8 *animadversa* and 6 *nec . . . in animo*, thus distinguishing between the things to which one should direct one's mind and those to which one should not. *Pace* Cizek (1992: 352), these *animus*-contrasts, and the parallel and contrast between *pro se quisque* and 3 *pro virili parte et ipsum consuluisse*, exclude any formal allusion here to the historian (though of course Livy the historian will in fact have to do this).

[44] To the famous *moribus antiquis res stat Romana virisque* ('The Roman state stands on the ways and men of old', 156(500)**1 Sk). This allusion helps to anticipate the subsequent Rome/building imagery. On the four pillars of Roman greatness—*vita, mores, viri,* and *artes*—see Ruch (1967) and (1968).

like Livy himself, for Livy has withdrawn temporarily from the contemplation of modern horrors to *prisca illa* (section 5) and made his own individual effort (*pro se quisque* in section 9 balances the *pro virili parte et ipsum* of section 3). Thus by a sort of sleight of hand Livy has conned the unsympathetic reader into adopting his own viewpoint. This effect is further assisted by the following survey of the whole *Aufstieg und Niedergang*, which, through its elaborate building metaphor, invites the reader to see Roman history as a continuous process, without the polarized distinction between old and new. Yet by the end of this survey Livy has himself to some extent shifted his own ground, in as much as his whole historical analysis will be geared to demonstrating the differences between the past and the present and highlighting the various stages of decline down to the present day: the past will be a mirror for the present, the present for the past—Livy will not in fact be shying away from full engagement with contemporary history. The escapism of section 5 has turned out to be a feint. Thus a sort of compromise has been achieved between the initially sharply divergent tastes of the historian and the majority of his readers.

The description of the disastrous present (*quibus... perventum est*) re-employs, and develops, the medical metaphor of section 4. Problems of interpretation and dating now become acute. What period does *haec tempora* refer to? What are the *remedia* for the *vitia*?

These questions raise fundamental issues about the interpretation of ancient texts 'in their historical context'. Henderson has had legitimate fun with traditionalist attempts to reconstruct, date, and thereby interpret, various stages of composition in Livy's *Ab urbe condita*, and with the various circularities often implicit in such attempts, particularly in relation to the lost books.[45] I agree—and I disagree. If Livy 1–5 has a given set of implications for its first readership and cannot have exactly the same implications for later readers, this is not to say that the implications it will have for the latter are valueless: a text is a text is a text. But if we can show that a particular portion of text was written at a particular time, then it may be the case that at that time it would have had to be read in a particular way. And such a finding would be of some interest and

---

[45] Henderson (1989).

some value: it would be *part* of the text's meaning—part of its meaning, because it would be absurd to claim that a text could only have meaning at a particular point in time. On the other hand, we can surely say that a particular piece of text has more meaning at a particular time: in a disquisition on British politics a passing allusion to toe-jobs meant more in 1992 than it would have done to earlier or later readers.[46] And in 'perpetual' works, like Livy's *Ab urbe condita* or Plutarch's *Lives*, there are bound to be tensions between topical and timeless meanings, and there are bound to be occasions when the writer redefines his earlier prospectuses (as e.g. in the second preface at 6.1.1–3).[47]

Livy's first pentad falls within the broad *termini* of *c.*35 (when Sallust died, leaving his *Histories* unfinished) and 25 (when Augustus closed the temple of Janus for the second time). The traditional view is that 27 is a *terminus post*, because of Livy's allusions to Augustus at 1.19.3 (his first closing of Janus) and 4.20.5–11 (the discussion of the *spolia opima*), but Luce,[48] following some earlier scholars, has argued that these two passages are later insertions. On the other hand, many scholars have seen *implicit* post-Actium allusions in the narrative of 1–5.

What, then, are the possibilities? On the traditional dating, *remedia* is generally taken as a reference to Augustus' failed marriage legislation of 28,[49] but Badian[50] has argued against that legislation's historicity. Woodman argues that *haec tempora* here denotes the civil-war period, that the preface and 1–5 are pre-Actium, and that the *remedia* are code for one-man rule, which is often imaged as the only cure for Rome's civil-war ills.[51] Unlike Woodman, Haehling accepts the traditional post-27 dating, but like him, he rejects any allusion to Augustus' alleged marriage legislation (though he believes it historical), and like Woodman he sees a reference to one-man rule.[52]

---

[46] I deliberately leave this reference unexplained: the fact that it will mean nothing to those unfamiliar with 'revelations' made in 1992 by the British gutter press is precisely the point.

[47] Kraus (1994*a*: Introduction).

[48] Luce (1965: 209–40).

[49] Following Dessau (1903) and W–M (1965: 80).

[50] Badian (1985: 82–98).

[51] Woodman (1988: 132–4 and nn. 65–79 on 152–4); Woodman does not commit himself on the question of the historicity of the attempted marriage legislation.

[52] Haehling (1989: 19, 213–15).

One has to choose. Luce's arguments for 1.19.3 and 4.20.5–11 as later insertions seem to me convincing. On the other hand, there are other, apparently non-detachable, passages in 1–5 which look post-27: 3.66–70 (the speech of T. Quinctius Capitolinus and the subsequent agreement by his colleague, Agrippa Furius, that Quinctius should have the chief *imperium*), a case analysed by Haehling and Briscoe,[53] is particularly challenging, and of course the portrayal of Camillus has often been seen as suggestively Augustan. Personally, I am not convinced by Badian's claimed demolition of Augustan marriage legislation in 28.[54] On the other hand, in our text *haec tempora* picks up the apocalyptic *iam* and *ad haec nova* of section 4, and a reference in any of these contexts to the failure of Augustus' marriage legislation would be both pathetic and bathetic. But this need not entail an actual civil-war dating. Livy surely could have written in such pessimistic terms even after Actium, just as Horace does, for example in *Odes* 3.6, because 'the present' can be a fairly elastic term when the perspective is the whole of Roman history from the foundation of the city,[55] and because, although Actium was indeed a decisive turning-point, the 20s were in fact a very tense political era.

If, then, reference to Augustan marriage legislation is excluded, the only concrete possibility that remains is one-man rule. Woodman and Haehling have produced positive arguments for this interpretation: (a) *remedium* is explicitly used of one-man rule in 3.20.8 and 22.8.5, both of which appear closely parallel to the present context; (b) Tac. *Ann.* 1.9.4 *non aliud discordantis patriae remedium fuisse quam ut ab uno regeretur* ('There had been no other cure for warring fatherland than that it be ruled by one man.') suggests that Tacitus understood Livy's preface in this way; (c) the metaphor of the sickness of the state and the consequent need for a single 'doctor' was extensively employed in the civil-war period.

---

[53] Haehling (1989: 191–215); Briscoe (1990: 195–7 [reviewing Haehling]).

[54] Nor is Williams (1990: 267 n. 19): 'his [Badian's] argument needs (and will receive) a reply'.

[55] Haehling (1989: 20 [without specific reference to the present passage]) reasonably regards 'the present' for Livy as consisting of the period between Caesar's dictatorship and the late 20s.

The case is a good one and can in my view be decisively strengthened from within the preface. For Livy's use of the verb *pati* surely
links with section 7: *patiantur... patiuntur*. That section, as we have
seen, sketched a hierarchical pyramid: gods and humans in general
intermixed at the beginning of time, foundation of Rome, humans
ruled by Rome, rule which they must 'bear', Rome the ruling power,
the gods above them and validating Roman rule. But in section 9 the
Roman state and the whole Roman empire are falling to bits, there
seems no prospect of divine aid, and yet the Romans cannot 'bear'
the *remedia* which would cure their sickness. What is required, then,
is another tier in the hierarchical pyramid, which the Romans must
'bear', just as their subjects 'bear' the Roman empire. A reference to
monarchy provides the requisite final link in the chain of command.
The repetitions of the verb *patior* seem to me to guarantee this
interpretation.[56]

Yet an important question remains (though it is rarely asked by
scholars): is monarchy the *only* remedy Livy has in mind, i.e. is
*remedia* a true plural or not? Section 10 gives the answer.

*hoc illud; hoc* refers forward, *illud* back in a general way to section 9,
whose moral implications Livy now brings out in detail. The juxta-
position and similarity of reference of 'this' and 'that', pronouns
which normally contrast and which have indeed been pointedly
differentiated earlier in the preface (4–5, 8–9), suggest the coherence
and unity of the moral programme to be announced. Livy now
addresses the reader in 2nd-person singulars, which replace the 3rd-
persons of section 4. We note the progression from the matter-of-fact
3rd-person plurals of section 4, to 3rd-person singulars of the individual in section 9, to 1st-person plurals at the end of 9, and now to
2nd-person singular. Thus Livy stresses the moral implications for his
readers in a direct personal appeal to the individual, an appeal,

---

[56] This chapter is concerned with the interpretation of the preface rather than with
problems of dating, but, since the former cannot be entirely divorced from the latter,
I should perhaps clarify my position on chronology: (a) Book 1 and hence the preface
are pre-27 (because 1.19.3 is an insertion); (b) the references in the preface to *haec
tempora* and the *remedium* of monarchy do not guarantee a pre-Actium dating; (c)
Book 1 cannot be much earlier than 2–5 (1–5 being in some sense a unit); (d) there
are post-27 elements in 2–5; (e) I have to conclude that Book 1 was originally
published separately, in (say) 29–28. A less messy picture emerges if one jettisons
(d), but I do not think one can.

moreover, so framed as to overturn the distinction between self-interest and national interest (in *tibi tuaeque rei publicae, publicae* unexpectedly redefines *tuae rei*; we remember Kitchener's notorious appeal: YOUR country needs YOU).

While the view of the function of history here—the provision of useful *exempla*, the good to imitate, the bad to shun—is conventional (e.g. Polyb. 2.61.3, Diod. 1.1.2–4, Tac. *Ann.* 3.65.1, and often in biography),[57] it is integral to the whole argument of the preface. Pleasure is a legitimate part of historiography—both for the writer (section 3) and for the reader (section 4)—but there is another *operae pretium* for the reader in the *salubre ac frugiferum* of *AUC* history. This imagery contrasts starkly with the imagery applied to the sick Roman state, but Livy is not now saying, as he seemed to be saying in section 5, that history provides salutary escapism: rather, history provides the healthful lessons which, along with the therapeutic imposition of monarchy, will cure the Roman state, provided that each individual plays his part. Again, Livy has greatly modified his own initial stance. It is now also clear that *remedia* in 9 was a true plural, alluding both to one-man rule and to the moral value of *AUC* history. The claim that 'we cannot bear the *remedium* of the knowledge of *AUC* history' might seem implausible, but that this is Livy's implication is supported not only by the imagery of *salubre ac frugiferum*, but also by the verbal parallel between *praecipites . . . ad haec tempora* in section 9 and section 4's *festinantibus ad haec nova*. The immoral identification of readers with the narratives of contemporary political disasters, and hence with the disasters themselves, must give way to identification with good *exempla* and alienation from bad ones. This will represent the right union of writer, reader, and subject-matter.[58]

---

[57] Chronology prevents Livy's *monumentum* from being influenced by the Forum Augustum, with its statues and *elogia* of great Romans of the past; rather, these *elogia* in some respects contested Livy's version of events: Luce (1990: 123–38). On the other hand, the common observation that Livy's 'exemplary' *History* accords with the general *Zeitgeist* is reasonable, provided that it does not obscure the fact that section 10 is the culmination of a complex argument.

[58] 10.31.15 'What man would find it wearisome to write or read the long duration of wars that did not tire those who fought them?' is a good parallel for the tripartite union of writer, reader, and historical agent.

The imagery *omnis... intueri* is also rich in implication. In so far as *AUC* history is a *monumentum* (the imagery picks up section 6), its 'commemorative' aspect has two functions: (a) to 'commemorate' the achievements of past generations; (b) to 'admonish' present and future generations.[59] In so far as it is an abiding monument, its solidity will help shore up the collapsing edifice of the Roman state—the message is the same as that conveyed by the health imagery.[60] And the fact that it is a *monumentum* which displays *every kind of exemplum* and to which *every individual among Livy's readers* should direct his gaze creates several implications: (a) the *monumentum* has to be taken as a whole: it allows neither self-indulgent escapism into the past, nor concentration only on what is good (this in implicit rejection of Livy's own attitude in section 5: *ut me a conspectu malorum quae nostra tot per annos vidit aetas... dum prisca illa tota mente repeto, avertam*), nor an unhealthy preoccupation with *haec nova* (section 4). (b) It makes a moral demand of each and every individual. (c) It should also evoke an intense emotional response, as in Sallust, *BJ* 4.5 *nam saepe ego audivi Q. Maxumum, P. Scipionem, praeterea civitatis nostrae praeclaros viros solitos ita dicere, quom maiorum imagines intuerentur, vehementissime sibi animum ad virtutem adcendi* ('For I have often heard that Q. Maximus and P. Scipio and also other distinguished men of our community used to say that, when they gazed at the images of their ancestors, their spirit burned intensely for prowess'), a passage surely in Livy's mind.[61] (d) This *monumentum*, in all its diversity, is the thing towards which one should direct one's gaze—not just *prisca illa* after withdrawal from *conspectu malorum quae nostra tot per annos*

[59] Mazza (1966: 92 n. 19) well cites Cicero *ap.* Non., 47L 'But I am reminded by the very word what the reason is for a monument: it ought to look to the future's memory of the past more than the good will of the present'.

[60] We should also, I believe, at some level hear the voice of Sall. *BC* 12.3 (quoted p. 53), with its contrast between 'decadent' modern buildings and the temples of old.

[61] Note also Cicero's use of *intueor* in the letter to Lucceius (*Fam.* 5.12.5 'For everybody else, however, who has had no part in anything troublesome but look on (*intuentibus*) others' misfortunes without any suffering, even pity is pleasurable'): if Livy's allusion to the letter is granted (p. 60), there would be further contrasts between Livy's conception of history and that there advocated by Cicero: serious moral contemplation and intense moral identification replace an emotional arousal which is merely pleasurable and which partly depends on alienation.

*vidit aetas* (section 5), nor just the 'bright light' of glory which the successful historian can expect to achieve (section 3): those things are legitimate but trivial and partial: one should be looking at the whole picture, and in this context 'the whole picture' is *AUC* history.

Finally, this *monumentum* has a double aspect.[62] On the one hand, it is *AUC* history in the abstract, whose moral lessons the present corrupt generation must 'bear' if they are to be cured of their ills; on the other hand, as we have all learned, 'il n'y a pas d'hors-texte', or in Livy's own words (6.1.2) *litterae... una custodia fidelis memoriae rerum gestarum* ('Writing... the one sure guardian of the memory of past actions.'). The *monumentum*, then, is *also* Livy's *Ab urbe condita* itself, product of the process *rerum gestarum memoriae principis terrarum populi consuluisse* (section 3), exemplar of the general category *incorruptis rerum gestarum monumentis* (section 6) and Livy's own *negotium* (section 11) or *opus* (13, cf. 4), a term which itself can gloss *monumentum*, or *res* (12, where *rei* = both 'Roman history' and 'my History').

Word play based on *capio* seems to delineate the again separate but complementary roles of historian and reader. Each has made his 'choice of life'. The historian has chosen (11 *suscepti) litterae* (which, however, in this context, represent not *otium*, but *negotium*); the reader has chosen an active life within the *res publica* (10); within the life of the *res publica*, the reader has further crucial moral 'choices' to make, based on the material the historian has provided for him. In the first place, he must 'choose' to rank history's exemplary value highest among its various qualities (10 *praecipue*); in the second place, he must direct his own behaviour by the examples of history, 'choosing' (*capias*) examples beneficial to himself and the *res publica*, avoiding examples repugnant both in their initial 'moral choice' (*inceptu*) and in their consequences.

The historian for his part has turned the *monumentum* of *AUC* history in the abstract, the raw material of section 4 (*res... quae... sua*), into a *monumentum* which teaches (*documenta*) by providing paradigms of behaviour, which exhibits order (*posita*), and is *illustre* not only because it is the 'big picture', the subject most worthy of contemplation, not only because for him the 'light' of his history

[62] Cf. Wheeldon (1989: 59); Cizek (1992: 356).

matters far more than the 'bright light' of personal glory, but because the historian's essential task is to uncover—and to create—light, or clarity. For this process too has a double aspect. Ultimately, truth is a matter of sight, what can be seen by the historian himself and his contemporaries (cf. 2 *videam*, 5 *nostra... vidit aetas*), or what has been seen by reliable witnesses in the past and faithfully transmitted in the historical tradition (6 *incorruptis rerum gestarum monumentis traduntur*). But to convey this truth to his readers the historian has to put it under the light, to highlight it, so that they in turn can see it, or, sometimes, feel it, more clearly. It is important in this context to resist Woodman's exclusively 'aesthetic' interpretation of historiographical canons such as σαφής, ἐνάργεια, *clarus*.[63] Livy here is surely imitating Thucydides, who applies the process of σκοπεῖν both to himself (explicitly at 1.1.3, implicitly at 1.22.2–3) and to his readers (1.21.2 and 1.22.4), and behind the words *inlustri monumento intueri* lie (besides Sall. BC 4.5)[64] τὸ σαφὲς σκοπεῖν... κτῆμα ἐς ἀεί ('to see clearly... a possession for all time'). Similarly, the second preface at the beginning of book 6 (6.1.1–3) uses the vocabulary of light and darkness to make a strong truth-claim in direct imitation of Thucydides.[65]

[63] Woodman (1988: 25–8, 30, 59–60, 89–90, 108 [restricting such ideas to 'vivid', 'probable', 'realistic']). I do not deny that descriptions exhibiting such qualities are *in fact* very often merely imaginative reconstructions or that *sub oculos subiectio (vel sim.)* was a recognised rhetorical technique often exploited by ancient historians, as by others, or that the implications of ancient historians' rendering their narratives in visual terms can be very complex, cf. e.g. Hartog (1980), tr. J. Lloyd (1988); Davidson (1991: 10–24 [whose insights could usefully be retrojected to earlier historians and applied also to aspects of Livy]); Feldherr (1991); Morgan (1993: 184–5 [on Duris of Samos]). I do, however, argue that sometimes (as in Livy here and in 6.1.1–3 [n. 65] and in Thuc. 1.22.4) the use of light/sight words makes a strong and serious truth-claim. See my 'Truth and untruth in Herodotus and Thucydides' in Gill and Wiseman (1993: 107 and 109–10).

[64] Cf. Kraus (1994a) on 6.14.2 for other historiographical examples of *intueri*.

[65] *Quae ab condita urbe Roma ad captam eandem Romani sub regibus primum, consulibus deinde ac dictatoribus decemvirisque ac tribunis consularibus gessere, foris bella, domi seditiones, quinque libris exposui, res cum vetustate nimia obscuras, velut quae magno ex intervallo loci vix cernuntur* [cf. Thuc. 1.1.3], *tum quod parvae et rarae per eadem tempora litterae fuere, una custodia fidelis memoriae rerum gestarum, et quod, etiam si quae in commentariis pontificum aliisque publicis privatisque erant monumentis, incensa urbe pleraeque interiere. clariora deinceps certioraque ab secunda origine velut ab stirpibus laetius feraciusque renatae urbis gesta domi militiaeque exponentur.* For discussion see W–M and Kraus (1994a: *ad loc*). It is important to understand the nature of Livy's 'redefinition' of his project in this passage: he has changed the *application* of his terminology, not the terminology itself, whose implications remain constant.

In important senses, therefore, it may be said that for Livy *AUC* history *is* his own work, the *Ab urbe condita*, and that in reconstructing Roman history he is in a moral sense reconstructing contemporary Rome.[66] By this stage Livy is in effect making tremendous claims not only for the value of *AUC* history in general but also for his work in particular, 'a possession for all time' of Thucydidean greatness on several levels, but incomparably greater than Thucydides' work in the enormity of its moral and political potential.

So much in purely historiographical terms. But the marked poetic and Ennian aspects of the preface (1, 9, 13 [below]) must suggest the possibility of another important resonance. And it seems virtually certain that in Book 16 of his *Annales* Ennius (in Skutsch's words) 'contrasted the transient nature of fame based on the monuments with the eternal glory which his poetry would bestow on his heroes'.[67] Moreover, there is a strong possibility that in some context Ennius actually used the word *monumentum* of that immortal poetry.[68] It is, therefore, exceedingly likely that in characterizing his work as an imperishable *monumentum* (10, 6), Livy is imitating—and trumping—Ennius' claims for his *Annales*.

But because these tremendous claims for his own work are only one element, although a complex element, in a dense, composite, overall meaning, they are much less strident, much less vainglorious, than the historiographical norm, and they are therefore both more insidious and more persuasive. (More persuasive, that is, if you see that they are being made, as many scholars do not.) Nevertheless, the majesty of Livy's claims and the deep seriousness of his purpose dwarf the petty ambitions and concerns of the *novi semper scriptores* of section 2: Livy has indeed something profoundly different and incomparably greater to offer his readers. While *novi semper scriptores* come and go, his history will be a *monumentum* for ever.

*ceterum* (11): the logic is: 'I ended section 10 by stressing the foul deterrent examples provided by history, especially recent history, but

---

[66] Cf. Wheeldon (1989: 59).

[67] Skutsch (1985: 568).

[68] Cf. Lucr. 5.311 *monimenta virum dilapsa*, 328–9 *facta virum... aeternis famae monimentis* (cited by Skutsch 1985: 568 as illustrative of the Ennian motif), Hon. *C.* 3.30.1 *exegi monumentum aere perennius* (!), with Lucr. 1.117–18 *Ennius... perenni fronde coronam*, 121 *Ennius aeternis... versibus.*

in fact Roman history provides an overwhelming preponderance of good examples and it is only recently that vices have predominated.' Here Livy tacitly rejects the possibility that love of his task has distorted his view of Rome's virtues. All the stress falls on the second *aut*-clause, which introduces the theme of Rome's moral greatness— *moral* greatness, for *maior* redefines the negative implications of 4 *magnitudine laboret sua*, just as *bonis exemplis ditior* offers, proleptically, a moral redefinition of 'riches' in place of *divitiae* (12) in the literal sense.

Nevertheless, in section 11 Sallustian pessimism has the last word and by the middle of section 12 we are back on the theme of universal Roman self-destruction and destruction (the wording picking up that of section 4). There is of course no inconsistency here: it is precisely because of the dreadful present that everybody has to direct their attention to the whole expanse of Roman history, which can provide the necessary *bona exempla*. But there has again been something of a shift in the argument: olden times have again been redefined: they began as a disadvantage for the historian to overcome (*veterem rem ... rudem vetustatem*), they then became a source of escapist comfort (section 5), they now have positive moral value as being particularly rich in good *exempla*, and their scope has been considerably enlarged: section 11 is about Rome's past but it is a past which extends nearly into the present. So there has been a yet further blurring of the initial *prisca (vetus)* ∼ *nova* polarity.

This heavily Sallustian context[69] seems to crystallize the earlier Sallustian 'markers'. Why, then, is *ambitio*, so prominent in Sallust's analysis of Roman decline, absent from the list of recent 'immigrant' vices? Is this a case of *imitatio cum aemulatione* ('imitation combined with rivalry')?[70] Doubtless, but an explanation which in itself has no content. Is it because Livy was a hill-billy who did not, could not, attach much significance to *ambitio*?[71] That would make him an imbecile. The real reason is that on Livy's historical analysis *ambitio* came, not *sera*, but as early as the reign of Tarquinius Priscus, an

---

    [69] Ogilvie (1965: 27–8); Sall. *BC* 7–12; *BJ* 4.5, 41.2, etc.
    [70] Woodman (1988: 131).
    [71] Ogilvie (1965: 24 [his second paragraph: this is strangely inconsistent with his first paragraph, which states the essential truth]).

immigrant into Rome (cf. 11 *immigraverint*, 12 *invexere*), who, amidst other demagogic behaviour, *primus...petisse ambitiose regnum* ('the first to canvass for the throne', 1.35.2): the absence of *ambitio* from the preface and its presence in the body of Book 1 is itself, therefore, a fine illustration of the historical programme set out in section 10, which requires Roman history to be seen as a continuous process, past illuminating present and vice versa. The *ambitio* which was a major factor in the revolutions of the late Republic came early, and so even early history may reflect upon contemporary history. This pointed transference of Sallust's *ambitio*-motif also functions as a cogent proof of the gross oversimplification in Sallust's analysis of Roman decline: Livy is engaging in a sharp implicit debate with Sallust, and this too is important to the overall argument. The preface ends (12–13):

> Sed querellae, ne tum quidem gratae futurae cum forsitan necessariae erunt, ab initio certe tantae ordiendae rei absint: cum bonis potius ominibus votisque et precationibus deorum dearumque, si, ut poetis, nobis quoque mos esset, libentius inciperemus, ut orsis tantum operis successus prosperos darent.

The thought of the first sentence is perfectly clear: enough of *querellae*, especially at the beginning of the *History*: they may be necessary to emphasize the dreadful dangers of the present political situation but they will not give pleasure (*gratae*); instead—and there follows the last sentence of the preface. Such an invocation to the gods, even if hypothetical, is unparalleled in historical prefaces and hence highly challenging.[72]

Livy makes a sort of link between poetry and history—*si, ut poetis, nobis quoque mos esset*, then we would start off with good omens, prayers etc. He does not say that is the *mos* (because it was not) nor does he say that he is beginning with the prayers (he does not). On the other hand, he has expressed enough *querellae* (a characteristic, as Woodman has shown, of a certain general tradition in ancient historiography, and one to which Sallust, imitated in sections 11–12,

[72] Oppermann's widely accepted interpretation (1967: 179), that Livy is appealing, via Virg. *Geo.* 1.21–40, to Octavian, is untenable, (a) because of the plurality of reference of *deorum dearumque* (which echoes section 7), (b) because of 1.19.3 (pp. 81–2): Augustus is distinct from the gods.

certainly belongs);[73] and the hypothetical alternative to *querellae* receives considerable stress. Up to *dearumque* the reader must suppose that Livy is actually going to begin with prayers, and a lot of them, not just a quick invocation to the Muse, but then the *si*-clause raises a doubt, yet then in turn the *ut*-clause seems to give the hypothetical a certain substantiality.[74] Indeed, it is precisely because this sentence hovers between the hypothetical and the actual that it is so rich in implication.

Besides the obvious parallel with the practice of epic poets, there are other formal considerations to take into account: Livy is alluding to the religious formula *absit/abesto omen*—the *querellae* are 'bad omens'. It may also be relevant that it was the *mos antiquus* of early Roman orators to begin speeches with invocations to the gods (Servius on *Aen.* 11.301) and it is certainly relevant that such invocations were regular practice at the start of great enterprises.[75] Furthermore, the sentence obviously makes a neat transition from the bad present to the good beginning of Roman history. None of this, however, addresses the essential problems.

Livy cannot align poetry and historiography directly because they *are* different things: in section 6 he himself has distinguished them. On the other hand, there was an ancient debate about their relationship and some critics all but asserted their identity.[76] Livy himself begins the preface with a virtual hexameter, as Sallust had done in the *Jugurthine war* (*BJ* 1.5, 5.1) and Tacitus was to do in the *Annals* (1.1.1), and Thucydides had done at 1.21.1 (a passage which picks up the beginning of the preface through ring structure). Hexameters are the metre of epic, epics are about war, Thucydides, Livy and Tacitus write about war, Thucydides, like Herodotus, to some extent sees Homer as his literary model, etc. etc.[77] One can make some sense of the poetry-historiography link in general terms. More specifically, almost certainly in Livy and perhaps also in Tacitus, at the precise point when they are talking about very early Rome, there is direct

[73] Woodman (1988: 40–4, 125–8, 205–6); cf. e.g. Sall. *BJ* 4.9.
[74] Cf. Cizek (1992: 358): 'even though he says that he does not invoke the gods, Livy does so, precisely in expressing his regrets in this regard.'
[75] Ogilvie (1965: 29), cf. Livy 22.9.7; 38.48.14; 45.39.10.
[76] Woodman (1988: 99–100, 114–16).
[77] Cf. e.g. Strasburger (1972: 1057–97); Woodman (1988: 1–7, 23–4, 40–51).

imitation of Ennius, the great epic poet of early Roman history; the Roman annalistic tradition was much influenced by the epics of Ennius and Naevius; and in Livy this Ennian imitation also helps bring out the double application of *operae pretium*. But none of this really explains section 13, especially after the distinction made in section 6.

One point must be that Livy is making something of the old distinction, already prominent in the preface, between usefulness/work and pleasure, *querellae* are more characteristic of gritty Sallustian contemporary history—perhaps indispensable but certainly depressing; let us at least begin with a bit more pleasure (for it is implied that Livy's alternative procedure *will* promote *gratia*): hence the associations of poetry, a more 'literary' form than historiography, more beautiful, more pleasurable etc.; cf. 6 *decora*. It is true that historiography is both pleasurable and useful, but if you want to play up the pleasurable element, it is appropriate to invoke poetry, the form more naturally associated with it. In one sense, then, Livy is here readjusting the balance slightly towards the 'escapist' pleasure of history that he treated in sections 3 and 5, a pleasure which is obviously more legitimate when one is dealing with very early history. We should note, however, that yet again Livy is manipulating his readers' tastes: they want lots of pleasure: Livy makes something of a concession to this, but he is going to give them this by his treatment of early history or of prehistory, which actually they rather dislike (section 4), though traditionally such *fabulae* were regarded as highly pleasurable (Thuc. 1.21.1, 1.22.4). *gratae* therefore in the first instance reflects, rather, Livy's own perspective (and perhaps his personal dislike of the doom and gloom of Sallustian prefaces), which he tacitly invites his readers to accept.

Another point is that, because section 6 has made some distinction between poetry's free use of *fabulae* and historiography's more solid concern with truth, Livy seems to be extending, or redefining, the licences he claimed in section 6. Maybe his *History* is going to be rather more 'poetic' than it earlier seemed: maybe this poetic element is going to extend into the post-foundation narrative as well, as it surely does. And it is appropriate that just as licence is granted to *antiquitas ut miscendo humana divinis primordia urbium augustiora faciat* (7), so Livy invokes the gods *ab initio. . . tantae ordiendae rei*.

Another point surely is that the epic poet is acutely conscious of the magnitude of his task, asks the gods for help and acts only as their mouthpiece.[78] Thus the poetic analogy reinforces the reader's sense of the magnitude of Livy's task and his personal modesty (however disingenuous), and, taken together with the poetic opening words of the first sentence and the other verbal parallels between the beginning and end of the preface, it frames the preface in a sort of poetic ring structure, a ring structure which further increases the impact of Livy's already unconventional *captatio benevolentiae*.

There are still other things to be said about this marvellous sentence. It foregrounds the moral importance of religious observance. And, by evoking section 7's link between the gods and primeval Rome, it reinforces the idea that moral regeneration means precisely that.[79]

But most important of all, the final sentence of the preface helps to define more precisely the nature of Livy's *opus*. Clearly, the last sentence rings in various ways with the beginning of the preface: *ab initio tantae ordiendae rei* picks up *a primordio... res* of section 1 and *res... est... immensi operis* of section 4; *orsis tantum operis*, in the second half of the last sentence, picks up not only *ab initio... tantae ordiendae rei* in the first half, but also *a primordio urbis* and *res est... immensi operis*. But the rings are not merely repetitions: the nature and implications of the *res* or *opus/opera* upon which Livy is engaged are progressively redefined as the preface proceeds. Hence the *successus prosperi* for which Livy prays (or might pray) are not merely the physical completion of a huge assignment but the successful promotion of the moral lessons of section 10: Livy's *History* will ultimately be a success only if it actually works, if his readers make the right moral choices in public life and Rome is cured.

The use of the 1st person plurals (*nobis... orsis*) is also noteworthy. Of course *nobis* can be understood as 'me, Livy the historian'. But it can also be understood as 'us historians', *rather than* 'me, Livy the historian'. On that reading, the generalizing plural seems to direct our attention away from the intense historiographical debate which has characterized

---

[78] *Formally*: in practice the epic poet's voice is far more complex: see e.g. Goldhill (1991: esp. 56–68).

[79] On this general theme see Miles (1986: 1–33) and (1988: 85–208); Serres (1991).

the preface so far, lifting our gaze to a higher plane: the importance of the enterprise itself and of its achieving a successful outcome.

But also, given the preface's concern to create a unity between the tastes and interests of readers and writer and given also its pointed variation of person in its references to readers, the 1st person plural here should surely be understood not merely as 'us historians' but as 'us, who both are engaged with history, writer and reader alike'. This move from the singular to the plural, from the poet/writer to poet/writer *and* audience/readers has an impeccable epic precedent: 'Sing to me of the man, Muse . . . daughter of Zeus, sing for our time too' (Homer, *Od.* 1.1–10). At the end of the preface the moral interests of the two groups are one, as they both look hopefully to the future, when the success of Livy's gigantic *Ab urbe condita* would go hand in hand with a successful cure of Rome. It is this, not the pleasure of historian or reader, not the glory that accrues to the historian who pleases his readers, not even the fact that history provides moral *exempla* for emulation or rejection, that will be the ultimate *successus*. Or indeed the ultimate *operae pretium*, for the words *successus prosperos* provide the final 'solution' to the original problematics of *operae pretium*. Of course, if this is the criterion by which Livy's *History* is to be judged, it was a failure, since the Roman Empire fell in CE 476! But Livy himself recognises that his own efforts cannot guarantee those ultimate *successus*, and in this sense also the hypothetical form of the final sentence rings with the indeterminate first sentence. Only the gods can guarantee the salvation of Rome. Did they? Not ultimately, but at one point in Livy's lifetime they seemed to go some way to doing so.

Following Luce, I see 1.19.3 as a later insertion:

Bis deinde post Numae regnum clausus fuit, semel T. Manlio consule post Punicum primum perfectum bellum, iterum, quod nostrae aetati di dederunt ut videremus, post bellum Actiacum ab imperatore Caesare Augusto pace terra marique parta.

Twice since the reign of Numa it has been closed, once in the consulship of Titus Manlius after the end of the First Punic War, and a second time, which the gods granted our age to see, after the war at Actium when the emperor Caesar Augustus established peace over land and sea.

But it is one that is directly linked to the preface. The wording *nostrae aetati di dederunt ut videremus* seems to pick up, and contrast with, section 5 of the preface: *malorum quae nostra tot per annos vidit aetas.* So also *imperatore ... Augusto pace terra marique parta* echoes 9 *domi militiaeque et partum et auctum imperium sit,* and seems to suggest that Augustus was the culminating instantiation of the whole *augeo-*process of Roman history as outlined in the preface. Contrary to the sickness of the civil-war period, the gods have now intervened beneficently, as they did at the beginning of Rome's history; not only has the *imperium* been saved but universal peace achieved, and this through the agency of the *imperator* Augustus, the word *imperator,* as often, hovering between the meanings 'C-in-C' and 'emperor',[80] and here suggesting that this *imperator* has saved the *imperium.*

1.19.3 is thus no mere chronological updating for a rudimentary second edition: it suggests a significantly different perspective, so that readers of the 'second edition', as opposed to readers of the original, must see the current political situation in a very positive light. It seems also as if peace through the agency of Augustus, *quod nostrae aetati di dederunt,* must be an element of the *successus prosperi* for which Livy and his readers invoked the gods *ut darent.* Augustus is in part the answer to their prayers. So, if one-man rule is one of the two indispensable *remedia* for contemporary ills, do the preface and 1.19.3 suggest that Livy's whole narrative of Roman history will he directed towards advocacy—of course a nuanced and critical advocacy—of one-man rule? The answer, surely, is yes.

I should like to pull this analysis together by posing the simple question: what is Livy's main aim in this preface? Three factors must be taken into account.

First, Livy's protracted negotiations with the reader to agree on the proper subject-matter of history. Second, Livy's ambiguous, disingenuous, but formally striking, modesty. Thirdly, Livy's relationship to Sallust. There are the close verbal parallels with Sallust's *Histories,* which come thick and fast from the very beginning and continue all the way through; there is also the Sallustian analysis of Rome's decline in sections 9 and 12, perhaps the idea in sections 4 and 12 of Rome collapsing under the weight of her own greatness,[81] and

---

[80] Syme (1979–91: i. 361 ff.); Horsfall (1989: 103).
[81] Though cf. n. 23.

indeed the general rather confessional tone of the preface, somewhat reminiscent of Sallustian prefaces.[82] Also, as we have seen, Livy is engaging in fashionable 'double allusion', looking back as well to the programmatic remarks of Sallust's own model, Thucydides.

For Cizek the explanation for this heavy evocation of Sallust lies in irony. 'Livy is ironic, amusing himself on the subject of these rhetorical tirades about morals, of this attack on the times [*convicium saeculi*].' While Livy recognizes the moral crisis of the first century BCE, he thinks that 'Sallust had exaggerated the real evil', he is fundamentally hostile to Sallust's approach to history, as the ancient tradition averred, and in contrast to Sallust manifests 'a shaded optimism'. From this initial ironic reading Cizek develops an eloquent and complex interpretation, which need not detain us here.[83] For its starting-point is wholly unconvincing. Where, for example, is the irony in the Sallustian 'collapsing-building' metaphor of section 9? If the moral analysis of sections 9 and 12 is not completely serious, then the moral justification of Livy's whole enterprise is badly undermined.

Woodman's interpretation is very different. Ancient historiography falls into two main categories: positive, optimistic, encomiastic, as represented by Herodotus; negative, pessimistic, critical, as represented by Thucydides and his follower Sallust. By imitating Sallust Livy underlines his pessimistic attitude to Roman history, whereas later, when he saw the benefits of Augustus' rule, he became a Herodotean/Ciceronian optimist.[84]

This categorization of ancient historiography seems to me *broadly* acceptable. But its application here does not sufficiently explain the sharp differences between Livy and Sallust: (a) Livy's formal modesty, which is much greater than the nearest Sallustian equivalents in *BJ* 4.2 and *Hist.* 1, fr. 3M. (b) The essential fact that Livy is writing an *AUC* history; the verbal reminiscences of Sallust's *Histories*, which went from 78 to perhaps 40, and his *Bellum Catilinae*, are thus very challenging, e.g. while Livy's *a primordio urbis* recalls Sallust's *a principio urbis (Hist.* 1, fr. 8M) and *res gestas populi Romani carptim*

---

[82] On the whole topic see Ogilvie (1965: 23–9); Mazza (1966: 70–5); Paschalis (1982); Korpanty (1983); Woodman (1988: 130–40).

[83] Cizek (1992: 361–4).

[84] Woodman (1988: 124–40).

*perscribere* (*BC* 4.2), it emphasizes that Livy is doing the exact opposite. (c) The exclusion (section 12) of *ambitio* from the list of recent vicious immigrants into Rome, which is strikingly divergent from Sallust's analysis. (d) The proportions of optimism and pessimism in the two writers. In one way Livy's attitude is more pessimistic (*ambitio* was a very early import), in other ways more optimistic: there is Livy's very positive emphasis in sections 10–11 on the sheer length of time when Rome was uncontaminated by vices, his tremendous stress on the usefulness of history in section 10, his belief that contemporary ills can be cured, if only the Romans will take their double dose of medicine (monarchy and *AUC* history) like men. Of course Sallust suggests history's value in providing worthy *exempla* (*BJ* 4.4–6), but in Sallust it is far from being the climax of the argument.

Interpretation of the Sallustian influence must form part of the interpretation of the preface as a whole. So we return to the basic question: what is Livy's main aim? Livy wants to argue that knowledge of *AUC* history down to the present day is one of the two indispensable cures for a nearly terminal Rome. However, there are two problems: (1) there have always been, and always will be, too many *AUC* histories; (2) most readers prefer contemporary history anyway. The latter problem becomes the more urgent the earlier we date the preface, because Livy would be in very direct competition with Sallust, but it remains acute on any dating, because Livy is certainly going against recent trends. Besides Sallust, we may think of Caesar, Asinius Pollio, the mass of literature about Cato in 46–45, Oppius on Caesar and perhaps Cassius, Bibulus and Volumnius on Brutus, Messalla's memoirs, the memoirs of other military men, etc. etc. The only major exceptions to this general picture, apart from Livy himself, are Tubero, and, earlier, Varro, and maybe Valerius.

Livy's solution to these problems is first to soft-soap his reader: instead of saying 'my subject is supremely great: I am too' (the usual opening gambit), he resorts to *captatio benevolentiae*, here the 'inadequacy-of-the-speaker' commonplace, particularly suited to great but hackneyed themes.[85] He also describes the whole business of

[85] Perhaps with specific allusion to the preface of Cicero's *Orator* (n. 5). It is sometimes suggested (e.g. by Ogilvie 1965: 26) that Livy's 'modesty' is to be explained by the august senatorial tradition of historiography, to which he himself does not belong. But while section 3 alludes to this tradition, it does so with irony and it is in any case only a single reference: the real motivation for Livy's 'modesty' lies elsewhere.

historiographical rivalry with irony and a degree of detachment—a further ingratiating device no doubt, but also preparing for the thought that it is not particular histories that matter but *AUC* history itself. Yet he obviously has to justify himself to some extent—to convey his own merits—otherwise why should the reader be reading Livy (as opposed to anyone else) at all? These merits consist above all in the greatness and seriousness of his purpose.

Secondly, he employs extensive Sallustian parallels. On one level these convey homage to a distinguished predecessor, whose intense moral engagement with the political crisis of his age Livy clearly approves and whose moralising analysis of the causes of Roman decline Livy substantially accepts. Yet, as usual in ancient literature, the extensive parallels suggest not only the close similarities but also the sharp differences between the two writers. To Livy Sallust is the most distinguished recent exponent of contemporary history and thus a suitable opponent for anyone who wants to argue the merits of *AUC* history. From that point of view, the essential differences between the two historians are as follows: while both are concerned with contemporary history and the fact of Rome's near-catastrophic decline, Sallust writes only contemporary history, and, as it were, only writes about it; whereas Livy will treat the past extensively from the very beginning (even before the foundation), but this whole treatment will have a direct bearing upon contemporary history, and he will also treat contemporary history directly; furthermore, his whole history will help towards the resolution of contemporary problems: he will not merely write about them—his writings will help to cure them.

For Livy, therefore, Sallust's stance as critic and moralist has three weaknesses. First, while he proclaims the moral value of Rome's great past, he does not actually write about it, unlike Livy. Second, and partly as a consequence of his failure to write about that past, his emphasis is much too negative, unlike Livy's, whose choice of *AUC* history enables him to maximize good *exempla*. Third, his conception of the moral value of that past is itself excessively rosy, unlike Livy's, who recognizes the destructiveness of *ambitio* from very early in Roman history. So, in so far as he is a rival (rather than a follower) of Sallust, Livy defeats Sallust in every single particular.[86] Thirdly,

---

[86] Livy's rivalry with Sallust acquires even more resonances if we accept Livy's engagement with Cicero's letter to Lucceius. For while Lucceius did not respond to

Livy frankly and disarmingly acknowledges the apparently vast gulf between his own tastes and those of most of his potential readers— but he then proceeds with a good deal of adroitness progressively to narrow this gulf. His ambiguous modesty, his extensive imitation of Sallust, his manipulation of the readers' prejudices—all these are simply the tools of his essential argument: that knowledge of *AUC* history down to the present is one of the only two things that can save Rome from disaster. Whether he really means this—whether, that is, his primary motive in writing the history was moral rather than literary or self-interested[87]—is a question about Livy the man which is not very important: what is important is to unravel the complexities of the formal argument of this great historiographical preface.

## ADDENDUM

Livy's preface is generally seen as essential for any interpretation of the historian, and as the references in Moles's second footnote indicate, it has attracted a corresponding volume of scholarly attention. Indeed, its interpretation is intimately connected to the interpretation of the narrative. For a general treatment of authorial self-presentation see Marincola (1997), with extensive bibliography. On the types of history written in antiquity see Wiseman (1981) and Fornara (1983); on intertextuality, double allusion, and related issues see the comprehensive treatment by Hinds (1997), with Bloom (1973) for a general study of competition with one's (poetic) precursors. Wilkinson (1963) has an excellent discussion of the poetics of prose.

---

Cicero's request for a monograph treatment of the Catilinarian affair and its aftermath, Sallust did produce a monograph on that theme but with an entirely different color from that requested by Cicero. Whether or not Sallust had read the letter (Woodman 1988: 125: '*it is almost as if* Sallust had read Cicero's letter and, in the standard rhetorical manner, treated the same subject with a different *color...*' [my italics; I take it that this means 'I think he did but I cannot prove it']), from Livy's point of view Sallust's *Bellum Catilinae* is, as it were, the wrong 'answer' to Cicero's letter.

[87] Cf. n. 19.

On more specific issues raised by this dense close reading: for novelty claims and the Hellenistic aesthetic, see Clausen (1964); for the historian as epic hero see Marincola (2007*b*); for Livy's irony and humour see Catin and Addendum. On the relationship between Livy and Cicero see the Addendum to McDonald; on *exempla* see Solodow and Addendum, adding Roller (2004) and Lowrie (2007); and for the notion of the historian adding *certius aliquid* see especially Miles (1995), chapter 1, who also treats the problem of Livy's prefatorial modesty. For historiographical autopsy and its roots in Greek practice (which, as Moles shows, was directly influential on Livy) see the illuminating studies by Schepens (1980) and (2007); for Livy's religious sentiments see Liebeschuetz and Addendum. Finally, for the problems and challenges faced by writers in the Triumviral period, see Osgood (2006).

# II

# Structure

# 3

## The Structure of Livy's History

### P. A. Stadter

## I. INTRODUCTION

The loss of three-quarters of Livy's history makes it difficult to understand the pattern according to which the great historian of republican Rome planned his work. Various studies have been made,[1] but a comparison of those most often cited suggests that the authors, rather than defining Livy's pattern, have been establishing in which books of the *Ab urbe condita* were treated certain periods recognized by modern historians of Rome. Their inability to define a plan becomes most apparent when we list the divisions of the work made by each. Thus Klotz would divide after Books 5, 15, 30, 45, 80, 90, 103, 108, and 116; creating the following units of books: 5, 10, 15, 15, 35 (?),[2] 10, 13, 5, 8, 26. Bayet, on the other hand, would mark a break after the following books: 5, 15, 20, 30, 40, 47, 52, 70, 76, 90, 96, 103, 108, 116, 133, and 142; producing the following units: 5, 10, 5, 10, 10, 7, 5, 18, 6, 14, 6, 7, 5, 8, 17, and 9. Most recently, Syme divides after Books 5, 15, 20, 30, 40 (?), 48 (?), 52, 59 (?), 70, 80, 89, 99, 108, 116, 124, 133, 142,[3] with the resulting pattern, 5, 10, 5, 10, 10 (?), 8 (?), 4, 7 (?), 11, 10, 9, 10, 9, 8, 8, 9, and 9. It is at once apparent that in these three schemes only the first forty books are divided equally: 5, 15 (= 10 + 5), 10, 10. These books are clearly divided by pentads and

---

[1] See especially Klotz (1926: 819–20); Bayet (Budé, 1961: xii–xv); and Syme (1959: 30–7). There are others, e.g., Bornecque (1933: 14) and Zancan (1940: 17–23).

[2] Klotz is uncertain how to divide the long span between Books 45 and 80.

[3] The question marks denote some uncertainty on Syme's part.

decades, whereas from the fifth decade on utter confusion reigns, except for the eight books 109–116, which are treated by all as a single unit. More recently, P. G. Walsh has argued, too briefly to convince, that Livy wrote both extant and lost books according to groups of fives.[4] Thus it seems necessary to reconsider the problem, and especially the method by which we can infer the structure of the lost books.

Two difficulties present themselves: first, why is it that it is universally agreed that for the first quarter of his work, including the thirty-five extant books, Livy is using a readily defined and regular structure of fives and tens, but at the very point where the evidence of the extant books deserts us, it is asserted that Livy has abandoned this system or any regular plan? It is one thing to state that 'if Livy began his works with decades in mind, they cracked and broke under pressure of the matter'.[5] It is another to say that this system broke down at exactly the point where the extant books give out, and the *Periochae* become the one dim lamp to guide us.

Second, as noted by Syme, 'artistic design should certainly be looked for'.[6] The schemes of Klotz, Bayet and Syme himself are notably lacking in this quality. The careful arrangement of Virgil's *Aeneid* makes us hesitate before accepting such a random grouping of books as 6, 7, 5, 8, 17. Livy after all was an Augustan: could he write with so little sense of proportion? The books of the *Ab urbe condita* are the work of the writer himself, not a later editor.[7] Furthermore they were shaped according to artistic criteria, and not by arbitrary features such as the length of a papyrus roll or the number of years covered.[8]

The table of the extant books presented in the appendix is revealing. Book 1 encompasses the longest period, from Aeneas to Tarquin the Proud, over five hundred years in a long book of sixty-five pages, two of which are devoted to the general prologue. However, the longest extant book of Livy is 3, which narrates but twenty-two years of early

---

[4] Walsh (1961*a*: 5–8).

[5] Syme (1959: 31).

[6] Syme (1959: 30).

[7] Livy refers frequently to various *volumina* ('volumes') or *libri* ('books') of his work.

[8] It is not my intention here to consider the books as artistic units. For Books 21–30 see the appendices in De Sanctis (1907–23: vol. iii, part 2). For Books 1–5 see Burck (1934).

Republican history. The length of the books in pages, in fact, varies from seventy-six and a half for 3 to forty-one and three-quarters for 32.[9] Even adjacent books can vary widely: forty-three pages for 36, sixty-two, or half again as much, for 37, though each covers exactly one year. The average length of a book in a pentad could vary from forty-eight pages in 31–5 to sixty-seven in 1–5.[10]

We must not accept too readily, therefore, statements suggesting that Livy was forced out of his plan by his material. For him the book was an extremely flexible unit, and we may expect that he could also manage larger units as well. Thus Book 5 ends with the recovery of Rome from the Gauls, and the third decade exactly embraces the Second Punic War, from the first attack of Hannibal to Scipio's triumph.

The most useful guide to understanding the subdivisions of Livy's immense work are the preambles which the author himself prefixes to certain books.[11] Where the original text is lost, we must depend on the skimpy outline of the *Periochae* and what little derivative works such as Florus and Julius Obsequens can reveal. To supplement them, our method must be inference, that is *to proceed from the known to the unknown.* Therefore we must first recognize the organization in the extant books, then consider the value and nature of the testimony of the *Periochae* for these books concerning Livy's organization, and finally on the basis of the *Periochae* and Livy's known practice determine the organization of the lost books. Logic demands that we refuse to postulate differences of method and structure between extant and lost portions unless they are clearly required by the evidence.

## II. THE EXTANT BOOKS

1–5. No one doubts that these books form a unit. The preface to Book 1 is really an introduction to the entire work, and does not

---

[9] Excluding Books 41 and 43 as defective.

[10] Recently Packard (1968: vol. i, p.v. note) has furnished scholars with a word count of the extant pentads of Livy: 1–5: 88,400 words; 6–10: 70,800; 21–5: 76,000; 26–30: 76,700; 31–5: 62,600; 36–40: 74,300; 41–5: 56,200. Note the remarkable differences between the two halves of the first and fourth decades. The halves of the third decade, on the other hand, are surprisingly equal.

[11] Bayet (Budé, 1961: xii n. 3).

contain any statement on the subdivisions into which the work will be divided. But the preface to 6 is explicit: *Quae ab condita urbe Roma ad captam eandem Romani ... gessere, .... quinque libris exposui. .... clariora deinceps certioraque ab secunda origine ... renatae urbis gesta domi militiaeque exponentur* ('I have presented in five books what the Romans have done from the foundation of the city of Rome to its capture.... From this point the more glorious and more certain actions at home and abroad of the reborn city, starting from its second beginning, will be presented,' 6.1.1–3). The barrier of time and lack of records sets apart the period prior to the attack of the Gauls. Book 1, of course had represented a special unit, the regal period, within this larger span. The preface of 2 reminds us that this also was a conscious decision of the author: 'Now I will trace the actions of the free Roman people, in peace and war' (2.1.1).

6–10. The preface to 6 clearly indicates the beginning of a unit, but its end is made uncertain by the loss of Books 11–20. Discussion therefore must be postponed until after the consideration of the remaining extant books.

21–30. The first words of 21, 'It is suitable for me to preface this part of my work', and the statement that he will now treat the war conducted by Hannibal against the Romans[12] establishes beyond doubt that Livy is beginning a new division of his work. The unit covering the Hannibalic war ends with Book 30, as is apparent from the preface to Book 31: 'I am indeed pleased ... to have arrived at the end of the Punic war' (31.1.1). For the sake of dramatic effectiveness Livy gives a brief flashback of Hannibal's early years and rise to leadership which fall outside his annalistic scheme. The historical account is meant to begin with the year 218, P. Cornelius Scipio and Sempronius Longus consuls.[13]

Although the decade forms a unit, it is divided artistically and historically into two halves at the end of Book 25. Book 26 begins as the consuls of 211 and the Senate consider the problem of Capua, which will be extremely important in determining the fate of the

---

[12] *Bellum ... me scripturum, quod Hannibale duce Carthaginienses cum populo Romano gessere* ('I am about to write the war which the Carthaginians, under Hannibal's leadership, waged with the Roman people,' 21.1.1).

[13] Cf. 21.6.3. Livy later discovered the difficulties of this date and tried to correct it in his text: see 21.15.3–6.

whole war.[14] Capua was a turning point in the war; when Hannibal was dislodged from there, he attempted his last great move, the march on Rome to within three miles of the city (26.10.3). The Romans held firm, the tide turned, and the second five books become an account of the steady efforts of the Roman people to overcome their resourceful opponent.[15] To achieve this division, Livy covers only seven years in the first five books, but ten and a half in the second five.

31–40. The preface to 31, in noting the end of the Punic Wars, also marks a new beginning: the Macedonian War.[16] To achieve this division between the Punic and the Macedonian Wars, Livy is willing to divide the year 201 between the two units. The year begins at 30.40.7 and ends in 31.4 with the typical annalistic notices. In this way Livy could complete the Punic War with the triumph of Scipio, and begin the Macedonian War with the story of the legates from Attalus and the Rhodians (31.2). The loss of the beginning of 41 deprives us of the preamble it may have contained, but it appears quite reasonable to suppose that the unit ended with the death of Philip V at the end of Book 40.[17]

Like the third decade, this one also is divided into two after the fifth book. The first five, covering 201–192 BCE, treat the Second Macedonian War and its aftermath; the second five, 191–179, the Antiochean and Aetolian War. The last chapter of 35 is devoted to a small and relatively unimportant encounter between the Romans and the troops of Antiochus, but this is sufficient to be an excuse for war.[18] Book 36 begins with the first actions of the consuls of 191

---

[14] Note 26.1.3–4 'That preoccupation [Capua] at that time especially held the attention of the Romans, not so much because of their anger . . . , as because they thought that the recovery of such a famous and powerful city would influence other minds to return to their respect for the previous rule, as its defection had alienated some communities'.

[15] On the artistic effectiveness of this book see De Sanctis (1907–23: iii. 379). For the division after 25, see also Walsh (1961a: 173).

[16] Cf. 31.1.6 'The Macedonian war followed on the heels of the Punic peace'. Some manuscripts actually have the title 'The first book concerning the Macedonian War'.

[17] The death of a foreign ruler could be an excellent division for a Roman annalist, despite Syme's doubts (1959: 30). At this time the history of Rome is chiefly one of external wars, and in fact the accession of Perseus to the throne marks a new stage in Roman activity in Greece.

[18] 35.51.5 'That occasion, considered as a loss of soldiers, was grievous, but seemed to strengthen the justification for *waging war on Antiochus*'. I am indebted to Prof. T. Robert S. Broughton for calling this passage to my attention.

BCE: sacrifices seeking good omens for the war, the senate's rogation of the people on the war, the assignment of provinces, and finally the official declaration of war (36.1.1–2.5).

Consideration of the second half of this decade reveals another facet of Livy's method. His presentation varies greatly in detail and length as he treats more or less important subjects. The four and a half years of the war, 191–187, are treated at some length (169 pages) in Books 36–8. The following eight and a half years are covered much more quickly (110 pages) in only two books. Moreover, the events of 191 BCE had been narrated in an account apart, a short book of only forty-three pages. These figures confirm the hypothesis that Livy intended to end 40 where he did, with the death of Philip V and the accession of Perseus.

41–5. The loss of the beginning of 41 denies us the preamble which we might have expected to clarify the structure of the preceding books. Nevertheless it is apparent that these books are devoted to the war of Perseus with Rome. Almost all of 45 is devoted to the final capture of Perseus and Aemilius Paulus' triumph.[19] With the triumph over Perseus, Livy ends an important division of his history, as he had in 30 with the triumph over Hannibal. Once more the statistics confirm the division and indicate that Livy was aiming at 167 as the last year of the pentad. Book 41 covered five years, and 42 (a long sixty-three pages) two and a half years, but the remaining three books cover the period of the Third Macedonian War (171–168), only four and a half years. The generalization that Livy treats the years in more detail as he progresses toward his own time must be tempered by the knowledge that in any particular decade or pentad—and even in a particular book—the years can be treated in widely differing proportions. The overall rhythm from 36 to 45 (3 books = 4.5 years, 2 books = 8.5 years, 2 books = 7.5 years, 3 books = 4.5 years) is additional evidence, if that is needed, that Livy intended to mark a division at the death of Philip V at the end of 40.[20]

Livy by his preambles and his arrangement of events and distribution of years divides his historical work into units of ten and five

---

[19] The year-end notices in chapter 44 do not weaken the effect of the preceding chapter.

[20] Those who have argued that the unit begun in 41 ends not at 45 but at 47 or 48 can give no good reason for their choice other than their feeling that the beginning of the Third Punic War should mark the beginning of the new unit. But 41 itself is an indication that Livy did not always begin with wars, since the Third Macedonian War was not treated until 43.

books, at least in the extant books. Yet if we study the *Periochae* which provide a guide to the contents of these books, we discover that those preambles and slight turns of emphasis which are so valuable for determining structure are completely lacking.

No mention of the extremely valuable preface of 1 has been preserved; *Periocha* 1a begins with the arrival of Aeneas, and the beginning of 1b is missing. The preambles to 2 and 6 are passed over in silence. The *Periocha* of 21 does suggest that there might be a preamble to 21 ('He relates the origin of the Second Punic War') but does not refer to those lines in which Livy states explicitly that this book is a new beginning. After a few words the summary passes on to Hannibal's crossing of the Ebro (cf. 21.7), omitting the portraits of Hamilcar and Hannibal. Similarly the *Periocha* of 31 states that the causes of the war against Philip were presented (actually Livy is very brief on this point: 31.1.6–3.6) but neglects Livy's specific reference to the milestone to which he had arrived and his computation of volumes and years covered. A fire in the temple of Vesta opens *Periocha* 41, with no sign of the preamble that might have headed the book.

Thus from the very succinct statements of the *Periochae* of the extant books we can learn very little of the structure which Livy intended for his history. We must deduce from the distribution of the events—for which the *Periochae* are very valuable[21]—the structure which Livy meant his work to have. Under such circumstances, good method requires that we give special importance to the structure of the extant books. In default of more information we must presume that Livy continued the pattern of organization of the early books, unless it can be shown that such a structure is impossible. The burden of proof must always remain with those who deny that the structural pattern of the extant books was continued in the lost volumes.


III. THE LOST BOOKS

In keeping with the conclusions just stated, in this part of my chapter I will consider whether it is possible to see an organization by decades

---

[21] See most recently the conclusions of Begbie (1967: 332–8).

98 P. A. *Stadter*

and pentads in the lost works of Livy. Note that I do not wish to
present my own arrangement of republican history, but to search out
from the meager evidence available what scheme was used by Livy.
Livy had a clearly formulated plan for books 1–5 and 21–45;[22] could
this plan have been continued in the lost books? If it could have been,
we must assume that it actually was, until new evidence presents
itself. The great danger lies in insisting that Livy must have seen the
same units in Roman history as we do. The modern disagreement as
to the nature of such units has been the chief cause for the variations
in the different outlines of Livy's works heretofore presented.[23]

6–20. After the disaster of 390 BCE one landmark stands out
clearly: 16 begins the account of the First Punic War. The hint in
*Periocha* 16, 'The origin of the Carthaginians and the beginnings of
their city are reported', is confirmed by Livy in the preamble to 31.[24]
From the same passage it is apparent that Livy considered that the
two Punic Wars followed one another with only a few unimportant
events in between. The pentad 16–20 must therefore represent the
First Punic War, as 21–30 the Second. In fact the *Periochae* of 16–20
reveal the following distribution of events:

16: 264–261 BCE, Origin of the War and the Sicilian
   Campaigns of 263–261
17: 260–256 BCE, to Regulus' crossing to Africa
18: 256–252 BCE, to the death of Regulus
19: 251–241 BCE, to the end of the war
20: 241–219 BCE.

These books cover a period of some forty-four years, which is most
unequally divided among them, the successive books covering ap-
proximately four, six, nine and twenty-one years respectively. One
has no difficulty in recognizing that Livy has arranged his books not

[22] The problems of 6–10 must await consideration of Books 11–20.
[23] Strangely enough, various analysts of Livy have marked unit endings at the end
of certain decades, yet only Walsh (1961a) has argued that Livy's units regularly
follow the decades. In their analyses, Klotz (1926) sees breaks after 80 and 90; Bayet
(Budé, 1961) breaks after 70 and 90; Syme (1959) after 70 and 80.
[24] 31.i.2–4 'When I think that thirty-six years—there are that many from the first
Punic war to the end of the second—have filled the same number of volumes as filled
the four hundred eighty-eight from the foundation of the city to the consulate of
Appius Claudius, who declared the first war with the Carthaginians...'.

by the number of years to be covered, but by the material: first the
outbreak of the war and the initial successes, then the disaster of 260
and Roman attempts to recover their position, next the epic of
Regulus from his initial invasion of Africa (note the serpent portent
at the beginning of *Periocha* 18[25]), to his death, and finally the slow
reduction of Carthage to an imposed peace. The last book of the
pentad hastily sketches the intervening years down to the outbreak of
the new conflict, the subject of the following decade.

As 16 marks a new beginning, 15 marks the end of the long series
of wars which resulted in the Roman conquest of Italy. More exactly,
the death of Pyrrhus in 272, narrated at the end of 14, removed any
threat to Rome from the Italians, and 15, like 20, is devoted to
skimming over the seven and a half years before the outbreak of
the next important conflict. Books 6–15 thus can be seen as one unit
covering the growth of Rome from its recovery after the Gallic attack
to its domination of Italy.[26]

Considering the pattern of the extant books, a division should also
fall at the end of 10. 'But the end of Book 10 in 294 B.C. seems devoid
of any significance. The historical break surely came a little later, in
290, with the two triumphs of M'. Curius.'[27] These triumphs mark the
end of what modern historians call the Third Samnite War. However,
whatever we may think, Livy did not consider 290 a good break;
Book 11 covers from 292 BCE down to at least 287, that is, until after
the secession of the plebs and several years after the so-called Third
Samnite War. For Livy the end of the 'Samnite Wars' is not the end of
a unit, as in fact its beginning had not begun a unit.[28] Yet there is a
discernible break at the end of 10. The whole last third of the book is
devoted to the battle of Lucius Papirius Cursor against the Samnites
in 293. The importance of this battle is enhanced by the historian's
account of the special Samnite preparations, the formation of the
Lintean Legion, the awesome rituals and oath, and Papirius' exhortation to his troops. The account of the battle and its results ends in

---

[25] The drama of Livy's account here is evident from Livy fragment 10 (Valerius
Maximus 1.8 ext. 19).

[26] Thus, e.g., Klotz (1926), Bayet (Budé, 1961), and Syme (1959).

[27] Thus Syme (1959: 30). According to the Varronian chronology used by *MRR*,
Book 10 ends with the events of 293, including the election of magistrates for 292.

[28] The Samnite Wars began at 7.29.

chapter 46; the last brief chapter, 47, completes the year with the customary annalistic notes. This great battle which asserted convincingly though not finally the supremacy of the Roman forces, appears to have been selected by our author as a moment of particular import, if not a turning point in the Roman conquest of Italy.[29]

The first forty-five books of Livy therefore, are organized in tens and fives: 5, 10 (5 + 5), 5, 10 (5 + 5), 5, 5, 5. Since the succeeding twenty-five books present unusual difficulties, which have caused most commentators to despair of finding a scheme of organization, let us pass over these temporarily and go on to Books 71–142.

71–80.[30] Book 71 begins with the tribunate of Livius Drusus (91 BCE) or more exactly—since his activity as tribune had already been treated in 70—with his decision to stir up 'the allies and the Italic peoples with the hope of Roman citizenship' (*Per.* 71). This would appear an excellent choice for the beginning of a unit in Roman history. There is no sure chronology for Drusus' activity but it is probable that the events treated at the end of 70 occurred immediately after he entered his tribunate on December 10, 92. Thus 70 probably ended with 92 and 71 began the new and crucial year of 91.[31] Book 80 ends with the death of Marius (January 15, 86) and an analysis of his character and influence on Rome for good and bad. In this case Livy determined to run over into the new year to record the last infamous act of the popular leader, the execution of S. Licinius, and then his death. With the death of Marius, the end of an epoch: the *populares* were now leaderless, and our attention must focus on Sulla and the conservative opposition. Five years are covered in ten books: is any further analysis of the structure possible? 71 traces the activity of Drusus to his death (presumably at the end of the book),

---

[29] Note that Livy had already (10.31–2) lamented the length of the Samnite struggle and urged the reader to persevere. Certainly Rome's problems with the Samnites did not end in 290 in any case: Samnite defections and wars occur regularly in *Periochae* 12–14. The phrase in 10.31.10 cannot be taken as a reference to a separate unit on the Samnite wars: cf. Bayet (Budé, 1961: xii, n. 4).

[30] Syme (1959) and Bayet (Budé, 1961) consider 71 the beginning of a unit, Syme (1959) and Klotz (1926) see 80 as the end of one.

[31] It is possible that Livy divided the year 91 between Books 70–71, as he did 201 BCE (30–31). The notice of Sentius' defeat in Thrace is placed between that for the trial of Rutilius and the action of Drusus. Since notices of external matters occur at the end of the year, this may mean that the account of Drusus' tribunate began the new year.

72–6 the Social War (91–88 BCE), 77 the return of Sulla in 88 and his laws, 78 the Mithridatic War, 79–80 the regime of Cinna and Marius at Rome (87 BCE). The individual books effectively cover significant blocks of material, but no large division is apparent, unless the last sentence of *Periocha* 75 furnishes a clue: 'L. Sulla mastered the Hirpini, put to flight the Samnites in several battles, accepted a number of peoples into citizenship, and, having done as much as hardly any other before the consulship, set out for Rome to seek the consulship.' Certainly a pregnant ending for a book, and perhaps for a pentad. Sulla's consulship and the reaction of Marius and Cinna to it, in fact, will form the subject matter of the following books. After the victories described in Book 75, the Social War was almost won, the great threat over. Of greater importance were the enmities at Rome between the two parties, the chief subject matter of the next five books. The *Periocha* of 76 gives this theory no support, filled as it is with minor events and never mentioning the consulship of Sulla. Yet such an argument from silence is not sufficient: the disinterest of the composer of the *Periochae* in preambles or statements by Livy of the importance of certain themes in his treatment has already been noted.

81–90.[32] With the death of Marius, the focus shifts from Rome to the East, from Marius to Sulla. Book 81 begins with Sulla at Athens, 90 narrates Sulla's death and its aftermath, the tumult of Lepidus and the rebellion of Sertorius. The unit is eminently plausible, devoted to those years (86–78 BCE) when Sulla's influence was dominant. It may seem convenient to divide the decade in two parts at the end of 84, since 85 begins with Sulla's crossing to Italy in 83 BCE, but an equally important break could be made after 85, and has the support of Livy's observable structure. Book 86 and the second pentad would begin with the election of the younger Marius to the consulship, and open the account of that gruesome year, 82 BCE, which was to occupy the historian for some three and a half books (86–9).

91–100. The first sentence of *Periocha* 91 may give a clue to the organization of these books: 'Cn. Pompey while he was still a Roman knight was sent with proconsular imperium against Sertorius.' The

---

[32] Syme (1959) and Klotz (1926) see 81 as the beginning of a unit; Bayet (Budé, 1961) and Klotz (1926) see Book 90 as an end.

spectacular rise of Pompey undoubtedly was the most important single aspect of the period after Sulla's death. Book 100 records his arrival at the top: the extraordinary powers granted him under the Manilian law of 66 BCE, his Parthian alliance, and his first victory over Mithridates. Sallust had already seen the importance of Pompey's progress in these years, though his unfinished *Histories* did not go past 67. Others have attempted to see different units in Livy: Bayet suggested breaks after 96, the end of Pompey's Spanish campaigns, and after 103, with Pompey's triumph of 61. Syme has correctly rejected the latter division, noting that the triumph must have been recorded in the early part of 103,[33] since the book carries the narrative as far as Caesar's victory over the Helvetians in 58 BCE. Syme himself marks a break after 99—a plausible suggestion, but contrary to the other indications of Livy's organization. A unit devoted to the meteoric rise of Pompey could reasonably satisfy our historian, steadily toiling to bring some semblance of order to the account of these hectic years. The division of the events of 66 and the postponement of the flight of Mithridates to a new book and a new unit may trouble some, yet even after the king's escape no completely satisfactory break is reached, since there still remained the organization of Pontus and other expeditions in Asia Minor and Palestine. Another five years were needed before Pompey could celebrate his triumph over Mithridates, a point to which Livy arrives only in the middle of 103. The historian must take the bull by the horns and be willing to cut the thread of history. If Livy before had organized by decades, there is every reason to think that he still did so in Books 91–100.

101–110. Of the previous decades the eighth has presented Drusus, the Social War and Marius, the ninth Sulla, the tenth the rise of Pompey. The years which follow encompass the conspiracy of Catiline, the first triumvirate, and the outbreak of turmoil; yet there is no reason to believe that Livy's pattern of organization broke down. Book 101 begins with a second victory by Pompey over Mithridates; 105 ends with the year 55, the year of the second consulship of Pompey and Crassus, of Caesar's daring raid across the Rhine and the prorogation of his powers, and of the Trebonian law granting Crassus Syria and Pompey both Spains for five years. Rome dances to

---

[33] Syme (1959: 78, n. 29). The notice is introduced by *praeterea*.

the tune of the three pipers. Pompey especially was at the height of his glory, thanks to the construction of his theater and other monuments. Velleius remarks that if he had died in 55 BCE, he would have been 'fortunate in the opportuneness of his death' (*felix opportunitate mortis*, 2.48). The pentad 101–105 would narrate the events of those twelve years from 66 to 55 BCE when it seemed that nothing could destroy Pompey's power.

If this pentad were the first part of a decade, the next group of books would end with 110, with Caesar's crossing to Greece in the spring of 48 BCE. The choice may seem strange, but it would not be so unreasonable as it appears on first glance. Book 106 opens with the year 54. The first item is the death of Julia; the last the death of Crassus, cut down in Parthia. Julia's death removed any bond of affection or affinity which might have stayed a conflict between Pompey and Caesar; Crassus' broke the tense triangle which had held the dynasts so carefully in balance. At once the animosities came to the surface, and it was only a matter of time until the battle was joined. That moment came not on January 1, 49, when Caesar's tribunes fled Rome—there was still a possibility of a peaceful settlement, as Cicero's correspondence makes clear[34]—but a year later, when the two dynasts met at the head of their armies, first at Dyrrachium, then fatally at Pharsalia. The pentad 106–110, then, would cover the collapse of the triumvirate and the chaos that followed, through the year 49, ending with Caesar's decision to pursue Pompey to Greece.

Two considerations have led almost all scholars treating the matter to view as a single unit, the fundamental one of this part of the histories, Books 109–116, beginning January 1, 49 and ending in 44 BCE with the assassination of Caesar. The first and most influential reason is the subtitle given each of these books in the *Periochae, qui est civilis belli primus, secundus*, etc. ('which is the first of the civil war, second, etc.') to 116, *qui est civilis belli octavus* ('which is the eighth of the civil war'). Second, the beginning of 49 is frequently considered by both ancient and modern writers as the beginning of the civil wars. Caesar's *Commentarii de bello civili* began there, as did Lucan's *Pharsalia* and the fifth decade of Cassius Dio. Sir Ronald Syme speaks

[34] See especially the conference at Capua on January 25 (Cicero *Ad Atticum* 7.15.2).

of 'the artistic propriety—not to say necessity—of making a new start in 49 B.C., with the recurrence of an epoch of civil wars'.[35] But both necessity and propriety are determined by the individual artist. The greatest historian of the civil wars, Asinius Pollio, chose to begin his account with the establishment of the triumvirate in 60 BCE, eleven years before the Rubicon.[36] Livy may well have chosen to begin his unit with the collapse of the *amicitia fatalis* in 54 BCE.

The titles in the *Periochae* present a different problem. If they represent Livy's own conception, they must have been suggested to the author or editor of the *Periochae* by something in Livy's preamble to Book 109 or 117. Yet I have noted that the *Periochae* have little interest in reporting these preambles.[37] There is in fact no reason to believe that these were not the work of someone, the epitomator or one of his readers, who wished to mark out the books which treated the period which he had learned to call the *bellum civile*. The desire was shared by Florus, who in his notices of various wars, derived from Livy, includes a 'Civil War of Caesar and Pompey', from 49 to 44 BCE. But no certain reflection of Livy's organization is seen by scholars in the other wars treated by Florus, nor is it necessary to do so here. Moreover, it may be questioned whether the titles of the *Periochae* are in fact meaningful historically. It seems puzzling that the events of late 45 and early 44 described in Book 116 should be considered part of the civil war: certainly that ended with the defeat of the sons of Pompey at Munda in 45. It might well be argued that the civil war, if it does not end at Munda, does not end until Philippi, for certainly the death of Caesar meant not an end but a new beginning to Rome's trouble.[38]

[35] Syme (1959: 34).

[36] Syme (1939: 8): 'The breach between Pompeians and Caesar and the outbreak of war in 49 B.C. might appear to open the final act in the fall of the Roman Republic. That was not the opinion of their enemy Cato: he blamed the original alliance of Pompey and Caesar. When Pollio set out to narrate the history of the Roman Revolution he began, not with the crossing of the Rubicon, but with the compact of 60 B.C....that formulation deserved and found wide acceptance.' Cf. also Plutarch, *Caesar* 13.3.

[37] Syme (1939: 291).

[38] There were various ways of reckoning the civil wars. For one computation, see *Per.* 133, when Octavian celebrated his three triumphs (August, 29 BCE): 'having ended the civil wars in their twenty-second year'. In this reckoning, the wars began in 50 BCE. On the whole problem of the scope of the civil wars and the unreliability of the titles of *Per.* 109–116, see Bruère (1950: 217–35, especially 221).

Books 101–110 therefore may be seen as a decade intended by Livy to narrate the ascendancy of Pompey, and the chaos which followed his attempt to maintain his position after the collapse of the triumvirate. At the end of Book 110 the outcome is not clear: Caesar has won small victories and consolidated his rear, but the decisive battle against Rome's greatest general, aided by most of the senatorial order and all the forces of the East, is yet to be joined.

111–120. Book 111 records the direct conflict of Pompey and Caesar in Greece, ending with Caesar's victory at Pharsalia. The civil war occupies the following books, to 115, which ends with the final collapse of the Pompeian resistance at the battle of Munda in the spring of 45.[39] The second half of the decade moves from the triumph and death of Caesar (Book 116) through the remaining events of 44 (Book 117) to the dismal progress of 43 told in the last three books. Book 120 completes the narrative of the proscriptions with the death of Cicero, his severed hands and head fixed upon the rostra. Livy's moving account of Cicero's murder and his Stoic evaluation of his life are preserved by the elder Seneca.[40] The death of this last fighter for the republic may be considered as a fitting close for a unit which began with 48 BCE and the Pompeian fight against Caesar.

Indeed the dramatic climax of Book 120 appears to mark the end of Livy's original project for his *Ab urbe condita libri*. At the end of 119 Octavian had assumed the consulship; the augury of the twelve vultures had marked him as a new Romulus.[41] The death of Cicero completed the account of the year with a dramatic turn, and the sense of regret for the lost republic tempered with an awareness of its weaknesses to be expected of Augustus' 'Pompeianus'.[42] The deeds of Octavian and Antony, and later of Augustus, require an account different in nature and subject to far more pitfalls than the history of the free republic.[43] These considerations lend a certain

---

[39] On the unity of 111–115, see also Walsh (1961a: 7).

[40] *Suasoriae* VI, 16 and 22 (= fr. 50 Weissenborn).

[41] *Per.* 119 and Julius Obsequens 69 'six vultures appeared. As he (Octavian) left the rostrum, having been made consul, six vultures again were seen and gave a sign for him to found a new city, just like the auspices of Romulus'. Cf. Livy 1.7.1.

[42] Cf. Tacitus *Annals* 4.34. For Livy's carefully tempered praise of Cicero, note the phrase concerning Cicero in the fragment just mentioned: 'he suffered nothing more ruthless from the victor than he would have done if he had the same success.'

[43] Syme (1959: 57–76).

credibility to the caption to *Periocha* 121, *qui editus post excessum Augusti dicitur* ('which is said to have been published after the passing of Augustus'). The notice could be based on a preamble by Livy to the continuation of his work (the kind of notice being rather different from those of *Periochae* 109–116 discussed above) or on a note of a grammarian. The pattern of organization I believe can be recognized in Livy would certainly suggest the end of Book 120 as a natural conclusion to Livy's history, according to his original conception. The *Ab urbe condita* would range from Romulus to the new Romulus, from the foundation of the city to these times, *quibus nec vitia nostra nec remedia pati possumus* ('in which we can endure neither our vices nor their cures', Pref. 9) in twelve units of ten books each.

121–142. The extreme brevity of the summaries of the *Periochae* of these books, which treated the period 42 to 9 BCE, makes judgment particularly difficult. If the theory advanced above is correct, these books were written as a supplement to Livy's great work, somewhat in the manner of books 16–18 of Ennius' *Annals*.[44] Such a division would help explain the statement of Servius that Livy's work comprised both annals and history, using the term history for narrative of contemporary events.[45] One is tempted to place at the beginning of this supplement the passage cited by Pliny from a preface, in which Livy, we are told, stated that '[he said] he had won sufficient fame for himself, and could have stopped, except that his restless mind grazed on the work'.[46] Syme (1959) has amply explored the unusual quality of these later books. Subject matter, source and treatment change with the end of the republic. With the establishment of the second triumvirate, power comes to reside in the hands of a few—after Actium, one—whose decisions are made secretly, in consultation with close

---

[44] Cf. Vahlen (1963: cxlv–clxvi).

[45] See Servius *Ad. Aen.* 1.373, under the lemma *annales*: 'The difference between history and annals is this: history is about those times which we either have seen or were able to see, derived from *historein*, that is to see; annals, however, concern those years which our own times have not known. Thus Livy consists of both annals and history.' Servius' division of Livy, of course, may not rest on any indication of the author, but on a grammarian's rule. Gellius 5.18 gives a similar explanation of the precise meanings of the terms *historia* and *annales*.

[46] Pliny, *Nat. Hist.* 1.16 (= Livy fr. 58 Weissenborn)

advisers. Roman history becomes in large part a biography of the *princeps*, and an attempt to understand his ways, a fact recognized first by Tacitus.[47] The supplement does not seem to have had the same formal organization as the main body of the history. I can see no sign of the arrangement by decades and pentads apparent before 120.

Let us return to the twenty-five books, 46–70, earlier passed by. It is worth stating once more that the divisions suggested of this problematic section are meant only to test whether it was possible that Livy continued the divisions by pentads and decades apparent in the first third of his work.

46–50.[48] Book 46 must begin a unit, since 45 ends one. Book 50 is concerned chiefly with Scipio Aemilianus, first in connection with the death of Masinissa, later when he was extraordinarily elected consul. *Periocha* 50 also notes the end of the last Macedonian War: 'The false Philip was defeated in Macedonia and captured.' The seventeen years up to the beginning of the Third Punic War (166–150 BCE) are covered in three books; the last two years occupy two books. Livy's interest clearly lies in the Punic War, not the dull years preceding it. But is it possible that Livy could have broken the account of the war into two parts? The destruction of Carthage and Corinth in the same year has been seen as an epochal date in Roman history ever since Polybius. Did Livy see 146 as the beginning of an era, rather than the end of one? Sallust shared this opinion, as did others.[49] The special attention given to Scipio could be intended to prepare us for the preeminent role he will play in the following ten books.

51–60. Book 51 begins with Scipio's consulship in 147. Carthage was caught in a fatal siege, and by the end of the book Livy can record the fall of the city and the victory games of 146. Book 60 begins with 126 BCE, or perhaps earlier, but is chiefly devoted to the laws enacted by Gaius Gracchus in 123 and (perhaps) 122.[50] The decade moves from the fall of Carthage to the legislation of Gracchus. If Livy chose

[47] See his boast, *Hist.* 1.1.2. Cassius Dio was aware of the problem: see 53.19.

[48] Our study of Books 48–55 is now immeasurably aided by the fragment of a rigidly annalistic *periocha* found in Oxyrhynchus (Oxy. Pap. 668).

[49] Cf. *Jugurtha* 41.2; *Histories* fr. 10–12 Maurenbacher, esp. fr. 11: 'But strife and avarice and ambition and the other evils which are accustomed to arise in prosperity increased especially after the destruction of Carthage.'

[50] The exact date of certain items of C. Gracchus' legislation is uncertain; see *MRR* i. 515, n. 4.

to continue his organization by decades, this unit would certainly permit the reader to follow, as he says in his Preface, 'as discipline broke down bit by bit, morality at first foundered' (Pref. 9). Once more the statistics of the books reveal that Livy has purposely rushed forward to an important year (see Appendix I). In the last two books he covers from 133 to the end of 123 or the first part of 122: eleven years, compared with the fourteen and a half years (147–133) of the preceding eight books. The early books of the decade are full of events and closely united:[51] 51, the fall of Carthage (146); 52, the destruction of Corinth (146), the Lusitanian massacre (146) and Roman reprisals (145);[52] 53–55, the battles against the Lusitani, the death of Viriathus, and final victory. In 55 and 56 the Numantines succeed the Lusitanians as opponents of Rome, in 57 Scipio assumes control of the war (134). Book 58, according to the *Periocha*, is devoted almost entirely to Tiberius Gracchus. Book 59 records the remaining events of 133, especially the fall of Numantia and Scipio's triumph, and hastens through the following years, at least to 129. Thus the great figures of this decade, if Livy made this an organizational unit, would have been Scipio (especially in Books 51, 57 and 59) and the Gracchi (58 and 60). I have not detected any obvious division into two pentads.

61–70. Book 61 marks a new beginning after the account of Gracchus' reform legislation in 60. It included the events of 121, comprising Gracchus' death, since Livy's annalistic method forced him to choose a particular time to end a period. Unlike a modern historian, he could not 'complete the story' by running ahead several years to report, e.g., the death of a protagonist, and then return to cover intervening events. Book 70 ends with the tribunate of Livius Drusus, so that the decade spans the period between two revolutionary tribunates. The end of Book 65 could mark a middle point, on the precedent of Sallust. That author broke the Jugurthine War into two parts, before and after Marius assumed command.[53] Book 66 is

[51] Here the Oxyrhynchus papyrus is especially helpful.
[52] Bayet (Budé, 1961) and Syme (1959) mark a break after 52, 'the end of an epoch' (Syme 1959: 30). Yet 52 does not end with the triumphs of Aemilianus, Metellus, and Mummius in 145, as suggested by Syme, but continues through 144 and Q. Metellus' election to the consulship (see the Oxyrhynchus fragment).
[53] The division is emphasized by the insertion of the speech of Marius, *Bell. Jug.* 85.

devoted to the Jugurthine War from Marius' appearance to its conclusion. The following three books continue to focus on Marius, the
conqueror of the Cimbri and the supporter of Saturninus. Finally in
the last book of the decade Livy hastens through seven years (98–91)
to arrive at Drusus' tribunate.[54]


## IV. CONCLUSION

This extended study of the extant books of Livy and the *Periochae*
shows 1) that Livy's history was clearly organized by pentads and
decades in 1–45, and 2) that it is eminently reasonable to assume that
Livy continued the same practice in books 46–120.[55] The divisions
thus formed are no less satisfactory intrinsically than others which
have been proposed, and have the advantage of conforming with the
known practice of our author. These conclusions are corroborated by
the evidence of late antiquity for the decades. Pope Gelasius in 496 CE
cites the historian with the words 'Livy says in the second decade'.[56]
Similarly a martyrology of the fifth or sixth century, 'If you review
the decades set out by Livy's stylus...'.[57] Of course the manuscripts
also show this traditional division in decades.[58] Yet any hypothesis
that Livy used such a scheme to organize his history has in the past
been rejected as artificial and mechanical.[59] These objections neglect
the natural element of artistic structure necessary in any literary
work. The longer the work, the more evident become the main
outlines of its form. Few now would challenge the carefully balanced
design of the *Aeneid*. Ronald Syme has ably demonstrated the artful
design by which Tacitus has disposed both the *Histories* and the

---

[54] The first nine books of the decade had covered the years at a rate of rather less
than three per book.

[55] For Books 121–142, see above, pp. 106–7.

[56] *Corpus scriptorum ecclesiasticorum* 35, p. 456, 23 (= fr. 63 Weissenborn).

[57] Cf. Klotz (1926: 820).

[58] Cf. also the suggestion of a division by fives in the Symmachan edition (Bayet
(Budé, 1961: xvi, n. 1 and xcv)).

[59] e.g., Klotz (1926: 820): 'no mechanical principle', and Bayet (Budé, 1961: xv)
'the artificial nature of the division into Decades'.

*Annals* in hexads and the first hexad of the *Annals* in two triads.[60]
Tacitus, while remaining true to inherited annalistic methods, refines
the literary artistry of his presentation so that, for instance, 'The first
hexad (of the *Annals*) embraces the principate of Tiberius, in two
equal portions, sharply and explicitly divided.'[61] Organization by
decades is apparent in other historians, such as Dionysius of Halicarnassus and Cassius Dio.[62]

Livy's occasional indications of despair in his task might suggest a
lack of plan, as in 31.1.5:[63]

Already I see myself, with every step I take, like those who have started
walking into the sea in the shallows near the shore, being born in a vaster
and profound depth, and the work almost seems to grow, which as I
completed the first parts seemed to diminish.

But this passage must be taken as another statement of Livy's
characteristic pessimism toward his work and its immensity.[64] The
prefaces to 2 and 6 had revealed a certain pleasure in the progress of
his work, as he turned first to the history of a free people after the
*superbia* of the kings, and then to *clariora certioraque* after the Gallic
sack. Book 21 he began with a pride in the importance of the war, an
old theme. Now, after treating this war in ten carefully articulated
books, he feels once more the immensity of his task, which seems to
grow as he works. The sentiment is not uncommon.

Several observations might be made on the basis of the results of
this study. First, the annalistic method of writing history did not
prohibit the artistic effort which the ancients considered essential to
the genre. The books and larger units into which Livy shaped his
works did not have to correspond exactly with the ends of the years.
Livy, as Tacitus, was not hampered by traditional schemes.[65]

---

[60] Syme (1958: i. 253–270; ii. 586–687).
[61] Note that the number of years in each half is quite unequal (9 vs. 15),
confirming Tacitus' conscious purpose.
[62] See Millar (1964: 39).
[63] The passage is so interpreted by Klotz (1926: 820).
[64] Cf. Pref. *passim*, 10.31.10–15, and Ogilvie (1965: 24).
[65] Syme (1958: i. 191) writes on Tacitus' *Histories*: 'On a superficial view annalistic
tradition and the necessity to begin where a year began, tolerable and even helpful for
the more rudimentary forms of narration, might appear to hamper and debilitate an
historian who expounds the crisis, not of a city, but of an empire. Tacitus betrays no
sign of discomfort.' Cf. Carney (1959: 1–9).

Second, Livy's focus shifts from foreign wars (Books 51–65) to domestic politics (especially after 66). Particularly apparent is the biographical quality of the later sections, which follow one by one the great political leaders across the stage: Marius (66–80), Sulla (81–90), Pompey (91–100), the triumvirate and its dissolution (101–110). Events regarded as epochal are the fall of Carthage, the tribunates of the Gracchi and of Drusus, the deaths of Marius and Sulla, the passing of the Manilian Law, the dissolution of the triumvirate in 54, the year 49, Caesar's last year, and the death of Cicero. Some periods he considered as merely transitional and to be treated more briefly: thus the years 241–219 (Book 20); 187–174 (Books 39–41); 166–153 (Books 46–7), 98–92 (Book 70) and 62–58 (Book 103). The effort to give form and structure to the steady flow of years and events is unmistakable throughout. Though without the subtlety of understanding and the ability to make all elements of the narrative combine to express a single vision, as Tacitus, Livy has left far behind those early annalists, described by Cicero, who know only how to record the bare order of events.[66]

# APPENDIX I
## LENGTH OF BOOKS AND
## SPAN OF YEARS

This table has been compiled on the basis of the Weissenborn and M. Müeller Teubner text. The years listed are the consular years as divided by Livy, with the (Varronian) BCE dates used by Broughton, *MRR*. A year split between two books is listed as half for each book; without regard to the length of treatment in either book or the period of time covered.[67] Similarly years spread over three books are counted as one third for each, etc. The last column, which marks all books known to end in the middle of a year, provides an excellent demonstration of Livy's free use of the annalistic method, especially

---

[66] Cicero, *De oratore*, 2.52–5.

[67] e.g. 201 BCE is considered half in 30 and half in 31, although the segment in the former is six pages, in the latter only three.

in that counterpoint of book endings and year endings normally recognized only in Tacitus.

The analysis for the lost books is based upon the *Periochae*, which, the Oxyrhynchus fragment excepted, are not satisfactory witnesses to chronological order within books. I have presumed, however, that they are correct in ascribing the particular events to the various books. The list is designed as a tool for evaluating Livy's distribution of his material, and absolute precision in dating of historical events has not been attempted.

TABLE

| Book | Pages | Years Spanned | Total Years | Ends in Midyear |
| --- | --- | --- | --- | --- |
| 1 | 65 | | | |
| 2 | 67 1/2 | 509–468 | 42 | |
| 3 | 76 1/2 | 467–446 | 22 | |
| 4 | 65 | 445–404 | 42 | |
| 5 | 61 | 403–390 | 14 | |
| 6 | 51 | 389–367 | 23 | |
| 7 | 50 | 366–342 | 25 | |
| 8 | 50 | 341–322 | 20 | |
| 9 | 61 | 321–304 | 18 | |
| 10 | 58 | 303–293 | 11 | |
| 11 | | 292–287 | | |
| 12 | | 283–281 | | |
| 13 | | $280–278^1$ | 2 1/2 | x |
| 14 | | $278^2–272^1$ | 6 | x |
| 15 | | $272^2–265$ | 7 1/2 | |
| 16 | | 264–261 | | |
| 17 | | $260–256^1$ | 4 1/2 | x |
| 18 | | $256^2–252$ | 4 1/2 | |
| 19 | | $251–241^1$ | 10 1/2 | x |
| 20 | | $241^2–219$ | 22 1/2 | |
| 21 | 58 | $218–217^1$ | 1 1/2 | x |
| 22 | 63 1/2 | $217^2–216^1$ | 1 | x |
| 23 | 55 | $216^2–215^1$ | 1 | x |
| 24 | 53 | $215^2–213^1$ | 2 | x |
| 25 | 54 1/4 | $213^2–212$ | 1 1/2 | |
| 26 | 63 | $211–210^1$ | 1 1/2 | x |
| 27 | 65 | $210^2–207^1$ | 3 | x |
| 28 | 62 1/2 | $207^2–205^1$ | 2 | x |
| 29 | 47 | $205^2–204$ | 1 1/2 | |
| 30 | 52 | $203–201^1$ | 2 1/2 | x |
| 31 | 48 1/4 | $201^2–200$ | 1 1/2 | |
| 32 | 41 | $199–197^1$ | 2 1/2 | x |
| 33 | 44 1/4 | $197^2–195^1$ | 2 | x |
| 34 | 56 | $195^2–193^1$ | 2 | x |
| 35 | 47 1/2 | $193^2–192$ | 1 1/2 | |
| 36 | 43 | 191 | 1 | |
| 37 | 62 | $190–189^1$ | 1 1/2 | x |

| | | | | |
|---|---|---|---|---|
| 38 | 64 | $189^2-187^1$ | 2 | x |
| 39 | 55 | $187^2-183$ | 4 1/2 | |
| 40 | 55 | 182–179 | 4 | |
| 41 | 28 1/2* | 178–174 | 5 | |
| 42 | 63 | $173-171^1$ | 2 1/2 | x |
| 43 | 21 1/2* | $171^2-169^1$ | 2 | x |
| 44 | 47* | $169^2-168^1$ | 1 | x |
| 45 | 49 | $168^2-167$ | 1 1/2 | |
| 46 | | 166–160 | 7 | |
| 47 | | 159–153 | 7 | |
| 48 | | 152–150 | 3 | |
| 49 | | $149^1$ | 1/2 | x |
| 50 | | $149^2-148$ | 1 1/2 | |
| 51 | | $147-146^1$ | 1 1/2 | x |
| 52 | | $146^2-144$ | 2 1/2 | |
| 53 | | $143-141^1$ | 2 1/2 | x |
| 54 | | $141^2-139$ | 2 1/2 | |
| 55 | | 138–137 | 2 | |
| 56 | | 136–135 | 2 | |
| 57 | | 134 | 1 | |
| 58 | | $133^1$ | 1/2 | x |
| 59 | | $133^2-129$ | | |
| 60 | | 126–123(?) | | |
| 61 | | 122–120 | | |
| 62 | | 118–115 | | |
| 63 | | $114-112^1$ | 2 1/2 | x |
| 64 | | $112^2-110$ | 2 1/2 | |
| 65 | | $109-107^1$ | 2 1/2 | x |
| 66 | | $107^2-105^1$ | 3 | x |
| 67 | | $105^2-103$ | 2 1/2 | |
| 68 | | $102-101^1$ | 1 1/2 | x |
| 69 | | $101^2-98^1$ | 3 | x |
| 70 | | $98^2-92$ | 6 1/2 | |
| 71 | | $91^1$ | 1/2 | x |
| 72 | | $91^2$ | 1/2 | |
| 73 | | $90^1$ | 1/2 | x |
| 74 | | $90^2-89^1$ | 5/6 | x |
| 75 | | $89^2$ | 1/3 | x |
| 76 | | $89^3-88^1$ | 2/3 | x |
| 77 | | $88^2$ | 1/3 | x |
| 78 | | $88^3$ | 1/3 | x |
| 79 | | $87^1$ | 1/2 | x |
| 80 | | $87^2-86^1$ | 5/6 | x |
| 81 | | $86^2$ | 1/3 | x |
| 82 | | $86^3-85^1$ | 5/6 | x |
| 83 | | $85^2-84^1$ | 1 | x |
| 84 | | $84^2$ | 1/2 | |
| 85 | | 83 | 1 | |
| 86 | | $82^1$ | 1/4 | x |
| 87 | | $82^2$ | 1/4 | x |
| 88 | | $82^3$ | 1/4 | x |
| 89 | | $82^4-80^1$ | 1 3/4 | x |
| 90 | | $80^2-78^1$ | 2 | x |
| 91 | | $78^2-76$ | 2 1/2 | |
| 92 | | 75 | 1 | |

(*Continued*)

| Book | Pages | Years Spanned | Total Years | Ends in Midyear |
|---|---|---|---|---|
| 93 | | $74^1$ | 1/2 | x |
| 94 | | $74^2$ | 1/2 | |
| 95 | | 73 | 1 | |
| 96 | | 72 | 1 | |
| 97 | | $71$–$70^1$ | 1 1/2 | x |
| 98 | | $70^2$–$67^1$ | 3 | x |
| 99 | | $67^2$ | 1/2 | |
| 100 | | $66^1$ | 1/2 | x |
| 101 | | $66^2$–65 | 1 1/2 | |
| 102 | | 64–63 | 2 | |
| 103 | | 62–58 | 5 | |
| 104 | | 57 | 1 | |
| 105 | | 56–55 | 2 | |
| 106 | | $54$–$53^1$ | 1 1/2 | x |
| 107 | | $53^2$–$52^1$ | 1 | x |
| 108 | | $52^2$–50 | 2 1/2 | |
| 109 | | $49^1$ | 1/2 | x |
| 110 | | $49^2$–$48^1$ | 5/6 | x |
| 111 | | $48^2$ | 1/3 | x |
| 112 | | $48^3$ | 1/3 | |
| 113 | | $47^1$ | 1/2 | x |
| 114 | | $47^2$–$46^1$ | 1 | x |
| 115 | | $46^2$–$45^1$ | 1 | x |
| 116 | | $45^2$–$44^1$ | 5/6 | x |
| 117 | | $44^2$ | 1/3 | x |
| 118 | | $44^3$–$43^1$ | 2/3 | x |
| 119 | | $43^2$ | 1/3 | x |
| 120 | | $43^3$ | 1/3 | |
| 121 | | $42^1$ | 1/4 | x |
| 122 | | $42^2$ | 1/4 | x |
| 123 | | $42^3$ | 1/4 | x |
| 124 | | $42^4$ | 1/4 | |
| 125 | | 41 | 1 | |
| 126 | | $40^1$ | 1/2 | x |
| 127 | | $40^2$ | 1/2 | |
| 128 | | 39–37(?) | 3 | |
| 129 | | $36^1$ | 1/2 | x |
| 130 | | $36^2$ | 1/2 | |
| 131 | | $35$–$34^1$ | 1 1/2 | x |
| 132 | | $34^2$–31 | 3 1/2 | |
| 133 | | 30–29 | | |
| 134 | | 27 | | |
| 135 | | 26 | | |
| 136 | | ? | | |
| 137 | | ? | | |
| 138 | | 12 | | |
| 139 | | ? | | |
| 140 | | $c.$12–10 | | |
| 141 | | 12–9 | | |
| 142 | | 9 | | |

*Books 41, 43, and 44 have large lacunae.

APPENDIX II

DIVISION OF LIVY'S *AB URBE CONDITA*
BY DECADES AND PENTADS

1. 1–10        From the origins to 293 BCE (Aeneas to 293)
               A. To the sack by the Gauls (390)
               B. Recovery and wars of conquest in Italy

2. 11–20       Conquest of Italy and First Punic War (292–219)
               A. Wars in Italy, defeat of Pyrrhus (272), events to 265
               B. First Punic War (264–241), events to 219

3. 21–30       Second Punic War (218–201)
               A. The victories of Hannibal, to 212
               B. Hannibal controlled, war in Africa, Scipio's triumph (201)

4. 31–40       Wars with Philip V and Antiochus (201–179)
               A. Second Macedonian War, and events to 192 BCE. Aetolian-Syrian War, and events to death of Philip V (179)

5. 41–50       War with Perseus and Carthage (178–148)
               A. Third Macedonian War to triumph over Perseus (167)
               B. Fourth Macedonian War, Third Punic War I, Scipio (to 148)

6. 51–60       From the fall of Carthage to the Gracchi (147–123)
               A. Carthage, Corinth and the Lusitanians, to 137
               B. The Numantines, Scipio and the Gracchi (123)

7. 61–70       From the death of G. Gracchus to the Tribunate of Drusus (122–91)
               A. Domestic crisis, unsuccessful war with Jugurtha, to 108.
               B. Marius' victories over Jugurtha and Cimbri, the tribunate of Saturninus, and events to 91

8. 71–80       Social and Civil War (91–86)
               A. Social War to election of Sulla to consulship (89)
               B. Civil War to death of Marius (January 15, 86)

9. 81–90      The domination of Sulla (86–78)
             A. Sulla in the East, opposition at home, to 83
             B. Civil War, Sulla's victory, the proscriptions, new
             legislation, to Sulla's death in 78
10. 91–100    Pompey's rise to power (77–66)
             A. The war with Sertorius to 73
             B. The war with Mithridates, to Manilian law (66)
11. 101–110   The formation and collapse of the triumvirate (66–48)
             A. From the victories over Mithridates to the
             second consulship of Pompey and Crassus (55)
             B. From the deaths of Julia and Crassus (54) to
             Caesar's crossing to Greece (48)
12. 111–120   Civil War and the last struggles of the republic
             (48–43)
             A. From Dyrrhachium and Pharsalia to the battle
             of Munda (45)
             B. Caesar's triumph and assassination, the struggle
             of Antony, Cicero, and Octavian, the formation of
             the second triumvirate and the death of Cicero
             (December 43)

*Addendum*: B. M. Marti has recently restated the case for taking
Books 109–116 as a unit (1970: 1–38, esp. pp. 7–10).

# ADDENDUM

Jal (Budé, 1971: vii–xix) and (1975) gives evidence that Livy considered Books 41–50 a decade, a structural unit focused on the end of
independent Macedon, but does not see indications that the decades
continued after Book 50. Wille (1973) argues that Livy's major
structural unit was fifteen books, most clearly visible in Books
15–30 and 31–45 (cf. 31.1.1), although he admits that he used
pentads and decades as well. Crosby (1978) likewise thinks of groups
of fifteen books, and even of thirty books. Walsh (1974: 8–10) accepts
my argument for continuing use of pentads and decades after

Book 45, and notes that the Preface indicates three stages of Rome's decline, which seem to match the periods from the fall of Carthage to the tribunate of C. Gracchus (Books 51–60), then to Drusus' tribunate (Books 61–70), and finally the collapse which followed, to the end of the republic in 43 BCE (Books 71–120).

Luce (1977: 3–32) made a substantial advance in a chapter devoted to 'The Structure of Livy's History'. He notes the subtlety of Livy's use of pentads and decades in Books 1–45, and suggests that the pentad, rather than the decade or Wille's fifteen-book group, is Livy's fundamental unit (1973: 6). For the books after Book 45, he accepts a continuing 'pentad-decade pattern' (1973: 17), but suggests a rather different handling of the internal structure of the pentad pattern from that found in the earlier books, one which tended to emphasize continuity rather than division. The rest of the book treats the narrative technique and compositional method revealed in the internal structure of the pentads in Books 31–45.

Jal (1994) revisits the question of Livy's organization, without reference to Stadter or Luce, concluding that Livy planned from the beginning a flexible structure which would permit him to present events from a 'Roman perspective'. Kraus (1997) supports the idea of arrangement by pentads and includes excellent observations on the necessity and nature of Livy's structural organization. Oakley (1997–2005: i.111–12) doubts whether it is possible to establish Livy's overall scheme, though he recognizes that there do seem to be divisions by decade and pentads in the extant books. Henderson (1989) plays with the implications of Livy having a planned ending point at Book 120 when he began his history, and of his decision to continue beyond that point.

I believe that my argument for a continuing structure in Books 46–120 still holds. Any detailed analysis falters for lack of evidence, but the use of pentads and decades is highly probable, though we can only hope to see darkly the specific reasons for the shape of each unit. Livy may have thought of an overlay of 15-book units as well, as is likely for Books 1–45. Like Vergil and Tacitus, Livy did not write formlessly, but employed a carefully considered structural framework in composing his history.

P. A. S.

# 4

## Structuring Roman History: The Consular Year and the Roman Historical Tradition

*J. Rich*

### 1. INTRODUCTION

By comparison with historians today, Roman historical writers had little freedom to decide what to write about and how to organize their material. For those who aspired to write full-dress Roman history the choice was largely made by the tradition in which they worked. They could, if they wished, write a monograph, normally on a war. Alternatively, they would follow the majority of their predecessors in writing annalistically, and in that case their subject matter was clearly defined as the deeds of the Roman people, at home and at war (*domi militiae*), arranged by consular years. The aspiring annalistic historian had merely to decide which of the two main branches of that tradition he should join—whether, like Livy, to take as his subject the whole history of the Roman people from the origins to their own time, or, like Tacitus, to confine himself to a limited period of relatively recent history.

Their handling of the formal requirements of the genre is therefore a topic of central importance for the understanding of writers working within the Roman annalistic tradition. Yet there has been little detailed study of how such historians shaped their material within the framework of the consular year. The most important contribu-

This is a revised and somewhat shortened version of the original published in the online journal *Histos* (*http://www.dur.ac.uk/Classics/histos/1997/rich1.html*).

tion is Ginsburg's monograph on Tacitus, which mainly confines itself to the first six books of the *Annals* (Ginsburg 1981). Regrettably, there has been nothing comparable on Livy. Studies of Livy's compositional techniques, like those of Burck (1934, 1950) and Luce (1977), have focused primarily on the shaping of individual books and groups of books and deal only incidentally with his treatment of the consular year. The main reason for this neglect appears to be a general assumption that we understand perfectly well how Livy handled the consular year. In what follows I seek to challenge this consensus.

The generally accepted view may be summarized as follows.[1] Livy, it is held, organizes his annual narratives on a standard pattern structured round the consuls' movements, with a central section of external events sandwiched between opening and closing domestic sections, and these domestic sections include detailed accounts of various recurrent topics, some of a ceremonial character. This standard pattern is perceived as playing an important part in setting the tone of Livy's work: although it was monotonous and much of the recurrent material was jejune, it made an appeal to Roman tradition, emphasized the regularity of Rome's constitutional processes and served to lower the tension between the great episodes. Livy, it is supposed, took the pattern over from his annalistic predecessors, and it has usually been thought that it derived ultimately from the *Annales Maximi*, the record of events kept by the *pontifex maximus*. Until recently it was held that the full impact of the Annales Maximi on the historical tradition followed their publication by P. Mucius Scaevola in the 120s. However, the ancient evidence shows only that the keeping of the record ceased with Scaevola, and, if a published version ever appeared, this is more likely to have taken place under Augustus, as Frier (1979) argued.[2]

---

[1] See e.g. McDonald (1957: 155–6); Walsh (1961*a*: 30–1, 174–6) and (1974: 23); Frier (1979: 270–4). For more nuanced views, noting variation in Livy's practice, see Burck (1992: 50–2); Kraus (1994*a*: 9–13) and (1997: 61–2); Oakley (1997–2005: i.122–5); Feeney (2007: 190–3). On official notices in Livy see Packard (1968); Phillips this volume and (1974). The best overview of the annalistic tradition and its use of archival material is now Oakley (1997–2005: i.21–108, iv.475–92).

[2] For attempts (in my view unconvincing) to defend Scaevolan publication see Forsythe (1994: 53–73) and (2000), Petzold (1999: 4–94, 252–9).

This view of traditional annalistic practice, as exemplified by Livy, is adopted by Ginsburg and plays an important part in her argument.[3] Tacitus' methods, as she shows, are quite different from those she attributes to Livy. Livy, she holds, adhered to chronological order and faithfully recorded recurrent domestic events, whereas Tacitus sometimes departs sharply from chronological order and reports routine items only when it suits him. Moreover, while he sometimes uses Livy's internal-external-internal pattern, Tacitus also deploys a variety of other patterns for the ordering of internal and external sections within the annual narratives. Tacitus, Ginsburg concludes, was adhering to the annalistic form only to subvert it. Annalistic form was traditionally associated with the Republican past, but in his hands it served to demonstrate the hollowness of the façade of republican government in the early principate.

I have no quarrel with Ginsburg's analysis of Tacitus' selection and ordering of his material or with her demonstration of the way in which he used these techniques to reinforce his historical interpretation. However, I hope to show that her conception of Livy's practice and of the annalistic tradition needs reconsideration.


## 2. ANNALISTIC FORM IN LIVY, BOOKS 21–45

Let us begin by looking at Livy's methods in the later extant books, namely Books 21–45, covering the years 218–167. As examples, analyses of Livy's narratives of two years from the fourth decade, 193 and 189, are given in the Appendix below. Both of these sample narratives exhibit some of the principal features which have customarily been identified as characteristic of the 'annalistic form', and the same is true of all the annual narratives in Books 21–45. For each year covered in these books the activities of the consuls provide a chronological and structural framework, from their entry into office, which at this period took place on 15 March, and their early activity in Rome, to their departure to their provinces and activity there, and finally to the return of one or both consuls to Rome and

---

[3] For her view of Livy see especially Ginsburg (1981: 7, 29, 33–4, 53, 78–9, 84–6.)

the election of their successors. A number of routine topics regularly figure in the domestic sections of these annual narratives. For virtually every year Livy supplies information on the initial disposition of provinces and armies and on the election of consuls and praetors. Other topics which frequently appear include the reporting and expiation of prodigies, the games and other activities of the aediles, and the death and replacement of priests. Prodigies are usually reported in the opening domestic section, as having been dealt with before the consuls' departure, while the notices about the aediles and the priests usually occur at the end, out of chronological sequence, as further events occurring 'in that year'.

Livy's practice is, nevertheless, a good deal more flexible than some modern accounts suggest. There is plenty of variety even within those parts of the annual narratives which derive from his annalistic sources, and Livy uses this material freely to serve his own compositional purposes.

Levene (1993) has shown how much variation there is in the selection, location and treatment of the prodigy notices. He perhaps underestimates the extent to which these variations may derive from Livy's sources, but he must be right in explaining at least some of them as narrative devices of Livy himself. Study of other categories of routine material would yield similar results.[4] The notices of the deaths and replacement of priests may serve as an example. These are not always confined to the end-of-year location and are sometimes linked to a broader theme, as when the deaths of three *pontifices* at Cannae are grouped with other consequences of the disaster (23.21.7) or priestly deaths form part of a pestilence narrative (41.21.8–9). The bald death notice is occasionally elaborated, as for Fabius Maximus, accorded a laudatory obituary (30.26.7–10), or Q. Fulvius Flaccus, of whose death we are given grim details (42.28.10–12). Livy gives a nearly complete record of changes to the pontifical college, but a number of deaths and appointments of augurs and rather more of *decemviri sacris faciundis* (religious overseers) must have been omitted.[5] Between 196/5 (33.42.1–6, 44.3) and

---

    [4] Cf. Luce (1977: 191–2). On Livy's handling of prodigies and other religious material see now Davies (2004: 21 ff.).
    [5] For the membership of the priestly colleges in this period see *MMR* i, (especially 282–3, 393–4); Hahm (1963); Szemler (1972: 70 ff., 101 ff.); Palmer (1997:

184/3 (39.45.8–46.1) there are no priestly notices, except for the appointment of Q. Fabius Pictor (the historian's son) as Flamen Quirinalis, only mentioned à propos of his election to the praetorship (37.47.8). This lengthy gap must owe something to authorial choice as well as the accidents of mortality.

Although some years do fall into a simple internal-external-internal pattern, the alternation between internal and external events is often more complex even within the sections deriving wholly from annalistic sources. Accounts of developments in war zones sometimes break into the opening domestic section before the consuls' departure.[6] Sometimes the scene shifts back to Rome during their absence.[7] Reports of one or both consuls' activities in their province sometimes dwindle almost to vanishing point.[8] Livy's account of the year 193 (see Appendix) is an extreme example of what Luce (1977: 52) has termed 'interlocking' structure.

Some events are reported as occurring simply 'in that year' (*eo anno*), but most purport to be narrated in chronological sequence. Sometimes Livy gives precise dates or (more rarely) intervals, but usually he just gives vague indicators of time such as 'at the beginning of the year', 'in that summer', 'near the end of the year' (*principio anni, ea aestate, exitu prope anni*) or links events by loose temporal connectives such as 'during those days', 'about the same time', 'next' (*per eos dies, sub idem tempus, inde*). All this serves to convey the impression that the narrative is moving through the busy and varied events of the Roman year, but this is to some extent an illusionistic effect. In the sections deriving from annalistic sources, we seldom have the evidence to control Livy's chronology, but, when we do, we are sometimes able to puncture the illusion, revealing Livy as ready to invent chronological links or displace events within the narrative when it suited him. Each of our sample years supplies an example.

---

107–14 [*decemviri*]); Rüpke (2008: 80–98). The pontifical and augural colleges had nine members each, one fewer than the *decemviri*, but in Books 21–45 Livy reports the death of 21 *pontifices*, but only 13 augurs and 10 *decemviri*. The one pontifical change which Livy certainly omits is the death of Q. Fulvius Flaccus and appointment of C. Sempronius Tuditanus to his place c.204 (Rüpke (2008: nos. 1762, 3016) ).

[6] e.g. 31.10.1–11.3; 34. 46.1; 35.1.1–12, 21.7–11; 37.57.5–6; 40.47–50.

[7] e.g. 35.6.1–7.5, 23–24; 36.21.6–11, 39.1–2 (doublet); 38.28.1–4.

[8] e.g. 32.7.7–8, 9.5, 26.1–3 (doublet); 37.46.10–47.2; 39.44.11, 56.3; 40.35.1; 42.26.1; 45.44.1.

Calendars show that the shrine of Victoria Virgo was dedicated on 1 August 193, less than half way through the consular year, but Livy mentions the dedication near the end of his account of the year (35.9.6). This in itself is not misleading, for the only explicit indication of time Livy gives for the dedication is that it occurred 'in the same days' as the procurement of some prodigies, which are themselves reported merely as occurring 'in that year' (35.9.2–5). However, one may doubt whether there was any basis for the chronological link between the prodigies and the dedication, and in any case it tells the reader nothing, since the prodigies are undated.[9] For 189 Livy reports the foundation of Bononia and the triumphs of L. Cornelius Scipio and L. Aemilius Regillus in the opening domestic section, yet he himself supplies the dates of these events, all of which occurred near the end of the consular year (37.57.7–8, 58.3–59.6).[10] His reason for extending the opening section so far was evidently to get the triumphs of Scipio and Regillus out of the way before narrating the activity of their successors in the command against Antiochus.[11] A false link to another domestic event slips in: Regillus' triumph is said to occur 'during the same days' as the censorial elections, but these must in fact have happened earlier, since Livy later reports the censors' activity during the year (37.57.9–58.2; 38.28.1–4).[12]

It was from one or more of his Roman annalistic predecessors that Livy drew the chronological sequence which gave him the structure of his annual narratives in Books 21–45. However, much of his material in these books came from sources of a different kind, and it was above all this blending of material from such diverse sources that gave his history of the period its novel character. Books 21–30 are dominated by the great campaign narratives of the Second Punic War, much of them taken from Coelius Antipater's monograph on the war and from Polybius, whom, in my heterodox view, he used directly from Book 21 on. In Books 31–45 their place is taken by the

[9] For the calendar evidence see Degrassi (1947); Briscoe (1981: 157).

[10] The dates of the triumphs are also given by the Fasti Triumphales (omitting to state that Scipio's took place in an intercalary month): Degrassi (1947: i.554).

[11] Cf. Luce (1977: 86–7).

[12] A consul had to preside over the election of censors (Gell. 13.15.4), so these elections must in fact have been held before the consuls of 189 departed for their provinces, *contra* Lintott (1999: 12–13), who overlooks Livy's distortion.

copious material which Livy drew from Polybius on the Greek East. Now Polybius' history was itself organized annalistically, but his years, being based on Olympiad reckoning, began in the autumn, and he subdivided his annual narratives by regions. Incorporating material from this work into his own structure based on the consular year posed considerable problems for Livy. To cope with these problems, he devised a range of strategies, which have been well analysed by Luce (1977).

The chronological indications with which Livy links Polybian to annalistic sections are frequently misleading. Thus when, as he often does, Livy starts a Polybian section with a reference to winter, he sometimes correctly brings out which winter is intended (e.g. 33.27.6), but elsewhere conveys the impression that the events took place a year later than their true date (32.32.1 ff. 35.13.4 ff.). Notoriously, Livy implies that Galba and Villius campaigned in Macedonia during their consulships in 200 and 199 respectively, whereas their campaigns actually took place a year later.[13] Livy links his account of the triumphs of L. Scipio and L. Regillus, which, as we saw above, occurred towards the end of the consular year 189, with his Polybian narrative of their successors' arrival in Asia by the words *eodem fere tempore* (37.60.1: 'at about the same time'), but in reality he has reverted at this point to the early part of the year. These and other similar chronological misstatements have earned Livy a good deal of criticism, and he clearly did not find chronology easy.[14] However, the main reason why such false chronologies occur so frequently is surely not incompetence, but the fact that chronological accuracy was not of great importance to him. Livy was more concerned in Books 31–45 with conveying the *impression* of the interweaving of Eastern and other events.

Only five year-narratives in these books contain no Eastern material (and one of these is lacunose), and several have two Eastern sections.[15] The majority of the Eastern passages are located in the central external section of the annual narratives, but Eastern material

[13] Livy 31.22.4–47.3, 32.3–6. Cf. Luce (1977: 59 ff.), who seems unduly confident that Livy himself was not taken in.

[14] In the third decade a number of Polybian sections are assigned to the wrong year, for example those on the First Macedonian War, on which see Rich (1984).

[15] No Eastern material: 187, 186, 180, 177, 176 (lacuna). Two Eastern sections: 200, 196, 192, 191, 189, 171.

occurs in other locations as well. In several of the year-narratives of the 190s Livy interrupts the opening or closing domestic sections with an Eastern passage.[16] For 193 and 192 he brings the final domestic section to what Levene (1993: 85) has called a 'false close', and then adds Eastern material pointing ahead to the coming war with Antiochus (35.12–19, 42–51).[17] For the years 185–181 Livy develops a new technique by which a report of Eastern embassies at Rome at the start of the year leads into an extended Eastern section, and this serves to unfold the story of the last years of Philip.[18]

As Luce (1977: 3–9) has shown, Livy planned Books 31–45 as a single span, whose principal theme was the defeat of Macedon and the extension of Roman supremacy over the Greek East. The wide range of techniques which he deployed for interweaving Eastern and Western events all served to emphasize the primacy of the Eastern theme. The framework of the consular year which Livy took over from his Roman source or sources divided events according to the traditional polarities of *domi* and *militiae*—domestic and military affairs. Livy in effect superimposed a new set of polarities: East and West. This becomes explicit in the remarkable narrative for 184, which opens with an extended Greek and Macedonian section and then returns to make a new beginning for the other events of the year.[19]

Thus, to my mind, even for Books 21–45 the contrast which Ginsburg draws between Livy and Tacitus is too sharp. It is true that throughout those books Livy's annual narratives are structured round the chronological sequence of the consular year and include a

---

[16] Eastern events interrupting the opening domestic section: 31.14–18 (200); 33.27.6–35.12 (196); cf. the year 191, where an extended narrative of events in Greece and the consul Glabrio's campaign there (36.5–35) is followed by events at Rome before the departure of his colleague Scipio Nasica (36.36 ff.). Eastern events interrupting the closing domestic section: 33.38–41 (196); 36.41–45.8 (191).

[17] Two of Livy's accounts of the First Macedonian War also stood at the end of year-narratives: 26.24–26.4 (211); 29.12 (205). In each case the reason is that the commander returned to assume the consulship for the following year.

[18] 39.23.5–29.3 (185: uniquely, the normal year opening material is omitted); 39.33–37 (184); 39.46.6–53 (183); 40.2.6–16.3 (182); 40.20–24 (181).

[19] Eastern events of 184: 39.33–37, from Polybius' sections on Italian, Macedonian and Greek events for the year. Other events of the year: 39.38–45.1, introduced by 'at Rome at the beginning of that year' (39.38.1), and with the consuls carrying out 'nothing memorable at home or at war' (39.44.11).

good deal of routine domestic detail. But Livy manipulates this
framework with a much freer hand than Ginsburg suggests and
makes it serve his narrative purposes.


## 3. ANNALISTIC FORM IN THE REST
## OF LIVY'S WORK

In Books 21–45, then, Livy took over a standard pattern from one or
more of his annalistic sources but deployed it flexibly, notably in the
way in which he combined it with Polybian material. This gives his
account considerable diversity, but the underlying framework is
nonetheless unmistakeably present. The consuls' movements between
Rome and their provinces provide a chronological structure, ensuring
that the main accounts of domestic events generally come at the
beginning and end of the year, and these domestic sections contain
extensive routine material. It is commonly implied that Livy used the
same structure for the annual narratives in the rest of his work. 'We
find this pattern in *any* book of Livy,' wrote McDonald in what is
perhaps the classic statement of the orthodox view of the 'annalistic
form'.[20] We must now consider the validity of this claim.

McDonald's statement is patently not true for Book 1, on the
kings, for which Livy does not use an annalistic framework at all.
But is it true for Books 2–10? If we read these books without
preconceptions, the answer must be negative.[21]

From Book 2 on Livy's narrative does provide an annalistic record
of the civil and military affairs of the Roman people arranged by the
years of office of the chief magistrates. This is announced in programmatic fashion at the beginning of Book 2, associating the transition to the annalistic mode with the establishment of political
liberty (2.1.1): 'Henceforth I shall recount the achievements of the
now free Roman people, their annual magistrates...'. Only at two

[20] McDonald (1957: 156).
[21] On annalistic form in the first decade see especially Kraus (1994a: 9–13); Oakley
(1997–2005: i.122–5).

points in Books 2–10 does Livy not record the year transitions, namely the Coriolanus saga, where he omits the consuls of 490 and 489 (2.34–9), and the anarchy preceding the Licinio-Sextian reforms, in which for a *quinquennium* only plebeian magistrates are said to have been elected (6.35.10). The significance of the latter case is well brought out by Kraus (1994*a*: 281): 'Without (annual magistrates) there can be no historiographical narrative.... By eliminating the authorities by whom time is measured the tribunes effectively take control of narrative authority as well.'[22]

There are, however, striking differences between the annual narratives of Books 2–10 and those of Books 21–45. In important respects the first decade year-narratives do not conform to the pattern familiar from the later books. Indeed, they do not exhibit a standard pattern at all.

Elections are frequently noticed, but the other recurrent domestic topics which get such detailed treatment in the later books play much less part in the first decade. It is true that the machinery and responsibilities of the Roman state in the period covered by the first decade were much simpler than later, and so there was no occasion for such detailed information on provinces and armies. However, this explanation cannot account for the fact that only twenty year-narratives in Books 2–10 yield prodigy reports, with many of those being much more integrated into the surrounding narrative than in the later books.[23] Deaths of priests are reported only twice, each time in pestilence narratives, while it is only in Book 10 that we start to get reports of aediles' activities comparable to those in the later books.[24]

It is true that many of the year-narratives in these books do purport to narrate events in chronological sequence, and it is not uncommon for us to find narratives which offer in embryonic form a pattern not unlike that found in the later books. Many year-narratives end with reports of elections. An account of a campaign

---

[22] Livy shows no knowledge of the 'dictator years', on which see Drummond (1978).

[23] MacBain (1982: 82–6).

[24] Priests: 3.7.6 (463); 3.32.3 (453). Aediles: 10.23.11–13 (296); 10.31.9 (295); 10.47.3–4 (293). Livy's selectivity with these and comparable items in the first decade is noted by Oakley (1997–2005: i.48 ff.).

may open with information on the sharing of commands between
the consuls or consular tribunes and on the conduct of the levy
and close with the commander's return in triumph. A number of
the year-narratives consist of accounts of campaigns followed by
notices of internal events which took place in the same year. Year-
narratives of this type are sometimes heavily compressed, as for 332
(8.17.5–12), sometimes relatively lavish, as for several years of the
Third Samnite War in Book 10.[25]

However, many of the year-narratives of these books conform to
quite different patterns. There is, for example, what one might call
the minimalist model: heavily compressed notices which merely list a
few items in a sentence or two, with little or no attempt to establish a
chronological or thematic sequence.[26] Twice Livy merely reports that
nothing worth mentioning happened.[27]

The extreme variety of the year-narratives is in fact one of the
hallmarks of the first decade. The amount of space accorded to
individual years varies hugely: Livy passes rapidly over some years
and sometimes over a whole series of years in order to make space
available for extended treatment of key episodes. Livy feels under no
obligation to report both internal and external events under each
year, and for many years only a single topic is mentioned. When he
does include both internal and external sections, there is no set order
of presentation. In the first pentad, where the relationship between
internal discord and external threats is a key theme, the narratives of
individual years sometimes switch repeatedly between domestic and
external settings. By contrast, the second pentad is heavily dominated
by external events.[28]

Thus the year-narratives of Books 2–10 do not conform even in
rudimentary fashion or as a norm to the standard pattern for the
year-narratives which we know from Livy's later extant books, with
its regular internal-external-internal structure based on the consuls'
movements and copious routine domestic detail. There was in fact
no standard pattern to the year-narratives in this part of his work.[29]

---

[25] See especially 10.16–23 (296) and 10.38–47 (293).
[26] e.g. 2.40.14 (487); 3.31.1 (456); 6.5.7–8 (387).
[27] 2.19.1 (500: contrast D.H. 5.52–7); 4.30.4 (429).
[28] Briscoe (1971: 18) gives statistics for military and domestic material in Books 2–10.
[29] See further the online version of this chapter, with illustrative analysis of Book 4.

Traces of the pattern familiar from the later decades begin to appear in the Third Samnite War narratives in Book 10, and no doubt it emerged as standard in the course of the lost second decade.

The difference in the structure of Livy's year-narratives for the Early and for the Middle Republic is obviously related to the discrepancy in their scale. The Middle Republic narratives are generally extended accounts covering a wide variety of topics, whereas those for the Early Republic are usually much more modest in their size and range. There are a number of reasons for these differences in the scale and structure of the year-narratives for the two periods.

One factor is the scope of Livy's work. He must have decided from the outset to allot less space to the early history of Rome, and this obliged him to select and compress his material much more than for later periods. Comparison with the parallel account of Dionysius reveals numerous occasions where Livy must have shortened what he found in his sources. It has often been held that his brief notices of events derive, albeit indirectly, with little alteration from the Annales Maximi, but this is a questionable assumption, and their compression may often owe much to Livy himself. However, there is no reason to think that a standard pattern like that of Livy's later books could be found in any of his predecessors, and so the explanation for its absence must be sought mainly in the nature of the available material.

The Republic's business was itself less complex in the early period than in the Middle Republic when the Romans had imperial responsibilities and were commonly fighting on several fronts at once. In addition, the quantity of archival material available must have been much smaller. Livy himself evidently consulted only earlier historical writers, but the chronological structure and the wealth of domestic detail which he provides for the Middle Republic must derive ultimately from archival sources, exploited by one or more annalistic intermediaries and with a good deal of distortion and invention creeping in in the process.[30] It is likely enough that such material

[30] The extent to which annalists distorted archival evidence for the Middle Republic or supplemented it by invention is a matter of dispute, as, for example, on the much discussed question of the legionary lists, for which see especially Gelzer (1935); Brunt (1971: 644–60); Gschnitzer (1981); Seibert (1993: 368–95). However, there can be no question that a good deal of Livy's domestic material on the period derives ultimately from archives.

was preserved in increasing quantity from about 300 BCE on.[31] It may be, as has often been suggested, that the Annales Maximi became more detailed from about that time. However, the Annales Maximi were at most only one of the archival sources from which Livy's Middle Republican material derived. Much of it is cast in the form of reports of the decisions of the senate, and the record of senatorial decrees was probably the most important archival source.[32] It may well be that few or no senatorial decrees survived from the period covered by the first decade.

We must now go on to enquire how long Livy continued to conform to the standard pattern established for the Middle Republic year-narratives in the lost books from 46 on. The answer to this question is largely a matter of speculation, although some help is afforded by the brief summaries of the individual books in the *Periochae*.[33]

Down to 91 BCE, Livy's year-narratives probably continued to conform to his mid-republican pattern. However, from the outbreak of the Social War in 91 BCE, nearly half way through Livy's work, the scale of the narrative became much ampler, particularly for the periods of civil war: the remaining books (71–142) covered just 84

---

[31] Lack of records does not, however, appear to be the reason for the shortage of notices of priestly appointments: fragments survive from an early imperial inscription from the Forum which gave what purported to be an inscribed list of appointments to a priestly college (probably the augurs) extending back to the early Republic (*ILS* 9338; Vaahtera 2002).

[32] So rightly Klotz (1940–1) and Bredehorn (1968), although these writers fail to recognize the extent of invention and distortion in apparently archival material. The conventional doctrine that the Annales Maximi were the primary source derives from Nissen (1863: 86 ff.). Much of Livy's information on prodigies may come ultimately from *senatus consulta* (Rawson 1971: 1–15, points out difficulties in ascribing this material to the Annales Maximi, though see also MacBain 1982). His information on aedilician activity and on priests cannot derive from the senate record, which may explain why these notices are introduced simply as events occurring 'in that year' rather than in chronological sequence. The ultimate source of the notices relating to priests was probably not the Annales Maximi but the records of the priestly colleges (Vaahtera 2002). The material relating to aediles and censors may perhaps derive from records held by those magistrates.

[33] Study of the *Periochae* for the extant books shows that they are generally accurate on the assignment of events to books but sometimes re-arrange events within books: Jal (Budé, 1984: lxi–lxii). On the question how far Livy's lost books were grouped by pentads and decades see (e.g.) Syme (1959; 29–37); Stadter (1972); Wille (1973); Luce (1977: 9–24). Stadter (1972: 304–6) gives a table showing the years covered in each book according to the *Periochae*.

years. In view of this change of scale and still more the nature of the subject matter, the structure of Livy's annual narratives must now have undergone radical modification. Livy doubtless continued to record routine administrative items, although with some changes: for example, traditional prodigy reports will have become less frequent, since expiation appears to have declined in the Late Republic, and Livy himself represented them as redolent of antiquity.[34] However, the standard internal-external-internal pattern based on the consuls' movements would henceforth have been quite unsuited to the character of Livy's material.

The twenty books (Books 71–90) which Livy devoted to the years 91–78 were mostly taken up with the internecine warfare in Rome and Italy and the conflict with Mithridates in the East. The disarray of Republican institutions in those years would have made it impossible to retain the old regular pattern for the annual narratives. Moreover, there are indications that in this part of his work Livy may have permitted himself, probably for the first time, to depart occasionally from the strict annalistic principle to narrate in a single section events taking place in one region over two or more years.[35]

A superficial stability returned between Sulla's death and the renewal of civil war in 49, and the *Periochae* indicate that for this period Livy adhered once again to the strict annalistic principle, dividing the campaigns of Pompey, Caesar and others into annual sections. However, changes in administrative practice will have prevented Livy from reverting to the old internal-external-internal pattern based on the consuls' movements between Rome and their provinces, for the consuls now spent most or all of their year of office in Rome, and the elections were normally held in July, in the middle rather than near the end of the consular year (which since 153 had begun on 1 January).[36] For many of these years Livy may have contented himself with a single urban section.

---

[34] Livy 43.13.1–2; Liebeschuetz (1979: 57–8); Davies (2004: 46–8).

[35] Implied for the Italian and Eastern events of 87–84 by the *Periochae* of Books 79–83, while Book 90 appears to have included a flashback on developments in Spain (so not only the *Periocha*, but also Eutropius 6.1 and Orosius 5.22.16–23.4, both deriving from Livy). Tacitus resorted to this expedient much more freely in the *Annals*, using it first at 6.31–7 and frequently thereafter.

[36] Elections: Mommsen (1887–8: 584–5). Giovannini (1983: 83–90) shows that consuls in the Late Republic sometimes left for their provinces while still in office, but always towards the end of their term.

All semblance of republican order collapsed once again in 49, and for much of the ensuing period of civil war and despotism (again narrated by Livy on a very ample scale) Rome and the republican political institutions played only a peripheral role. Livy could, if he chose, have reverted to a more traditional narrative mode to recount Augustus' new order, but how far he did so we cannot say. The meagre *Periochae* of the Augustan books are concerned mainly with external events.[37]

From Book 2 on Livy's work was a record of the domestic and external affairs of the Roman people arranged by the years of office of the chief magistrates. Although his later books charted both the collapse of political liberty and a corresponding reduction in the magistrates' importance, he doubtless continued to organize his material in this way to the end of his work, noting the transition to the new consuls and narrating events under their consular year, with only occasional departures from this strict annalistic principle. However, the foregoing discussion has, I hope, shown that the character and structure of Livy's annual narratives varied considerably between the different parts of his work. One factor making for change was Livy's use of different sources and the nature of the material available to his sources. However, the most important factor was the nature of the events themselves: the vast changes in the fortunes of the Roman people had their necessary counterpart in the structure of Livy's annual record.

The standard pattern for the annual narrative which is familiar to us from Books 21–45, with its underlying internal-external-structure based on the consular year and wealth of routine detail in the opening and closing domestic sections, was not, as is commonly supposed, a norm which Livy attempted to observe throughout his work. It was rather a distinctive feature of Livy's account of the period from the early third century to the Social War, and so of about two-fifths of his 142 books. Its adoption for his account of the Middle Republic helped him to convey the special character of that period, in which Rome's affairs were more complex than they had been in the early centuries and the republican system was more stable

---

[37] For speculation about the character of Livy's Augustan books see Syme (1959: 57–76); Badian (1993).

than in both the earlier and later periods. The collapse of republican order from 91 BCE on was reflected in the narrative structure.

## 4. ANNALISTIC FORM IN LIVY'S PREDECESSORS

Livy took over his annual pattern for the Middle Republic, with its regular chronological structure centred on the consuls' movements and ample routine domestic detail, from one or more of his predecessors. In origin it was a literary creation. Although it must have been based on documentary research, the archival material did not supply the pattern. As we have already noticed, the usual view that the pattern derived from the Annales Maximi probably exaggerates its importance as a source, and in any case it disregards the likely character of the pontifical record. As Cicero (*De Or.* 2.52) and Servius Danielis (*Aen.* 1.373) tell us, the *pontifex maximus* displayed the record on a whitened board, but it must have been preserved in a more compact and durable format, either bound wax tablets or papyrus rolls.[38] According to Servius Danielis, the *pontifex maximus* 'had been accustomed to note down events worthy of record which happened at home and at war, on land and on sea, day by day'. Thus the pontifical record probably consisted of a series of notices of events, recorded simply in the order in which they occurred (or the *pontifex maximus* learned of them) with no grouping by topic or distinction between domestic and external matters.

The annalist who first established the pattern not only undertook a good deal of archival research, but also imposed thematic and chronological order on the results. Two further, related questions now arise: to which writer should this considerable achievement be credited, and from which source or sources did Livy himself derive the pattern?

The first history of Rome was written in Greek by Q. Fabius Pictor at the close of the third century BCE, and in the early and mid second century three further Roman histories in Greek appeared, by L. Cincius Alimentus, A. Postumius Albinus and

---

[38] Surely not on bronze tablets, as suggested by Bucher (1987 [1995]).

C. Acilius. Cato was the first to write a Latin prose history, but his *Origines* were highly distinctive, incorporating not just Roman history, but extensive treatment of other Italian communities. Histories of Rome from the foundation in Latin were produced in the later second century by such writers as Cassius Hemina, L. Calpurnius Piso and Cn. Gellius, and this tradition was to be continued in the early first century by the writers of whom Livy made most use, Valerius Antias, Claudius Quadrigarius and C. Licinius Macer.[39]

It is disputed how early in this tradition historians began to arrange their material by the consular year. Some have argued that Piso was the first to organize his work annalistically from the foundation of the Republic.[40] That Piso's work was organized in this way is shown by the fact that it is almost invariably cited as *annales* and by fragments giving consular dates for events in 305, 158 and 146 (26, 36, 39 *HRR*).[41] However, Piso cannot have been the pioneer of annalistic arrangement. His predecessor Hemina gave consular dates.[42] So already, in the early second century, did Ennius in his great Roman historical epic, whose title, *Annales*, surely alludes to its annalistic organization.[43] Ennius was most likely following the ex-

[39] *HRR* has long been the standard edition of the fragments of the Roman historians, but new editions of the early writers are now provided by Chassignet (1996–2004) and Beck and Walter (2001–4), and Cornell *et al.* (see Addendum to Briscoe, this volume) will provide a comprehensive replacement for Peter. Valuable discussions of the early historians include Badian (1966); Timpe (1972), (1979); Rawson (1991: 245–71, 363–88); Forsythe (2000); Suerbaum (2002: 345–458); Walter (2004: 212–356). On the language and style of the verbatim fragments see Briscoe (2005). For the fluidity of ancient usage of the terms *annales* and *historiae* see Gell. 5.18; Verbrugghe (1989). The flexibility of Roman, as of Greek, historical genres is well stressed by Marincola (1999).

[40] So especially Wiseman (1979a: 9 ff.), and Forsythe (1994: 38 ff.), followed in the first, online version of this paper.

[41] I cite the Roman historical fragments throughout by the numeration of *HRR*. Piso's *annales*: cited thus ten times in Latin writers, and by circumlocutory Greek equivalents at Dion. Hal. 4.7.5, 4.15.5, 12.9.3.

[42] 26, 37, 39 *HRR* (events of 219, 181 and 146); cf 20 *HRR* (= Gellius 25 *HRR*), consular tribunes of 389. Forsythe (1990) fails to refute Hemina's priority over Piso. Fornara (1983: 25) regards Hemina as the earliest annalist.

[43] Entry into office of consuls of 214 and 204: *Ann.* 290, 304–6 Skutsch. Allocation of provinces to consuls of 200, at the start of the Second Macedonian War: *Ann.* 324. The title is given as *Annales* by Lucilius 342 M, and always thereafter.

ample of the first Roman historian, Fabius Pictor.[44] Ennius may have used an annalistic arrangement only for relatively recent history: a complete magistrate list could hardly be accommodated in the two books (Books 4 and 5) which he devoted to events from the establishment of the Republic to the Samnite Wars.[45] Fabius, however, may well have organized his material by the consular year from the inception of the Republic: citations show that he treated both the early years of the Republic and the Samnite Wars in some detail, and Livy's citation of his account of the warfare of 294 surely indicates annalistic organization at that point.[46] Fabius will certainly have sought Greek readers and been influenced by Greek models, but this is not, as has sometimes been thought, a reason for doubting his use of year-by-year arrangement: many Greek histories were, of course, organized in that way.

In constructing the first historical account of the Roman past, Fabius must have made considerable use of archival sources, including the annual record compiled by the *pontifex maximus*. That record

[44] It is most improbable that Ennius himself pioneered annalistic arrangement, as is maintained by Beck and Walter (2001–4: i.35 ff.); Walter (2004: 258 ff.). The case for Fabius as the originator of annalistic organization in Roman historiography is well made by Frier (1979: 255 ff.). Northwood (2007) refutes attempts to demonstrate the contrary. See also Oakley (1997–2005: iv.475–7).

[45] Little survives of Books 4 and 5. Book 6 may have been devoted wholly to the Pyrrhic War: so Skutsch (1985: 84 ff., 305 ff.) and (1987); Suerbaum (1995). Cornell (1986b), (1987) argues that the book may have started earlier.

[46] Livy 10.37.14 (= Fabius 19 *HRR*): 'Fabius writes that both consuls campaigned in Samnium and near Luceria and an army was led across into Etruria (but by which consul he does not add) . . .'. Although Fabius did not indicate which consul commanded in Etruria, the passage surely implies that he did name the consuls. Other citations relating to the Samnite Wars: 18, 20 *HRR*. Events in the early years of the Republic: 17–19 *HRR*, to which should be added Livy's citation of 'the most ancient authors' at 2.18.5. Dionysius' statement (1.6.2) that Fabius and Cincius 'narrated the events of their own time in detail . . ., but ran over the early events after the foundation of the city in summary fashion' is not evidence against Fabius' use of annalistic organization for the early Republic. The passage means merely that he and Cincius, like many of their successors (including Livy), treated recent events in greater detail than earlier times, and does not, as often supposed, imply a contrast between their coverage of the regal and early Republican periods (the context shows that 'foundation' here must refer to Romulus' foundation of the city). A fragment of the Latin history of Fabius Pictor (probably just a translation of the Greek original), cited by Gell. 5.4.3, shows that the year 367 occurred in its fourth book, so confirming the density of treatment for the early period (the use of an interval date in this fragment is not evidence of non-annalistic organization).

included fairly routine domestic items such as prodigies and famines. The inclusion of some material of this kind is known to have been a feature of annalistic accounts of the Roman past from Ennius on, and most likely went back to Fabius himself. Thus in Fabius' account, like those of his successors, rather dry notices including some routine domestic events probably alternated with more fully narrated episodes.

Cato in his *Origines* reacted against the tradition which Fabius and Ennius had established. His declaration (77 *HRR*) that 'I do not wish to write what is on the tablet at the home of the Pontifex Maximus, how often grain was dear, how often darkness, or something else, has obscured the light of the moon or sun' is surely a polemic against his predecessors. He seems to have accorded the early Republic only brief treatment. He adopted the remarkable policy of not naming Roman commanders, and, if he did not name the commanders, he cannot have named the consuls. Probably his work was not organized annalistically at all.[47]

Cato's successors followed him in writing in Latin prose, but in their annalistic arrangement, as in their subject matter, they reverted to the tradition established by Fabius. It does not, however, follow that the distinctive pattern of Livy's Middle Republic narratives, with their regular chronological structure based on the consuls' movements and mass of routine domestic detail, was already established in the tradition at that point. On the contrary, what we know of their book structure shows that, with one exception, the histories of Rome from the foundation composed in the later second century narrated the Middle Republic on too small a scale to accommodate a treatment like that with which we are familiar from Livy: Cassius Hemina's history filled only four (or perhaps five) books, and Piso's only seven.[48] We know hardly anything of the book structure of the histories of Fabius and those who followed him in writing Greek histories of Rome, but it is most unlikely that any of their

---

[47] Structure of the *Origines*: Nepos, *Cato* 3.3; Astin (1978: 212 ff.). For an eclipse recorded in the Annales Maximi and by Ennius see Cic. *Rep.* 1.25 (= *Ann.* 153 Skutsch).

[48] Hemina reached at least 281 in Book 2 (21 *HRR*); his fourth book began with the Second Punic War (31 *HRR*) and continued at least to 181 (37 *HRR*). Piso treated an event of 304 in Book 3 (27 *HRR*) and of 158 in Book 7 (36 *HRR*).

accounts of the recent past conformed to the ample pattern of Livy's Middle Republic year-narratives.[49]

One late second-century historian of Rome did write at greater length, namely Cn. Gellius, whose work appears to have been on a more ample scale than that of Livy himself: he had already reached Book 33 by 216 BCE (26 *HRR*) and his cited book numbers go up to 97 (29 *HRR*). This obscure writer is thus a possible candidate to be the originator of the annual pattern for the Middle Republic used by Livy. However, Livy can hardly have derived it from Gellius directly: since Livy never cites him, he is unlikely to have made much use of his work and may well not have consulted it at all. Moreover, other possible explanations are available for the huge scale of Gellius' work: it may simply be the result of rhetorical invention and elaboration.[50]

Livy must, therefore, have taken his annual pattern for the Middle Republic from one or more of the first century annalists, and this narrows the choice to Valerius Antias and Claudius Quadrigarius, the only such writers cited by Livy in Books 21–45. It is usually supposed that Valerius' and Claudius' works were broadly similar in character and that both organized their year-narratives on the pattern which we find in the later extant books of Livy. However, it is unlikely in principle that the two works were so similar, and what little we know about them suggests that they were not. Valerius' work began with the origins of Rome, but Claudius seems to have taken the original step of starting with the Gallic Sack. Claudius found a distinctive source in his second-century predecessor C. Acilius (57a, 64a *HRR*). Transmitted book numbers suggest that Valerius wrote on a more ample scale than Claudius: the episode of Mancinus' dishonourable treaty with Numantia in 137 and the political storm to which it gave rise figured in Book 9 of Claudius (73 *HRR*) but in Book 22 of Valerius (57 *HRR*), and only a few of Valerius' additional books can have been devoted to the early period omitted by Claudius.[51] Fronto

---

[49] One book number is cited for the Latin version of Fabius: above, n. 46.

[50] So Wiseman (1979*a*: 20 ff.).

[51] Valerius treated events after 137/6 on a still more ample scale, since his work extended to at least 75 books (62 *HRR*). Forsythe (2002) holds that 57 *HRR* comes not from Valerius' narrative of the Mancinus affair, but from a reference forward in his account of the parallel episode of the Caudine Forks treaty of 321. This would produce a more even book distribution, but the proposed interpretation of 57 *HRR* is not tenable.

(134 van den Hout[2]) singled out Claudius' style for praise, saying that he wrote 'pleasantly' (*lepide*), but criticized Valerius for writing 'without charm' (*invenuste*). Fronto's friend Aulus Gellius shared his taste for Claudius and gives a number of verbatim extracts, which reveal him to have been an attractively simple and vivid writer.[52]

One of Gellius' extracts from Claudius happens to include a transition to a new consular year. The passage recounts the great Fabius' encounter with his son in 213, at which the son as consul obliged his father to dismount (57 *HRR* = Gell. 2.2.13). It opens as follows:

> Then were made consuls Sempronius Gracchus for the second time and Quintus Fabius Maximus, the son of the man who was consul the previous year. His father, as proconsul, came to meet that consul riding on a horse and did not want to dismount, because he was his father....

Claudius passes straight from the younger Fabius' election to the story of their meeting. However, the meeting took place after the consul Fabius' arrival in his province, and thus in Livy's narrative, in his usual manner, it is separated from the notice of his election by a chapter of information on administrative arrangements at the end of the old and start of the new year, as follows:

| | |
|---|---|
| 24.43.5–6 | Election of Fabius and Gracchus and of the praetors for 213 |
| 24.43.7–8 | Games in 214 |
| 24.43.9–44.6 | Entry into office of consuls of 213; provinces and armies |
| 24.44.7–8 | Prodigies expiated |
| 24.44.9–10 | Departure of consuls for their provinces. 'The father came to the camp at Suessula as legate to his son. When the son came to meet him...'[53] |

---

[52] On Claudius' style see Briscoe (2005: 66–9).

[53] Livy is right that the elder Fabius was *legatus* to his son. If he had been proconsul, as Claudius states, and so an independent holder of *imperium*, he would have been under no obligation to dismount.

Thus Claudius handled this year transition in a fashion quite different from the standard pattern used by Livy for the Middle Republic.
A single passage cannot in itself be conclusive, since it might be
untypical. However, it seems unlikely that an annalist whose year
transitions were normally a record of administrative formalities
would have passed over such matters as completely as Claudius
does here. Thus, in the light of this passage and the other considerations about the two authors noted above, we should conclude that it
was only Valerius, and not Claudius, who organized his annual
narratives for the Middle Republic on the uniform pattern which
Livy took over. I suspect that Claudius, and probably also earlier
annalists such as Piso, treated the period in a manner much more like
Livy's first decade, with its lack of fixed pattern for the annual
narratives and less comprehensive coverage of routine domestic
affairs.

Valerius Antias was thus Livy's source both for the bulk of his
domestic material on the Middle Republic and for the chronological
framework of the consular year. Livy will, of course, have used other
Roman authorities as well on domestic events, just as he drew on
Polybius for events at Rome relating to the Greek East. Occasionally
we may detect Livy blending domestic material from other annalists
with his Valerian framework, as in his notices on dramatic festivals in
the 190s.[54]

The question remains whether it was Valerius himself who carried
out the research in the archives (particularly of the senate) and the
subsequent shaping of material needed to produce annual narratives
with the standard pattern and copious domestic detail which Livy
took over from him, or whether Valerius was following Cn. Gellius,
who, as we have seen, is the only possible candidate among earlier
annalists. The fragments of Gellius' work contain nothing to suggest
that he deserves the credit, but are too meagre to decide the question.
I suspect, though, that, if Valerius was so heavily dependent on
Gellius, Gellius' work would have had wider influence and Livy

---

[54] At 34.44.5 and 36.36.4 (= 40 *HRR*), Livy follows Valerius on this topic, but at
34.54.3–8 he draws on another source (perhaps Claudius): see Asconius 69–70 Clark;
Briscoe (1981: 118, 134, 276).

would have used him directly. Thus on balance it seems more likely that Valerius did the work himself.

If this conclusion is correct, Valerius Antias emerges as a much more remarkable figure than is commonly allowed: he was all too ready to distort and invent, but combined this with diligent research in the archives (either in person or through assistants), which he then turned to creative use. It now becomes easier to comprehend Livy's heavy dependence on Valerius, despite the mistrust which he more than once expresses. Valerius, like Polybius, offered Livy a much more detailed account of the Middle Republic than was provided by the other annalists Livy consulted, and much of this account had at least the appearance of reliability.[55]

## 5. THE ALTERNATIVE TRADITION: FANNIUS, ASELLIO, SISENNA, AND SALLUST

While Hemina, Piso, and Gellius reverted to Fabius' model, other writers of the later second century BCE pioneered new modes of Roman historiography. L. Coelius Antipater wrote a monograph on the Second Punic War in seven books, while C. Fannius wrote a history which appears to have been limited to the recent past, so founding a new genre whose many distinguished exponents culminated in Tacitus himself.

Fannius' example was followed at the beginning of the first century by Sempronius Asellio. Asellio was explicitly critical of *annales*, whose writers, he tells us, merely reported 'what happened and in which year it occurred' (*quod factum quoque anno gestum sit*), whereas those who, like him, sought to recount the 'deeds' (*res gestae*) of the Romans, aimed not only to tell what happened but also to explain the planning and reasoning behind it (*quo consilio quaque ratione gesta essent*).[56] His critique was presumably aimed at the tradition founded by Fabius and in particular against recent exponents such as Piso. Asellio's view of how history should be

---

[55] On Valerius Antias see further Rich (2005).
[56] 1–2 *HRR* = Gell. 5.18.

written recalls and may have been influenced by Polybius' conception of 'pragmatic history'. We should not, however, infer from this polemic that Asellio did not arrange his material by years. That, after all, was how Polybius himself had organized his work. The next Roman writer of recent history was L. Cornelius Sisenna, whose subject was the Social War and the ensuing civil wars. His *Historiae* (the title is well attested) may have been a continuation of Asellio's work. A fair number of fragments survive, and in one Sisenna remarks on the arrangement of his material: 'I have treated together the events which occurred in Asia and Greece in a single summer, to avoid confusing readers by picking out items or hopping about' (127 *HRR*). The fragment shows that Sisenna's material was arranged by years, and within the year by regions.[57] For other years he may have treated Asia and Greece as separate regions, but at least for the summer in question (probably 88 BCE, when revolt from Rome spread from Asia to Greece) he found it preferable to treat them together.

Next in this tradition come the *Histories* (*Historiae*) of Sallust, composed a generation after Sisenna's and very likely conceived as a continuation of his work. Here we are on much firmer ground, for about five hundred fragments survive from the five books of Sallust's *Histories*, many with book numbers.[58] The work's opening words (1.1) declared its scope precisely and in traditional annalistic terms as the civil and military deeds of the Roman people from 78 BCE: *res populi Romani M. Lepido Q. Catulo consulibus ac deinde militiae et domi gestas conposui* ('I have compiled the military and civil deeds of the Roman people for the consular year of M. Lepidus and Q. Catulus, and for the years thereafter'). The fragments show that, although much of Book 1 was taken up with prefatory material, the rest of the work gave an account of the period from 78 to 67 BCE organized by consular years, and in general, and certainly for the major wars, Sallust adhered to strict annalistic arrangement, assigning events to the appropriate year-narrative. Valuable indications of

[57] So rightly Beck and Walter (2001–4: ii.306); *contra*, Rawson (1991: 374).
[58] Maurenbrecher (1893) remains the standard edition of the text, though see also now Reynolds (1991: 151–201) and Funari (1996). McGushin (1992–4) provides a translation and useful commentary, but his treatment of the structure of the *Histories* is not wholly satisfactory: see my reviews in *CR* 43 (1993: 280–2) and 46 (1996: 250–1).

how Sallust organized his year-narratives are given by surviving
portions of three double leaves from a palimpsest, dealing with the
period from the end of 76 to early 74 BCE (2.42–3, 45, 47, 87, 92–3,
98, 3.5–6 Maurenbrecher): the overall impression which this material
conveys is of a writer handling his year-narratives with a freedom and
informality which contrasts markedly with the manner which Livy
adopted from Valerius Antias for the Middle Republic.[59]

Later accounts of the recent Roman past included Asinius Pollio's
history of the civil wars, and the histories by imperial writers such as
Aufidius Bassus and Cremutius Cordus, and their successors Servilius Nonianus, Pliny the Elder and Fabius Rusticus. We have no
information on the arrangement of any of these works, but most,
and perhaps all, were probably organized by the consular year.[60]

## 6. CONCLUSION

If the arguments advanced above are correct, the handling of the
consular year in the Roman historical tradition developed on broadly
the following lines.

The use of the consular year as an organizing principle probably
went back to the first Roman historian, Fabius Pictor. Cato reacted
against the tradition which Fabius had established in various ways,
including the rejection of annalistic arrangement. In the next generation, Hemina, Piso, and Gellius reverted to the Fabian model. Soon
afterwards Fannius and Asellio pioneered a new genre of Roman
historiography which, instead of starting with the foundation of the
city, dealt only with a period of the recent past, but they too probably
and their successors Sisenna and Sallust certainly organized their
material by the consular year.

We may surmise that the year-narratives of the early historians,
from Fabius to Piso, followed no fixed pattern and varied between

---

[59] See the online version of this paper for a detailed discussion.
[60] The nature of his material may perhaps have induced Pollio to dispense with or
at least modify annalistic organization. For Pliny the Elder annalistic organization
seems likely for his 31-book continuation of Aufidius Bassus' history, but less so for
the 20-book work on the German wars.

extended episodes and brief notices, whose style perhaps echoed that of the Annales Maximi themselves. Much the same was true of some of their first-century successors, such as Claudius Quadrigarius. However, the work of Valerius Antias constituted a major new departure. By diligent research in the archives, particularly of the senate, he amassed a good deal of new material, much of it concerned with matters of routine domestic administration and ceremonial, for the years from about 300 BCE on. Valerius incorporated this into his work along with much distortion and invention and shaped it into a narrative with a regular, formal structure which purported to follow the progression of events through the consular year and in particular the consuls' movements between Rome and their provinces.

Livy used Valerius Antias' work as the framework for his own account of the Middle Republic, although he also drew on other annalists and introduced much material from Coelius Antipater's monograph on the Second Punic War and from Polybius. His year-narratives for the period exhibit the regular pattern and wealth of routine domestic detail which he took over from Valerius, but he also manipulated the pattern for his own purposes and in Books 31–45 transformed its character by combining it with extensive Polybian material on the Greek East. In the rest of Livy's work, his year-narratives had a different character. Those for the Early Republic have no fixed pattern, and are probably closer in manner to those of Piso and Claudius. (Valerius' narratives for this period were probably much the same.) We cannot tell how Livy organized his annual narratives for the period from the Social War on, but a number of factors will have ensured that they differed from those for the Middle Republic: the use of different sources, the still ampler scale of Livy's account, and above all the collapse of republican order and stability, of which the uniform pattern of Livy's third and second century year-narratives had served as an emblem.

Livy's work was the culmination of the long tradition of histories of Rome from the foundation. However, before Livy wrote, the alternative models of the monograph on a war and the history of a limited recent period, pioneered by Coelius, Fannius and Asellio, had each found a great practitioner in Sallust. What survives of Sallust's *Histories* suggests that the year-narratives in that work had a free and informal structure quite unlike the regular Valerian pattern.

When Tacitus came to write annalistic history, he undoubtedly devised his own ways of handling the annalistic form and made it serve his own purposes. However, he should not be thought of as reacting against a uniform traditional pattern. A wide range of models was available to him of how the annual narrative might be structured, most notably in Sallust's *Histories*, in the different phases of Livy's work and (the most obscure to us) in the earlier historians of the principate.

## APPENDIX: SAMPLE YEAR-NARRATIVES FROM LIVY, BOOKS 31–45

(1) 193 (34.55–35.19)

ROME

| | |
|---|---|
| 34.55.1–4 | 'At the beginning of the year', earthquakes and their expiation |
| 34.55.6–56 | Provinces and armies; bad news from Liguria leads to emergency measures; departure of consuls |
| 34.57–59 | Reception of eastern embassies, especially those from Antiochus [from Polybius' section on Italian events of the year] |
| 34.60–62 | Embassy from Carthage reports Hannibal's despatch of Aristo and complains about Masinissa; Roman embassy sent out [largely Polybian] |

SPAIN

| | |
|---|---|
| 35.1 | Warfare in Spain 'at the beginning of the year' |

ROME

| | |
|---|---|
| 35.2 | C. Flaminius, the praetor appointed to Hispania Citerior, fails to get additional troops in response to this news |

| | |
|---|---|
| NORTHERN ITALY | |
| 35.3–5 | The consuls' warfare against the Ligurians and Boii |
| ROME | |
| 35.6–7.1 | Despatches from the consuls and resulting senatorial discussions |
| 35.7.2–5 | Measures to alleviate debt |
| (35.7.6 | 'These events took place in Italy at home and at war. In Spain...') |
| SPAIN | |
| 35.7.6–8 | Warfare by the praetors |
| ROME | |
| 35.8 | Consul L. Cornelius Merula returns to hold elections; unsuccessfully seeks triumph |
| 35.9.1 | Censors close *lustrum* |
| 35.9.2–5 | Prodigies 'in that year' |
| 35.9.6 | Cato dedicates shrine of Victoria Virgo 'in the same days' [calendars give its foundation date as *kal. Aug.*] |
| 35.9.7–8 | Foundation of Latin colony 'in the same year' |
| 35.10.1–11 | 'The year was now at its end': election of consuls and praetors |
| 35.10.11–12 | Notable aedileship 'in that year' of Lepidus and Paullus: many cattle-drovers fined and public works constructed with the proceeds |
| LIGURIA | |
| 35.11 | 'At the close of that year', the consul Q. Minucius Thermus twice escapes from serious danger |

GREECE AND ASIA

| | |
|---|---|
| 35.12–13.3 | Aetolian approaches to Antiochus, Philip and Nabis [from Polybius' Greek events for 194/3] |
| 35.13.4–19 | Roman embassy to Antiochus; his war council. 13.4–5 'in that winter... at the beginning of spring...' implies that we have now moved into 192, and so there is no explicit reference to the consuls' entry into office at 35.20, but in fact this section is from Polybius' Asian events for 194/3. |

(2) 189 (37.48–38.35.6)

ROME

| | |
|---|---|
| 37.48–49 | Rumours of setbacks in the East; Aetolian embassy rebuffed |
| 37.50–51.7 | Provinces and armies; dispute over *flamen Quirinalis*; departure of consuls and praetors |
| 37.51.8–56 | News of battle of Magnesia; embassies from L. Scipio, Antiochus and others; senatorial decisions on the peace settlement |
| 37.57.1–6 | 'During those days' report of defeat and death in Liguria of L. Baebius on way to Spain; successor sent |

SPAIN

| | |
|---|---|
| 37.57.5–6 | Victory of L. Aemilius Paullus |

ROME AND ITALY

| | |
|---|---|
| 37.57.7–8 | 'In the same year' Bononia founded [*a.d. iii. kal. Ian.*] |
| 37.57.9–58.2 | 'In the same year' censorial elections |
| 37.58.3–59 | 'During those days' return and triumph of L. Aemilius Regillus [*kal. Feb.*] and L. Scipio [*mens. intercal. pr. kal. Mart.*], with *supplicatio* for Paullus between them |

THE EAST (from Polybius' Greek events and Asian events for 190/89)

| | |
|---|---|
| 37.60.1 | 'At the same time the consul Cn. Manlius reached Asia and the praetor Q. Fabius Labeo reached the fleet' [in fact doubling back to summer 189] |
| 37.60.2–7 | Naval activity of Q. Fabius Labeo |
| 38.1–11 | Events in Aetolia: the war there ended by consul M. Fulvius Nobilior |
| 38.12–27 | Cn. Manlius Vulso's Galatian campaign |

ROME

| | |
|---|---|
| 38.28.1 | 'While these events took place in Asia, peace prevailed in the other provinces' |
| 38.28.1–4 | Activities of censors |
| 38.28.4 | Floods |

GREECE

| | |
|---|---|
| 38.28.5–34 | Activity of Fulvius Nobilior, the Achaeans etc. [from Polybius' Greek events for first half of 189/8][61] |

ROME

| | |
|---|---|
| 38.35.1–4 | Return of Fulvius; elections; prorogation of Fulvius and Manlius |
| 38.35.4–6 | Dedications 'in that year' by the consul Fulvius, by a Cornelius and by the aediles from fines on corn-hoarders. Games repeated. |

[61] On the chronological problems of Fulvius' movements see Warrior (1988); Briscoe (2008: 104–6, 110).

# 5

# Design and Structure in Livy: 5.32–55

*T. J. Luce*

Livy's history has been criticized for its lack of design and structure.[1] The historian, it is affirmed, was not sufficiently in control of his material: the narrative wanders, and on occasion sags; there is a want of focus, of clarity, of balance, of continuity. Professor Syme has been particularly critical: 'He is betrayed by ignorance of politics and warfare, by lack of critical principles—and, above all, by incapacity to dominate the material with design and structure.'[2]

Numerous reasons may be advanced in explanation or extenuation. First, the great bulk of the history, as well as the huge time-span covered, militate against an easy conception of the whole. Aristotle's illustration of a creature of great size comes to mind (*Poet.* 1451a): 'Since the eye cannot take it in all at once, the unity and sense of the whole is lost for the spectator.'[3] A second reason stems from the prevailing view of how Livy used his sources. Almost totally dependent on them, yet unable adequately to criticize or master the

---

[1] The writer thanks the APA's anonymous referee and Professor W. V. Harris for their helpful criticisms and suggestions.

[2] Syme (1958: i. 139; compare also 148): 'Admirable as Livy is in the eloquence of a speech, in descriptive colouring, in narrative movement, he shows no comparable skill when events have to be grouped and interrelated—and no instinct for historical structure. For disposition as for material he is content on the whole to follow his sources.'

[3] Livy himself is in part responsible for this impression. At 31.1.5, with 112 books still to come, he compared himself to a man drowning in the vastness of his undertaking. But he should not be taken too seriously; the deprecation and self-effacing are largely a pose: see Hellmann's sensible remarks (1939: 19, n. 2). On Livy and Aristotelian canons see Burck (1964: 181).

difficulties of their use, the historian was generally content to reproduce their materials and the ordering of those materials, together with
their biases and occasionally even their language. Specifically, he
selected only two or three authorities as the chief sources for extended
sections, alternating between them; he seldom conflated, but usually
used one at a time, appending variant versions, usually statistical in
nature, at odd intervals. The resulting picture is of a compiler moving
back and forth between authorities somewhat randomly, uncertain as
to exactly what was coming up next, himself taking full charge of the
material only when opportunities for eloquence, high drama, or
moralizing presented themselves.[4]

Efforts have been made to alter or soften this view, but they have
been sporadic and fragmentary. Kurt Witte in a pioneering effort
showed how Livy adapted Polybius in order to achieve balance,
movement, and structure. His findings are instructive, but he maintained that Livy seldom looked beyond the single episode (the
'Einzelerzählung') in making his adaption. Witte may, however,
have been led to this conclusion as much from the fragmentary
nature of the Polybian text as from his analysis of Livy's narrative.
A number of other studies on individual episodes have confirmed
and extended Witte's findings.[5] In addition, analyses of special aspects of the narrative have demonstrated a high degree of structure;
the speeches comprise one such area, while style has been shown to
have influenced considerably the design of the whole and of special
types of episodes.[6] At the other end of the spectrum are analyses of

---

[4] Walsh (1961a: 110–72) gives a summary of the subject. Ogilvie's study on how Livy
used Licinius Macer in Book Four is an illustration of the prevailing view (1958: 40–6).
Only a few have demurred; most vehement is Laistner (1947: 83–102). Zimmerer (1937)
is one of the few who have attempted to explain *why* Livy used his sources as he appears
to have done (see esp. 36–43, 65–8); she believes that for Books 31–45 his manner of
alternating between Claudius Quadrigarius, Valerius Antias, and Polybius was due to
the effective contrast which they offered among themselves in content, outlook, and
style. Since she believes Livy intentionally mirrored *all* these features in his narrative, his
own contribution, in her view, would appear to have been slight.

[5] See, for example, Walsh (1961a: 191–7); also Walsh (1954: 97–114) on sieges and
naval battles. Not all estimates have been wholly favorable; for example, Jumeau
(1939: 21–43) finds much unevenness in a stylistic analysis of 30.18–26.

[6] On the speeches see Walsh (1961a: 219–44). McDonald's discussion of style in Livy
is excellent (1957: 155–72). On particular episodes see McDonald for the Hercules and
Cacus story (1.7.4–7), and Walsh (1961a: 250–1) on Manlius and the geese (5.47.1–6).

the large-scale structure of the 142 books of the *Ab Urbe Condita*. From the extant books and the Periochae it is clear that Livy designed and composed the early part of his history by the pentad and groups of pentads. But as the narrative of the later years became increasingly detailed, such exact grouping became difficult, and ultimately impossible, to achieve.[7]

The most significant study on design and structure in Livy is that of Erich Burck, *Die Erzählungskunst des T. Livius*. Using the parallel narrative of Dionysius for comparison, Burck was able to show clearly that in the first pentad Livy gave great attention to the development of overall structure and thematic unity. The full implications of this study for Livy's method of composing and his use of sources have not yet been properly appreciated, although thirty-seven years have passed since the book first appeared. Nor, surprisingly, have others gone on to analyze the later pentads and decades along similar lines. As a result, much remains to be done before an adequate conception of the design and structure of the *Ab Urbe Condita*, or the lack of it, can be gained.

This essay is an effort to fill in a small part of this considerable gap. The last half of Book Five, comprising the defeat at the Allia and the sack of Rome by the Gauls, has been chosen for analysis. Although Burck treated it in his book, he did so in a somewhat summary fashion, reserving as he did the fifth book to near the end of his study, and using it chiefly to confirm his earlier findings. Yet the design of this section is more complex than Burck apparently realized, and illustrates in brief compass how intricate structure can be in Livy, what a wide variety of narrative techniques were employed to that end, and how free and thorough his adaptation of source material could be at times.[8] In fact, it appears to be one of the most polished and carefully written parts of the history, and hence is probably not typical of the whole. But only further investigation of the rest can confirm this impression.

---

[7] See Walsh (1961a: 6–9); Bornecque (1933: 11–23); Syme (1959: 27–87, esp. 28–42).

[8] The following discussion is arranged according to types of narrative techniques and structural devices; it does not follow the narrative sequentially, section by section.

## I. STRUCTURAL DEVICES AND TECHNIQUES

Book Five as a whole was composed in two contrasting sections. The first (1.1–32.5) recounts the fall of Veii, Rome's greatest victory up to that time; the second relates her greatest defeat, the defeat at the Allia, and the sack of Rome. The two are linked by the commanding presence of Camillus, *the fatalis dux*, the leader fated to destroy Veii and save Rome (5.19.2). A prominent theme is that of religion: due observance of the gods brings success, neglect, disgrace and defeat. In his final speech Camillus sums up the lesson (51.5): 'You will find that everything the gods favored turned out well, everything they opposed did not.' The symmetry of the book is further emphasized by matching Camillus' concluding speech (51–54) with the oration of Appius Claudius at the start (3–6). In the middle stands the digression on the Gallic migrations (33.2–35.3).[9]

## 1. The peripeteia

The chief structural device is the peripeteia, or reversal of fortune. Two of them are employed. Leading up to the first is the 'Affair at Clusium', the defeat at the Allia, and the beginning of the siege of the Capitol. The dominant theme is the collapse of Roman values, effort, and nerve which affects all classes of society and all departments of life. The peripeteia itself is sudden and unexpected, the contrast with the preceding events emphatically signalled.

A complete change had come over the city during the night and in the course of the following day: the Romans were not the same as those who had fled in such panic at the Allia. (39.8)

Thereafter, as a parallel and in contrast to the first part, begins the account of Rome's gradual recovery of her former military, religious, and moral strength. This chain of events leads to the second peripeteia, the sudden intervention of Camillus at the last possible moment as the ransom in gold is being weighed (49.1). The complete victory

---

[9] See Burck (1964: 109–36); Ogilvie (1965: 626).

which follows is the counter-balance to the defeat at the Allia. Once again, the contrast is made explicit:

> At the first clash the rout of the Gauls was accomplished with as little effort as they themselves had expended in their victory at the Allia. (49.5)

## 2. Exaggeration and paradox

Livy takes great pains to make the contrast on either side of each peripeteia as sharp and as striking as possible. One method is by exaggeration, even to the point of paradox.[10] Contrast is carried so far that on occasion Livy comes near to depicting a reversal of identity. Before the first peripeteia the Romans are more like the Gauls than themselves:

> It would have been a peaceable embassy had not the bellicose envoys behaved more like Gauls than Romans. (36.1)

> On the other side no one behaved like a Roman, not the commanders, not the troops. (38.5)

Similarly, Roman characteristics belong (temporarily) to the Gauls:

> And so the barbarians were blessed not only by fortune but also by fore-sighted leadership. (38.4)

But at the final denouement the reversal is complete:

> The Gauls were alarmed by this unexpected turn of events: they seized their weapons and attacked the Romans more in anger than good judgement. (49.5)

Before the first peripeteia Roman decline is sudden, unexplained, and absolute:

> No extraordinary measures are taken in face of the unknown and numerous enemy. (37.1–2)

> The levy is half-hearted, while the military tribunes actually belittle the danger. (37.3)

> At the Allia no camp is secured, no defense raised, no auspices taken, no sacrifice made, no adequate battle plan devised. (38.1–2)

---

[10] On the technique in general and this episode in particular, see Burck (1964: 224–6).

At the first onslaught the Romans, leaders and soldiers alike, flee 'almost before they saw the unknown enemy', making no attempt to fight and not even raising a battle cry. (38.6–7)

Part of the army is so stricken with fear that they forget their wives and children at Rome and rush off to Veii, where they post no guard and send no messenger to Rome. (38.5, 9)

The other part flees at once to the city, but in such panic that they rush to the Capitol without shutting the city gates behind them. (38.10)

Livy makes no real attempt to explain Roman behavior, save to invoke fate (*fatum* 32.7, 33.1, 36.6) and Fortune (*fortuna* 37.1, 38.4). During Rome's recovery and final victory, however, *fatum* is conspicuous by its absence, and *fortuna* is no longer blind or negative, but purposeful— a co-partner with divine aid and human wisdom (49.5): 'Now Fortune had reversed her course, now the favor of the gods and man's intelligence were on Rome's side.' ('Iam verterat fortuna, iam deorum opes humanaque consilia rem Romanam adiuvabant'.[11])

The plight of those in Rome as the Gauls approach after their victory at the Allia is similarly exaggerated.

The Romans fail to close the gates, station guards, or defend the walls. (39.2)

The people first fill the city with cries of grief (39.4). Then, as they wait in suspense for the expected attack by the Gauls, their minds become numb with fright. But suddenly, when the sight of the enemy entering the gates has put them beside themselves with fear, their attitude completely reverses:

Finally, with dawn approaching they were beside themselves with fear, and close upon this fear came what they were dreading: the enemy's standards were seen moving through the gates. Yet a complete change had come over the city during the night and in the course of the following day: the Romans were not the same as those who had fled in such panic at the Allia. (39.8)

The contrast could scarcely be more abrupt or more contrived. No explanation is given for the sudden change of heart; Livy's sole aim

---

[11] Cf. Kajanto (1957: 58–60). The repetition *iam . . . iam*, particularly with the plpf., is used to signal climactic moments with impressive and portentous effect. The echo with the passage announcing the doom of Veii earlier in the book is doubtless deliberate (5.19.1). Cf. the fall of Alba at 1.29.4 and the impending death of Galba in Tacitus (*Hist.* 1.39). The device lends itself to narrative parody, as in Petronius 8.4.

seems to be to achieve the sharpest possible contrast at the moment of reversal. The peripeteia, therefore, has been created purely as a structural device.

Thereafter Roman recovery is the chief theme. Certain features here are exaggerated also:

The self-sacrifice of the patrician elders: 'They gazed as in veneration at the beings seated in the vestibules of their homes, for their attire and bearing surpassed those of mortal men, and in majesty of countenance and gravity of expression they were most like to deities. They approached them as if they were statues...' (41-8-9)

The daring act of Fabius Dorsuo as the Gauls looked on and did nothing: 'either because they were overawed by this amazing act of courage or because they, too, were sensible to the claims of religion'. (46.3)

The complex and dangerous procedure of nominating Camillus dictator in conformity to all constitutional requirements: 'so great was the respect for proper procedure, so sensitive were they to the niceties of the situation when their own situation was well-nigh hopeless'. (46.7)

The reward to Manilius on the Capitol of extra food, despite near-starvation. (47.8)

The peripeteia which follows also illustrates Livy's desire to achieve balanced structure at the expense of probability. While Camillus is joining his forces at Veii and Ardea and is equipping and training them, the desperate situation on the Capitol forces the Romans to offer a ransom in gold to the Gauls (48.5–8). Camillus with his whole army intervenes suddenly. How they were able to enter the forum unseen and unchallenged by the Gauls is not explained. The peripeteia thus makes exciting reading, but little sense.[12] The reversal is completed by Camillus' immediate victory amid the rubble of the city and his second victory on the Via Gabinia, where not a single Gaul survived to report the disaster (49.6).

Livy has thus deliberately created a black and white contrast on both sides of each peripeteia. Rome's decline and defeat could scarcely be more absolute, her recovery more pronounced, the final reversal more surprising.

---

[12] See Burck (1964: 221–2) for similar techniques in Hellenistic historiography.

## 3. Leitmotif

Livy makes it clear that the disaster at the Allia was not caused solely, or even chiefly, by military mistakes; it was the result of moral guilt, religious neglect, and political folly on the part of all classes: leaders, Senate, and people. The military mistakes are therefore explicable only in terms of the general failure. The neglect and the subsequent recovery of 'human and divine' aid is thus the chief theme. It is introduced at the start in the form of two prefatory anecdotes: the disregard of the divine voice on the Nova Via which warned of the approach of the Gauls (32.6–7), and the exile of Camillus: 'The one citizen was expelled whose presence would, if anything in this life is certain, have prevented Rome's capture' (33.1).[13] A simple statement of theme links the two:

Not only were the warnings of the gods disregarded, as destiny began to run her course, but the only human that could save the city, Marcus Furius, was driven out. (32.7)

'Gods and men' becomes thereafter a leitmotif which appears at each crucial stage of the story, the repetition reinforcing and unifying the basic structure. At the Allia:

Paying no heed to the gods much less to the men they faced. (38.1)

Introducing the first reversal:

They decided . . . to defend gods and men, and the very existence of Rome. (39.9–10)

When Roman fortunes begin to recover:

Preserving the respect to gods on the one hand and to men on the other. (40.10)

Introducing the second reversal:

But gods and men forbade the Romans be a ransomed people. (49.1)

---

[13] The use of a prefatory anecdote, chiefly to foreshadow and to characterize, appears elsewhere: e.g., the story of the young Hannibal swearing eternal enmity to Rome at the start of the third decade (21.1.4–5); note that in Polybius it is delayed considerably (3.11.5–12.6). Compare the anecdote of the centurion before the senate-house which concludes Book Five: *hic manebimus optime* (55.2); the advice was taken, and contrasts with the unheeded voice on the Nova Via.

At the point of final victory:

> Now Fortune had reversed her course, now the favor of the gods and man's intelligence were on Rome's side. (49.5)

Finally, the two prefatory anecdotes are recalled in the aftermath and are united: first, when Camillus orders a temple to Aius Locutius to be built on the Nova Via (50.5), and second, in his great speech which closes the pentad (51.7, 52.1).

## 4. *Terrarum orbi documento* ('an object lesson for the entire world')

The events before and after the first peripeteia are contrasted most strongly in the themes of moral collapse and regeneration. Livy takes great pains to make the contrast as forceful and thoroughgoing as possible.

After the two prefatory anecdotes, the 'Affair at Clusium' recounts the moral guilt incurred by the Fabian ambassadors: *contra ius gentium* ('contrary to the law of nations', 36.6). The idea is repeated twice more in as many pages (36.8, 37.4), and is picked up by Camillus in his last speech: *gentium ius ab legatis nostris violatum* (51.7, cf. 6.1.6). The disapproval of the Senate is noted (36.9–10), and the historian puts his own opinion on record: 'The Gauls reacted with justifiable anger' (36.11). At the same time he is at pains to show that the defeat at the Allia was not a case of the sins of the Fabii being visited upon the state. The Senate and the people are implicated also. When the Gauls demand satisfaction, the Senate deplores the violation and admits the justice of their demands. But political favoritism (*ambitio*) for the Fabii prevails.[14] In order to avoid responsibility for a possible future defeat (36.9–10), decision is passed to the people, among whom the influence and wealth (*gratia atque opes*) of the Fabii is so great that the three are elected military tribunes with

---

[14] In Plutarch's version the majority of senators is described as denouncing Q. Fabius (*Cam.* 18.1) and the blame is laid almost exclusively on the people (18.2). Diodorus (14.113) goes so far as to depict the Senate voting to hand over Q. Fabius to the Gauls, but being overruled by the people (cited as the first example of the people overruling the Senate).

consular power for the coming year (36.10–11). The state as a whole is thereby involved in moral guilt, as Camillus makes clear in his final speech (51.7).

This theme thus accounts for the division of material on each side of the first reversal: Senate, leaders, and people are treated each in turn. In the first part the Senate shirks its duty and is therefore responsible by default; in the second it redeems itself by the sacrifice of its elder statesmen. Their intention to atone for their failure earlier to set the plebs a good example is made explicit (39.13).

Roman leadership is a second theme of contrast. In the face of an unknown enemy who had 'stirred up war from the Ocean and the furthest shores of the world,'

the state that against Fidenae, Veii and other nearby peoples named in many a crisis a dictator as a last resource looked on this occasion to no extraordinary command or safeguard. (37.1–2)

Contrasted with this is the appointment of Camillus as dictator (46.10), as well as the help of the Latins (46.4) and the Ardeates (43.6–45.3, 48.5). In the first part the three Fabii forget their status as ambassadors; in the sequel the centurion at Veii, Q. Caedicius, rejects any thought of himself leading the troops to Rome and is the first to ask for Camillus as dictator ('mindful of his status', 46.6), while the appointment of Camillus conforms to every constitutional requirement despite great danger, involved procedure, and the 'well-nigh desperate state of affairs' (46.7); moreover, the historian is sure his hero did not set out from Ardea to Veii before the actual news of his appointment was given him, 'because he could not return to Roman territory without permission of the people nor possess the auspices to lead the army without having been named dictator' (46.11). Similarly, the rashness (*temeritas*) of the Fabii (37.3) balances the actions of the Romans on the Capitol: 'they did nothing rashly or in fear' (43.2). Failure to hold an accurate levy (37.3) parallels Camillus' levy at Ardea (48.5). Failure to secure a campsite or defensive rampart at the Allia (38.1) corresponds to the Roman defense of the Capitol (43.2), as well as the death penalty meted out to one negligent guard (47.10). Finally, failure to anticipate the nature of the Gallic attack, 'even making light of the rumored gravity of the danger'

(37.3, cf. 38.1–2) balances Camillus' strategic foresight in the night attack on the Gauls at Ardea, for it turned out 'just as Camillus had predicted' (45.2).

The third group, the people, are responsible for the election of the Fabii as military tribunes, panic on the field of battle, and disorder and confusion in the aftermath. In the second half, when they flee the city as the Gauls approach, L. Albinius, a plebeian, orders his wife and children from his wagon in order to carry the Vestals and the sacred objects to Caere. Confusion and panic no longer prevail: 'Though afflicted and weighed down by great misfortune, their spirit was not crushed' (42.7).

The loss and recapture of divine aid is a counterpart to that of human help. The warning voice on the Nova Via was ignored, the violation of *ius gentium* went unpunished (cf. 51.7), while at the Allia the auspices were not taken nor a sacrifice made (38.1). In the second half great attention is given to strict religious observance: the care of sacred objects by the Flamen Quirinalis and the Vestals; the anecdote about L. Albinius; the story of Fabius Dorsuo's daring journey through enemy lines to perform a family sacrifice: 'He placed his confidence in the favor of the gods, whose worship he had not forgotten even under the threat of death' (46.3); sparing the sacred geese of Juno on the Capitol despite the lack of food, 'which proved Rome's salvation' (47.4). Divine aid is on the Roman side at the final victory (49.1, 5), and in the aftermath the religious theme is strongly emphasized both in the acts of Camillus, 'a man of great religious feeling' (50.1), and in his final speech:

The power of the gods has been so clearly revealed in Rome's affairs in these past days that mankind, I believe, will never again disregard any aspect of their worship. (51.4)

Livy's desire to teach a moral lesson is clearly responsible for the selection, ordering, and emphasis of material. The narrative corresponds to the program announced in the Preface: 'The chief merit and benefit of history is to behold in the record of a great nation examples of every sort of conduct; from it you may select for yourself and for your country those things worthy of imitation and those which, whether wrongly begun or wrongly concluded, you should avoid.'[15] This paradigmatic view of history is implicit throughout in the choice and treatment of material (cf. 40.10, 46.7). In his concluding speech Camillus passes in review the chief examples of vices and virtues that the state had just beheld. He also reiterates forcefully the sentiments of the Preface:

> The conclusion is inescapable. The penalty we paid to gods and men in suffering defeat, capture and ransom is so great that we stand today as an object lesson to the entire world. (51.8)

Yet it is the first peripeteia at 39.8 which testifies most clearly to Livy's decision to structure his material as he did. One might have expected him to make the defeat at the Allia central and pivotal. But he did not. The Allia was merely one of a series of events which were 'wrongly begun, wrongly concluded'; the defeat itself was accordingly reduced in importance and made to take its proper place in the grand design (see section 6 below).

Yet the balancing series of exemplary behavior needed an introduction of *some* sort. Hence the peripeteia. It is true that it is sudden, unexplained, and unmotivated; but since it was created solely as an introductory device, for Livy to have searched out or manufactured an immediate cause for the Roman change of heart would serve no really useful purpose. It would contribute nothing to the lesson, and might impair the economy of structure and the narrative pace. What would be gained, in fact? Nothing, except a certain specious verisimilitude (see Part III below).

## 5. Methods of narration

The first peripeteia allows Livy to create a structure based essentially on thematic contrasts. No event is presented as climactic or as important solely as a piece of action. The things which happen are not closely connected circumstantially; they are treated as a series of 'closed wholes' (Witte's 'Einzelerzählungen'), narrated as *exempla*, and arranged around a central dividing point. The rather chiastic nature of the design is somewhat static in conception. It would seem

---

[15] Praef. 10 (quoted above). On the meaning of *monumentum* see Ogilvie (1965: 28).

unsuited for narrating what is, after all, a linear progression of events through time.

But, of course, the story does move forward and great changes do come about. Hence the second reversal at 49.1, which is solely the product of 'action', and whose only function is to make exciting reading. What Livy has done, in fact, in the last half of Book Five, is to blend two disparate approaches to the narration of events. It cannot have been an easy task. But the finished product is clearly successful. There is little feeling of incongruity. Nor is the transition obvious; indeed, it is impossible to say just where the one leaves off and the other begins. This is because after the first reversal Livy uses the series of *exempla virtutum*, examples of virtuous actions, both as a foil to the events of the first half and as pieces of action increasingly important simply as action, building in a temporal sequence to a climax of pure 'situation'. Hence the differing treatment of material in the various parts of the story. The account of Rome's recovery takes over twice as much space as that of her decline (omitting the digression on the Gauls). Events before the first reversal are brief and not particularized; the only participant named is Quintus Fabius, and this only because Livy could not resist pointing to an example of foreign valor (*peregrina virtus*, 36.6) on the battlefield at Clusium.[16] The succeeding part is much different; anecdotal *exempla* abound, generalized description is reduced, and individual exploits are detailed: the self-sacrifice of the elders (with individuals named: Marcus Folius at 41.3 and Marcus Papirius at 41.9), the religious piety of Lucius Albinius (40.9–10) and of Gaius Fabius Dorsuo (46.1–3), Camillus at Ardea (43.6–45.3), Quintus Caedicius at Veii (45.4–8,46.6), Pontius Cominus' journey (46.8–11), Marcus Manlius on the Capitol (47.1–11), Quintus Sulpicius (47.9–10, 48.8–9), and Camillus' final victory (49.1–7).

## 6. Expansion, omission, subordination

Livy's picture of Roman decline before the first reversal is uniformly black, and is described only in general terms; everything (save Quintus

---

[16] Compare the treatment of Flaminius in Books 21–22. Despite bad character, neglect of religion, and foolhardiness (e.g., 21.63, 22.1, 3–4), he displayed great *virtus* on the battlefield at Lake Trasimene (22.5–6).

Fabius' *peregrina virtus*) which did not contribute to this was omitted. Hence various episodes in the parallel accounts of Diodorus, Plutarch, and Dionysius find no place in Livy: for example, the speech to the people by the father of the Fabian ambassadors urging rejection of the Gallic demand for satisfaction (Diod. 14.113); the recommendation of the fetial priests that the ambassadors be surrendered (Plut. *Cam.* 18); the preparations made by the Gauls for a night attack on the Capitol (DH 13.7–8; Plut. *Cam.* 26–27). A speech by the elder Fabius is necessary only because in Diodorus' version the Senate acquiesces in the Gallic demands for handing over of the chief offender, Quintus Fabius. But since Livy wants to stress the implication in guilt of *all* elements in the state, he has the Senate refuse to make any recommendation; a speech by the elder Fabius can thus be dispensed with. The fetial priests are excluded from the story on similar grounds: Roman decline must be total, even in matters of religion. Finally, to detail the preparations of the Gauls for a night attack on the Capitol would only distract from the central focus: the recovery of Roman spirit. Before the first peripeteia Livy feels free to dwell at some length on Gallic psychology (39.1–3) and attitudes (36.8–10). But not afterward, when events are told almost entirely from the Roman point of view.[17]

Since the disaster at the Allia comes before the first peripeteia and is designed primarily as one of a number of episodes illustrating Rome's moral decline, Livy has chosen not to make it climactic or pivotal.[18] Patriotic feeling doubtless contributed to this decision as well. The account of the battle is accordingly quite brief (38.1–10); it requires as much space to bring the combatants to the site (37.1–8), and as much to narrate their dispersal (39.1–8). Moreover, after first adverting to the preparations of the Romans (or the lack of them: 38.1–2) and of the Gauls (38.3–4), and then returning to the Romans again (38.5), he abandons the temporal sequence. By stating baldly the outcome (38.5) he forestalls any attempt to build to a climax;

---

[17] When their reactions are noted, they are used to point up Roman *virtus*: e.g., their reactions to Dorsuo's daring act of *pietas* (46.1–3).

[18] Bruckmann's treatment of the Allia (1936: 41–4) is disappointing and unsatisfactory because he discusses the defeat alone (35.4–39.2 only) and fails to see how it relates to the narrative which precedes and follows. This proves doubly unfortunate, since Bruckmann selects the Allia as one of three archetypal patterns for Roman defeats in general.

then, as if in retrospect, he sketches in briefest outline what generally befell the Romans on the field (38.6–8).[19] The magnitude of the disaster is cleverly underplayed. To be sure, 'a great slaughter took place' (38.8), but no numbers are given, and we read immediately: 'the entire left wing fled after throwing down their arms . . . yet most fled safely to Veii' (39.9), and then 'all those on the right wing . . . headed for Rome' (38.10). There seems little left to constitute the 'great slaughter'. Moreover, the fight itself is leached of all interest or excitement:

> As soon as the Gauls' battle cry was heard those nearest on the flanks and those furthest away at the rear ran from this enemy they had barely seen, without even trying to fight or to raise a battle-cry of their own, without having suffered a scratch or having even been touched. (38.6)

This colorless account of one of the best known episodes in Roman history is remarkable. And daring. Indeed, it is something of a tour-de-force, for in effect Livy denies that there was any battle at all: 'Men were not killed while fighting' (38.7).[20]

Events leading up to the second peripeteia are narrated chiefly to create suspense. It is characteristic of Livy to delay the moment of reversal as long as possible. In certain shorter episodes this takes the form of what can be termed the '*nisi*- or had-not-technique': i.e., Livy pushes the reversal not only to the brink of disaster, but a bit over the edge: 'The worst was in the process of happening, had not . . .'[21] A similar technique is also used on a large scale. The last third of Book Five not only is designed to create this effect as a whole, but is itself composed in part of smaller such units. The self-sacrifice of the elders (41.1–10) is an illustration. Their preliminary preparations are given swiftly, with economy, and in the past tense. The arrival of the Gauls in the forum, which sets the scene in the historic present (*in forum perveniunt*), marks the first step leading to the climax. Excitement is generated by giving the psychological reactions of the Gauls

---

[19] His account is quite close to that found in Diodorus, as Schachermeyr (1929: 292–4) and Ogilvie (1965: 719) note. But Livy's compression results in some puzzles and inconsistencies (noted by Schachermeyr).

[20] Cf. Burck's remarks (1935: 473).

[21] e.g. 2.47.8, or 3.1.4. See further Burck (1964: 215); Hoch (1951: 19 ff.); Jumeau (1939: 23–4).

to the sights they see or imagine. The verbs continue in the historic present: *ruunt, petunt*. The confrontation is delayed as long as possible: arrival at the Colline Gate, gathering in the forum, dispersal for booty, return to the forum, hesitant glances into the open doors of the patrician houses, the final entrance. Note that verisimilitude is sacrificed for the sake of suspenseful delay. When the Gauls first scatter for booty, we must suppose that in passing by the doors of the patrician houses they either deign not to notice them or choose not to. The climax is further delayed by noting every step in their approach after their return to the forum: 'they hesitated to enter... they gazed as in veneration at the beings seated in the vestibules of their homes... they approached them as if they were statues.'[22] The account of the actual assault is very brief; Augustan sensibilities as well as the historian's own predilection forbade scenes of blood and carnage. Furthermore, the climax has been reached at the point when the first blow is struck; elaboration would be anticlimactic and would contribute nothing further to the effect or the point of the episode. Hence the conclusion is swift (41.10): 'After killing the leading statesmen no one was spared. The houses were ransacked, emptied, set afire.'

The same technique operates on a larger scale as events build to the second peripeteia. The episodes involved were complex not only in number and variety, but also because attention must focus on three different places at once: Rome, Veii, and Ardea. Although Livy normally strives for unity of time and place (see below), here he accepts and even exploits the complexity in order to prolong the suspense and heighten the excitement.[23] After the first peripeteia a lengthy scene at Rome is devoted to the (now) exemplary behavior of

---

[22] Burck (1964: 202, n. 1) sees a contradiction in that Livy speaks of a number of houses (*in aedium vestibulis*), but the final scene can take place in only one. It would seem most natural (though not mandatory) so to view the final scene. Plutarch's version (*Cam.* 21–2) puts all the elders together in the open forum where the Gauls could not possibly have overlooked them on first gathering. This, together with the apparent contradiction, suggests that Livy himself may have transferred them to their respective houses in order to delay the confrontation, although he narrated the last scene as if the elders were all together.

[23] Burck (1964: 218) notes that Livy uses a similar technique to create suspense when switching from events *domi* to events *militiae*.

senators, plebeians and leaders. The scene then moves to Camillus at Ardea (43.6):[24]

As the Gauls set out from the city, Fortune herself brought them to Ardea...

Then to Veii (45.4):

In the territory of Veii there was a similar massacre—this time of the Etruscans...

Back to Rome for the episode of Fabius Dorsuo (46.1):

At Rome meanwhile...suddenly a young Roman...

Then to Veii and the decision to appoint Camillus dictator (46.4):

At Veii meanwhile not only had morale improved, but numbers and strength also...

Back to Rome for the episode of Manlius and the geese (47.1):

While these things were going on at Veii, at Rome in the meantime the citadel and Capitol...

That Livy is here deliberately exploiting 'division by place' is shown by his making the Dorsuo exploit into a separate episode; it could easily have been included in the first scene at Rome (39.9 ff.) or in the next (47.1 ff.).

From 47.1 on the scene remains focused on the Capitol, where famine and exhaustion lead to the final decision to capitulate. The hopelessness of the situation is brought home forcibly in a masterful periodic sentence of great length. For the last time the reader glimpses the proceedings at Ardea and Veii, but they seem too late. The steady piling up of participial and adjectival phrases, combined with numerous subordinate clauses, reinforces the long waiting and ultimate exhaustion (48.5–7):

---

[24] Since he does not want Camillus' victory at Ardea to overshadow the final reversal, Livy has Camillus sketch the battle plan and foretell its outcome in a speech to the Ardeates. The encounter itself can thus be reduced to a few lines. The subsequent victory at Veii under the centurion Q. Caedicius cannot, in turn, be allowed to overshadow Camillus' exploit (45.4–8). Hence it is narrated very summarily, and the centurion firmly 'put in his place' (*par Camillo defuit auctor*).

While the dictator was holding a levy of his own at Ardea (having ordered his master of the horse Lucius Valerius to fetch the army from Veii) and was making preparations and exercising the troops with the aim of enabling them to oppose the enemy on equal terms, the army on the Capitol in the meantime, exhausted from standing guard day and night, having surmounted every misfortune save starvation, which alone nature would not let them overcome, looking day after day for help from the dictator, and, in the end, as both hope and food failed them, seeing the guards staggering to their posts, their wasted bodies barely able to support the weight of their arms—the army finally bade the authorities negotiate surrender or ransom on whatever terms they could, the Gauls having made no secret that they could be persuaded to lift the siege for no very great price.

The senate is thus forced to treat for peace. The gold is weighed out. While the tribune futilely protests, a Gaul insolently throws his sword on the scale, 'uttering words intolerable to Roman ears, "Woe to the vanquished!"' (48.9), Livy can postpone the reversal no longer:

But god and man forbade the Romans be a ransomed people. For by some chance, before the unspeakable business could be carried through... (49.1)

The climax has been reached and the goal achieved. Livy characteristically ends the story as rapidly as decency will allow. In fifteen lines he recounts two battles and a triumph. In effect the intervention itself and this 'conclusion' form a single unit by virtue of their brevity and the continued use of verbs in the historic present. The manner in which Livy builds to and concludes the reversal reveals, perhaps better than any other passage, how much skill and self-discipline he exercised in composition. The subject matter immediately preceding the peripeteia was complex and inviting: the pestilence which attacked the Gauls (48.1–3); the first futile attempt at negotiation (48.4); the hurried levy at Ardea; the final last days on the Capitol, made terrible by famine, despair, and exhaustion; the difficult decision to offer ransom; the concluding scene of capitulation, with all its pathos, ignominy, and final insult. The material offered an almost unparalleled opportunity to indulge in a kind of writing of which he was particularly fond: crowd psychology, speeches, and 'tragic' scenes of pity and fear. Moreover, the concluding events must have tempted him to glorify at length one of his favorite heroes—Camillus— and his favorite heroine—Rome. But Livy yielded to none of these temptations. His skill as a narrator is seldom shown to better advantage than in what he chose not to say.

Particularly characteristic is his habit of introducing and concluding episodes as quickly as possible. Sometimes a mere phrase suffices for transition; 'by some chance or other', 'suddenly', 'through those days perchance', 'in the meantime' (*forte quadam, repente, per eos forte dies, interim*), and the like are frequent. The technique operates on a very large scale as well. For example, he plunges *in medias res* almost at once at the start of the Hannibalic War in Book 21, and concludes the decade so swiftly that Scipio's famous triumph (30.45.2) is described quite sketchily (compare Appian's fuller account at *Pun.* 66).[25] Occasionally, however, at the start of a grand sequence of events which requires a large canvass and generous treatment, Livy will vary his practice. Hence the placement of the excursus on the Gallic migrations. It is not merely a 'pleasant diversion' (*diverticulum amoenum*, 9.17.1), nor a vehicle to display the results of historical research, nor the conscientious fulfillment of the ethnographical digression which was traditional in ancient historiography. The 'Affair at Clusium' is carefully gotten under way (and in the historic present) *before* the excursus is inserted (33.1):

After Rome had expelled the one citizen whose presence would, if anything in this life is certain, have prevented her capture, and with the fateful disaster bearing down on upon the city, envoys from Clusium come seeking aid against the Gauls. Tradition says that these peoples...

Hence the digression serves in part the purpose of delaying the (announced) end of the story and of whetting the reader's interest in this 'hitherto unseen and unheard of enemy that had stirred up war from the ocean and ends of the earth' (37.2).[26]

---

[25] On the technique in general see Walsh (1961*a*: 178–9); Münzer (1910: 340); Burck (1964: 183 and n. 1); Witte (1910: *passim*, esp. 290–2, 299–301, 370–7). Failure to sketch necessary background material at the start of new enterprises has brought justified criticism: e.g., Syme (1958: i. 148), on the start of Book 31 and Rome's entrance into eastern affairs.

[26] See Ogilvie's remarks (1965: 700–1). Bayet's belief that the excursus is a later insertion is ill-founded (Budé, 1954: 96, 157–8). Compare the inclusion and the placement of the digression on the *vallum* just before the decisive engagement at Cynoscephalae is joined (33.5.5–12 = Polybius 18.18); Livy usually omits or sharply curtails this type of Polybian material (see Walsh 1961*a*: 158 for examples).

## 7. The unities

Normally Livy tries to achieve as much coherence and simplicity as he can in his narrative; this is particularly true for unity of time and of place.[27] At times this takes the form of straightforward telescoping, at others of glossing over and blurring in order to gain greater cohesion and simplicity.

In the versions of Polybius (2.18), Diodorus (14.115), and Plutarch (*Cam.* 22) the Gauls do not arrive in Rome until the fourth day after the Allia.[28] Livy brings them to the city gates on the very afternoon of the disaster (39.2).[29] This produces a tightly-knit story, but creates difficulties. The Gauls on arriving invest the neighborhood (39.3). But before they enter the gates the following events occur: the Romans decide to defend the Capitol and proceed to make necessary preparations, the emotional scene of separation takes place, the plebs including Albinius and the Vestals flee to surrounding towns (apparently while the Gauls looked on), and the elders have time to prepare themselves for sacrifice and to take their places in the houses surrounding the forum. The end of the story is similarly treated. According to one tradition the siege of the Capitol lasted seven months. Livy gives no hint of time, except that it was long enough to produce near starvation. But why the Gauls, who were doing the investing, should also have been afflicted with famine is not made clear (48.1), nor is Camillus' delay month after month at Ardea accounted for.

It has been noted above that in order to create suspense and narrative excitement Livy made the exploit of Fabius Dorsuo into an episode separate from the others which occur at the site of Rome. His usual practice, however, is to eliminate such separate scenes. For example, the story opens at Clusium (33.1), is interrupted by the digression on the Gauls, and resumes again at Clusium (35.4).

---

[27] See Witte (1910: 359–68).

[28] See Walbank (1957–79: i. 2.18.2 n.). Wolski (1956: 44) is surely mistaken in believing this to be the preservation of an authentic detail; cf. Ogilvie's remarks (1965: 720).

[29] Not two days and two nights as Burck (1964: 126) understands it. W–M 5.39.2 n., rightly notes that *insequenti die* of 39.8 means the day after the Allia and that *lux appropinquans* refers to the same day.

But the Clusine embassy to Rome, which comes next, requires three shifts: Clusium—Rome—Clusium. In order not to expand or complicate unnecessarily he avoids any real scene in Rome by first stating that the three Fabii were dispatched to Clusium and by then giving as if in retrospect the instructions of the Senate (partly in a *qui* clause, partly in *oratio obliqua*). In effect, a scene at Rome is eliminated. The impression is further reinforced by the tenses; all verbs following the resumption of the story after the digression are in the past tense until we are settled in Clusium for the main scene, where the historic present is used (*datur.* 36.1). A similar device is used at the site of Veii (46.4–11) when Caedicius and his men vote to summon Camillus from Ardea, but not before Pontius Cominus can make a journey to Rome in order to secure Camillus' election. The procedure was involved: it entailed originating the idea at Veii, sending Cominus to Rome, returning him to Veii, and then forwarding a message to Camillus at Ardea to inform him of his election. Livy's intention to retain as much unity of place as possible is clear, for *Veiis interim* ('meanwhile at Veii…') begins the section and *dum haec Veiis agebantur, interim arx Romae* ('while these things were going on at Veii, the citadel in Rome, meanwhile…') begins the next. Hence the journey of Cominus is given in short, simple sentences and in the historic present: it is not described in stages or separate scenes (the usual practice: see below), but follows Cominus continuously throughout the trip: *inde… et… inde*. The 'scene' at Rome is relegated to an ablative absolute (*accepto inde senatus consulto uti…*), and a participle suffices for sending legates to Camillus at Ardea. But further difficulties are involved; since Livy prefers to believe that Camillus did not set out from Ardea until the *lex curiata* (the law passed by the Curiate assembly) was actually enacted, Pontius would have had to take *two* journeys, the second to relay the actual passing of the law.

## 8. Division and division 'headings'

The most characteristic feature of Livy's narrative technique is the division of material into separate units based on groups of people, stages in a developing sequence of events, themes, or differing places.[30] He seldom narrates events as a continuous, uninterrupted sequence; only when aiming at a special effect, such as that concerning the journey of Pontius Cominus, does he violate this fixed technique of composition. Action is narrated in discrete scenes as in a stage-play, rather than following it continuously as in the manner of a movie camera. The technique is everywhere present in the *Ab Urbe Condita*, operating both on a very small and on a very large scale.

Its use on a small scale functions chiefly to mark the developing stages in action or to divide a large group into smaller units so that both actions of individuals and the general course of events can be easily conceived and followed. An example of the former is at 39.1–2, describing the reactions of the Gauls after their victory at the Allia: 'at first they stood rooted in shock... their next fear was that this was a trap... they then turned to gathering the spoils... at last they reached Rome' (*ipsi pavore defixi primum steterunt, ... deinde insidias vereri..., postremo caesorum spolia legere..., tum demum...ad urbem Roman perveniunt*). In parallel fashion the reactions of the Romans after the same event are thus described (39.4 ff.): 'The Romans, when most of the army... private grief was then... soon the howls and the cries... then throughout the whole time...'(*Romani cum pars maior... privatos deinde... mox ululatus... omne inde tempus...*); and beginning a new sequence: 'at the Gauls' first approach... then at sunset... then in the darkness itself... finally, with dawn approaching...'(*primo adventu... deinde sub occasum solis... tum in noctem... postremo lux appropinquans*). An example of division by group is at 40.4 ff., which describes the actions of those in Rome as the Gauls approach: 'when a great many of the women followed their relatives into the citadel... another group consisting mostly of plebeians... headed for the Janiculum hill, from which some scattered through the countryside, others to neighboring cities...' (*magna pars tamen earum* [sc. *mulierum*] *in arcem suos persecutae sunt... alia maxime plebis turba...petit Ianiculum. Inde pars per agros dilapsi, pars urbes petunt finitimas*). At the Allia (38.9–10) the parallel division between *pars incolumis Veios perfugit*

---

[30] See Walsh (1961*a*: 185–96); Burck (1964: 182–95); Witte (1910: *passim*, esp. 288–305, 368–80).

('most fled safely to Veii') and <u>*ab dextro cornu*</u>...*Romam omnes petiere* ('all those on the right wing...headed for Rome') is reinforced by *ne...quidem* phrases in each division: *ne nuntius quidem* ('not even a report...'), *ne clausis quidem portis* ('not even when the gates had been closed', cf. 41.5).

The 'Einzelerzählungen' which Witte first noted are the result of the same narrative technique operating on a larger scale. Thus we find 'The Affair at Clusium', 'Manlius and the Geese', 'Camillus' Victory at Ardea', and so forth. But equally pervasive and significant is a division technique intermediate between the 'Einzelerzählung' and the short passage of a few lines. In this group division is based on persons and places more often than on themes or temporal sequence. In most cases the first words of each division form a kind of 'heading' which functions like modern boldfaced type used to mark topics and sub-topics. Once the basis for division had been determined (e.g., groups or places), Livy usually adhered to the appropriate 'heading' throughout; he seldom abandoned the basis for division until it came to a natural end, or mixed different types together. The 'Affair at Clusium' is divided as follows (the principle of division being the group):

1. '*Clusini* novo bello exterriti...': the plight of Clusium (35.4).
2. '*Mitis legatio*, ni...': violation of *ius gentium* by the Roman legates (36.1).
3. '*Tribuni* quorum temeritate bellum contractum...': the Romans prepare for the Allia (37.3).
4. 'Interim *Galli*...': the Gauls do likewise (37.4).
5. 'Ibi *tribuni militum*...': the Romans at the site of the Allia (38.1).
6. 'Nam *Brennus regulus Gallorum*...': the Gauls at the Allia (38.3).
7. '*In altera acie* nihil simile Romanis...': the defeat itself (38.5).
8. '*Gallos* quoque...': reaction of the Gauls to victory (39.1).
9. '*Romani*, cum pars maior...': reaction of the Romans to defeat (39.4).

Once one becomes aware of such 'headings' they fairly leap to the eye; at times they can seem somewhat obtrusive and mechanical. After the first peripeteia Livy recounts the plans which the Romans make for their defense. The plan is given first for the defense of the Capitol (39.9–10), second for the preservation of religious rites and objects

(39.11), and third for the self-sacrifice of the elders (39.12–13). The following sections recount, in the same order, how each of these decisions was carried out:

1. Versae inde adhortationes *ad agmen iuvenum* quos in Capitolium
   ...(exhortation to the young fighters going to the Capitol, 40.1).
2. *Flamen* interim *Quirinalis virginesque Vestales*...(the escape to Caere of the priest of Quirinus and the Vestals, 40.7).
3. Romae interim... *turba seniorum*...(the fate of the elders back in Rome, 40.1).

The last division serves as both the conclusion to the previous section and the introduction to the last unit before the second reversal; the division is based on place. Hence, picking up the previous section:

3. *Romae* interim...('meanwhile at Rome')[31]
4. Proficiscentes Gallos *ab urbe*...fortuna ipsa *Ardeam* ubi Camillus exsulabat duxit...('as the Gauls set out from the city...fortune itself brought them to Ardea where Camillus was in exile', 43.6).
5. Similis *in agro Veienti* Tuscorum facta strages est...('in the territory of Veii there was a similar massacre', 45.4).
6. *Romae* interim...('meanwhile at Rome', 46.1).
7. *Veiis* interim...('meanwhile at Veii', 46.4).
8. Dum haec Veiis agebantur, interim *arx Romae*...('while these things were going on at Veii, at Rome in the meantime', 47.1).

## 9. Style

Livy employs various stylistic devices to give shape and design to his narrative. 'Division headings' are one example. His treatment of short, self-contained sequences in which action and movement predominate is another. In this kind of episode sentences of transition or of introduction are customarily brief and given in a past tense (the pluperfect is common). Sentences preliminary to the main piece of action are regularly periodic, lengthy, and also given in a past tense (but these seldom in the pluperfect); they are also few in

---

[31] Further subdivided into Romani *ex arce*...(42.3) and Galli *quoque per aliquot dies*...(43.1).

number—often one will suffice. As the action gains momentum the sentences shorten, parataxis becomes frequent, and the historic present often appears. If the action becomes particularly violent or hurried the sentences may reduce to only a few words apiece and historic infinitives take over. The self-sacrifice of the elders has already been cited in another connection for some of these characteristics. Save for Livy's brief interjection of a variant version at 41.3, two complex sentences set the scene: *expectabant... sedere* (third pl. perf.). Historic presents take over when the action speeds up: *perveniunt... ruunt... petunt*. When the pace slows temporarily past tenses reappear (*redibant... tenebant*), before the action builds to a second and greater climax in historic infinitives: *parci... diripi... inici*.[32] The episode of Manlius and the geese (47.1–6), as Walsh has observed, is another illustration.[33] A brief sentence serves as transition and introduction, given in a past tense: *dum haec Veiis agebantur... fuit*. The actions of the Gauls preliminary to the main scene come next in a lengthy periodic sentence: *Namque Galli... evasere*. A brief sentence denotes the reversal: *anseres non fefellere... quae res saluti fuit* ('the geese heard them..., which proved Rome's salvation'). The next division concentrates on Manlius and his acts: *M. Manlius... vadit... deturbat... trucidat*. The sentences then become even shorter and historic infinitives take over: *proturbare... deferri*. The conclusion is given in a single short sentence and in a past tense: *quieti datum est*.

But style is not confined to reinforcing sense chiefly or solely in such 'action' sequences. It has been noted how the lengthy and complex sentences describing the conditions which forced the Romans on the Capitol to treat for peace reflect the length of the siege and the exhaustion of the defenders. And style is also used to structure much larger units. The 'Affair at Clusium' is an illustration. The events involved in this sequence are numerous and complex. Involved are four shifts in locality (Clusium—Rome—Clusium—Rome), and extended length of time, four different meetings (two of the Roman Senate, one of a Roman assembly, one of the Gallic

---

[32] See also the first abortive attack by the Gauls on the Capitol (43.1–2), Camillus' victory at Ardea (45.1–3), and Pontius Cominus' journey to Rome (46.8–10).
[33] Walsh (1961*a*: 250–1).

council), three embassies, an argument about policy among the Gallic chieftains, and a battle. Livy tackles the task of narration simply and directly. Since for his purposes the most significant single event in this section is the violation of *ius gentium*,[34] he makes it the focal point. He does this not by dwelling on the act itself (the fact of violation is stated in a few words, followed by a brief comment on its most flagrant feature), but by causing two different narrative styles to meet at the point which he wishes most to emphasize (36.6). Prior events are therefore introductory in nature and are given summarily. Four lengthy sentences covering a page of text are needed to give the preliminaries. The first and last (35.4, 36.5) are hypotactic and periodic. The second (35.5–6) is a series of brief phrases forming a single stylistic unit which is asyndetic, paratactic, and elliptical, with both a verb to introduce *oratio obliqua* and all auxiliary verbs (*impetratum, missi*) omitted. The third sentence (36.1–4) is of great length and combines both hypotaxis (*ni, quibus, etsi,* or. obl., *quorum, quoniam, si, quam, si, ut*) and parataxis (*et, et*). Variety is thus achieved (four long sentences all paratactic or hypotactic would have been monotonous), but together they form a prefatory unit by virtue of their length and great compression. Indeed, Livy has compressed so drastically that at 35.4 we read of the Clusini that 'they enjoyed no right of alliance or friendship with Rome,' whereas in the next sentence the Senate warns the Gauls 'not to attack the allies and friends of the Roman people'. His method of avoiding in this section a separate scene in Rome has been noted above. The violation of *ius gentium* is thrown into relief when the long sentences of introduction are broken by a simple statement in the historic present: 'With the fates beginning to bring down ruin on the city of Rome, the envoys take up arms, contrary to the law of nations' (36.6). Each important stage in the action which follows is given briefly in the historic present; each of these in turn is followed by one or more equally brief statements in a past tense which elaborates what has been said in the historic present:

1. legati . . . arma capiunt / potuti . . . eminebat.
2. Q. Fabius . . . ducem Gallorum . . . occidit / agnovere . . . datum est.
3. receptui canunt / erant qui . . . vicere . . . placebat . . . videbantur . . . obstabat.

---

[34] The 'telos': Burck (1964: 184).

4. ad populum reiciunt / plus gratia atque opes valuere.
5. infensi Galli . . . ad suos redeunt / tribuni militum cum tribus Fabiis creati.

Thus compression, subordination, and—above all—style serve to give these complex events a relatively simple structural pattern and to emphasize the most important idea. Four lengthy sentences serve for introduction: one for sending the Clusine embassy, one for sending the Roman embassy, one for a statement by the Gauls, one for a reply by the Romans. Brief sentences in the historic present follow, giving the chief stages in the action: the Fabii take up arms, Q. Fabius kills a chieftain, the Gauls sound retreat, the Senate refers judgment of the Gallic claims to the people, the Gallic legates return to Clusium threatening war. Each of these in turn is followed by short sentences amplifying what has taken place. The most important point in the episode is placed where the two styles meet.

## II. SOURCES AND INNOVATION

Livy's narrative of the disaster at the Allia and of the sack of Rome is the product of a long and complex tradition. Numerous scholars have made attempts to separate the authentic elements from the fabrications, and then to trace the provenance and order of these later accretions. The initial study of Mommsen still holds first place, despite being superseded on this or that point by work of later scholars. For example, many believe that an appeal by Clusium to Rome in this period is out of the question; it would have been brought into the story *circa* 225 BCE when the city played a role in the Gallic turmoil.[35] Hence the Fabian embassy would also have been an addition made around the same time, doubtless to explain why the Gauls advanced on Rome and to give an *aitia* ('cause') for Rome's

---

[35] Cf. Polyb. 2.25–31; see Nap (1935: 8–9, 46); Wolski (1956: 36); Ogilvie (1965: 699–700). Some believe that there were two towns of the same name in this early period (Plin. *N.H.* 3.5.52: Clusini Novi, Clusini Veteres): for example, Richardson (1964: 23–4, 70–1). But the Clusini Novi more probably comprised a settlement of Sullan veterans near or at the site of the old town. Moreover, doubts about early contacts between Rome and Clusium may not be justified: cf. the saga of Lars Porsenna.

defeat.[36] The episode involving Q. Caedicius, the centurion at Veii, also seems to have been modeled on events of the third century.[37] The *devotio* of the elders has overtones of the death of the consul Octavius in 87 as well as certain borrowings from Greek literature.[38] Other Greek reminiscences have been noted.[39] And almost all scholars are agreed that the introduction of Camillus into the legend came relatively late (see below).[40]

Münzer, following Pais and Niebuhr, suggested that perhaps the saga did not progress in a single, linear development, but that two differing, but equally early, versions existed: one, popular and transmitted chiefly by word of mouth, in which the city was 'saved'

[36] See Mommsen (1879: 303–5); Nap (1935: 326–7); Ogilvie (1965: 716). Wolski (1956: 33–4) believes that the killing done by the legates was modeled (in reverse) on the murder of Roman legates by the Gauls in 283 (cf. Ogilvie 1965: 715). But violence done to or by legates is a common enough *casus belli* that the origin of the story need not have been prompted specifically by Gauls. One thinks, for instance, of Queen Teuta and the Coruncanii in 230 (Pol. 2.8).

[37] His election seems to be a throwback from events in Spain in 212, his name from the military tribune of 258 (Cato fr. 83 *HRR*). See Mommsen (1879: 322–6); Ogilvie (1965: 730). Caedicius, as if from *caedes*, suits both the one who hears the forecast of disaster (32.6) and the one who inflicts it (45.8 *caedi nocturnae... maiorem caedem*). The views of Basanoff (1950: 13–26) are far-fetched.

[38] See Ogilvie (1965: 720, 725–6); Nap (1935: 117, 196 n. 1). The core of the story, however, is based on ancient and authentic Roman practice: see Ogilvie (1965: 725) and Magdelain (1964: 435–6).

[39] e.g. see Mommsen (1879: 302–3, 321–2); Thouret (1880: 136–41); Täubler (1912: 219); Wolski (1956: 42–3).

[40] One of the chief stumbling blocks in tracing and evaluating the development of the saga is the problem of identifying the source(s) of Diodorus. Almost every possible solution has been proposed, but nothing approaching a consensus has been reached. Mommsen (1879: 297–9) opted for Fabius Pictor; Münzer (1910: 324, 330, 337) judged the source to be old and reliable, but was not so certain of its identity. Some advocate a date as late as Sulla (e.g., Wolski 1956: 25–6; Momigliano (1942: 112 n. 7) demurs); some find references which seem to date to the Caesarian period: e.g., Hirschfeld (1913: 276–8); Ogilvie (1965: 699). Inevitably, intermediate theories have been advanced: i.e., Diodorus used *two* sources, one early and one late: e.g., Schachermeyr (1929: 284–9). Schachermeyr is one of the few who have tried to imagine just what types of information later historians had to hand and how they might have worked from them. His picture of Fabius Pictor using the pontifical notices may not be particularly convincing (he believes, among other things, that these notices were quite full for the sack: 299, n. 1), but the questions he asks are challenging and fundamental. Parts of Diodorus are clearly confused (e.g., shifting the battle site from the left to the right bank of the Tiber), and certain parallels with Livy are striking: see Wolski (1956: 29 and n. 2); Schachermeyr (1929: 292–4); Ogilvie (1965: 719).

and Camillus played a prominent role; and a second, featured in the earliest histories, which took no account of him.[41] The theory has much to recommend it, although a few have demurred.[42] Certainly the chief piece of evidence in its favor is the testimony of Aristotle as reported by Plutarch (*Cam.* 22.3). The philosopher not only recorded the sack, but reported that the city had been 'saved'—the savior being a certain Lucius. The name must be an error, since Camillus' praenomen was Marcus (nor are there other Lucii in the saga who are likely candidates).[43] But this is no reason to reject the whole of Aristotle's testimony.

Nevertheless, even if this 'popular' legend be reckoned very early, it is clear that it did not become incorporated into the *written* historical tradition until late—possibly not until Sullan times. Hence the many differing versions. Polybius (2.18.22), who was most probably following Fabius Pictor,[44] mentions nothing about recovery of the gold or of a role for Camillus. On the other hand, some versions knew of the recovery of the ransom money, but not by Camillus: Strabo (5.2.3) and Diodorus (14.117.7) report that the Caeretans defeated the Gauls on their retreat northward and sent it back, Justin declared that Massilia replaced, but did not recapture, it (43.5.9), while Suetonius says that it was the progenitor of the Livii Drusi who recovered it (*Tib.* 3.2).[45] When Camillus was introduced into the legend he was reported to have seized the gold from the Gauls as they

[41] See Münzer (1910: 334–5) and his references there; cf. Cocchia (1922: 17–32). Recently scholars have uncovered an apparent third version which held that the Capitol itself was captured. Skutsch (1953: 77–8) believes this was probably Ennius' version. Other scholars have subsequently found possible allusions to it in later writers: McGann (1957: 126); Clarke (1967: 138). But perhaps not enough consideration has been given to the possibility of poetic or rhetorical exaggeration in these instances.

[42] For example, Momigliano (1942: 113) accepts it and Täubler (1912: 231–2) rejects it.

[43] I am not convinced by the suggestion that L. Albinius was the 'savior' in this early version: Sordi (1960: 49–52); Ogilvie (1965: 723–4); Palmer (1970: 162–4). Although Albinius may have been the flamen Quirinalis himself in the original version, the Romans do not appear to have equated the preservation of the *sacra* with the saving of the city itself (cf. his elogium *CIL* 6.1217 = *ILS* 51), nor is it likely that the Greek Aristotle would have equated them. I agree with Momigliano (1942: 113) that a distorted report of the Camillus legend is the best solution.

[44] See Walbank (1957–79: i. 184–5) and references there.

[45] *Abnepos* of the tribune of 122. Münzer (1926: 853–5) believes the date to be 283 and the story to be a late fabrication. Sordi (1960: 149–51) considers it to be early.

were withdrawing northward, but the location was identified variously from source to source.[46] Finally, Livy's version brought Camillus into the rubble of the forum itself, and before the gold had been completely weighed out. There are additional indications of a late date. For example, the night journey of Pontius Cominus was originally intended merely to open up the lines of communication between Veii and Rome (as in Diodorus: 14.116); later it was found ideal for reporting the request for, and granting of, the dictatorship.[47] But the appointment itself created problems. In one version (Dion. Hal. 13.6), Q. Caedicius, the centurion in Veii, after election as commander by his soldiers, appointed Camillus dictator. But this was clearly irregular on several counts.[48] An alternate and more satisfactory solution was to secure the election at Rome itself, but it is significant what form this took. Instead of one of the consular tribunes appointing Camillus dictator in the normal fashion (note that Quintus Sulpicius was present and available), Camillus was popularly elected. This, as Täubler has argued, is probably modeled on Sulla's election (and there are other features of Camillus' dictatorship and career with parallels in the Sullan period).[49] Moreover, further difficulties appear in the story, for Cominus left before the actual *lex curiata de imperio* was passed; Livy preferred to believe that Camillus would not have quit Ardea until formal announcement of its actual passage had been given him (46.11).[50]

Livy's version clearly represents a late stage in the development of the saga; his source or sources can be dated no earlier than the Sullan period. Valerius Antias, Licinius Macer, and Claudius Quadrigarius

---

[46] Pisaurum according to Serv. *ad Aen.* 6.825; a certain οὐεάσκιον according to Diod. 14.117. See Münzer (1910: 336–7). Livy (5.49.6) reports a second battle, following the one in the forum, *ad octavum lapidem Gabina via.* See Sordi (1960: 148–9).

[47] See Ogilvie's summary (1965: 732).

[48] Vestiges of this version are evident at Livy 5.46.6–7.

[49] It must at least date to after 217, when Minucius was popularly elected. But the Sullan period is probably responsible for the whole procedure. Although some of Täubler's parallels (1912) are not particularly convincing (e.g., the recall from disgrace and 'exile', the battle before the city, the championing of senatorial interests), the manner of election, and the scope and duration of the dictatorship (cf. Livy 6.1.4) seem to me most telling. Cf. Ogilvie (1965: 728, 732).

[50] See Mommsen (1887–8: iii.1.41 n. 1) and n. 70 below.

have been suggested.[51] Of these, slight preference can be given to Claudius.[52] He is the only one of the three whose surviving fragments (1–7 HRR) concern these events; meager as they are, they coincide with Livy's version. If Livy did indeed use Claudius, however, he must have elaborated the material considerably. Claudius covered the period from 390 to 218 BCE in only three books;[53] his treatment of the Gallic catastrophe must therefore have been quite abbreviated. All critics have assumed that Livy adhered quite faithfully to his sources. He might abridge, omit, or embroider for artistic or didactic purposes, but he seldom, if ever, made sweeping changes or invented outright. The finished product was thus likely to preserve clear traces of the political bias, special interests, and even stylistic peculiarities of the sources used. This view is based chiefly on the observable methods which Livy employed in adapting Polybius for large portions of Books 31–45.[54] But the present study suggests that in the early books—or, at least, in certain parts of these early books—Livy

[51] See Ogilvie (1958: 42–4) and (1965: 699, 716, 720, 742). Ogilvie considers Licinius Macer 'unlikely' (716), although he sees his influence at 5.46.11 (732). The digression on the Gauls (33.2–35.3) is certainly not from the same source; Ogilvie has shown that the source was undoubtedly Greek, Timagenes and Posidonius being equally probable (1965: 700–2; 1958: 43 and n. 49). Mommsen (1879: 345–6, cf. 324 and n. 64) believed Livy used two sources, chiefly because of the 'variant' at 46.11 on the election of Camillus as dictator.

[52] See Zimmerer (1937: 140 ff., esp. 144–50); cf. Thouret (1880: 148 ff). Ogilvie (1965: 736, 738) believes that since Dionysius (13.13) puts the ransom gold at 2,000 lbs., while Livy, Diodorus, Plutarch, and Zonaras all give 1,000 lbs., he must have taken the figure from the 25 talents (= 2,000 lbs.) taken from the throne of Jupiter Capitolinus in 52 (Pliny NH 33.14, Varro ap. Non. 338L): 'It follows that whereas D.H.'s source must be later than 52, L's must be earlier.' But this argument seems to assume that information cannot be added by an extant writer, but only by his source. If a source *must* be postulated, Varro is known to have made the connection in his De Vita Populi Romani, as Nonius 338L reports. The work probably dates to 48–46 BCE: see Riposati (1939: 84–86, cf. also 165–67, 250, 298). Moreover, Dionysius is known to have used Varro, and particularly Valerius Antias through Varro: see Palmer (1970: 29–32). It is also generally admitted that Livy used Varro very little, if at all: Ogilvie (1965: 6). Note that Pliny, loc. cit., rejected Varro's inference about the amount of ransom gold. Cf. also Mommsen (1879: 330 n. 75).

[53] See Zimmerer (1937: 5–10), who suggests that these books were chiefly introductory to the main narrative, as are Books 1–2 of Polybius. Note the number of 'lower class' individuals: M. Caedicius (32.6), L. Albinius (40.9), Q. Caedicius (45.7), Pontius Cominus (46.8; cf. Plut. Cam. 25.1).

[54] Nissen (1863) and Witte's long article (1910) are the chief studies on this important subject.

took a much freer hand than in the later Polybian sections. First of all, the structure which he imposed on his material dominates it completely, dictating both the scope and the emphasis of each part. Since it corresponds to his moral purpose as stated in the Preface, and since it is intricate and highly artificial—arising neither 'naturally' nor logically from the events described—it seems almost certain that it was Livy's own invention. It did not therefore derive from a source. Consequently, a great many events in the tradition had to be sharply curtailed, or omitted entirely; for others the historian resorted to expansion and free invention (as, for example, in the occupation of Rome, which he gives almost entirely in emotional and psychological terms: 42.1–43.5).[55] It might be argued that such changes, however pervasive, are of degree and not in kind: Livy can nowhere here be shown to alter the basic *facts* reported in his sources (reducing the Gallic march on Rome from four days to one, for example, or introducing scenes of 'pity and fear' are neither basic nor extraordinary—both procedures can be paralleled in the 'pure' Polybian sections). But a strong case, I believe, can be made for showing that Livy indeed was responsible for at least one basic alteration in the received tradition.

To begin with, however, we should not expect a priori that Livy (or any other of the late annalists, for that matter) effected very many *fundamental* changes. Indeed, studies in such early legends as the sack of Rome or the Coriolanus saga show that the process of transformation was generally gradual and took place over a long period—each generation of writers adding to, or improving, different parts of the story according to its particular concerns and prejudices. In time a 'tradition about the traditions' grew up: the major episodes of early Roman history assumed certain canonical outlines with which most readers were familiar. Hence the historians of early Rome could not reasonably expect, or want, to create surprise very often in the readers' minds. The question is seldom 'What will happen?', but 'How will it happen?' The pleasure of reading was in recognition of the familiar, realized not so much in the fulfillment of a story, but in expectation of its fulfillment—suspense of anticipation, not of revelation. Hence

---

[55] See Ogilvie's comment (1965: *ad loc.*); Burck (1964: 127).

Livy's fondness for delaying a climax as long as he can; hence, too, the swift introductions and conclusions to almost all episodes, large and small, throughout the *Ab Urbe Condita*. This partly accounts for the affinity many have felt between certain Livian episodes and the techniques, if not the plots, of Greek and Roman tragedies. Indeed, the techniques of so-called 'tragic' history of the Hellenistic period were particularly suited to retailing the stuff of early Roman history.[56] Foreshadowing is one of them, and is a Livian hallmark. The disaster at the Allia is presaged by the warning voice on the Nova Via, with Livy himself reinforcing the foreboding as the main story gets under way (33.1). Similarly, the outcome of the sacrifice of the elders is anticipated at the outset (41.1). Indeed, it is imperative that the reader know in advance the outcome of such episodes; otherwise he cannot properly feel or appreciate the force of the narrative. Rarely a story might be so little known that a different kind of suspense—the surprise of revelation—was possible. Even less frequently would a major episode lend itself to this sort of treatment. Yet this appears to be the case with the ending of the present story. Note that the 'saving' of the city by Camillus' last-minute intervention is never foreshadowed or hinted at. Quite the contrary; the story seems to be moving relentlessly to a shameful conclusion. Moreover, later versions which bring Camillus into the ransom scene in the forum seem to have been taken directly from Livy alone.[57] What particularly encouraged him

---

[56] On history and tragedy see the fine article by Ullman (1942: 25–53); on its influence on Livy see Burck (1964: 176–233) and Walsh (1961*a*: 22–34, 176–90). For a more cautious appraisal see Jumeau (1936: 63–8); cf. also (1966: 561–2).

[57] Chief among them is Plutarch in his life of *Camillus* (28–9), the sources for which are still in dispute. Klotz (1941) reviews the various theories (282–5), but his attempt to deny that Plutarch used Livy at all is unconvincing. After all, Plutarch *cites* Livy at 6.2 (= 5.22.3), and even mistranslates a technical Latin word (*prosecuisset* at Livy 5.21.8 means 'to cut out a victim's entrails', which Plutarch understood as *prosecutus esset*, hence his κατακολουθήσαντι at 5.4): on both Livian passages consult Ogilvie's valuable notes (1965). Klotz assumes that Plutarch used only a single source, and rarely added or incorporated information from other sources—a much too rigid and mechanical conception. It seems to me more probable that for the Gallic catastrophe Plutarch used Livy and at least one other source (quite possibly several others), not merely alternating between them, but using one to supplement the other(s) as he went along. Certainly his account of Camillus' intervention in the forum contains nothing which could not have come from Livy and Plutarch's own pen. Livy also seems to be the only, or the chief, source for the encounter at Clusium (*Cam.* 17), the battle at the Allia (18.4–6: but not the preliminaries), the flight after the Allia

to aim for a surprise ending in this instance, of course, was the existence of a great variety of conflicting versions concerning the ransom. Some apparently recorded that even the Capitol fell, while others know of no recovery of gold or of a part for Camillus. Some claimed that the gold was subsequently recovered (again with no role for Camillus), but each disagreeing on the agent and the date. When Camillus was injected into the proceedings, he was permitted to defeat the Gauls on their retreat northward, but there was no consensus on the site or on the circumstances. Here, then, was a rare opportunity to build to a surprise ending: which will he choose? The preceding narrative does not anticipate the outcome. If anything, it prepares the reader for the sort of ending one finds in Diodorus. Hence the surprise—really a *double* surprise, for by bringing Camillus into the forum itself he created an ending *no one* was quite prepared for. This grand and daring conclusion to the first pentad was doubtless meant chiefly as exciting reading. No one could take it very seriously, given the story's many improbabilities. Indeed, in some later references to the ransom gold Livy unblushingly represents it as paid, ignoring his earlier tampering with the canonical version (10.16.6, 22.59.7, 34.5.9: all in speeches). In fact, he permits Camillus in his final speech to describe the Romans as 'defeated, captured and ransomed' (*victi captique ac redempti*, 51.8); and there may be more than a hint of correction and of apology when he acknowledges Camillus' later victory over the Gauls on the via Gabinia to be 'a more regular battle' (*iustius proelium*: 49.6).

(18.7), the episode of Albinius (21.1–2), Camillus at Ardea (23.2–24.3), Manlius and the geese, together with the aftermath (26.1–27.5), and the events leading to and including the ransom scene (28–29). For certain other events he has not relied exclusively or largely on Livy, although some details may be added from him: Camillus' trial, the meeting of the Senate concerning the actions of the Fabii at Clusium, the arrival at the Allia, the *devotio* of the elders, arrival of the Gauls in Rome after the Allia, and the journey of Cominus. It must be admitted, however, that no single passage in Plutarch points unequivocally to Livy as a *chief* source: (1) the citation of Livy at *Cam.* 6.2 is slightly inaccurate and may merely be an isolated variant which Plutarch did not recall exactly, (2) since *proseco* is a technical term, it quite likely appeared in other Latin versions, (3) no other change which Livy himself can clearly be shown to have made in the story appears in Plutarch. Hence *non liquet* might be a proper verdict. If it is maintained that Livy was *not* a source, then the date of Plutarch's source becomes important. If before Livy, then the final scene cannot be Livy's invention; if after, the source could have been based partly on Livy.

## III. VERISIMILITUDE

Livy's account of the Gallic catastrophe shows beyond doubt that he turned his back on any attempt to retail these events 'wie es eigentlich gewesen' ('as it really was'). In fact, he has not even bothered to narrate them 'wie es am wahrscheinlichsten gewesen' ('as it most probably was'). This deserves further scrutiny, since the many improbabilities in the narrative appear at just those places where he can be shown to have taken a free hand in adapting his material. Critics have occasionally remarked on his disregard of realism and verisimilitude in his account of early Rome, but none has recognized it for the pervasive and characteristic phenomenon it is. How can we account for it?

Some seem to assume that he was careless in matters such as these, with the further implication that if he had not been so inattentive or hurried he would have corrected them.[58] This is possibly the explanation for certain minor inconsistencies: for example, when he depicts the Gauls investing Rome a few hours after the Allia was fought, the subsequent departure of the Vestals and other citizens must have taken place under their very noses. But inadvertence cannot explain most examples. Indeed, Livy flatly avoids devising rational explanations or understandable motives. The behavior of the Romans prior to the Allia is highly exaggerated and irrational; at no point does he attempt to say *why* they behave so deplorably, except to invoke *fate* (32.7, 33.1, 36.6) and Fortune (37.1, cf. 38.4): 'So completely does Fortune blind our minds when she wants to remove all obstacles to her growing power.' The sudden change of heart recorded at the first peripeteia is even more mysterious; the Gauls (and the reader) can only view the Allia as a 'miraculous victory' (39.1) and the behavior of the Romans thereafter as 'another miracle, like the earlier one' (39.2). The second peripeteia also illustrates Livy's willingness to sacrifice likelihood and realism for the sake of structural parallelism and narrative excitement. Camillus' long delay at Ardea is not

---

[58] Münzer, for example (1910: 334): 'It is characteristic of him, that he unmindfully skirts around all unevenness, contradictions, and implausibilities, to make the dramatic peripeteia more effective.' Cf. also Meyer's lament (1903: 151).

explained, and only chance (*forte quadam*) accounts for his last minute intervention in the forum.[59] Moreover, the picture of him and his men picking their way over the rubble and through the ranks of the assembled Gallic army, apparently unnoticed and unchallenged, has much in common with the final scene of the 'Pirates of Penzance'. No, the answer must be that Livy was well aware of many such improbabilities in his narrative. And it is also clear that he was not much bothered, if bothered at all, by their presence.

Another explanation might be that he was indifferent to the sort of writing that aims for verisimilitude. But even a cursory examination of his adaptation of Polybius in the later books disproves this notion. Gone are most of the romantic improbabilities prevalent in the first decade; realistic details (*enargeia*) are added everywhere.[60] For example, when King Philip mounted the hill at Cynoscephalae where a preliminary clash of light-armed troops had taken place, Polybius says he found the summit deserted (18.24); Livy distributes a few corpses and arms over the field (33.8.9)—a neat touch, and quite convincing (there probably *were* a few casualties in the earlier skirmish). Again, at the conference at Nicaea between Flamininus and Philip, Livy depicts the king striding to the prow of his ship as it approached anchorage near shore where the Romans awaited (32.32.12)—whereas Polybius merely says 'he remained afloat' (18.1); and after some preliminary words Livy (32.33.1) has an embarrassing silence fall between the two men as each waits for the other to begin in earnest—an effective detail not in Polybius. Examples can easily be multiplied.[61]

It is in his account of early Rome that Livy's disregard for verisimilitude and realism seems most prevalent. The reason is doubtless due in part to his attitude toward the nature and reliability of the early tradition. That he viewed the whole of it with the gravest misgivings is abundantly clear. It was not merely that particular inventions and fabrications had intruded,[62] or that individual stories were improbable (e.g., Horatius at the bridge earned 'greater fame than credibility'

[59] 'Il deus ex machina del dramma': Funaioli (1934: 127).
[60] See Walsh (1961a: 181 ff.).
[61] See Witte (1910: *passim*).
[62] Often to enhance the family history of this or that historian: e.g., 4.16.2–4, 7.9.1–6, 8.40.

for his exploit, 2.10.11); more important, the entire picture was *uniformly* suspect. This was particularly true of events before the sack, in which most of the few records that did exist were destroyed; at the start of Book Six (6.1.2) he compares a man of his own time looking back on these events to one who catches only a glimpse of objects from far away. General shapes alone are discernable; their details are lost, and can only be guessed at. Some particulars handed down by tradition were probably authentic, but how could one be sure which were true and which not? Livy does not know, and admits it (7.6.6): 'I would spare no effort if there were any way of ascertaining the truth; as it is, one must hold to tradition when antiquity prevents us from attaining sure knowledge.' Hence he usually refuses to estimate the truth or falsity of what he relates, since particulars are not recoverable;[63] in matters so remote and so uncertain, approximations to the truth must be accepted in lieu of the truth itself.[64]

Perhaps this helps to explain the particular antipathy Livy felt toward his bête noire, Valerius Antias. Of course the man was a liar (*nullus mentiendi modus est*: 26.49.3), but no more so than the other annalists Livy used (he impartially points to exaggerations and outright inventions on all their parts).[65] No, what particularly nettled him about Antias was the latter's fondness for inventing precise

---

[63] See, for example, Praef. 6–9, 5.21.8–9, 8.18.3, 29.14.9, for his general attitude. For examples of his remarks on particular problems see 1.3.2, 4.23.3, 27.1.13. It must be admitted, however, that his attitude is partly affected by the belief that, even if some particulars *were* knowable, the discovery would be negligible; for example, on the disputed cognomen of a consul, 'in this it matters little what the truth is' (8.18.2). I do not mean to suggest that Livy worked according to a set of predetermined critical principles; I agree with Hoffmann (1942: *passim*, esp. 19, 36–40) that he took each case as it came and, if he was moved to criticize at all, did so according to intrinsic probability.

[64] e.g., 5.21.9 *in rebus tam antiquis si quae similia veris sint pro veris accipiantur, satis habeam.* But he goes on to draw the line at the particularly outrageous *fabula* in question: 'In events as old as these I would be quite prepared to accept approximations of the truth in place of the truth itself. But it is not worth my approving or rejecting this particular story, since—far from inviting belief—it seems more suited to the stage, where miracles are at home and appreciated.' Moreover, symbolic truth can have as high a value as literal truth. In the Preface (7) he suggests that the military glory of the Romans makes their claim of Mars as their progenitor perfectly acceptable, even if he is not reckoned as the literal ancestor.

[65] On Licinius Macer 7.9.3–6; Coelius Antipater 21.47.4–5, 29.25.1–4, 29.27.13–15; Claudius Quadrigarius 25.39.12, 38.23.6–9; Antias 30.19.11–12, 32.6.5–8.

details which would give his narrative the appearance of truth and authenticity.[66] He was especially fond of numbers—exact numbers (body counts made for propaganda purposes are not a recent invention: Antias made a specialty of them).[67] But Livy did not respect a historian who could unblushingly number the raped Sabine women at precisely 527 (fr. 3 *HRR*).[68] His attitude is best illustrated by the following remarks on an early battle (3.5.12–13): 'For an event as old as this it is difficult to give trustworthy figures on just how many fought and died. But Valerius Antias presumes to work up the totals: 5,800 Romans fell in Hernican territory; of the Aequi who entered and plundered Roman territory 2,400 were killed by the consul A. Postumius; another band, while driving off plunder, fell in with Quinctius and was slaughtered on an even grander scale, for the number of casualties amounted to four thousand three hundred and—keeping his count running down (*exsequendo*) to the very last corpse—thirty.'[69]

Livy saw nothing wrong with taking a somewhat free hand in narrating the history of early Rome; since it was uncertain and suspect, what else could one do? But he seems to have considered efforts to invest these events with a false appearance of exactitude not only misleading, but—perhaps more important—inappropriate to

[66] Antias reproduced, or appears to have reproduced, official information found in the pontifical notices of the Annales Maximi. In general see Cic. *de Or.* 2.52, Cato fr. 77 *HRR*, and McDonald (1957: 155–9); on Antias in particular see Klotz (1940–1: 24–49); Zimmerer (1937: 17–21, 36–43, 79 ff.). Fronto described his style as *invenuste* (114N; cf. Cic. *de Leg.* 1.26). To begin with, then, his history had the appearance of an 'official' chronicle in content and in style. Livy's distrust, if not disinterest, in the minutiae of ancient days may help to explain his failure to incorporate more antiquarian material than he did; for example, he did indeed consult Cincius the antiquarian at 7.3.7 (see Heurgon 1964: 432–7), but is no sign of use of Varro, save possibly at 7.2.

[67] See, for example, 26.49.1–6, 30.19.11–12, 33.10.7–10, 36.38.6–7, 38.23.6–9. Walsh (1961*a*: 121 n. 2) suggests that these figures may represent the exaggerated claims of commanders in their official reports to the Senate. But Antias' obvious inventions in early Roman history (where official reports are out of the question) and the failure of annalists to agree on casualty totals in the later period make this hypothesis unlikely.

[68] Livy does not give a number, except to say that he thinks it was higher than thirty (1.13.7). Ogilvie believes that Livy cannot therefore be using Antias here as a source. But if Livy *had* cited Antias' figure, it could only have been to reject it.

[69] Is it possible that Livy is using *exsequor* ambiguously here (i.e., both in its meaning of 'follow to the grave' and 'bring to completion')? If so, the picture of Antias as the self-appointed *vespillo* to ancient battlefields is a marvellous touch.

the spirit which animated, or ought to animate, them.[70] Livy states his view at the very start (Pref. 6): 'Events before the city was founded or planned have been handed down more as pleasing poetic fictions than as reliable records of historical events.' Quite clearly he considered that this applied with equal force to events after the actual founding: in fact, down to the sack, and in gradually diminishing measure thereafter (6.1.1–3). The historian was therefore entitled, and possibly even obliged, to narrate the grand and stirring legends of early Rome in the spirit of the poet or the story-teller. Exaggeration and the miraculous were permissible and entirely at home in such contexts, provided they were not overdone. But throughout the historian must have a serious purpose. Since the stories embodied national ideals and moral values, he must strive to bring out these qualities clearly and forcefully. The *details* were untrustworthy, but the spirit which breathed through the legends, he believed, was decidedly not.

## ADDENDUM

Many of the issues discussed here Luce treated at greater length in his 1977 book on Livy's working methods and composition, which focuses on the fourth and fifth decades (Books 31–45). Recent treatments of Livy's scale and narrative economy include Moles, Henderson (1989), and Vasaly (2002). On the question of Hellenistic

---

[70] There is a puzzling exception to Livy's general avoidance of overnice precision. After the senate has voted that a *lex curiata* should be passed recalling Camillus from exile and naming him dictator, Pontius Cominus leaves for Veii to relay the news. From there legates summon Camillus to Veii. But, says Livy (46.11), he prefers to believe that Camillus did not set out until the news reached him that the law had actually been passed. This bit of nit-picking has brought justified exclamations of puzzlement and exasperation from several quarters (e.g., Mommsen 1879: 324 n. 64; Täubler 1912: 224): why couldn't Cominus wait for an extra hour or two until the curiate assembly met and passed on the law?—difficulties have been created where none exist, or need to. The answer must be due partly to Livy's desire to show his hero in the best possible light and partly as a contrast with the general disorder which led up to the Allia; there may also be a bit of self-advertisement in appearing to ferret out such subtle constitutional irregularities. Almost all scholars assume that Livy must have taken the quibble over from a source; but full responsibility could easily be his.

historiography, its nature, and its influences—all relevant to Luce's discussion of *peripeteia*—see Humphreys (1997) with Levene (1997) and Marincola (2003) on historiographical emotions, and Wiseman (1993) on *enargeia*.

On the religious issues raised by Livy's use of the leitmotifs of divine and human aid, see Feeney's (1998) discussion of the place of religion in Roman literature; on religion in Livy see Liebeschuetz and Addendum. For temporal and transitional markers, tense variation, *nisi-* clauses, and their effect on the structure and meaning of a historiographical narrative, see Chausserie-Laprée (1969). Suits (1974) is a fine structural study of a whole Book of the *AUC*.

For Livy's use of his sources in the first decade, see Oakley and Forsythe (1999), a meticulous study of Livy's editorial comments, also in the first decade; Damon (1997) examines a section of Book 34. For the invention of early Roman history see Wiseman (*passim*, but especially 1979*a* and 2004), in continuing dialogue with Cornell (especially 1986*a* and 1995).

In the debate about verisimilitude in historiography, Woodman's 1988 book is essential; its conclusions remain fruitfully controversial. On the larger question of the effects of narrative on the representation of reality, see also White (1978) and (1980). For Antias, see Rich; for the often spurious precision in numbers in war narrative there is an interesting discussion by Rubincam (1991).

For more on Book 5 see Kraus (1994*b*). The figure of Camillus has generated many studies: e.g. Hellegouarc'h (1970) and Miles (1995) chapter 2 on Augustus and Camillus; and Wiseman (1979*b*) and Jaeger (1993) on Camillus and Manlius. Finally, the role of topography in Livian narrative has been well treated by Horsfall (1982) and (1985); see further the Addendum to Joshel.

# III

# Language and Style

# 6

Comedy, Wit, and Humour in Livy

*L. Catin*

We have noted in an earlier discussion a digression 'which caused me to lose sight of events in the Peloponnese' (39.53.1). Just what was this digression? The observation of a coincidence, pure and simple, that Livy noticed and found curious: Hannibal, Scipio, and Philopoemen are all three dead and all three buried away from their homelands (39.52.7–9). Livy, then, is no longer the historian, but the bystander observing history. The bystander seeks profound causes where they have no place, at the cost of not seeing them where they are present. Hence those comparisons that strive to create the illusion of a predestined connection between independent events, to awaken that feeling of the supernatural which dreams in the heart of crowds. The bystander likes being sententious. 'In war', Livy exclaims, 'there is nothing so insignificant that does not at times entail serious consequences' (25.18.3). He is fond of obvious truths. One need not read Livy to know that 'there are things easier said than done' (31.38.3). It is probable that 'it is easier to beat Antiochus and Philip separately than both at once' (33.19.7). It is certain that 'the qualities that make a good soldier do not necessary make a good general' (35.19.13), and it is obvious that 'a horseman goes faster than a man on foot' (31.37.10). The bystander is also fond of giving an opinion on technical questions that lie outside his expertise. During the battle of Pydna the Romans send elephants against the Macedonians, but 'most human inventions have only a theoretical value; in practice, when it is time to act, not to discuss how to act, there is no sign of a result. Thus, for all their reputation, elephants in battle turned out to be useless' (44.41.4). Next thing, Livy informs us that these elephants led the Latin allies to smash the enemy's left wing. Then he undertakes to explain to us the advantages and disadvantages of the phalanx. His explanation is clear and probably correct, but Livy's tone reminds us of the 'armchair' generals of whom he can on occasion make fun: 'In every gathering, at every dinner-party, there are people who can lead the armies to Macedon, who know where to pitch camp, where to post our garrisons, when and by what pass we should enter Macedon, where to set up our stores, the right land and sea routes for our supplies, when to give battle and when it is wiser to decline it' (44.22.8).

Moreover, Livy likes a laugh at others' expense. He is quick to detect the ridiculous in an attitude or a character. The great comic figures, a *miles gloriosus*, a *bourgeois gentilhomme*, excite ridicule not for their respective cowardice and stupidity, but because they have striven to build splendid houses of lies that collapse at the first confrontation with the real world. In Livy, we see the elite of the Samnite youth swear with great ceremony the solemn oath neither to retreat nor to allow anyone else to retreat. May the gods' wrath descend on him who is forsworn, his ancestors, and his descendants! Well, once battle is joined, 'whether they have sworn or not', all the Samnites have a single pressing concern: to run away (10.38.10–11; 10.41.10). Philip of Macedon has heard that from the summit of Mount Haemus a single glance reveals the Black Sea, the Adriatic, the Danube, and the Alps. From such a vantage-point, what plans will he be able to form with a view to his next campaign! Those who know the country point out in vain the difficulties of the climb; he sets off with a large escort; with great effort he approaches the summit; the panorama turns out to be a fog so thick that he no longer knows his way. 'When they had come back down, they made no contradiction of the popular belief, rather, I think, to avoid mockery of this mad expedition than because they had been able to see at a glance so many seas, mountains, and rivers so far distant from each other' (40.21–2).

Livy also has a taste for caricature. He is like those serious authors who for relaxation pencil into the margins of their manuscripts little men who are masters at tumbling and grimacing. One stroke of the pencil calls for another, and lo and behold, a rapidly drawn sketch, burlesque and yet true to life—for burlesque is simply a parody of the truth that expresses discordant reality; like a speech out of turn, it startles and arouses laughter. Here are the flute players who decamp to Tibur when deprived of their privilege of feasting in the temple of Jupiter; but the locals get them drunk and heap them up on carts that take them back to Rome, where daylight comes upon them, with their hangovers, in the middle of the Forum (9.30.5–9). There is the schoolmaster of Falerii, the victim of his own trick. Having taken the children of noble families on a country walk, this treacherous scoundrel leads them all the way to the Roman camp, where he means to hand them over as hostages; but it is he, stripped naked with his hands tied behind his back, whom the consul Camillus hands over to the children, who with stout strokes of the cane drive him straight back to Falerii (5.27.1–9). We have seen that most ambassadors who come to Rome behave there with great humility, making plentiful bows and obeisances before they dare to address their supplications to the Conscript Fathers; contrariwise, those from Rhodes come one day threatening to take up arms if the Romans do not stop making war on Perseus. The senators' only response is to read them a decree granting freedom to the Carians and Lycians, their enemies; whereupon the haughty ambassadors faint (44.15.1–2). Quinctius, to make fun of King Philip's vaunts of sending into action 'clouds of footsoldiers and cavalrymen and of covering the seas with his fleets', tells the story of a banquet given for him by an inhabitant of Chalcis, an estimable man, who was doing the honours of his house to great effect. 'Having been entertained at his place as well as could be wished, we asked him, not without surprise, where at that season (it was the summer solstice) such abundant and varied game came from. Less of a braggart than those fellows, our host laughed heartily and said that this splendid variety of game was simply a piece of pork seasoned a certain way…' (35.49.6–7; the snippet recurs in Petronius, *Satyricon* 70). Near Apollonia, this vainglorious Philip, surprised in his camp by a night attack, 'fled half-naked, in a state hardly befitting a soldier, and even less a king' (24.40.13). Near Heraclea, Perseus, heir to his father's bad luck, 'was reportedly in the bath when he was informed that the enemy was coming. At this news, he leapt panic-stricken from the tub, shouting that he had been

beaten without a fight' (44.6.1). Majestic persons losing all their
majesty at a stroke, that schoolmaster whose turn it is to be thrashed,
those arrogant ambassadors who faint, those Oriental despots whose
armies are like pork and who run away in the nude—all are good
fodder for folk humour.

Livy does not even eschew coarser merriment. If the occasion arises,
he hardly hesitates, in the midst of the most serious narrative, to give
us an example. Hence, sometimes, we find a curious mixture of
nobility and broad humour. The ex-consul Servilius urges the soldiers
to grant Aemilius Paulus, who has beaten Perseus, the honour of a
triumph. He has the right to speak (his speech has already covered
over 200 lines), because he knows all about courage; his body is
covered in scars, and every blow was delivered from the front. 'It is
said that he bared his wounds and recounted the various occasions on
which he had received them. During this exhibition, he had the
misfortune to reveal what he would have done better to hide, a
swelling on the groin, at the sight of which those standing near him
burst out laughing. "But what of it?" he said. "This had happened to
me from sitting whole days and nights on horseback, and I did not
blush at an ailment that had never prevented me from serving the
Republic."' (45.39.17–18).

Often, the anecdote brings more refined relief. The narrative comes
with a riddle to which the denouement provides the solution.
Sometimes the theme is the interpretation of an oracle or the revelation of a mysterious thought. Book 1, where legend is rarely far
from history, exhibits more than one example. Tarquin's sons go off
to Delphi together with their cousin Brutus, who offers the god a
golden staff hidden in one of cornel-wood, a symbol of his mind, for
Brutus has the wisdom to play the fool. They ask the oracle who will
succeed to Tarquin's throne. 'The first to kiss his mother.' Then
Brutus, pretending to fall, kisses the earth (1.56.9–12). To mock the
augur Attus Navius, King Tarquin exclaims: 'Hey, Mr. Diviner, ask the
augurs whether what I have in mind at the moment is possible.'
Navius consults the auspices and answers in the affirmative. 'Well',
said the king, 'I had the notion that you would cut this stone with a
razor.' The story goes that Navius, without hesitation, cut the stone
(1.36.3–4). In his garden, in the presence of his son's messenger,
without a word Tarquin the Proud knocks off the heads of his finest

poppies with his stick, and his son understands that he must put to death the leading men of Gabii (1.54.6). It is with a play on words that Titus Tatius has Tarpeia killed. Before betraying the Roman citadel to the Sabines, the girl had asked them, as the price of her treason, to give her what they had on their left hands, meaning 'heavy gold bracelets, rich bejewelled rings'. But in their left hands they also carried shields, with which on their leader's command they crushed her (1.11.6–9). In Book 5, we see soldiers digging a mine, while the king of Veii offers sacrifice. 'The voice of the *haruspex*, promising victory to whoever should cut up the victim's entrails, was heard in the mine, and persuaded the Romans to breach the tunnel, seize the entrails, and carry them to the dictator' (5.21.8). Finally, at the beginning of Book 9, the drama of the Caudine Forks is preceded by a brief comedy in which the main character remains true to his viewpoint even though he appears to contradict himself. Not knowing what to do with the Roman army caught in the defile, the Samnites write for advice to their general's father, Herennius Pontius, 'an old man in a worn-out body, who retained great powers of intellect and judgement'. He advises them to let all the Romans out as soon as possible without doing them the slightest harm. That opinion is not to their taste. He then advises them to kill the lot. They begin to think his mind is wandering; however, they ask him to come and explain himself. He arrives in his cart, and confirms his two pieces of advice: 'The first course of action, through a great good deed, would establish forever peace and friendship with the most powerful of peoples; the second would put off war for several generations, which would hardly be enough for the Romans to restore their forces after losing two armies.' Having spoken he goes back home in his cart (9.3.10).

Sometimes the anecdote boils down to a quip that pithily expresses a vivid sentiment. Occasionally this quip may be no more than fatuity imagining itself to be ingenious and appealing to the bystander's taste for obvious truths. Fabius Cunctator blithely observes that if Livius Salinator had not lost Tarentum, he would not have had to retake it (27.25.5; already quoted by Cicero, *De senectute* 4). But usually it is a short or long remark that says much about the character of the person uttering it. Those directed by Papirius Cursor at his cavalry and at a praetor of Praeneste plainly reveal his

brutal yet sly severity (9.16.15–16). Likewise, the morose Livius
Salinator's rancour towards his fellow citizens is perfectly expressed
in his words to Fabius before leaving for his province (27.40.9). One
saying is enough to suggest the tyrant Nabis' mixture of cynicism and
hypocrisy: 'It is in their own interest that he has suspects arrested;
that way he prevents them from plotting, which is better than
punishing them' (34.27.6). In Macedon, Marcius and Perseus are
going to have a parley. Separated by the river Peneus, they come
face to face, each accompanied by a magnificent escort; but which is
to cross the river first? There they are, stranded beside the water by
their concern for national prestige. A word from Marcius puts an end
to the embarrassment: 'It is for the younger to seek out the elder, and
the son the father' (42.39.5): for Marcius—like Perseus' own father—
was called Philippus. Taken by itself, the utterance might not deserve
to be handed down to posterity, but it helps to give detail to Marcius'
portrait; it comes from the same improvising spirit of which soon
afterwards he gave a serious proof, when, unable to make war, he
pretended to want peace (42.43.1–3). Livy's skill, or rather tact, is to
slip into his narrative words that make us ready to smile but at the
same time give us insight into character.

These sayings are probably not Livy's invention, but they cheer and
enliven him; wit comes to him from others' wit. In many a more
sarcastic mockery, where anger tries to control itself without man-
aging to achieve the subtlety of wit, we shall recognize Livy's stamp,
in particular his taste for antithesis, sometimes a little blatant. We
have already mentioned the Rhodian ambassadors who faint at the
announcement that the Senate is granting freedom to their enemies,
the Carians and the Lycians. In another version, the Senators supposedly replied to their arrogant threat: 'Since the Rhodians are now
the arbiters of peace and war for the whole world, from now on the
Romans will take up and lay down their arms at the slightest sign of
their will and will recognize as the guarantors of treaties, not the
gods, but the Rhodians' (44.15.5). Hanno, commenting before the
Carthaginian Senate on a message from Hannibal, who after a victory
asks for reinforcements, parodies his old antagonist thus: '"I have
destroyed two armies, send me troops.... I have taken two camps
from the enemy (two camps no doubt full of plunder and provisions!), send me money and corn..."' (23.12.13–14).

Nevertheless, especially in the last two decades, Livy also goes in for a more discreet form of mockery. 'We are sparing you the trouble', his Quinctius says to Nabis, 'of becoming angry in our stead' (34.32.6). This line, ingeniously prepared, is slipped into a carefully contrived speech, as is shown by the evocation of Lycurgus and the cities of Argos and Sparta, 'of old the two lights of Greece, whose enslavement would tarnish the title of liberators of the Greek world' that the Romans claim to deserve. But Livy's irony also expresses itself without special preparation, in short phrases that follow quietly at the end of a preceding narrative development. The praetor L. Furius, having defeated the Gauls in the consul's absence, is granted the honour of a triumph. 'He paid into the public treasury 320,000 *librae* of copper and 170,000 of silver; but there were no prisoners or booty before his chariot, nor soldiers behind it: it was plain that everything except the victory was in the consul's hands' (31.49.2–3). In Macedon, the praetor C. Marcius Figulus had conceived a stratagem for capturing Cassandrea that did not come up to expectations. So, 'the victim of his own scheme, he was slower to come up with new devices' (44.12.4). The miserly Perseus, soon to be defeated by the Romans, retains in his treasury part of the sum he had promised his ally Gentius. 'He seemed to be striving only that the Romans should gain the maximum possible booty from his defeat' (44.27.12). Sometimes, even more discreetly, the mockery takes the form of a simple litotes. Antiochus, preparing his campaign against the Romans, makes his way towards Thermopylae. 'This place is renowned for the Spartans' resistance even to death against the Persians–resistance which has remained to this day more memorable than the battle. It was certainly not in that same frame of mind that Antiochus, already encamped within the gates, decided to close the defile with fortifications; a double palisade, a double ditch, and lastly, at the critical points, a wall built with the stones collected in large quantity from the area fortified the complex' (36.15.12–16.2).

Not even humour is alien to Livy. Humour consists of a judgement that pretends to reduce to common experience an event that exceeds it. Thus, when Livy shows us the usurer who wishes to seduce, and does do violence to, his debtor's son, 'taking this flower of youth for additional interest' (8.28.3), or the general who 'for want of an enemy, makes war on his fellow citizens' (4.49.9), he dresses scoundrels in the everyday clothes of the upright. At first sight, the one is merely a creditor demanding the payment of compound interest, the other an active soldier who does not mean to waste his time. In humour there is, so to speak, a brief intention to deceive that is very soon unmasked. The drama is put not in its rightful place, but closer. The effect of this displacement is all the stronger for marking a reaction opposite to the spontaneous one of pity, indignation, or astonishment. The reader soon recognizes this coquettish play of shame by an emotion that dissimulates, only to reveal itself in the end as scornful of commonplace displays. Besides, in its studied unconcern, humour implies a sensibility already subject to judgement and soon to be governed by it: if it is right that we should be indignant at the usurer's brutality and the general's crime, let us not forget that the young man had a timely escape from dishonour, and that Rome was not destroyed. This is not Tarquin raping Lucretia, or Brennus burning the city, but misfortunes so limited that it is not indecent to wear a smile. Such, too, are the woes of the Bergistani. One fine day, this people of Tarraconnensis rebels; Cato arrives; they submit; Cato departs; they rebel again. 'Then Cato had them all sold at auction, to save them from seeking peace too often' (34.16.10). The successful effect is due to the antithesis we detect between Cato's brutal decision and his claim of charitable motivation. The two terms of the antithesis, instead of crashing into each other, melt into the mould of the sentence in which the idea as a whole is worked out: the subordinate comes back to the principal without a clash as naturally as the mind ascends from effect to cause. Livy simply disdains to show the subsidiary movements of a Catonian wrath. Like true elegance, humour is sober.

Finally, it happens in Livy that a well-constructed sentence gives the impression that the author is playing with words even though play is not involved. For example, verbal juggling such as the following, presented in riddle form: 'She had a series of rendez-vous with a married man during which she did not spare outrageous words about her husband, whose brother he was, nor about her sister, whose husband he was' (1.46.7); 'One boat was seen to capture two more easily than two had taken one' (36.44.9). At one point Livy even amuses himself by posing us a little problem in elementary arithmetic: four conspirators each recruit six accomplices; thinking this number still insufficient, they double it. What is the total number of conspirators? Into how many groups should they divide for the groups to be equal? (38.1.6–7).

No doubt these flashes of wit are few and far between over the thirty-five surviving books. Livy is the craftsman of his Roman history, a long and dramatic work, and also an edifying one. These anecdotes, these quips, these humorous or ironic reflections suffice none the less to prove that, although he is serious, Livy is not starchy. He shows enough wit to let us know that, given the chance, he could have shown more.

## ADDENDUM

In the introduction to his great *Commentary*, Ogilvie famously wrote, 'No touches of humour are to be found in the history (32.34.3, 24.34.16)' (Ogilvie (1965): 4; the references to Livy's text are presumably to places where another writer might have added such a touch). This extract from Catin's short but enlightening book, *En lisant Tite-Live* ('Reading Livy'), written 20 years before Ogilvie made this pronouncement, presents a very different Livy—but one who has not, regrettably, caught on much in the Anglo-American world until relatively recently. Livian scholars are now alert to the historian's sometimes pervasive use of irony, plays on words, and *paraprosdokian* (the 'unexpected'); for good examples see Moles and Kraus (1994*a*), *passim* in the Commentary. Dutoit (1956) examines Livy's word-play and etymological puns, especially in relation to Virgil. What is at stake is not merely that the historian (and his readers!) shows a heightened sensitivity to language, though that is important; irony and wit play a crucial role in the shaping of historiographical interpretation. On the latter, see Plass (1988) and Bartsch (1994), though neither of them focuses on Livy.

On the importance of bystanders as guides and focal points in Livian narrative, including the figure of the historian or historian-substitutes, see Solodow, Jaeger (1997) chapter 4, and Levene (2006); on crowds see Canetti (1960). On characterization in Livy see Luce (1977) chapter 7, Vasaly (1987), and Bernard (2000); in general, on characterization in historiography see Pitcher (2007). Jaeger (2007) has a close reading of the scene on Mt. Haemus.

# 7

## The Literary Techniques of Livy[1]

*P. G. Walsh*

Over forty years ago, Kurt Witte published two articles on Livy's narrative-form which must furnish the basis of any appraisal of Livy, whether considered as historian or literary artist.[2] Using the narrative of Polybius, whom Livy followed closely in the Fourth and Fifth Decades when reporting Eastern affairs, Witte was able to illustrate in detail Livy's methods of transcription. He showed that the more dramatic sections of the *Ab Urbe Condita* were narrated in 'scenes' ('Einzelerzählungen'), each with an abbreviated introduction and conclusion but with an elaborated central description. Further, he demonstrated how Livy, following a procedure well established amongst historians, had stock methods of describing battle-accounts, dialogue-scenes, and other specialized narrative-genres. Witte's researches in this field were not, however, exhaustive. First, there are some other types of scene for which Livy had particular methods of presentation: and secondly, there are certain interesting features in the narrative-genres discussed by Witte which are worthy of attention.

---

[1] I wish to thank Professor F. W. Walbank, of the University of Liverpool, for much helpful criticism.
[2] Witte (1910: 270–305, 359–419).

## SIEGES

In ancient warfare, sieges and blockades were common events. For the historian whose chief aim was to interest his audience and his readers, they posed a difficult problem, for unless there were some unusual method of attack, the description of stereotyped operations would clearly become monotonous. Livy attempted to solve this problem by focusing the attention on the persons under siege, a solution consonant with the increasingly humanitarian outlook of the Augustan Age. By adopting the standpoint of the besieged, he exploited his facility for *psychological observation*, especially in the description of the fall of a town.

The attacking party is usually mentioned briefly, followed by an extended account of the defenders, and especially their state of mind. This predilection for psychological observation can be seen in Livy's adaptation of Polybius' account of the fall of Abydus. Polybius describes the conduct of the townsfolk, surveying the scene from the outside through the eyes of Philip: Livy avoids the narration of the grisly facts, and ponders instead the motives of the besieged.

Polyb. 16.34.9 But when he saw the number and the fury of those who destroyed themselves and their women and children, either by cutting their throats, or by burning or by hanging or by throwing themselves into wells or off the roofs, he was amazed...

Livy 31.18.6 For sheer fury (*rabies*) suddenly (*repente*) gripped the population of Abydus. They thought the men who had fallen in battle had been betrayed, and they accused each other of perjury. Above all they accused the priests, for these had delivered alive to the enemy the men whom they had by sacred oath marked out for death. They all suddenly (*repente*) ran off to butcher their wives and children, and then committed suicide themselves, seeking every possible path to death (*per omnes vias leti*).

In this analysis of mental strain and the suddenness of its effects, the word *rabies* is important. In the previous chapter, it is used to compare the plight of the Abydenes with that of the Saguntines (31.17.5 'turned to the *rabies* of the Saguntines'); and in the account of the siege of Corinth, when some Italian deserters repelled the Romans, we read: 'these men had no hope of salvation in the event of a Roman victory, and this incited them to frenzy (*rabiem*) rather than reckless defiance' (32.23.9).

Another striking example of the psychological approach can be seen in the account of the siege of Ambracia. The Romans attempted to enter the city by digging a subterranean passage, but the rising heap of earth betrayed the stratagem to the townsmen, and they began to dig a trench. So much Polybius tells us. But Livy imaginatively dramatizes the suddenness of the moment of discovery, and stresses the mental reaction of the besieged:

Polyb. 21.28.7 But when the heap of earth became considerable and visible to those in the city, the leaders of the besieged set vigorously to work to dig a trench...

Livy 38.7.7 But then the rising heap of earth that suddenly (*repente*) appeared gave away the operation to the townspeople. Frightened that the wall might already be undermined and a way into the city opened up (*pavidique ne iam subrutis muris facta in urbem via esset*), these proceeded to dig a ditch.

Almost all siege-descriptions show this same tendency to concentrate the attention on the besieged, and especially on their state of mind.[3] In many descriptions, Livy so far identifies himself with the besieged that he describes the Romans as 'the enemy'.[4]

The second tendency which characterizes Livy's siege-descriptions is that of simplifying, if not ignoring, technical devices used. Here we are presented with an interesting facet of his make-up: he had no grasp of, or interest in, the specialized machines of war. In this there is a marked contrast between the avid curiosity of Polybius his source, who delighted in explanatory passages about such contraptions, and his own 'lay-man's' approach. In the siege of Ambracia, Polybius tells us, the townsfolk had discovered that the besiegers were building a tunnel, so they dug a trench parallel to the city-wall and lined it with thin sheets of brass (21.28.8 'they lined the side of the trench next the wall with exceedingly thin plates of brass'), and then advanced along the trench with their ears close to the brass sheets, the

---

[3] See, for example, 32.17–18 (the siege of Atrax), 36.22–4 (Heraclea), 38.28–9 (Same), 29.6.10–17 (Locri), 28.22–3 (Astapa).

[4] See 36.22–4 (three times), 38.29.1, 38.6.7 (Ambracia), 2.17.3 (Pometia).

reverberation of which indicated the position of the Roman miners. We find that Livy has said nothing of the brass plates, but has substituted a general explanation:

38.7.8 They remained silent, placed their ears to the soil at several points, and tried to catch the sound of the enemy digging.

In the narration of the ensuing scuffle in the tunnel, Livy has made a ludicrous mistake in translation. The townsmen rushed into the tunnel with shields ($\vartheta\upsilon\rho\epsilon o\upsilon\varsigma$), but Livy confusing this with $\vartheta\upsilon\rho\acute{a}\varsigma$, has written: 'hurriedly barring it with doors' (38.7.10⁵). Polybius later described how the Ambraciots were to 'smoke out' the Romans by means of a corn-jar full of feathers ignited by charcoal. In this jar a hollow tube was to be placed, and fitted to the tube a blacksmith's bellows. As the feathers caught fire, the tube was to be removed. Livy has omitted some of these details. Perhaps they would have been too complex for the comprehension of his audience, but the omission also reflects the author's aversion from technicalities.⁶

If we examine Livy's narration of the siege of Syracuse (24.33.9), and compare it with the account of Polybius, we again observe this difference of approach.⁷ Polybius (8.4) has a long explanation of the construction of the $\sigma\alpha\mu\beta\acute{u}\kappa\alpha\iota$, the harp-shaped ladders which were attached to quinqueremes and had a platform from which attackers could mount the city-wall. None of this appears in Livy's account.⁸

In brief, Livy's narration of sieges virtually excludes extended mention of attackers or of technical apparatus: he concentrates

---

⁵ See Sage (*LCL*, 1936: 23).

⁶ Polybius narrated this part of the account in the form of a suggestion made by someone (i.e. in the didactic manner), and explained that the event accorded with the suggestion (Polyb. 28.12.16 'Upon all those instructions being followed....'). Livy has described the operation as it actually happened; thus his version is more lively and vivid.

⁷ It is doubtful whether Livy used Polybius (8.3 ff.) directly. But the two accounts are similar in outline (whilst differing in one or two details) which suggests that a common source was used.

⁸ Though it is not strictly relevant to the discussion of sieges, we find another example of Livy's aversion from technical explanations in 37.11.13, where he mentions some Rhodian fire-ships without describing details of their mechanism. Appian (*Syr.* 24), who also follows Polybius (not always faithfully, it must be admitted), describes the details, which he must certainly have obtained from Polybius' account.

instead on the situation of the besieged, assessing the effects of the attack in terms of human emotions and sufferings, and thereby affecting his audience with that 'pity and fear' at which the rhetorical historians, no less than the tragedians, aimed.

## SEA-BATTLES

It will be remembered that Witte drew attention to the many stock situations in Livy's battle-accounts, and under headings such as 'The Outbreak of Battle', 'The Commencement of Defeat', 'The Outbreak of Flight', he convincingly showed that these accounts are in many cases identically constructed. These comments were confined to battles on land, but a similar technique is found in the narration of some sea-battles.

In the fourth decade there are three main sea-engagements, that off Cissus (36.43–5), that off Phaselis (37.23–4), and that off Myonnesus (37.29–30).[9] Livy's accounts of these are constructed almost identically, and the terminology is often similar. There is accordingly an astonishing resemblance between these accounts which can hardly be accounted for entirely by any similarity of situation.

In the descriptions of the *preparation for battle*, the fleet of Antiochus is invariably mentioned first, and the procedure is identical in each case. Livy starts with the left wing in each passage.

36.44.1 When Polyxenidas was brought the news that the enemy was approaching, he was delighted at having the chance to fight. He himself extended his left wing towards the open sea, and ordered his ships' captains to deploy the right towards the shore. They then advanced to do battle with a level front.

37.23.7 In the king's fleet the left wing, which was on the side of the open sea, was commanded by Hannibal, the right by Apollonius, one of the king's courtiers; and they now had their vessels drawn up in a line.

---

[9] I omit detailed reference to the battle off Gytheum between Nabis and Philopoemen (35.26), since there was no real engagement.

37.29.8 The king's fleet, which was approaching in a long line, two ships abreast, also formed up facing their enemy, and extended the left wing far enough to enable it to overlap and surround the Roman right.

The reactions of the Rhodians or Romans are then described:

36.44.2 when he saw this, the Roman
37.23.9 after Eudamus saw the enemy's line
37.29.9 when Eudamus saw this

In each case the Rhodian and Roman fleets convert their column into a line, and in two cases this rearrangement causes confusion:

36.44.2 [The Roman admiral] furled his sails, lowered his masts and, stowing the tackle, awaited the ships coming up behind. There were now about thirty ships in his front line and, to make it extend as far as the enemy's left wing, he put up the foresails and proceeded towards the open sea, ordering those following behind to turn their prows towards the enemy right wing close to the shore. Eumenes was bringing up the rear but, *as soon as the scramble to stow the tackle began,* he also brought up his ships with as much speed as he could.

37.23.9 [Eumenes] too moved out into open water, ordering the ships that were following to form a straight line while maintaining their order. *Initially, this move caused confusion...*

37.29.9 Eudamus...saw that the Romans were unable to make their line equal to the king's...Making his ships put on speed...he made the flank equal to the enemy's and then set his own ship in the path of the enemy flagship.

*The battle* itself in each case has as its main feature clashes between individual ships or small groups, and the main engagement is described baldly. In two of the accounts the use of the pluperfect is designed to plunge us into the middle of the battle without tiresome preliminaries:

36.44.10 By now the fleets had engaged in all sectors, and the battle raged everywhere as the ships became mired with each other.

37.30.1 By now battle had been joined in every quarter by the entire fleets.

Above all, Livy, with his love of generalization, is at pains to demonstrate that the courage of the Romans and the superior naval tradition of the Rhodians were decisive factors.

36.45.1 For Polyxenidas, seeing that he was unquestionably outclassed as regards the valour of the fighting men... proceeded with a headlong flight.

37.30.2 The Romans were far superior to the Rhodians in the robustness of their vessels and the courage of their men.

37.30.6 But, as usual, what counted most in the fighting was the courage of the men.

37.24.1 But in a trice the quality of their vessels and their accomplished seamanship removed all fear from the Rhodians.

37.30.2 The Rhodian ships had the advantage in mobility, the helmsmen's skill, and the proficiency of the oarsmen.

Finally, we find that *the flights* of the fleets and of the commanders are described in similar phraseology:

36.45.1 [sc. Polyxenidas]... raised his foresails and *proceeded with a headlong flight.*

37.30.7 [sc. The ships]... hurriedly raised their topsails and *fled.*

35.26.9 Philopoemen himself made his escape in a light spy-boat and *did not arrest his flight* until he reached Patrae.

36.45.4 Polyxenidas *did not end his flight* until he reached the harbour of Ephesus.[10]


## CONFERENCES

Apart from the narration of wars, the dramatic sections of Livy's history are chiefly concerned with meetings and discussions, whether between individuals or at councils and assemblies. In our consideration of the stylistic features of these descriptions, we must remember that Livy had written philosophical works before beginning the *Ab Urbe*

---

[10] Other sea-engagements are reported in 21.49–50, 22.19–20, 25.27, 26.39, 28.30, 30.10, 44.28, but many of these are assaults on land-fortresses or have other unusual features which prevent a clear-cut engagement. The others are so rare and so widely separated that a common technique of description could hardly be expected. The fact that the three engagements reported in the fourth decade are close to each other has obviously (consciously or subconsciously) made for a similar presentation.

*Condita.*[11] It is likely that the structure of 'conference-scenes' in his history has been affected by earlier dialogue-compositions.

Perhaps the most obvious structural device of dialogues composed after the Aristotelian model is that of *artistic division* between speeches or between sections of the argument. The method commonly used by Livy to achieve this effect can be called the '*silentium* device': he has invented a dramatic silence which has the effect of a curtain. (Similar usages in Cicero's dialogues suggest the source of this device.[12]) Thus the Nicaea conference (32.32–6) is divided into five sections. Night intervenes between the third and fourth, and the fourth and fifth. Between the second and third sections there is an interval whilst Philip (who was speaking from a boat) moved closer to the shore. To allow for a similar division between the first and second sections, Livy has invented a silence not recorded in Polybius:

Polyb. 18.1.10 He seemed to them all to have opened the conference with little dignity, but Flamininus, however, begged him to state his reasons for attending it. Philip said it was not his own business to speak first, but that of Flamininus...

Livy 32.33.1 After this there was silence, the Roman thinking it appropriate for the man who had requested the meeting to speak first, and the king that the opening words belonged to the party dictating the terms of peace, not the one being given them.

Whereas Polybius related how they bade each other speak first, Livy has converted this into a dramatic silence which effectively breaks up the continuous conference.[13]

Again, in the famous trial scene when Perseus indicts Demetrius before their father Philip, the king's speech is followed by a silence, and another is inserted between the speeches of the two brothers:

---

[11] See Seneca, *Ep.* 100.9: 'Include Titus Livius also, for he wrote both dialogues, which you can classify as historical as much as philosophical, and books explicitly containing philosophy.'

[12] See Cicero *De Or.* 3.35.143: 'After Crassus had spoken, he kept quiet for a moment, and there was silence amongst the others'; see also *De Rep.* 2.38.64.

[13] In this passage Livy omits reference to the vulgarity (φορτικῶς) of Philip's conduct because it is not consonant with his notion of the dignity of kingship.

40.8.20 After Philip uttered these words in a fit of raging temper, tears came to everyone's eyes, and a gloomy silence long hung in the air.

40.12.2 But there followed a long silence, during which it became clear to everyone that he was bathed in tears and could not speak.[14]

Many of Livy's conference scenes (like those of other ancient historians, notably Thucydides and Tacitus) are constructed around antithetical speeches. He went to extraordinary lengths to balance these speeches, so far as was possible, both in length and order of topics. If we examine the accounts of the Lysimachia conference in Polybius (18.50–2) and in Livy (33.39–40), we see that Livy has effected major changes. Polybius reported a speech by Antiochus two and a half times as long as that of the Romans which preceded it: Livy effectively reduced the one and extended the other to make them more equal in length. An exordium and a peroration are inserted into the speech of the Romans; we also see some conventional rhetoric.[15] The speech of Antiochus has been rearranged so that the points raised by the Romans are answered in the same order. Most interesting of all, whereas Polybius reports additional speeches from the representatives of Smyrna and Lampsacus (which were interrupted by Antiochus on the grounds that the matter should be referred to the Rhodians[16]), Livy completely omits reference to these speeches: instead he focuses attention on the antithetical speeches of the Romans and of Antiochus, so that this scene is symbolic of the impending enmity between the two powers.

We find a similar balancing technique elsewhere. In the description of an assembly addressed by Eumenes and by the Rhodians, (Livy 37.52–6; Polybius 21.18–24) Livy reduced the speech of Eumenes and increased that of the Rhodians to equate them in length; further, he inserted into the speech of the Rhodians an answer

---

[14] The '*silentium* device' can also be found in 3.47.6, 9.4.7, 30.30.2, 32.20.1, 34.59.1. Dutoit (1948) draws attention to the prevalence of these silences but does not comment on their structural function.

[15] e.g. 33.39.6, where the words of Polyb. (18.50.6: 'For it was a ridiculous thing, he said, that Antiochus should come in when all was over and take the prizes they had gained in their war with Philip') become in Livy, 'it was quite unacceptable that the Romans should have experienced *such perils and hardships by sea and by land over all those years* only to see Antiochus reaping the profits of the war.'

[16] i.e. by the regular Hellenistic method of arbitration.

to a point raised by Eumenes,[17] as well as more general topics. There is no doubt that here, as elsewhere,[18] he has tried to equate the two speeches in length and content.

Witte has drawn attention to another technique in these conference-scenes, by which Livy fuses a number of speeches to form one coherent, non-redundant statement. He illustrates this by an interesting passage in which Hannibal is represented as giving his views at a war-conference of Antiochus. Now Hannibal was not present at this conference, and Livy has added Hannibal's comments to those of the other speakers to include every element in the camp hostile to Rome.[19] In 38.8.3 the Aetolians are depicted as agitating for peace. Their own council proceedings are first described: their envoys then make supplication to the Roman consul. When the consul replies, it is clear that he is answering not only the petition of the envoys but also the points made at the council at which he was not present.[20] Here Livy is more concerned to present a contrast between the Aetolian and the Roman viewpoints than to achieve complete consistency.

One other feature of conference-scenes can be considered here— Livy's refusal to insert personal comments as judgment of any situation leads him to attribute judgments made by Polybius to the

---

[17] 37.54.26–7. This referred to the cities which had sided with Antiochus. In Polybius the Rhodians make no reply to this point.

[18] e.g. 31.29–32 (the Aetolian Council). Of the four speeches, the first two are equal in aggregate length to the second two. The two main speeches are in direct speech, the others in indirect speech. Thus an obvious balance is attained. In 37.35.2 ff. there is a long speech followed by a short one, then a short followed by a long. Livy has himself added to the first speech the topic of Lysimachia and certain commonplaces in order to make it comparable in length with the other long speech.

[19] Livy 35.17–19; see Witte (1910: 377).

[20] 38.8.3 'The opinions of all coincided on one point: *peace was to be sought*, on favourable terms if possible, and failing that on conditions they could bear. *It was because of their confidence in Antiochus that the war had been undertaken*, they said, and now that Antiochus had been defeated on land and sea and driven practically from the whole word beyond the Caucus range, what hope was there...?' [The envoys address the consul] 'They begged the consul to spare their city and pity a people which had once been an ally and which had been driven to insanity by the misfortunes, not to say the injustices, she had suffered.... In reply the consul observed that the Aetolian *requests for a peace-treaty* were more frequent than they were sincere. *In seeking a treaty, he said, they should follow the lead of Antiochus, whom they had dragged into the war*—Antiochus had relinquished not just a handful of cities...but all of Asia this side of *the Taurus range*.'

historical personages involved.[21] An important example of this change is to be found in 37.25.4, where an observation of Polybius is converted by Livy into *a letter* sent by Antiochus to Prusias. Remarkably enough, this letter is a forthright condemnation of Roman imperialism, and is markedly similar to the letter recorded in Sallust and allegedly written by Mithridates to Arsaces.[22]

Polyb. 21.11.1 [Antiochus] ... sent frequent messages to Prusias inviting him to enter into alliance with him. Prusias previously had not been disinclined to join Antiochus, for he was very much afraid of the Romans crossing to Asia with the object of deposing all the princes there.

Livy 37.25.4 Antiochus ... had also sent emissaries to King Prusias of Bithynia with a letter of complaint about the Romans' passage into Asia. They were coming, Antiochus said, to wipe out all monarchies, so that there would be no empire left anywhere in the world but that of Rome. Philip and Nabis had been conquered, and he was the third to be under attack. As each lay next to a defeated neighbour, the fire next door, as it were, would sweep through them all. After him, the Romans' next step would be into Bithynia, since Eumenes had already acquiesced in voluntary servitude.

Sallust, *Histories* 4.69 (Maurenbrecher): In fact the Romans have ever and always had but one reason for making war on all nations, peoples, and kings: a deep desire for power and wealth. For this reason first they undertook war with Philip, king of the Macedonians ... and subsequently, when Philip had been crushed, Antiochus was stripped of all land this side of the Taurus Mountains as well as 10,000 talents ... Eumenes, whose friendship they boastfully promenade, they first betrayed to Antiochus as the price of peace; afterwards, having treated him as the guardian of captured territory, by their expenses and scorn they turned him from a king into the most wretched of slaves ...

There are a number of other examples of Livy's 'indirect exposition'. In 38.10.3 he converts the *thoughts* of Philip (in Polyb. 21.31.3) into complaints sent *through embassies and letters*. In 33.8.1–2 Philip's *mental* reaction to the reports of his men (Polyb. 18.22.8) is converted into *an expression of his doubts*. In 33.31 Livy has described a conference between Flamininus and the Roman commissioners. Polybius

---

[21] This *indirect* exposition is discussed in Bruns (1898). See also Witte (1910: 274).
[22] See Ernout (1947: 299). Bikerman (1946: 131) states that the letter is not authentic.

(18.45) stated that Flamininus urged the liberation of Greece, but the commissioners hesitated because they had no definite instructions, and they feared a possible invasion by Antiochus. In Livy's account, these doubts attributed to the commissioners have become their own words expressed at the conference:

Polyb. 18.45.10 The hesitation felt in the conference was due to the fact that, while a decision had been reached in Rome about all other questions, and the commissioners had definite instructions from the Senate on all other matters, the question of Chalcis, Corinth, and Demetrias had been left to their discretion owing to the fear of Antiochus....

Livy 33.31.10 The others did not oppose his arguments with respect to the independence of the cities, but they argued that it was safer for the Greeks themselves to remain a short while under the protection of a Roman garrison rather than accept Antiochus' overlordship in place of Philip's.

## DIALOGUES

Livy's method of reporting dialogues is designed to convey a dramatic effect for the purpose of depicting the character of the personalities concerned. Usually the disputants are major figures: where less significant persons are involved, Livy has attempted to recount attitudes which reflect national characteristics, and in some cases the dialogue becomes symbolic of the antipathy between nations.[23]

The favourite dialogue-form used by Livy has been demonstrated by Witte very effectively.[24] Both protagonists make short statements. A's first statement causes B no concern: it may even encourage a certain complacency, and B replies with assurance. A's second statement is the vital one—an unexpected comment or demand which causes the utmost fear or anger or confusion in B. This effect of peripateia, as Witte calls it, often exists in Polybius, and Livy has merely embellished it to accentuate the contrast. For example, in

[23] In 36.28.1 Phaeneas is the personification of the Aetolian attitude. In 31.18 the discussion at Abydus is symbolic of the antipathy between Rome and Macedon (see McDonald 1938: 25–6).

[24] Witte (1910: see especially 284, 288, 304), commenting on Livy 36.28, Polyb. 20.10, Livy 39.34, Polyb. 22.13, Livy 31.18, Polyb. 16.34.

32.10 Philip and Flamininus are depicted as exchanging views from opposite sides of the Aous. Though Polybius' account is lost, that of Diodorus, who followed Polybius closely in dialogues, has survived.

Diod. 28.11 Flamininus held that Philip must completely evacuate Greece, which should thereafter be ungarrisoned and autonomous, and that he must offer satisfactory compensation for damage done to those who had suffered from his breaches of faith. Philip replied that he must have assured possession of what he had inherited from his father, but that he would withdraw the garrisons from whatever cities he had himself won over, and would submit the question of damages to arbitration. To this Flamininus replied that there was no need of arbitration, that Philip himself must make terms with those whom he had wronged; furthermore he himself was under orders from the senate to liberate Greece, the whole of it, not merely a part. Philip retorted by asking: 'What heavier condition would you have imposed if you had defeated me in war?', and with these words he departed in a rage.

Livy 32.10.3–7 The consul's terms were essentially as follows: the king was to withdraw his garrisons from the city-states, and restore to those peoples whose land and cities he had pillaged any retrievable assets, the value of the rest to be estimated through non-partisan arbitration. Philip's response was that the status of the various city-states differed from one to another. Those which he had captured himself he would liberate, but in the case of those passed down to him by his ancestors he would not relinquish possession because they were legitimately his by right of inheritance. In the case of grievances lodged by states with which he had been at war over damage suffered during the conflict, he would defer to any arbiter whom they might choose from amongst the peoples with whom both parties were at peace. The consul replied that there was no need for an arbiter or judge in this matter, since it was clear to anyone that responsibility for injury lay with the aggressor, and Philip had in every case been the first to resort to force, without provocation. Then, when discussion arose of which states were to be liberated, the consul first of all named the Thessalians. At this the king was so incensed that he cried out: 'What heavier condition could you impose on a defeated enemy, Titus Quinctius?' and with that charged from the meeting.

Livy here appears to have added one significant sentence not contained in Polybius—the reference to the Thessalians as the first people to be freed: this makes more specific the words of the consul 'to liberate Greece, the whole of it, not merely a part,' and makes more explicable the angry reaction of Philip. Notice how the anger is more forcefully expressed; ἐχωρίσϑη is rendered 'charged', φησί as 'cried out', and the question of Philip, a generalization in Diodorus, is in Livy directly put to Flamininus.

There are of course many conversations recorded by Livy which do not contain matter lending itself to the peripateia technique. In these other dialogues Livy has concentrated on producing a lively and stimulating effect, free from wordy connections and explanations, as for example in 32.32.13 (compare with Polyb. 18.1.6) and 38.14.7 (Polyb. 21.34.6). He is so addicted to the dialogue form that sometimes he creates dialogues where none existed in the source. Witte has shown how Livy coalesced the conversation of two different days into a single dialogue.[25] Elsewhere he has added some purely common-place conversation to create a dialogue. In Polybius' account of a conversion between Cn. Cornelius and Philip there is merely one remark made on each side; Livy converts this into his normal structure with two remarks on each side.

Polyb. 18.48.4 . . . and [Cn. Cornelius] advised [King Philip] to send an embassy to Rome to ask for an alliance, that they might not think he was watching for his opportunity and looking forward to the arrival of Antiochus. Upon the king's accepting this suggestion. . . .

Livy 33.35.3 [Cornelius] asked Philip if he could bear to listen to advice that was not just serviceable but truly to his advantage. The king replied that he would even demonstrate his gratitude if the Roman furnished any advice to improve his position. . . .

The conversation then proceeds as in Polybius.

In 33.8 (the description of a meeting between Philip and some of his troops at the battle of Cynoscephalae) Livy has created a dialogue from the words of the soldiers and some comments of Polybius (18.22.8) which Livy has transferred, with a little elaboration, to the mouth of Philip.[26]

Livy's use of *oratio recta* ('direct speech') and *oratio obliqua* ('indirect speech') in dialogue-scenes gives a clue to the much controverted problem of their use generally in the *Ab Urbe Condita*. In the passage just quoted (33.8.1) Livy has converted the comments of the soldiers from *oratio recta* in Polybius to *oratio obliqua*. This has

---

[25] See Livy 39.34.3 and Polybius 22.13.8 (the Maronea incident).
[26] This passage is discussed by Lambert (1946: 58–9).

the effect of lessening the prominence of the soldiers in the dialogue, and thus the attention is focused on Philip, confronted with the necessity to take a vital decision. Usually Livy has followed Polybius in the use of *oratio recta*: both authors use it to convey a more emphatic effect, and to concentrate attention on the speaker. Occasionally statements made by Polybius in *oratio obliqua* have been converted into *oratio recta*: Bornecque, quoting Kohl, says that it is the ideas of Livy, or those which he approves, which are related in direct speech.[27] In some passages it appears to be the *opinion which prevails* which is so expressed.[28] Such precise formulations however are dangerous, and it is safer merely to observe that Livy puts into *oratio recta* the statements to which he especially wishes to draw attention.

## SPEECHES

The research which has been made into the approach of Livy to speeches has not always sufficiently availed itself of the opportunity to compare such speeches with those still to be found in Livy's sources.[29] Such a comparison shows considerable changes in Livy's account, occasionally for moral or patriotic considerations, but almost always with stylistic motives. In other words, Livy imitates Thucydides in adhering to the spirit of what was said whilst encasing it in his own literary framework.[30] Such changes have the effect above all of more vivid characterization of the speaker concerned.[31]

Livy's method of indicating that his rendering only approximates to the original is the insertion of a vague phrase at the commencement of a speech. Thus in 37.45, where he reproduces a speech of Scipio Africanus, he writes: 'Africanus *is said to have spoken* more or

[27] Bornecque (1933: 158).
[28] e.g. 31.25, 32.10, 32.34, and the speech of Menippus in 35.32.7 ff.
[29] See Canter (1917); Ullmann (1929) and (1927); Lambert (1946), Kohl (1872); Bornecque (1933: 155–74).
[30] See Thuc. 1.22. This attitude is condemned implicitly by Polybius' attack on Timaeus in 12.25.5.
[31] See Johnson (1929: 36–7).

less as follows.' The speech bears little resemblance in form to the original in Polybius, which is merely a catalogue of peace-terms expressed prosaically in *oratio obliqua*. Livy's version, in *oratio recta*, is more rhetorically expressed, and Scipio's pre-eminence as the *doyen* of Roman generals is brought out by the increased emphasis on Hannibal. One sentence with its bold use of anaphora, congeries, and antithesis is sufficient to show the difference from the original:

Polyb. 21.17.2 Therefore they would now give them the same answer as they had formerly received, when before the battle they came to the Hellespont.

Livy 37.45.13 After we crossed the Hellespont and before we saw the camp of the king and his line of battle, at a time when we both faced the same chances in war and the outcome of the conflict was uncertain—at that point you made overtures for peace and we put before you terms as equals to equals. Now as conquerors to conquered we are offering the same terms.[32]

Livy's speeches are regularly constructed with an exordium and a peroration, sometimes composed by himself, sometimes elaborated from a topic found in his source. Thus in 33.12.5, as Witte has shown,[33] the most effective argument in a speech of Flamininus is converted into an exordium. In 32.34 a speech of Philip in Polybius 18.5 is rearranged so that the point on which Philip was most indignant is brought forward from the end to form a more effective introduction. In 33.39–40 there is an exchange of speeches between the Romans and Antiochus. In the speech of the Romans, Livy has inserted as introductory topic a general expression of senatorial displeasure, and the possibility of a future invasion of Italy as the peroration. Antiochus' speech commences with an expression of

---

[32] Another illustration of the amplification of a speech with the aim of characterization can be seen in the speech of Hannibal in 36.7. A comparison with Appian (*Syr.* 14) suggests that Livy's prefatory remark ('Hannibal used the following speech to bring the king and all present to think about the war in general') conceals considerable changes. Rearrangement of topics, insertion of exordium and peroration, introduction of the topic of Pyrrhus, omission of the fact that the Lacedaemonians refused to ally themselves with Antiochus, all help in building up a picture of the gigantic threat facing Rome, with Hannibal indirectly depicted as the implacable enemy, a courageous and consummate leader of the anti-Roman forces.

[33] Witte (1910: 296–9).

indignation at the Roman inquisition. None of these topics appears in Polybius.[34]

Frequently Livy has changed the order of topics to give the speech greater cohesion and rhetorical force. In 18.4–5 Polybius reported a section of Philip's speech at the Nicaea council. The first topic was Lysimachia, previously annexed by Philip: then Cius, which he had attacked: then the law permitting the Aetolians to support as individuals either of two external powers in conflict: and finally the Aetolian demand for the evacuation of Greece by the Macedonians. Livy's rearrangement in 32.34 has brought the final topic to the beginning, the Aetolian law next, and finally Cius and Lysimachia. The speech is skilfully planned to give the smoothest continuity by ingenious inter-connection of topics.[35]

*Speeches before battle* are as we should expect a specialized genre. In this type of speech the elaboration made by Livy lies chiefly in examples—apposite references to previous battles or hardships overcome. In 33.8, for example, Livy has summarized a speech of Flamininus from Polybius 18.23.3–7. The Roman general reminded the soldiers of their victory in Epirus, when the Macedonians were routed, in spite of their holding 'hopelessly difficult terrain'. Livy has amplified it: 'At the same time he reminded them that the Macedonians they would be fighting were the ones they had dislodged and defeated in battle at the gorges of Epirus where, though the enemy had the protection of mountains and rivers, the Romans had surmounted the natural obstacles of the area.' Such praise for one's own troops and emphasis on the weaknesses of the enemy naturally form the basic topics of such speeches.[36] So much for the matter of Livian speeches. As regards the *form*, Livy imposes on all speeches his own literary polish, whatever the source. His version of a speech by Africanus in 38.51.7 can be compared with the original speech recorded by Aulus Gellius (4.11.4). Here Livy has been careful to retain the matter of the original but he has embellished it by copious use of rhetorical figures—congeries, isocolon, apostrophe,

---

[34] 18.50.5 ff. Another example can be seen in 37.52 (Polyb. 21.18).

[35] There are many examples of such transposition of topics: see, for example, Livy 33.31 (Polyb. 18.45) and 37.36 (Polyb. 21.15).

[36] e.g. 21.40–1, 23.45.2, 26.41, 3.62.2, etc.

antithesis.[37] Abundant research has however been made into the form of Livy's speeches, and no more need be said here.


## BATTLE-ACCOUNTS


Witte's demonstration of Livy's stock techniques in the narration of battles, perhaps the most important section of all, does not include a number of features which are noteworthy.

There is first what we may call the 'switch-technique'. Perhaps the most notable difference to the ordinary reader between the accounts of Livy and Polybius is that Polybius writes much more episodically. He devotes his attention to a particular topic in a particular locality, and having disposed of it, he commences a fresh narration about the new topic. Livy avoids this episodic effect by skilful linking-up of scenes, so that his narration assumes a more cohesive aspect. This 'switch-technique' is obviously of particular value in the description of widespread warfare. The method of transition consists in relating the journey of a person or persons from the locality being described to the locality where the next operations to be narrated are enacted. For example, in 31.24 there is a description of Philip's speedy offensive from Chalcis to Athens, a plan which would have succeeded, says Livy, 'but for a scout...who caught sight of the king's army from a watch-tower. He set off ahead of Philip and reached Athens in the middle of the night. In Athens there was the same indolence and the same heedlessness that had let down Chalcidice a few days earlier....The Athenian praetor and Dioxippus... galvanized to action by the alarming report....'. Thus the transition is accomplished without wearying the reader, and it is made all the smoother by the comparison between the unpreparedness of the two cities.[38]


[37] See Marouzeau (1921: 165–6). This speech of Africanus is not recorded in Polybius, and it is fortunate that Aulus Gellius has preserved it, since it disposes of the over-zealous contention that Livy has invented the speech to glorify his hero (see Carcopino, quoted by Bornecque (1933: 122)).

[38] An almost identical example is found in 31.33.5–6.

In 32.23 a similar treatment is observed. Livy passes from the narration of the Sicyon Council to that of the siege of Corinth. To avoid the bald change of topic, he mentions the decision of the Council to send troops to Corinth, and accompanies them, so to speak, to that city, describing the scene as it met the eyes of the Achaean contingent. Again, in 36.6 Livy describes the journey of Antiochus to Boeotia before commenting on Boeotian affairs; Polybius (20.7) passes directly to the new topic.[39]

Another technique occasionally used in battle-accounts can be labelled the '*deus ex machina*'. A comparison of the accounts of the battle of Thermopylae in Livy (36.15–19) and Appian (*Syr.* 17–20) shows how Livy has made more dramatic use of the forces of Cato. Appian tells us that the Roman commander Glabrio sent Cato and Flaccus with chosen forces, and immediately proceeds to relate their success and failure respectively before embarking on an account of the operations of the main Roman force in the Pass. Livy has at the outset (17.1) mentioned merely the despatch of these forces. In chapter 18 the main battle is described: the preliminary success of the king's forces, the later advance of the Romans, and the final stalemate. Then, when the Romans appeared far from success ('the Romans would have withdrawn in failure, or suffered heavier losses' 18.8) Livy suddenly introduces the victorious Cato in the rear of Antiochus.[40]

[39] It is obvious that this technique can be used more widely than in battle-accounts; cf. also 36.21.6.

[40] Another example of this '*deus ex machina*' technique can be found in the description of a battle in Epirus in 32.12. Livy has superimposed his usual 'stages' on the battle: 'They surged forward in their eagerness for combat and fought outside their fortifications, but the Roman soldiers enjoyed no small advantage...After suffering many wounds and much loss of life, however, the king's men withdrew to positions that were either fortified or protected by natural features, and the danger recoiled upon the Romans...Indeed, they would not have pulled back from that position without paying for their recklessness but for a loud shout from the rear, followed by fighting breaking out, which drove the king's men out of their senses with sudden panic.' (Notice that this sentence is constructed as in the passage in 36.18.8 with a conditional clause.) The account of Plutarch (*Flamininus* 4.6) suggests that Livy has exaggerated the danger to the main force, and the suddenness of the appearance of the task force in the rear: 'then the Romans below raised shouts of triumph and dashed upon their foes and crowded them together into the roughest places, while the Romans behind the enemy sent down answering shouts from the heights.'

Another instructive feature of these accounts is the emphasis laid by Livy on the part which fear plays in the destiny of a battle. This 'fear-complex' has a clear correspondence with Livy's sympathy with the besieged party in siege-descriptions, and with the defeated force in battle-accounts. It is part of his psychological approach. For example, in 33.7.8 he writes: '[sc. Philippus] was in a panic for a time; then...he thought that he had to throw everything into the fight...he sent Athenagoras...'. There is no record of this fear in Polybius 18.21. In 31.34.5 we read of Philip's panic after a skirmish with the Romans: 'the king himself, never yet having met the Romans in pitched battle, was also panic-stricken'. The account of Diodorus shows that Philip, on the contrary, was reassuring his troops with the utmost indifference to danger.[41] There are many other examples of Livy's emphasis on the fears of participants in battle.[42]


ADDENDUM

Since the 1950s Walsh has made major contributions to Livian scholarship, most notably *Livy: His Historical Aims and Methods*, which was first published in 1961 and reissued in 1989. It remains the one general study of Livy written in English. The article reprinted here is not particularly representative of Walsh's work on Livy, but it is extremely useful, especially given the current interest in *topoi*. The latter are the object of some of the most revealing of recent studies on ancient historical narrative: see, for example, Woodman (1998, especially chapters 5, 10, and 11), Rossi (2004), and for Livy see Kraus (1994*b*). Fussell (1975), Keegan (1976) chapter 1, and Lendon (1999) discuss the role and effect of *topoi* in military historiography.

Walsh (1961*a*) chapter 10 elaborates on the treatment here of Livy's psychological observations. For speeches generally, see the Addendum to Burck. For a start on paired speeches ('antilogy') see Rodgers (1986) and Ginsburg (1993), a reading of Tacitus and Livy. For the use of indirect discourse (*oratio obliqua*) in the historians see

---

[41] Diodorus 28.8.
[42] e.g. 31.27.10, 32.5.2, 33.15.6, 35.27.16, 36.16.6.

Utard (2004); and for the specific case of speeches before battle see Hansen (1998), with references to earlier (and on-going) discussion. Lendon (1999) treats fear in battle narratives, though with a focus on Caesar. Luce (1977) chapter 7 discusses Livy's view of national characteristics. Walsh (1958*b*) discusses Livy's errors in translation from the Greek, though this should be read in tandem with Levene (2010). For Livy's adaptation of Polybius see further Tränkle and Burck and Addenda thereto.

# 8

## The Style of Livy

### A. H. McDonald

Dedicated to Hugh Last

The immense detail of the work that was devoted to the study of Livy's style during the last century brought Livian scholarship almost to a standstill, as it were, by its own bulk. Historians still needed to analyse his subject-matter, and there was scope for examination of the manuscript tradition; but the literary critic who considered treating Livy's style, syntax, and diction could hardly expect to do more than refine on the results of his predecessors. And who, un-aided, would set himself alongside Madvig or Weissenborn? More recently, however, three separate lines of research have given us a fresh perspective.

First, since Livy used the Annalistic form, with its traditional authority and its firm framework of construction, and this also influenced the tone and manner of his expression, the historians working on the Annalistic tradition have helped to interpret the general character of his narrative.

Secondly, within the Annalistic framework, Livy was free to compose the major episodes of his history according to the rules of rhetorical and dramatic elaboration. Here we may benefit from the study of Hellenistic historiography as well as Roman rhetoric, with special reference to Cicero's literary theory, in examining his technique of narration.

Thirdly, the historical treatment of Latin syntax and the important advances in Latin lexicography have thrown new light on Livian usage. If Roman historians enjoyed a certain licence in their syntax and diction, and Livy had the power to write freely as the spirit of his work moved him, what is the place of archaic, poetic, or colloquial expression in his style to reinforce and colour the regular prose usage? When we consider the evidence throughout the surviving Decades, there arises the problem whether Livy's style shows development from an 'epic' First Decade to more regular prose usage later. These are general matters which are relevant to the understanding of his narrative and to the appreciation of his writing at any particular point. It is timely, therefore, to take up again the discussion of Livy's style in its main features, as a basis—one may hope—for further research on its details.[1]

## I. THE ANNALISTIC FORM

The form of Livy's history was Annalistic. From the time when the pontifical records were published, certainly after the publication of the *Annales Maximi* (*c.*123 BCE), the history of the Roman Republic rested upon an authoritative collection of material, set in a chronological framework, that imposed its tradition upon Roman historiography. The Gracchan and Sullan Annalists elaborated it and gave it literary style, Livy accepted the convention, and—after the Imperial Annalists—not even Tacitus could depart from it.

The Annalistic form bore the marks of its official origin in arrangement and content. Servius (*ad. Aen.*, 1.373) refers to the *tabula* of the Pontifex Maximus, 'on which [the chief priest] was accustomed to write the names of the consuls and of other magistrates and to make a day-by-day record of activities worthy of note, at home

---

[1] Based on a paper read to the Joint Meeting of Greek and Roman Societies at Oxford in August, 1955. The writer would express his thanks to Prof. U. Kahrstedt, Prof. Sir Frank Adcock, and Prof. E. Fraenkel for the benefit of discussion and advice over many years, while the material was being developed. As the aim is to work directly from the original evidence, bibliographical references have been limited to those which are immediately relevant. For a survey of the recent work on the subject (with a fuller bibliography) see McDonald (1954).

and abroad, on land and at sea'; from the records of which in the archives the editors of the *Annales Maximi* compiled their material. The *tabula* had included matter of priestly significance, as Cato indicates (fr. 77 *HRR*): 'When grain was expensive, how often mist or something else obscured the light of the moon or the sun.' In contrasting *annales* and *historiae* Sempronius Asellio defines *annales*: '"Annales" are books that showed only these matters, namely what was done in which year, that is to say in the manner of those who keep a diary... further, to write repeatedly under which consul a war began and under which it ended and who had a triumphal entrance because of it and what happened in the war...' (frs. 1–2 *HRR*). This definition, it would seem, had particular reference to the *Annales Maximi* and to those Gracchan Annalists who followed it strictly in composing their material. The Annalistic form, then, was based upon the annual divisions of the official year, marked by ceremonial notices of the business of state; and it included not only constitutional and military but sacral items, because both magistrates and priests played their part in the administration of the Republic.[2]

We find this pattern in any book of Livy. Each year closed with a report of the elections and priestly notices; the next year opened with a statement of the entry of the magistrates on office, the allotment of provinces and voting of troops, the expiation of prodigies, and the reception of embassies; then, when their administrative business in Rome was finished, the consuls left for their provinces, and Livy's narrative turns to events outside Rome; after which, at the end of the year, we find the next annual round of official notices.[3]

32.8–9 Once the consuls had begun their term of office, they convened the senate on the Capitol, and the senators decided that the two consuls should decide their provinces by lot ...; the consuls next brought the envoys before the senate ...; after the draft was held, the consul was delayed in Rome by news of prodigies and by the expiatory rites for them ...; the consuls devoted themselves to the necessary religious ceremonies, setting out for their provinces only after appeasing the gods.

[2] *HRR* I².iii ff.; Rosenberg (1921: 113 ff.); Gelzer (1934: 46) and (1954: 342); cf. Crake (1940: 375); McDonald (*OCD*², s.v. 'Annals'). See also Fraccaro (1957: 59–65).

[3] *HRR* I².xxv ff.; cf. Nissen (1863: ch. 5); Kahrstedt (1913a: ch. 2), aptly naming the pattern 'Jahreswechsel'.

It was jejune material, recurring monotonously, and often tedious. Yet, apart from providing a chronological system, the Annalistic form made an appeal to Roman tradition, through its immediate civic associations, as long as the ceremonial procedure of the Republic was observed. At least, in reporting prodigies, Livy admitted its appeal: 'Nevertheless, as I write about bygone affairs, my mind in some way takes on an antique cast, and a certain spirit of religious respect prevents me from regarding as unworthy of recording in my history matters that the deeply sagacious men of old deemed meritorious of public attention' (43.13.2); and he aimed at instilling the same patriotic awe in the minds of his Augustan readers. Further, in a sweeping narrative that covered the centuries, the Annalistic form allowed a certain play of literary variety, by which the regular ceremonial passages not only held together but pointed the contrast and eased the tension of the great dramatic episodes of Roman history.[4]

The literary form which the Annalists had developed out of the pontifical records owed something to conventional elaboration along technical, antiquarian, and sacral lines. The record of an official event need not amplify the details of routine procedure. In reporting a well-known type of official occasion the historian, too, may content himself with a bare statement. But if the ceremony is not familiar, he must recount it fully, at least once, for the sake of the reader, and this may call for reconstruction of the conditions, on the basis of research or by analogy with contemporary institutions. The Annalists certainly had to elaborate the material of the *Annales Maximi* to make it historically intelligible.[5] They were also stimulated by political considerations. It was not for nothing that the Gracchan age saw a struggle about constitutional precedent or that Sulla forced a return to the principles of senatorial government.[6] Then, on the literary side, a ceremonial description could heighten the tone of the narrative at important places. The Annalists applied the principles of rhetorical composition in reconstructing Roman history with circumstantiality, and Livy followed them in the spirit of the Augustan appeal to the past.[7] We find phraseology in Livy that is technical to

---

[4] Kroll (1924: 362, 370).
[5] Gelzer (1934: 46), (1954: 342), and (1935: 269).
[6] Rosenberg (1921: 139 ff).
[7] McDonald (1954: 396, 409–10).

the point of legalism; it may also bear the marks of antiquarian research; and where the augural aspects of a ceremony become significant, the religious associations are heightened by the sacral vocabulary. Livy exploited these elements of archaic formalism, as Cicero accepted them for laws about religion: 'There are certain legal phrases, Quintus, which, though not yet as old as those in the ancient Twelve Tables and Sacred Laws, are yet somewhat older than the style of our present conversation so as to carry greater authority' (*de leg.* 2.7.18).

It will be worth illustrating the procedure of formal elaboration, with special reference to style and diction. The opening of a great war, for instance, called for description with full-dress ceremony. Our best illustration is Livy's account of the declaration of the Syrian War under 191 BCE (36.1–3), which is not complicated by details of the immediate political situation; it may be compared with the similar treatment of the Second Macedonian War (26.5–9) and the Third Macedonian War (42.30–5). The passages are too long to quote verbatim, but we may note the chief parallels in phraseology. First, the initial sacrifices and prayers (31.5.4; 36.1.1–2); then the report on the sacrifices (36.1.3; 42.30.9); after this the war-vote and decree to allot provinces (31.6.1; 36.1.4–6; 42.30.10–31.1). The vows follow:

36.2.3–5 That vow, dictated by the pontifex maximus Publius Licinius, was pronounced publicly by the consul in the following words: 'In respect to the war which the people have ordered undertaken with King Antiochus, should this be concluded as the Senate and people of Rome desire, then the Roman people will celebrate great games for ten successive days in your honour, Jupiter, and gifts will be presented at all the couches, finances for them being drawn at the discretion of the Senate. Whichsoever magistrate celebrate these games, and whensoever and wheresoever he do so, let it be deemed that the games have been celebrated and the gifts duly presented.'

Then the consultation of the *fetiales* (31.8.3–4; 36.3.7–12); and the expiation of prodigies (31.12; 36.37.1–6). Finally, the ceremonial departure of the consuls for their provinces (31.14.1; 36.3.13–14; 42.35.3).[8]

---

[8] Cf. Halkin (1953).

The pattern of description is ceremonially explicit, correct, and emphatic, and the material has been arranged with great care so as to present the formal character of the declaration of war, constitutional and ritualistic. The elaborate description does not recur purely for documentary purposes; for many of the details are conventional and there was no need, in terms of factual reporting, to enlarge repeatedly upon the procedure. The historical moment in each instance was important: the passages referring to the declaration of the Second Macedonian War and of the Syrian War stand conspicuously at the opening of the Pentads of books that describe the two wars. The occasion is treated with special literary attention not only to mark its historical significance but to make an appeal to the patriotic sentiment of the Roman reader. We may feel the emotional overtones of the formal expression of the ceremonial details, with the apt quotation of ritual in archaic style and diction (36.2.3–5; cf. 22.10.2–6; Cic., *de leg.* 2.8.21).

The following parallel accounts of the same religious procedure provide an instructive comparison:

35.40.7 In this period there were two particularly terrifying incidents at Rome, one of which lasted longer than the other but was not as damaging. There were earth tremors for thirty-eight days, and these suspended business for the same number of days, which were spent in an atmosphere of anxiety and fear. A three-day period of public prayer was held because of the phenomenon.

34.55.1–4 At the start of the consular year of Lucius Cornelius and Quintus Mucius, earthquakes were reported so often that people grew tired not just of the phenomenon but also of the holidays declared on the occasion. Meetings of the Senate could not be held and public business conducted because the consuls were busy with sacrifices and expiatory rites. Eventually the decemvirs were ordered to have recourse to the books, and on their ruling public prayers were held over three days. People made supplication to the gods, couches with garlands on their heads, and a proclamation was made that all members of the same household should worship together. Furthermore, on the authorization of the Senate, the consuls issued a decree forbidding the further reporting of an earthquake on a day on which a holiday had been proclaimed following a previously reported earthquake.[9]

[9] *HRR* I².xxvii–xxviii.

In the first passage we have a bare report of the expiation of serious earthquakes. In the second—even allowing for additional details in the original record—we may note the conventional features of the ritual which it was possible to work up for literary effect. The vocabulary is formal; at the same time the sentence structure is more complex than one usually finds in formal sections. Livy has combined the appeal of traditional procedure with some personal interest, and has written his account in smooth contemporary style.

There is not the space in this chapter to take further the discussion of Livy's technical vocabulary, as it is revealed in connection with the despatch of Roman envoys and their reports, the reception of foreign embassies, the records of censors' activities, the founding of colonies, the celebration of triumphs, and so on. A glance at the footnotes of Mommsen's *Staatsrecht* (1887–8) will suffice to show how the official mode of expression was followed by historians as well as orators. This is a subject that would repay linguistic study in Livy's work, if it were treated in the first instance with special reference to his formal sections as a legacy of the Annalistic tradition. That Livy was interested in presenting the full constitutional subject-matter in its appropriate style is proved not only by the length of his Annalistic sections but by the care with which he reproduces the Polybian details of Roman negotiations and settlements in the East. As far as he can, he preserves the language of diplomacy in his general narrative. Our chief purpose here, however, is to stress the influence of the traditional style which came to him from the *Annales Maximi* through the Annalists, above all where the vocabulary of the State religion, in its 'augural' and 'sacral' forms, appeared to him to evoke the spirit of early Roman history.

Two examples will make the point. When Scipio Africanus was charged with misconduct in the Syrian War, according to Gellius (4.18.3), he spoke as follows:

Roman citizens, I recall this is the day on which I defeated Hannibal the Carthaginian, the greatest enemy of your empire, in a great battle in Africa and brought forth a glorious peace and victory for you. Therefore, let us not be ungrateful to the gods and, so I think, let us leave this scoundrel; let us go straight from here to give thanks to Jove Optimus Maximus.

These words may not be authentic—they probably represent a composition of the Sullan period—but they allow an instructive comparison with Livy's account, which derived through Valerius Antias from the same report.[10]

38.51.7–9 Tribunes of the people and citizens of Rome: this was the day on which I fought a pitched battle with Hannibal and the Carthaginians in Africa, and did so meritoriously and successfully. It is therefore proper to avoid litigation and strife today. I shall go forthwith from this place to the Capitol to pay my respects to Jupiter Optimus Maximus, to Juno, to Minerva, and to the other deities who protect our Capitol and citadel. I shall thank them for having granted me the will and the occasion to render outstanding service to my state both on this very day and on many other occasions.

We need only note in passing the effect of Livy's full 'periodic' style, alongside the direct Latin of the first passage, the latter with its strong key words, placed emphatically. For the simple 'I defeated in a great battle' he had the formula 'I fought a pitched battle and did so meritoriously and successfully'; for the contemptuous 'scoundrel', the balanced phrase 'litigation and strife'; and the reference to Jupiter is ceremonially elaborated. This passage is not only rhetorical; it represents Livy's formal conception of the event.[11]

In the light of our argument we may now turn to the celebrated description of Valerius Corvinus' combat with a Gaul. It will be convenient for later reference to treat the general features of style briefly before coming to the significance of Livy's description of the climax. The Gaul, according to the Annalist (Gellius 9.11), had arms resplendent with gold: *armisque auro praefulgentibus*. He advanced haughtily: *grandia ingrediens... incedebat*; note the alliteration and the neuter plural used adverbially as in Greek. He was brandishing his spear: *manu telum reciprocans*, a 'poetic' verb; and he gazed with extreme arrogance all around him: *perque contemptum et superbiam circumspiciens despiciensque omnia*. The padded expression and the play of related compounds here show a certain care for realistic detail. The sentence piles up present participles to make its final effect, as the Gaul advanced to issue his challenge. Valerius asked

[10] Malcovati (1955: 7–8); Scullard (1951: 298–9).
[11] Marouzeau (1921: 165–6).

leave to fight the Gaul *tam inmaniter adrogantem* ('who was so fiercely presumptuous'), and came forward *intrepide modesteque obviam* ('fearlessly and modestly in his path')—the strong contrast reflected in the words. Then the champions come to grips: *et congrediuntur et consistunt et conserebantur iam manus*, in a triple statement of their moves; note the alliteration and assonance of *con-*, adding verbal emphasis to the precision of the description.[12]

Livy (7.26.1–5) arranged his account in 'periodic' structure. As the Gaul advances, a *cum* clause sets the sentence in shape, instead of the Annalist's accumulation of participles. The diction loses its archaic colour. The word *praefulgentibus* disappears, and the Gaul is simply *atque armis insignis* ('and notable for his armour'); *manu telum reciprocans* gives place to *quatiens scutum hasta* ('banging his shield with his spear'), a more explanatory phrase; the fighting is merely *conserenti iam manum Romano* ('as the Roman now came to grips'); and Livy drops the phrases emphasizing arrogance. The sentence, in fact, is not highlighted, because Livy will work up more gradually to the climax of the story.

The climax comes with the intervention of the raven. As the Annalist says, 'some divine power is on hand': a raven flies up and settles above the tribune's helmet and thence begins to fight against the face and eyes (*os atque oculos pugnare*) of his adversary. Now it flew at him, and threw him into confusion, and clawed his hand, and blocked his sight with its wings and, when it exhausted its rage, flew back to the tribune's helmet (*insilibat, obturbabat et unguibus manum laniabat et prospectum alis arcebat, atque ubi satis saevierat, revolabat in galeam tribuni*); thus Valerius was able to kill the Gaul. The hero of the duel is the raven, and this powerful sentence, stressing each detail, gains its effect from the series of vivid verbs in the imperfect tense linked by *et* or *atque*. Livy aims at a significantly different effect, which influences both his construction and his diction.

---

[12] *HRR* I².1.211–12 (but not Claudius Quadrigarius); Marouzeau (1921: 164–5). In using the Annalistic passage to illustrate archaic Latin, as Mr. R. M. Ogilvie has pointed out to me, one must take more account than hitherto of Greek influence on the vocabulary and style, possibly through the rendering of a Greek original.

7.26.3–5. Minus insigne certamen humanum numine interposito deorum factum; namque conserenti iam manum Romano corvus repente in galea consedit, in hostem versus. Quod primo ut augurium caelo missum laetus accepit tribunus, precatus deinde, si divus, si diva esset qui sibi praepetem misisset, volens propitius adesset. Dictu mirabile, tenuit non solum ales captam semel sedem sed, quotienscumque certamen initum est, levans se alis os oculosque hostis rostro et unguibus appetit, donec territum prodigii talis visu oculisque simul ac mente turbatum Valerius obtruncat; corvus ex conspectu elatus orientem petit.

The human combat was made less remarkable by the intervention of divine will; for, when the Roman was already in close combat, a crow suddenly landed on his helmet, facing his opponent. The tribune first joyfully accepted this as an augury sent from heaven and then prayed that, whatever god or goddess had sent the well-omened bird be at his side with good will and favor. Marvelous to say, the bird not only kept its captured perch but whenever fighting started, raising itself by its wings, attacked the face and the eyes of his opponent with its beak and claws until, when the man was terrified by the sight of such a prodigy and confused in his vision and his mind, Valerius lopped off his head; the crow rose out of sight flying east.

The combat loses its vivid details, so that the reader may feel the force of divine intervention. As Livy says, *minus insigne certamen humanum numine interposito deorum factum.* There is little need to stress the place of sentimental piety in his traditionalism. What is striking here is the use of 'augural' idiom to evoke a direct response from the Roman reader. Valerius reacts with propriety to the appearance of the raven: *ut augurium caelo missum laetus accepit,* and his prayer is ritualistic: *si divus, si diva . . . volens propitius adesset.* Note the technical term *praepetem* for the auspicious bird. The attack is a miracle—*mirabile dictu*—and Valerius kills the Gaul *territum prodigii talis visu;* after which the raven returns to the heaven which was its home. In style Livy has reduced the archaic robustness of the original story to the fashion of his times; yet he is able to play on the 'archaizing' appeal of current priestly usage, fitting it appropriately to his theme. The 'sacral' associations heighten the literary effect of his narration.

In this section we have attempted to show how Annalistic historiography, as it grew out of the *Annales Maximi* under the hands of the Gracchan and Sullan Annalists, established the framework of full-scale history for Livy and provided the means of expression by which he could evoke a response to the appeal of political and religious traditionalism. The effect was precise and powerful, working through the associations of technical vocabulary, especially in its constitutional and 'sacral' aspects. It was produced by conventional elaboration of the formal records when the historical moment called for literary emphasis; but we also find its influence elsewhere in the narrative, where Livy felt that he should display a theme in its deeper implications. This procedure covered not only the construction of an account, but its circumstantial detail and its diction. There is an organic relationship between the 'ethos' of Livy's work, its Annalistic form, and the influence of Annalistic expression upon his style. At this point, in treating the more broadly descriptive parts of his narrative, we must turn to the rules of rhetoric for historical composition, as laid down by Cicero.

## II. RHETORICAL HISTORIOGRAPHY

Livy, it is well known, stood under the influence of Cicero. In the first place, he was a rhetorician, professionally in debt to Cicero's work. As he wrote in the form of a letter to his son, he recommended the reading of Demosthenes and Cicero so that one should speak like them. He opposed Sallust and those who attempted a severe style by writing obscurely, using 'old-fashioned and unrefined language'. This is an echo of the battle which Cicero waged for a pure Latinity, without archaism or vulgarity, and it indicates Livy's place in the literary tradition.[13] Livy, too, wrote philosophical dialogues that smacked rather of history—perhaps like Cicero's *De re publica*. His traditionalism in historical thought associates him with Cicero in the ardent feeling for Rome that moved the best Italian citizens. The two men had the same conception of historiography—'history truly the witness of time, the illumination of truth, the lifeblood of memory, the guide of life, the messenger of the past, with what voice other than that of the orator is it entrusted to immortality?'—especially

---

[13] Norden (1915–18: i. 234).

with reference to the Roman tradition. These words are from Cicero (*de or.* 2.9.36), and Livy's *Preface* furnishes an Augustan commentary on the pronouncement. If history, then, was 'the genre especially close to oratory', Livy could look to Cicero, who had drawn upon the experience of Hellenistic criticism and adapted its theories to a programme of Roman historiography. In Cicero's view Rome had no historical work worthy of her greatness: 'Our literature is lacking in the field of history' (*de leg.* 1.2.5). For though the first law of history was to tell the truth, and the whole truth, this established only the *fundamenta* (foundations): the result would be no more than a plain *narratio* (statement of the facts). It was necessary to build up the historical narrative (*exaedificatio*) and embellish it (*exornatio*), so that it should take on a form befitting its dignity and importance. By rhetorical standards the first Roman historians had been mere chroniclers: 'not elaborators of deeds but mere reporters', that is, writers 'who left unornamented records of dates, men, places, and deeds' (*de or.* 2.12.53–4).[14] Although Greek rhetoric had come to Rome by the Gracchan period, and the Sullan Annalists could apply the principles of systematic elaboration, yet in Cicero's opinion the earlier writers lacked style. The task of presenting Roman history called for greater rhetorical skill and a finer literary style. Cicero defined the programme, Livy carried it out.[15]

*Exaedificatio* and *exornatio*—the rhetorical technique in historiography must first undertake the construction of the narrative, along with the literary elaboration that naturally accompanied it. Cicero's words on this subject (*de or.* 2.15.63) are worth quoting for their detailed indication of the method which Livy would follow:

The completed structure, however, rests on substance and words: the nature of the substance requires temporal order and a description of the geography; in truth, since for deeds that are great and worthy of record, the nature of the substance means that first the planning, then the actions, and last the consequences are expected; in the case of the planning, what the writer approves of should be indicated; and for the actions, not just what was done or said, but also how; and in the discussion of the outcome, the causes should be explained, all of them, whether accidental or carefully foreseen or

14 Gelzer (1934: 53).
15 Rambaud (1953: 9 ff., 121).

rash; and for those men who stand out by reputation or name, not just their deeds but also their way of life and character.

This kind of narration will be clear, since it is systematic; it may be full, but it should practise economy; above all, being circumstantial, it should produce an impression of reality, of essential probability, in the mind of the reader. These are the *virtutes narrandi* 'virtues of description' of rhetorical composition in narrative: 'lux, brevitas, fides' ('clarity, concision, fidelity'). The last point is further explained by Cicero (*de inv.* 1.21.29):

A narrative will be plausible if it seems to consist of things which usually appear in reality; if the appropriate qualities of the characters are observed; if the reasons for their deeds are apparent; if the resources for committing the deeds seem to have been present; if, for the matter to be narrated, suitable opportunity, enough space, and a proper location are shown to have been present; if the subject suits the nature of those who are doing it, the behavior of the general population, and the attitude of those who hear it. Then verisimilitude can arise from these principles.

The historian, then, should master his material, interpret it, and describe it in such a way that it will make sense to the intelligent and critical reader. As part of his general composition he may insert speeches to dramatize or characterize a situation or a person: 'History is related ornately, with an occasional description of a country or a battle; public addresses and exhortations can also be included' (*Or.* 20.66). For all the brilliance of Livy's speeches and the fame which they have justly earned on their own account, it is wrong to take them out of their carefully ordered context.

The professional historian would normally receive his material as *commentarii* ('notes', Greek ὑπομνήματα), which would be the better prepared if the author had borne in mind the requirements of the final literary form. Cicero prided himself on taking the material about his consulship well on the way towards the point at which Posidonius should publish it (*ad Att.* 2.1.1–2):

My book, however, exhausted Isocrates' entire container of unguents and all the boxes of perfume of his followers and even some of Aristotle's rouge... Posidonius has already written to me at Rhodes that, when he read my journal, which I had sent to him to write up a more elaborate

version of the same subject, not only was he not roused to write something
but that he was distinctly frightened off...

and Lucian (*Hist. conscr.*, 48) shows that rhetorical arrangement was
regular even in *commentarii* ('notes').[16] Livy was fortunate in succeeding to Annalistic subject-matter that was already well elaborated,
and where he had recourse to Polybius he found a detailed narrative
which he need only reproduce in good literary order. The strictness
with which he applied the rhetorical rules of composition can be seen
throughout his narrative, but the most instructive examples occur in
the parts where we can control his procedure by reference to the
original text of Polybius. Witte and others have profitably analysed
the literary character of Livy's adaptation of the material provided by
Polybius; yet they have not related it sufficiently to the rules of
rhetoric, and we may briefly illustrate the main features.[17]

Military operations always gave rise to descriptive elaboration in
terms of time, place, plans, action, and results.[18] In treating the siege
of Ambracia (Livy, 38.3–7; cf. Polyb., 21.25–8) Livy emphasizes the
topographical conditions and the strategical difficulties, adds circumstantial details of the first assault, and explains the conduct of
the defenders, all more explicitly than we find in Polybius. The
account of the tunnelling operations is vivid and precise, as he
visualizes the scene, but inaccurate, because he lacked technical
knowledge. At Cynoscephalae (Livy, 33.5–11; cf. Polyb., 18.18–33)
the terrain and the weather were decisive factors. Polybius had
indicated how a heavy morning mist brought Philip to a halt and
how a clash of Macedonian and Roman outposts on the ridge in dim
light led to the engagement of the full armies. Livy intensifies these
indications. Darkness like night held the Romans in fear of ambush
and caused the Macedonians to lose their way in desperate confusion. He then visualizes the topography on the basis of Polybius'
account and attempts to define it; after which he sets about reducing
to a more or less formal disposition what was originally a disorderly
engagement. The description gives a superficial clarity which makes

---

[16] Bömer (1953: 210); McDonald (1954: 393); cf. Adcock (1956: 7ff.).

[17] Nissen (1863: ch. 2); Witte (1910: 270, 359); cf. Walsh (1954: 97) and (1955:
369).

[18] Cf. Plathner (1934); Bruckmann (1936).

nonsense of Polybius, until it pays the penalty with one of the worst 'howlers' in history. As the phalanx lowered its pikes for action, Livy states: '[Philip] ordered the men of the Macedonian phalanx to lay down their spears (the length of these proving an encumbrance) and fight with their swords' (33.8.13). At the same time he explains with his own emphasis the motives of the generals, especially those of Philip, who is shown becoming involved unwillingly, step by step, in the battle that was to lose him the war.

It is not only Livy's fresh interpretation of Polybius but the errors which this introduces that make the point of the illustrations. Livy will take up the implications of his subject-matter and bring them out, as he believes, effectively for the sake of his readers. In military matters we see the blind leading the blind, and this may also be true of his treatment of motives, except where they represent general human reactions. It is the kind of thing for which Polybius criticized Timaeus (12.25), and Timaeus provided the model for rhetorical composition. Livy's very mistakes stress the effect of a literary method that worked from the writer's desk.[19]

The scene of a conference had to be clearly set before describing the course of negotiations. When Flamininus and his allies, for instance, met Philip V at Nicaea (Livy, 32.32–7; cf. Polyb., 18.1–12), the time was important, the place was picturesque, and the action contained more than one dramatic incident. Following the indications of Polybius, Livy depicts vividly Flamininus' group on the beach and Philip on the prow of a ship, the silence that fell after the king's reference to treachery, the moving of the ship nearer the shore so that he could hear better, and later the private meeting of Flamininus and Philip on the beach, the shouting of the allies on hearing the terms, and the effect of the noise on Philip at a distance. The dramatic point of Flamininus' taunt that Philip was afraid is heightened: 'to which Philip replied with the pride of a king: "I fear no one apart from the immortal gods, but I do not have confidence in the integrity of all the men I see around you, least of all the Aetolians"' (32.32.14). The main speeches are reported in ceremonial style to suit the character of the conference, and Livy disapproves of any frivolity: he omits a joke of Flamininus and rebukes Philip for

---

[19] Nissen (1863: 31 ff.); cf. McDonald (1954: 387).

his jibe at Phaeneas: 'Philip was, in fact, of a wittier disposition than was appropriate for a king' (32.34.3). But the literary art does not detract from Livy's practical object of presenting the sober details of the negotiations.[20]

Again, Livy turns all the resources of his technique to the description of the Isthmian Games, when Flamininus proclaimed 'the freedom of Greece' (Livy, 33.32–3; cf. Polyb., 18.46). In setting the stage he explains the importance of the Isthmus as a centre of Greek life and, following Polybius, stresses the particular interest of this meeting. Then, with a glimpse of the seated assembly and the ceremony of a trumpeter's call for silence, we see a herald proclaim the freedom of Greece. There follows a brilliant description of the crowd's response and their rush to acclaim Flamininus. The comments of Polybius are reproduced in the objective form of a report of the thoughts of the Greeks themselves, as they rejoiced in the occasion. Then Livy proceeds with the business of the Roman commissioners in Greece.

The course of an action might allow variety in treatment. When the Aetolians sued for peace in 191 BCE (Livy, 36.27–9; cf. Polyb., 20.9–11), the issue turned on the implications of the phrase 'the Aetolians surrendered themselves and all their possessions unconditionally to the Roman people' (36.28.2), which the Aetolians did not understand to mean unconditional surrender. Polybius explains their difficulty at the outset. Livy leaves it to appear as the climax of a description which is marked by strong dramatic irony. In reply to Phaeneas' protest that they had committed themselves 'to surrender not slavery' (36.28.4) and that there must be some mistake, the consul explains the Roman procedure; then 'ordered the lictors to bring chains and stand around the Aetolian delegation' (36.28.6). Here Livy modifies the normal 'interpretative' method of rhetorical practice and uses the form of dramatic arrangement.

To take an example of another convention, the choice of policy before Prusias is elaborately presented (Livy, 37.25; cf. Polyb., 31.11). Polybius described Antiochus' invitation to join in an alliance, Prusias' fear of Roman action against kings, and the letter of the Scipiones pointing out the Roman policy of supporting kings and

---

[20] Cf. Holleaux (1923: 115).

urging him to enter on the side of Rome. Livy balances the Scipiones'
letter with a letter of Antiochus, for which he draws on Polybius'
reference to the fears of Prusias: 'The Romans were coming, said
Antiochus, to wipe out all monarchies, so that there would be no
empire left anywhere in the world but that of Rome' (37.25.5). The
letter of the Scipiones, too, is arranged in formal composition. By the
literary convention of balanced letters Livy has attempted to clarify
and heighten the effect of the alternatives facing Prusias.

The 'letter' to Prusias is not the only reference to a natural
antagonism between a 'free state' and 'monarchies'; it can be paralleled in Perseus' appeal to Antiochus Epiphanes (Livy, 44.24;
cf. Polyb., 29.4): 'A free city and a king were inimical to each other
by nature' (44.24.1). Along with the idealized Augustan conception
of Roman imperialism Livy stresses the fundamental antagonism of
republicanism and monarchy. At the same time he recognizes the
rights of monarchical government and has a consistent view of regal
spirit and dignity as well as arrogance and vanity. We have noted
above his remark on Philip's kingly pride (32.32.14), and he is careful
to explain any point of protocol. When Attalus refused to appear in
the Athenian assembly (Livy, 31.15; cf. Polyb., 16.26), on the
grounds, according to Polybius, that it would be 'vulgar' to refer to
his favours in person, Livy enlarges upon his attitude in Roman
terms: 'it was deemed more appropriate to his status for him to
write a letter about any matters of concern to him. Rather this, it
was felt, than that he be present in person and be put in the
embarrassing situation of listing his services to the state of Athens,
or receiving applause and acclamation from a crowd that would tax
his modesty with extravagant flattery' (31.15.1–20). This is to preserve the *dignitates personarum* for the reader. Accordingly, a king
should not be undignified, and we have noted Livy's criticism of
Philip. Note, too, the characterization of the miserly tyrant Moagetes
(Livy, 38.14; cf. Polyb., 21.34), where Livy adds dramatic details of
Moagetes' sordid appearance and contemptible conduct, and sums
up his impression with the word 'niggardly'. As regards Livy's conception we may recall the importance of the client kings and their
ceremonial entertainment at the court of Augustus (cf. Suetonius,
*Aug.* 48). From the literary point of view this was the setting in which

Livy would explain the significance of the Hellenistic rulers to his Roman public.[21] In presenting an argument the rhetorical method laid down rules of procedure, which were as useful in the narrative as in the composition of speeches. One example will serve to illustrate the method. When the young Attalus came to Rome (Livy, 45.19.1–20.3; cf. Polyb., 30.1–3), some leading Romans attempted to win him away from Eumenes, while Stratius urged him to remain loyal to his brother. The situation allowed broad characterization, and Livy handled the Polybian material freely. In particular, he stresses the form of Stratius' appeal. If it is glorious both to save a kingdom for a brother and to seize it from him, the former as the loyal course is the more praiseworthy, the latter disgraceful. This is the rhetorical topos of *honestas* ('integrity' or 'what is honourable'). It is followed by an appeal to *utilitas* ('expedience' or 'what is useful'): there was no practical advantage in revolt. Polybius' summary becomes the report of a full argument, systematically constructed on rhetorical principles. This is the kind of thing which Livy does, if usually with less emphasis, in his arrangement of any discussion. The rhetorical treatment of his narrative as a whole must be taken into account in appreciating the part of *oratio obliqua* in reporting speeches where it was undesirable to interrupt the sweep of his description by a formal speech.[22] As regards the formal speeches, the most spectacular elements in Livy's writing, there is no need here to enlarge on their composition. Taine showed their significance, and R. Ullmann has analysed them in strict rhetorical terms.[23]

One special point must be made. Witte spoke of Livy's 'episodic' handling of scenes:[24] that is, Livy set out to elaborate and interpret major episodes, not to provide the discussion of political and strategical questions which Polybius regarded as the chief function of a historian. He will explain the time and place with only enough detail to clarify the scene itself, and often abbreviates the introductory details in Polybius so drastically that he misrepresents them. Tacitus, it may be

---

[21] Cf. McDonald (1955: 177–8).
[22] Lambert (1946).
[23] Taine (1904); Ullmann (1927) and (1929).
[24] 'Einzelerzählungen': Witte (1910: 273).

recalled, does the same thing in order to focus his dramatic treatment, so that in terms of strategy he appears 'the most unmilitary of historians'. In fact the rhetorical rules were directed merely towards immediate understanding by superficial clarity, and literary presentation might gain effect at the expense of genuine historical interpretation.

These examples have been chosen not to illustrate Livy's literary art in general but to show how he applied the accepted methods of historical composition, in the light of the canons defined by Cicero. Of course, a powerful writer will be the master of his technique, and Livy had an interest in human motives deeper than the considerations which were necessary to explain a story. His feeling will intensify the impression of an account; his emphasis will heighten the effect of one factor and reduce another to insignificance. In short, his personal concentration led to selective use of the conventional methods. This overriding principle will be appreciated by contrast with the painstaking, uninspired, and often tedious elaboration of material by Dionysius of Halicarnassus.

It is in this setting that we may treat Livy's use of dramatic methods of emotional appeal. Hellenistic historiography included a 'tragical' school which is now, somewhat confusingly, called 'Peripatetic', because it appears to have adapted Aristotle's theory of tragedy to historical writing. If one applies the theory of 'catharsis' to the exposition of the tragic events of history, then the historian may arrange his material in dramatic form in order to inspire the reader directly, as a spectator, with feelings of pity and horror. In the framework of his narrative he will develop episodes as dramatic scenes, with vivid affecting detail, and he will refrain from personal comment, which would spoil the illusion of the action; any observation will appear in the reactions of the characters themselves. Among the Greeks Duris and Phylarchus practised these methods, and Cicero refers to the technique as a standard form of historiography (*ad Fam.* 5.12.4–5).[25] His words have particular significance for Livy's style:

[25] Polyb., 2.56–63; Walbank (1938: 55) and (1955), cf. McDonald (1954: 386–7).

Nothing indeed is more suited to the pleasure of the reader than changes of circumstance and vicissitudes of fortune... For chronological order does not hold our attention very much, like a recitation of the official record of magistrates; but the doubtful and varying fortunes of a great man contain wonder, suspense, joy, worry, hope, fear...

Recent research has found evidence for 'Peripatetic' influence on Livy and Tacitus.[26] As regards Livy, who was primarily a rhetorical historian, we should note that if the subject-matter was tragic in itself, its presentation by rhetorical methods might naturally take on a dramatic form and move the emotions directly. Livy might differ from a strict 'Peripatetic' writer only in giving his personal analysis of motives and reactions, and indeed he often leaves the action to speak largely for itself. We may assume that he was as familiar as Cicero with the dramatic technique—the arrangement of the Aetolian episode mentioned above, for instance, shows a practised hand—and the feeling and force of his style would readily admit an emotional appeal. One need only refer here to Burck's work on the First Decade.[27] We should look for 'Peripatetic' influence, however, not so much in conventional application of the Hellenistic technique as in the dramatic concentration of effect in his handling of the rhetorical methods, aided by the imaginative power of his description and interpretation. For an illustration we shall turn later to the analysis of Livy's account of the siege of Abydus, after we have considered the other factors of style and diction.

## III. STYLE AND DICTION

Within the traditional Annalistic framework, as formally elaborated, we have seen how Livy constructs the leading episodes of his narrative, political or military, according to rhetorical principles. At the same time, he controls the technique and adapts it for greater concentration in the descriptive effect and emotional appeal of his

[26] Kroll (1924: 351); Norden (1952: 93); Mendell (1935: 3).
[27] Burck (1934).

history. In this context we may take up the more conventional questions of style and diction.

According to Cicero, *exaedificatio* stood not only *in rebus* (as we have quoted above) but *in verbis* (*de or.* 2.15.64): 'It is, moreover, necessary to strive for a kind of discourse and a style of speech that is expansive and drawn out and flows evenly with a certain mildness, without the edge of legal discourse and without the barbs of political speech.'

The ideal in presentation was 'abundance and richness of phrases and words', as one found in Timaeus: 'extremely rich in the abundance of his material and in the range of his views, and not unpolished in the organization of his words, he brought great eloquence to his writing' (*de or.* 2.14.58); and Cicero emphasizes his definition in criticizing Coelius Antipater: 'he did not distinguish his history with a range of hues, nor did he polish that work with his marshalling of words and a smooth and even style' (*de or.* 2.13.54).

The style of historical writing, then, in the first place must be smoothly flowing, equable and extensive, that is 'periodic'. The 'periodic' style belonged organically to the process of arranging historical material. When the accompanying circumstances were set syntactically in their subordinate place, the action could be clearly defined. The stream of narration should not run low with Attic harshness, nor swell its surface with Asianic word-play, nor break violently with irregularity of expression, as in Sallust. One should be able to formulate a complex statement with logicality and force, so as to relate its elements one to another and present the whole in a comprehensive form, and then move forward to the next stage. To the orderly narrative could then be added the refinements of word-play and rhythm that completed the impression by satisfying the ear. All this should be designed to give not only coherence and clarity but strength and momentum, and Cicero's emphasis upon the flow did not lessen the need for force in 'periodic' style.

We have already noted Livy's place in the literary tradition, where he supported Cicero and opposed Sallust and the school of 'obscure severity'. Quintilian would praise him for his *clarissimus candor* ('brilliant transparency', 10.1.101) and *lactea ubertas* ('creamy richness', 10.1.32), the virtues of the 'periodic' style. Yet *lactea*—the word is suspect:

They write a verse, as smooth, as soft, as creame;
In which there is no torrent, nor scarce streame.

But *ubertas* reminds us of the style that was associated (in Roman ears) with *amplitudo* and *dignitas*.[28] Livy showed in his writing that he recognized the need to concentrate the 'periodic' style in order to carry his vast theme in a strong and sweeping narrative. Sentence structure, of course, need not be 'periodic' at all. One can present a theme elegantly in a series of simple sentences, leaving the reader to grasp their logical coherence. Often in an analytical passage it makes for clarity to do so. Yet in a long descriptive narrative one needs greater momentum, and this calls for comprehensive sentences, the 'periodic' style, in which the major stages are presented emphatically, and minor steps are reduced to syntactical dependence. Between the two extremes there is scope for considerable variety. Just as few would write only in simple sentences, so the 'periodic' style does not consist entirely of 'periods'. Not only the immediate subject-matter but its larger context, and the emphasis which the writer wishes to place at any point, will determine the relative importance and syntactical arrangement of the details—together with the consequent play of words and the demands of prose rhythm.[29]

As we have remarked earlier, Livy tends to visualize scenes as a whole, in an 'episodic' manner, and the opening and closing circumstances are subordinated to the vivid detail of the central action. This treatment leads to the elaborate sentences, packed with dependent phrases and clauses, that lead rapidly into and out of his most brilliant pieces of description. The action is often presented in short sentences. Sometimes the pressure of his massive 'periodic' style on the details of writing causes difficulty. Livy had set himself, with strong sentiment and a free style, to present Augustan Rome with the epic of her past, and he raised his narration to the level of the heroic episodes of Roman history. His conception of a theme was urgent. Its expression was powerful and often unrestrained, and he

---

[28] Gellius 6.14.3, Marouzeau (1921: 150 ff.).
[29] Kroll (1924: 366). Compare the different treatment of similar actions in Caesar, *BG* 4.14–15 (where he dismisses the Usipetes and the Tencteri from his pages in a closing 'period') and *BG* 7.88 (where he describes the critical stage of the victory at Alesia in a striking series of short sentences).

did not hesitate to force the details of his 'periodic' construction into the main pattern of his thought.

Nearly a hundred years ago Madvig pointed out the danger of awkward combinations of words and harsh syntactical constructions in an elaborate 'periodic' style, a danger which Cicero avoided but which Livy is inclined to take too lightly.[30] In reference to the cult of Hercules on the Palatine both Livy (1.7) and Dionysius of Halicarnassus (*Rom. Ant.*, 1.39) describe the encounter of Hercules and Cacus. Dionysius sets out the story in a series of simple sentences. Livy's story runs as follows, and must be read as a whole:

1.7.4–7 Herculem in ea loca Geryone interempto boves mira specie abegisse memorant, ac prope Tiberim fluvium, qua prae se armentum agens nando traiecerat, loco herbido ut quiete et pabulo laeto reficeret boves et ipsum fessum via procubuisse. Ibi cum eum cibo vinoque gravatum sopor oppressisset, pastor accola eius loci, nomine Cacus, ferox viribus, captus pulchritudine boum cum avertere eam praedam vellet, quia si agendo armentum in speluncam compulisset ipsa vestigia quaerentem dominum eo deductura erant, aversos boves eximium quemque pulchritudine caudis in speluncam traxit. Hercules ad primam auroram somno excitus cum gregem perlustrasset oculis et partem abesse numero sensisset, pergit ad proximam speluncam, si forte eo vestigia ferrent. Quae ubi omnia foras versa vidit nec in partem aliam ferre, confusus atque incertus animi ex loco infesto agere porro armentum occepit. Inde cum actae boves quaedam ad desiderium, ut fit, relictarum mugissent, reddita inclusarum ex spelunca boum vox Herculem convertit. Quem cum vadentem ad speluncam Cacus vi prohibere conatus esset, ictus clava fidem pastorum nequiquam invocans morte occubuit.

The tale goes that Hercules, after slaying Geryon, drove the monster's magnificent cattle to this spot, and after swimming across Tiber's stream, driving the kine before him, he lay down on a grassy bank so that this serene setting with its lush pasturage might refresh his cattle and himself, exhausted as he was from his journey. When sleep overtook Hercules, heavy with food and drink, a local shepherd, by name Cacus, a creature of ferocious strength, when he was much taken by the beauty of the beasts and wished to steal them, since if he drove off the herd and forced it into his cave, the tracks would lead their inquiring owner in his direction, he selected the handsomest bulls, turned them around, and dragged them into the cave by their tails.

---

    [30]  Madvig (1875: 356); Riemann (1885: 309–10).

When the first flush of dawn roused Hercules from sleep and his gaze swept over the herd, he realized that some of them were missing. He headed for the nearest cave to see if perchance their tracks might direct him there. But when he saw that all the hoof marks pointed away from the cave and nowhere else, befuddled and uneasy, he began to drive the herd away from the alien spot. At this point certain of the heifers, as they were moving off, mooed because they missed, as is natural, the males left behind. The bulls shut up in the cave lowed in response, and Hercules turned back. When Cacus saw him striding toward his cave he tried to resist by force but, smitten by the hero's club and calling in vain for his fellow shepherds, he expired.

While Dionysius gives a leisurely story, Livy concentrates his material as a graphic episode. It was conventional in history as in epic—one thinks of Virgil's technique—to treat such episodes as highly polished insertions, giving variety and colour.[31] Yet an episode should not be unduly distracting—it must be compact as well as picturesque; and Livy has arranged his material in what he regarded as its main stages. In the long introductory sentence, he brings Hercules and the oxen on the scene. Then, in a complicated sentence, he shows Cacus dragging some of the oxen into the cave. Now the action quickens at its critical point. Hercules went to the cave. Deceived by the tracks he began to move away. The lowing turned him back. In resisting Hercules, Cacus met his death. The pattern is clear enough and Livy regularly gathers the preliminary circumstances of any action into an elaborate opening statement. Further, he aims at strengthening the action itself by parallel placing of the rival subjects: Hercules arriving, Cacus stealing, Hercules to the cave, Hercules leaving, then—the impersonal subject at the climax—the lowing of the oxen, and finally Cacus slain. This alternation of action, represented syntactically, is the key to much of Livy's 'periodic' composition.

What of the second sentence? Madvig argued that the introductory clause, 'when sleep overtook Hercules', requires as its main statement, 'a local shepherd, by name Cacus, wished to steal the oxen'. Livy makes this statement subordinate, 'when he wished to steal them'; then he is left with the dragging of the oxen backwards into the cave as his main statement. But this needs to be explained; so he is

---

[31] Heinze (1928: 442 ff., 485 n. 1).

committed to yet another subordinate clause, namely 'because the tracks would have led Hercules to the cave', before he can complete his period. The end of the sentence is out of touch with the opening words.[32] Now it is quite true that *in the sentence itself* one might best stop at Cacus' wish to steal. Yet *in the whole account* Livy might well desire to put Hercules to rest and the stolen oxen appropriately in the cave, in two comprehensive sentences, before he proceeded to the rapid stages of the actual encounter. He should probably have divided the sentence. Yet his awkwardness here is the defect of powerful composition, where it meets local complications. This kind of overcharged sentence, though one finds other examples in Livy, is not typical: he writes for the most part with a notable combination of strength and ease. The interest of the example lies in illustrating the principles of 'periodic' composition where a writer's conception of his material bears heavily on the stylistic conventions. As Norden has pointed out, even Cicero may pack his sentences when he is carried away by a piece of spirited historical description (cf. *ad Fam.* 15.4.8).[33]

In Livy's story of Hercules and Cacus we also meet the problem of his stylistic diction. He writes of Hercules on his arrival at the Palatine, *fessum via procubuisse*; and Cacus stole the cattle *cum eum cibo vinoque gravatum sopor oppressisset*. The noun *sopor* is not regular in prose before Livy, though it carries a specific meaning, stronger than *somnus*; the prose usage seems to be based on the verb *sopire*. One should perhaps not argue that *sopor* had to be avoided in Ciceronian prose; but its appearance here is linked with the use of the metaphorical phrase *sopor oppressisset*. The impression of the whole clause is poetical. We may recall Virgil (*Geor.*, 4.190): *fessosque sopor suus occupat artus*; and again (*Aen.*, 6.520): *curis somnoque gravatum... pressitque iacentem... alta quies*.[34] In the morning Hercules awakes *ad primam auroram*. Although this expression has lost its original force, it is still poetic, and occurs only here in Livy for the regular *prima luce*. Hercules is *confusus atque incertus animi*, the genitive closer to poetry than to prose. So the story goes on, concise but

[32] Madvig (1875: 359–60).
[33] Norden (1952: 78).
[34] Stacey (1898: 38); Gries (1949: 60–1).

elevated in style, until by another striking phrase *Cacus morte occu-buit.* One can hardly mistake the poetic colouring of the entire account. A glance at Virgil's description of the encounter of Hercules and Cacus (*Aen.*, 8.190–267) will show verbal similarities which need not be attributed entirely to coincidence.[35] Elsewhere in the First Decade Livy displays agreement with Virgil. Norden has argued, for instance, that Virgil's lines on the sack of Troy (*Aen.*, 2.486–95), which according to Servius (*ad* 2.486) were transferred from the destruction of Alba Longa, are so similar in tone and expression to Livy's account of the siege of Alba Longa (1.29) that we may attribute both passages to the same original authority. Virgil appears to have been drawing upon Ennius at this point (e.g. *fit via vi . . . et late loca milite complent*, 494–5). Though we need not assume that Livy used Ennius directly, his Annalistic source may have done so; for there seems little doubt that Ennius influenced early Roman historiography almost as strongly as he inspired the Virgilian epic.[36] In any event, where his subject-matter lay in the legendary past— 'material fitting for the stories of poetry'—Livy was ready to present his history as a prose epic, in the high poetic manner.

No one reading with a sense of style will deny that Livy's First Decade is poetically coloured. What has caused discussion is the development of a general theory about Livy's style which Eduard Wölfflin suggested and his pupil S. G. Stacey attempted to elaborate in their joint lexicographical work on Livy. In examining parallel instances Wölfflin found that Livian usage tended to vary from Decade to Decade, and that the First Decade in particular contained variations which reflected the initial uncertainty of a powerful new writer. Stacey made a survey of what he termed 'poetic diction' in Livy. He concluded that Livy began by writing 'Silver' Latin, with free use of poetic expression, and then, as he gained command of his style, turned to a more regular 'Ciceronian' manner, thus reversing the main trend in Latin prose. The evidence for this view rests upon the comparative occurrence of words that appear earlier only in the poets, e.g. nouns ending in -*men*, frequentative verbs and certain

---

[35] Stacey (1898: 39–40).

[36] Norden (1915: 154 ff.), after Stacey (1898: 40). Note also the value of Norden's edition of Vergil, *Aen.* 6, in studying this question.

compound verbs, *-ere* for *-erunt* in the third person plural of the
perfect indicative, and so on—usages which characterize his style in
the First Decade and then occur less often.[37]

Recently, in a thesis significantly called *Constancy in Livy's Latinity*,
Konrad Gries has re-examined Stacey's work and challenged his
conclusions. Why should an Augustan writer, he asks, while literary
Latin was still very much alive, refer to an arbiter in the past? In
reference to 'poetic diction', even though a word lack the authority of
Cicero or Caesar, may it not represent prose usage? Indeed, what
Stacey termed 'poetic' may often be archaic or colloquial. How can
we talk firmly about development in Livy's style when we find 'poetic'
usage, albeit less frequently, in the later surviving Decades?[38] Gries
has done useful service in modifying Stacey's over-simple view of
'poetic diction', but he pays too little attention to the formal developments of Latin style and diction. He tends to dismiss a word too
readily from the 'poetic' class if it can possibly be taken as archaic or
colloquial. Must words that we find elsewhere only in Plautus or
Terence be taken as colloquial but not poetical? And he ignores the
form of expression, e.g. *cum . . . sopor oppressisset*, that gives a phrase
poetic colour. Norden, for instance, refers to Livy's style in the First
Decade as contemporary but touched with archaic colour, and
Löfstedt speaks of 'the light poetic colouring which, though sometimes overestimated, is noticeable'.[39] Gries, however, has raised an
important issue, which will be worth further consideration, in connexion with the development of Latin prose style from the earlier
historians to Livy himself.

We have seen in the episode of Valerius Corvinus and the Gaul
how Livy adapted the archaic material of his Annalistic source to the
demands of contemporary writing, yet added the 'archaizing' appeal
of 'sacral' diction to heighten the significance of the event. His
description of the duel between Manlius Torquatus and a Gaul,
where he was using Claudius Quadrigarius (Gellius, 9.13), shows
his tendency to give a poetical colouring. There advanced (wrote
Claudius) a naked Gaul who was outstanding in strength and valour.

---

[37] Wölfflin (1933: 1 ff.); Stacey (1898: 18); cf. Löfstedt (1933: 294 ff.).
[38] Gries (1949: 4 ff.).
[39] Norden (1952: 77); Löfstedt (1933: 295).

He waved to both sides to be quiet. There was a pause in the fighting. On gaining silence he immediately issued a loud challenge (*cum voce maxima*). None dared to take it up on account of his size and ferocious appearance. Then the Gaul began to jeer and put his tongue out (*linguam exertare*). To cut the story short—Manlius took up the challenge: *metu magno ea congressio.* They fought shield to shield (as Claudius tells us twice), and Manlius stabbed the Gaul with his Spanish sword and overthrew him. When he had overthrown him, he cut off his head, removed his torque, and placed it all bloody (*sanguinulentam*) on his own neck; hence the *cognomen* Torquatus. The account is marked by short sentences, by simple connexion through personal pronouns, and by the repetition of words, which are the features of Claudius' archaic style.[40]

In Livy's words (7.9–10) the Gaul came forward and loudly (*quantum maxima voce potuit*) issued the challenge (in a well-rounded sentence). There was a long silence amongst the Roman *primores iuvenum*, since (says Livy) they did not wish either to reject the challenge or to take it up. Then Manlius asked permission from the general, and this was granted (in two well-chosen direct statements). Only now, with an apologetic reference to his authority, Livy mentions the Gaul putting out his tongue (*linguam etiam exserentem*). So the duel begins, 'with the spirits of so many mortal spectators hanging between hope and fear', and the death of the Gaul is described more elaborately—though the actual moves are the same. From the body, otherwise untouched, Manlius took a torque as spoil: *corpus…uno torque spoliavit* (the formal phrase), and placed it spattered with blood (*respersum cruore*) on his own neck. Amidst the triumphal chants, states Livy, was heard the *cognomen* Torquatus—a final touch of Roman ceremony. We need not emphasize further the greater formality of Livy's conception or his rhetorical devices, especially in the use of direct speech. He has arranged the story so that the main sentences represent its main stages, in 'periodic' style, with a number of present participles, avoiding the simple repetition of words—but enough has been said about sentence structure. Note, however, as regards syntax, that Livy corrects the vulgar *cum voce maxima*. On the point of diction he

[40] *HRR* I[2].208–10; Zimmerer (1937: 88 ff.).

writes *exserentem* for the frequentative *exertare (linguam)*, and the
phrase *respersum cruore* for the adjective *sanguinulentam*: that is, he
prefers the literary vocabulary to colloquial and realistic words. Livy's
mode of expression, like his conception of the scene, belongs to the
cultivated literary fashion of his day.

On the other hand, the description is heightened in tone, as the
gigantic Gaul is overthrown by the noblest of the Roman 'aristocratic
youth', who was ready (in Livy's alliterative phrase) *praecipuam
sortem periculi petere* ('to seek the short straw of danger'). Along
with the rhetorical composition and the use of ceremonial phrases
associated with the heroic traditions of Roman warfare, we have to
appreciate a colouring of expression and diction that is epic in
character. In such a context words take on what one may properly
call 'poetic' effect. At the central point of the story the phrase *tot circa
mortalium animis spe metuque pendentibus* keeps much of its metaphorical force in the intense feeling of the context, and the impression is increased by the appearance of *mortalium*. As Gellius remarks
(13.29), *mortales* was frequently used as a synonym of *homines*
especially in the form *multi mortales*, but in this sense it was too
'poetic' for regular prose and might be regarded as 'inept and frigid',
unless it was chosen for special effect. It was, in fact, a coloured word
that had faded in popular usage yet still presented a question of taste
for the purist. Livy employs it freely, sometimes as much for sound as
for sense; but he recognized its appeal as a solemn synonym for
*homines*, especially in a group, and we may attribute its use here to
his feeling for the epic tone of his description.[41]

Our examples have shown how Livy presents his material stylistically according to his conception of its significance. But we have
been quoting from the First Decade, where he may have thought of
his work as the 'prose epic' of Rome. The evidence does not help in
deciding whether he modified his treatment later. It will be important, therefore, to consider a passage from a part of his narrative in
which he is following Polybius; for, while the content might move
Livy to develop its presentation stylistically, Polybius was the least
likely of all writers to influence his feeling or manner of expression.
The example, too, will serve to illustrate the intimate connexion

[41] Marouzeau (1921: 160–3); cf. Heinze (1933: 97 ff.).

between Livy's general attitude to history, his rhetorical methods of arrangement, and his style and diction.

In 200 BCE the city of Abydus fell to Philip V of Macedon (Livy, 31.17–18; cf. Polyb., 16.30–4). The siege of Abydus, states Polybius, was remarkable for the strategic importance of the city on the Dardanelles, for the military operations, and especially for the gallantry of the people of Abydus. They first resisted the Macedonian attack from land and sea; then, when the outer walls had fallen, they attempted to negotiate. Philip demanded unconditional surrender. The citizens resolved to fight to the end and perish with their families, and the elders were instructed under oath to put them to the sword. The men of Abydus fought desperately, until the Macedonians breached the inner walls; but the elders betrayed their trust and offered to surrender the city. Philip was astounded to find the people committing suicide, and gave three days' grace 'to those who wished to hang or stab themselves'; which they did, family by family. Polybius comments on their spirit, which (he says) outdid that of the Phocians and Acarnanians, and on the unfairness of Fortune, since the Phocians and Acarnanians were able to win the day. The description is precise and detailed; the praise is detached and objective.

Yet how dramatic the scene, how passionate the action, how horrible and pitiful the climax! Livy feels the tragedy of it. In his account there is no preliminary discussion. He recounts the course of events, but his concern is with the demonstration of mass hysteria. There is no tone of admiration for vigour and courage and a great resolve: it is not the εὐψυχία ('nobility') of Polybius, but *rabies* ('insanity'), bringing worse evils than the Macedonians would have inflicted. The people's determination arose from anger and desperation; their resistance was terrifying in its frenzy; the elders had a more dreadful task than the soldiers; the final massacre was an act of madness. And the comparison was not with the fortunate Phocians and Acarnanians but with Saguntum: it was *Saguntina rabies*, the most famous instance in Roman history of insane self-destruction. We see here the profound sympathy of Livy. He takes up the drama, with its tragic content, and displays it, and interprets it in terms of human behaviour under intolerable stress. Let us consider the stylistic means which he employed.

The stages of the action are clearly defined. First (*primo*) the people of Abydus resisted the Macedonian attack from land and sea; then (*postea*), when the outer walls had fallen, they attempted to negotiate; they (*autem*) proposed terms. 'When Philip had replied that no terms short of unconditional surrender were acceptable and the report of the embassy was brought back to the people of Abydus, their resentment and despair roused them to such fury that they resorted to action as insane as that witnessed at Saguntum', and in a long sentence Livy sets out all the preparations for final self-destruction. There (he continues) first (*primum*) were chosen those who when the time came should carry out the destruction of the citizens, and they swore the oath; then (*tum*) the soldiers swore to fight to the death. The latter (*hi*) fought desperately; the leaders (*principes*) sent to Philip offering surrender. Philip gained the city but lost the citizens. For (*enim*) such madness invaded the people that—and Livy tells how it happened—they carried out their self-destruction. Astounded by their fury, Philip gave them three days for dying (*triduum ad moriendum*), and scarcely anyone fell into his hands alive. This outline gives the structure of the account in its sentences, and we may appreciate the well-organized, sweeping narrative of the best 'periodic' style.

The diction is striking. Livy's feeling for the tragic events has led him to raise his style. In the first resistance *Abydeni . . . adeuntes aditu arcebant* ('the Abydeni kept those entering from the entrance')— note the pressing alliteration. Philip's rejection of the negotiations is epigrammatically stated: *nihil pacati nisi omnia permittentibus* ([there would be] 'no peace unless they allowed everything'). Tacitus highlighted this kind of phrase; Livy fits it into the sweep of his narrative. As for the effect of the reply (*renuntiata haec legatio . . . iram accendit*), the participial phrase increases the force of the expression as subject of the active verb, and moves the action forward. Livy inserts the interpretative abstract words: *ab indignatione simul ac desperatione* ('out of indignation and at the same time, desperation'). He plays on Roman feelings by adding to mothers and children also *pueros ingenuos virginesque* ('freeborn youths and maidens'), the jewels of Roman society. Then he has priests and victims brought forward and altars set up in the middle—a sacral elaboration of the scene. Those who are to destroy the citizens have to swear *praeeuntibus exsecrabile carmen sacerdotibus* ('with the priests dictating to them the formulae of execration')—the words of the ritual formula giving overtones to the description; while those of military age—note the collective *militaris aetas*—swore *neminem vivum nisi victorem acie excessurum* ('that none would leave the battle alive if not victorious'), and the conventional alliterative formula takes on life in the sweep of the style. The soldiers, in a direct phrase, *memores deorum pertinaciter pugnaverunt* ('mindful of the gods fought tenaciously'); the elders offer to surrender in a sentence with falling rhythm: *luce prima sacerdotes cum infulis ad urbem dedendam Philippo mittunt* ('at dawn they sent their priests, wearing fillets, to surrender the town to Philip').

The style rises yet higher with the surrender: [*Philippus*] *hominum praedam omnem amisit* ('Philip lost all the human booty')—a figurative transference of *praeda*; and we again find the impersonal phrase used as subject for force and effect: *tanta enim rabies multitudinem invasit* ('For such insanity overtook the crowd'). Then for those who have died, and are now betrayed, note *qui pugnantes mortem occubuissent* ('who had fallen in battle')—the epic expression, we may recall, for Cacus' death. As the description reaches its climax we find the people *periurium alius alii exprobrantes* ('accusing one another of perjury') and so blaming the priests, in a sentence notable for its antithetical structure, balanced and bound by alliteration: *quos ad mortem devovissent, eorum deditionem vivorum hosti fecissent* ('for they had delivered alive to the enemy the men whom they had by sacred oath marked out for death'). The statement of destruction is poetic in conception: *seque ipsi per omnes vias leti interficerent* ('they committed suicide themselves, seeking every possible path to death'); note the figurative phrase and the more formal verb (as against *occidere*). The conclusion is epigrammatic and alliterative: *plura facinora in se victi ediderunt quam infesti edidissent victores, nec nisi quem vincula aut alia necessitas mori prohibuit, quisquam vivus in potestatem venit* ('In that period of time the defeated townspeople inflicted more atrocities on themselves than a bloodthirsty conqueror would have done, and nobody fell into Philip's power alive with the exception of those for whom imprisonment or some other duress made suicide impossible'). We need not labour comment on this piece of writing. It draws on the resources of

Latin expression outside the limits of normal prose, and plays on associations and overtones with epic effect; yet it is regular and direct. Livy still has the imaginative fire of the First Decade, now refined in an equally powerful and evocative style, the achievement of his mature development. We need not suppose that he has changed his canons of prose style in history. That is, Stacey was right in pointing out the 'poetic' features of Livy's writing, though he exaggerates them, but he was wrong in generalizing about a return from 'Silver' to 'Ciceronian' Latin. Gries underestimates the 'poetic' quality of Livy's narration, but he is right in arguing that Livy was constant in his own principles of prose writing. Constant in inconstancy—if we apply the canons of Ciceronian prose usage; yet historians were permitted a certain licence in their style. We may close by setting the evidence in the perspective of the developments in literary Latin.

## IV. LIVY'S STYLE IN THE LITERARY TRADITION

In Cicero's time—and under Cicero's leadership—the attempt was made to establish general rules of linguistic and syntactical procedure so as to set in order the variations of archaic Latin in word-formation, gender, declension, and conjugation as well as in syntax.[42] The aim was to achieve consistency, as an aid to clarity in expression, where one had to be effectively understood. The development also involved the selection of vocabulary. Cato, for instance, had not hesitated to build up his sentence with powerful synonyms, aided by assonance and alliteration, often poetical, sometimes colloquial, always impressive in his use of words. When he said, robustly, *rem tene, verba sequentur* ('grasp the substance; the words will follow'), this implied not necessarily baldness of speech but, in an imaginative man, a free disposal of the whole wealth of Latin.[43] It was the Scipionic circle that began the cult of elegance, and their influence gathered force in a widening milieu, under the influence of Greek literature and Roman rhetoric, until Cicero and his contemporaries

---

[42] See now in general Palmer (1954: 118 ff.).
[43] Norden (1915–18: i. 164 ff.).

were able to establish a 'classic' form. One must, in Cicero's phrase, choose 'words that no one could justly criticize' (*de or.* 3.2.40). Who would judge, and by what standards? The judgment was that of contemporary good taste in the Roman capital, based on appropriate usage and idiomatic expression for the sake of purity and elegance in diction: 'nothing but the pure and well chosen' (*Or.* 8.25). One must, as Caesar said, avoid like a rock the 'strange and unfamiliar word' (Gellius, 1.10.4). On one side lay the archaic words that had become obsolete; on the other crowded the colloquialism of familiar speech and the vulgarism of the masses—'unusual words' in the view of literary society; and ahead stretched the way of correct usage, where one should take up the 'suitable words' in their strict sense. Then let the writer look to the ordering of expression, so that his sentences should formulate his thought and affect the reader by sense, sound, and rhythm: 'placement of words' involving 'composition, elegance, rhythm'; here the 'periodic' style, as we have seen, provided a method of comprehensive organization. The self-conscious practitioners and critical public, whose activity and reactions promoted this development, were found predominantly in Rome, while local usage maintained itself outside the city. This strict Latinity represented *urbanitas* in contrast to *rusticitas*. At the same time, we may note, Cicero's procedure was not final. His rules became important because they represented sound Latinity, and Augustan *urbanitas* in style was not less vital for its debt to his work.[44]

This development covered prose writing in general, but, as Cicero admitted, his rules applied in particular to oratory. Historical prose appealed to deeper feelings and broader imagination: it called for a greater variety in expression, more colour, and a freer use of language. The vocabulary of regular prose could be heightened to gain effect, and the historian had licence to draw upon archaic diction, colloquial usage, and poetic word-play for the purposes of his narration, as might seem appropriate to him. In Cicero's view the poet was close to the orator in methods of literary composition: 'for the poet is a very close relative of the orator: rather more restricted in rhythm, more free by contrast in the choice of words, but an ally and

[44] Marouzeau (1949: ch. 1); Riemann (1885: 13 ff.); Bornecque (1933: ch. 16).

almost an equal in many types of ornamentation' (*de or.* 1.16.70).
Following Cicero's canons Quintilian (10.1.31) stressed the closeness
of history to poetry: 'for it is very close to the poets and in some sense
a prose poem'; and the common feature again was stylistic licence.
Both might employ words which the practical orator would rule out
for immediate effect, because they aimed at making a different
literary impression: 'Equally, it is written to create a memory for
the future and to glorify the author, and it avoids the tedium of
chronicles by its out-of-the-way words and its freer rhetorical features.' Not that a historian would depart basically from the established Latinity of Cicero; for the virtues of consistency, clarity, and
elegance always command respect. But there was scope, within the
bounds of literary taste, for the evocative and figurative phrase.
Where did the imaginative writer look for his linguistic reinforcement? Although the regulated prose of strict *urbanitas* was not as
limited in expression and effect, well handled, as we sometimes
assume, it was on the whole a sober manner of writing. It lacked
spontaneous warmth and feeling. For these qualities the historian
had to dip into the broad stream of popular Latin, which Cicero had
only in part diverted and filtered for his oratorical purposes. The
historian, like the poet, was allowed stylistic licence to borrow,
refurbish, and even coin appropriately from the living language of
his day as well as to play on the literary associations of the past.[45]

Consider the scope of Roman history. In treating the early traditions, one might accept the emotive poetical word: the epic influence
of Ennius could be perpetuated in prose. Or on matters of constitutional significance against the background of Roman religion, recall
the phrase with 'sacral' associations? Or again, in vivid dialogue, use
a colloquial expression?[46] The question, in fact, is not whether Livy
was specifically writing a 'poetic' style in the First Decade. He was
always free to accept a poetical phrase that pressed for admittance. In
the First Decade, indeed, Livy did not resist the spell of the distant
past, as it reached him through his authorities. His style was in its

---

[45] Löfstedt (1933: 365).
[46] To take two examples. Is *sinere* with the subjunctive 'poetic' or 'colloquial'
(Gries 1949: 59)? At 34.24.2, it seems 'sacral'. Or *per ambages*—'poetic' (Stacey
1898: 36) or variable in regular use (Gries 1949: 20–1)? At 34.59.1, it seems colloquial.

beginnings, and he may not have quite decided upon his own principles of expression: Wölfflin was surely right in detecting Livy's gradual development of his style in the early books.[47] But this was a matter of discretion, not of difference, in prose style. As he moved forward, he wrote with less exuberance, though with equal power, and stood more firmly in the main current of literary Latin. This did not prevent him enlarging his scope of expression. As he drew on the resources of the language, he made a wide choice for colour and heightened effect, and so his style shows elements which we may identify (if we wish) as archaic, 'sacral', colloquial, or 'poetic'.

If a writer extends his vocabulary in response to his feeling for sound and sense, the critic may be in difficulties when he tries to specify the sources of the new material. In Latin usage, as Löfstedt has pointed out, one may find archaic terms going underground, so to speak, in Ciceronian literature, and coming to the surface again in later Latin. If a non-Ciceronian usage in Livy, for instance, has a parallel in Old Latin, is it therefore archaic, restored for its traditional associations, especially if these are 'sacral' in character? But 'sacral' usage may have survived in formulae which are of literary interest only to the historian. Or the older usage perhaps remained current colloquially, to be gathered in from the contemporary language? Indeed, as Cicero remarked (*de or.* 3.2.42), 'rustic' speech may smack of the archaic. We may not beg the question by referring to 'archaic and colloquial' usage; for, strictly, the one term excludes the other. As for the term 'poetic', a historian might choose a word that is paralleled both in the poets and in colloquial speech. Was he writing under poetic influence? Or did he borrow independently from colloquial usage, for the same reason as the poet? We can only judge in the light of the context. Here we may leave the question for further research in detail. For the most part Livy's borrowings from so-called 'non-classical' usage help in giving warmth and colour to his style, with the greater stylistic freedom of historical writing.[48]

Livy, we may conclude, aimed at writing a style that would be acceptable under the canons of Augustan *urbanitas*, taking into account the licence which a historian was allowed in order to

---

[47] Wölfflin (1933: 18).
[48] See Löfstedt (1933: ch. 12); cf. Palmer (1954: 148–9).

heighten the effect of regular prose composition. Even if he took a little time to gain control of his style, it must—all in all—have proved fashionable in Augustan Rome.[49] Why, then, should Asinius Pollio charge him with 'Patavinitas'? As Quintilian states, 'Asinius Pollio thought that there was a certain 'Patavinity' in Titus Livius, a man with wondrous gift for words' (8.1.3; cf. 1.5.56). Any discussion of this question must now rest on Latte's analysis of the evidence. In the context Quintilian is dealing with expressions that betray a lack of *Latinitas* and *urbanitas*, which Pollio apparently, in some degree, found lacking in Livy. The term 'Patavinitas' need not point specifically to *Paduan* idioms. By a form of literary polemics which may be paralleled in Hellenistic criticism, Pollio referred to Livy's home in order to sharpen his charge that Livy still showed signs of his original *rusticitas*.[50] If Pollio was thinking in terms of style, he presumably felt that Livy sometimes exceeded even the licence permitted to historians. But, since Quintilian is hardly precise about the significance of Pollio's remark, he may be mistaken in relating it to literary style. The point may have been personal, or, more likely, it was directed against what Pollio regarded as historical naiveté, or political 'rusticity', on the part of Livy. In any event, we need not set a jibe of Pollio against the evidence for Livy's place in the development of Roman historical prose.[51] Our analysis has shown him in the Annalistic tradition, adapting the technique of rhetorical and dramatic composition, and drawing freely upon the ordered resources of the Latin language after Cicero—all in a manner that we may believe found acceptance in the literary taste of Augustan Rome.[52]

---

[49] Cichorius (1922: 261), on the popularity of Livy's readings.

[50] Latte (1940: 56).

[51] See Riemann (1885: 13 ff.); Bornecque (1933: 194–6); Syme (1939: 485–6); and in general André (1949: 89 ff.).

[52] One of the urgent needs in Latin studies is a re-examination of Livy's narrative style in detail, with reference to the particular kinds of context—formal Annalistic, rhetorical composition, dramatic, simple reporting—apart from the oratorical style of the speeches. As regards his sources of diction, Löfstedt (1933: ch. 12) has shown the method of study; cf. Leumann (1947: 116). Consult also Cousin (1951: 253, 297, 308).

ADDENDUM

We have mixed feelings about including this classic article. On the one hand, it offers a convenient introduction to, and close analysis of, Livian style, in a way that is not readily available elsewhere in English. On the other hand, we disagree with many of McDonald's premises.

Most notably, his characterization of Livy's relationship to Cicero misrepresents the status of Cicero's theorizing (and probably its aims) and disregards the ways in which historiography incorporates the oratorical, as just one part of its multi-faceted style. Most damagingly, in affiliating Livy with Cicero and over-emphasizing his tenuously attested rhetorical and philosophical interests, McDonald encourages readers to evaluate Livy apart from the other historians, as if he somehow should not be assessed on the same terms.

Though valuing his close reading of Livian style, much recent scholarship on Livian historiography has moved away from McDonald's position. For samples of close reading see Kraus (1997) and Jaeger (2007); Oakley (1997–2005) i: 111–51 provides a thorough introduction to Livy's style in the context of the second pentad. Woodman (1988) chapter 3 discusses the relationship between Cicero and Livy (though we disagree with some of its conclusions); for the background to the *De oratore* see now Fantham (2004). For the development of Latin prose style see Rosén (1999); for its poetics see the Addendum to Moles, and for the differences between kinds of periodic sentence see Kraus (1994*a*) 20–1. Hine (2005) and Coleman (1999) discuss the question of the 'poetic' and the 'prosaic', while Mayer (2005) investigates the difficulties of writing 'periodic' Latin. For the intersections between poetry and historiography see Levene and Nelis (2002) and Foucher (2000); for *urbanitas* see Ramage (1973) and—with intricate discussion of the relationship between diction and self-presentation—Krostenko (2001). Hays (1987) considers the meaning of Quintilian's phrase *lactea ubertas* in the context of rhetorical education. Finally, Oakley (1985) discusses the various episodes of single combat in Livy, among others (see further, Addendum to Solodow).

# 9

# Form and Language in Livy's Triumph Notices

## J. E. Phillips

Many scholars have discussed the annalistic style of Livy, especially the way he and his predecessors developed and expanded the bare records of the Roman past in accordance with the principles of rhetorical historiography.[1] It has often been pointed out how marked a stylistic distinction there is between the historian's elaborate accounts and the curt, bald notices with which he begins and ends each consular year—elections, the inauguration of new magistrates, provincial and troop allotments, prodigies, and the like. And the conclusion is generally drawn that the notices in the plain manner faithfully reproduce the official *Annales Maximi* in style as well as in substance.[2] However, students of Livy, preferring to concentrate on the rhetorically more interesting sections, have had little or nothing further to say about the stylistic features of the annual notices. Consideration of them from an artistic point of view has confined itself to explanations for their inclusion in the history. Reasons

---

[1] Most important, Burck (1934); Klotz (1940–1); cf. also Walsh (1961*a*: 110 ff., esp. 120 ff.); Badian (1966: 11–23).

[2] Nissen (1863: 89–91, 101); Cichorius (1894: 2256); Soltau (1897*b*: 27–8, 85–6); Bornecque (1933: 72); Walsh (1961*a*: 30–1, 121). For the style of the pontifical annals, Cic. *De or.* 2.52–3, *Leg.* 1.6. Cf. also Quint. *Inst.* 10.2.7.

The belief that Livy's annual notices substantially reproduce the content of the *Annales Maximi* has been recently challenged in the case of prodigy reports by Rawson (1971: 158–69), but her conclusions, even if accepted, do not affect the stylistic question.

suggested are Livy's desire to give an impression of authenticity, or to establish an effective contrast with the more ornamental passages, or to show his love for the traditions of the Roman past.[3]

Yet it would seem that more might be said. Granted that the annual notices reflect the style of the pontifical annals, is this similarity only because their ultimate source is the pontifical annals? It is hard to believe in a Livy who was merely a copyist (and that sporadically), and who exercised not even editorial control over his material. It seems more reasonable to assume that as a serious writer Livy was capable of controlling what he wrote at all times, not just when he faced the composition of an important speech or the narrative of a critical battle. True enough that the annual notices are written in a flat, rather monotonous fashion; we may still ask by what means this monotonous effect is achieved and to what degree it is done deliberately. A second question is how 'official' Livy's language in these reports actually is; how far does he maintain the linguistic appearance of state records?

The following essay will give a close examination of repetitive elements and technical vocabulary in one of the kinds of annual notices, the triumph reports. Triumphs, of course, do not necessarily occur annually, but they do occur frequently enough to have a regular place in the annalistic material in Livy, and triumph reports are drawn from the same ultimate source as the strictly annual material, the *Annales Maximi*.[4] Furthermore, for one part of the triumph reports, we possess a parallel official record, the *Fasti Triumphales*, as comparative material.

Discussion will be limited to a review of the triumphs reported in Books 21–45. The accounts of Livy's predecessors for the period covered by these books would have been much fuller than for the period of the first decade. And the earlier historians themselves would have had much more complete documentary material as their source. The consequence for Livy of this relative abundance is that he had much more freedom of choice: he could develop, concentrate, omit, or emphasize as he saw fit, within the relatively wide

---

[3] Walsh (1961*a*: 30–1); McDonald (1957: 155–7).

[4] Sempronius Asellio fr. 2 *HRR*; cf. Cichorius (1894: 2256 and col. 2250); Soltau (1897*b*: 27–33, 85–97).

bounds set by the material available. We have no cause to assume that he would merely have accepted the judgment of previous writers in these matters, instead of making his own decisions. What he did in fact do when the possibility was before him is the question that concerns us here.

In these two and a half decades, then, Livy reports the celebration of thirty-eight triumphs or ovations, in thirty-seven separate notices.[5] His treatment covers the whole range, from a sparely written notice only one or two sentences long (e.g., 40.16.11) to detailed accounts of political conflicts attendant on some general's request for permission to triumph (38.44.9–50.3, 39.4.2–5.6, 45.35.4–39), or lengthy descriptions of especially impressive displays of captured wealth (34.52.4–10). Broad as the scope of treatment is, there are regularly recurring elements that give structural definition to the triumph notices.

A full triumph or ovation notice falls into two halves with a total of five standard parts; all the parts do not necessarily appear in every notice (see Table).[6] The first half describes the preliminaries to the celebration, and begins with the formal report to the senate made by the returning general and his request for a triumph. The announcement of the senate's decree follows, with any discussion that may have accompanied the decision. The second half concerns the triumphal ceremony itself, in which the actual statement of the triumph is given, followed by the list of booty carried in the triumphal procession or, what amounts to the same thing, deposited in the treasury; there may be additional details about the spoils, the captives, or other extraordinary features of the procession. Finally any

---

[5] Triumphs: 26.21.1–10, 28.9.7–20, 30.45.2–5, 31.47.6–49.3, 33.22.1–23.9, 33.37.9–12, 34.10.6–7, 34.46.2–3, 34.52.3–12, 36.39.4–40.14, 37.46.1–6, 37.58.3–5, 37.58.6–59.6, 38.44.9–50.3 and 39.6.3–7.5, 39.4.1–5 and 17, 39.42.2–4, 40.34.7–8, 40.38.8–9, 40.43.4–7, 40.59.1–3, 41.7.1–3, 41.13.6–8, 42.21.6–7, 45.35.4–40.5, 45.42.2–3, 45.43.1–8. Ovations: 26.21.1–10, 31.20.1–7, 33.27.1–2, 34.10.3–7, 36.21.10–11 and 39.1–2 (a repeated notice), 39.29.4–7, 40.16.11, 41.28.1–3 and 6.

[6] The Table shows the division into parts, as defined here, for each notice. Examination of the chart will give an idea of the regularity with which the several parts recur. Text references to all the items in each category will be found in the Table rather than in the notes; irregularly or rarely appearing items are reviewed in the main body of the chapter.

**Table**  Occurrence of Structural Elements in Triumph and Ovation Reports, Livy
21–45

| Report/Request | Senate Proceedings | Celebration | Parade | Donative |
|---|---|---|---|---|
| 26.21.1-2 | 26.21.3-5 | 26.21.6 | 26.21.6-10 | |
| 28.9.7 | 28.9.8-10 | | 28.9.11-16 | 28.9.17 |
| | | 30.45.2 | 30.45.3, 4-6 | 30.45.3 |
| 31.20.2 | 31.20.3-6 | 31.20.6 | 31.20.7 | 31.20.7 |
| 31.47.6-7 | 31.48.1-49.1 | 31.49.2 | 31.49.2-3 | |
| 33.22.1 | 33.22.2-23.2 | 33.23.4 | 33.23.4-7 | 33.23.7 |
| 33.22.1 | 33.22.2-10 | 33.23.8 | 33.23.8-9 | 33.23.9 |
| | | 33.27.1 | 33.27.2 | |
| | 33.37.9 | 33.37.10 | 33.37.11 | 33.37.12 |
| | 34.10.5 | 34.10.3 | 34.10.4 | |
| | | 34.10.6 | 34.10.7 | |
| | | 34.46.2 | 34.46.2 | 34.46.3 |
| 34.52.3 | 34.52.3 | 34.52.3, 10 | 34.52.4-10 | 34.52.11 |
| | | 36.21.10 | 36.21.11 | |
| | | 36.39.1 | 36.39.2 | |
| 36.39.5 | 36.39.6-40.10 | 36.40.11 | 36.40.11-12 | 36.40.13 |
| 37.46.2 | 37.46.2 | 37.46.2 | 37.46.3-6 | |
| 37.58.3 | 37.58.3 | 37.58.4 | 37.58.4 | |
| 37.58.7 | 37.58.7-59.1 | 37.59.2 | 37.59.2-5 | 37.59.6 |
| 38.44.9-10 | 38.44.11-50.3 | 39.6.3 | 39.7.1-2 | 39.7.2 |
| 39.4.2 | 39.4.3-5.6 | 39.5.13 | 39.5.14-16 | 39.5.17 |
| 39.29.4 | 39.29.4-5 | | 39.29.6 | |
| | 39.42.2 | 39.42.2 | 39.42.3 | |
| | 39.42.2 | 39.42.4 | 39.42.4 | |
| | | 40.16.11 | 40.16.11 | |
| | | 40.34.7 | 40.34.8 | 40.34.8 |
| | 40.38.8 | 40.38.9 | 40.38.9 | |
| | | 40.43.5 | 40.43.6 | 40.43.7 |
| | | 40.59.1 | 40.59.2 | 40.59.2 |
| | | 41.7.2 | 41.7.2 | 41.7.3 |
| | | 41.7.2 | 41.7.2 | 41.7.3 |
| 41.13.6 | 41.13.6 | 41.13.6 | 41.13.7 | 41.13.7-8 |
| | 41.28.3 | 41.28.6 | 41.28.6 | |
| 42.21.7 | 42.21.7 | 42.21.7 | | |
| | 45.35.4 | | 45.40.1-4 | 45.40.5 |
| | 45.35.4 | 45.42.2 | 45.42.2 | 45.42.3 |
| | 45.35.4 | 45.43.1 | 45.43.4-6 | 45.43.7 |

bonus or donative given to the soldiers and officers as part of the
celebration is reported.[7]

The general's report to the senate and request for a triumph is
handled with only a moderate amount of substantive expansion. Livy

---

[7] Livy refers to two triumphs without actually reporting them. The naval triumph
of Q. Fabius Labeo is mentioned at 37.60.6 and again at 38.47.5; the report proper

264     *J. E. Phillips*

may summarize points that the general was supposed to have made
in his speech (26.21.2, 37.58.3), or specify the location of his campaigns (39.4.2, 41.13.6, 42.21.7), or subordinate the fact of the
request proper to the questionable motives of the person making it
(31.47.6). But such additions are not frequent nor always very striking when they are made. The vocabulary of the report and request is
fairly regular. Livy uses the exceedingly common phrase *res gestae* for
the 'deeds' of the general, a standard usage in military contexts.[8]
The verbs used for delivery of the speech are *disserere* (26.21.2,
36.39.5, 37.58.7, 39.4.2; *edisserere* at 34.52.3) or *exponere* (28.9.7,
31.20.2, 31.47.7, 42.21.7), with one appearance of *commemorare*
(38.44.10). The word for making the formal request is regularly
*postulare*, although *petere* is used twice, and in fact *postulare* seems
to be the usual Latin term for submitting a formal request to a
governing body.[9] The fullest form of the request itself, as seen at
38.44.10, is 'that the immortal gods be appropriately honoured and
he be permitted to ride in triumph into the city'. The first part, 'that
the immortal gods be appropriately honoured', is found in several
other places in Livy (e.g., 37.59.1, 38.48.16, 41.17.3), not always with
reference to a triumph, but always in the context of a victory. It
cannot be precisely paralleled in documentary material, but its un-
varying appearances in Livy suggest that, if it is not itself borrowed
from ritual language, it certainly imitates an official style.[10] The
second part, 'he be permitted to ride in triumph into the city', is
also not supported by evidence outside Livy, though it is found often,
and usually without the first part.[11] Three times Livy says simply

may have been overlooked as Livy changed from one source to another. He also quotes
a dedicatory inscription put up by Ti. Sempronius Gracchus in which Gracchus
mentions a triumph not reported in the extant text of Livy (41.28.8–10); the report
evidently was in a now lost part of the text, since it is mentioned in *Per.* 41.

[8] The use of the phrase in the standard authors is too well known to require
documentation; cf. *TLL* vi.1944.31 ff. Other occurrences: *CIL* I².626.6; Sempronius
Asellio f. 1 *HRR*; Claudius Quadrigarius fr. 48 *HRR*.

[9] Cf. *Lex Vrs.*, *CIL* I².594.100 and 105; tribunician decree from the trials of the
Scipios, Gell. *NA* 6.19.5. Less conclusive are Cic. *Balb.* 34 and *Fam.* 1.2.1. For its use in
civil and criminal law, Berger (1953: *s.v.*).

[10] Cf. Laqueur (1909: 215–18), who regards the whole phrase as official; for
*honorem habere*, *TLL* vi.2922.83–4.

[11] The phrase is found at 26.21.2 (*inire*), 28.9.7 (*inire*), 31.20.2, 31.47.6, 36.39.5,
38.44.10; cf. W–M's note on 39.4.2. Also in a refused request, 35.8.9, and W–M *ad*

'make a request for a triumph' (33.22.1, 39.29.4, 42.21.7), and once 'request that they [the senators] give the order for a triumph' (39.4.2).

Because the decree granting the triumph or ovation concerns the senate and therefore involves politics, this is the place where Livy has the greatest opportunity to apply his rhetorical talents and present his readers with stirring speeches for and against the proposed triumph. More or less full descriptions of the debate are given in twelve of the instances, and some of them are very full indeed.[12] In the other reports of senatorial action only the decree is mentioned. The point to note here is that Livy regularly uses the same few expressions to indicate the decree itself, whether he is writing the extended or the abbreviated accounts. *Decernere* is much the most common, appearing in sixteen reports; Livy also uses *consensus (consentire)* and *ex senatus consulto*.[13] All three are familiar from their application to senatorial procedure in the literary sources, but they are also found often enough in documents to substantiate their attribution to bureaucratic language.[14] In three cases Livy avoids altogether the standard words. At 31.20.5 he describes the decision thus: 'nevertheless they resorted to the compromise of . . .'; at 26.21.4 he says 'a compromise was reached'; and at 39.29.5 'was none the less granted the compromise honour'. In each case a triumph was

*loc.* Versnel (1970: 163) regards it as not only the official request form but also the correct expression for 'to triumph', solely on the basis of its frequency in the first decade of Livy. But cf. the discussion below on *triumphare*.

¹² Course of the debate reported at 26.21.3–4, 28.9.8–10, 31.20.3–6, 31.48.1–49.1, 34.10.5, 36.39.6–40.10, 37.58.7–59.1, 38.44.11–50.3, 39.4.3–5 and 6 (with further discussion after passage of the decree, 39.5.7–10), 39.29.4–5. The conflict over the triumph of L. Aemilius Paulus, 45.35.4–39.20, occurs in the *concilium plebis*, not the senate; nonetheless it is formally a member of this class.

¹³ *Decernere*: 28.9.9, 31.49.1, 33.23.1, 33.37.9, 34.52.3, 36.40.10, 37.46.2, 37.58.3, 37.59.1, 38.50.3, 39.5.6, 39.42.2, 40.38.8, 41.13.6, 41.28.3, 45.35.4. *Consensus (consentire)*: 33.23.1, 33.37.9, 36.40.10, 37.46.2, 37.58.3, 39.42.4. 'By senatorial decree': 31.20.6, 33.27.1.

¹⁴ *Decernere*: SC de Bacch., CIL I².581.6; Lex Ant. de Termess., CIL I².589.2.13; CIL II.1569.9; Res gestae div. Aug. 14. Of a municipal body: Lex Vrs., CIL I².594.64, 99, 103, 125; Res gestae div. Aug. 21. Of a pontifical college: CIL X.8259. Cf. TLL v.142.22 ff. *Ex senatus consulto*: e.g., Sentent. Minuc., CIL I².584.4; SC de Asclep., CIL I².588.5. For these two expressions, see Mommsen (1887–8: iii. 994–7). *Consensus (consentire)* is usual of the senate only from the time of Cicero on; e.g., Ad Brut. 1.18.2, Marcell. 3; also SC of 11 ʙᴄᴇ *ap.* Frontin. Aq. 100.

requested but only an ovation granted, a situation which may have led Livy to a search for alternate expressions (though *decernere* is used of an ovation at 41.28.3). On the other hand, he does not use *censere* or *placere* here, words known from their procedural application in other sources and in other parts of Livy's history.[15]

The core of the triumph and ovation reports is the announcement that the triumph or ovation was held.[16] In the triumph statement (ovations will be considered shortly), there is a basic full expression of which nearly all the notices are merely variants. An example is 36.40.11 'Publius Cornelius then triumphed over the Boii during his consulship'. The information provided is the name of the triumphator, his rank or the note 'during his magistracy', the name of the conquered people, and the statement that a triumph was celebrated. The form may be varied by the addition of 'on the Alban Mount' or the day of the triumph,[17] or by the omission of the name, the office, or the conquered people.[18] In the case of omissions, the reader would usually be able to supply the missing parts from the immediate context. In general, Livy achieves a remarkably consistent tone in the statements of the celebration, chiefly owing to the presence of the verb *triumphare*, almost always in the form *triumphavit*. There are four occurrences of a variation on *triumphavit* modeled on the request form, but in two of these *triumphare* appears as a participle (*triumphans urbem est invectus*, 37.46.2 and 40.43.5; cf. 30.45.2, and

[15] For *censere* and *placere* in Livy, see Packard (1968: *s.vv.*); some examples are (*censere*) 22.61.4, 32.1.13, 45.20.7; (*placere*) 23.32.16, 38.35.3, 42.31.7. Documentary use: *censere*, e.g., in *SC de Bacch.*, *CIL* I².581.3, 9, 18, 25, 26; *SC* of 99 BCE *ap.* Gell. *NA* 4.6.2; *Lex Tarent.*, *CIL* I².590.13, 20, 25. *Placere*: *SCC ap.* Frontin. *Aq.* 100, 104, 106, 108, 125, 127; *SCC* quoted by Caelius *ap.* Cic. *Fam.* 8.8.6–8.

[16] A straightforward statement that a general triumphed or had an ovation is omitted only in the elaborate report at 28.9.11 and at 39.29.5. At 34.10.6 the statement is in a subordinate clause ('before he celebrated his triumph'), but this is the only such example.

[17] 'On the Alban Mount' (clearly not a capricious addition): 26.21.6, 33.23.8, 42.21.7. The date: 37.58.4, 37.59.2, 39.5.13, 39.6.3, 45.42.2, 45.43.1; perhaps 40.59.3 should be added.

[18] Omission of name: 26.21.6, 30.45.2, 33.37.10, 37.46.2, 37.58.4, 37.59.2, 39.5.13, 40.38.9, 41.13.6, 42.21.7. Omission of people conquered: 26.21.6, 30.45.2, 34.10.6, 34.52.3 and 10, 37.58.4, 37.59.2, 40.38.9, 40.43.5, 42.21.7. Omission of rank: 26.21.6, 30.45.2, 34.10.6, 34.52.3 and 10, 37.46.2, 37.58.4, 37.59.2, 39.5.13, 39.6.3, 39.42.3 and 4, 40.38.9, 41.7.2, 42.21.7, 45.42.2, 45.43.1.

34.52.10, where *triumphavit* had occurred at 34.52.3).[19] Another variation is found at 45.42.2, where Livy says *navalem triumphum egit*.[20] The historian here chooses to use one expression almost exclusively, with an infrequent variant deliberately reminiscent of his own language in an earlier stage of the triumphal process. He also chooses not to use other common Latin expressions adequately attested in bureaucratic language and found in other parts of his own history.[21]

A most interesting question is how Livy's celebration statements compare with those of the triumphal *fasti* known from inscriptions. The best known and best preserved of these are the *Fasti Capitolini*, which date probably from between 19 and 11 BCE. Each notice in these lists gives the following facts: the name and filiation of the general, his office, the name of the conquered people, and the day and Capitoline year of the triumph. There is no verb; the very appearance of a name on the *Fasti* is statement enough that a triumph was celebrated. Additional information is given when necessary, such as the number of times a general had held office or celebrated a triumph, whether the triumph was a naval one, or whether it was 'on the Alban Mount'.

Plainly these *Fasti* are more detailed and more standardized in their presentation than Livy's triumph reports. Livy does not usually give the date and, since he writes annals, does not need to give the year. He omits filiations and notations of how often a man had been

---

[19] A similarly constructed expression in an alleged votive inscription: *triumphans in urbem Romam redit*, 41.28.9. Cf. *Romam redieit triumphans, CIL* I².626.4–5 (Mummius inscr.), and Sempronius Asellio f. 2 *HRR, quis triumphans introierit.* Perhaps *triumphare* in the bureaucratic language of the first century BCE had replaced an older expression; cf. nn. 11 and 24.

[20] There is another naval triumph at 37.58.4; here Livy simply uses *triumphavit*, but he had just said *triumphus navalis est decretus* in the preceding sentence. *Triumphum navalem agere* is the regular official expression; see, e.g., the *Fast. tr. Cap.* for the years 260, 257, 254, 167 in Degrassi (1947); the *Fasti Vrbisalvienses* for 167 in Degrassi (1947) 339; Plin. *NH* 34.13.

[21] e.g., *triumphum agere* not referring to a naval triumph: *CIL* I².652.5; *Res gestae div. Aug.* 4; Cic. *Phil.* 14.23, *Rep.* 6.11, *Fam.* 3.10.1; Suet. *Aug.* 22. For its use in Livy, see Packard (1968); some examples are 7.11.9, 38.17.6, 41.7.1, 45.38.11. Other ignored possibilities: *triumphum inferre, SC* of 8 BCE ap. Macrob. *Sat.* 1.12.35; *triumphum ducere*, Plin. *NH* 7.98.

magistrate or held a triumph. On the other hand we do find in his notices the general's name, his office, and the names of the people he defeated, all with varying degrees of regularity, and the note, where appropriate, 'on the Alban Mount'. The most definitive feature of Livy's reports, the verb *triumphare*, does not appear in the Capitoline *Fasti*; one might well wonder whether *triumphare*, *triumphum agere*, or some other expression is meant to be supplied. On the whole, comparison of Livy's notices with the Capitoline *Fasti* shows only a partial stylistic correspondence between the two.

Livy's practice may also be compared with fragments of two other sets of *fasti*, the *Fasti Vrbisalvienses*, from a small town in Picenum, and the *Fasti Barberiniani*, most probably originating in Rome.[22] The remains of the former set preserve material only incompletely covering the years 195 to 158 BCE, and the latter 43 to 21 BCE. The *Fasti Vrbisalvienses* contain the name and office of the general, without filiation; the names of conquered peoples and the dates of the triumphs also occur with special notations of naval triumphs and the number of triumphs to each man's credit, but no year is given. The *Fasti Barberiniani* omit filiations, years, and even offices, but they conclude each notice with the words 'he triumphed, he made an offering of his victory palm'.[23] The use of *triumphavit* here, as well as its frequent occurrence in other inscriptions and in literary sources, strongly suggests that it is the verb to supply in the *Fasti Capitolini* and *Vrbisalvienses*.[24]

Another point of comparison is the way in which Livy on the one hand and the inscriptions on the other refer to the peoples and lands whose defeat was the subject of the triumphs. Livy generally says *de* with the name of a people and *ex* with the names of countries (e.g., *de Gallis*, 31.49.2; *ex Hispania*, 34.46.2); the prepositions are occasionally interchanged (*de Aetolis et de Cephallania*, 39.5.13; *ex Liguribus*,

---

[22] Degrassi (1947) 338 ff. and 341 ff.; for the *Fasti Barberiniani*, see also n. 23.

[23] The reference to offering the palm is taken to mean the ritual presentation at the temple of Jupiter Optimus Maximus at the end of the parade; from that it is inferred that the *fasti* may come from the temple itself, the only place where anyone would care about a ritual offering. See Henzen in *CIL* I².76–8; Degrassi (1947) 345.

[24] *Triumphare*: *CIL* I².763*b* and *c* (Scipio inscr.); *Lex Iul. munic.*, *CIL* I².593.63; inscr. (?) of Pompey *ap.* Plin. *NH* 7.98; Degrassi (1937) *elogia* 78, 80, 81; Cic. *Phil.* 11.18, *Mur.* 15; Sall. *Iug.* 114.3.

40.59.1). All the *fasti* show exactly the same pattern: *de* for people and *ex* for places, with a fair number of exceptions (e.g., *ex Parthineis, Fast. tr. Cap.*, 39 BCE; *de Illurico, Fast. tr. Cap.*, 42 BCE).

The Barberini *Fasti*, then, present the closest relationship to the form of Livy's triumph notices; at the same time both they and Livy show ties to the other extant *fasti*. Livy is apparently drawing on a familiar tradition and its accepted variants in the composition of his triumph statements. He displays more variation than the inscriptions do, but with only a few exceptions it is variation on a recognizable model, to be explained by the greater freedom in composition possessed by the writer of books over the writer of inscriptions. Even in the occasional case where Livy discards the dominant form, the departure is patterned on a model he has already established in another part of the whole report.

The situation with the ovation notices is not quite so clear. Nine ovations[25] are reported in Books 21–45 (see note 5), all with essentially the same form: the basic phrase is *ovans urbem ingredi (inire)*. The participle alone appears at 26.21.6. The name of the general is omitted only at 26.21.6 and 34.10.3, but his office never appears. Only two contain the name of the subject nation (36.39.1, 41.28.6). There are no dates. For variation Livy adds 'by senatorial decree' (31.20.6, 33.27.1), or 'thanks to his successful operation' (34.10.3), or reports only the decree, not the celebration (39.29.5).

None of this is different in principle from the treatment of the triumph notices. The difficulty in discussing the ovations arises from the nature of the comparative material. The occurrences of the expression *ovans urbem ingredi* and its variants are from authors later than Livy.[26] In all the extant *fasti*, including the *Fasti Barberiniani*, ovations are indicated by the participle *ovans* (as in

---

[25] The ovation report at 36.39.1–2 is a very similarly phrased doublet of the one at 21.10–11; see Klotz (1915: 500–2), who attributes it to Livy's absentmindedness in changing sources. The differences are slight—a relative clause at 21.10 is a prepositional phrase at 39.1, the booty lists diverge slightly (see Klotz, *loc. cit.*, and W–M for the reading), the verb in the booty lists is *prae se ferre* in the first and *transferre* in the second. These variants are just further indication that Livy is exercising choice in the composition of the notices.

[26] e.g., Plin. *NH* 15.125; Tac. *Ann.* 3.19 and 47; Suet. *Aug.* 22 and *Tib.* 9; Gell. *NA* 5.6.20–1 and 27.

Livy), but with no verb following. The only comparable reference to an ovation in inscriptions appears in Augustus' *Res Gestae: bis ovans triumphavi* ('I celebrated two ovations', 4.1). There seems to be no reason why the elliptical statements of ovations on the *fasti* could not be understood as the same expression, especially if the notices of triumphs proper are to be completed with this word. G. Rohde states, on the basis of the literary evidence alone, that *ovans urbem* with a verb of entering reflects the formulation of the senatorial decree authorizing the ovation;[27] that may be so, but it does not really explain what word or phrase is intended to complete *fasti* announcements that an ovation was held. Whatever the situation in technical language, however, Livy does select a model for his notices and use it, with minor variations but without serious divergence.

The reports of captives and booty in the triumphal procession are, along with the announcements of the celebrations, the element that appears most consistently in the triumph notices. In a formal sense they are found in every notice but one (42.21.7), for even when there is little or no booty, Livy reports its absence (31.49.3, 40.34.8, 40.38.9, 40.59.1–3, 45.42.2). There is room here for some rhetorical expansion: some particularly magnificent processions are described in considerable detail, such as that of Flamininus (34.52.3–10), or presumably the one of L. Aemilius Paulus, though the text is damaged and the account is not complete (45.40.1–4). The spoils of Cn. Manlius Vulso are the occasion for some moralizing remarks on the dangers of luxury (39.6.7–9). Sometimes not the booty but other aspects of the procession call for comment: for instance, the unusual double triumph and relative merits of M. Livius Salinator and C. Claudius Nero at 28.9.11–16, the African triumph of P. Cornelius Scipio (30.45), the invidious comparisons made at the triumphs of L. Scipio (37.59.2) and L. Anicius (45.43.1–4). From time to time there are remarks on the fate of distinguished captives (30.45.4, 37.46.5, 45.43.9–10), or on the attitude of the soldiers or other participants (33.23.6, 34.52.12, 39.7.3, 41.13.8).

In the midst of all this variety there is the same underlying consistency noted in other parts. The very presence of the parade description is a constant element, however much it may be varied by

---

[27] Rohde (1942: 1891).

the kinds of additions just mentioned. Certain features of Livy's language are also constant. The captives and sacrificial victims are regularly said to be led before the triumphal chariot, *ducere ante currum*, a phrase also found in inscriptions and literary sources.[28] There is one occurrence of *traducere* (36.40.11). For the captured treasure of all kinds, Livy much prefers the verb *ferre* (usually as *tulit*), or occasionally *prae (se) ferre*.[29] He may add to *ferre* the phrase *in aerarium*, when the booty is given as money or coin-metal (28.9.16, 31.49.2, 34.10.4, 41.28.6). The only other alternative to *ferre* is a surprisingly frequent occurrence of *transferre* or *transvehere*. The choice of *trans-* compounds may have a basis in sacral or official usage; the prefix in these two verbs and in *traducere* seems to refer to the ritual crossing of the *pomerium*, the formal start of every triumph.[30] In any case, it is evident that Livy is once again limiting himself to a few expressions and avoiding other possibilities, even though his dependence on an official model cannot be suggested with certainty.

The same is true of the remaining part of the triumph notice, the report of bonuses given to soldiers and officers. Livy says either *dare* or *dividere* for the distribution.[31] There is no evidence to support these words as part of an official vocabulary, but it is clear enough that Livy chooses not to use a wider range of expressions.

To sum up, then: a study of Livy's triumph notices in Books 21–45 shows that he has two main techniques for handling this typically annalistic material. First, there is a basic structure for the standard or 'ideal' triumph notice. All the parts together account for the whole

---

[28] *Ducere ante currum*: 31.49.3, 33.23.5, 34.52.9 (no verb), 37.59.5, 39.7.2, 40.34.8, 40.38.9, 45.43.6. *Ducere* alone: 26.21.9, 34.52.9, 37.46.4, 40.38.9. The phrase in other sources: Degrassi (1937) *elogia* 89 and 17; *Res gestae div. Aug.* 4; Cic. *Verr.* 5.67; Sen. *Brev. vit.* 13.8; cf. *TLL* iv.1521.11 ff.

[29] A form of *ferre* in every report, except when varied as noted. *Prae se ferre*: 31.49.3, 36.21.11, 37.46.3, 39.42.4.

[30] *Transferre*: 33.23.9, 34.52.4 and 8, 36.39.2, 36.40.12, 37.58.4, 40.16.11, 40.34.8, 40.59.2, 41.7.2, 45.40.1, 45.43.4. *Transvehere*: 33.23.4, 33.37.11, 36.40.11, 39.7.2. Dictionaries and translators invariably understand these verbs as 'carry in procession, parade', but cf. Phillips (1974: 54–5).

[31] *Dividere*: 28.9.17, 30.45.3, 31.20.7, 33.23.7, 34.46.3, 34.52.11, 36.40.13, 39.5.17, 39.7.2, 40.34.8, 40.59.2, 41.7.3. *Dare*: 33.23.9, 33.37.12, 37.59.6, 39.7.2, 40.38.9, 40.43.7, 41.13.7, 45.40.5, 45.42.2, 45.43.7.

constitutional procedure of a triumph, from requesting it through obtaining and actually holding it. Even though all the parts may not appear in every notice, each notice, whatever its individual features as a result of omission, addition, or elaboration, recognizably belongs to the standard type. The elements of the triumph report, then, are repetitive enough to allow the definition of a standard structure; but they are varied enough by omission or substantive or rhetorical addition to avoid unrelieved uniformity.

Uniformity is imposed on the reports in another way. Livy has a carefully selected vocabulary for reporting the facts of each part of the notice. Insofar as his language can be compared with that of public documents and of literary sources which presumably owe something to such documents, he does choose words characteristic of the bureaucratic style. But he does not use the entire range of bureaucratic language open to him. And even where official models cannot be adduced, his linguistic range is small, much smaller than the Latin language requires: consider, for example, the possible synonyms for and compounds of *ferre* which are not used in the procession reports. This selectivity must be deliberate, and its aim must be the uniformity which is in fact its effect.

If it is accepted that Livy gives his annual notices the character of the pontifical annals by the repetition of certain kinds of information about recurring events, by conscious restriction of vocabulary, and by the employment of technical terms, then perhaps a few more general speculations about the practice of annalistic historiography may be permitted. It is true that a dry, monotonous reporting makes the elaborately composed episodes stand out more impressively; this contrast is effective within the triumph notices as well as between annual notices and other material. It is also true that the flavor of the old *Annales Maximi* would evoke a patriotic piety in the reader. But there is a more positive aspect to annalistic repetitiveness. Livy chose to write annals at a time when the development of Roman historiography and the events of the recent past combined to make his choice hardly inevitable. Annalistic history, even more than history generally, is not only an account of individual events, but of events that are formally similar or even identical. The Roman annalist offers his readers the regular repetition of constitutional processes. Each triumph may have unique features, of course, as may each election, each allotment of provinces and troops, and so on. But in the end, there remains an impression of uniformity, of a pattern. The reader is invited to contemplate the annalistic framework, not only each stirring speech or each outstanding individual. The yearly pattern— which is the Republican constitution in its continuing operation—is meant by Livy to be seen as subsuming the vicissitudes of men and events to itself. A decision to write annalistic history is more than a matter of style or tradition; it is the choice of an interpretation of history as well.[32]

ADDENDUM

This article offers a concrete, specific analysis of so-called 'annalistic material'. Levene (1993) does the same in a book-length study of Livy's prodigy notices. The most creative discussions of annalistic material remain those focused on Tacitus; for a start, see Ginsburg (1981). For Livy's relationship to his annalistic precursors, see Rich and Northwood (2000). On Livy's vocabulary see Adams (1974), Moore (1989), Kraus (1994*a*): 17–24 and, for readers with German, Tränkle (1968).

The standard collected edition of the Roman annalists remains *HRR*, with commentary in Latin; a new version, with English translation and commentary, is being prepared by a team of scholars under the direction of T. J. Cornell. There are bilingual versions in French (Chassignet (1996–2004) and German (Beck and Walter (2001–4)). Forsythe (1994) is a text, with commentary, of the fragments of L. Calpurnius Piso. The most extensive discussion of the *Annales Maximi* is Frier (2nd edn., 1999); see also Bucher (1987) and Verbrugghe (1989).

The basic discussions of the triumph and the ovation in Versnel (1970) and Rohde (1942) have now been supplemented by Beard

---

[32] This essay is a revision of a chapter of my dissertation, Jane Phillips Packard, 'Official Notices in Livy's Fourth Decade: Style and Treatment' (Diss., University of North Carolina at Chapel Hill, 1969). I owe special thanks to Prof. T. Robert S. Broughton for support and advice in its preparation.

(2007), which is sure to change the way historians understand the surviving ancient representations of the ceremony. On triumphs in Livy see Pittenger (2009).

The epigraphical evidence to which Phillips refers is not easily consulted without access to a research library. For *CIL*, see our Abbreviations list. The *Fasti Capitolini, Barberiniani,* and *Vrbisalvienses* were all published together in one volume of *Inscriptiones Italiae* (XIII.1: Degrassi (1947)); the *elogia* are found in *Inscriptiones Italiae* XIII.3, Degrassi (1937). A text and translation of the *Res Gestae* is most conveniently found in Brunt and Moore (1967).

# IV

# Narrative

# 10

## An Introduction to Books 29 and 30

*E. Burck*

### THE RECEPTION OF THE MAGNA MATER
### (29.10. 4–11. 8, 29.14)

Book 29 begins with Scipio's arrival in Sicily, where he prepares
for his crossing to Africa. Livy deliberately expresses himself more
emphatically than he has before: 'the plans he already had in mind
embraced nothing less than the destruction of Carthage' (1.13).
In the very first chapters he continues the progressive development
whose initial phases we admired at the end of Book 28: through the
justice of his administration Scipio wins the trust of this province
too, and all Sicilians support his preparations for war the more
eagerly (1.18). Livy brings the aim of the war to the reader's attention
more insistently in chs. 3–4, where he describes how Scipio's friend
Laelius leads on his orders a commando raid on the North African
coast as far as Hippo Regius; this causes untold consternation in
Carthage. The Carthaginians' worried reflections (3.10–13) on the
dreadful change in the military circumstances serve to characterize
the threatening situation and—as we have often seen in this
Decade—work as indirect praise of Rome while also hinting at the
final Roman victory. On this occasion Livy also mentions a conversation between Laelius and the Numidian prince Masinissa, who at
the end of the Spanish war had come over to the Romans; the latter
insistently demands that Scipio invade. He has already made considerable preparations in support of them in North Africa. In this way,
Scipio's sphere of influence and trust is further expanded, this time

right up to the immediate neighbourhood of the enemy heartland. The enemy, aghast at the expected Roman attack, in turn take their first countermeasures. The reader impatiently awaits Scipio's final command to depart. But an opportunity to capture Locri, currently occupied by the Carthaginians, diverts him temporarily from his African plans: he sends an expeditionary corps into Bruttian territory. There is fighting with mixed results, in which Hannibal himself intervenes; in the end Scipio captures the town and then returns to Sicily. The battle between the two great leaders, which now seemed imminent, has been put off and reserved for the African theatre.

However, before the year comes to an end Livy once again—now increasing expectation for the last time in this long sequence—refers to the impending decision in Africa. Consultation of the Sibylline books reveals the prospect of Hannibal's expulsion and defeat if the cult image of the Idaean Magna Mater is transported from Pessinus to Rome. Livy ends his account of 205 BCE by describing the execution of the necessary religious and diplomatic measures, and begins the next year with the arrival and solemn reception of the image (10.11–11.8, 29.14). This religious innovation has a decisive significance similar to that of the first *lectisternium* for the Twelve Gods in 217: for the first time they are admitting to Rome an Oriental divinity with a form of worship and a priesthood essentially alien to the ancient Roman religion. Soon other deities from Asia Minor, Syria, or Egypt would follow the great Mother of the Gods and their foreign religious notions and cult practices would increasingly dilute ancient Roman religion and the native form of worship. Augustus was the first person to bring this unending influx of Oriental cults to a temporary halt and to revive ancient Roman rites and priesthoods. Livy supported Augustus' religious restoration with the same conviction as when in his history he blamed the spread of Oriental cults in Rome for a deleterious undermining of native strictness and morality. In our context, however, he does not use his account of the Great Mother's reception in Rome to deplore the beginning of this unhealthy development, but merely asserts the significance of this cult procession for the contemporary state of the nation. For with the reception into Rome of this new object of worship came, so to speak, divine sanction for Scipio's plan (still viewed with distrust by the Senate) for a crossing to Africa: the gods have spoken and assented to

Hannibal's expulsion and defeat. Now at last Scipio can put to sea, once a senatorial commission has reviewed his preparations in Sicily and declared them to be exemplary.

## SCIPIO'S CROSSING TO AFRICA; FIRST ENGAGEMENTS (29.24.10–29.4, 34.3–36.3)

Scipio's crossing resolves almost all the tensions and expectations Livy has deliberately been stirring up more forcibly and intensifying constantly since the victory at Silpia. It is only natural that his manner of narration also gives this moment its due prominence. This is one of the few departures in the whole work to which he pays special attention, emphasizing the uniqueness of the current drama by comparing similar situations (in particular the embarcations of the fleet in 256 and 255 BCE), as well as by referring to the previous course of the war and by emphasizing Scipio's personality (26).[1] These reflections are underlined by the description which immediately follows of the vast crowd that had flocked together to watch the spectacle. Around this personal perspective Livy places two sections of narrative, from which the importance and special character of these historic days may be indirectly inferred (24.10–25.13; 27.1–29.4). He so structures these scenes that the reader is drawn less into fearful expectation of the battles to come in Africa than into the joyful enthusiasm of a victory parade: 'such was the ardour in every breast to set sail for Africa that it seemed as if the prize of certain victory rather than a hard campaign awaited them' (24.11).

The troops are reviewed, a scene enlivened by the portrait of the Cannae legions (24. 10–25. 4); they then receive their final orders, issued by Scipio with exemplary care (25. 5–13). Where everything has been thought out in such detail, success cannot fail to follow. But all human plans, if they are to succeed, must include—so the ancient

[1] Klotz (1940–1: 193) assumes the source of this section to be Valerius Antias. In the background must ultimately be the famous description at Thucydides 6.31–2 of the Athenian fleet's departure in 415, which is also recalled by Scipio's sacrifice and prayer.

Romans held—a prayer to the gods for their protection and assist-
ance. Accordingly, after personally appraising the enterprise right at
the centre of the narrative in the way I have mentioned (26), Livy
follows the great council of war by a solemn prayer, which he has
formulated in close imitation of the ancient sacral style and which
he rounds off with a description of the accompanying sacrifices
(27.1–5). At his first sight of Africa Livy has Scipio turn to the gods
with the prayer that he may cast eyes on this land to his and the state's
wellbeing (27.9). Another incident points in the same direction,
when Scipio takes the name of the 'Fair Promontory' [sic] as a
favourable omen for the entire enterprise (27.13).[2]

The final paragraph stands in stark contrast to this hopeful atmosphere of religious solemnity (28. 1–29. 5). Livy heightens the effect of
Scipio's landing with a prolonged and vivid depiction of the horror
aroused in the fleeing civilians and in the Carthaginian capital.[3] This
impression of Scipio's overwhelming power is heightened still further
by the speed of his initial expansionary moves and reaches its first
apex in the rendezvous with Masinissa and his cavalry. This union
will soon lead to a greater success, when the Carthaginians send
Hanno with a cavalry detachment against the Romans once they
have disembarked, and Hanno is defeated at Salaeca by the combined
Roman and Numidian cavalry under Scipio and Masinissa (34.3–17).
Once more Scipio makes use of a tactical ruse, but once again Livy
avoids speaking of *insidiae, dolus,* or *fraus* ('ambush', 'trickery', or
'fraud') as he had so often done for similar surprise manoeuvres on
Hannibal's part. The aggressive energy that has marked all Scipio's
undertakings infuses this first engagement, too, and finds an unusual

---

[2] This is in complete accord with Scipio's character: Livy had reported that at the
capture of New Carthage he interpreted the onset of the ebb-tide as a favourable
omen (i.e. that he had personally believed it): *hoc cura ac ratione compertum in
prodigium ac deos vertens* (26.45.9). At the same time, this interpretation may be
intended as a compositional and thematic reference back to the beginning of the war,
where Scipio *père* had regarded the favourable outcome of the cavalry battle by the
Rhone as a good omen for the conclusion of the war (21.29.4). These are not religious
humbugs or ruses.

[3] Once again, the effect is heightened by division into individual groups and
by intensification: *hominum modo turba...pecora...urbibus vero...praecipue
Carthagini...eo maior tum fuga* ('a crowd of men...flocks...but in the cities...
especially in Carthage...therefore the rout was greater at that time', 29.28.3–7).

liveliness of expression in his cry of superiority over his opponent's sluggishness and inexperience. A setback follows, however, for the planned capture of Utica is thwarted by the approach of Syphax, who in the meantime had broken his earlier ties with the Romans and fought on the Carthaginian side (35.3–12). Nevertheless, Livy does not emphasize the failure of this Roman plan, but masks this disappointment for the reader by reporting the construction of a permanent camp and the provision of necessary food and clothing, once again demonstrating Scipio's energy and prudence (35.13–36.3). Almost at once the book calmly ends with brief reports on the battles in southern Italy and the elections of magistrates in Rome—a deliberate winding-down of tension after the crossing and before the great decisive events of 203 to 201 BCE, which Livy has reserved for the last book.

## SCIPIO'S FIRST VICTORIES IN AFRICA, UP TO THE CARTHAGINIANS' FIRST SUING FOR PEACE (30.3–8; 30.16–17; 30.21.11–23.8)

The last book of the Decade, apart from brief reports of the usual civil affairs in Rome at the end of each year (elections, prodigies, etc.) and some notices on the collapse of Carthaginian power in Italy, is exclusively devoted to the Romans' final conflict in North Africa. The primary source for these African battles is Polybius.[4] The breaks between years do not mark any deeper ruptures in the composition, so that the unitary flow of these tremendous events can still be clearly perceived despite repeated changes of arena. The first major division in the book comes after the defeat of Syphax and the Carthaginians' ensuing entreaty for peace (ch. 17), the second after the collapse of the peace-negotiations and the change of year from 203 to 202 before the final battle between Hannibal and Scipio (ch. 27).

The report on the distribution of magistracies and provinces at the beginning of the book at once shows that the situation has changed

---

[4] Klotz (1940–1: 117–19).

from the previous year. At the end of ch. 1 we read: 'As for Scipio, the period of his command was not limited by a definite date but was to continue until the successful conclusion of his African campaign; and a decree was passed ordering a day of prayer that his crossing to Africa might bring a blessing to the Roman people and to him and his army' (30.1.10–11). The last objections in the Senate to Scipio's offensive strategy have thus fallen away. The army, the people of Rome, and the Italians were already convinced, and now finally the Senate, after hesitating in the previous two years, is also sure that the decisive battle is about to be fought, that it will take place in Africa, and that Scipio is the only general competent to fight it. Hence the eyes of all magistrates and provinces—indeed, of the entire state—are on Scipio, and supplies are sent to him from all sides (3.1–2). That is the endpoint of the process of rebirth that Livy has elaborated again and again ever since Cannae, that mighty unification of all forces and their concentration on the destruction of Hannibal and the Carthaginians. At the same time, however, these introductory sentences, which are not found in Polybius' parallel account, effectively focus the reader's sense of suspense on the significance of the coming battles.

The new year sees Scipio full of activity: 'Nor had Scipio, for his part, at any moment during the winter allowed any relaxation in his efforts; the number of tasks and anxieties he had simultaneously on hand were many' (3. 3). He arms himself to counter the Carthaginians' war-plan, i.e. that Syphax and Hasdrubal, encamped not far from Scipio, should cut off the invading Roman army by land while a blockade prevents its reinforcement by sea, so that it may be starved and crushed like Regulus' army before it. Besides securing his troops and providing them with weapons, food, and clothing, Scipio embarks on an active round of diplomacy aimed at bringing back into his camp the Numidian chieftain Syphax, with whom he had already made contact from Spain. These efforts failed in the end because Syphax, having for a time attempted to mediate between the Romans and the Carthaginians, was repeatedly kept on the Carthaginian side by his wife Sophonisbe (the daughter of the Carthaginian Hasdrubal), to whom he was passionately devoted (7.8–9). Scipio, however, makes exceptionally adroit use of the diplomatic interlude and his resulting knowledge of Syphax' camp, and forms a plan for setting fire to the two enemy camps by night. Livy has not a word that Scipio conceived this plan (as Polybius 14.1 explains) on the grounds that he realized he was in no position to meet the superior enemy force in open battle. Not an embarrassed second-best, then, but the expression of the highest inventiveness and boldness, skilled at exploiting every opportunity. Accordingly Livy makes Scipio the chief actor in the entire narrative, concentrating the reader's interest on him, without considering in detail (as Polybius does) the hopes and calculations of Syphax and Hasdrubal. For Polybius, both are on a par with Scipio as agents of history; for Livy, they are utterly subordinate to him. In Polybius, Scipio's character exactly corresponds to the picture the Greek historian had drawn of him at the capture of New Carthage: superior cleverness that keeps up appearances before his negotiating partner, but that in fact soberly calculates and exploits every opportunity; a man who clear-sightedly creates an atmosphere of trust even in his dealings with the enemy and knows how to create in his own troops a devoted faith in his divine visions, but who takes his decisions in total coolness and unsullied rationality. This consistency of characterization is lacking in Livy, although he develops every phase of the preparation and execution of the night attack with obvious pleasure and deep sympathy. This begins with the report of Scipio sending officers in disguise (4. 1)—not merely Polybius' common soldiers, which runs counter to Livy's idea of Roman hierarchy and of the proper distribution of functions in the army. There follows the breaking-off of the truce, which Livy represents as justified by the Carthaginians' unreasonable counter-demands, of which Polybius knows nothing (4.8). Now Scipio may act *libera fide* (4.10)—a quite deliberate formulation in accordance with Roman thinking— without any inner inhibitions. And now the night action quickly unfolds, every scene of fighting and every frightening situation (note the repeated *primo-deinde*) developed with dramatic tension. The articulation of this rapidly told story results naturally from the course of events: a brief description of the camp by way of introduction (3.3–7); the preparations for attack (Scipio's ruse and deception: 3.8–4.12); the military measures (5.1–7); and—without a sharp break, so as to match the speed of the night's events—the execution (5.8–10; 6.1–9).[5] The entire enterprise constitutes a *ruse de guerre* that with all its carefully considered details (4.4; 4.7; 5.1; 5.9) and lack of moral scruple (4.10) would be worthy of a Hannibal, but in his case would undoubtedly have been expounded by Livy as testimony of the Punic perfidy we all know. But obviously, in his satisfaction with the success of what Polybius, too, praises as Scipio's finest and boldest exploit, Livy was not in the least aware of applying a double standard.

This great victory which, standing at the beginning of the book, forms an impressive counterpart to Scipio's final victory at Zama, does not merely lead to the destruction of the two encircling armies. It also confers on Scipio freedom of movement and plunder; furthermore, it causes voices to speak out at Carthage for the first time in favour of concluding peace. Just as Livy exploited Scipio's initial measures in order to stress Roman *clementia* towards the inhabitants of a city said to have voluntarily (!) surrendered (7.2), so now in reproducing the various opinions in the Carthaginian senate he finds a welcome opportunity to hint at model Roman *constantia* (7.6). Neither detail is in Polybius. The advocates of peace at Carthage, however, do not prevail, since a fresh army is formed out of Syphax' relief force and 4000 Spanish mercenaries and immediately ordered to march against Scipio. Livy very cleverly uses Syphax' reported speech (7.11–12)—absent in Polybius—to represent the calming of the worried Carthaginians' morale.

These fresh formations come up against Scipio on the 'Great Plain'. In contrast to the night attack, Livy reports this battle soberly and briefly (8.3–9). Nevertheless, due emphasis is given to the ferocity of the struggle and the magnitude of the victory, especially through the closing sentence, which is absent from Polybius.

This battle finally puts paid to the Carthaginian attempt to cut off the Roman invasion force, and under the impact of this defeat minds in Carthage turn again to making peace with Scipio. But the majority

---

[5] Paragraphs 6, 7–9 are another addition to the Polybian original, and must come from Valerius Antias, already cited as a subsidiary source at 3. 6. The precision of the figures (11 Carthaginian senators; standards, elephants) serves to augment the Roman glory and is very typical of Valerius.

still rests its hopes in the navy and in the possibility that a blockade can keep reinforcements from the Romans. It is resolved to recall Hannibal from Italy to protect the capital, and to deploy the fleet to meet the attack on Utica. Here, by destroying some Roman transport ships, the Carthaginians gain a slight advantage; this, however, in no way hinders Scipio from carrying out his further plans. He now sets out for his major objective, the siege of Carthage. He advances on Tunis (some 22 kilometres from Carthage), occupies it, and makes it into his base of operations against the enemy capital. He sends Laelius and Masinissa with a portion of the army to pursue Hasdrubal and Syphax and to conquer the kingdom of Numidia. Both meet with complete success: they take Syphax prisoner, destroy the last enemy troops, and capture the Numidian capital. Scipio honours Masinissa by granting him the title of king and restoring him to his father's kingdom; Laelius he dispatches to Rome with the captive Syphax and an embassy from Masinissa to deliver a report. The Carthaginians now decide—*nullo auctore belli ultra audito* ('they refused to listen any longer to anyone who urged a continuation of the war' 16.2)—to open peace negotiations.

These are the preconditions for four transactions that Livy relates in quick succession in effective contrast to each other towards the end of 203 BCE. First is the Carthaginians' plea to Scipio for peace (16.4–15), introduced by the ambassadors' prostrations, which Livy finds as disgusting as the Carthaginians' attempt to shift the blame for the war onto Hannibal and to recall the Roman *beneficium* of the first peace. In Scipio's answer Livy does not conceal his striving for fame and the honours due a conqueror, but it is nevertheless in the spirit of Roman *clementia* and *iustitia*; the peace-terms, however, are harsh enough. Secondly, there follow Laelius' and P. Aelius' reports to Senate and People in Rome: the successes are succinctly stated, the effect on the audience described more expansively (17.1, 5–6). Scipio's exemplary behaviour is matched in the third episode by that of the Roman Senate and People when immediately afterwards honours are bestowed on Laelius in the Roman popular assembly, and Masinissa's ambassadors are received in the Senate (17.7–14). All line up behind Scipio—what a telling contrast to the Carthaginians, who totally abandon Hannibal!—ratify his decisions, and honour Masinissa and his envoys in accordance with the majesty of the Roman people. Lastly, comes the Senate's reception of the Carthaginian ambassadors outside the city (21.11–23.8): from beginning to end full of mistrust towards those notorious 'treaty-breaking' Carthaginians (22.6; 23.5–7), whom they now wish—such is their confidence in Scipio's successes and plans—to see completely ruined. That is the other side of the oft-vaunted Roman *clementia*, the readiness to spare opponents who voluntarily submit. The Carthaginians have left their surrender too late; now fate must take its course—all the more so since the Carthaginians, even before their envoys' return, had broken the truce with Scipio by recovering a number of Roman cargo vessels that had been wrecked in a storm.

HANNIBAL'S RETURN TO AFRICA<br>(30.19.10–20.9; 25.11–12)

Simultaneously, Hannibal's position in southern Italy collapses: the allies desert him, and he receives the order from Carthage to embark and return. Livy presses upon us Hannibal's embittered disappointment, but does not refrain from once again emphasizing his brutality: only fear (not *fides*—as in the Roman case!) has still bound some cities in Bruttian territory to him, and his last action on Italian soil is the murder in the temple of Juno Lacinia of the Italians who do not wish to follow him to Africa. However, for Livy the climax of Hannibal's self-reproach is where with utmost bitterness he contrasts himself with Scipio, who is resolutely making the attack on the enemy capital that Hannibal himself, to his detriment, had omitted. Thus this scene, too—like the character-sketch of Hannibal—is far from an objective appreciation (for which this would be the right place); and in the last analysis, it does not support the assessment of Hannibal as the great and equal opponent of the Roman commanders, but serves the glory of Rome and, above all, of Scipio. We are confronted by this contrast once more in Livy's description of the crossing. Whereas Scipio had first caught sight of the 'Fair Promontory' from the sea and seen in it a good omen (29.27.13), Hannibal's ship is making for a ruined tomb—an evil omen in every ancient reader's eyes, and one which already anticipates the Carthaginians' ruin in the battles to come. In both cases the invention is due not to Livy but to his source, probably Coelius, who had a particular taste for dreams, portents, and omens. But what Coelius derived from tradition—or even invented—mainly for the sake of certain tragic effects, Livy bathes in human warmth and sympathy and tells with a tender respect for celestial signs and expressions of will.

## SHOWDOWN BETWEEN HANNIBAL AND SCIPIO: THE BATTLE OF ZAMA (30.28–38.5)

With Hannibal's arrival in Africa and the start of 202 the last act of the great drama begins. In striking contrast to the parallel report in Polybius, which is fully preserved (15.1–19),[6] Livy has turned it into an independent and entirely self-contained narrative. The narrative acquires especial weight from this shift in compositional emphasis, which the content merits and which Livy, as we shall see, most artfully further strengthens in the introductory portions of this section. The narrative falls into two extended main sections, the speeches of the two commanders (30–32.3) and the battle (32.4–35); these are framed by two shorter sections. The first of these offers a very judicious introduction (28) and portrays the conditions for the parley (29); the second describes the military consequences of the battle and the negotiations for a truce (36–38.5).

After the customary official report at the beginning of the year, Livy (following Coelius?), in an unusually extended climax, describes at length the mood then prevailing in Rome after Hannibal's

---

[6] The comparison between the two accounts is highly instructive and, especially in the last few years, has been undertaken from various points of view. While Witte (1910: 300 ff.), and Ullmann (1927: 127 ff.)—like Taine before them—saw Livy's achievement as essentially in the independent quality of the narrative and, in the two major speeches, the rhetorical transformation of Polybius' train of thought, the differences in the two speeches' starting points and purposes, their emotional values, the point of their historical arguments, and the Roman tenor of Livy's version have been brought out with great success: see Hoffmann (1942: 93 ff.), and in addition the joint treatment by A. Lambert, the author of the painstaking dissertation *Die indirekte Rede als künstlerisches Stilmittel des Livius* (1946), and Cavallin (1948: 54 f.). Cf. too Walsh (1961a: 219–44 (Livy's speeches)).

departure from Italy, which oscillated between joy and fear. However, he does not go into the joy at all, but—beginning with a threefold antithesis (*aut, aut, aut* 28.3)—lays out a menacing list of the dangers that Hannibal and his troops present to the Romans. From the mouths of the worried citizenry, who recall his life and his achievements from childhood onwards, Hannibal's personality and accomplishments here receive unqualified recognition, of a kind that Livy has never given before. To this—in a two-part statement for heightened effect—Livy adds the danger represented by the battle-hardened army as a whole, accustomed as it is to victory, and by the numerous individual warriors distinguished by outstanding exploits (28.5–6). But it is essentially on artistic grounds, as with Hannibal, that these champions receive their recognition here, both to increase the tension and to enhance the magnitude of Scipio's impending victory through the glory of his great opponent. The same purpose is served by the ensuing paragraphs, especially the brief portrayal of the mood in Carthage at the end, with the last words of which (*velut fatalem eum ducem*, 'as the destined leader of their destruction', 28.11) Livy refers back to the beginning of the Decade (21.46.8, 22.53.7). This twofold depiction of mood is intended to give due prominence to the magnitude of the impending decision (28.8), a purpose considerably strengthened subsequently in the sentences introducing the battle (32.4) and above all in the colloquy between the two commanders. By their content and compositional arrangement these again recall the beginning of the Decade, echoing both the proem and especially the great paired speeches of Hannibal and Scipio's father before the battle of the Ticinus (21.39.7). Lastly, the brief episode of the captured Carthaginian spies being led through the Roman camp and the announcement of Masinissa's arrival (29.2–4) reflect something of Scipio's confidence in victory and Hannibal's concern; at the same time this gives an explanation of why Hannibal, despite his manifest guilt,[7] should propose a parley with Scipio. Whereas in Polybius (15.5–8), whose Carthaginians press for a decisive battle, Hannibal

---

[7] This too is a significant reference back to Livy's account of the causes of the war at the beginning of the decade. Once again, just before the end of the entire conflict, he emphasizes Hannibal's guilt.

admires the 'high intelligence and daring' that Scipio has just demonstrated to the spies, and 'from an inexplicable compulsion' takes the decision to bring about a parley with him, in Livy serious concern about the outcome of the impending battle induces him to attempt to change fate by negotiations with Scipio.

It may seem surprising that Livy, unlike Polybius, did not make the two commanders' speeches equally long. The reason must simply be that the person who makes a request needs to support his proposal with more extensive justification and argumentation than the person who refuses it. In addition, the brevity of the refusal matches Scipio's elation and self-confidence, which he had so convincingly demonstrated just before the parley by leading the Carthaginian prisoners through his camp.

Hannibal's speech, one of the most impressive in all Livy, would need a sentence-by-sentence commentary to exhaust the depth of human experience, the wealth of feelings, and the abundance of connections between it and the history as a whole. To these must be added the choice nature of the language and of the style, which moves artistically between spacious and sometimes emphatic periods and succinct maxims such as we never find again in Livy in this profusion, and in which Livy's careful word-placement brings out the most delicate nuances. Hannibal begins with the fateful quality of the hour and a contrast between his own person[8] and Scipio, an opening which is more than a *captatio benevolentiae* and which, while stressing his own achievements, powerfully enhances the importance of Scipio (3–5). These paragraphs are a significant Livian addition to the arguments taken from Polybius and developed in what follows, but it is now already becoming clear how in the last analysis the entire speech is directed toward paying respectful homage to the achievements of Rome and Scipio. Livy puts in Hannibal's mouth his own conviction that fate itself had brought about this encounter, and by the unreserved praise that Hannibal bestows on the Romans Livy constructs this scene as a unique triumph of the Roman cause willed by fate. The effect of this triumph is all the more lasting in that in the speech Livy takes every opportunity to refer to the war's chief

---

[8] Note the use of *Hannibalem*, not *me* at the beginning and end of the speech (30.30.4. and 29).

events. In this he shows a substantial divergence from Polybius, whose Hannibal argues chiefly from general human experience. In the Greek events are primarily interpreted through a philosophical world-view. Livy, on the other hand, uses the historical facts of Rome's rise to heighten Roman self-confidence. This is even more noticeable in the rest of Hannibal's speech. He first indicates in pointed antitheses how both peoples have been led by the war to the edge of the abyss, and how the lessons of this and of the First Punic War urge the conclusion of a lasting peace, for whose permanence he and Scipio offer the best guarantees (6–9). Now follows an impressive comparison between the two commanders. Hannibal, taught wisdom by the alternation of good and bad luck, warns Scipio, whose successes and great qualities (*virtus, pietas, honos, gloria*) he acknowledges with praise (here the entire course of the war, represented by its leading moments, passes in review before the reader) against want of moderation and against presumption: a significant warning in the Augustan spirit, intensified by the experiences of the civil wars (10–15; 16–17). Luck quickly changes, and a good peace is better than a victory anticipated from a battle that may, given the uncertainty of all human calculations, turn any situation into its opposite (18–22). Proof: the fate of Regulus (23)—again, a historical argument lacking in Polybius. And now Hannibal ends by proposing the peace-terms whose observance he himself is ready to guarantee (24–30).

Scipio begins by rejecting Hannibal's plea for peace, lest the Carthaginians' breach of the treaty bring them any benefit (1–3). Once again in these paragraphs, which are not inspired by Polybius, Livy pillories Punic perfidy. He then makes Scipio counter Hannibal's historical objections by saying that the Carthaginians were to blame for the war, whereas in both Punic Wars the Romans had simply taken up arms in defence of their allies. These *pia ac iusta bella* ('pious and just wars') had enjoyed the protection of the gods, who would continue to stand by the Roman cause (4–5). That is entirely the language and conviction of the Roman Senate, as developed by Livy right at the beginning of the Decade in his treatment of the question of who was responsible for the war, and made the basis of his entire description of the Second Punic War. Hannibal's warning against the vicissitudes of fate, by contrast, Scipio regards as completely misguided in the current circumstances: they could not impose on him any obligation towards the Carthaginians. Only an appropriate atonement by the Carthaginians can afford a basis for fresh negotiations (6–9). Scipio's counterproposal is rejected by Hannibal, and both commanders are now content to leave the decision to the gods. This last expression (10) underlines yet again Livy's view of the impending decision, in which he sees a divine confirmation, so to speak, of the Roman victory.

Three main themes are pursued by Livy in this pair of speeches. The first is the emphasis he lays on the world-historical significance of this encounter, which by its contrast with the paired commanders' speeches before the battle of the Ticinus encapsulates in two focal-points the immense change in the war situation over these seventeen years. This change is presented as the will of the gods and the decree of fate. The impact is intensified by resonances in both speeches, since Livy puts prognostications of future events in the mouths of the two commanders (32.1–3), as well as by the superlatives with which he emphasizes the two leaders' and the two armies' strengths as the battle begins (32.4). The second theme is the human tragedy of Hannibal, which is all the more powerful for his recognizing it himself. It is a shock to see how strongly Livy—again in contrast to Polybius—hammers into the reader the pleading quality in Hannibal's speech, ending with the pointed oxymoron *Hannibal peto pacem* (30.29). The third of these controlling viewpoints is the evaluation of Hannibal's fate as a proof of Rome's endurance and of Scipio's greatness. The many references to the vicissitudes of both Punic Wars and to Scipio's astonishing rise are a unique mirror of Roman self-confidence. Rome's true nature is constantly reconfirmed by its ability to transcend in victory all its defeats, however painful they may have been individually. It is that which gives this speech its peculiar Roman shade, which takes on its Augustan hue through Livy's stress on moderation, self-mastery, and independence from the blows of fate.

After the end of this parley Livy hastens to describe the battle—but not without first briefly mentioning the two leaders' addresses to their troops. If here he is substantially more succinct than Polybius (15.10–11), this is above all because he does not wish to let these speeches weaken the effect of the imposing colloquy between the generals just before. It is significant, however, that Scipio again pillories Carthaginian faithlessness and emphasizes the gods' protection of Rome (32.7–9). His words ring out in total confidence of victory, which Livy further underlines by an addition of his own without any precedent in Polybius: 'Scipio, as he spoke, stood so erect and wore on his face an expression of such calm happiness that you might have thought the victory already won' (32. 11). The details of the two armies' formations have the effect of slowing down the narrative before the battle begins. This in its essential features matches the battle in Polybius. It differs, however, quite significantly in its objective manner from the descriptions of battles in the early books of the Decade, in which graphic individual scenes and passionate impulses, mood-swings, and pathetic exclamations, seemed to determine the outcome more strongly than any particular tactical manoeuvres, which Livy disposed of quite briefly. Here, with his peculiar clarity of articulation, he follows Polybius closely in distinguishing three phases of the battle, each of which—unlike Polybius—he introduces with a brief insistence on Roman superiority (33.12–13; 34.1–2; 34.13).[9] The first phase depicts the battle of the elephants and cavalry and leads to the exposure of both armies' wings (33.12–16). The second section begins with the clash of the first two lines and ends with the scattering of the Carthaginians' front line (in Polybius, of their first two) (34.1–8). Then comes the Romans' formidable regrouping and a fierce battle between the two sides' remaining infantry, a battle decided in Scipio's favour by the Roman cavalry attack on the Carthaginian rear. To this is attached a brief appreciation of Hannibal's qualities as a general. In judging him Livy follows Polybius, only going wrong in again failing to see the high value of the third line (see n. 9). Hannibal's admission of

---

[9] In 33.6 he returns to the notion of the unreliability of Hannibal's Italian allies, mentioned on his departure from Italy (30.19.10 ff.), thus creating the impression that Hannibal's third rank had not stood its ground. The opposite was the case: the battle formation alone shows this, and it is confirmed by the parallel passage in Polybius (15.11). Here stood Hannibal's most experienced core units, who were expected to deliver the decisive blow. Livy's alteration, which actually brings him into contradiction with his account of Hannibal's departure (see above), causes a further divergence from Polybius: according to Livy, in the second phase of the battle only the Carthaginian first rank is annihilated and in the final phase the struggle is carried on by their second and third ranks.

his definitive defeat, of which Polybius says nothing, concludes the battle narrative as impressively as Scipio's confidence in a successful outcome had introduced it (32.11; 35.11).

For the history of tactics, the notable contribution of this battle is that Hannibal—who once again planned to fight this as a battle of encirclement—was defeated by Scipio with his own stratagem. Hannibal had intended to encircle the enemy with his third line, which he had separated from the other two and held back as they advanced. But Scipio, who had seen through Hannibal's intention during the battle, thwarted him by a stroke of genius, regrouping his lines after the second phase. This success was the fruit of Scipio's new tactics of manoeuvre, steadfastly practised ever since the Spanish wars. The decisive movements that Scipio executed to this end are well brought out in Livy's description (34.11), though he does not indicate as such the ensuing tactical effects of 'halting' the first encounter and of deploying of the *principes* and *triarii* to the wings in order to encircle the Carthaginians.

Scipio at once recognizes the opportunity afforded by his great victory by setting out immediately by sea and land to besiege the enemy capital (36.1–3). Further operations, however, are rendered superfluous when the Carthaginians sue for peace. Livy gives full weight to the reproaches of unmanly servility and faithlessness that rain down on the Carthaginians (36.5, 9; 37.1). Here too he recalls the opening chapters of the Decade, in which he had awarded the Romans such a high testimonial of their loyalties to their allies. In Polybius Scipio, on the one hand, demands that the Carthaginians understand, as they must, their guilt and that they accept the Romans' unavoidably harsh conditions. On the other, he wants the Romans' human feeling to be recognized, as they grant the Carthaginians certain national rights and freedom from an army of occupation (15.17–18). In Livy, by contrast, Scipio dispenses almost entirely with explanations of the terms for an armistice. As Livy sees it, a Roman *imperator* has no need of such a thing; he dictates, and what he dictates sounds harsh enough (37.2–6). But just as so often Livy had put praise of Roman courage in enemy mouths, so here he has the justice of the Roman demands confirmed by no less a person than Hannibal himself: 'he spoke at length about the peace, showing that it was far from unfair and must be accepted' (37.11). This is a

complete triumph for Roman *iustitia* and *aequitas*: the belated and
shattering admission that Hanno's position at the start of the war had
been right, put in the mouth of the man against whom he had then
been arguing (21.10. 4–13).


## END OF THE WAR AND CONCLUSION
## OF PEACE (30.42.11–45)

The Carthaginian peace mission arrived at Rome at the end of the
year, but was admitted to the Senate only by the new consuls. In his
account of this session (42.11–21) Livy presents an adroitly executed
counterpart to the earlier debate on the same topic (30.21.11–23.8).
Whereas there he had given the Carthaginians less to say than the
Romans, and the entire debate had been dominated by the charge of
Punic perfidy, now the Romans are silent, and the Carthaginian
Hasdrubal speaks—hardly for the benefit of his own people, more
in praise of the Romans. He praises Roman self-control and moderation in good fortune, Roman power of victory, and Roman mercy
towards the defeated, and does so almost more highly than Hannibal
had just done in his parley with Scipio. Here a fair amount of the
Augustan view of life and traditional political ideology breaks
through. Moreover, the further treatment of the envoys in Rome
and the course of the peace negotiations add up to a sustained
illustration of Roman *benignitas* and *pietas* (43.5–9).

From Rome attention now returns once more to Carthage, to the
first effects of the peace treaty (44.4–12). And here for the last time
Livy allows Hannibal to be heard, in a bitter complaint against his
fellow countrymen for their narrow short-term view and the selfish
materialistic canons by which they judge public and political events.
He foretells that no good will come to his people. But the key
sentence of his speech also contains, in masterly ambiguity, a fearful
warning to Rome, which with the destruction of Carthage has robbed
itself of its last great opponent and thereby runs the risk, if it has no
more external enemies to fear, of splitting into cliques and parties
and tearing itself apart through internal conflict: 'Peace can never
stay for long in a great country. It will find an enemy at home if it

lacks one abroad, just as a powerful body appears immune from any external infection but is drained by its own strength' (44.8). We know this argument very well from the polemics that broke out at Rome in the middle of the second century when the Senate held ever more lively debates on whether the Romans should allow Carthage, now flourishing again, a new living-space and a new expansion, or destroy their hostile rival once and for all. Then it was principally Scipio Nasica who objected to Cato's famous 'Carthage must be destroyed', arguing that Rome ought not to get rid of its last opponent, who compelled it to remain on its mettle militarily and morally, and thus to keep itself strong and powerful not only for a possible conflict with that opponent, but also for its own development.[10] For otherwise, he argued, Rome would turn its energies, as they became free, against itself and thus wear itself out in internal turmoil and division. Livy generalizes this argument and boldly transfers it into Hannibal's mouth, a man whom fate's heaviest blows had matured into far-sighted prophecy. And in it is expressed a deep insight into the reasons for Roman decadence, which after the destruction of Carthage spread at an alarming rate. We sense a reminder of the dark sentences of the proem to the entire work, in which Livy conjured up the individual phases of that decline in their terrifying weight and strength. At the same time, however, in their sententious generality these last words of Hannibal are an urgent warning to the Romans against *hubris* and an admonition to use their powers rightly and to maintain internal cohesion.

It is natural that attention should be redirected from Hannibal to Scipio and that the book should end with the homecoming and triumph of the victor of Zama. The account closes with the explanation of the honorific cognomen Africanus: not with a loud fanfare of victory and triumph, but muted and controlled in the true Augustan way. Scipio's unique greatness and importance are raised beyond his momentary success to historic validity through a comparison with later celebrators of triumphs—a conclusion truly worthy both of the great conqueror and of the historian.

---

[10] Cf. Gelzer (1931: 261 ff.). Cato's remark is more famous to English speakers in the inexact version, *delenda est Carthago.*

ADDENDUM

Burck's approach to Livy as a serious author whose aims and ideology merit scrutiny has become so pervasive that its pioneering nature
is, ironically, hard to appreciate. In a sense all of the work in this
volume depends on that approach. Readers with German can avail
themselves of the entirety of Burck's book on the third decade as well
as his study of Livy's narrative technique in the first five books, *Die
Erzählungskunst des T. Livius* (1934, repr. 1964). There is also a
historiographical study of the second pentad by Lipovsky (1981),
a student of Luce. The third decade remains, mysteriously, under-
studied as a narrative unit (though there are articles on individual
books and episodes); Levene (2010) will fill a large gap in the
scholarship with an analysis of Livy's historiographical technique in
all the Hannibalic books.

Throughout the selection Burck alludes to Livy's Augustan values.
For more recent views on Livy as an Augustan, see Luce ('Dating')
and Feldherr with Addenda.

Burck's references to Livy's sources represent the former orthodoxy of the 'Quellenforschung' approach to the historian, where
Livy's text was divided and analysed according to which source he
was believed to have been following. The contributions of Rich,
Tränkle, Briscoe, and Oakley in this volume offer more up-to-date
thinking on this subject.

Burck's discussion of the speeches of Hannibal and Scipio before
Zama has stood the test of time. As noted in the introduction, this
area of Livian studies lacks a treatment that is both nuanced, such as
that of Luce (1993), and thorough, such as Ullmann (1927). There is
an important German dissertation focusing on indirect speech by
Lambert (1946); for a theoretical discussion of the use of speech in
narrative see Laird (1999) chapter 4, and for a good, recent overview
of the general function of speeches in historiography see Marincola
(2007a) chapter 9. Further suggestions may be found in the
Addendum to Walsh.

# 11

## Livy and the Story of Horatius I.24–26

### J. B. Solodow

The value of history, Livy says, lies in offering the reader instructive moral examples, these being of two sorts: 'thence you may draw, for your own benefit and that of your state, examples to be imitated; thence too examples, wicked in origin and wicked in outcome, to be shunned' (Pref. 10). Nor does Livy leave it in doubt to which class each of the stories he recounts belongs, for the moral is most often clear: the bravery of a Mucius Scaevola deserves imitation, the lust and ambition of an Appius Claudius are execrable. Livy expresses such unequivocal judgments not so much by direct statement as through narrative: he focuses his narrative upon the moral and highlights it with every device of literary art. This is now an accepted truth in Livian criticism.[1] And yet there are occasions when, despite his stated goal, to present 'instructive examples set in a perspicuous historical account',[2] the historian also deals with the inescapable complexities of man's life, in which deeds do not always lend

---

[1] See, for example, Walsh (1961a: 66): 'Livy's history is dominated by ethical preconceptions... His idealisation of the past depicts such [i.e., moral] qualities in sharp outline.'

[2] The hyperbaton emphasizes *inlustri* ('perspicuous'). This common form of the figure, whereby a syntactically obtrusive word intervenes between an adjective and its noun, in Livy at least regularly emphasizes the adjective, which is left suspended for a moment in the reader's mind. The most probative examples are those where the emphasized adjective contrasts with another word, as at Pref. 4: *ab exiguis profecta initiis eo creverit ut iam magnitudine laboret sua* ('starting from *small* beginnings, it has grown to such a point that it now labors under its own *vastness*'); or at 38.17.13

themselves to such neat classification. Livy seems to me a man of greater moral imagination and wider human sympathies than he is usually held to be. I will discuss here one episode from his history where he dwells precisely on the absence of clarity and on the resulting complexity of moral judgment. My argument is based on a close examination of his narrative style, those habits of language which are the truest clues about a writer.

The episode is the famous one of the Horatii and Curiatii, in which a Roman saves his country but then outrages it morally by murdering his sister. I first describe the moral problem of the story, indicating the narrative devices by which Livy focuses attention on it and illuminating some of them through comparison with Dionysius of Halicarnassus and other writers. This analysis then leads to some general remarks on Livy's work, particularly its engagement of the reader.[3] Afterwards in a second part, in order to prove that Livy, and no one else, is responsible for the manner in which the story is told, I review its possible sources and also the modern historical interpretations of it, which tend to deny Livy any responsibility.

---

*generosius est, in sua quidquid sede gignitur; insitum alienae terrae in id, quo alitur, natura vertente se degenerat* ('whatever grows in its *own* soil is more excellent; transplanted to a *foreign* land, where it is altered by nature, it degenerates towards its source of nourishment').

[3] An indication of this is found in the sentence already quoted from the Preface, where Livy employs the second-person singular pronoun and adjective: *tibi tuaeque rei publicae* ('for your own benefit and that of your state'). The address is direct, almost personal. Livy nowhere else addresses the reader this way; Sallust and Tacitus never do. (Liv. 9.18.11 and Sall. *Cat.* 1.6 and 3.2 are rather impersonal; second-person potential subjunctives, like *discerneres* ['you might discern'], are virtually impersonal too.) And, as Livy draws close to the reader, so he leaves a certain distance between himself and the Roman state. He speaks to the reader of *tua res publica*, 'your state', (not *nostra*, 'our'—contrast Sall. *Jug.* 4.5: *civitatis nostrae*, 'our state'). Other historians talk freely of *nos* ('we'), i.e., 'the Romans' (Caes. *Gal.* 3.28.4, Sall. *Jug.* 8.1, Curt. 6.3.8, Tac. *Hist.* 1.2, *Ann.* 13.55, etc.). Livy's use of the word is very restricted: as Leeman (1963: i. 296) remarks, he never uses *nostri* ('our men') to mean 'the Roman troops'; and in the Preface, the only place he does use the adjective, it has a strong temporal reference (*nostra... aetas*, 'our generation', 5; *vitia nostra*, 'our weaknesses', 9). The historian affects a certain impartiality.

I

The story is straightforward. In order to conclude a war between their cities Tullus Hostilius, king of Rome, and Mettius Fufetius, dictator of Alba Longa, agree to have two sets of triplets meet in a duel; the survivor will bring victory to his side. One of the Romans, Horatius, after losing both his brothers, succeeds in killing the three Albans. Upon his triumphant return to the city, however, angered to see his sister weeping over one of the slain Curiatii, to whom she had been betrothed, Horatius kills her. Tullus is obliged to bring him to trial. Specially appointed *duumviri* find him guilty; then on appeal the people acquit him, whereupon he expiates his crime in certain ritual acts.

An outline, of course, does not convey the riveting effect which the story has from start to finish. But it does reveal how Livy has carefully divided the action into halves, the duel abroad and the trial at home (and the halves are about equal in length, 52 lines and 57 lines in the Oxford Classical Text). By this division he effects a sharp contrast between Horatius' heroic deeds and the murder of his sister. In Dionysius (3.21–2) any contrast between the halves is obscured by a cloud of incidental scenes: an exchange of longish speeches between Horatius and his sister (Livy gives nineteen words to Horatius alone, and this after the murder, not before); the burial of the sister (Livy alludes to this at the very end of the story, so as not to interrupt the narrative here); the celebration of Horatius' victory (absent in Livy); and Tullus' address to the vanquished Albans (Livy places this directly after the duel, closely attaches it to the duel with the words *priusquam inde digrederentur* ('before departing from there')— the subjunctive binds the two events by imputing intention—and gives the content in a brief piece of indirect discourse).

Livy, moreover, draws our attention to the contrast between the halves through verbal echoes. By prominently repeating certain words he invites us to see the two episodes as in some ways parallel to each other. *Ferox*, for instance, is often applied to Horatius.[4]

---

[4] R. M. Ogilvie, in his indispensable *Commentary on Livy: Books 1–5* (Oxford 1965) 105–6—henceforth simply 'Ogilvie'—remarks that Tullus Hostilius is

He and his brothers go forth to duel *feroces* (1.25.1); when left alone against the three Albans he is still *ferox* (25.7), as he is again when facing the last of them (25.11). We might translate the word as 'fierce'. In the corresponding scene of the second half, where Horatius slays his sister, Livy says: *movet feroci iuveni animum comploratio sororis* ('his sister's lamentation arouses the ire of the *ferox* young man', 26.3). In this context the word has a different ring to it and connotes 'savage'. The echo leads to the important suggestion that it is the same quality which causes him to act on each occasion. In the duel itself events are picked out with words that will recur in the next half. *Increpuere arma* ('the arms clattered', 25.4), an odd phrase since *increpo* is used of arms nowhere else in Latin,[5] is found at the opening of the battle. The verb is echoed in Horatius' reproaching his sister: *increpans* ('reproaching', 26.3). The dread felt by the army during the contest (*horror ingens spectantes perstringit*: 'enormous dread comes over the spectators', 25.4) is matched by the dread which the law inspires in the citizens attending the trial (*lex horrendi carminis*: 'the law embodied in this dread formula', 26.6).[6] With *defigit* ('pierced', 25.12) Horatius dispatches the last of the Curiatii, with *transfigit* ('pierced', 26.3) his own sister.[7] And the

---

distinguished for his *ferocitas* ('fierceness') and that this is the key word of the section. He passes over the interesting fact that the word is used now for the king (22.2, 23.4, 23.10, 27.10, 31.6), now for Horatius, the leading hero of his reign (25.1, 25.7, 25.11, 26.3). Dumézil (1942) thinks that the two men are identified because in origin they were one: Tullus–Horatius represents at Rome the warriors, the second of the three social classes, or 'functions', into which Dumézil believes Indo-European society was divided. (On Dumézil, see below, pp. 316–18). But Erb (1963: ch. 1), shows how in general Livy tailors his description of the wars waged to fit the picture of the reigning king; thus the wars are chiefly an expression of the king's character; hence the *ferocitas* of both Tullus and Horatius.

[5] Ogilvie points out the oddity, which is great enough to have persuaded H. J. Müller (in W–M) to read *concrepuere* ('clashed') instead. Here, as elsewhere, Livy strains language for effect: the unfamiliar use of a word helps to fix it in our minds and alert us to the following echo.

[6] *Horrendus* ('dread') is an unusual word. Found once in tragedy (*Trag. inc.* 198 R; 'contextu dubio', says TLL vi.2981) and once again in Cicero (*Tusc.* 2.2; *vi potius verbali*, TLL ibid.), the word is first brought into use by Virgil and Horace. It is not found in prose before Livy. In any case, the collocation *horrendi carminis* ('dread formula') is unparalleled in Latin.

[7] *Defigo* ('pierce') may be a special word here, for both its meaning and its construction. In classical prose generally *defigo* in its physical sense is uncommon

field on which Horatius' brothers fell (*corruerunt*, 'they fell', 25.5) is recalled by the spot where his sister fell (*corruerat*, 'she had fallen', 26.14).[8]

Through the composition of the story and these verbal echoes Livy draws our attention to the problem which lies in the contrast between the halves. Horatius in the first half is a typical Roman hero, courageous and patriotic. But in the second half this same patriotic feeling leads him to kill his sister. The problem then is this: what are we to think of such a man, of such patriotism? Let us look into this more closely. Not only does Livy describe Horatius' heroism in the first part, but he also shows on what principle it is founded, the willingness to sacrifice oneself for the good of the commonweal. Of all the combatants in the duel he says: *nec his nec illis periculum suum, publicum imperium servitiumque obversatur animo* ('neither the ones nor the others have any thought for their own peril, only for the supremacy or servitude of their nation', 25.3). The striking asyndeton and chiasmus throw into greater relief the words *suum* ('their own')

---

outside of agricultural contexts (the usual word is *transfigo*, 'pierce'). As for its construction, Ogilvie reports that '*defigo* with the plain ablative is only found in poetry'.

[8] I give two other examples of Livy's use of verbal echo. (1) In the account of Porsenna an echo suggests a parallel between Horatius Cocles and Mucius Scaevola, who are the heroes of successive stories. Livy says of the former's brave deed, *ipso miraculo audaciae obstupefecit hostes* ('by the marvel of his boldness he stunned the enemy', 2.10.5); and of the latter's, *prope attonitus* miraculo *rex* ('the king, practically thunderstruck by the marvel', 2.12.13). (2) Coriolanus in the first episode of his career distinguished himself by his bold attack on the inhabitants of Corioli, *quos* [sc. *exercitus Romanus*] *intus* clausos *habebat* ('whom [the Roman army] kept beseiged', 2.33.6). Shortly afterwards the Roman people are beset by hunger: *fames deinde* [sc. *civitatem invasit*], *qualis* clausis *solet* ('hunger then [attacked the city], as usually happens to the beseiged', 2.34.2). The Romans are, in a sense, 'besieged' themselves. And since it is Coriolanus, now prominent, who most bitterly opposes distributing to the people what grain is available, he is seen as the people's enemy. Livy represents the people as thinking: *fame se iam* sicut hostes *peti* ('that, like enemies, they were now being assaulted by hunger', 2.35.1). The two comparisons, *qualis clausis* ('as usually to the beseiged') and *sicut hostes* ('like enemies'), are gratuitous and deliberate. Their words, echoing the siege of Corioli, remind the reader that Coriolanus has gone from attacking Rome's enemies to attacking his fellow citizens, from being Rome's champion to being her enemy. And, lo and behold! the implicit image comes to life in the next episode, in which Coriolanus leads a Volscian army against the city.

and *publicum* ('of their nation'),[9] and this opposition lies at the heart of the episode.[9a] For the basis of Horatius' heroism is precisely his subordination of himself to the public good, which may be considered the cardinal Roman virtue. In the second half, however, the repeated word *ferox* at the beginning (26.3) and the phrase *ipsius* [i.e., *Horatii*] *parem in omni periculo animum* ('[Horatius'] courage, unchanging amidst every peril') near the end (26.12) remind us that the same moral character which caused Horatius to enter eagerly into battle also led him to kill his sister. Though it was obvious that his loyal subordination of himself to the state merited the highest praise before, it is far from obvious now, when he murders his kin. Perhaps, from a different point of view, we could formulate the problem thus: are the qualities important to war and empire compatible with civil society, with ordinary life? In any case we can see that Livy engineers the contrast between the halves of the story for the purpose of putting such a question. Dionysius, by comparison, not only clouds but also trivializes the contrast between the two parts of the story. He says only that envious Fortune did not allow Horatius, a mere man, to continue long in good luck, but as it raised him, so it cast him down swiftly (3.21.1): not a useless moral, but a hackneyed one.

Livy now amplifies his theme by sounding it in a new quarter. He projects onto the king the same natural conflict between personal and patriotic motives that might have arisen in Horatius but did not. Tullus Hostilius, as depicted by the historian, is caught in a dilemma when Horatius appears before him, and this dilemma in turn highlights the problematic character of Horatius himself. For, while

---

[9] Even without chiasmus such sharp adversative asyndeton is extremely rare in Livy. W–M cite: *non iuvenem, vicesima iam stipendia merentem* ('not a youth, a soldier already serving on his twentieth campaign', 3.71.6). But of the twenty-two examples given by Kühnast (1872: 287), not one is so sharp and violent as ours; most are made up of entire clauses in which the first words are opposed, as at 5.22.2 *ex qua* [sc. *familia*] *filius ad senatum rettulisset, pater tam popularis sententiae auctor fuisset* ('from this [family], the son had proposed to the senate, the father had sponsored so popular a measure').

[9a] Cic. *Inv.* 2.78–79 and DH 3.27.1, 3.30.4 both give the hero's *praenomen* as Marcus; Livy, however, presumably followed by Zonaras 7.6, calls him Publius. Ogilvie is no doubt correct in assuming that the earliest legend knew him simply as Horatius. Capitalizing on this, Livy may have been the first to name him Publius, in order to bring out his devotion to his country.

Horatius feels only the patriotic motive, the king is sensitive to both the patriotic and the personal. On the one hand, Tullus is the dispenser of justice before whom Horatius is brought: *raptus in ius ad regem* ('he was hailed into court, before the king', 26.5). On the other, he is a man unwilling to incur the displeasure of the citizens: 'the king, lest he should himself be responsible before the people for so grim and unpopular a judgment, and then, after the judgment, be responsible for punishing Horatius...' (26.5). In this dilemma he chooses to create a new institution, the *duumviri*, whom he charges with the judicial responsibility.[10] Livy in effect attributes the origin of this institution, not to any social or legal need, but to the personal moral predicament of the king. The *duumviri* embody the difficulty for him in judging Horatius. Livy quotes the law appointing them, which begins *duumviri perduellionem iudicent* ('let the *duumviri* try him for treason', 26.6), and then he adds: 'the *duumviri* created by this law, believing that it did not allow them to acquit even an innocent man, when they had condemned him...' (26.7).[11] He is careful to explain the motivation of the *duumviri*: they thought they had no choice, but would need to condemn even an innocent man. By telling us that they execute their commission in this wholly unreflective manner, he prevents us from taking their verdict as any kind of independent judgment on their part, and so maintains

---

[10] No other source records the king's appointment of *duumviri*. Indeed, scarcely any other source records the existence of these *duumviri* at all. The *duumviri* of his own day mentioned by Cicero (*Rab.* 12) imply the earlier ones, to be sure. And these are expressly named in Festus (p. 380 L) and the *De Viris Illustribus* (4.9). But neither Cicero (*Inv.* 2.78–9) nor Dionysius nor Valerius Maximus (6.3.6, 8.1.1) nor Florus (1.1.3.3–6) nor Dio Cassius (= Zonaras 7.6), to name only the authors of the longer accounts, mentions the *duumviri* at all. Valerius in fact describes Horatius as *a Tullo rege damnatus* ('condemned by king Tullus', 8.1.1). And the scholiast on Cic. *Mil.* 7, who was well supplied with antiquarian learning, knows no *duumviri*; instead, appeal from the king's sentence is made directly to the people. Perhaps Livy revived an obscure tradition about them for his own purposes.

[11] It seems odd that the *duumviri* should be appointed simply to condemn a man. To the other explanations that have been offered for this, mostly of a legal nature, I add my own. Perhaps the king's words, *duumviri perduellionem iudicent*, meant 'let them try him for *perduellio*', but were understood as 'let them convict him', for *iudicare* can have either meaning. Seeley (1881) also suggests this possibility; he thinks, however, that it was Livy, not the *duumviri*, who misunderstood the words!

the ambiguity concerning Horatius. No character within the story, neither the king nor his surrogates, is made to declare his belief in the guilt or innocence of the accused. Finally, upon the *duumviri's* pronouncing Horatius guilty, the king urges him to appeal: 'then, at the urging of the king, who interpreted the law leniently, Horatius declared "I appeal" [*Provoco*]' (26.8). Here too Livy suggests the conflict within the king, by having him keep to both the forms of law and his own sympathetic spirit.

The way in which Livy has related the king's predicament to the central moral question shows more clearly in a comparison with Dionysius. At the corresponding point in his version (3.22.5) Dionysius gives a description of the king's situation very different from Livy's straightforward one. Instead of a single pair of conflicting motives he gives us a heap of arguments, three for punishing Horatius, two for acquitting him. Some of these are intricate and legalistic: for instance, that Horatia ought not to have been punished with death, for her offense was not capital; or that nothing further should be done to Horatius, since the father, who had the right to avenge his daughter, had already acquitted him. In Livy the king's thought is less abstract, more personal. We can see this in a small but telling difference: Dionysius' Tullus simply wants to avoid condemning a national hero, Livy's wants to avoid the popular odium he would incur by doing so. Livy, by selecting clear and concrete details (or by inventing them), brings out vividly the king's dilemma in judging.

In the next scene of the drama, which takes place in court, Livy uses the appeal delivered by Horatius' father to recall to mind the same complexity of judgment: the man you are judging now, the father says, is the same who brought you victory over Alba Longa. The speech is short and effective. The only line of defense open was what the rhetoricians called *constitutio iuridicalis*, the argument that the deed was just.[12] Of this there were two forms: the pleader could either argue that the deed in itself was just or defend the deed by

---

[12] Since the crime was *caedes manifesto* ('flagrant murder', 26.12), the fact could not be denied: this would have been *constitutio coniecturalis*. And the law itself did not allow controversy: this would have been *constitutio legitima*. These distinctions between the defenses are found in *Rhet. Her.* 1.18–25.

reference to something extraneous.[13] Livy has the father use both forms. The elder Horatius gives the former argument in indirect discourse: *se filiam iure caesam iudicare*, etc. ('that he judged his daughter justly slain', 26.9). The latter argument is presented at greater length, and with it the father breaks into direct discourse: ' "Can you tolerate, citizens, the sight of this man chained and flogged, beaten and tortured—the very man whom a short while ago you saw marching home covered in glory and rejoicing in his victory?" ' (26.10). The effect of this device, the switch from indirect to direct discourse, can readily be assessed here. The second part is the more important to the father's audience (and to the historian's), in that it keeps before their minds the earlier instance of the son's devotion to the state. The very form in which Livy reports the speech, with greater weight placed on the second argument, underlines the complexity of the issue.

Nor does the story have a clear resolution. The people initially had been ambivalent about Horatius upon his slaying of his sister: *atrox visum id facinus patribus plebique, sed recens meritum facto obstabat* ('this crime seemed hideous to the senators and common people alike, but it was offset by his recent service', 26.5).[13a] And at the end they are still of two minds. After the father's speech, to be sure, they acquit Horatius, more on account of his previous valor than the justice of his cause, Livy says (26.12). But at the same time his acquittal apparently does not satisfy their sense of justice: his deed must be expiated. So a beam is erected under which Horatius is sent, *velut sub iugum* ('as if under the yoke', 26.13). The once victorious hero is forced to submit like a defeated enemy. Even at the end of his

---

[13] *Rhet. Her.* 1.24: '[a juridical issue] is absolute when we claim that the act itself was a thing rightly done, no external consideration being relied on . . . ; it is assumptive, when the defense on its own merits is weak and the case is made by relying on an extraneous matter.' Cicero also describes this defense, at *Inv.* 1.15 and then again at 2.78–9, where he calls it *relatio criminis* and gives as an example Horatius' plea, without mentioning the father.

[13a] The phrase not only reminds us of those who witnessed the events, but also provides a transition between Horatia's murder, in the previous sentence, and Horatius' being brought before the king, in the next. Livy strives for this kind of continuity, which might be termed 'cinematic', since it could easily be filmed by a camera without the need for cutting away to a new scene. Homer too strives for a continuous texture, as is well known, but neither Sallust nor Tacitus does.

story, we, like the people of Rome, cannot be sure how to judge Horatius.[14]

Through a final device Livy brings this indecision home to us, his readers: he narrates the climactic scenes from the point of view of the spectators. This perspective of narration has often been remarked in the battle;[15] it is also found in the trial scene, though it is less striking. At the beginning of the duel, Livy writes: 'as their fellow-soldiers urged each set on... they advanced into the area between the two armies, their ears ringing with shouts of encouragement' (25.1). Then the whole of sections 2, 4, 5, 6, and 13 in chapter 25 refer to the spectators and their reactions. Livy twice singles out their anxiety, *cura* (25.2, 25.6). In the trial Livy reminds us of the citizen bystanders at 26.5, 9, and 12, and the elder Horatius is made to invoke them as witnesses in 26.10 and 11. By means of these sentences, reminding us of the presence and the reactions of the spectators, Livy induces us to view the story through their eyes.[16] We seem to feel the same trepidation as the army, the same uncertainty about Horatius as the king and people. Livy's narrative, that is to say, contains within itself both a moral problem and an *awareness* of the problem, an awareness which is transferred from the characters in the story to the reader.

[14] Machiavelli, in his *Discourses on the First Decade of Livy*, Book 1, chapter 24, strongly disapproves of the people's acquitting him. No state, he observes, can afford to balance crimes with merits; law and liberty will inevitably suffer.

[15] In this aspect of his battle description, as scholars have noted, Livy resembles Thucydides. But there is an important difference: the example always cited from Thucydides (7.71) is an isolated one; in Livian narrative this is a regular feature. Livy's predilection for the word *spectaculum*, which he uses 91 times altogether, three times in this very passage (25.2, 25.5, 26.10), indicates his concern for adding spectators to his narrative. See following note.

[16] For one among many other instances we may turn to the story of Manlius Torquatus, for which Livy's direct source was Claudius Quadrigarius. Claudius (fr. 10b *HRR*) makes no mention whatever of the bystanders. Livy, by contrast, mentions them frequently: *duo in medio armati spectaculi... more... nequaquam visu ac specie aestimantibus pares*, etc. ('two armed men *in the middle*, as at *a show*...not at all matched in looks and appearance *in the eyes of those judging them*', 7.10.6). *Aestimantibus* ('in the eyes of those judging them') is otiose but subtly alludes to the spectators. (It is not accidental that the use of the participle in the dative to designate the standpoint of judgment only becomes frequent with Livy: cf. Hofmann and Szantyr 1965: 96). I hope to publish soon a separate essay on Livy's use of spectators.

Again the contrast with Dionysius is instructive. Dionysius does portray the spectators of the battle-scene (not the trial-scene, however), and he does so at length, especially in 3.19. But his description of their state of mind, as of Tullus Hostilius', is sometimes so abstract that its effect is to distance us from the scene, not draw us into it: 'there were continuous cries expressive of every emotion experienced in battle, some caused by what the men on each side did and saw, others by what they suspected was going to happen; and the imagined events were more numerous than the real' (3.19.1). Such remarks are so general that they could be applied to almost any suspenseful situation. Sometimes Dionysius' description of feelings is just pedantically obvious: 'everyone gave a shout—the Albans as if already victorious, the Romans as if defeated, since they took it for granted that their two men would be easily overwhelmed by the three Albans' (3.19.5). Livy is briefer, more subtle, and more persuasive; unlike Dionysius, he succeeds in making us feel that we too are present at both scenes as silent judges of Horatius.

Through all of these narrative devices—symmetrical composition of plot, verbal echo, word placement, creation of subordinate scenes and characters, handling of speeches (direct and indirect), choice of vocabulary, and perspective of narration—Livy brings out the ambiguities of Horatius' career.

This analysis suggests some more general thoughts about Livy as a historian. The catalogue of his deficiencies is familiar: ignorance of geography and warfare, confusion on legal and constitutional matters, willingness to sacrifice accuracy to clarity, etc. His greatness as a historian evidently does not lie in searching critical investigation of the past.[17] It lies rather in his own imaginative reconstruction of the past and his representation, or rather evocation, of it to the reader. His book therefore, especially in its earlier parts, is a document not so much of Roman history as of his own view of that history (and no doubt, to some extent, the view of his contemporaries). Livy's main engagement is not so much with the records of the Roman past as with the mind of his reader. It is to affect the reader that he draws on those resources of narrative art which I have described. By such means, and without necessarily changing the overall form of the

---

[17] But see now Luce (1977) for a strong defense of Livy.

story, Livy is able subtly to direct the reader's attention to what is important. He also makes the story more vivid to the reader by providing spectators to his history. Taking their point of view, the reader is drawn into the story. He participates both in the events and in the feelings about the events. And when, as usual, the story has a moral point, he is thereby invited to take a certain moral stance as well and to share the admiration for a Mucius Scaevola, the scorn for an Appius Claudius, the bewilderment at a Horatius.

Amidst these stories we must not lose sight of Livy himself, the narrator of them. The vision of the national past impressed so subtly and yet so forcefully upon the reader is Livy's own. And the greatness of his history is finally the greatness of the vision, which is not merely chauvinistic, but has many noble aspects, not all exemplified in our passage. It is marked, for instance, by generosity: Livy's sympathy and understanding are not confined to the Romans, but extend even to enemies. Thus Hannibal near the end of his career is made to seem good, perhaps even tragic;[18] besieged foreigners are regularly portrayed with tenderness;[19] and Livy often momentarily makes us take the point of view of the enemy by calling the Romans *hostes*.[20] Though he frequently flaunts his patriotism, Livy can also maintain a kind of impartiality. This aspect of his work is apparent if we compare our passage with other Roman versions of the story. Florus, for example, writes of the duel: *tribus... illinc volneratis, hinc duobus occisis* ('when three men had been wounded on that side and two men slain on this', 1.1.3.4). And Festus speaks of *Horatius noster* ('our Horatius', p. 380 L). That *hinc* and that *noster* ('our') betray the author's point of view; each one lets us know he stands 'here', on the side of the Romans. Florus, furthermore, passes explicit judgment when, after saying *ille mox parricidio* [sc. *victoriam*] *foedavit* ('he soon besmirched [victory] with honor', 1.1.3.5), he finally declares: *abstulit virtus parricidium, et facinus infra gloriam fuit* ('his courage abolished the murder, and his crime was less than his glory', 1.1.3.6). It is precisely this kind of formulation that is lacking in Livy. Usually, of course, his moral feelings and judgments

---

[18] See Burck (1971: 33).
[19] See Walsh (1961a: 193).
[20] To the examples adduced by Walsh, add 7.10.9.

are clear to the reader. But judging well and knowing when not to judge may be equal testimonials to the moral faculty. It seems to me a final and not insignificant measure of Livy's greatness that on occasion, when the material warrants it, he is capable of suspending judgment altogether. This is what he does in the story of Horatius. Refusing either to condemn or to approve, he lays before his readers a moral problem which they must resolve themselves.

There can be found in Livy other examples of moral complexity or deliberate unresolvedness.[21] (1) During the Second Punic War, L. Pinarius, prefect of the garrison at Henna, fearing an attack on his men, massacres all the inhabitants while they are attending an assembly unarmed (24.37.1–39.7). Livy concludes his account: *ita Henna aut malo aut necessario facinore retenta* ('so Henna was retained by a deed that was either wicked or necesssary'). (2) When L. Marcius Philippus and A. Atilius report their dealings with Perseus, some senators approve the results as useful, while others are more struck by the un-Roman underhandedness through which they are achieved (42.47). Again, as in our passage, Livy chooses to embody the different views in the persons of the story rather than enunciate them himself.[22] (3) The consul Manlius Torquatus has his own son put to death for disobeying orders and fighting a duel outside the ranks, though he was victorious. The soldier-spectators feel the awfulness of the sentence, while Livy observes its salutary effect upon discipline (8.7.1–8.2). Like the young Manlius, the reader is *ignarus . . . laus an poena merita esset* ('not knowing whether he had deserved praise or punishment'). Yet none of these stories is so rich in unresolvedness as ours, and we may wonder whether special circumstances led Livy to write it in the way he did. In answer I offer the following speculation. Much of recent Roman history had been made by generals returning to the city after military victories abroad. The fall of the Republic is traced in the careers of Marius, Sulla, Pompey, Caesar, and Octavian: all won distinguished victories

---

[21] Professor T. J. Luce of Princeton University has pointed these out to me and has in other ways improved this essay by his kind and valuable criticism.

[22] Bruns (1898) called attention to this technique, and Witte (1910: 274–80) elaborated. Perhaps the most famous example is found in Tacitus, when, after the death of Augustus, antithetic views of that emperor are put into the mouths of anonymous speakers (*Ann.* 1.9–10).

for the state; all upon their return inspired fear for the future in many of their fellow citizens.[23] Perhaps then it was as his thoughts dwelt on such figures that Livy composed the remarkable story of Horatius.

## II

The analysis of the Horatius episode rests on the assumption that Livy himself is responsible for the story's form. Yet someone may well object: 'Livy could not have intended the episode of Horatius to be a tale of moral ambiguity; he had little to do with shaping the story, which was simply handed down to him; the elements that create moral complexity were present all along in the traditional version.' This is a serious objection and seems well taken, for indeed the story does appear to be very strongly determined, containing perhaps as much that is 'given' as any other in the early books. The objection is answered in part by the previous section, in which we saw that key features of the narrative are characteristic of Livy and so probably originate with him. But it will be useful also to investigate the sources of the story and consider to what extent they may have determined the story's form.

One important determinant of the traditional version was aetiology. The desire to establish the origins of things was so strong in the Romans that, when they did not know the origin of some name or custom, they often created a story that would embody an aetiology of it; such aetiologies therefore played a large role in shaping the stories told about early Rome.[24] As presented by Livy this brief tale includes aetiologies for four topographic names, two legal

[23] Montesquieu, for one, blamed the fall of the Republic on such men: 'those warriors, so fierce, so bold, so frightening outside the state, could not be very moderate within it' (*Considerations on the Causes of the Greatness of the Romans and Their Decline*, ch. 10).

[24] Ogilvie's commentary collects many examples of this process. For topographic aetiologies see his notes on the *ficus Ruminalis* (1.4.5) and the *fossa Cluilia* (1.23.3)— he scouts both of Livy's explanations. For 'episodes constructed to illustrate the provisions of Roman law' consult his General Index under 'stratagems'. (The entries under these heads have been mistakenly transposed.)

institutions, and (probably) one law, all presumably known to the Romans of the day. These are: the tombs of the Horatii and Curiatii, the two Roman together, the three Alban closer to Rome and separated from one another; the *pila Horatia* (either 'Horatian Column' or 'Horatian Spears'), whether a column or a set of spears; the *tigillum sororium* ((apparently) 'Sister's Beam'), under which Horatius passed in expiation; the sepulchre of Horatia outside the Porta Capena; the institution of the *duumviri perduellionis* (a two-man board that judged cases of high treason); the Roman citizen's right of *provocatio*, or appeal to the people; and the law forbidding the mourning of a public enemy. I myself think the genesis of the story lies almost wholly in these aetiologies. But other determinants have been proposed. Scholars have located the origins in the political disputes of the second century, in pre-historic Indo-European myth, and even in early Roman poetry. In assessing these historical interpretations we meet one error common to all: a failure to recognize Livy's hand in his own work. A study of the sources, however, will vindicate the historian's responsibility for his version. Indeed, the very abundance of determinants, far from restricting or preventing any judgment on Livy himself, gives us instead a measure of his ability to rise above his given material and to make of it what he wanted.

We meet one difficulty right away. Source criticism in the traditional sense, tracing the written accounts on which our author drew directly, is impossible here, as Münzer recognized sixty-five years ago.[25] Though we have many scattered notices of the story, they are nearly all late and tell us nothing about the tradition before Livy. Dionysius, despite his full account, is silent about his sources. We may take as a sign of the difficulty the fact that even Ogilvie, who usually advances strong claims for Livy's sources, here makes a very mild one: Valerius Antias 'suggests himself as a possible source' for Tullus' reign (1965: 106); the justification is that one of the fetials is named M. Valerius. Although then we cannot hope to identify Livy's direct sources, we can nevertheless identify the original elements out of which the story was constructed. And that some of the constructing had been done long before Livy's time (centuries before, I should

---

[25] Münzer (1913: 2323).

say) is implied by two pieces of evidence: Ennius had related the story on a large scale (*Annals* 120–36 Sk.);[26] and Livy himself testifies 'no other ancient deed is nearly so well known' (24.1).

What can we know about the genesis of this story? Let us start with aetiologies, which are still so prominent in Livy's account, not only for their number but also for their position. Each half of the story is closed by a notice, phrased in the present tense, of those monuments still existing which are explained by the story: first the tombs of the five fallen warriors, then the *tigillum sororium* and Horatia's tomb. (The *pila Horatia* is worked into the elder Horatius' discourse, just before the reader needs to be reminded of it.)[27] Accordingly Münzer and Ogilvie, among others, have suggested that the various aetiologies, topographic and legal, are primarily responsible for the form of the story. They were assembled into a coherent version, one bit affecting the other until a smooth narrative was produced. Without a doubt the *gens Horatia* played some part in preserving and shaping the tale.

This theory, which I think correct, assumes nothing about the truth of the aetiologies: they may be right or wrong. It would be an error to insist that the story is as it is because the aetiologies truly record the series of events. This is the mistake made by van den Bruwaene, for instance, who believes that the reality of the events is vouched for by the monuments: 'the fact is attested, since traces remained: the tombs, the *tigillum sororium*, the *pila Horatia*.'[28] I would say, 'traces remained, and *voilà*—a "fact"!' It is probable that the desire for aetiologies produced the story and the desire for a coherent story gave the aetiologies their present shape; so the monuments attached to them may prove nothing about what actually happened. The weak connection between monuments and actual events perhaps accounts for certain features of the preserved story. It is uncertain, says Livy (and no one else), which were the Albans,

---

[26] Of course not all of Skutsch's nine verses need to be taken as referring to the tale of Horatius: other editors attribute many of them to other passages.

[27] It is curious that Livy 'announces' none of the three legal aetiologies. He could have stated, for instance, as Cicero did (*Mil.* 7), that this was the first capital case tried by the people. Perhaps he was uncertain of the legal implications and so left the matter alone.

[28] Bruwaene (1952: 153).

which the Romans—surely names on monuments would have settled this. Uncertainty also surrounds the *pila Horatia: pila* is either singular and means 'column' or is plural and means 'spears'.[29] Furthermore, the aetiology of *tigillum sororium* is certainly wrong: the beam is to be connected with the rites of Juno Sororia, the goddess of female puberty—whose parallel on the men's side by an astonishing coincidence bears the name of Janus Curiatius![30]

Münzer and Ogilvie are right then, against van den Bruwaene, in thinking that the monuments gave rise to some of the story—and this not because the aetiologies were true, but because they were unknown. I do not believe the genesis of the story is fully recoverable, and in any case I am more interested in how Livy treated the material which had reached him, but let me sketch a reconstruction. I do not offer this with any confidence that it is correct, but rather as one example of how the monuments may have determined the story. (I make the extreme assumption that none of the aetiologies is true.) This is the reconstruction: the course of a duel was provided by an imaginative contemplation of five probably anonymous tombs;[31] the *pila Horatia*, located near the Forum, associated the hero's name with a legal proceeding; the tomb of Horatia and the *tigillum sororium* gave material for such a proceeding; the misunderstood adjectives *sororium* and *Curiatius* created an expiation for Horatius' crime and a name for his opponents. Some such sequence of steps, taken over a period of time, not by any single writer but by popular tradition, produced, I believe, the outlines of the Horatius story.[32]

---

[29] Singular in Liv. 1.26.10, Schol. *ad* Cic. *Mil.* 7, DH. 3.22.9; plural at Liv. 1.26.11, Prop. 3.3.7.

[30] See Ogilvie 117, who gives full details and bibliography.

[31] There was likely some reason for believing the one group of tombs Roman, the other Alban. For, otherwise, why would the Romans be closer to Alba and vice versa? I suspect that in the words *nocte praeteritis hostium castris* ('during the night they made their way past the enemy's camp', 23.4) Livy or some predecessor has invented a maneuver to explain this feature of the monuments.

[32] I might mention here the suggestion of Alföldi (1965: 102–4) that the fight between the Horatii and Curiatii is symbolic of Roman claims to sovereignty over the Latins. If true, this would explain the fact of the Roman victory in the story, but none of the details. By providing another motive for the creation of the story, it would supplement my account. Though Alföldi is concerned mainly with early Roman history and I with Livy, we agree on the probable fictiveness of this episode.

Legal aetiologies also undoubtedly had a role in the formation of the story: Horatius' trial is the first instance both of the employment of *duumviri perduellionis* and of the exercise of *provocatio ad populum*; also a law forbidding the mourning of a public enemy may be glanced at in Horatius' words, 'the same to whichever Roman woman mourns an enemy' (26.4).[33] The legal aspect of the story has been most recently and most elaborately investigated by R. A. Bauman.[34] For Bauman, Livy's version contains within it clues to the gradual development of the story before Livy. According to the genesis he proposes, nearly every detail, as related by Livy, is a trace of tendentious accounts put forth in the second century by one or another political faction. If his reconstruction is right, then Livy had nothing to do with the story's form, and my interpretation is wrong. In fact, however, it has grave flaws, most of which rest on a general misunderstanding of Livy. Because the misunderstanding is instructive and because, so far as I know, Bauman's book has not been reviewed at length, I discuss it in some detail.[35]

At the beginning of the trial Horatius' father asserts 'that he judged his daughter justly slain' (26.9). On the basis of the present tense of the infinitive Bauman (1969: 27) discerns a 'striking contrast' between Livy's version of the story and others in which the *paterfamilias* had made a prior adjudication. Leaving aside his unwarranted division of the extant accounts into two groups (cf. n. 35), we see that Bauman has overlooked a fundamental trait of Livian narrative. Livy aims at making his narrative dramatic; unlike Dionysius, he strives for concentration and avoids diffusing the power of his story with

[33] Following Mommsen (1889), Ogilvie 115 cites Ulp. *Dig.* 3.2.11.3: 'it is not customary for enemies or those convicted of treachery to be mourned'; also Marc. *Dig.* 11.7.35 and Suet. *Tib.* 61.2. Quint. 3.6.76 may refer to the same law.

[34] Bauman (1969). The first essay, on the nature and function of the *duumviri* in historical times, has little bearing on the second and need not concern us here.

[35] I indicate two other serious flaws which do not rest on this misunderstanding. (1) On p. 23 Bauman founds a crucial series of arguments upon a mistaken inference from the use of *denique* in Ulp. *Dig.* 1.13.1 pr. In juristic Latin the word does not always mean 'next' but can mean 'in point of fact' or 'for instance'; see Hand (1829–45: ii.274–5); *TLL* v.1.533–4. (2) The passages cited on p. 26, n. 33, far from confirming, give the lie to Bauman's theory, most improbable in any case, that there existed a *parricidium* version of the story, in which quaestors tried Horatius beside the *perduellio* version with *duumviri* which we find in Livy.

too many details and separate scenes. One way of his achieving this has often been noticed: he regularly 'telescopes' into one event several that he found in his sources, either fusing several scenes into one more complex or alluding to an earlier in a later scene.[36] He may well have done that here, eliminating an entire earlier scene in his source, replacing it with this brief phrase, and so consolidating the narrative. The present infinitive then can hardly bear all the weight of argument that Bauman places on it.

In the same scene Bauman points to other details which were, in his view, determined by the tradition before Livy. First, he claims that the people's acceptance of *deprecatio* ('plea for clemency'), the father's final plea, amounts to a deliberate rejection of the notion *iure caesam* ('justly slain'); this would reflect Gracchan concerns of 110 or 109 BCE, when, after the *quaestio Mamiliana* allowed Opimius' slaying of C. Gracchus to be re-examined, Opimius offered in plea not the rightness of his deed but his other good services to the state (1969: 30–1). But Livy's phrase was *absolveruntque admiratione magis virtutis quam iure causae* ('they acquitted him more because of their admiration for his courage than the justice of his case', 26.12), in which one motive, though stronger than the other, does not eliminate it. More importantly, the connection between Horatius and Opimius is simply too far-fetched to be believed. And this is true of other alleged connections, such as between the plea of *maiestatem auxi* ('I increased [the state's] sovereignty') and Saturninus' career (1969: 31–2) or between the murder outside the *pomerium* (the sacred boundary of the city of Rome) and an event of 193 BCE (1969: 33–4). Furthermore, Bauman never relates the second-century political influences which he reconstructs to any historical writer upon whom Livy might have drawn.

The underlying error here is his failure to allow for the historian's own elaboration of the story. Neglecting altogether Livy's dramatic narrative and the purposes he might have had in telling a story, Bauman unhesitatingly assumes that Livy is but the faithful recorder of whatever was handed on to him, a kind of preserving fluid which embalms even precise verbal formulations derived from a series of

---

[36] See all of Witte's justly renowned article (1910: 270–305, 359–419); also Walsh (1954: 105).

differing versions. Bauman states his view as follows: '[Livy's] account bears all the marks of a conceptual chain made up of successive accretions, each of which was shaped by the contemporary political climate. In transmitting this chain to us Livy has in effect presented us with a string of beads, each of which bears a clear chronological imprint and tells an unmistakable story'(1969: 27). Such a view is untenable. Had there existed only one written version on which all changes were made? Would not rival authors have written separate versions? And, above all, even if such a single version had existed, would Livy have taken it over completely unaltered? We may be certain that he would not. The renowned comparison between a fragment of Claudius Quadrigarius (10b *HRR* = Gell. 9.13.7–19) and Livy 7.9.6–14 demonstrates how many small, purposeful changes Livy might make in the material before him.[37] Lacking any sense of such transformation, Bauman's understanding of Livy is mistaken and misleading, and it is for this reason chiefly that his reconstruction of Horatius' trial fails.

Georges Dumézil, though his view of the Horatius story is in a sense opposite to Bauman's, shares the same fundamental weakness. In his book, *Horace et les Curiaces* (1942), he explains Livy's tale as the Roman reflection of an ancient Indo-European initiation myth. He claims that nearly every detail either represents the original myth or can easily be explained as a Roman divergence from it. Bauman could see actual Roman political strife as the only aetiology of the story, or at least its second half; Dumézil is blind to all Roman aetiologies, not only political but legal and topographic as well. Despite this he is at one with Bauman in his misunderstanding of Livy, and so in his misuse of him: he too treats Livy as a mere transparent preserver of tradition.

His method is comparative. He first recounts an exploit from the life of the Celtic hero Cuchulain. The young Cuchulain, setting out from his city, comes upon three monstrous brothers who have killed many of his own people; one by one, in single combat he kills all three; but upon his return, the women of the city, fearing that in his

---

[37] Schibel in his recent book (1971), which itself digests nine other comparisons of the two historians, nevertheless leaves still more to be said. I touch upon one or two of these points below; the rest I save for some other time.

state of fury he is a threat to the city, show themselves to him naked, whereupon Cuchulain is seized and three times dipped into vats of water that cool his fury. Dumézil explicates this story as a warrior's initiation, comprising his first great deeds, his battle-fury, and his necessary restoration to society. He then compares this with the story of Horatius and discovers many parallels. He concludes that the story of Horatius originated in the same way, as a myth of initiation. The method itself is problematic, for the parallels are not always persuasive. To be sure, some general resemblances between Cuchulain and Horatius can be caught even from a summary. But Horatia is not 'a loose woman' like those who greet Cuchulain. Horatius displays *ferocitas* ('fierceness'), not *furor* ('fury'). And the two heroes can hardly be considered parallel, as Dumézil argues (1942: 103), on the grounds that each one's opponents had killed many from the other side: this is no more than an obvious detail which motivates enmity.[38]

Dumézil's interpretation is open to still other objections. He neglects other explanations of how the story took shape, even those which lie close to hand. He makes no mention of the numerous legal and topographical aetiologies which the story itself gives. This neglect leads to absurdities. Thus, on pp. 103–4 he attempts to account for the Roman version of the combat by elaborate and incredible hypotheses. It does not occur to him that the position of the five tombs outside Rome, to which Livy calls our attention, might be responsible. But he neglects more than the specifically Roman explanations which Livy's text offers; he altogether neglects Livy himself. Like Bauman, Dumézil treats the historian as if he were a recorder who neither added to the story nor subtracted from it, who had no interests of his own, no purpose but to hand on the tradition. Only through ignoring both the Roman background and the individual historian who gave shape to the material can Dumézil look

---

[38] A Greek story which is strikingly similar to Horatius' can offer no support for Dumézil's hypothesis of an origin in Indo-European myth. Told by pseudo-Plutarch (*Parallela minora* 16) and repeated in Stobaeus (*Flor.* 39.32), it is a pure fabrication made for the sake of the parallel with the Roman story. The authorities cited are spurious. See Ziegler (1951: 867–70) on the whole essay. Peytraud (1939: 32–5) discusses the two Greek passages briefly and uncritically.

back to an alleged Indo-European myth for his interpretation of the Horatius legend. Though I doubt the reconstructed myth in its detailed form, I can see one contribution which Dumézil may make to understanding the legend of Horatius: I am willing to believe that the basic plot of such a story may have served as the kernel around which the fuller Roman version was formed. Even given the monuments, given the institutions which lacked that origin in concrete events which the Romans desired, other plots could have been imagined which would have suggested an origin. Perhaps then a story like Cuchulain's did play some part in the formation of the Horatius legend. Nevertheless, this can be true only in so restricted a sense that it does not affect our understanding of Livy's account.[39]

Let us consider briefly one last explanation for the genesis of the Horatius story. Wilhelm Soltau claimed that there existed from early times certain obscure family traditions about both Horatius' heroic deeds and his murder of his sister, the latter tied to certain monuments, the former elaborated with the help of Herodotus 1.82; then Ennius in the *Annals* gave the duel a poetic coloring; and finally the same poet, on the model of Aeschylus' *Eumenides*, wrote a *praetexta* (a play on a Roman historical subject) about Horatius, at the end of which a reconciliation was achieved, as the crime of shedding kindred blood was justified in the name of higher duty. The arguments with which Soltau supports this view are weak, however: the evidence, for instance, on Ennius and his alleged source Naevius is nil; and Livy resembles Homer, Herodotus, and Aeschylus distantly, if at all.[40] Soltau's purely literary origin for the story is not persuasive.

Yet it is useful to recognize what urged him to put forward so improbable a hypothesis. He defends it on the grounds that 'it provides a solution to the puzzle of how so highly dramatic an

---

[39] Dumézil (1956) returned to Horatius and Tullus. This is not the place for a general discussion of his stimulating but highly controversial theories, which, if right, must have the most serious consequences for early Roman history and religion. See the work of Dumézil's supporter, Littleton (1973). I remain skeptical of the thesis in *Horace et les Curiaces* at least, as was H. J. Rose in his sober review (1947: 183–6).

[40] Ogilvie 112 does note some reminiscences of the Homeric duel, which, though convincing, affect only the tiniest portion of the story; they merely lend some touches of epic coloring.

incident could be laid in Rome's obscure, pre-historic period'.[41] It is a puzzle, but other solutions lie closer to hand. First, Soltau underrates the extent to which aetiologies could have generated the story. While not wholly ignoring them, as did Dumézil, he yet omits several of the topographic monuments and all of the legal precedents from his account. He ought to have followed Livy more closely, who carefully relates events and aetiologies. Second, he too, like the others, gives Livy himself no share in creating the story that has come down to us; again the historian is taken for a mere preserver of earlier material. Most readers no doubt agree with Soltau in finding the story highly dramatic. Yet, if this is a sign of literary art, why must it be Ennius' and not Livy's? To take a modern parallel: German or French history in the pages of Leopold von Ranke is remarkably dramatic, but the historian himself is responsible, not some playwright predecessor.[42] Comparison of Livy with other writers shows that he too generally strives to cast his stories in dramatic form.[43] So he is likely to be the one who gave to the traditional story of Horatius its gripping character as well as those features of narrative by which its meaning is indicated.

## ADDENDUM

On the episode in general: Meusel (1988: 66–90) and Mensching (1966: 102–18). On the second-person singular: Gilmartin (1975: 99–121). On *ferocia*: Eckert (1970: 90–106). That *ferox* does 'not necessarily have bad connotations in republican Latin': Harris (1979: 51, n. 2). On Horatia: Watson (1979: 436–47). On the origins of the *duumviri*, including Livy's account thereof: Tyrrell (1978: 10–25). On 'spectacularity' in Livy: Feldherr

---

[41] Soltau (1909: 107). This is a slightly expanded version of Soltau (1908).

[42] On this feature of von Ranke's work see Gay (1974: 59–67).

[43] See, for example, Witte (1910: *passim*). Dionysius twice (3.18.1, 3.19.3) explicitly compares the events he is describing to a tragedy, whence Soltau infers that his source was a tragedy. Yet how undramatic, in every sense, is Dionysius' account! Münzer was right to reject a tragic source for it.

320     *J. B. Solodow*

(1998). A thorough comparison of Livy's and Claudius Quadrigarius' versions of Manlius and the Gaul: Oakley (1997–2005 ii.113–23). Dumézil (1970: 12–28) returned to Horatius and the Curiatii one more time.

*J. B. S.*

# 12

## Livy's Comic Narrative of the Bacchanalia

### *A. C. Scafuro*

Livy's account (39.8–19) of the suppression of the Bacchanalia in 186 BCE. has been the subject of many studies that either focus upon its connection with the famous *Senatusconsultum de Bacchanalibus* ('Decree of the Senate about the Bacchanalia') or else elucidate its religious significance.[1] In view of the obvious importance of the events narrated by the historian, it may seem odd, if not irreverent, not to pursue one of these foci and to offer instead a literary and sociological analysis that concentrates almost exclusively on the romantic strand of the narrative. The justification for this orientation is that its comic elements have never been fully explored. Since nowhere else in his surviving books does Livy avail himself of what we might call a comic strategy,[2] it has seemed worthwhile to

---

[1] For the extensive bibliography, the reader should consult North (1979: 99, n. 13) for religious issues and (1979: 99, n. 17) for historical issues. Tierney (1947: 89–117) examines both the historical and religious problems.

An exception to the more traditionally-oriented studies referred to in the preceding paragraph is the article by Cova (1974: 82–109). Cova's aim is not to authenticate the historical information of the episode, but rather to identify the structure of the Livian narrative (109). Cova's article is illuminating, and I will have frequent occasion to advert to it in the course of this essay. Although our assessments converge at certain points, our procedures are quite different.

[2] One other episode in Livy suggests a comic or romantic structure in a nutshell with due focus on the alignment of character and status, and shows, moreover, one point of resemblance to the story of Hispala. Hispala's fearful reaction upon viewing the consul's entourage is similar to the reaction of the younger daughter of Marcus Fabius Ambustus when she was visiting her elder sister: a lictor of Servius Sulpicius

322 A. C. Scafuro

explore in detail this lesser-known twin sister of Hellenistic tragic history.[3]

Faecenia Hispala plays a leading role in Livy's account; presented as a *scortum nobile* ('prostitute of repute') at the beginning of the episode, she is rewarded with privileges of citizen rights by senatorial decree at its end. Status transformation thus likens her to a number of the heroines of New Comedy; like some of her comic prototypes, moreover, she becomes a focal point for the personal and social tensions of her community. As in New Comedy, so in Livy's narrative, plot is bound up, inextricably, with civic ideology.[4] At a crucial point in the narrative, however, Livy disrupts the comic paradigm. Here, I will argue, the historian has reworked the tradition and presented his own view of the sociopolitical significance of these events for Rome. To demonstrate that Livy's narrative does function in this way, I first will summarize Livy's plot (Part I); next, I will delineate the comic elements of the episode, its comic frame, and ideology (Part II); then I will argue that the comic paradigm is disrupted; in this section, I examine the inner tensions in the narrative by focusing on Hispala's status as witness and by considering the motifs of place, isolation, quarantine, and inform-ing (Part III); finally, I will suggest why Livy created the disruption (Part IV).

(a military tribune and the husband of the elder sister) arrived at the house unex-pectedly, beating at the door with the rods of office (Livy 6.34). The younger sister was terrified (*expavisset*), while the elder sister laughed at the younger's lack of sophistication: had she not been married to the plebeian Gaius Licinius, she, too, would know the meaning of this sound. The insult to the younger sister becomes the catalyst for the struggle between the patricians and plebeians, which results in the passage of the Licinian Sextian laws admitting plebeians to the consulship. Livy uses the sibling rivalry over status only to motivate the conflict; he does not return to the sisters, nor to a picture of Licinius returning home as consul and banging on the door with the rods of office to the smiles of his wife. Yet the beginning of the story suggests a comic or romantic structure in a nutshell, in which the plebian Gaius Licinius is the marginal character.

[3] Strasburger (1982: 801–34).
[4] For the interrelation of New Comedy and civic ideology, see Whitehead (1986: 338–45) and Konstan (1983).

# I. THE PLOT

The account of the suppression of the Bacchants is composed of two narrative strands: (1) the account of the Senate's response (its meetings and decrees) and of the consular investigation, and (2) the story of Faecenia Hispala and her lover Aebutius. The first narrative strand contains some authentic elements and has been shown, by comparison with the so-called *Senatusconsultum de Bacchanalibus*, to represent a tradition based on official information.[5] The second narrative strand, written in a romantic Hellenistic style and showing the influence of New Comedy,[6] has fallen sometimes under suspicion, although at least one Livian scholar has opined that 'this need not in itself discredit the main lines of the story'.[7] Indeed, the historicity of Aebutius and Hispala is supported by Livy's mention of their names in the *Senatusconsultum* reported in 19.3–6.[8] Both narrative strands (the actions of the State and the romantic story of Hispala and Aebutius) have been thoroughly integrated with 'all the appearance of a well-knit episode, which has been taken from one source'.[9] What this source (or principal source) was, we do not know; in the following analysis, I sometimes refer to it as 'the transmitted story'. I assume that the two narrative strands had been integrated before Livy, and that the basic outline of the romance had already taken the shape of a comic plot—indeed, such treatment would have been hard to avoid, given the decree (19.3–6) that united the names of Aebutius and Hispala and ensured the former at least 'acceptability' if he

---

[5] The decree may be found in *CIL* I$^2$: 581 = *ILS* i.278. A reassessment of the historicity of Livy's narrative through the comparison of the inscription with Livy's account began with Fraenkel (1932: 369–96); Keil (1933: 306–12); Krause (1936: 214–20); Gelzer (1936: 275–87). Tierney (1947: 89–117) summarizes and criticizes these earlier treatments.

[6] The influence of New Comedy on the episode has long been noted by scholars: for example, Kroll (1964: 361); Fraenkel (1932: 388 n. 2); Meautis (1940: 477); McDonald (1944: 26); Bruhl (1953: 98); Son (1960: English summary, 193–207), esp. 200–1); Kern (1960: 99 ff.).

[7] See McDonald (1944: 26). Other scholars are not so generous in their estimation of the tradition's value: for example, the verdict of Heitland (1923: ii. 229): 'The story of the discovery in Livy 39.8 ff. is an interesting romance.'

[8] This point is made by Son (1960: 203).

[9] McDonald (1944: 26); so too Cova (1974: 83–7).

married the latter.[10] Livy's personal contribution may be seen in extended metaphors, highly dramatic moments, psychological characterizations, elaborated speeches, niceties of plot, and suggestions of contemporary ideologies.[11] There is no litmus test, of course, to demonstrate scientific certainty in these matters of source criticism.[12] But there is enough material to suggest that Livy used the techniques and devices that I have listed to exploit the 'dramatic potential' inherent in the transmitted story.

Before delineating the plot of Livy's account, it will be useful to consider the approaches of two scholars, David Konstan and Elaine Fantham, in their studies of New Comedy. Konstan has recently demonstrated how New Comedy reflects the social codes of the city-state;[13] concentrating on the marriage code, he points out that, in Greece, the Periclean legislation of 451 BCE had provided that only

---

[10] I endorse Treggiari's interpretation of the *Senatusconsultum* that Livy cites in 19.3–6 (1969: 85); she considers it in the light of the Augustan legislation and concludes that 'we cannot take the *Senatusconsultum* to mean that marriages between *ingenui* and *libertinae* were invalid. But we can understand it to mean that they were discouraged by the censors, who might penalize freeborn men who married freedwomen, just as they penalized senators who had freedman fathers. There was no law against the sons of freedmen taking part in political life, but they might be excluded from the Senate by the censors. Just so, the intermarriage of freeborn and freed might be perfectly valid, but the ingenuous partner might be penalized by a censorial *nota*'. By this interpretation, the *Senatusconsultum* of 186 BCE did not legalize a marriage between Hispala and Aebutius, but, in fact, made the marriage more acceptable within the political (and moral) community.

[11] Tierney (1947: 116 with nn. 85–8) concludes his detailed study about Livy's historicity with this assessment of Livy's twelve chapters (8–19): '... there are major portions of good, even though distorted, tradition in cc. 8, 10 and 13, and lesser portions of same value in 9, 12, and 18. A further large portion of c. 18 was previously authenticated by the inscription . . . the speech of the consul in cc. 15–16 is a Livian expansion in Gelzer's sense. We are left with the bare framework of the Livian narration regarding Hispala, Aebutius and his relations, and the list of names, Campanian, Roman and Etruscan, of the priests and priestesses of the sect. [Admitting that] . . . parts concerning religion contain authentic historical information . . . a good reason no longer exists for regarding the framework of his narrative as a free annalistic elaboration. The dramatic presentation of the story of Aebutius and Hispala is probably due to Livy, but not necessarily the story itself. I believe we see Livy's hand in the refined psychological analyses and in a certain overelaboration of detail which is often to be noticed in his work.'

[12] For discussions of Livy's use of non-Polybian sources in the fourth and fifth decades, see Luce (1977: 221–29); Klotz (1940–1: 24–100); Nissen (1863: cc. 3 and 5).

[13] Konstan (1983).

the children of two parents of citizen status could themselves be citizens. Viewed from this perspective, one type of comic plot reflects a profound tension in society. In Konstan's words:

The impulse to marry outside the group, common among the youths of ancient comedy, thus threatened to dissolve the boundary that separated citizens from strangers. The tension between father and son, which as a personal problem might find expression in the conflict between passion and duty, reflected on the social level an ambiguity or ambivalence in the status system itself.[14]

Konstan's interpretation of Plautus' *Cistellaria* demonstrates particularly well the working out of these tensions. The plot is quite conventional. Alcesimarchus, the young man, is in love with a courtesan named Selenium, the foster daughter of the bawd Melaenis. He has just been told by his father that he must marry a relative from Lemnos, and is on the verge of suicide, torn between obedience to his father and passionate love for Selenium. The summons to obedience seems to win out, and Selenium's foster mother, Melaenis, chastises the young man for utter faithlessness, breach of promise, and perjury. After a number of complications, however, Selenium's true origin is discovered: she is not really Melaenis's daughter, but Demipho's Sicyonian daughter, the exposed daughter of his recent bride and former rape victim; hence, she has the proper credentials for marriage: acknowledged paternity and, presumably, qualifications for citizen status in Sicyon where the play is set.[15]

Konstan emphasizes the contrast between the recognition plot—which he sees as a frame for the *Cistellaria*—and the inner panels involving the confrontation between the foster mother Melaenis and Alcesimarchus. The recognition plot had been announced in the delayed prologue at the beginning of the play, as well as enacted at its end—hence, his description of the plot as a frame. The recognition plot reveals a conservative ideology: 'distinctions of caste are

---

[14] Konstan (1983: 18).

[15] We do not know the qualification for citizen status in Sikyon and Lemnos. It is possible that the two states had the right of intermarriage. Fredershausen (1912: 207) briefly alludes to the problem of the play's location; likewise, Fantham (1975: 58 and n. 36).

represented as grounded in nature,' so that 'Selenium proves in fact
to be of the class for which she is fitted by feeling'.[16] More interesting
to Konstan is the inner panel of the comedy, the Melaenis–
Alcesimarchus confrontation; this transcends the comfortable ideology of the Selenium–Alcesimarchus frame. Konstan writes about this
part of the play:

Melaenis' liberal aspirations for her foster daughter, her defense of
Selenium's dignity and security against the impulsive but unreliable love of
Alcesimarchus undermine the contrast between the orders. It is not so much
that the barrier to marriage between citizens and outsiders is in question
here . . . but rather that any relations between the orders must be predicated
on good faith and respect for the common values of both.[17]

Konstan suggests that the conflict between the young man's passion
and the needs of the socially disadvantaged woman whom he has
seduced may reflect another tension: this is the (political) tension
between Roman citizens and their Latin allies 'who occupied an
ambiguous status which might pose problems of ideology not entirely dissimilar to those of the Athenian metics'.[18]

Fantham's article, unlike Konstan's work, is not an interpretation
of comedy.[19] As an analysis of the legal status of women in New
Comedy, however, it provides information that is helpful for the
interpreter of New Comedy who must often identify both the status
of the woman (which often will depend upon recognizing the
Athenian locale), and consider then whether it provides a legal or
conventional obstacle to the young couple's future. Fantham distinguishes two major categories of females in comedy: the respectable
citizen, who may be maiden, wife, or widow; and the noncitizen, who
may be music girl, courtesan, concubine, or procuress, and who may
be free, freed woman, or slave.[20] Fantham has carefully identified
these different categories in Menander, Plautus, and Terence, and has
demonstrated how the status of the female affects typical comic-plot
patterns. Sometimes, as in comedies of citizen love and marriage, the

[16] Konstan (1983: 110).
[17] Konstan (1983: 110).
[18] Konstan (1983: 124).
[19] Fantham (1975: 44–74).
[20] Fantham (1975: 71).

material is unpromising: 'The young man is told that he is to marry X's daughter, whom he has never or barely seen; it was virtually impossible to generate a plot based on romance from such material.'[21] Aside from introducing rapes and pregnancies to provoke romantic citizen marriages, Fantham shows that 'there was a way out of the dramatist's dilemma; love between a youth and girl was easier to contrive if the girl, though both a citizen and eligible for marriage, had lost her identity through kidnapping or been rescued as a foundling and was already living as a noncitizen'.[22] Fantham's focus on status and its function in the comic plot allows us to go a step further and to suggest a likeness between the unravelling of the complication in a recognition comedy and the unravelling of a mystery's complication: the strategy of the mystery writer is to set up a series of clues and false leads that will eventually lead to the resolution of the mystery, usually the identification of a criminal; similarly in comedy, the playwright not infrequently sets up a series of clues that may be used by the audience to identify the real status of one of the players. It might be possible to argue that Livy or his source for the narrative of Hispala and Aebutius has borrowed such a strategy from the writers of New Comedy.

Let us turn now to Livy's account (39.8–19) of the suppression of Bacchanalian cult activities in 186 BCE. This follows closely upon his report of Marcus Fulvius' triumph over the Aetolians and Gnaeus Manlius' triumph over the Gauls in Asia. Here, Livy especially stresses certain signs of Roman cultural degeneracy: for example, the growing laxity in the army's discipline and, closely connected with this, the spread of Asian luxury to Rome (bronze couches, tapestries, female lute and harp players, gourmet foods, and the upgrading of the Roman cook). Yet all this, he says, hardly even provided the seeds for the luxury that was to come. We probably are to imagine that one of these poisonous blossoms was the arrival or renewal of the Bacchic cults. In Livy's story, the Bacchants are immoral and dangerous—sex addicts, criminals, will-forgers, and murderers.[23]

---

[21] Fantham (1975: 52 with n. 24).

[22] Fantham (1975: 56).

[23] It is not my purpose here, as stated above, to discuss the historicity of Livy's account of the activities of the Bacchic cult. The reader should consult Tierney (1947: esp. 104–17).

Chapters 8 and 9 in Book 39 introduce the episode. The first sentence rather abruptly brings the major action to the forefront: 'The following year saw the consuls Spurius Postumius Albinus and Quintus Marcius Philippus turning their attention from the army, and from the sphere of military and provincial affairs, to disciplinary measures against an internal conspiracy.'[24] The rest of the introductory material provides all the background information that the reader needs to understand the stage action: not only the origins of the conspiracy (8), but also the origins of Aebutius' difficulty with his mother and stepfather, and the origins of his relationship with Faecenia Hispala (9). About Aebutius, we learn that his father had performed his military service with a horse supplied by the State, and that Aebutius was left a ward. When his guardians died, he was brought under the tutelage of his mother Duronia and his stepfather, Titus Sempronius Rutilius, who, when the story begins, is unable to render an account of Aebutius's money. Duronia and the stepfather decide that the son must either be done away with or compromised in such a way as to be unable to make trouble about his lost inheritance. The latter plan is decided upon; the Bacchanalia is to provide the opportunity; Aebutius is to be initiated. The mother concocts a story. During an illness of Aebutius, she had vowed that upon his recovery she would have him initiated. She must fulfill her vow: now, he must be continent for ten days, then attend a banquet and the purification at the shrine. Next, we learn of Aebutius' romantic interest: 'a prostitute of repute, the freedwoman called Hispala Faecenia. . . . While she was not worthy of the profession to which she had inured herself as a young slave,' Livy writes, 'still, after obtaining freedom, she maintained herself in the same old way' (39.9.5). Hispala developed an intimacy with Aebutius, 'from their being neighbours'. This intimacy was damaging neither to Aebutius' property nor to his reputation. She, after all, supported him, and not only that, she also had petitioned for a guardian from the tribunes and praetor, so that she could make out a legitimate will leaving all her belongings to Aebutius. These were their 'pledges of affection'. So ends the introduction; the stage is set for action.

<hr/>

[24] All passages from Livy Book 39, are cited from the 1966 Teubner reprint edition of W–M.

Chapters 10–11.3 concern Aebutius' perilous position and end with his expulsion from his family. When Aebutius informs Hispala of his mother's religious plans for him, she reveals that she herself had once been initiated, and after telling of its terrors, she begs him not to participate. Aebutius returns to his mother's house and says he will not be initiated. Reproaches follow; the mother blames Hispala: her son has been polluted by the magic charms and poisons of a snake; he cannot stand to be chaste, not even for ten straight nights; he has no reverence for a parent, a stepfather, or the gods. The section concludes as Aebutius, fighting with his parents, is driven from the house: 'Pouring reproaches on him from both sides, mother and stepfather drove him from the house with four slaves.'[25]

Chapter 11.3–7 may be termed the wanderings of Aebutius and the verification of his story. First, he brings the story to his aunt's house. She recommends that he bring it to the consul. He goes the next day, 'when no witnesses are at hand'; he tells the story and is bid to return in three days. The consul meanwhile asks his mother-in-law, Sulpicia, whether she knows the old woman Aebutia. Sulpicia responds yes, and speaks respectfully of her ('a decent woman with traditional values'). Postumius says he must meet her, but Sulpicia should make the arrangements and do the inviting; then he would interrupt, as if by chance, to ask about Aebutius. The meeting takes place; the consul's 'chance' intrusion occurs; aunt Aebutia reiterates her nephew's story: Aebutius had been despoiled of his fortune by those who least of all should have done so; he was staying with her, having been ejected by his mother because—good lad that he was— he refused to be initiated into obscene rites. The consul is convinced finally that Aebutius' story is reliable, that he is no 'unreliable source'. Chapter 11 ends with the reader's just expectation that some real action can now take place to correct the plight of poor Aebutius.

---

[25] The vivid detail here—of the mother quarreling on one side and of the stepfather with the aid of four slaves on the other, all of whom drive Aebutius out—has a comic effect. The positioning of the characters around Aebutius suggest a *flagitatio* (perhaps modeled after comic scenes rather than real life); compare, for example, Plautus, *Pseud.* 357–68, where a *flagitatio* begins as Callipho and Pseudolus surround Ballio at Callipho's suggestion. For *flagitatio*, see Usener (1901: 1–28).

Chapters 12–14.3 contain Hispala's confession. The consul has Sulpicia invite Hispala for questioning. Hispala, disturbed because she does not know the reason why she is summoned by so noble and dignified a woman, almost faints away when she sees the lictors, the consul's entourage, and the consul himself. She is brought to an interior part of the home, and in mother-in-law Sulpicia's presence, the consul asks her to tell what she knows about the nocturnal celebrations of the Bacchant rites. Sulpicia—'a lady of great dignity'—and Postumius offer pledges of safety. After some initial fear and trembling, Hispala admits to having been initiated as a young slave while in the company of her mistress; but from the date of her manumission, she knows nothing more. The consul threatens her with vague threats; he says that he had heard everything from the person who had heard it from her. Hispala, after some more hedging and after casting aspersions on the perfidy of Aebutius, expresses great fear of the gods, whose secret rites she is about to reveal, but greater fear by far of the men who, with their own hands, would cut up and mangle the limbs of an informer. She beseeches both Sulpicia and the consul to send her away, somewhere outside of Italy, where she might spend the rest of her life in safety. The consul bids her be of good spirit; he will see to it that she may live safely in Rome. Then Hispala provides the information. When she finishes, she falls on her knees and again begs the consul to send her far away. The consul asks Sulpicia to vacate some part of her house so that Hispala might move in there. All of Hispala's belongings, including the domestics, are transferred here, and Aebutius is asked to move into a house belonging to a client of the consul.

Chapters 14.3–17.3 contain Postumius' report of the matter to the Senate, the Senate's response and its decrees (which forbid the celebration of Bacchic rites except under well-defined and special circumstances), and the speech of the consul to the assembly.

Chapters 17.4–19.7 provide the finale for both the political action and the personal story. Further decrees against the Bacchants are proposed. There is great panic and terror in Rome and throughout Italy. A report indicates that more than 7000 men and women were involved in the conspiracy. There are trials, punishments, and the destruction of Bacchic shrines. There are more decrees of the Senate. The final scene unfolds as Sp. Postumius brings a motion to reward

Aebutius and Hispala. Each is to receive 100,000 bronze coins from the treasury. Furthermore, Postumius proposes that Aebutius be given military status such that he will not have to serve in the military, and that Hispala be granted certain rights: the right to alienate her property (*datio, diminutio*), of marriage outside her *gens* (*gentis enuptio*), the option of a *tutor*, just as if a husband had granted her one in his will, and the right to marry a man of free birth without any slur or disgrace attaching to that man. Last of all, he proposes that the consuls and praetors, both those in office now and those in the future, should take care that she be safe and not come to any harm.

## II. COMIC ELEMENTS

The comic elements are the following:[26]

1. Comic diction. There is an accumulation of diminutive forms: *meretricula* (9.7), *corruptela* (8.6, 9.3, 10.6), and *ancillula* (9.5).[27] Duronia, Aebutius' mother, calls Hispala an *excetra*, literally, a snake or serpent, a word that becomes an abusive epithet for a woman in some of Plautus' plays.[28] While all these words appear

---

[26] I have included here only those elements that can be reasonably called comic as opposed to, more generally speaking, dramatic. Among the latter, I single out only one: Livy's beginning the episode with the notice of the consuls' activity: 'The following year saw the consuls Spurius Postumius Albinus and Quintus Marcius Philippus turning their attention from the army, and from the sphere of military and provincial affairs, to disciplinary measures against an internal conspiracy' (8.1)... 'Both consuls were assigned the task of investigating clandestine seditious activity' (8.3). Cova (1974: 91–2) has noted this chronological inversion as an example of Livy's 'dramatic economy'.

[27] In Plautus: *ancillula: Cas.* 193; *Cure.* 43; *Men.* 339; *Mil.* 794, 795, 912, 987, 1133; *Rud.* 74; *Truc.* 93. *corruptela: As.* 867; *Truc.* 671; *Poen.* 830. *meretricula: Rud.* 63; *Truc.* 309. In Terence: *ancillula: Heaut.* 252, 293; *Ph.* 665, 838; *Eun.* 166. *corruptela: Adel.* 793. Tränkle (1968: 103–52) does not single out diminutives as a category of archaic or poetic diction; the only diminutive he notices (121–2) is *terricula*, which occurs twice in Livy (5.9.7 and 34.11.7). Before Livy, the word appears only in Afranius (com. 270) and Lucilius (fr. 484).

[28] *excetra: Cas.* 644; *Ps.* 218; at *Per.* 3, the word may be either 'water snake' or 'malignant woman'.

in prose, their accumulation and repetition in this episode is significant: they appear nowhere else in Livy.[29]

2. Comic intrigue. Postumius' stratagem, by means of which he pretends to walk in by accident on a conversation between Aebutia and Sulpicia, is a common device of New Comedy (see, for example, *Andria* 4.3).

3. Stereotypical characterization: the protagonists in Livy's narrative resemble comic characters. Besides the more general similarities, for example, between the wicked stepfather, who appropriates his son's wealth, and misers in such comedies as *Aulularia*, or between the *scortum nobile* of Livy's narrative and courtesans of noble nature such as Thais in *Eunuchus*, there are more particular comic colorings:[30]

(a) Before Aebutia is summoned to Sulpicia's house, Postumius asks his mother-in-law whether she knows the old woman and is told that she is 'a decent woman with traditional values' (11.5). The quick characterization of moral uprightness is reminiscent of characteriza-

---

[29] The word for priest (*sacrificulus*) appears twice in the episode (39.8.4 and 16.8); both times it is joined with oracle monger (*vates*). The word is not found in comedy. It is derogatory here and may also be so at 25.1.8 concerning the influx of foreign rites into Rome at a critical time, and at 35.48.13, where *sacrificulus* is used to modify *vates*. When Livy does not use the term in a derogatory context but uses it instead to refer to an official Roman priest, he, of course, uses *sacrificulus* as a modifier of *rex*: 2.2.2; 6.41.9; 40.42.8.

[30] It is interesting to observe how Livy presents Hispala as a *scortum nobile* in the early part of his narrative: far from being the stereotypical grasping and greedy prostitute set on devouring the property of her client, she instead supports Aebutius: 'While his own family was niggardly in every respect towards him he was actually supported by the harlot's generosity. In fact, her affair with him had taken Hispala even further: since, on her patron's death, she was under nobody's legal authority, she petitioned the tribunes and the praetor for a guardian, made a will, and appointed Aebutius her sole heir' (9.7). In other words, it is her generosity to Aebutius that makes her a *scortum nobile*. Because we must assume, on the basis of Livy's account, that Aebutius has no funds of his own, we must conclude that Hispala supports her lover from her earnings as a prostitute: 'the prostitute of repute, a freedwoman called Hispala Faecenia, who was too good for that occupation, which she had taken up as a slave-girl, but she continued to keep herself by the same line of work even after her manumission' (9.5). Hispala's relationship to Aebutius therefore somewhat resembles Thais' relationship to Phaedria at the close of the *Eunuchus* (1072–80), where it is envisioned that Phaedria's rival, the rich soldier Thraso, will continue to be Thais' client and hence support Thais, thereby assisting Phaedria himself. Livy has glossed over the implications of Hispala's breadwinning activities on Aebutius' behalf, passing judgment upon them only fleetingly in his description of Hispala as 'too good for that occupation'.

tions in New Comedy—in *Adelphoe*, for example, when Demea sees
Hegio approach, he describes him as a 'a man of traditional virtue
and honour' (442).

(b) Aebutius is presented as conducting himself in a seemly manner
in regard to his relationship with Hispala; it was a 'sexual relationship...in no way damaging to the young man's finances or his reputation' (9.6) conducted with discretion. The concern for the protection
of a young man's reputation when conducting an affair with a courtesan is characteristic of New Comedy: in the *Andria*, Davos tries to
persuade Simo that Pamphilus' affair with Glycerium was of a similar
character: 'he took care that this affair was in no way a disgrace to him,
as is proper for a decent young man' (444–5). And the concern that a
courtesan will extort the wealth of a young man is so pervasive in New
Comedy that one need only refer to the last act of *Heauton timorumenos*, where Chremes is only dissuaded with the greatest difficulty from
disinheriting his son because of his fear of Bacchis' potential for
extortion.

(c) When Hispala is summoned to Sulpicia's house, she is
surprised and fearful; her anxiety appears to arise not merely from
the unexpected sight of the lictors, the consular entourage, and the
consul himself at her door, but from her perception of the difference
between their status and her own:

On receiving the message, Hispala was frightened—without knowing why,
she was being summoned to the presence of a woman of great dignity and
distinction—and when she caught sight of the lictors in the forecourt, and
then the consul's retinue and the consul himself, she almost fainted. (12.2)

The self-consciousness of lowly status is frequently articulated by the
concubines and courtesans of New Comedy—Habrotonon in
*Epitrepontes* and Glykera in *Perikeiromene* come easily to mind.[31] In
*Hekyra*, when Bacchis is summoned before Laches, the father of her
former lover, she is fearful as Hispala is, and her anxiety stems from
the explicit recognition of her status:

LA: By Pollux, Bachis, I imagine that you are truly amazed
    Why I ordered my slave to summon you out here.

---

[31] For *Epitr.*, see especially 855–77 (Sandbach (1972)), with Gomme and Sandbach
(1973: *ad* 860). For *Perik.*, see especially 708–19.

BA: By the god I am also somewhat apprehensive when I think who I am,
Lest the reputation of my profession be prejudicial to me; I can easily
defend my conduct. (732–5)

4. The domestic plot with its happy ending: an upper-class young
man falls in love with a prostitute; the young man has lost his money,
the prostitute is generous and kind; in the end, the young man will
get back his money and will be able to marry the prostitute: a way will
be found legally for her to marry the young man, and so the marriage
will be beyond reproach. A similar pattern (the comic paradigm)
appears in those comedies in which a young woman thought to be of
humble or servile origin is discovered to be a citizen; sometimes,
quite happily, she will turn out to be the daughter of the next-door
neighbor and will thus be eminently qualified for marriage. This is
the pattern, for example, in Terence's *Andria*. Glycerium, the
thought-to-be sister of the now-dead courtesan Chrysis, is the mistress of Pamphilus. As soon as the audience is alerted to the relationship between these two in the opening scene, it awaits the clues that
finally will reveal Glycerium's true status and provide the necessary
sanctioning for the marriage.[32]

In Livy's episode, we might note the insertion of certain details at
the beginning of the story that create expectations for its conclusion.
A reader trained by comedy to put together such details as clues to
citizen recognition will be particularly apt to notice them. Thus,
Hispala's generous nature, described by Livy as soon as he introduces
her into the story (9.5–7), creates the expectation that her sociopolitical status will be changed, that character will be rewarded by
status, that the 'prostitute of repute' will become a 'woman of repute'.
This, after all, is the comic ideology, and it appears to be in effect
when Hispala is given the option of a *tutor* as if a husband had

---

[32] The experienced spectator/reader of New Comedy will have picked up the clue
in the first scene when Simo describes Glycerium's appearance at Chrysis' funeral: . . .
'since her dignified and ladylike appearance surpassed all the others' (122–3).
Menander's audience would perceive the clue more easily if, as generally thought,
there were a divine prologue containing the recognition plot: see, for example, Drexler
(1938: 32). But Terence's audience will certainly be on the alert by 1.3, when Davos
gives away the plot of the play in lines 220–4, which have been ascribed to Menander's
divine prologue; so Oppermann (1934: 262–85), and so, to my knowledge, all scholars
since, with the vocal exception of Büchner (1974: 48–50).

provided her one in a will. Clearly, the former status of 'slave-woman freed by patron' is thus changed to 'woman left heiress by husband'. This bit of manipulated legality makes her a legitimate and dignified widow, an attractive candidate for marriage. In one detail, however, this represents a departure from the comic paradigm of New Comedy, for New Comedy never allows for a resolution based on the actual granting of citizen rights to a courtesan or to a member of that class—or to any noncitizen, for that matter.[33] The person who ends up with citizen rights was a citizen from birth, although knowledge of that status may have been lost or forgotten through various complicated circumstances. Thus, noble nature and citizen birth coincide in New Comedy. Not here. In Livy's account—and most likely in the transmitted story—the comic paradigm is changed to fit the historical situation of the heroine. The comic ideology is not thereby disturbed, however, so long as good character and citizen rights are aligned in the end.

We have, therefore, the comic elements in Livy's story.[34] Why has Livy used them? If we assume that the basic outline of Livy's story has a historical basis—that a prostitute named Faecenia Hispala and her equestrian lover Aebutius provided information to the consul Postumius about the celebration of the Bacchanalia, and that the two were rewarded with the privileges outlined in c. 19—then we must admit that the comic paradigm and its ideology to some degree fit the historical situation and were probably present, in however nascent or developed a form, in the transmitted story. The accumulation of comic elements in Livy's narrative suggests that Livy welcomed, embellished, and deployed them purposefully to mark the narrative as comic. To the question posed at the beginning of this paragraph, I will now offer a slightly paradoxical answer. Livy sets up the comic paradigm in order to disrupt it: the more he marked the narrative with comic elements, the more marked their dissolution would become.[35] In the next section of this essay, I will focus on the

[33] The author owes this observation to David Konstan.
[34] For comic *flagitatio*, see n. 25 above.
[35] Cova (1974: 85) poses a similar question when he points to a contradiction between Livy's statements about his method in his preface and the *praxis* in this episode. His answer is that Livy invents in this episode in order to fill in the gaps of the historical record, especially those that were made more obscure by Livy's modern

inner tensions in the narrative, and show how their emergence
disrupts the comic paradigm.


## III. THE DISRUPTION OF THE COMIC PARADIGM

Little has been said here so far of the conspiracy of the Bacchanalia, as
it seems to form only the background for the domestic comedy. It is
necessary, however, to call attention to the fact that Livy presents the
successful discovery and suppression of the conspiracy as a result of
manifold secret meetings, that is, through a kind of counter-conspir-
acy led by the consul Sp. Postumius. Thus, the forces of immorality
and wickedness, the infectious growth of the Bacchanalia, are coun-
terbalanced and overcome by the counter machinations of a 'moral
majority'. Viewed in this light, the evil forces in society are also the
mirror reflections of its moral forces. Hispala makes explicit this
notion when she calls the assemblage of Bacchants a 'second city-
population' (13.14). The consul Postumius expresses the same notion when he addresses the citizen assembly:

Unless you take precautions, my fellow-citizens, their nocturnal assembly
will soon be able to rival this daylight meeting which has been legitimately
convened by a consul. At present they are individuals standing in far of your
unity; soon, when you have slipped away to your homes and farms, and they
have assembled, they will be discussing saving themselves and destroying
you—and then it is *their* assembled numbers that *you* as individuals will
have to fear. (16.4–5)

---

juridical concepts. There may be some truth here, but not the whole truth; Cova does
not give enough weight to the role of the transmitted story. I would extend Cova's
answer and say that Livy did not lose his eye for a good story after the first decade; if
we drop our distinction between 'history' and 'legend' and consider 'story' as a
rendering of an action that is uniform, consisting of a beginning, middle, and ending
that are causally related to one another, we shall see that Livy constantly expanded
material with a view to creating story—even the unpromising story material of the
rest of the fourth decade. Concerning these matters, see my article (1987: 249–85).
Livy's artistic achievement in this episode should not go unremarked—for example,
the effect of the language concentrating on informing and secrecy that are outlined in
the next section of this essay. Such composition can only be the product of Livy's *own*
artistic project, which may, of course, have something to do with Livy's view of the
distant—and not so distant—past.

The daytime assembly, the consul suggests, has its counterpart in a nocturnal rally of perversion. We could follow through other implications: that the trials with their consequent imprisonments, sufferings, and deaths are the 'moral majority's' mirror image of the initiation rites and the crimes associated with them, and that the consuls and other magistrates in charge of the trials mirror the 'priests' and 'oracle-mongers'. These, of course, are only implications, but we must keep in mind that Livy has set up the image that makes them available—the mirroring worlds of the daytime (moral) assembly and the nocturnal rally of perversion.

It will be useful at this point to present some of the conclusions of J. A. North concerning the religious organization that Livy is describing. He compares the standard form of association in Republican Italy, the *collegium*, with the Bacchic organizations, and argues about the latter:

By the mere fact that it consists of individuals who have chosen a particular worship, it evades the normal basis of State control and supervision of religion at all its levels. What is more the external escape from State control echoes the internal escape of the Bacchist in the practice of his religion from the normal regulations and structure of the life of the city.[36]

According to North, the Senate saw the Bacchic groups as a threat to stability; what the Bacchic groups really presented was 'a change in the nature of religious organization, that is the creation for the first time of groups of specifically religious function'. This change, he observes, was 'obscured by Livy's implicit belief that the arrival of the cult of Bacchus was sudden, that it was essentially a foreign invasion shallowly rooted, easily eradicated and hence without any significance in the long term religious history of Italy'.[37] Yet Livy's narrative does not conceal the inner tensions and discomfort that resulted from the competing power structures and from the almost total annihilation of one of them. These tensions are revealed most strikingly in an inner panel (12.1–14.3) that disrupts the frame (to borrow Konstan's terms) that tells of the conventional romance of an equestrian lover with a noble prostitute who is rewarded with citizen rights in the end. In order to clarify this ideology and its disruption, we will consider

[36] North (1979: 93–4).     [37] North (1979: 95).

(a) Hispala's status in relation to her functions as witness and narrator; (b) the prominent motifs of place, isolation, and quarantine; and (c) the function of informing in the episode.

## A. Hispala's Status as Witness and Narrator

Hispala's knowledge of the Bacchic rites stems, she claims (39.10.5–6, 12.6), from an earlier period in her life when, a slave, she had been initiated in the company of her mistress; since her manumission, she has learned nothing further. The limitation of her knowledge to the period of her slavery has two important implications.

1. It implicates both the slave and slave-owning classes in the celebration of the rites.[38] While the participation of the upper class is further maintained by Hispala during her confession ('a number of men and women of repute' 13.14), it is also corroborated within the story by the access of Aebutius' mother to the rites and by the fears of the senators concerning possible participants in their own families (9.4 and 14.4). The persons whom Hispala fears therefore include members of the slave-owning class. The two 'mirroring worlds' are not distinguished by class, but rather by morality: the consul represents the morally upright concerns of the daytime State, the Bacchants the immoral forces of the nocturnal assembly. Morality, not class, is the distinguishing feature of the participants in the daytime State.

2. Hispala is free of guilt: as a slave, she must do what her mistress commands. Had she been free at the time of her initiation, her innocence would be more difficult to maintain, and therefore her appearance as a witness (that is, a guilty witness) would be less plausible within the story. Her former slave status therefore assists in the maintenance of her innocent character, which is corroborated within the story by her attempt to deter Aebutius from initiation.

Hispala, then, is a perfect witness for the State—even as she is a perfect narrator for the tale—precisely because of the marginality

---

[38] Cova (1974: 82 n. 1) observes the heterogeneity of the class backgrounds of the Bacchants.

and fluidity of her status. As a former slave, she appears free of guilt, and as a witness and narrator, she can win her inquisitors' sympathy as well as our own. Paradoxically, status comes to be marked in the narrative, even though it does not mark the Bacchants *per se.*[39]

Livy's embellishments through the comic paradigm mark status even further; they also augment the readers' reservoir of sympathy for Hispala and create expectations for the ending of the story. At its beginning, when the State is in disarray, moral character does not coincide with status, but is, instead, independent of it. Hispala, though a prostitute, is a *scortum nobile*; the Bacchants, although they include 'a number of men and women of repute' (13.14), are immoral. In accordance with the comic paradigm, however, character and status finally should coincide. At the end of Livy's story, the Senate will confer what nature is discovered to have conferred at birth in the comic paradigm. As long as both nature and the Senate reward character, the comic ideology is not really disrupted: a person will have citizen rights as the guerdon of her character. But the comic ideology will be disrupted if citizen rights are conferred for some other reason. That, I think, happens in the inner panel of Livy's account of the Bacchanalia. Because the disruption occurs in the most highly dramatized portion of the account, it is most likely that the disruption is Livy's alteration of the transmitted story. In the next two sections, I will pinpoint the disruption and argue that Livy has altered the transmitted story for ideological reasons.

## B. Motifs of Place, Isolation, and Quarantine

Livy's sense of place is especially important in this narrative. First, we might notice that in c. 8 the different types of crimes—widespread

---

[39] Cova (1974: 94–6) sees extensive Livian invention here. He imputes to Livy a modern juridical view of the past that required a *delatio* ('accusation') to make public the threat of the Bacchants; since *delatio* is an odious action, it had to be carried out by an informer who was not a member of the elite—hence, the entrance of Hispala into the story; once she appears, the romance, with its incongruities, becomes inevitable. According to Cova's view, Livy would have had to make up either the *Senatusconsultum* of c. 19, or the reasons for the rewards it provided. I do not think either possibility is tenable.

sexual perversion and promiscuity, forgeries and use of false witnesses—are all imagined as having their origin in the same metaphorical workshop, an *officina*. The metaphor is repeated in c.
10, in Hispala's speech to Aebutius, in which she tries to discourage her
lover from being initiated. The celebrations, she says, are an *officina*
for every kind of corruption. In c. 9, Livy says that the evil from
Etruria has entered deep (*penetravit*) into Rome in the manner of an
infectious disease (*veluti contagione morbi*). We might infer that it
were better, metaphorically speaking, had the factory been quaran-
tined. Indeed, we will soon see that the notion of quarantine informs
the inner panel and is intimately connected with the motif of place.
After the mention of the disease-like entrance of the Bacchic rites
deep within Rome, Livy continues: 'At first the size of the city—being
larger it was also more tolerant of such immorality—kept the cult's
practices hidden. But eventually information about them reached the
consul Postumius, in a manner more or less as follows' (9.1). The
very spaciousness of the city had concealed the evil until now; at last,
knowledge of it will initiate a counter-effort to restore a valetudinous
respectability. The conspirators must have no accidental knowledge
of the consul's knowledge until his diagnosis is confirmed and a
remedy is ready; hence, the emphasis on the secrecy and isolation
of Aebutius' visit to Postumius 'when no witnesses are at hand'
(11.3), and on the consul's method of achieving the corroboration
of his story by Aebutius' respectable aunt (11.4–12.1).

More significant, however, is the final isolation of Hispala, who is
conducted to 'the interior part of the house' (12.3). Here begins the
inner panel. The romantic beginning of the narrative of Hispala and
Aebutius and the happy ending cannot conceal the tragedy of this
inner story—Aebutius' betrayal of Hispala and Hispala's defeat
before the consul. Indeed, Livy explicitly marks his account at the
important point where the comedy ceases or, rather, is suspended for
a time:

Convinced that it was Aebutius who had given away her secret (as was,
indeed, the case), the woman threw herself at Sulpicia's feet. At first she
began to beg her not even to take seriously, and certainly not turn into a
capital charge, the words spoken by a freedwoman to her lover – it was only
to scare Aebutius that she had said these things, not because she really knew
anything. At this Postumius flew into a rage. Hispala evidently thought she

was even then exchanging pleasantries with her lover Aebutius, he said, instead of conversing in the home of a lady of great dignity, and with a consul. Sulpicia raised up the frightened woman, offering her words of encouragement while simultaneously calming her son-in-law's anger. Eventually Hispala pulled herself together and, after a long tirade against the disloyalty of Aebutius for thus repaying her for her devoted services to him, she declared that she greatly feared the gods whose secret rites she would expose, but much more did she fear the men who would tear her apart with their own hands for informing on them. As a result, she said, she had this appeal to make to Sulpicia and to the consul, that they would remove her to some place outside Italy where she could live out the rest of her life in safety; but the consul told her to cheer up and said that he would personally see to it that she should live safely in Rome. Now Hispala disclosed how the rites began (13.1–8).

Aebutius' treachery—his informing the consul of Hispala's participation in the Bacchic rites—has placed his beloved in a precarious situation before the consul. She has two obvious alternatives: she can either keep quiet and suffer whatever punishment lies behind the consul's intimidating words,[40] or become an informer too and seek, in some way, to escape the certain punishment of her former associates. Once she makes her decision, her future is by no means secure. It is not as if informing against her past associates will gain her easy acceptance into the society to which Aebutius belongs by birth, nor, to be sure, that silence about the activities of her associates will provide her any comfort among them in the future. Caught in the tragic *nexus*, a dilemma of place and no place, of status and no status, she falls on her knees before Sulpicia, choosing neither of the obvious alternatives. Instead, she equivocates: the conversation of a freedwoman with her lover in a matter of no importance ought not be turned into a capital charge; she had spoken in order to frighten her lover, not because she knew anything in particular. The consul's response is immediate and angry. 'You are playing the wrong role' is the gist of Postumius' words—Hispala behaves as if she were teasing a lover, instead of speaking with a consul in the house of 'a lady of great dignity'. The narrative is thus yanked out of its comic frame and set on the 'tragic

---

[40] 'Hispala said she knew no more, at which the consul declared that she would not receive the same indulgence or favour if she were refuted by the testimony of another as she would if she made a clean breast of it herself' (39.12.8).

stage' as Hispala realizes that her equivocation will not work, that the appeal of a 'freedwoman' to 'a lady of great dignity' has no effect, that she must face alone Postumius' consular authority; the comic frame returns only at the conclusion, for the 'happy ending', the marriage.

Before yielding to the consul's request, Hispala casts aspersions on her lover, and then speaks of her fear of the gods whose secret rites she has been asked to expose and of her great fear of the men who will mangle their informer. Finally, she begs her inquisitors to send her away, outside Italy. Her request makes sense, and not only psychologically, as arising out of her fears. It is a solution to the tragic dilemma of place and, as such, it fits in with the related motifs of isolation and quarantine. There is no *place*, so Hispala thinks, in all of Italy for such a person as she: the person who has straddled the boundary between daytime society and the nocturnal one, the cultivated society and the orgiastic, the moral and the immoral—that paradoxical creature, the *scortum nobile*, must, in the end, become the outcast of both societies. The consul responds to her request with an assurance of safety in Rome. Then follows Hispala's information and her second plea for expulsion. This time, the consul responds with a surprising suggestion: his mother-in-law, 'such a dignified lady', should make some part of her house vacant for Hispala. Postumius' action, small but nevertheless grandiose, is the tragic *lusis* of the inner panel, an alternative solution for Hispala's dilemma of place: rather than becoming society's outcast, she now will be cast inside a small apartment at the top of the safest building in all of capacious Rome, the home of the consul's mother-in-law. The public stairs are blocked, and interior access alone permitted: 'Hispala was given a loft above the house, with the stairs from it to the exterior sealed off and access to the loft brought inside the building' (14.2). The motifs of isolation and quarantine thus come to a climax as we see Hispala kept apart from all community and from her blurred allegiance, as if she were to be purified, reminding us of the ten-day period of sexual abstinence that precedes initiation into the Bacchic cult. Similarly Aebutius, first having been driven out of his mother's house, is now relegated to a house owned by a client of the consul's. Both outcasts—Hispala, who had envisioned her future outside of Italy, and Aebutius, who had been literally cast out by his family—are now cast for roles inside the consul's society. When the two lovers reemerge from their isolation, their status, we shall see, will have been transformed; the two will be purified and initiated into the 'moral majority'.

While the period of internal isolation certainly is due to the requirements of safety, Livy has depicted it as a period prior to initiation, with consul and consul's mother-in-law presiding—priest and priestess, as it were—over the couple's readmittance into society. Having once set up the image of mirroring worlds in Hispala's speech where the Bacchants are the 'second city-population' (13.14) and, later, in Postumius' speech where the 'nocturnal assembly' is set explicitly against the daytime assemblage (16.4–5), it is easy for Livy to suggest the resemblance between initiation into illegitimate rites and reentry into legitimate society. This he does by his focus on place and isolation, by his careful description of Hispala's new abode almost as if it were a shrine, by his reference to the blocking of public access to Hispala and to the separation of the lovers. While the transmitted story may well have mentioned the temporary asylum offered to the two lovers, it is not likely that it would have been so attentive to the details of place and isolation, to the presentation of mirroring worlds. This is surely Livy's elaboration; it is artful and dramatic, but it also disrupts the comic paradigm. Asylum for purification before admittance into society surely implies the adulterated state of the initiates; if so, then the offer of asylum becomes an example of the consul's generosity to its impure and placeless inhabitants, and the Senate's subsequent rewards to Hispala can no longer be seen as rewards for character; the comic ideology that aligns citizenship and character fissures. That the comic ideology has in fact been altered deliberately in the inner panel will become more evident in the following discussion of informing.

## C. Informing

Informing plays an important role in Livy's narrative, both in the frame and inner panel. Here, I first will examine the references to informing throughout and see how they serve to structure the narrative; then I will focus on the import of informing for the inner panel.

The size of the city, Livy wrote in c. 9, had at first concealed (*celavit*) the disease; at last, 'information' (*indicium*) came to the consul. The rest of the story followed as an explanation of how (*hoc maxime modo* 9.1) the consul acquired 'information'. We recall that Hispala recognized Aebutius as the informant (*index arcani*, 13.1); she showed her awareness of her own role as *index* when she expressed a fear of those 'who, with their own hands, would cut up and mangle the limbs of an informer' (13.5). Her finished story was an *indicium* (*peracto indicio* 14.1) and Livy thus frames the informing section with *index* at 13.1 and *indicium* at 14.1. Personal betrayal (*indicem arcani* 13.1; cf. 10.1 'Such were the pledges of affection between the two, and they kept no secrets from each other.') induced Hispala's loyalty to the State, but she did not give up her information until first she had acquired assurance of personal safety.

An incipient conflict between personal and State loyalties is perceptible among the Senators. When the consul, with the informants now under his control ('having both informants at his disposal' 14.3), came before the Senators, they feared first for the danger of the State, then 'privately they each feared for their own relatives, in case one of them should be party to the villainy' (14.4). Their personal qualms appear to have been quickly quieted in the interests of the State, and they decreed an investigation: the consuls were asked to protect the two *indices* and to encourage still other *indices* with rewards (14.6). A senatorial decree is enacted: 'they posted a reward for any informer bringing an offender before them or denouncing him in his absence' (17.1). Apparently, loyalty to the State had a heyday: 'Many were reported by informers. Several of these committed suicide, both men and women' (17.5–6). Many others were put to death (18.5).

Rewards for the original informers become the Senate's concern, too (19.1). The consul introduces a motion for the reward of Aebutius and Hispala 'since it was thanks to them that the affair of the Bacchanalia had been brought to light' (19.3). Now the two are enabled to marry legally (or at least to marry with respectability). The State, which had separated the two lovers and which had made Aebutius an informer against his lover and Hispala an informer against her past associates, now gives sanction to the marriage bond of the two *indices*. The hierarchy of loyalty has been reestablished through the process of informing, which first fissures the relationship between Hispala and Aebutius and then reconstructs it anew: what had been the personal but unlegitimized relationship between a man and a prostitute, confirmed by 'pledges of affection', becomes a state-sanctioned relationship between one informer and another who are joined together by virtue of their act of loyalty to the State. *Indicium*, the discovery of information that was announced as the subject of the story in c. 9, has been completed as the indices of c. 19 get their reward.

Let us now consider Livy's depiction of informing in the inner panel. After Hispala's realization that her lover has betrayed her, she equivocates even on bended knee ('the woman threw herself at Sulpicia's feet. At first she began to beg her not even to take seriously, and certainly not turn into a capital charge, the words spoken by a freedwoman to her lover – it was only to scare Aebutius that she had said these things, not because she really knew anything', 13.1–3) until the consul's anger forces her to see her precarious position; then she asks for protection; and upon receiving assurances, she informs. This is the most highly charged moment of the episode—for its protagonists and readers, too. Until now, the narrative has sympathized with both Hispala, the *scortum nobile*, and with Postumius, the energetic and concerned consul. But at this moment, the narrative is surely constructed on the side of the consul. There is no question but that the Bacchants are immoral and dangerous and must be eradicated, no question but that the consul is right. What is remarkable in Livy's narrative is that, with all its attention to informing, there is little recognition of the moral issues involved in it; there is no pondering, for example, of such questions as which is to take precedence—personal loyalties or loyalty to the State? Personal safety or the safety of the State?[41] Aebutius had informed on Hispala—and

---

[41] It is interesting to note here how easily Livy, had his focus of attention been different, could have exploited the comic paradigm differently. If Livy had chosen to focus on the moral issue of the conflict of loyalties involved in informing, then a pattern of comic conflict was ready to hand: it is a common motif in New Comedy for a young man (and sometimes, a young woman) to be torn between love for, and loyalty toward, a beloved of questionable status and the obligations owed to a father: for example, the situations of Pamphilus in the *Andria*, 260–4, 277–80, 896–8, and Alcesimarchus in *Cist.*, of the young women in the opening scenes of *Stichus*. A comic conflict between loyalty toward a beloved and obedience to a father could easily have shaped a conflict between a beloved (Aebutius) and obedience to the Roman State as emblematized in its patriarchal leadership, the consul. But Livy has not shaped his

probably on his mother, too—incidentally, in his attempt to regain his paternal inheritance;[42] Hispala informs on her past associates because it is the lesser of two evils (to be protected by the consul rather than to be mangled by her past associates). Only the Senators are portrayed as perceiving the potential for conflict when Livy reports their public fear for the State and their private fears that their own families might be involved. Yet Livy gives no explanation of how the Senators resolved the conflict which could so easily have stalemated their exertions. Instead, he portrays the Senate as quickly going into action in the State's behalf; their conflict is depicted on the side of the consul—in terms that assume the guiltiness of Bacchants ('privately they each feared for their own relatives, in case one of them should be party to the villainy', 14.4) and the crisis to the State.

How do we respond to Hispala's moment of equivocation before she accedes to the consul's demand for information? To her falling to her knees to repudiate the tale she had told Aebutius? If we attempt to critique her conduct according to the norms of comedy, surely we will find ourselves at a loss. For the women of New Comedy who undergo transformations of status usually are not dramatized on stage at so crucial a moment in their lives on the basis of which the audience can determine their character.[43] There are a few occasions,

---

narrative with precisely the same moral questions that shape New Comedy. This is, I think, a very striking point to observe. We might observe it even more clearly by comparing Konstan's analysis of the frame and inner panels of *Cist.* with my analysis of Livy's account of the Bacchanalia. Recalling Konstan's interpretation cited in Part I of this essay, it was 'the socially disadvantaged woman' who strives (in the inner panel of *Cist.*) to make Alcesimarchus see that 'any relations between the orders must be predicated on good faith and respect for the common value of both'. In the inner story of Livy's account of the Bacchanalia, clearly the role of insisting on good faith belongs to the consul: it is both his intimidation of the woman *and* his promise of protection that elicit her act of loyalty to the State.

⁴² Both Son (1960: 201) and Cova (1974: 96) allude to this possibility; for the latter, it is one of the incongruities (in fact, one of the 'paradoxical consequences') that follow, inevitably, from the introduction of romance into the story.

⁴³ Sometimes the women never appear on stage. The audience, for example, never sets eyes on Glycerium in the *Andria*; but her character is assured by reference to her good upbringing (*Andria* 274–5). Pamphila only appears in the *Eunuchus* when she is delivered to Thais' house (*Eun.* 265–6); she does not speak, but Thais' attestations to her upbringing certify her character (*Eun.* 116–17, 748). In *Heauton timorumenos*, Antiphila's character is proven in 2.3 before her brief appearance in 2.4: whereas in the later scene she speaks only two lines and utters five short exclamations, in the

however, when women who will later undergo status transformations are portrayed at a critical moment, and had we more of New Comedy, their number might increase.[44] Glykera in *Perikeiromene* certainly shows heroic defiance to Polemon in her proud speech to Pataikos,[45] and she keeps a noble silence about her relationship to Moschion;[46] Selenium, in *Cistellaria* (based on Menander's *Synaristosai*), appears in person to speak of her monogamous love for Alcesimarchus at the very moment when he appears to have deserted her to obey his father's command to marry a relative;[47] Philoumene, in *Sikyonios*, certainly shows mettle in her reported appearance before the citizenry at Eleusis, even if she does not herself address the crowd.[48] Granted that a woman's opportunity to display her character at a critical moment in New Comedy appears to be infrequent; granted, too, that in none of the examples that I have adduced is the heroine in fear for her life, although Philoumene in *Sikyonios* certainly fears for her virtue; nevertheless, none of them responds in the way that Hispala does—with equivocation. Torn between fear and a demand for loyalty to the State, she collapses. Instead of a triumphant moment of proud *nobilitas*—and *nobilitas* (whether it finally would take the shape of silence or informing) stems from principle, not from fear of punishment—we see in Hispala's equivocation that utterly humiliating moment when fear takes over, that transparent moment of human weakness when all one can do is save one's skin.

Livy uses the comic frame to depict a situation in which status and character are out of alignment; granting special citizen rights to Hispala and punishing the Bacchants will bring about the realignment

---

earlier scene her conduct is reported by Syrus, who has visited her by surprise and found her weaving. Livy's famous depiction of the surprise visit to Lucretia shares similarities with Syrus' report (279–84).

[44] I have limited this statement to women of New Comedy who undergo status transformation. There are some other women who are dramatized in what are, arguably, dangerous situations: for example, Khrysis in *Samia*, who is expelled from the house of Demea. Pamphile in *Eptrepontes* and the two sisters in the opening scenes of *Stichus* are put in very trying circumstances (in both plays, the fathers— unlike the father in *Hecyra*—are actively trying to persuade their daughters to leave their husbands). These women, however, do not undergo status transformations.

[45] *Perik.* 709 ff.   [46] *Perik.* 147–50.
[47] *Cist.* 98–112.   [48] *Sik.* 187 ff.

of moral and social status—that is the comic ideology and it cajoles the reader into the comfortable belief that noble character will be rewarded in the end.[49] The inner panel, however, puts an end to that fiction, just as Postumius puts an end to Hispala's equivocation: her life in Rome henceforth will be a result of his generosity; the State, not nature, confers status, in exchange for information.

Why does Livy allow Hispala to be a *scortum nobile* in the frame and then allow her *nobilitas* to slip at so crucial a moment? Why avail himself of the comic paradigm—and then drop it here?

## IV. SOLUTIONS

The ideology of New Comedy is limited—its heroines, unlike those of Old Comedy, are not asked, and do not take it upon themselves, to interest themselves directly in the larger political community, the State. The paradigm and ideology of New Comedy supply too slender a thread for these weightier matters. Asked to subordinate private concerns to public ones, Hispala falls to her knees, equivocates, and the plot-line snaps. No longer allowed to be the *scortum* familiar to her own neighborhood and interested in protecting her lover alone from the viciousness of cult participation, she is compelled to widen her horizons to become, in effect, State's witness and catalyst for the deliverance of all of Rome and Italy from harm. Thus are Hispala's new loyalties created for her. Attentive readers of New Comedy will feel the disruption most of all. Livy, I would argue, has composed his narrative with these strategies in mind. By first erecting and then

[49] It perhaps needs pointing out that the narrative strand about Aebutius and Hispala could function just as well without the latter's equivocation. In that case, Hispala, in response to the consul's request for information and his hint of Aebutius's revelation to him, might answer in martyr-like fashion: while aware that informing lays her open to life-threatening danger from the Bacchants, she will inform anyway, because it is in the interests of the State. Impressed by her courage and forthrightness, the consul offers her protection. The rewards of the Senate follow. Noble nature is thus rewarded by the conferment of status, and there is no effective disruption of the comic paradigm. It is not inconceivable—only unable to be proved—that Livy's source provided such a story.

dissolving his own comic edifice, he calls attention to the shortcomings of the comic ideology with its focus on private interests and relationships. The dissolution allows him to focus on the moment of resurrection, when private individuals must enter the public arena, when hierarchies of loyalty must be rearranged or created, when officers of the State must engineer and protect the State's existence. Against such a background, the flawed *scortum nobile* of New Comedy is transformed into a witness for the State, a fully competent Roman *matrona*.

If we should pose the question of whether there is any ideological point to the story that reflects the historical situation of Livy's own day—an ideological point that might suggest why Livy told the story with the particular motifs and emphases that appear in his narrative—we might be tempted to point to the Augustan legislation on marriage and, in particular, to the Julian law on marriage between the orders of 18 BCE. But here we are on slippery ground for two reasons. First, we cannot know for certain whether Livy reached Book 39 before or after the legislation was enacted,[50] and, secondly, the precise provisions of the law are difficult to elucidate.[51] However, if the law did deal with the relation of status and marriage (which is self-evident), and if the law had been passed before Livy wrote Book 39

[50] Syme (1979–91: i.400–54) examines Bayet's dates (Budé, 1940: xvii), and concludes that the latter's argument (that the third decade was finished by 19 BCE) is not conclusive. Syme appears to favor an earlier date (p. 425). According to his general calculations, the fourth decade would have been completed before 18 BCE: 'Nothing therefore forbids the notion that Livy, by going to work about 29 BC had reached Book cxxxiii and with it the end of the Civil Wars by AD 1—if not some years earlier' (415–16). Syme thus calculates at least 4.4 books per year; at this rate, Livy would have finished almost 53 books by 18 BCE.

[51] A clear presentation of the evidence and of opposing views may be found in Corbett (1930: 31–9). One view is that the law permitted marriage with freedwomen to all except senators: see Corbett (1930: 31). Against this view is the fact that jurists speak elsewhere of the 'provisions of the *lex Julia* as prohibitions, not as permissions, which they could hardly do if they had known the law as one allowing marriage between *libertini* and *ingenui* with the exception of senators and their descendants' (Corbett 1930: 32). If, as Treggiari (1969: 85) argues, the *Senatusconsultum* of 186 removed a moral and not a constitutional *fraus* and *ignominia* between *ingenui* and *libertinae*, then the Augustan legislation both 'permitted marriages which had previously not been officially approved' (p. 85 with n. 2, citing Watson), and prohibited marriages between persons of the senatorial class and freedpersons. See, further, Watson (1967: 32–7) and Treggiari (1969: 82–6). More recent bibliography: Raditsa (1980: 278–339) and Gardner (1986: 31–2 and 77–8).

(which we will grant only for the sake of argument), then Livy's narrative might have had a certain relevance for a contemporary audience whose loyalties may have been divided between personal affection and the dictates of status. Yet, while Livy may be attentive to certain details about class rank in his narrative because of the legislation, I think I have shown that the question of divided loyalties was not, in fact, of great significance in Livy's account of the Bacchanalia; moreover, it is not likely that the legal agenda of 18 BCE was responsible for Livy's particular shaping of the motifs of place, isolation, and quarantine, nor for the vivid depiction of Hispala's fear for her future in Italy when she is asked to inform. Indeed, my analysis has pointed out remarkable emphasis on informing, on the State's exaction of personal loyalties for its preservation as a political entity. If we are to conjecture events of Livy's epoch that may have left their mark on the historian's narrative, instead of pointing to the marital legislation of 18 BCE, we might look instead to the proscriptions and conspiracies of the last century of the Republic that engendered so much anxiety over personal survival in Rome—and the survival of the State; these more general events are likely to have given life to Livy's account of Rome in the early second century BCE.


## V. CONCLUSION

Part II of this study demonstrated that Livy (and probably the transmitted story) applied elements of New Comedy (stereotypical characterizations, intrigue, diction, the domestic plot or comic paradigm, together with its comic ideology that equates citizen status with character) in the story of Hispala and Aebutius. In Part III, it was argued that the comic paradigm was disrupted. New Comedy, Livy's frame, and probably the transmitted story share the ideology that good character is rewarded in the end with citizen status (by birth: New Comedy; by the State's award: Livy's frame and the transmitted story). Livy's inner panel (12.1–14.3) is not in accord with the ideology of the outer frame, however: Hispala's ignoble equivocation signalled the abrogation of the comic paradigm. Her safety, henceforth, will be the consul's gift, not a reward for character;

her asylum resembles purification before initiation and, as such, implies Hispala's adulteration which her all-too-human equivocation has made tangible. In Part IV, an explanation was sought for the disruption. It was argued that the comic paradigm confined itself too narrowly to private relationships; the paradigm is dropped so that a new hierarchy of relationships can be established, in which the individual's relation to the State is most important. Hispala's equivocation, her request for expulsion outside Italy, the description of her temporary asylum are Livy's elaboration of the transmitted story of Hispala and Aebutius, added to extol the generosity of the Roman State. The relevance of the story for Livy's contemporaries probably reaches back to the generation at the end of the Republic that had feared for survival in Rome amid a city torn apart by intimidating proscription lists and conspiracies.

Before leaving the episode, it is worthwhile to focus a moment longer on the heroine of the story. Hispala is made to carry a great deal of narrative weight. She was the source of information that allowed Postumius to come forward in the Senate to demonstrate the danger of the Bacchants to the State. She thus provided the narrative bridge by means of which the Bacchants are viewed, on one side, as a threat to private households (Hispala's view), and, on the other, as a threat to the entire State (Postumius' view). Hispala is likewise made to assume an important historical role: it was her act of informing that initiated the State's eradication of the Bacchanalia and the reestablishment of order in Rome and Italy. Moreover, Hispala is used to mark the narrative at the point where Livy has chosen, at the expense of Hispala's character, to disrupt the comic ideology in order to elaborate his own ideological view of the State. Viewed from these perspectives, Hispala resembles a number of the other leading ladies in Livy's account of early Roman history—women like Lucretia and Verginia who are raped or killed at critical moments in the development of the Roman State. These women, too, unite private household and State, set in motion significant re-orderings of the State, and permit the opportunity to display the strength of the New Order, although at the expense of their lives. Paradoxically, it is the comic paradigm and not a tragic one that provides the heroine the role of catalyst for the reestablishment of Roman order when threatened by the Bacchants: a former slave who could cross the boundaries between daytime society and nighttime society, a prostitute who could provide a bridge between the private discourse of lovers and public discourse of men in assembly. The exploitation of the individual female figure as a narrative device to mark a critical turning point in history attests for us, in exemplary manner, a traditional method of Hellenistic historiography in the hands of its greatest and most creative Roman epigone.[52]

## ADDENDUM

This article provides gateways into multiple aspects of Livian scholarship. The Bacchanalian conspiracy has most recently been treated by Robinson (2007) chapter 1. Walsh (1996) also analyses the dramatic elements of Livy's account, but with the aim of establishing what actually happened in 186 and how the story evolved to the form it takes in Livy. On Livy's sources, see Briscoe (2003) with further references. For a more comprehensive treatment of conspiracies in Roman historiography, including a typology of shared elements, there is now a book-length discussion by Pagán (2004); and for drama and historiography see Wiseman (1998). Geffcken (1973) is a valuable discussion of the rhetorical and literary deployment of the 'great comic figures' in Roman literature, with special analysis of their use in establishing argument and manipulating audience expectations.

For women in Livy, see Joshel as well as Kraus (1991) on women as pivotal characters in Roman politics, Santoro L'Hoir (1992) for a lexical treatment, Moore (1993) and Calhoon (1997) on Lucretia, and McClain (1998) on sisters.

---

[52] I would like to thank all those who offered criticisms of earlier drafts of this essay: E. Gruen, D. Konstan, K. Raaflaub, A. Richlin, E. Stehle, T. Tuozzo. My earliest debt is to the late Alison Elliott, who encouraged the first version of this essay five years ago. Thanks are also owed to S. Oberhelman, general editor of *Helios*.

# V

# Cultural History

# 13

## The Religious Position of Livy's History

*W. Liebeschuetz*

The History of Livy is extraordinarily full of references to the gods and their worship. In this way it differs strikingly from the writings of Sallust and Tacitus, not to mention the Commentaries of Caesar. This fact has been interpreted in various ways. Kajanto has argued that, the frequent references to religious matters notwithstanding, events in Livy's History are mainly determined by human beings, not by gods and fate.[1] Bayet sees in Livy a pure agnostic who has grasped the importance of the religious factor in history.[2] On the other hand, Stübler maintains that Livy was traditionally orthodox and supplemented tradition with a belief in the mission of the emperor Augustus as a god and son of a god to save Rome.[3] An intermediate position is taken up by Walsh who sees in Livy a Stoic who can continue to respect traditional beliefs and practices because they have been given a symbolic place in a comprehensive philosophical system.[4]

A considerable part of the difficulty in penetrating to Livy's personal attitudes lies in the fact that Livy's History has been profoundly influenced by earlier narratives. The narrative of numerous events of Roman history had long been shaped into a pattern which would teach a civic or religious moral. It was an important function of

I should like to thank Dr. P. G. Walsh and Professor A. D. Momigliano for suggestions and corrections.

[1] Kajanto (1957). Use of this work has been made throughout this chapter; cf. Fowler (1914: 134–58).

[2] Bayet (Budé, 1940: xxxix, 5, 137–8).

[3] Stübler (1941).

[4] Walsh (1961a: 46–81); also (1958a); also (1966).

historiography at Rome to convey such lessons[5] and Livy, when rewriting the earlier narratives, will have been reluctant to omit or change beyond recognition too many of the well known *exempla*.[6] In addition, it has been shown that earlier histories not only furnished Livy with a factual basis for his narrative but also strongly influenced the whole character of sections based on them.[7] On the other hand Livy's most individual contribution to the History is generally agreed to consist of the episodes, single scenes, or sequences of scenes, into which he has organized the traditional material.[8]

In the present paper a number of Livy's episodes are examined in detail. I shall argue that thoroughgoing rationalism and earnest advocacy of religion are closely associated. Livy would appear to have been unaware that one was inconsistent with the other and to have made no attempt to save Roman religion by associating it with a more rational system such as that of the Stoics. It will be suggested that Livy's attitude, a reflection of the overwhelmingly public character of Roman religion, was shared by many educated Romans of the age and survived into much later periods.

## I. LIVY'S THOUGHT REVEALED IN EPISODES

Livy's handling of an episode can be studied in the narrative of the Caudine Forks disaster. Livy based his version on an elaborate older

[5] Cf. Cicero, *de Or.* 2.36; *Or.* 120. His use of *exempla*: Rambaud (1953: 25–54). Augustus collects *exempla*: Suet., *Aug.* 39.2. Polybius noted that Roman history contained many stories of exemplary patriotic behaviour like that of Horatius Cocles: Polyb. 6.54.6–55.4. On the ways *exempla* were used by Livy and in politics, and the range of lessons, sometimes contradictory lessons, that might be drawn from the same famous incident see now Chaplin (2000).

[6] Some older *exempla*: Dream of Latinius, Liv. 2.36.1 ff. and Cic., *Div.* 1.55; Macr., *Sat.* 1.11.3. Defeat of Flaminius, Liv. 22.3.4 ff. and Cic., *Div.* 1.77. Temple of Locri, Liv. 29.8.9 ff.; 29.18.1–16 and Diod. 27.4.

Camillus' generosity to Falerii already an *exemplum* in 171: Liv. 42.47.6; Diod. 30.7.1; Momigliano (1942: 110–20, esp. 113).

[7] Walsh (1961a: 124–6, 131–5). See also McDonald (1960: 43–8, especially 45 on 'scissors and paste' composition); Ogilvie (1965: 7–16).

[8] Burck (1964 [reprint with up-to-date bibliography]: 182 ff.); Ogilvie (1965: 17 ff.); Witte (1910: 270 ff. and 359 ff.). A single scene, death of Romulus: 1.15.6–16.8. A sequence of scenes forming a unit: 1.8.4–13.8 (Sabine women).

account, with many details derived from the events connected with the Numantine treaty of 137—an exceptionally clear example of the reconstruction of the Roman past on the model of more recent events.[9] This account had already suggested that the Roman disaster had been incurred as retribution for the arrogant refusal of a Samnite offer of peace.[10]

We can conclude from his many references to *fetiales*, or the justness or otherwise of war,[11] that this was a lesson which Livy considered important. It is not surprising therefore that he developed it to the best of his ability. The arrogance of the Romans, the injustice of their cause and the appropriateness of the punishment are made abundantly clear.[12] But the episode does not end with the lesson. The second and longer part, the description of how the Romans reacted to disaster and humiliation, is developed to provide an impressive example of Roman character, of the pride and sense of honour which made the Samnites' rejection of the advice of Herennius Pontius a disastrous mistake.[13]

In this second half of the episode the topic of the just war is still relevant but Livy has handled it differently so as to allow no clear lesson to emerge. He insists that the agreement which the Romans renounced was a *sponsio* not a *foedus* and thus eliminates the offence against the gods.[14] He reports two speeches in which the ex-consul Postumius proposes and defends the renunciation of the treaty. But

---

[9] 9.1–12.4. See Nissen (1870: 43 ff.). While there can be no doubt that the detail of the renunciation of the Caudine treaty is based on events of 137/6, the surrender of the sponsors of the Caudine treaty was already considered a precedent in 136: Plut., *Ti. Gracchus* 8; App., *Ib.* 83.

[10] DH 15.9 (13). Dio 8.8–10; Zonar. 7.20. App., *Samn.* 1–2.

[11] 1.24.3 ff.; 1.35.5 (cf. Ogilvie 1965: 127); 3.71; 4.30; 7.31 ff.; 21.5 ff.; 21.10.9; 21.19.6, 31.8.3; 35.16.1; 36.3.9; 38.42.7; 39.2.1–3. See now Petzold in Lefèvre and Ohlshausen (1983: 241–66); von Albrecht in Lefèvre and Ohlshausen (1983: 295–9); Rich (1967); Rüpke (1990). This concern for the justness of wars was already found in Livy's predecessors. See Erb (1963); Gelzer (1933: 129–66). Polybius' interpretation: Polyb. 36.2.

[12] 9.1.3–11; end of lesson, 9.7.12.

[13] 9.3.5–13; ibid. 12.2–4.

[14] 9.5.2 'not as is commonly believed, and as Claudius even wrote, was the Caudine peace made by means of an official treaty [*foedere*], but by a personal pledge [*per sponsionem*].' Cf. Cic., *Inv.* 2.30 *foedus summae religionis*. See now Crawford (1973: 1–7).

he also records the objections of certain tribunes and repeats them in a speech assigned to the Samnite leader, Gaius Pontius himself.[15] The moral issue has thus been turned not into a lesson but into a debate—a debate whose outcome is inconclusive.

After the renunciation of the treaty, the surrendered sponsors are rejected by the Samnites and return home 'having possibly fulfilled the national pledge, and having certainly fulfilled their own'.[16] This cautious phrase surely implies that Livy felt considerable doubt as to the morality of the Roman action. It is necessary to add that the inconclusiveness of the debate is hardly allowed to reflect on the Roman decision. The reader has already been fully convinced that a people such as the Romans have been shown to be could not possibly live at peace after so great a humiliation. The Romans are felt to be humanly if not morally justified.

Taking the episode as a whole, we see that the moral interest is central throughout—surely there is very little constitutional or historical interest—but the straightforward moral lesson occupies only a portion of the episode. Livy has shown himself eager to build up suitable material to teach an appropriate lesson but also aware that much history is not suitable and that issues like the renunciation of the Caudine treaty are too complex for simple approval or condemnation.

An example of an episode in which religion occupies a central place is provided by the narrative of the deification of Romulus. This brilliantly evokes the psychological atmosphere in which a new cult becomes accepted.[17] The disappearance of Romulus in the midst of a sudden storm, followed shortly after by a return to bright sunshine, leaves the actual fate of Romulus mysterious, while the accompanying natural phenomena suggest supernatural processes.[18] The explanation that Romulus has been taken up to heaven is assigned to senators who were standing nearest and is represented as evoking an

---

[15] 9.8.3–9.19; cf. Cic., *Off.* 3.10.109; *Rep.* 3.18.28. C. Pontius: Liv. 9.11.1–13.

[16] 9.11.13.

[17] 1.15.6–16.8; cf. Richard (1966: 67–78); Ogilvie (1965: 84–7); Porte (1981: 300–42).

[18] Not only the thunder but also the rapid restoration of 'a calm and tranquil sky' (cf. 2.62.2 and 26.11.3). According to DH 2.56.2 such detail is found in accounts that are 'rather mythical'. Livy uses it to make his rationalist account psychologically plausible.

outburst of religious emotion in the frightened people.[19] Nowhere does he state that it was an illusion. Nowhere does he state that an alternative version, which had darkly survived to his time, according to which Romulus had been killed and dismembered by the senators, was the true one.[20] But indirectly he unmistakably shows that this was the version he favoured. Early in his account he states that Romulus was dearer to the people than to the senators and that he kept a bodyguard.[21] This information in this position must be intended to prepare the reader for Romulus' murder by the senators. Next the report of his apotheosis is expressly assigned to senators, and the fact that it prevailed is ascribed to the panic of the moment and to the admiration of Romulus' qualities—nothing is said about its truth.[22] Finally Proculus Iulius claims that the deified Romulus has appeared to him. But this action is motivated or at least its circumstances are indicated by 'since the state was troubled by desire for their king and hostile to the Senate',[23] which strongly suggests that the vision was made up with the political aim of calming the people and reconciling them to the senate, an aim which, we are expressly told, it achieved.[24]

So Livy did not believe that Romulus was actually raised to heaven.[25] But this does not mean that he refused him divine honours. The section dealing with his death begins by asserting that none of the actions of Romulus' life was in contradiction of the belief held after his death of his divine origin or of his divinity.[26] This statement is echoed by the phrase which opens the last scene of Romulus' life, 'after these eternal labors had been completed',[27] and again by the statement that 'marvel at the man' induced people to believe in his apotheosis.[28] Moreover the supposed vision is given a

[19] 1.16.2–3.
[20] 1.16.4; cf. DH 2.56.3; Cic., *Rep.* 2.10 (20).
[21] 1.15.8.
[22] 1.16.4.
[23] 1.16.5 continues 'and by the plan of a single man, *fides* is said to have been added to the event.'
[24] 1.16.8; cf. Cic., *Rep.* 2.10 (20).
[25] There is not even an assurance of the survival of the soul of Romulus, which seems to be accepted by DH 2.56.6; ibid. 2.56.3; Cic., *Leg.* 2.8.19; ibid. 2.11.27; *ND* 2.24.62; but mocked by Cotta in *ND* 3.15.39. Also DH 2.63.3 seems to be acquitting Julius of inventing the vision.
[26] 1.15.6; cf. Cic., *Rep.* 2.10 (17).
[27] 1.16.1.     [28] 1.16.4.

perfectly valid divine message for the Roman people: 'the gods thus willed it that my Rome be the capital of the world: for that reason, let them tend to military matters.' It is plain that Livy did not consider that to show the purely human origin of a cult was enough to discredit it. Quite the contrary. Great public benefits deserved religious commemoration. It is quite consistent that the religious rite described after the account of the foundation of Rome is not directed towards one of the great gods but to Hercules, represented as a deified man.[29]

Another episode in which religion plays a great part is the narrative of the great Latin War,[30] culminating in the *devotio* of the consul Decius in the decisive battle. The religious features were already in Livy's source, but we can observe some of his modifications.

After hearing the impudent demands of the Latins the consul Manlius turns to the image of Jupiter with the words: 'Hear these wicked proposals, Jupiter, hear them, Law and Right (*ius fasque*)! Will you, Jupiter, observe foreign consuls and a foreign senate in your consecrated temple, yourself a prisoner and defeated?'[31] The language is religious but also demagogic and recalls the arguments used to oppose the political advance of the plebeians.[32] Livy is critical of this particular example of demagogy. He describes Manlius as 'equal in ferocity' to the Latin envoys, and thus recalls his condemnation of the Roman envoys who had provoked the great attack of the Gauls.[33] The traditional account, or Livy's particular source, then moved to a climax: the Latin envoy scorns Jupiter and receives instant and dramatic punishment. Livy tones down the supernatural elements with 'according to tradition' and states as a fact only that the envoy fell down the steps of the temple. A miracle is reduced to an omen. As for the rest he comments, 'these things could be true, and they could be invented to represent the wrath of the gods fittingly'. But the traditional point remains. The war whose successful outcome

[29] The message: 1.16.7; Hercules: 1.7.15. Does Livy's attitude imply a readiness to deify the living Augustus? This is not clear; cf. 4.20.7 (Ogilvie (1965: 563–4)), 'well-nigh sacrilegious' not to accept Augustus' version of the Cossus inscription—but this is perhaps humorous and Livy did not alter his version. See also 9.18.4 'the lie of his boasted origin' (of Alexander the Great) and 26.19.6–8.
[30] Liv. 8.3.8–11.1. On the location of the battle see Oakley (1997–2005: ii.486).
[31] 8.5.8.      [32] 6.41.4 ff.      [33] 5.36.1.

proved a turning point in Roman history was a thoroughly just one.[34]

In the account of the *devotio* Livy first reveals his rationalism by dissociating himself from the account of a vision seen by each of the consuls with 'it is said'.[35] Then the consul's self-sacrifice is described in terms of the effect it has on the soldiers of the two armies. Charging into the enemy on horseback, the consul appeared 'a victim sent from heaven to appease all divine anger and to turn destruction away from his side to that of the enemy', for fear and panic accompanied him into the Latin ranks and there first upset the front line and then the rest of the army. Thus the *devotio* achieved its effect— but this could be explained in purely psychological terms.[36] This is also true of its effect on the Romans, who, we are told, 'with their minds released from religious doubt' renewed their attack. The sight of the ritual victim freed the Romans from worry about the intentions of the gods.[37]

But in Livy's account the *devotio*, though beneficial, is not decisive. Even after the death of Decius, in some parts of the battle the Latins were still superior and the Roman victory was only achieved by a well-timed charge of the reserves on the orders of the surviving consul.[38] Either side might have won if it had been under the leadership of T. Manlius.[39] So Livy leaves the possibility open that the battle was decided by purely military factors.

To sum up the outlook revealed in the episodes examined so far, Livy has shown himself very much interested in morality, especially the observation of *fides* in private, public and international affairs,[40] but also aware that moral issues are not always straightforward. We

---

[34] 8.6.3. Livy regularly dissociates himself from narratives of miracular occurrences, e.g. 1.31.4 *traditur* followed by *certe* when he resumes his account of facts; cf. 1.55.3 and 1.55.5; 2.7.2 and 2.7.6. See also 2.20.12 with Ogilvie's commentary (1965) and Cic., *ND* 2.2 (6); and Liv. 45.1 and Cic., *ND* 2.2 (6). On the whole subject see Kajanto (1957: n. 1, 25 ff.).

[35] 8.6.9; 8.9.1.

[36] 8.9.9–13. Other examples of psychological effectiveness of ritual acts: 1.12.5–6; 10.26.11; 10.19.17; 2.62.1–2; 26.11.2–3.

[37] 8.9.13.

[38] 8.10.4 ff.

[39] 8.10.8. On Livy's description of *devotiones* see now Feldherr (1998: 85–92).

[40] Cf. nn. 11, 45, and 46.

have also found Livy a strong supporter of religion and prepared to develop certain events as examples of the advantages of religious observance. But he is also willing to explain the effectiveness of religious rites psychologically or sociologically.

The sociological approach to religion is very prominent in Livy's treatment of Numa. When we compare his account with that of Dionysius of Halicarnassus we see that Livy has magnified Numa's share in the establishment of the state religion,[41] perhaps primarily from the literary motive of gaining a sharp character-contrast between Romulus, the great military leader, and Numa, the man who founded the state anew 'with justice and laws and moral practices'.[42] But the result of this method of composition, that Roman religion appears as something deliberately established by a king to serve as a foundation for the social order of a state at peace, must be intended. It is likely that this widely held view of the origin and purpose of Roman religion was already found in Livy's source, perhaps Antias.[43] But Livy does nothing to obscure it. On the contrary he states it as clearly and unambiguously as possible: 'once the worries about dangers coming from outside were laid to rest, to prevent their minds from growing soft from leisure, minds which fear of the enemy and military discipline had kept under constraint... he decided to instill in them fear of the gods, which is highly effective when dealing with an inexperienced and relatively unsophisticated people.'[44] And since this fear could not be made to descend into their minds without the aid of 'some invented marvel' he pretended that he had nocturnal meetings with the goddess Egeria and that it was she who had inspired his religious regulations.

And Numa achieved his aim. The people, the *multitudo*, became so preoccupied with appeasing the gods in the correct way that their thoughts turned away from force and violence. More positively, since it was felt that the gods took an interest in human affairs, such piety

---

[41] DH 2.18–23 assigns basic religious regulations to Romulus. Livy 1.7.3 'he performed rituals to the other gods in the Alban ritual, but to Hercules in Greek ritual, as they had been established by Evander.'

[42] 1.19.1; Ogilvie (1965: 30–1).

[43] Cic., *Rep.* 2.14; *Leg.* 2.7 (16); DH 2.63 ff. cf. Ogilvie (1965: 90–1); Walbank (1957–79: i. 41–2); Fowler (1914: 81 ff.).

[44] 1.19.4.

filled the hearts of all that *fides ac ius iurandum* ('trustworthiness and respect for oaths') could regulate social relationships without the support offered by the penalties of the laws.[45] Livy returns to the topic of *fides* when he describes Numa's institution of the cult of that goddess. By including in the chapter on Numa's religious innovation, alone of numerous perhaps equally picturesque rites, a description of part of the ritual of *Fides*, he once again emphasizes that this is the most valuable product of Roman piety—in the private field at any rate.[46]

It has been suggested that Livy's rationalism is restricted to the superstition of the lower orders,[47] but of this there is insufficient evidence. Admittedly, he provides many examples of the social use of religion to keep the people in order,[48] or to oppose political change,[49] and gives no indication that he considers this an abuse. But neither does he at all suggest that he distinguished between aspects of the religion of the Roman people which were merely socially useful and those which had a more truly religious or philosophical significance.

In Livy's history there are few examples of that higher religion implied in Varro's saying that the superstitious man fears the gods but the truly religious person reveres them as parents.[50] He will not even allow religious merit to the contemplative vigils of Scipio Africanus in the temple of Jupiter. There is no place in this history for knowledge of the gods derived from contemplation of the regular motions of the heavens, which according to Stoic doctrine can be the source of piety and justice and of a happy life.[51] Livy did not develop the idea of Natural Religion,[52] although the account of religious acts before Numa might have given him an opportunity.

Livy certainly appears to criticize some manifestations of religion; all forms of religious hysteria or excess,[53] religious individualism,

---

[45] 1.21.1–2. Similarly Polyb. 6.56.13–15.
[46] 1.21.4 on *fides*; cf. 3.20.5 and two famous *exempla*, *Per*. 18 (Regulus), 24.18.5 (prisoners of Cannae).
[47] Walsh (1961*a*: 48).
[48] 5.55.1; 6.1.10.
[49] 4.2.5 ff.; 5.14.2; 6.41.4 ff.; 7.6.10.
[50] Varro in Aug., *CD* 6.9.
[51] Scipio: 26.19.9; contemplation of heavens: Cic., *ND* 2.61 (153); *Div*. 2.72 (148–9).
[52] Cic., *Leg*. 1.8 (24); Dio Chr. 12.39; Varro in Aug., *CD* 4.31.
[53] e.g. 6.5.6; 7.3.1–4; 25.1.6 ff.; 26.9.7–8; 27.23.2; 27.37.1 ff.; 28.11.1; 29.10.4; 29.14.1–2.

even on the part of a national hero,[54] mystery cults,[55] the excesses of foreigners.[56] But in rejecting these things he is merely restating the traditional Roman distinction between religion and superstition,[57] not introducing a philosophic distinction between higher and lower forms of religion. Livy's rationalism must therefore be taken to operate over the whole range of the religion of the Roman people. But it would nevertheless be a mistake to deduce that Livy intends to invalidate Roman religion. Surely the piety of so many heroes of Livy's History is pointed out as not the least of the exemplary features of this most exemplary period of Roman history.

## II. BOOK 5: ELABORATE ADVOCACY OF RELIGION

Any doubts as to whether Livy is not after all using religion for purely literary purposes that may remain in the mind of the reader of Books 1–4 of the History are surely removed by a reading of Book 5. This book, which has as its double theme the capture of Veii by the Romans and of Rome by the Gauls, is not only by far the longest sustained religious episode in the History, but also one which through its place at the end of the first pentad, concluding the obscure early history, occupies a particularly emphatic position.[58] But in this episode each of the three main happenings, the capture of Veii, the capture of Rome, and the Roman recovery, follows a narrative in which the impious acts of the defeated and pious acts of the victors have been carefully recorded.[59] The moral, that national piety

[54] 1.31.7; cf. 1.20.6–7; also on Scipio Africanus 26.19.9.
[55] 39.8 ff. (Bacchanal scandal); cf. Reitzenstein (1927: 101 ff.); Latte (1960a: 270 ff.).
[56] In the episode 10.38 ff. Livy contrasts the Samnites' barbarous abuse of religion (38.5–13) with the good sense of the Roman who acts on the report of favourable auspices even though the report is proved false (40), and vows a thimbleful of mead (42.7). See also abuse of religion in mass suicides: 28.22.5–11 (Astapa); 31.17 (Abydos). On Abydos contrast Polybius 16.31–3, cf. Walbank (1965: 11).
[57] Cic., *ND* 2.28 (72); *Div.* 2.72 (149). On the origin, Latte 1960a: 268).
[58] Klotz (1926: 819); Walsh (1961a: 173). Second Preface: 6.1.1–3.
[59] Analysis: Burck (1964: 109–36); Ogilvie (1965: 626) and the subsequent detailed commentary; Levene (1993: 175–203).

leads to success, is made to follow quite naturally from the narrative, but Livy also makes the point explicit, as in the sentences that herald the capture of Veii.

'And now the games and the Latin festival had been repeated, now the water had been let out from the Alban lake upon the fields and now her fate was seeking Veii out. Accordingly, the leader fated to bring about the destruction of that city and to save his country, Marcus Furius Camillus, was appointed dictator. The change in command instantaneously changed the entire situation.'[60] In this summing up, which is surely Livy's own, the contribution to victory of various ritual acts and of the generalship of Camillus are put absolutely parallel and on the same level. Each contributes to victory in the same way and to the same degree.

A similar tendency is implicit in the treatment of the second episode of the book, the capture of Rome by the Gauls. Before the disaster the Romans replaced a deceased censor, took no notice of a divine warning, and expelled their ablest general Camillus. Finally, Roman ambassadors, in flagrant breach of international law, took part in fighting against the Gauls and were subsequently not surrendered to the Gauls but elected to office.[61] The ensuing disastrous war is thus shown to have been a thoroughly unjust one.

The theme that the Romans defeated at the Allia were fighting in an unjust cause Livy found in his sources.[62] But he used all the resources of his art to impress it on his readers. 'Now even though so heavy a weight of calamity was looming over them—to such an extent does fortune blind men when she does not want her gathering might to be resisted and scattered...', the Romans did not appoint a dictator, did not levy adequate forces, did not fortify a camp before battle, consulted neither auspices nor entrails before engaging the enemy and were defeated almost without a fight.[63] Even though Livy never makes the point explicit, a reader familiar with the idea of dramatic justice[64] cannot avoid feeling that the Romans were defeated because

---

[60] 5.19.1–2.
[61] 5.31.6; 32.6; 36.8.
[62] 5.36; cf. Diod. 14.113.3–7, DH 13.12.
[63] 5.37.1–3; 38.1; 38.5 ff. This detail is not found in other versions.
[64] For Greek tradition: Ogilvie (1965, on 5.37.1); cf. also Livy 44.6.14; 6.17 (from Polybius?); 29.8.11; 18.12–15 (temple of Locri).

they had acted impiously and that the blindness inflicted on them was an act of just retribution.[65] But with the entry of the Gauls into the city a complete reversal of Roman morale took place. Henceforth, the Romans showed the utmost respect for all matters concerned with religion.[66] Now the Gauls have put themselves in the wrong.[67] They are then defeated as effortlessly as they had previously conquered the Romans.[68] Finally, the moral of all these events—that the Romans fare well when they heed the gods but badly when they spurn them—is drawn in Camillus' great concluding speech.[69]

But the fact that Livy has composed his narrative to teach a religious moral does not mean that the form of this or similar narratives is to be taken at its face value, as a literal account of the way the gods reward piety and punish impiety. Such naivety would be unthinkable on the part of the author of the episodes discussed earlier. Then, many of the religious topics, the prophecies and their appeasement, the acts of piety after the battle of the Allia, perhaps the arguments for not moving the city to Veii,[70] were so tightly bound up with the subject matter of Book 5 that only an aggressive secularist could have written the book on a purely profane plane—and we know that Livy was not that. Finally, Book 5 is by far the longest passage in which metaphysical reward and punishment plays such a central role. Such passages become progressively rarer in the later books.[71] This in itself suggests that Livy felt most free to use such motifs when the events he was describing contained a considerable proportion of myth—as he believed to be the case with Roman history up to the capture of Rome by the Gauls[72]— and could thus be shaped more freely into effective examples.

[65] Cf. Cic., *Har. Resp.* 39. Blindness as gift of fortune: Cic., *Am.* 15 (54).

[66] 5.39.8 ff.; cf. 5.47.4 and Plut., *Camillus* 27.3 on sacred geese.

[67] 5.48.9.

[68] 5.49.5 'Now their luck had turned, now divine resources and human counsels aided the Roman cause. Accordingly, the Gauls were routed in the first charge with hardly more exertion than it had taken them to win at the Allia.'

[69] 5.51.5–10. But Kajanto (1957: 35–7) argues that Livy merely gives Camillus the arguments which a pious Roman of the old times would have used.

[70] Cf. Plut., *Cam.* 31.3; 32.1.

[71] Walsh (1961*a*: 55); Kajanto (1957: 52–3, 62–3, 98–100).

[72] *Praef.* 7 (cf. Cic., *Leg.* 1.1–5); Liv. 6.1.2 ff.; 7.6.6, 'one must rely on oral tradition when antiquity has detracted from unimpeachable certainty'. On the First Decade as 'prose epic' cf. McDonald (1957: 166–8).

One must also consider literary convention. Since the Hellenistic period, or even earlier, historians had used religious motifs without theological implications for moralising or even purely literary ends.[73] Thus the history of Agathocles found in Diodorus, but probably derived from Duris,[74] employs many of Livy's themes: divine signs,[75] the political use of religion,[76] and the psychology of crisis religion.[77] The account also includes a fulfilled oracle[78] and examples of supernatural retribution.[79] Another section of Diodorus' History, probably based on Philinus, presents the disaster suffered by Regulus at the hands of the Carthaginians as a punishment for his earlier arrogance in refusing terms of peace.[80]

Even Polybius made use of the full machinery of tragedy, furies, blindly self-destructive actions and agony, to make the unhappy last years of Philip V of Macedon appear to be a retribution for the crimes of the earlier years of his reign.[81] But in Polybius the features are clearly not meant to be statements about the moral government of the universe, but similes, impressing the reader that his particular history was as terrible and sad as any he might see on the stage.

This use of religion also came to Rome. Roman historians took over many of the dramatic devices of the 'tragic' historians, and among them metaphysical causation. Livy's predecessors had already presented the Caudine disaster and the defeat of Regulus[82] as retribution for arrogance. The defeat of Gaius Flaminius at Lake Trasimene was shown to have been deserved by the consul's impiety.[83] Responsibility for the destruction of Carthage seems to have been assigned by Valerius Antias to Nemesis.[84] The capture of Rome in 390 appears to have been treated in one version as a punishment

---

[73] References to religion hold attention: Cic., *Inv.* 1.23. cf. Walbank (1955: 4 ff.) and (1960: 216–34); Ullman (1942: 25–53).

[74] Schwartz (1905: 1855); Barns *et al.* (1957).

[75] Diod. 19.2.2 and 19.29.

[76] Ibid. 20.7 and 20.11.

[77] Ibid. 20.14.

[78] Ibid. 20.29.3.

[79] Ibid. 19.103.5; 20.70.

[80] Diod. 23.15.1–6; cf. Pol. 1.35; Walbank (1945: 1–18).

[81] Walbank (1938: 55–68).

[82] Livy, *Per.* 18. On development of the *exemplum*: Klebs (1896: 2086 ff.).

[83] Livy 21.63.1 ff.; 22.3.7 ff.; Cic., *Div.* 1.35; Walsh (1961a: 68).

[84] App., *Lib.* 85, cf. Walsh (1961a: 122).

for an earlier act of hubris, the refusal by the Romans of a Veiian offer
to surrender.[85] This theme was not taken up by Livy, but that of the
guilty envoys which plays so important a part in his narrative had
also been previously used by one or more of his predecessors.[86] It
would seem that this particular feature of dramatic writing appealed
to Roman historians because it provided a convenient way of putting
into history the moral lessons which, as we have seen, it was one of
the functions of historiography at Rome to supply.[87]

Thus Livy's scheme of composition in Book 5 would not be
thought to have committed him personally to any particular view
about providence and its ways with men. Educated readers certainly
would have recognized it as part of his dramatic literary technique.[88]
As literary technique it is extremely effective. Livy's demonstration of
the benefits that result to the Roman people when Roman virtue and
Roman religion together determine the behaviour of Rome's citizens
is all the more convincing because it suggests an immediate if naive
explanation of why these benefits result. But as this explanation is not
explicitly stated, but in accordance with Livy's normal technique[89]
merely made to arise out of the events, the reader remains free to
supply his own more sophisticated explanation.


## III. LIVY AND STOICISM

It has been suggested[90] that the sophisticated explanation which
enabled Livy himself to argue the continued validity of traditional
cults was Stoic philosophy, in the form in which it was current at
Rome and is expounded in Cicero's *De Natura Deorum*: that Reason,
which according to Stoic doctrine pervades all nature,[91] might be

---

[85] Cic., *Div.* 1.44 (100); DH 12.13 (17).

[86] Diod. 14.113; Dion. H. 13.12 (18–19); cf. Ogilvie (1965: 716).

[87] The technique is likely to have fitted well with the theatrical aspect of Roman
state religion noted by Polybius 6.56.8–11 (cf. Walbank 1945: 9–10), and exploited by
Cicero before the people but not the senate, *Cat.* 3.18–23; cf. 2.13; Syme (1964: 247).

[88] On Livy's use of dramatic technique: Burck (1964: 176 ff.). On Tarquinius'
tragedy: Ogilvie (1965: 186–7, 196–7).

[89] Bruns (1898: 12–27).

[90] Walsh (1961a).          [91] Cic., *ND* 2.19 (end); cf. Fowler (1911: 365 ff.).

personified, as Ceres on the land, for instance, or Neptune in the sea, and could thus be thought to provide a rational justification of the gods of the city state.[92] Stoic doctrine could also provide a new basis for morality in that man by virtue of his share of the universal reason was in a position to harmonize his conduct with the end towards which the world was tending.[93] Finally the Stoic doctrine of providence[94] could be adapted to supply a higher justification for the Roman empire. Stoic philosophy was therefore well suited to serve Livy[95] as a metaphysical framework for his narrative as a whole, as well as to explain the effectiveness of religious acts. But it does not seem to me that Livy has used Stoicism, or indeed any other philosophy, in this way.

In spite of his method of indirect characterization Livy is always careful to make the point of his lesson perfectly, even pedantically, clear. If therefore he intended his story to be interpreted in terms of a system of philosophy, he would surely have provided some quite unmistakable indication that he had a particular system in mind. But there are no unmistakable references to Stoic philosophy in the History. Such Stoic themes as philosophical religion, natural religion, or the harmony of the natural order,[96] do not occur at all. Some expressions which can be understood in a Stoic sense are found. But they are too scattered, too obscure and too ambiguous to be taken for the philosophical key to the whole. These defects, for instance, limit the significance of certain final or comparative clauses which carry the implication that the endless succession of troubles suffered by the Romans in their early years were purposely sent to school the people for greatness.[97] Certainly a doctrine of providence can be read

---

[92] Cic., *ND* 2.28 (70–2).

[93] Cic., *Leg.* 1.7 (22).

[94] Cic., *ND* 2.13 (36).

[95] Leaving aside the problem of the depth to which a Roman's outlook might be affected by Greek philosophy. Obviously Lucretius was profoundly affected, but Cicero or Varro very much more superficially, cf. Fowler (1914: 81–2).

[96] See above, nn. 50–3.

[97] As argued by Walsh (1961a: 52–3). The relevant passages are 3.10.8 (cf. 6.21.2); 6.34.5; 7.1.7; 7.27.1; and 10.6.3; cf. also 1.46.3, the most significant. The relative insignificance of the final clauses is illustrated by 6.34.5 where after relating the failure of plebeians to stand for the consular tribunate Livy comments 'lest this go too well for the other side', and proceeds to relate the beginning of the Licinian-Sextian agitation. Surely providence was pursuing more profound aims in this matter than to prevent excessive joy over a political triumph.

into them. But in no case is it a primary[98] function of the passage to make a statement about providence.

More prominent, through numbers and context, are the forty references to fate, and it is indeed tempting to see in them a pointer to a Stoic doctrine of providence.[99] But examination of individual passages in their context does not suggest that the idea of a purposeful providential order is the central concept underlying them all. Instead, they naturally seem to fall into two groups: passages where fate represents the divine will as expressed in oracles,[100] and those where it personifies inevitable destruction, or the power responsible for sending it.[101] In the passages of the second group fate is often a near synonym for death.[102] In a number of passages fate represents the destiny of an individual, but mostly in contexts where the possibility at least of death is being contemplated.[103]

Fate is most prominent in Book 5 and here the passages fall very clearly into these two groups. The *libri fatales* are the books containing the oracular lore of the Etruscans, and the *fata* are the prophecies contained in them or in a reply of the Delphic oracle.[104] Secondly, *fatum* or *fata* appear in the role of remorseless and inevitably

<hr />

[98] e.g. 6.21.2 'the Volsci, who had been given as if by some divine lot to the Roman army for nearly continuous training' distinguishes Volsci from more occasional enemies. In 3.30.2, Livy's comment on the cessation of civil strife as a result of a hostile raid expresses his belief in the importance of *metus hostilis* for the preservation of internal peace at Rome. See Kajanto (1958: 55–63, esp. 61–2) with ref. to Liv. 2.54.2; 3.9.1; 1.19.4; cf. the debate over the destruction of Carthage: Plut., *Cat. Ma.* 27.3; App., *Lib.* 69; Diod. 34.33.4–6; Sall., *Cat.* 10. Of all the passages only the statement about the Ligurians (39.1.1) is part of a longer development (cf. the speech of Manlius, 38.17). But even this should probably be taken to mean no more than that Livy thought constant effort good for the Romans.

[99] Stoic interpretation: Walsh (1961a: 53–5); Ogilvie (1965: 48) on 1.4.1. A contrary view: Kajanto (1957: 53–63). The following argument owes much to Kajanto.

[100] e.g. 1.7.11; 8.6.11; 8.24.11; 21.22.9; 29.10.8. See also below, n. 104.

[101] e.g. 8.24.4; 10.28.12. See also below, n. 105.

[102] 3.50.8; 9.1.6; 10.29.3; 26.13.17; 42.11.5; 42.52.7.

[103] 1.7.15; 5.40.3; 8.24.2; 9.18.19; 8.7.12; but in 9.33.3 only the recurring feuds between the tribunes and the Claudii.

[104] 5.14.4 *fatalibus libris*; 5.15.4 *proprior interpres fatis oblatus*, a man to interpret a *prodigium*; 5.15.9 *excidium patriae fatale*, inevitable if the Romans were to drain the Alban lake according to the *libri fatales* and the *disciplina Etrusca*; 5.16.8 *desperata ope humana fata et deos spectabant*, *fata* is the reply from Delphi; 5.16.10 *ex his quae nunc panduntur fatis*—the decree of the gods revealed at Delphi.

approaching calamity—or the power responsible for it.[105] The relative prominence of *fatum* in Book 5 is a consequence of the relevance of each of the meanings to the subject matter of the book. In the narrative of no other event in Roman history do oracles play so essential a part as in the narrative of the conquest of Veii. On no other occasion were the Romans unable to avoid the crowning calamity of the capture and burning of their city. Each of the two aspects of fate logically presupposes a belief in predestination, but there is nothing specifically Stoic about either of them. Oracles and doom, after all, already occur in Homer.[106]

But in a few passages fate seems to have been assigned a wider and more positive role. So in four well-known passages the three greatest leaders of the Roman people, Aeneas, Camillus and Scipio Africanus are each in turn associated with fate.[107] At first sight it would appear that Livy wishes to demonstrate the special care of providence for the Roman people revealed by the gift of providential leaders at hours of national crisis. But a closer examination shows that fate does not play an identical role in all four passages. The providential association is very strong when, shortly after the battle of Cannae, Scipio is described as *iuvenis fatalis dux huiusce belli* ('the young man, predestined to command this war').[108] But when later in the war the Carthaginians are described as dreading Scipio *velut fatalem eum ducem in exitium suum natum* ('as if this predestined commander was born for their destruction')[109] the proximity of *exitium* detracts from the providential association. Scipio may still be the heaven-sent leader, but he is also the agent of inevitable destruction. The role of fate is shrinking to that which we have found so prominent in Book 5.

[105] Cf. (a) the impressive phrase *fato(-is) urgente (-ibus)*: 5.22.8; 5.36.6; 22.43.9 (for the same phrase rather than an echo: Virgil, *Aen.* 2.35; Lucan, *Phar.* 10.30, Tacitus, *Germ.* 33.2); (b) closely related: 5.19.1 *fata adpetebant*; 5.33.1 *adventante fatali... clade*; 5.37.1 *vim suam (fortunae) ingruentem*; 5.32.7 *ingruente fato*; (c) where fate is an agent of unavoidable destruction—or the destruction itself: 8.7.8; 25.16.4 (Gracchus could not avoid fate though forewarned); 26.29.9 (Marcellus driven by fate to meet Hannibal and his death). In 1.42.4 *fati necessitatem* in the immediate context refers to Servius' failure to appease the hostility which was to lead to his death—not to the expulsion of the kings and the introduction of *libertas* (otherwise Walsh 1961a: 54).

[106] Homer, *Il.* 22.303 μοῖρα or 365 κήρ. See also Kajanto (1957: 53) on μοῖρα.

[107] Cf. Walsh (1961a: 54); Ogilvie (1965: 671).

[108] 22.53.6.     [109] 30.28.11.

The context in which Camillus is described as *fatalis dux* is very similar.[110] A powerful implication is that he is the leader who will bring inescapable doom to Veii and its as yet quite unsuspecting citizens. Of course a providential interpretation is not excluded, but the author is in no way committed to it.

Aeneas is not given the epithet *fatalis dux*, but the fates are said to have led him 'in his wanderings to Italy and the beginnings of a greater development'.[111] Here the idea of a directing providence is clear. But a Roman reader confronted with the 'fates' was quite likely to think no further than the divine signs which directed Aeneas' movements and his settlement in Latium.[112] The purpose of this passage, like that of a number of other passages—including one 'fate' passage—in Book 1[113] is to add significance to the events described by forecasting the greatness which will be their eventual outcome.

To sum up the use of fate in the History: for Livy the strongest associations of the concept of fate are not with providential government of the world but with inevitable calamity and with oracles. He does not use *fatum* and *fatalis* as signposts to a providential interpretation of his history, but for limited literary aims. Of course a Stoic interpretation is not excluded, but it will be the reader's, not the author's contribution.[114]

It is true that the reader of Livy's history feels himself transported into 'an ordered and intelligible universe'.[115] But this, I would argue, is due to the subject-matter rather than to the cumulative effect of a comparatively small number of passages open to a Stoic interpretation. It would be hard to write an account of the steady growth of

---

[110] 5.19.1 'And *fata* began to attack Veii. Therefore, a commander destined (*fatalis*) to destroy that city and to save his country was named dictator.' The *fata... fatalis* effect is, surely, one reason for the choice of the epithet.

[111] 1.1.4.

[112] Cf. Servius on *fato profugus* in *Aen*. 1.2. On the signs, DH 1.55–7.

[113] 1.4.1. Other forecasting passages: 1.7.10; 1.16.7; 1.55.5–6.

[114] The only case with a definitely Stoic link is 25.6.6; but this is said by the survivors of Cannae, to evade responsibility—not by Livy. Contrast the much clearer use of *fatum* in a philosophical sense by Lucan, e.g. 1.33; 1.70 ff.; 2.2 ff.; 2.226. *Fortuna* is not given a providential role either: see Erkell (1952: 172–3); Kajanto (1957: 98–100).

[115] Walsh (1961a: 81).

Roman power over the centuries without making it appear preordained and inevitable. Moreover, the principal Roman institutions and ideals are presented so vividly and consistently that the reader is indeed transported into an orderly world signposted with stable institutions and civic virtues—but the order is that of a somewhat idealized Rome, not of an underlying philosophical system.


## IV. THE OUTLOOK OF LIVY

The fact that Livy felt able to commend religion without justifying it in terms of a more philosophical view of the world is in itself significant. Evidently Livy felt that a rationalist outlook on the world could coexist with complete affirmation of the religion of the Roman people. In contrast to his firm adherence to public religion Livy's personal religion remains elusive. We can be sure that he enjoyed traditional ceremonies and that he was capable of entering imaginatively into the state of awe and reverence induced by sacred objects or rites. I would suggest that it was this capacity, exercised on the ceremonial of contemporary religion, rather than an intellectual grasp of the importance of the religious factor in history, that enabled him to describe Roman religion in action in the early years of the Roman state. But further it is difficult to go. For a reader whose conception of religion is derived from the Bible it is almost impossible to assess the relative strength of strictly religious, as opposed to political, antiquarian, or literary elements in his outlook.

But the elusiveness of his personal religion is not peculiar to Livy. In the *De Natura Deorum*, Cotta, the representative of the New Academy, and Balbus, the Stoic speaker, while philosophically at opposite extremes, are agreed on the necessity of maintaining the Roman state religion. Cotta, who puts forward the agnostic view, is willing to engage in rational discussion of religion, but in practice he feels bound to follow the tradition of his ancestors, and the arguments of the philosophers are irrelevant.[116]

---

[116] *ND* 3.2 (5–6). On this cf. De Ste Croix (1963: 6–38, esp. 29–31); Weinstock (1961: 209–10).

Cicero himself was neither what we would recognize as a religious man, nor was he a firm adherent of any single philosophical sect.[117] Moreover he has written some devastating criticism of important aspects of Roman state religion.[118] Nevertheless in a public role he acted and spoke with strict orthodoxy, and when he came to draw up a constitution and laws for his ideal state, he went back to the combination of religious and secular institutions that he supposed to have existed in Rome in its golden age.[119] So the validity of the Roman state religion was common ground among Romans of otherwise very different religious or philosophical attitudes.[120] Livy's aims as a historian are comparable with those of Cicero as a political theorist, and his appeal is to the same common ground.

But while the precise character of the religion of Livy, and of men like him, may be debated, its existence cannot be ignored. Only a strong and widely shared sense that the traditional religion was an essential part of the Roman state can explain its long survival in the face of rational criticism. Some of the rites revived by Augustus may have declined into mere romantic masquerading by members of the Roman aristocracy,[121] but two hundred years later the paganism attacked by Tertullian was still, in the first place, the state cult of the Roman people, not the teaching of philosophers or the rites of mystery religions.[122] Moreover, even in this late age sceptical rationalism was not felt to be an enemy of traditional religion. Quite the contrary. In the *Octavius* of Minucius Felix the spokesman of paganism bases his unsuccessful case on the argument that, since reason cannot provide certainty about the nature of the government of the world, it is best to maintain the religion handed down by one's forefathers.[123] The combination of scepticism with respect for

---

[117] Ferguson (1962: 83–96); Cumont (1922: 31–3); Latte (1960a: 285–6).

[118] Notably in *Div.* 2.

[119] Cicero and public religion: II *Verr.* 1.46; *Font.* 46; *Har. Resp.* 18 ff.; *ad Att.* 1.18.3. The ideal state: *Leg.* 2.10 (23). *Ius divinum*: *Leg.* 2.18–22.

[120] Sallust was not a religious author, *Cat.* 30.2; *Iug.* 90.1. Yet *deos neglegere* is a symptom of decline, *Cat.* 12.3; 10.4 (on which passages see Syme 1964: 247). Cf. also Varro's attitude in Aug., *CD* 4.31.

[121] Latte (1960a: 309 ff.).

[122] Tert., *Ap.* 10.3 ff.; 13.1 ff.; 25.1 ff.

[123] Min. Fel., *Oct.* 6.1. In his case this includes the religious examples of Roman history, ibid. 7. Cf. Lieberg (1963: 62–79).

ancestral *auctoritas* recurs in the plea Symmachus delivered to the Christian emperor Theodosius for the restoration of the Altar of Victory.[124] This attitude has found its classical expression in Livy's History and this fact itself may have contributed to its power of survival.

Livy would certainly have wished his work to have such an effect.[125] Whether he really believed that the institutions he had revived in his narrative could be restored to life is another matter. The preface suggests a fundamentally pessimistic outlook.[126] The past had been better than the present. Moral decline came to Rome late, but it comes to all states. This mood recurs in several comments in the body of the History.[127] Descriptions like the *devotio* of Decius read like an attempt to evoke something which belonged to a long-vanished state of mind.[128] Such descriptions add archaic colour to the narrative. More significantly, they display valuable patriotic or moral attitudes.[129] But this does not necessarily mean that Livy thought that a revival of the rites would restore the attitudes in the very different Rome of his own time. The health of so political a religion could not be independent of that of the body politic as a whole.

This brings us to the question of Livy's attitude to Augustus and his revival of the Roman state.[130] The fact that Augustus remained on good personal terms with the historian by itself is enough to prove that Livy fully accepted the new system.[131] That Livy dared to continue his history into the present shows that he could not have been in any active sense an opponent of the Augustan principate.[132] One

---

[124] Symmachus, *Rel.* 3.        [125] *Praef.* 10.

[126] *Praef.* 4, 9, and 11. On this cf. Kajanto (1958: 55–63).

[127] As at 3.20.5; 4.6.12; 7.2.13; 7.25.9; note also 10.40. (This last is in a far from philosophical context: an *exemplum* to show that a magistrate is justified in acting on the report of favourable auspices even when the report is false, cf. Latte (1960a: 201–2). This is a moral which Livy cannot have taken quite seriously, and this reflects on every element of the narrative. A different view: Walsh 1961a: 51.) Again cf. 43.13.1. It has been noted that here Livy's pessimism exaggerates, cf. Latte (1960a: 289).

[128] 8.11.1.

[129] e.g. 1.21.4 (*fides*); 1.24.4–9; 1.32.5–14 (fetial procedure).

[130] See Walsh (1961a: 10–19), also in Dorey (1966: 118–20); also Mette (1961: 269–85) and Hoffmann (1954: 170–86).

[131] Tac., *Ann.* 4.34. Cf. his influence on the young Claudius: Suet., *Claud.* 41.1.

[132] Syme (1959: 27–87).

can understand the attitude. Like his contemporary authors, Livy was grateful for peace.[133] He will have sympathized with many of Augustus' measures; the establishment of order and the end of popular politics,[134] the moral legislation,[135] and the religious revival which was concerned with just the elements that had figured so largely in Livy's romantic reconstruction of an earlier Rome,[136] the restoration of temples and the resumption of long-interrupted rites. He had noted that the spirit of the old soldier-citizens had disappeared from the army and civil life, and is likely to have come to the conclusion that the size[137] of the Roman empire made a return to the old system impossible. Thus he may well have seen in the principate a further stage in the inevitable evolution of government which is the theme of two speeches in his narrative of the struggle of the Orders.[138] On the other hand, it is difficult to see how a man who gave so central a place to *libertas*[139] and to elected magistrates in his survey of Roman history, who ascribed Rome's greatness to a long succession of competent leaders rather than a few outstanding individuals,[140] and who in his account of the recent past had criticized Caesar and praised Pompey,[141] could have failed to recognize the true position of Augustus in 27 BCE. At first, gratitude and a real hope of the regeneration[142] of the Roman people may have been his dominant

[133] 1.19.3 (one of the remarkably few and widely separated compliments to Augustus. Others: 4.20.7; 28.12.12; *Per.* 59).
[134] Cf. the numerous unfriendly references to tribunes.
[135] See the extraordinary puritanism of 30.14.5; cf. also 10.23.1–10; the account of Lucretia, 1.57 ff.; of Verginia, 3.44–9; also 38.24, on the wife of Orgiago.
[136] Syme (1959: 55–6), including the fetial ceremony; Latte (1960a: 294 ff.).
[137] See Fraccaro (1956–7: i. 81–102). Size of empire: *praef.* 4.
[138] 4.4.4 (Canuleius)—cf. Syme (1959: 74)—and 10.8.9–12 (Decius Mus).
[139] 2.1.1–2.5.10; 2.15.3; 4.15.3; 6.19.6–7; 34.49; 45.17; 37.54. The point, often a very sharp one, is directed against *regnum*, which Augustus had been careful to avoid. But *libertas* had been the slogan of Brutus and Cassius. The relevance to Augustus could hardly be missed. Livy only qualifies his opposition to *regnum* by allowing it the task of training a people for liberty. 2.1.3–7 might justify a position like Augustus' for a limited period. 1.49.3–7 suggests what actions would make even such a position a tyranny.
[140] 9.17.5 ff.; 18.8 ff. (Alexander excursus). The point is also implicit in the strict annalistic form.
[141] Tac., *Ann.* 4.34.3. Sen., *QN* 5.184.
[142] In fact I know no passage suggesting the possibility of regeneration to balance the pessimism of passages cited in nn. 130–1 above, and some others in Fraccaro's paper (cited n. 137 above).

emotions. In the long run he can hardly have accepted the Principate as more than the inevitable solution to an intolerable situation.[143]


## ADDENDUM

It is around forty years since I wrote my chapter on Livy, published in 1967. Since then a lot has been written about Livy, but perhaps more important, the questions scholars ask have changed. My starting point was an interest in the author and the views that he was trying to communicate in his History. Meanwhile 'the author' has gone out of fashion and critics have been concerned to stress the inevitable ambiguity of any text, the near impossibility of gaining an objective reading of the author's original intention. What can be described objectively are the literary composition, and the rhetorical devices which the author has employed. Significantly Levene's *Religion in Livy*, the most substantial recent study of the subject, concludes that 'the search for the belief of Livy is illusory' (Levene (1993): 30). So by and large the search for the author has been abandoned, and research has concentrated on the construction of the work.

There also has been a change in the make-up of scholarly writing on Livy. Necessarily his History still is, and always will be, of interest to historians. The great historical commentary begun by Ogilvie (1965) and continued by Oakley (1997–2005) and Briscoe (1973, 1981, 2008) includes numerous commentaries on passages touching on religion. The recent synthesis on Roman religion, *Religions of Rome* by Beard, North, and Price (1998), necessarily draws a lot of material from Livy, and each of the passages cited in the source book, which is the second volume, is accompanied by a bibliography of relevant scholarly work. At the same time there has been a growth of interest in Livy as a literary artist. The majority of recent monographs have been concerned to analyse Livy's literary and rhetorical techniques,

---

[143] No book dealing with Augustus' Principate seems to have been published in Augustus' lifetime. Strangely enough the last published book dealt with the proscriptions, cf. Syme (1959: 39) on the superscription of *Per.* 121. Petersen (1961: 440–52) suggests that Liv. 1.49.1–7 on Tarquinius Superbus' relations with the Senate is an allusion to Augustus and hence advice and warning to the *princeps*.

and their effect on the reader. Luce's *Livy: The Composition of his History* (1977) has probably been the most influential work. It is a sensitive and perceptive discussion of the way Livy selected material from different and divergent older narratives to compose his own version of Roman history. Luce systematically illustrates how Livy's choice was often determined by considerations of historical probability, and sometimes with a view to literary effect. Forsythe (1999) has systematically examined all Livy's explanations of why he has preferred one version rather than another, and has thus put Luce's conclusions on a statistical basis.

In the last half-century the importance of religion in western society has declined to an extraordinary degree, with the result that it has become much less interesting to establish what notable figures in the past have thought about religion, even assuming it is possible to find out what their opinions were. The most substantial work on religion in Livy has been the book of Levene, mentioned earlier. It covers, if I may say so, more or less the same ground as my article, but does so on the basis of a wider and more systematic examination of Livy's text, and as a result has been able to reach more detailed and more fully documented conclusions. One important result is that as long as the supernatural plays any part at all within his work, he combines two equally strong indications: that the supernatural actually works within this world (as is established by the overall narrative), and that it is simply to be attributed to illusion or error on the part of those that perceive it (as established by explicit and implicit comments of an implied author with every claim to reliability: Levene (1993): 28). But this precise balancing of belief and scepticism is not maintained in the structuring of the narrative, for this gives the impression that impious or immoral behaviour almost invariably meets with punishment: 'Correct behaviour is identified with following of certain rules, both religious as narrowly defined, but also moral in a wider sense, such as appropriate behaviour in sexual and family matters, but above all in the political and military sphere. This morality is consistently linked with divine favour or disfavour, and consequent success or failure of Rome' (Levene (1993): 244).

The paradoxical combination of scepticism and full acceptance disappears in Davies (2004). For him Livy's treatment of religion is not a personal investigation into the question whether the claims of

Roman religion are true, but rather a full exposition of how Roman religion has worked in Roman history, as seen by someone fully committed to it. In the nature of things such a description necessarily includes many examples of abuse, misunderstanding, and political exploitation of the religion of the Roman people, none which however impairs its essential validity. The interpretation of Livy is argued against the background of a wider thesis on the place of religion in Roman historiography.

Livy's insistence that practice of the traditional religion and morality has been essential for Roman success is in line with Augustus' policy of religious and moral restoration, albeit that included a considerable amount of covert innovation. This might be taken to imply that Livy's History is Augustan propaganda, if it were not for the fact that the Roman political traditions upheld by Livy are so obviously republican. Haehling (1989) has argued that Livy's History supports Augustus, but only as an emergency regime. He is, as it were, a doctor who is forcing the Romans to take the remedies needed to cure vices which the Romans have found unsupportable, without being willing to accept the medicines they must take if they want to be cured (*Praef.* 9).

Livy's view of his duty as a historian is in some ways like, in others unlike, that of a modern historian. He genuinely tries to reconstruct the past, even the moral code of the past, as for instance in the greater prominence he has given to the virtue of *fides* as compared with *iustitia* (Moore (1989): esp. 35–50, 151–2). On the other hand he also values traditions for their own sake, and is anxious to record them irrespective of whether they correspond to what had actually happened Miles (1995). Moreover, Livy seems not to have discriminated against sources that had been compiled quite recently, and certainly long after the events that they purport to describe. But what from the modern point of view is a weakness made the work more interesting for its readers, because it gives the narrative of things long past contemporary relevance (Gutberlet (1985) and Wiseman (1979*a*): 1–139). For instance, by turning a blind eye to the date of his sources, Livy was able to introduce into his history of early Rome, the two opposing ideologies of the late Republic, that of the *populares* as well as that of the *optimates* (Wiseman (2004): *passim*).

W. L., *Nottingham*

# 14

## The Body Female and the Body Politic: Livy's Lucretia and Verginia

### S. R. Joshel

Brutus, while the others were absorbed in grief, drew out the knife from Lucretia's wound, and holding it up, dripping with gore, exclaimed, 'By this blood most chaste until a prince wronged it, I swear, and I take you, gods, to witness, that I will pursue Lucius Tarquinius Superbus and his wicked wife and all his children, with sword, with fire, aye with whatsoever violence I may; and that I will suffer neither them nor any other to be king in Rome!'

Livy 1.59.1, LCL[1]

Reality, robbed of its independent life, is shaped anew, kneaded into large, englobing blocks that will serve as the building material for a larger vista, a monumental world of the future... Empires can be built only on, and out of, dead matter. Destroyed life provides the material for their building blocks.

Klaus Theweleit, *Male Fantasies*

This essay has grown out of extended discussions with Amy Richlin, Avery Gordon, and Andrew Herman, and I have benefited from their insight, critical comments, and constructive suggestions. To each, a special thank you.

[1] Translations from ancient sources are the author's own, unless indicated otherwise. LCL refers to the Loeb Classical Library.

## PRETEXT: THE CONDITIONS OF A READING

I read Livy's history of Rome's origins, its earliest struggles with neighboring states, and the political events that formed the state that conquered an empire. The historian writes within an immediate past he regards as decadent, a fall from the glorious society of ancestors who made empire possible; he stands at a point where his Rome is about to be reinvigorated by a new imperial order. Raped, dead, or disappeared women litter the pages. The priestess Rhea Silvia, raped by the god Mars, gives birth to Rome's founder, Romulus, and leaves the story. The women of the neighboring Sabines are seized as wives by Romulus' wifeless men. When the Sabine soldiers come to do battle with the Romans, the Roman girl Tarpeia betrays her own menfolk by admitting their foes into the citadel. She is slain by the enemy she helped. By contrast, the Sabine women place their bodies between their kin and their husbands, offering to take on the violence the men would do to each other. Later, a young woman, named only as sister, is murdered by her brother Horatius because she mourns the fiancé he killed in single combat. 'So perish every Roman woman who mourns a foe!' he declares, and their father agrees that she was justly slain. Lucretia, raped by the king's son, calls on her menfolk to avenge her and commits suicide. The men overthrow the monarchy. Verginia, threatened with rape by a tyrannical magistrate, is killed by her father to prevent her violation. The citizen body ousts the magistrate and his colleagues. In these stories of early Rome, the death and disappearance of women recur periodically; the rape of women becomes the history of the state.[2]

I read Klaus Theweleit's study of Freikorps narratives, written by 'soldier males' who would become active Nazis. They write of World War I, of battling Reds, of living in a time they experience as chaotic and decadent in a Germany fallen from former greatness. Dead, disappeared, and silent women litter their texts. Sexually active

---

[2] Lavinia, daughter of King Latinus, married to Aeneas in order to cement an alliance between Latins and Trojans, disappears from the text (1.3.3), as do the politically and/or sexually active Tanaquil and Tullia (exiled 1.59.13). On this and related issues, see now Jed (1989) and Joplin (1990), which unfortunately appeared too late to be considered here.

working-class and communist women are slain brutally; chaste wives and sisters are made antiseptic, are killed tragically, or do not speak.

And I read Livy and Theweleit in the United States in the summer of 1987, at a time when the title of a recent Canadian film evokes what is often not explicit—*The Decline of the American Empire*. A time of concern about American power abroad and American life at home. The war against drugs and the battle against uncontrolled sex. Betsy North, Donna Rice, and Vanna White litter the TV screen, newspapers, and magazines. Betsy, silent and composed, sits behind her ramrod-straight husband, stiff and immaculate in his Marine uniform. Donna Rice appears in private, now public, photographs with Gary Hart; she has nothing to say. He gives up his candidacy for the presidency, guilty of extramarital sex. Vanna White turns letters on the popular game show 'Wheel of Fortune'. She does speak. 'I enjoy getting dressed as a Barbie doll', she tells an interviewer. An image on our TV screens gotten up like a doll that simulates a nonexistent woman named Barbie, she is rematerialized by her dress in some sort of fetishistic process: 'Speaking of *Vanna White*, a polyester magenta dress, one worn by the celebrated letter-turner, is on display at a Seattle espresso bar, where fans may touch it for 25 cents' (*Boston Globe*, June 9, 1987).

I look here at gender relations and images of women in Livy's history of early Rome, focusing on his tales of Lucretia and Verginia, but I do so within my own present. Freikorps narratives and the current mediascape are the 'conditions of my narrative', to borrow a phrase from Christa Wolf. I am not equating Rome, Fascist Germany, and the United States of the 1980s; nor am I making the images of women in their histories and fictions exactly analogous. By juxtaposing images, I raise questions about the representations of gender within visions of building and collapsing empires. As Theweleit suggests of fascism, the Roman fiction should be understood and combated not 'because it might "return again"', but primarily because, as a form of reality production that is constantly present and possible under determinate conditions, *it can, and does, become our production*' (1987–9: i. 221). Whether our own fictions include tales similar to Lucretia's and Verginia's with names changed or whether, as academics, we dissect Livy's tales, we retell the stories, bringing their gender images and relations into our present (cf. Theweleit (1987–9: i.265–89, 359)).

## LIVY AND THE CONDITIONS OF HIS NARRATIVE

Livy (64 BCE–CE 12) lived through the change from aristocratic Republic to Principate, a military dictatorship disguised in republican forms. For more than a century before Livy's birth, Rome's senatorial class had ruled an empire; by the time of his death, Rome, its political elite, and the empire were governed by one man. He grew up during the civil wars that marked the end of the Republic, and his adult years saw the last struggle of military dynasts, Octavian and Antony, and the reign of the first emperor, the victor in that struggle. Raised in a Padua known for its traditional morality, Livy was a provincial; he did not belong to the senatorial class and was uninvolved in politics, although he did have friendly relations with the imperial family (Ogilvie (1965: 1–5); Walsh (1961a); Syme (1959); see Phillips (1982: 1028), for bibliography).

Livy wrote the early books of his history after Octavian's victory over Antony and during the years in which Octavian became Augustus *princeps*—in effect, emperor (Phillips (1982: 1029), for the debate on the precise date). Shortly afterward came Augustus' restoration of the state religion and his program of social and moral reform which included new laws on marriage and adultery aimed primarily at the upper classes. The adultery law made sexual relations between a married woman and a man other than her husband a criminal offense. Ineffective and unpopular, the law nonetheless indicates the regime's concern with regulating sexuality, especially female (see Dixon (1988: 71 ff.)). The program was to return Rome to its ancestral traditions, renew its imperial greatness, and refound the state.

The state to be refounded was a Rome uncorrupted by wealth and luxury, greed and license, the supposed conditions of the late Republic. The stories in which Lucretia and Verginia figure record critical points in that state's formation, marking the origin of political and social forms which, along with the behavior of heroes, account for Rome's greatness and its rise to imperial power. The rape of Lucretia precipitates the fall of the monarchy and establishment of the Republic and the Roman version of liberty. The attempted rape of Verginia belongs to a struggle between privileged and unprivileged groups (patricians and plebeians) known as the

Conflict of the Orders; the event resulted in the overthrow of the
decemvirs, officials who had abused their original mission of codify-
ing the law, and began a long process of reform that eventually
changed the form of Roman political institutions.

To modern historians, Livy's stories of Lucretia and Verginia are
myths or, at best, legends that include some memory of actual events.
Current historical reconstructions of Rome in the late sixth and mid-
fifth centuries BCE, the society in which Lucretia and Verginia are
supposed to have lived, depend on archaeology, some early documents,
antiquarian notices in later authors (Heurgon (1973); Gjerstad (1955–
73); Bloch (1965); Raaflaub (1986b) for historical methodology), and,
as has recently been suggested, the 'structural facts' obtained when
Livy's accounts have been stripped of their 'narrative superstructure'
(Cornell (1986a: 61–76, esp. 73); Raaflaub (1986b: 49–50)). This evidence usually leaves us without a narrative or the names of agents (see
Raaflaub (1986b: 13–16)). But Livy invented neither the outline of
events nor the characters in his stories. First written down in the
third and second centuries BCE, the tales were perpetuated as part of
a living historical tradition by Roman writers of the early first century
BCE who were the major sources for Livy's retelling (for Livy's use of his
sources, see Ogilvie (1965); Walsh (1961a); Luce (1977)). The history of
the roughly contemporary Dionysius of Halicarnassus allows us to see
how Livy used the tradition.

This tradition 'was neither an authenticated official record nor an
objective critical reconstruction, but rather an ideological construct,
designed to control, to justify, and to inspire' (Cornell (1986a: 58)).
For historian and audience, the past provided the standards by which
to judge the present: the deeds of great ancestors offered models for
imitation and supported the claims of the ruling class to political
privilege and power. Each historian infused his version of events with
his own (and his class's) literary, moral, and political concerns. The
past, Cornell notes, 'was subject to a process of continuous transformation as each generation reconstructed the past in its own
image' (1986a: 58). For many modern historians, Livy's account of
early Rome better reflects the late Republic than the late sixth and
fifth centuries BCE (Raaflaub (1986b: 23)).

Even if we view Livy's 'description of the monarchy and early
Republic as prose epics or historical novels' (Raaflaub (1986b: 8)), we

should not ignore the power of his fictions of Lucretia and Verginia. For Livy, they were history, and, as history, they should inform a way of life in an imperial Rome ripe for refounding. In good Roman fashion, Livy views history as a repository of illustrative behaviors and their results: 'What chiefly makes the study of history wholesome and profitable is this, that you behold the lessons of every kind of experience set forth on a conspicuous monument; from these you may choose for yourself and for your state what to imitate, from these mark for avoidance what is shameful in conception and shameful in the result' (*Praef.* 10, LCL). Before he begins his historical narrative per se, Livy urges a particular kind of reading. His stories will proffer an array of subject positions, beliefs, and bodily practices. The reader should recognize and identify with them and should understand the consequences of assuming particular subject positions. Bodily practices fit into a vision of building and collapsing empire: some result in imperial power; others bring decadence and destruction. The reader should pay close attention to 'what life and morals were like; through what men and by what policies, in peace and in war, empire was established and enlarged; then let him note how, with the gradual relaxation of discipline, morals first gave way, as it were, then sank lower and lower, and finally began the downward plunge which has brought us to the present time, when we can endure neither our vices nor their cure' (*Praef.* 9, LCL).

Thus, the question for us is not whether victims, villains, and heroes are fictional, but the way Livy tells their story, offering up a blueprint for his imperial present.

## LIVY'S STORIES OF LUCRETIA AND VERGINIA: RAPE, DEATH, AND ROMAN HISTORY

### Lucretia and the Fall of the Monarchy (1.57–60)

In 509 BCE, the king of Rome, Lucius Tarquinius Superbus, wages war on Ardea in the hope that the booty will lessen the people's resentment at the labor he has imposed on them. During the siege of the city, at a drinking party, the king's sons and their kinsman Collatinus argue over who has the best wife. On Collatinus' suggestion, they decide to settle the question by seeing what their wives are doing. They find the princes' wives enjoying themselves at a banquet with their friends; Collatinus's wife, Lucretia, surrounded by her maids, spins by lamplight in her front hall. Lucretia makes her husband the victor in the wife contest. One of the princes, Sextus Tarquinius, inflamed by Lucretia's beauty and her proven chastity, is seized by a desire to have her. A few days later, without Collatinus' knowledge, he returns to Collatia, where he is welcomed as a guest. That night when the household is asleep, he draws his sword and wakes the sleeping Lucretia. Neither his declarations of love nor his threats of murder nor his pleas move the chaste Lucretia. She submits only when he threatens to create an appearance of disgraceful behavior: he will kill her and a slave and leave the slave's naked body next to hers, so that it will look as if they had been slain in the act of adultery.[3] After the rape, she sends for her husband and her father, instructing them to come with a trusted friend (Collatinus brings Lucius Junius Brutus). To her husband's question 'Is it well with you?' she answers, 'What can be well with a woman who has lost her chastity? The mark of another man is in your bed. My body only is violated; my mind is guiltless; death will be my witness. Swear that the adulterer will be punished— he is Sextus Tarquinius.' The men swear and try to console her, arguing that the mind sins, not the body. She responds, 'You will determine what is due him. As for me, although I acquit myself of fault, I do not free myself from punishment. No unchaste woman will live with Lucretia as a precedent.' Then she kills herself with a knife she had hidden beneath her robe. While her husband and father grieve, Brutus draws the weapon from Lucretia's body and swears on her blood to destroy the monarchy. Lucretia's body, taken into the public square of Collatia, stirs the populace; Brutus incites the men to take up arms and overthrow the king. Brutus marches to Rome, and in the Forum the story of Lucretia and Brutus' speech have the same effect. The king is exiled, the monarchy ended; the Republic begins with the election of two consuls, Brutus and Collatinus.

---

[3] By 'submits' (or, later, 'gives in'), I do not intend to imply consent on Lucretia's part (*contra* Donaldson (1982: 24) and Bryson (1986: 165–6)). To speak of consent in conditions of force and violence is meaningless; in Lucretia's situation, it seems perverse. She can die or live through the rape only to defend her honor by suicide.

## Verginia and the Fall of the Decemvirate (3.44–58)

In 450 BCE, the decemvirs have taken control of the state. They have displaced the consuls and the tribunes, protectors of the rights of plebeians. The chief decemvir, Appius Claudius, desires the beautiful young Verginia, daughter of the plebeian centurion Lucius Verginius. When Appius fails to seduce her with money or promises, he arranges to have Marcus Claudius, his *cliens* (a dependent tied to a more powerful man or an ex-master), claim Verginia as his (Marcus') slave while her father is away at war (apparently the client will give the young woman to his patron Appius). Marcus grabs Verginia as she enters the Forum. When the cries of her nurse draw a crowd, Marcus hauls her before Appius' court. The decemvir postpones his decision until her father arrives but orders Verginia turned over to the man who claims her as his slave until the case can be tried. An impassioned speech by Verginia's fiancé Icilius incites the crowd; Appius rescinds his order. The next day, Verginius leads his daughter into the Forum, seeking support from the crowd. Unmoved by appeals or weeping women, Appius adjudges Verginia a slave, but he grants Verginius' request for a moment to question his daughter's nurse in Verginia's presence. Verginius leads his daughter away. Grabbing a knife from a butcher's shop, he cries, 'In the only way I can, my daughter, I claim your freedom', and kills her. Icilius and Publius Numitorius, Verginia's grandfather (?), show the lifeless body to the populace and stir them to action. Verginius escapes to the army, where his bloodstained clothes, the knife, and his speech move his fellow soldiers to revolt. The decemvirate is overthrown, and when the tribunate is restored, Verginia's father, fiancé, and grandfather (?) are elected to office.

## FLOOD: BODILY DESIRE AND POLITICAL CATASTROPHE

Livy's narrative of Rome's political transformation revolves around chaste, innocent women raped and killed for the sake of preserving the virtue of the body female and the body politic; Roman men stirred to action by men who take control; and lustful villains whose desires result in their own destruction. Although the basic elements of Rome's early legends were present in Livy's sources, he could have dispensed with the tales in abbreviated fashion or minimized the role of women in stories of political change. Instead, he carefully constructs tragedies, drawing on all the literary techniques and models so meticulously noted by scholars (Ogilvie (1965: 218–32, 476–88); Phillips (1982: 1036–7) for bibliography). Why *this* writing of Roman history in Livy's present?

Livy's view of the immediate past engages him in Rome's ancient history. He elaborates that history, because he finds pleasure in it and relief from recent civil war, social upheaval, and military disaster:

> To most readers the earliest origins and the period immediately succeeding them will give little pleasure, for they will be in haste to reach these modern times, in which the might of a people which has long been very powerful is working its own undoing. I myself, on the contrary, shall seek in this an additional reward for my toil, that I may avert my gaze from the troubles which our age has been witnessing for so many years, so long at least as I am absorbed in the recollection of the brave days of old. (*Praef.* 4–5, LCL)

'The troubles' haunted male authors of the first century BCE— Sallust, Cicero, Horace, and Livy himself. As in the imagination of Theweleit's Freikorps writers, political chaos and military failure are associated with immorality. Although this vision is familiar to modern historians of ancient Rome, the strikingly similar images of chaos and men's experience in Weimar Germany compel reconsideration of the Roman images. I attend here only to how two elements, marked in these tales of origin, both deaden and kill: male excess and female unchastity.

Ancient authors attributed the crises of the late Republic to political ambition and to male bodies out of control in the social world, guilty of, in Livy's words, *luxus, avaritia, libido, cupiditas, abundantes voluptates* (luxurious living, avarice, lust, immoderate desire, excessive pleasures). Uncontrolled bodies bring personal ruin and general disaster (*Praef.* 11–12). For his contemporary Horace (*Odes* 3.6.19–20; cf. 1.2), disaster floods country and people. The body and its pleasures are present only as excess in this vision. The slightest infraction seems dangerous. A single vice can slip into another or into a host of moral flaws, as in Livy's description of Tarquinius Superbus and his son Sextus (Phillipides (1983: 114, 117)). Any desire becomes avarice or lust and must be rooted out.

> The seeds of vicious avarice
>     must be rooted up, and our far too delicate
> characters must be moulded by
>     sterner training.
> Horace, *Odes* 3.24.51–4 (trans. Clancy)

Men of the Freikorps feared a 'Red' flood affecting the entire society, 'piercing through the ancient dam of traditional state authority' (Theweleit (1987–9: i.231); see 385 ff., esp. 392, for Freikorps images of chaos). It 'brought all of the worse instincts to the surface, washing them up on the land' (Theweleit (1987–9: i.231)). Ultimately, comments Theweleit (231), this flood flows 'from inside of those from whom the constraint of the old order has been removed'. A man could feel 'powerless' and 'defenseless' before what flows—fearful yet fascinated. The flood solidifies in a morass; men can hardly extract themselves from a mire that softness produces within them (404, 388). Indulgence must be rooted out: 'If you want to press on forward, you cannot allow this mire of failure of the will to form inside you. The most humane way is still to go for the beast's throat, to pull the thing out by its roots' (388). The 'defense against suffocation in flabby self-indulgence and capriciousness' (389) lies in toughness and self-control: men should 'stand fast . . . think of, and believe in, the nation' (405).

Livy focuses on what he imagines to be the ancient and necessary virtue of the soldier: *disciplina*. Roman tradition offered him tales of discipline instilled by floggings, sons executed by fathers to preserve *disciplina* for the state, and men hardened to fight both the enemy without and the weakness within themselves (see Valerius Maximus, 2.7.1–15, esp. 2.7.6, 2.7.9, 2.7.10). Neither exceptional bravery nor victory should be allowed to undermine *disciplina*. When Livy's Manlius Torquatus orders the execution of his own son because, although successful in battle, he had ignored a direct order that no one was to engage the enemy, he makes the execution and the sacrifice of his own feelings a model for future generations of Roman men:

As you have held in reverence neither consular authority nor a father's dignity, and ... have broken military discipline, whereby the Roman state has stood until this day unshaken, thus compelling me to forget either the Republic or myself, we will sooner endure the punishment of our wrong-doing than suffer the Republic to expiate our sins at a cost so heavy to herself; we will set a stern example, but a salutary one, for the young men of the future. For my own part, I am moved, not only by a man's instinctive love of his children, but by this instance you have given of your bravery. ... But ... the authority of the consuls must either be established by your death, or by your impunity be forever abrogated, and ... I think you yourself, if you have a drop of my blood in you, would not refuse to raise up by your punishment the military discipline which through your misdemeanour has slipped and fallen. (8.7.15–19, LCL)

Whatever his motives (8.7.4–8), the son had not simply disobeyed his commander and father; implicitly, he had failed to maintain the necessary self-control.

In Livy's view, control must be absolute. A slight crack in the edifice brings down the entire structure. *Disciplina* resulted in conquest; its gradual relaxation precipitated a slide, then collapse (*Praef.* 9)— personal, social, political. A man, and Rome, would seem to have a choice between obdurate victor and pusillanimous loser, between fighter and pulp in the Freikorps vision (cf. Valerius Maximus, 2.7.9 and Theweleit (1987–9: i.395)).

The heroes of Livy's history, the men who act when women are made dead, are disciplined and unyielding. Noble Brutus chastised men for their tears and idle complaints (1.59.4) when they lamented Lucretia's death and their own miseries. He urged them as men and Romans to take up arms. Later, he would administer as consul and suffer as father the scourging and execution of his own sons as traitors. Founder of the Republic and the consulship, he is a model for future consuls and fathers, like Torquatus, whose defense of the state's tradition and existence will require dead sons and numbed affections. No *luxus* here or in the likes of Cocles, Scaevola, and Cincinnatus. These men are stern and self-controlled, bodies hardened to protect Rome and fight its wars. They must have been to have become the foremost people of the world (*Praef.* 3)—the rulers of world empire. Like Virgil's Aeneas, Trojan ancestor of the Romans, conceived within a few years of Livy's heroes, they endure pain and adversity to create a Rome whose imperial power is portrayed as destiny (*Aeneid* 1.261–79): 'so great was the effort to found the Roman race' (*Aeneid* 1.33). So disciplined, so self-controlled, so annealed, the body as a living, feeling, perceiving entity almost disappears.

Livy's instructions to imitate virtue and avoid vice invoke the *mos maiorum*—the way of the ancestors as a guide for the present. Bodily excess as manifested in the lust of Tarquin and Appius Claudius brings personal ruin and the collapse of their governments. Not incidentally, at the same time, Rome's wars with its neighbors are waged unsuccessfully. Tarquin desires Lucretia during the inactivity (*otium*) of a long siege which is blamed on the king's extravagance and his consequent need for booty. His avarice and his son's lust become 'two sides of the same coin, a metaphor of the City's moral sickness', and explain Rome's military failure (Phillipides (1983: 114–15)). For the sake of Rome's martial and moral health, father and son as desiring agents must go (Phillipides (1983: 114)). The actions of disciplined men like Brutus result in personal success and Roman power. They set the example for Livy's present: the male body must be indifferent to material and sexual desire.

So Woman poses a particular problem.[4] The Roman discourse on chaos often joins loose women with male failure to control various appetites.[5] Uncontrolled female sexuality was associated with moral decay, and both were seen as the roots of social chaos, civil war, and military failure.

> Breeder of vices, our age has polluted
> first marriage vows and the children and the home;
> from this spring, a river of ruin
>     has flooded our country [*patria*, lit. 'fatherland'] and our people.
> Horace, *Odes* 3.6.17–20 (trans. Clancy)

---

[4] I distinguish an individual woman or women from Woman, 'a fictional construct, a distillate from diverse but congruent discourses dominant in Western cultures' (De Lauretis (1984: 5)).

[5] Appetites include a decadent concern with food, table servants, and dining accoutrements. For discussion and sources on Roman luxury and decadence, see Earl (1961: 41 ff.) and (1967: 17–20); and Griffin (1976). Uncontrolled sexuality and decadent eating fit Lévi-Strauss's observation of a 'very profound analogy which people throughout the world seem to find between copulation and eating' (1966: 105). See Modleski's analysis of the 'ambivalence towards femininity' played out in a woman's function 'as both edible commodity and inedible pollutant' in Alfred Hitchcock's *Frenzy* (1988: 101–14).

Livy's view of control makes it appropriate that his narrative tends toward a simple dichotomous vision of female sexuality: woman is or is not chaste.

This vision may account for the satisfaction Livy's tales find in the point of the knife. Where he omits words about forced penetration, he offers a precise image of the dagger piercing Lucretia's body and her death (1.58.11; cf. Verginia, 3.48.5). Perhaps that knife is aimed at 'any unchaste woman', real or imagined, of Livy's age (cf. Freikorps worship of asexual 'high-born' women and attack on sexual 'low-born' women; Theweleit (1987–9: i.79 ff., 315 ff., esp. 367)). In Rome's imagined past, the knife constructs absolute control. It eradicates unchastity and kills any anomaly in female sexuality, such as the contradiction between Lucretia's violated body and her guiltless mind, or the blurring between the 'good' and the 'evil' woman (see Theweleit (1987–9: i.183)).

In Livy, the 'good' woman's threatening element is her attractiveness. While Livy never explicitly questions the innocence and chaste spirit of Verginia or Lucretia, the beauty of each woman is marked and explains the rapists' actions. Lust seizes each man, as if desire originated outside him in beauty (1.57.10; 3.44.2). If, as the object of desire, a woman's beauty is the condition of male lust, then good as well as evil men are potentially affected. Her existence threatens men's *disciplina*. 'The affective mode of self-defense in which [the annihilation of women] occurs seems to be made up of *fear* and *desire*' (Theweleit (1987–9: i.183)). Once Woman has played her role—to attract the villain whose actions set in motion other active males who construct the state, empire, and therefore history in the Roman sense—she must go.

As Theweleit suggests, what is at issue in this construction is male uncontrol. 'What really started swimming were the men's boundaries—the boundaries of their perceptions, the boundaries of their bodies' (1987–9: i.427). The dagger stems the flood, at least in the imagination. In effect, the aggression men visit on women is really aimed at their own bodies (note Theweleit (1987–9: i.427, 154–5)). Woman must die in order to deaden the male body. Aggression toward Woman and self produces *disciplina* (or is it the other way around?). The pathos of Livy's stories displaces the relief at the removal of the threatening element. 'How tragic!' sigh author and reader, finding pleasure in the pain of noble loss. Ultimately, the pleasure of the narrative lies in killing what lives: women, the image of Woman as the object of desire, and male desire itself.

Discipline was necessary not only for the acquisition of empire but also for ruling it. The denial of the body to the self speaks the denial of social power to others; a Roman's rule of his own body provides an image of Roman domination and a model of sovereignty—of Roman over non-Roman, of upper class over lower, of master over slave, of man over woman, and of Princeps over everyone else (note Livy's use of a Greek metaphor likening a disordered body to the plebs' revolt against the *patres*, 2.32.9–12). In particular, the morality of control served Rome's new ruler. Augustus presented the required image of control and sacrifice (*Res Gestae* 4–6, 34; Suetonius *Augustus* 31.5, 33.1, 44–5, 51–8, 64.2–3, 65.3, 72–3, 76–7; cf. 71); denial and the morality of control enabled his authority to be 'implanted into subjects' bodies in the form of a lack in overflowing' (Theweleit 1987–9: i. 414). In the Princeps' new order, there were to be no more selfish desires like those which had precipitated civil war. Woman was to be returned to her proper place. Marriage was to be regulated by the state; women's sexuality was to form the images and establish the boundaries so necessary to secure Rome's domination of others and Augustus' structuring of power. Harnessed, chaste, and deadened, Woman became the matter of a new order designed to control men and the free movement of all bodies. 'Women within the new state once again provide the building blocks for internal boundaries against life' (Theweleit (1987–9: i.366)).

## WOMAN AS SPACE: NOT A ROOM OF HER OWN

Within imperial constructions and the political context of the late first century BCE, Livy's account of early Rome creates Woman and her chastity as space, making her a catalyst for male action. She embodies the space of the home, a boundary, and a buffer zone. She is also a blank space—a void, for Livy effectively eliminates her voice, facilitating the perpetuation of male stories about men.

As is well known, a woman's chastity is associated with the honor of her male kin (Dixon (1982); Ortner (1978)). Lucretia's behavior makes her husband the victor (*victor maritus*) in a contest between men (1.57). The praise awarded her is for chastity, measured by conduct outside the bedroom. Lucretia, spinning and alone but for her maids, acts out the traditional virtues of the good wife; the princes' wives, banqueting with friends, presumably display Woman's traditional vice, drinking wine, an offense tantamount to adultery (Watson (1975: 36–8); MacCormack (1975: 170–4)). Verginia's fiancé Icilius (3.45.6–11) equates an assault on female chastity with violence done to male bodies and accuses Appius Claudius of making the eradication of tribunes (whose bodies were sacrosanct) and the right of appeal, defenses of men's *libertas*, an opportunity for *regnum vestrae libidini* ('a tyranny of your lust').

The association of male honor and female chastity makes a different kind of sense when we observe the narrative role of other women in Livy's early books. Women function as obstacles or embody spaces, often between and separating men. The Sabines put their bodies between their battling fathers and new husbands, offering to take on the anger the men feel toward one another and the violence they would inflict (1.13.1–4). Tarpeia fails to use her body in this way. Bribed by the Sabine king when she fetches water outside the city wall, the girl admits Rome's enemies into the citadel (1.11.6–9). The women whose actions preserve the physical integrity of both husbands and fathers are treasured by both; the girl whose treachery leaves her male kin vulnerable is crushed by the very enemy she aided.

As Natalie Kampen has pointed out, Tarpeia crosses the boundary of the city and appropriate behavior; the Sabines make themselves a boundary between warring men and observe appropriate behavior (1986: 10). If the issue is the control of female sexuality, control means the deployment of the female body in relations between men. Proper deployment founds relations between men, making society possible in Lévi-Strauss's terms (1969; cf. Mitchell (1975: 370–6)). Not surprisingly, friezes depicting these tales 'appeared at the very heart of the nation in the Forum', thus violating a convention that made women 'extremely rare in public state-funded Roman sculpture' (Kampen (1986: 1, 3)). Kampen dates the friezes to 14–12 BCE, arguing that these representations served Augustus' moral and social program (5 ff.). In effect, the friezes made visible the narrative role of women in Livy's story of origin: within an emergent imperial order, women are fixed within the frame as boundary and space.

The move from animate life to inanimate matter is repeated in etymology. In each case, the Romans used a story of Woman's body to explain the name of a fixture of Rome: from Tarpeia the name of a place, the Tarpeian rock associated with the punishment of traitors, and from the Sabines the names of political divisions of citizens (the *curiae*). Whether the story follows the naming or vice versa, women's bodies literally become building material—the stuff of physical and political topography. Women who are supposed to have lived are transformed into places and spaces.

The Sabines, *matronae* (respectable married women) who voluntarily take up proper control of their own bodies, are reflected in Lucretia, the noble wife who will herself act and speak the proper use of her body. Tarpeia, *virgo* (unmarried girl) in need of paternal control, finds her counterpart in Verginia, whose father administers the necessary disposal of his daughter's body. Livy's *matrona* and *virgo* become spaces within the husband's or father's home. Unlike Dionysius of Halicarnassus (4.66.1), Livy never moves Lucretia out of Collatinus' house. She appears fixed in every scene—spinning in her hall, sleeping and pinned to the bed by Tarquin, and sitting in her bedroom when her kin come to her after the rape. This fixity in space informs her identity in the narrative and constitutes the grounds for male praise (1.57.9). And Verginius (3.50.9) literally equates his daughter with a place within his home (*locum in domo sua*).

In both narratives, the space that is Woman is equated with a chastity that should render the space of the home or between men impenetrable. Thus, rape or attempted rape appears as the penetration of space. The chastity of both women is described as a state of obstinacy or immobility (1.58.3–4, 5; 3.44.4). However, alone or accompanied only by women, wife and daughter are vulnerable to non-kin males who can use force combined with the threat of shame or the power of the state in order to satisfy their lust. Lucretia is a place where Tarquin intends to stick his sword or his penis. She appears as an obstacle to his desire, impenetrable even at the threat of death. When she gives way at the threat of a shame worse than rape, Tarquin conquers (*vicisset, expugnato*) not a person but her chastity (*pudicitiam, decore*). The rape of a Lucretia fixed in and identified with Collatinus' home seems equivalent to a penetration of his private sphere, his territory.

Male heroes, not raped women, carry forward the main trajectory of Livy's work—the history of the Roman state (see De Lauretis (1984: 109–24) on Oedipal narratives). They lead citizen males to overthrow a tyrannical ruler, advancing from the sphere of the home to that of the state, from private vengeance to public action. The transition from domestic to political is represented in a shift in the scene of action from Collatia and the private space of Collatinus' home to Rome and the public space of the Forum. Brutus, not Lucretia (1.59.5; cf. Dionysius 4.66.1), effects the change of scene, just as he transposes her request for the punishment of the rapist to his own demand for the overthrow of the monarchy. His oath of vengeance begins with the determination to avenge Lucretia and finishes not with an oath to dethrone Tarquin's family but with the promise to end the institution of monarchy itself.

The connection between the rape of an individual woman and the overthrow of monarchy and decemvirate finds its model in the Greek stereotype of the tyrant whose part Tarquin and Appius Claudius play (Ogilvie (1965: 195–7, 218–19, 453, 477); Dunkle (1971: 16)): they are violent and rape other men's women.[6] Livy's rewriting of the Greek paradigm, however, has a particularly Roman subtext: imperial conquest and its product, large-scale slavery. In both tales, men complain that they, Roman soldiers, are treated as Rome's enemies (1.59.4), the conquered (3.47.2, 3.57.3, 3.61.4), or slaves (1.57.2, 59.4, 59.9, 3.45.8). In effect, king and decemvir behave as if citizen males, like slaves, lacked physical integrity. Very importantly, the 'slave' makes possible the victimization of both women. Lucretia gives in

---

[6] It is well known that Livy drew on other paradigms and stereotypes, literary genres, and Hellenistic historical practices; however, for my purposes, tracing the elements from diverse sources is less important than how they work within Livy's historical discourse. As Phillipides (1983: 119 n. 20) points out, 'the elements taken from a prior sign system acquire a different significance when transposed into the new sign system'. Following Julia Kristeva, she notes that 'this process of transformation involves the destruction of the old and the formation of a new signification'.

when Tarquin threatens to kill her in a simulation of adultery with a slave. Appius Claudius intends to rape Verginia by having her adjudicated a slave, thus legally vulnerable to a master's sexual use (cf. Dionysius 11.29–33, making clear the issue of the slave's lack of physical integrity). Tarquin, his father, and Appius Claudius are made to do to Lucretia, Verginia, and their male kin what Roman 'soldier males' do to the conquered. Roman wives and children are assimilated to the conquered and slaves (3.57.4, 61.4), and the physical vulnerability of the latter is unquestioned. This was the empire that needed *disciplina*.

Verginia's story sets out a logic of bodies: between the rape of a woman and direct violence to the bodies of her male kin lies male action. 'Vent your rage on our backs and necks: let chastity at least be safe', Icilius exclaims to Appius Claudius early in Livy's account (3.45.9). Verginia's betrothed offers to substitute male for female bodies. Appius' lust, inflicted on wives and children, should be channeled into violence, inflicted on husbands and fathers. The switch never occurs, because male action intervenes and removes the source of lust and violence. At the end, Icilius, Verginius, and Numitorius are alive, well, and sacrosanct tribunes; chastity is safe; Verginia is dead.

But Verginia's father makes clear that her rape poses a direct threat to the male body. After slaying her, he states that there is no longer a *locus* in his home for Appius' lust, and he now intends to defend his own body as he had defended his daughter's (3.50.9). The buffer between himself and Appius is gone.[7] Woman's chastity signifies her, and hence his, imperviousness to assault; her rape endangers his body. Thus, the raped woman becomes a *casus belli*, a catalyst for a male response which stems the threatened violence. Men halt the invasion before it gets to them.

Icilius' speech suggests the nature of the threat to the male body (see Douglas (1984: 133 ff.) and Donaldson (1982: 23–5), on the fear

---

[7] Ironically, the removal of Woman in both stories returns Roman 'soldier males' to the conditions of their mythical *patres* Romulus and Remus, two men without a woman, not even a mother, between them (1.6.4–7.3). Quite literally, the twins try to occupy the same space at the same time and do violence to each other. Like the Romans and the Sabines, they cannot coexist without the body of woman between them, without the space and place of 'not us'.

of pollution). His words effect a displacement.[8] As 'rage' (*saevire*) replaces rape, male necks and backs replace female genitals. Although rage and lust seem interchangeable, Icilius' proffered exchange excludes an assault on the body's most vulnerable place—its orifices (Douglas (1984: 121)). The very substitution of necks and backs for orifices masks an apprehension about male vulnerability: invasion of woman as boundary threatens penetration of the male body (see Richlin (1983: 57–63, 98–9)).

In Livy's accounts, men experience the offense of rape as tragedy. They grieve and are moved, but they do not directly suffer invasion; they remain intact. Moreover, they can feel like men, because they have taken out their own swords. In a most satisfying way, the invader loses ultimate control of the woman's body. While Appius Claudius and Tarquin wield their penises or try to, the father and, even better, the woman herself wield the knife.

Male action against the tyrant (it should be emphasized) begins not with rape but with the woman's death. Narratively, it appears as if Lucretia and Verginia must die in order for male action to begin and for the story to move on. Three logics seem to account for the slaying of the women and explain why the violence done to woman does not end with rape.

In the first place, a living Lucretia or Verginia would stand as evidence of disorder and chaos (see above on Horace *Odes* 3.6). Livy's Verginius and Icilius speak of the social disorder Appius Claudius' desire introduces for the men of their order and the destruction of the social ties between them. Verginius accuses Appius of instituting an order of nature—rushing into intercourse without distinction in the manner of animals (3.47.7). By killing his daughter, he halts the plunge into animality. Of course, animality and the disorder it signals mean that father and husband no longer control the bodies of 'their' women. Appius robs Verginius of the

---

[8] Tales of male bodies that suffer violence and penetration focus on those who occupy the place of the son *in potestate*—sons killed by stern fathers and young men raped (often unsuccessfully) by evil army officers and magistrates (Valerius Maximus 5.8.1–5, 6.1.5, 7, 9–12); see Richlin (1983: 220–6, esp. 225–6). In effect, Roman patriarchy associates all women with sons in paternal power. Apprehension about their vulnerability to aggressive non-kin males would seem to stem from the 'rightful' power that fathers (and husbands) wielded over their bodies.

ability to give his daughter in marriage to a man of his choosing
(3.47.7). Icilius loses a bride *intacta*, and the bond between Icilius
and Verginius would be flawed if Verginius offered him 'damaged
goods'. Icilius asserts that *he* is going to marry Verginia, and *he*
intends to have a chaste bride (3.45.6–11). He will not allow his
bride to spend a single night outside her father's home (3.45.7).
Appius denies plebeian males membership in a patriarchal order.
And where the decemvir offends an already existing patriarchal order,
only the political change motivated by his assault on the chastity of a
plebeian woman assures paternal power to the men of her social
class. In versions of the story earlier than Livy's first-century sources,
Verginia was a patrician. By changing her status, Livy's sources
invested meanings from current political struggles into the fifth-
century Conflict of the Orders (Ogilvie (1965: 477)). Yet the updated
political story is essentially a story about patriarchy, for the political
events turn on the control of a daughter's/bride's body.

   Second, alive, the raped woman would constitute another sort of
threat: once invaded, the buffer zone becomes harmful to what it/she
once protected. If women are boundaries, rape, which assaults an
orifice, a marginal area of the body, creates a special vulnerability for
the 'center', that is, men. The danger of a living Verginia is noted
above. Her life is dearer than her father's own, but only if she is chaste
and 'free' (3.50.6), a body intact whose access lies in her father's
control. A raped Lucretia, still alive, would display the violation of
her husband's home. The mark of another man in Collatinus' bed
apparently cannot be erased, at least not without his wife's death.
Livy's Lucretia speaks as if she and the marked bed are one: although
her mind is guiltless, her body is violated and soiled. Only death,
self-inflicted, can display her innocence (1.58.7). Soiled, the body
must go (see Douglas (1984: 113, 136), on inadvertent pollution and
efforts made to align inward heart and public act).

   For history to be a source of models for emulation (*Praef.* 10), it
must demonstrate an unequivocal pattern. The relation of a moral
present to its imagined origins constructs chastity as an absolute
quality (see Dixon 1982: 4). The pleas of Lucretia's husband and
father that the mind, not the body, sins frame her suicide as a tragic
martyrdom. Correcting them, Lucretia makes herself an *exemplum*:
'no unchaste woman will live with Lucretia as a precedent' (1.58.10).

On the surface, the pleas of father and husband imply that men do not require Lucretia's death: suicide appears as woman's choice. This construction of female choice and agency disguises the male necessity at work in Lucretia's eradication. Alive, even Lucretia would confront a patriarchal order with a model, an excuse, for the woman unchaste *by volition*. Lucretia's statement admits no distinction: her suicide leaves no anomaly for the patriarchal future.

Third, and perhaps most important for the narrative: dead, the female body has other purposes. Dead, the woman whose chastity had been assaulted assumes other values. Dead, her body can be deployed, and the sight of it enjoyed, by all men. Without the stabbing of Lucretia and Verginia, there is no bloodied knife, no blood to swear on, no corpse to display to the masses. Brutus, Icilius, and Numitorius use the dead female body to incite themselves and other men (1.59.3, 3.48.7). The woman's blood enlivens men's determination to overthrow the tyrant. Her raped or almost raped and stabbed body kindles thoughts of men's own sufferings and feeds mass male action (note Theweleit (1987–9: i.34, 105–6)); in an almost vampiric relation, the living are enlivened by the dead. He becomes free (i.e., comes alive) when she becomes an inert, unliving object.

Actually, Livy's narrative deadens both women before the knife ever pierces them (Theweleit (1987–9: i.90 ff.)). Lucretia is introduced as an object in a male contest, as Verginia is an object of contention, pulled this way and that by the men who would claim her body. In the rape scene, Lucretia is inert; appropriately, she sees death from the moment Tarquin enters her bedroom. The stories 'record the living as that which is condemned to death' (Theweleit (1987–9: i.217)). Narratively, Lucretia and Verginia become ever more dead, as action moves progressively further from them: from the sight of their deaths to the bloodstained knife to the raped, almost raped dead body to the story of that body told to men not present at the murder. The farther removed from the body, the wider the audience, the more public the action, and ultimately the larger the arena of Roman conquest and rule. Male action secures the form of the Roman state and *libertas*. Most immediately, this results in 'soldier males' winning wars that, until these episodes, were stalemated.

The tragic effects and pathos evoked by the woman's death veil the necessary central operation of the narrative: to create a purely public (and male) arena. Although presented as tragedies, Lucretia's suicide and Verginia's slaying remove the women from the scene, from between men. With the buffering space gone, there will now ensue a 'real' struggle between men, a struggle that moves forward the central narrative, that of state and empire (on the primacy of public and male concerns, see 3.48.8–9 and Theweleit (1987–9: i.88)).

While consulship, tribunate, Senate, and assemblies mark the shape of the state whose development Livy traces, each rape, each body willing to bear the wounds men would inflict on each other, and each dead body sets in place a block of a patriarchal and imperial order. The rape of Rhea Silvia gives the Roman state its *pater* (no room here for a queen mother). The rape of the Sabine women makes possible patriarchy by supplying it with its one necessary component: the women who produce children. Lucretia and Verginia precipitate the overthrow of a tyrant and the confirmation, or indeed establishment, of patriarchy for patricians and then plebeians. Assured at home that their wives and children will not be treated as the conquered, these men can go forth, conquer an empire, and do to other men and women what they would not have done to their own wives and children.

It is in this context that we should see the silence in Livy's narrative, the silence of Lucretia and Verginia, and the dead matter these women become. Verginia never speaks or acts. Livy remarks on her obstinacy in the face of Appius' attempted seduction, although, in fact, he speaks not of her but of her *pudor* (3.44.4). When Appius' client grabs her, her fear silences her; her nurse, not Verginia, cries out for help. The girl is led here and there by kin or grabbed by Appius' client. There is no notice of tears, clinging, or interaction with her father, as in Dionysius' telling (11.31.3, 32.1, 35, 37.4–5). Even the women who surround her are moving by the *silence* of their tears (3.47.4). At the moment she would become a slave, Appius shouts, the crowd parts, the girl stands alone *praeda iniuriae* ('prey to sexual assault', 3.48.3). A moment of silence. Her father takes Verginia's life; he acts and speaks the meaning of her death. Nothing of or from Verginia. 'From the start, indeed, she [a Freikorps bride] is no more than a fiction. She never appears in her own right; she is only spoken *about*' (Theweleit (1987–9: i.32)).

Throughout the events leading up to and including the rape, Livy's Lucretia is also silent. Although the rape scene is highly dramatic,

Livy gives us only Tarquin's actions: he waits until the household is asleep, he draws his sword, he enters Lucretia's bedroom, he holds her down, he speaks, pleads, and threatens. Lucretia is mute. Like Verginia's, her terror eliminates speech, and her chastity makes her obdurate: she is a silent stone.

Silence is what Tarquin demands of her: '*Tace, Lucretia, Sex. Tarquinius sum*' ('Be quiet, Lucretia, I am Sextus Tarquinius'). His speech could not connect silence and erasure more directly. The command and direct address (*Tace, Lucretia*) imply 'I give the orders,' and since he orders Lucretia's silence, the command is almost tauto-logical. Then he asserts his own name (*Sex. Tarquinius*) and existence (*sum*). The insistence on his own existence follows from his demand for her silence. Indicative, statement of fact, replaces imperative, command—here an order that she erase the fact of herself as a speaking subject; his name replaces hers. In effect, he says, 'I am; you are not, although since I must order your silence, you are and I shall have to make you not be.' Implicitly, his existence as a speaking (here, an ordering) subject with a name depends on her status as an object without speech (see Kappeler (1986: 49)). Like Brutus' later deployment of her body in the overthrow of the monarchy, Tarquin's words and act are vampiric: her silence (erasure), his existence.

Her silence constructs a pleasure of terror like that of the horror film, where the audience is held in expectation that what it fears will occur. Certainly, tension and terror cannot exist without Lucretia's silence, without her presence as an actionless body. The description of Tarquin's actions delays what every Roman would know to be the inevitable. Livy's account allows the reader to dwell on the details of power asserted—drawn sword, hand on breast, woman pinned to the bed, woman starting out of sleep to hear '*Tace, Lucretia, Sex. Tarquinius sum*.' The mute, immobile victim sets the escalating movement of violation in high relief. As in the cinema, the construc-tion of powerlessness provides a perverse thrill.

What are the pleasures of this silence for male author and reader? Did Livy, 'pen' in hand, identify with Tarquin and his drawn sword, experience the imagined exertion of force, and take pleasure in the prospect of *pen*etration with sword or penis (on pen and penis, see Gilbert and Gubar (1979: 3–16))? Is this the titillation found by the male reader? Or does Lucretia's silence also open a space for the flow of the reader's feelings, permitting his entry into the forbidden pleasure of the penetrated, imagined from the place of one required to be a penetrator (Silverman (1980) and Richlin (1992))?

About the act of penetration itself, no words and a gap filled with the language of chastity conquered. Despite rules of taste or convention, such language erases the moment of Lucretia's violation and silences her experience as a subject of violation. Livy comments only, and only after her violation, that she was *maesta* ('mournful'). The place of Lucretia's pain is absent. Without words about her experience at that moment and without that moment, Lucretia is dead matter—not feeling, not thinking, not perceiving. Present is Lucretia's chastity, but not Lucretia. Livy or convention—it doesn't matter which—creates rape as a male event, and an imperial one. Rape consists of male action and female space, the exertion of force and chastity.

After, and only after, the rape, Lucretia speaks and acts as Verginia does not. Donaldson sees Lucretia's act as a sacrifice of self, contrasting it with Brutus's sacrifice of his feelings and his sons (1982: 12). Brutus achieves political liberty, Lucretia personal liberty (8). Higonnet focuses on Lucretia's speech as an explanatory text for suicide (1986: 69). She argues that Lucretia's use of language is 'revolutionary' because she sets her own verbal constructs against those of Collatinus which make her a verbal boast and a sexual object (75). With Donaldson (1982: 103 ff.), she views the stress on Brutus' role as the 'masculine domestication of an essentially revolutionary heroic instance of female suicide'.

This assumes that we can return to some origin where women occupied some other role and misses the male production of origin. The sacrifices of Brutus and Lucretia are 'radically different', but not for the reasons noted by Donaldson (12). Brutus' words and actions bring a political order in which men like himself can act; his sacrifice preserves that order. Lucretia's actions result in her own eradication. She is sacrificed so the men of her class may win their liberty—their ability to act. Her language kills no less than her actions: like the Sabines, she 'asks for it'. Together, words and actions set an example for the control of female sexual activity; in other words, she founds an order in which her female descendants can only enact their own destruction. As with Rhea Silvia, the Sabines, Tarpeia, Horatia, and

Verginia, men's liberation and political advances require the sacrifice of Woman.

Moreover, both Lucretia's words and her act silence any difference that would disturb the structural boundaries of an ideal patriarchal order. I find it difficult to see Lucretia's speech (given her by the male historian, it should be emphasized) as revolutionary, when she is made to speak as well as act the absolute, objective quality of chastity and herself as a space invaded. Soiled is soiled: 'No unchaste woman will live with Lucretia as a precedent.' To see or hear anything else would make Lucretia anomalous—innocent yet penetrated—and alive. Patriarchy in Livy's good old days apparently cannot tolerate a subject whose speech would evoke the disorder of anomaly; it depends on woman's silence, or at most speech that enunciates the role men set out for her (note Theweleit (1987–9: i.123); Gilbert and Gubar (1979: 14)).

Theweleit's analysis of the 'mode of production of [his] writers' language' is instructive. Freikorps authors employ the postures of description, narration, representation, and argument 'only as empty shells' (1987–9: i.215). Rather, their linguistic process is one of transmutation. The events depicted serve a preconceived idea which is not directly described. The 'ideational representation' impresses itself on perceived reality and devours it (87). While every linguistic process 'appropriates and transforms reality' (215), Freikorps authors deaden what they depict. Theirs is a 'language of occupation: it acts imperialistically against any form of independently moving life' (215). The life that especially draws the onslaught is the 'living movement of women' and the whole complex of feelings and experiences, sexual and emotional, associated with women.

The thrust of Livy's narrative kills, but with certain effects. Women are made dead, and men come alive. Women as a presence disappear from the narrative and leave the stage of history to men struggling with one another, winning wars, and building an empire which, of course, means making other women and men physically dead in conquest or socially dead in enslavement. Lucretia and Verginia endure and are removed from the scene by the activities of the conqueror—rape, death, enslavement. In effect, Livy builds Rome's origin and its history with what deadens in the imperial present.

Where it would seem that women in Livy are made dead with the result that the men who make empire come alive, this operation of the narrative veils the deadness of the men who build imperial society. *Disciplina* requires bodies insensible to desire. Brutus holds aloft the bloody knife drawn from Lucretia's body and swears the overthrow of tyranny. He evokes the more recent image of his descendant, beloved by Caesar and one of his assassins. Livy seems simply to have replaced one dead body with another; Lucretia's corpse hides another, not of the past but of Augustus' emerging imperial order—Gaius Julius Caesar, a man who controlled neither his ambition nor his bodily desires.

## EPILOGUE: THE NEWS, HISTORY, AND THE BODY OF WOMAN

The story of Lucretia, Donaldson says, has disappeared from popular knowledge not on account of 'moral disapproval, but neglect: the explanation lies in the modern decline in classical knowledge and classical education' (1982: 168). We are too distant from ancient Rome and the eighteenth century that found meaning in its virtues. Instead, 'we celebrate the "heroes" of the sports field and the world of entertainment more readily than the heroes of the battlefield and the deathbed; the word is drained of its moral sense.'

I cannot share Donaldson's perception of distance and difference. The news, that raw material of political history, seems to belong to the 'world of entertainment': fiction and fact meld, working on and with the same images. Through them echo the women and gender relations in Livy's stories of early Rome, his narrative of origins constructed in apprehension of decadence and decline. The Iran-Contra hearings slip into the air time of the soap opera. The cases of Bernhard Goetz and Baby M become news and made-for-TV movies. In the newspaper, extramarital sex costs a politician his chance at the presidency; in the cinema, it nearly costs a man his family and his life. In Rambo films and *Fatal Attraction*, 'the world of entertainment' does offer us heroes of the battlefield and the deathbed (more precisely, death *and* bed). Daily, images of woman as space and void cross my TV screen. Often, the news seems written on the bodies of women; at least, she is there—a part of the landscape of what becomes history. This is not a Roman landscape. The women belong to seemingly different narratives: hostages, not raped women, catalyzed action in Reagan's White House. Women are not slain in current political narratives, yet seemingly different stories proffer words flooded with 'moral sense', implicitly urging correct bodily behavior, generally the practices of self-control—'just say no'. These stories, too, require the bodies of women, made dead by their silence and their allocation to a holding place in stories of men. And when these women speak, they enunciate this place or their pleasure as inanimate matter, like a Barbie doll available for purchase.

The 'decline in classical knowledge' has not spelled the disappearance of these features of Roman fictions, however unfamiliar the specific narratives. The deadening or silencing of Woman perpetuates the fictions and history of the bodies politic, female, and male. Since the eighteenth century, when some celebrated Lucretia's story, the commodity has taken the place of honor in systems of value as a bourgeois order replaced an aristocratic one, but the images of Woman have followed the displacement. 'Her image sells his products' (Pfohl (1990: 223–4)); it 'sells' Livy's history, too.

ADDENDUM

The political and cultural conditions in which this article was first written have changed in the last fifteen years or so. Instead of the 'Decline of the American Empire', we seem to have arrived at its explosion, literally and figuratively, in the war on terrorism following 9/11 and the American invasion and occupation of Iraq whose 'purpose' has become ever-changing—ridding the world of Iraq's weapons of mass destruction, taking down a dangerous dictator, eliminating a member of the 'axis of evil', bringing freedom to the Middle East, or participating in the 'global struggle against violent extremism', the Bush administration's new moniker for 'the global war on terrorism'. Yet 'decline' still haunts us—in the images of what American soldiers wrought at Abu Ghraib, in the campaign against gay marriage, or in the mounting deficit—all depending on one's point of view. Instead of the silent Donna Rice, the voluble Monica Lewinski gave intimate interviews of an affair that led to the impeachment of President Clinton. Dead bodies, male and female, American and Iraqi, pile up but rarely appear on our television screens—except in stolen pictures of flag-draped coffins and in simulation on 'Over There', Steven Bochco's drama about an Army unit in Iraq on FX. 'Desperate Housewives' and 'Sex and the City' (now in reruns) present American audiences with the images of women most discussed. And last but not least, the reports of the mass rape of women in Bosnia in the early 1990s and in Darfur, Sudan, have filled our print media and the web, but, unlike weapons of mass destruction or 'violent extremism', mass rape has not become a cause for war. Regardless of whether the present is more of the same or a changed landscape, however, in a volume on a Roman historian, it seems only fair to leave the conditions of this essay's writing in place, as Livy himself does in his own preface.

Scholarly work over the last fifteen years has addressed the Roman setting of the stories analyzed in this article. So prolific has this work been that only a few items can be mentioned here. Discussions of Zanker (1988) and Nicolet (1991), especially, have produced scholarly debate on the transition from Republic to Principate, Augustan ideology, and Augustus' use of history and its inscription on the city of Rome: Wallace-Hadrill (1981), (1986), and (1987); Raaflaub and Toher (1990); Kennedy (1992); Gurval (1995); Favro (1996). Beyond interesting work on Roman historiography and the sources of early Roman history in general (Cameron (1989); Fox (1996); Marincola (1997); Wiseman (1988), (1995), (1998)), many scholars have taken up, in Gary Miles' words, the 'complexity and originality in Livy's historiography and . . . his conceptualization of Roman history' (1995: 5): Miles (1986), (1988), (1995); Henderson (1989); Kraus (1994*a*) and (1994*b*); Moles; Feldherr (1998). In particular, Miles' (1995) astute observations on Livy's preface and Chaplin's fine analyses (2000) of Livy's use of *exempla* help to refine some of the points made in my article; Catharine Edwards' book on Roman immorality (1993) should be consulted on aspects of Roman moral discourse only touched on above. Lastly, scholars have explored the relations between texts and Roman topography: Edwards (1996); Jaeger (1997); Vasaly (1993).

*S. R. J.*

# 15

## Livy's Revolution: Civic Identity and the Creation of the *Res Publica*[1]

### *A. M. Feldherr*

In an essay on the cultural revolution that marks the coming of the principate, Andrew Wallace-Hadrill maps the intellectual frontiers of Augustus' *imperium*: the *princeps'* appropriation of political power coincides with and depends upon the rationalization and codification of knowledge about Rome and her institutions that made such information uniform, capable of dissemination throughout the empire, and independent of the social authority of the *nobiles*.[2] The result of this decoupling of systems of knowledge from local authority was nothing less than a 'new sense of being Roman'. At almost the same time that Augustus consolidated his political control over the Roman world, another similarly ambitious attempt at creating a unified and comprehensive picture of the totality of the Roman state was under way: the historian Livy, whose own city had just received full Roman citizenship in 49 BCE, and who from the beginning of his text advertises the fact that he is not a member of the *nobilitas*, nevertheless promises to 'write out in full the history of the Roman people from the origin of the city' (*Praef.* 1). The expression

[1] This chapter was developed from parts of my 1991 dissertation at the University of California, Berkeley. In that form it profited from the criticism of my advisers, E. S. Gruen, T. N. Habinek, T. G. Rosenmeyer. I am also grateful to my wife Deborah Steiner and to the participants of the 'Roman Cultural Revolution' conference at Princeton, in particular to Richard Sailer, for their many helpful suggestions. The flaws that remain are my own.
[2] Wallace-Hadrill (1997: 3–22).

not only suggests the comprehensiveness of his account but also lends it the character of a final, official version; the same verb, *perscribere*, is also used of the written record that gave legitimacy to senatorial decrees.[3] So too Livy ends his preface with a prayer to the gods that recalls the practices both of the poets who glorified Rome's origins and of a consul setting out on campaign.[4]

The place of Livy's text in an Augustan 'cultural revolution' has been among the most debated issues in Roman historiography and has yielded an astonishing variety of conclusions. Livy has appeared as Augustus' 'improving publicist', in Syme's notorious phrase, and conversely as a staunch republican.[5] What all such approaches share, however, is a presumption of the priority of political action over literary creation. Whether Livy approves or disapproves of the Augustan regime, he can only react. Yet not only does Livy's preface fail to mention any political figure; as we have seen, it also appropriates the language of political activity to describe the historian's task. Thus a more productive starting point takes seriously Livy's claim that his *History* can act autonomously as an instrument of social and political change.[6] The aim of this chapter is to illustrate how

[3] Cf., e.g., Caes., *B.C.* 1.6, Cic., *Cat.* 3.13, and for the procedure Mommsen (1887–8: iii.1003 ff.). The verb also helps define Livy's place in the historiographic tradition: Sempronius Asellio in his preface (fr. 1 *HRR*) contrasts authors of *historiae*, who attempt to narrate events thoroughly (*perscribere*) with the producers of *annales*, which merely recount 'what was done and in what year it happened'.

[4] Ogilvie (1965: 29). Cf. especially 45.39.10 *maiores vestri omnium magnarum rerum et principia exorsi a dis sunt, et finem statuerunt.*

[5] For recent surveys of the range of positions that have been taken see Badian (1993), Deininger (1985), and Kraus (1994a: 6–8). The phrase 'improving publicist' will be found in Syme (1959: 76).

[6] Cf. the comments of Kraus (1994a: 8–9): '. . . the historian's project parallels/rivals Augustus' own building of a new Rome via (re)construction of its past. . . . But a shared project does not necessarily mean a lack of independence.' Starting from a different perspective, Miles (1995: 8–74) has recently argued that Livy's demonstration of the ultimate unreliability of the records upon which any narrative of the past depends serves both to undermine any attempt to create an authoritative account of how things actually happened and correspondingly to emphasize the moral function of history, its capacity to shape and perpetuate an image of national identity. This strategy also redresses the inequality in social status which placed Livy the Paduan at a disadvantage in comparison with aristocratic historians.

Luce (1990) offers a particularly striking demonstration that Livy's *History* did not constitute an official Augustan version of the past by pointing out the variations between the *tituli* inscribed on the statues of Roman heroes in the Forum Augustum and Livy's accounts of their deeds.

Livy's text can perform such a function through an analysis of his narrative of perhaps the single most significant transformation to affect the Roman state in his text, the end of the monarchy and beginning of the republic. The 'revolution'[7] accomplished by L. Junius Brutus in 509 BCE was the event that brought into being a distinctively Roman ordering of political authority. However, as we shall see, the constitutional aspects of this change depend upon a more profound shift in each Roman citizen's sense of civic identity, the nature of which mirrors first-century anxieties about the individual's place in the Roman state. Within Livy's text, this revolution in consciousness can in turn be correlated with a change in the systems of communication and representation by which the individual is brought into contact with the collective authority of the state. The public spectacles staged and orchestrated by Brutus serve as the means through which the new state is built and finally provide a model for how Livy's narrative, by representing the same events, can itself generate 'a new sense of being Roman' among its own audience.

The fundamental principle of the new order that followed upon the expulsion of the Tarquins can be found in the first sentence, indeed in the first word, of Livy's second book, which begins just after the end of the *regnum: liberi iam hinc* (2.1.1). *Libertas*, the power of law exceeding the power of men, defines the Republic against the monarchy. Yet the semantic range of the word *liberi* extends beyond the simple absence of a tyrant to describe the civic status of each individual Roman as a free citizen as opposed to a slave.[8] Later in this introduction Livy highlights the interdependence between the transformation of the state as a whole and the personal development of each Roman as citizen, both of which are implicit in the word *liberi*. *Libertas*, according to Livy, was only possible when Rome had already been in existence long enough for the original population of shepherds and exiles to feel a sense of communal loyalty sufficient to survive the storms of faction (2.1.5). Thus the state cannot achieve its final form until its individual members

---

[7] Given the cautions of Wallace-Hadrill, the phrase is used advisedly. Livy's term for the transformation is '*libertatis origo*' (2.1.7).

[8] On the connections between *libertas* and *civitas* see especially Wirszubski (1950: 3 ff.).

develop a sense of belonging to the community, and correspondingly Livy's narrative integrates the creation of the Republic with the development on the part of the individual of a new sense of civic identity. Livy's *regnum* and republic epitomize radically different views of the hierarchy of social bonds that construct identity. This difference in turn affects every level of social organization and is particularly revealed in the tension between family and state as *loci* of loyalty and affection. For yet a third meaning of *liberi* is children, and it is through Brutus' execution of his own *liberi* for conspiring to recall the Tarquins, that the establishment of *libertas* is completed.[9]

Reasons why issues of belonging and civic identity should permeate accounts of Rome's origins written in the late first century are not far to seek. The citizen population had grown from 395,000 in 115 BCE to about 1.5 million in 28 BCE, according to a conservative estimate.[10] Not only did this vast population of new Romans, who were already *cives* of their own cities, have to think of themselves as members of the Roman *patria*, but in the face of such expansion the very term *civis*, which originally described a participant in a tangible community of peers, required redefinition for all citizens.[11] Nor is it inappropriate to adopt the perspective of the individual citizen here. The Romans themselves recognized that the subjective dimension, the individual's identification of himself as a Roman citizen, was fully as important as issues of law and public procedure in questions of citizenship. Thus Cicero in the *Pro Balbo* claims that 'our *ius civitatis mutandae*... depends not only on public laws but also on the will of the private citizen'. (*Pro Balb.* 27).

The choice to accept Rome as his *patria* is one that Livy as a new citizen himself would have faced. A member of a well-connected Paduan family, the historian was fully conversant with the local

---

[9] For another analysis of the implications of this passage for Livy's conceptions of 'the process of social unification', and particularly of how the importance of connections to family and locality for the consolidation of the state figures in Livy's narrative of the monarchy, see Phillips (1979).

[10] See Brunt (1971: 13–14) for the statistical evidence. The census figure for 28 BCE is given at *Res Gestae* 8.2 as over four million, which Brunt assumes is only conceivable if it includes women and children.

[11] On the vast problems of citizenship see the standard treatment by Sherwin-White (1973) and particularly Nicolet (1988: 21–3). The meaning and derivation of *civis* are discussed by Benveniste (1969: i. 335–7).

traditions and history of his birthplace, and, unlike any of the other non-Roman Augustan writers, he died in the city where he was born.[12] Livy's Paduan origins not only provided ammunition for his contemporary rival, Asinius Pollio, who criticized Livy's style for its *Patavinitas*,[13] they also manifest themselves in his text and give a particular significance to the starting point he chooses for his narrative. Livy begins his history of Rome with an account of two Trojan exiles: in addition to Aeneas' settlement in Latium, another Trojan, Antenor, successfully fled to Italy and became the ancestor of the Veneti. Therefore just as the Roman state has its origins in the loss of a previous fatherland, Troy, so too the creation of Livy's text depends on the historian's own decision to tell the story of his Roman *patria* rather than the alternative narrative of his native people the Veneti. The displacement of an earlier *patria* similarly affects other outsiders incorporated into the Roman state during the first book, most notably the Albans whose Romanization coincides with the actual destruction of their native city (1.29).

Cicero's philosophical writings show how the changing definition of citizenship could affect the individual and help to define the Romans' conceptualization of the relationship between patriotism and loyalty to the family and other social groups. Although Cicero was a Roman citizen by birth and even the *pater patriae*, he is still at pains to define what that *patria* is. As Book Two of the *De legibus* begins, Cicero and Atticus are wandering by the river Fibrenus on Cicero's native estate at Arpinum. Atticus is surprised to hear Cicero refer to Arpinum as his *patria*, and Cicero responds by asserting that 'everyone from the towns has two *patriae*, one of nature, and one of citizenship' (*De leg.* 2.5). The hoary distinction between law and

---

[12] The importance of Livy's ties to his native city are stressed by Leeman (1961) and especially Bonjour (1975*a*: 185, 249–50). Within the history, Paduan local traditions emerge not only at 1.1, but also in the description of the failed Laconian expedition into Paduan territory at 10.2.4–15, commemorated both by the spoils displayed at Padua in the temple of Juno, and by an annual reenactment of the naval battle. More strikingly, in his account of the battle of Pharsalus, Livy includes a description of the prodigies that announced the battle at Padua, and were interpreted by a local augur, C. Cornelius, who was a relative of the historian (Plut. *Caes.* 47).

[13] Quint. *I.O.* 1.5.56, 8.1.3. The scholarship on the precise implications of this charge is vast. A recent survey will be found in Flobert (1981), who argues that the primary thrust of the term lies in its contrast not to *latinitas* but to *urbanitas*.

nature has a special significance for the *De legibus*, but it also parallels the link between public laws and private will that we saw in the passage from the *Pro Balbo*. It would be one thing if Cicero's two *patriae* could be neatly divided into the spheres of legality and affection, if Roman citizenship simply constituted an extra level of obligation that was distinct from and not in competition with pre-existing loyalties to the natural *patria*.[14] But patriotism involves affections as well as obligations. 'It is necessary', Cicero continues, 'that the *patria*, where the name of *res publica* is a marker of our common citizenship, stand first in our affections; for which we ought to die and to which we ought to devote ourselves entirely and upon which, as upon an altar, we ought to set and as it were sacrifice all our goods. However, the *patria* which bore us is dear in almost the same way as that which receives us' (*De leg.* 2.5). Thus the same criterion of affection, *caritas*, is used to measure the bonds to both the smaller and the larger *patria*.[15]

It was not only the native town that could offer a challenge to civic identity. A passage of Cicero's *De officiis* locates the Roman male at the midpoint of a concentric pattern of social entities, extending from the family to the entire species, all of which placed demands on his affections and loyalties. In this passage too there is a tension between a motion inwards, by which the nearest bond of family ought to prevail, and a motion outwards, by which every outer layer of society, because it encloses the nearer bonds, requires greater obligations. 'No association is graver, none is dearer than that which binds each one of us to the Republic. Our parents are dear (*cari*), our children are dear, but one *patria* embraces all the affections of all men; on behalf of which what good man would hesitate to seek death, if he might benefit her?'[16] On the one hand civic loyalty is a natural extension of all other affections. If you love your wife and children

---

[14] This is the view of Nicolet (1988: 45–7), who claims that the Romans avoided such a conflict of obligations by creating 'two levels of citizenship'.

[15] For a further analysis of this passage and Cicero's treatment of the conflict of loyalties it reveals, see Bonjour (1975a: 78–86).

[16] Cic. *De off.* 1.57. Bonjour (1975a: 59–65) similarly describes the inherent ambiguity of terms like *pietas, caritas,* and *amor,* which were used to describe sentiments toward both the fatherland and the family. On the word *caritas* see Hellegouarc'h (1963: 148–9). Based largely on Cicero, *Part.* 88, scholars have proposed various distinctions between the terms *amor* and *caritas.* Both may be applied

you will necessarily love the Republic which encompasses and protects them. Except you have to love the Republic more. It is not enough to serve the Republic simply as a means of preserving your family; at a certain point you must measure the Republic on the same scale of *caritas* as the family, and the Republic must prevail.[17]

The schema put forward in Cicero's writings, by which *caritas* is built outward from the inner core of the family to include the state, directly informs Livy's discussion of loyalty to the *res publica* in the preface to Book Two. The factors that have sufficiently bound the wandering peoples to one another are 'love of wives and children and the *caritas* of the place itself' (*pignera coniugum ac liberorum caritasque ipsius soli*, 2.1.5). Livy's first book includes a clear illustration of how love of children and wives can bind citizens to one another. After the rape of the Sabine women, Romans and Sabines are united as a people because of their mutual affection for the Sabine women who are wives to the Romans and children to the Sabines.[18] And in the later books of Livy's narrative many mutinies will be quelled by the sight of wives and children, most famously Coriolanus' in the middle of the second book itself. *Caritas ipsius soli* will form the theme of Camillus' great speech at the end of the first pentad.[19]

---

to family, but while *amor* is the natural result of *usus* and *familiaritas, caritas* implies some choice and is therefore especially suitable to affections towards more distant or abstract persons and organizations. But for our purposes it is enough that *caritas* too describes an affective bond which is here applied both to the family and to the *patria*.

[17] Cf. Bonjour (1975a: 64) on the relationship of the two *patriae*: 'It is self-evident that *de legibus* (2.5) makes only a quantitative difference, not a qualitative one between *caritas* as it relates to the larger or the smaller *patria*' (trans. edd.).

My purpose is not to suggest that the family is an exclusively private entity. The work of Thomas (1984) in particular has demonstrated the extent to which family relations were always public in the sense that they were recognized, controlled by, and integrated into the public life of the state. The point is rather that according to the subjective terms used by Cicero and Livy, the integration of family and civic roles becomes a locus of tension and conflict; it cannot be taken to be self-evident and unproblematic.

[18] 1.13, a passage whose connection with the preface to Book 2 is confirmed by similarities in language. For example, with *animos... consociassent* (2.1.5), compare *regnum consociant* (1.13.4). So also Phillips (1979: 89).

[19] For appeals to wives and children cf., e.g., 7.40.12. On the Coriolanus episode, 2.39–40, see especially Bonjour (1975b). Bonjour (1975a: 66–8) gives other examples of how ties to family are accentuated in patriotic exhortations throughout Livy's text. *Caritas ipsius soli* is especially emphasized at 5.54.1–4.

But beyond simply reproducing the Ciceronian model of patriotism, Livy has devoted his second book to the tensions inherent in the conflicting claims of more immediate groups and the new conception of the *res publica*. Indeed in his narrative of the transition from monarchy to Republic, Livy also chronicles that crucial moment in the education of every citizen at which the Republic becomes dearer than family. The structure of the book highlights the individual's struggle between family loyalty and state loyalty. Thus Brutus' execution of his sons forms the beginning and Coriolanus' abortive mutiny occurs at the center. This event is followed ten chapters later by the scene in which the Fabian *gens* undertakes the Republic's war with Veii, almost at the cost of its own destruction (2.48–50). Livy also includes parables which are used within the text explicitly to educate citizens to think of the state not only as the protector of the family but in the same terms as family and even body. Thus in a kind of prelude to the education of Coriolanus, the plebeian Titus Latinius receives a prophetic dream warning him of a danger to the state if there is not a ritual repetition of improperly performed *ludi*.[20] Latinius is afraid that he will be laughed at if he tells anyone and so disregards the dream. A few days later his son dies. When he hesitates even longer, his own body is stricken with disease. The event implies more than the interconnectedness of family and state, it suggests an analogy between them. The *res publica* is a family or body in macrocosm. This is also the point of the famous parable of the belly and the limbs, which the patrician Menenius Agrippa tells to a group of plebeians who are trying to sever the bonds to the state which Livy stresses in his preface to the second book (2.32.8–12). When the limbs, or plebeians, begrudge food to the belly, which represents the patricians, they themselves begin to fail. Here again the image of the body is used as part of a rhetoric of inclusion.

Thus what is at stake in the transition between monarchy and Republic is not simply a system of government nor even liberty as opposed to tyranny but a fundamentally different interaction between the individual and the social entities that enclose him, and therefore a novel conception of individual identity. So too Livy's

---

[20] 2.36; cf., Cic., *De div.* 1.55.

portrait of the Tarquins emphasizes a sense of obligations that is directly the reverse of the Republican citizen's. The last Tarquins continually overprivilege the family against the state. When the Tarquins first appear in Book One, they are wanderers who have come from Corinth to Tarquinia to Rome (1.34.1–2). Thus they are just like all the other original Romans, also exiles. Yet the Tarquins ultimately fail to make the connection to place that other Romans have, and they leave the narrative just as they entered it, wandering among the cities of Etruria seeking aid for their clan. Tarquinius Superbus gains the throne by the deposition and murder of Servius Tullius. He justifies this act on the grounds that he is the son of Tarquinius Priscus. Tarquin claims that 'he has occupied the throne of his father, and much better the king's son be the heir to the kingdom than the king's slave' (1.48.2). Not only does he define public status on the basis of domestic status, but in so doing he reverses one of the great models of inclusion formulated under the monarchy, the adoption of Servius Tullius. Tarquinius Superbus is as devoted to his sons as he is to his father.[21] As a ruse to overcome the town of Gabii, Sextus Tarquinius pretends that his father the king has finally turned against his own family and forced him into exile (1.53.6). The young Tarquin's lie to the Gabines only highlights the essential closeness between father and son. The contrast between Tarquinius Superbus and Brutus in this regard receives its final illustration when, after Brutus has watched his own sons executed for plotting against the state, Tarquin is immediately described begging his Etruscan allies 'not to allow him to perish before their eyes with his adolescent sons'.[22]

The transition from monarchy to Republic could have been construed as a simple dynastic transition; both of the first consuls, Collatinus and Brutus, were related to the Tarquins.[23] What is

---

[21] The importance of this theme in Livy's account of the reign of Tarquinius Superbus is also highlighted by Dumézil (1949), who argues that the indulgence shown by Tarquin toward his sons contrasts specifically with Roman ideals of fatherhood and thus helps delineate the Etruscan character of their reign.

[22] *cum liberis adulescentibus*, 2.6.2. The same phrase was used to describe Brutus' sons two chapters before at 2.4.1.

[23] For Brutus and Collatinus as dynastic successors of Tarquinius Superbus, see Gantz (1975: 546–8). Bettini (1991: 48–52) uses the legends about Brutus and Collatinus as an illustration of the opposition between the affectionate *avunculus*,

more, Brutus' motive for hating Tarquinius could have been portrayed as revenge for the murder of his own father and brother.[24] Yet
unlike the accession of Superbus, the creation of the Republic is not
the result of either revenge or family ambition. In fact the first
appearance of Brutus in the narrative occurs in a context where his
values are explicitly contrasted with the Tarquins'. A terrifying portent occurs; a snake emerges from a wooden column and causes
panic in the royal palace.[25] Tarquin, typically confusing the boundary
between public and private, refuses to summon the haruspices, as he
ought to do for a public prodigy, and instead sends his sons to
consult the Delphic oracle.[26] Brutus, who has always pretended to
be a fool in order to protect himself, is sent along with them, as Livy
says, more as a source of fun, a *ludibrium*, than as a companion. The
oracle's response to the king's inquiry is not recorded. But when the
sons themselves ask who will be the next to rule at Rome, they are
told that it will be the next to kiss his mother. Brutus, correctly
solving the riddle of the oracle, realizes that the earth is the common

represented by Collatinus who desires to spare his sister's sons the Vitellii, and the
disciplinarian *pater*. What is remarkable is that Livy's version seems to de-emphasize
the role of family bonds. The two avuncular relationships sketched in Livy are those
between the Vitellii and the sons of Brutus (2.4.1), where I will suggest that it
contributes to the characterization of the conspiracy's anti-republican nature, and
that between Tarquin himself and Brutus' brother, whom he puts to death (1.56.7).
The latter case is treated by Bettini as the exception that proves the rule: Tarquin is so
monstrous that he even kills his sister's sons. The reference to family relationships in
this passage also perhaps contrasts with Brutus' perspective, if the point of the
Delphic embassy is the redefinition of the term *mater*. On this see below.

[24] Indeed the whole episode was the subject of a tragedy by Accius which seems to
have begun with Tarquin recounting a dream in which he sacrificed one of two brother
rams and was then butted and knocked down by the survivor (Acc., *Prae.* 17–38 Ribbeck
= Cic., *De div.* 1.44). But even here the emphasis seems less on revenge as such than on
the deceptive appearance of the sheep, which corresponds to Brutus' deceptively
harmless exterior.

[25] Ogilvie (1965: 216) suggests that the manuscript reading *in regiam* be retained
in place of Bauer's *in regia* and that therefore the portent did not occur in the *regia*
itself. He supports this on the grounds that there were no wooden columns in the
original *regia*.

[26] 1.56.4 ff. Ogilvie (1965: 217) points out that even if the prodigy did occur in the
*regia*, it ought still to have been considered public. However he attributes the error
not to the king but to the annalistic tradition. Thus the 'tendentious' language of
1.56.5 indicates that an earlier annalist felt the need to justify grafting the episode of
the Delphic embassy onto the occasion of the snake portent. I would argue that Livy's
emphasis serves to highlight the confusion of public and private within the narrative.

mother of all mortals, feigns stumbling and kisses the ground. The riddle is of course an ancient one, with parallels in Herodotus and elsewhere,[27] but in this context it takes on a particular significance; it drives home the point that whereas the Tarquins think only in terms of the family, Brutus has made the conceptual leap to apply the vocabulary of family to larger communities. Correspondingly the imagery of the family is transformed from something exclusive, which differentiates Tarquins from others, to a means of inclusion:[28] the earth is a common mother. In fact the language used to describe the earth, *communis mater omnium mortalium* recalls Cicero's argument for the supremacy of the larger *patria*.[29] Thus the passage may be related to the Ciceronian transition by which the largest community supersedes the smaller in the individual's affections.

The first two events of the Republic, the expulsion of Collatinus and the execution of Brutus' sons, confirm and extend the process of redefinition of state and family. In the versions of these events given by Plutarch and Dionysius the sequence is reversed: the banishment of Collatinus follows after and results from the trial of Brutus' sons for treason.[30] After Brutus has executed his own sons, Collatinus wishes to spare his nephews, who were also involved in the conspiracy. This is the reason that his own loyalty to the state came under suspicion. In Livy's version, however, Collatinus has done nothing to deserve banishment. His only offence is his *nomen*, Tarquinius. Thus the effect of Livy's order is to highlight the issue of family membership in the expulsion of Collatinus. Furthermore, the conspiracy of the sons of Brutus to recall the Tarquins is not simply a monarchist plot but results from the entire civic and social outlook that we have defined as typical of the last kings. Whereas Livy virtually defines the Republic as a time when the rule of law was more powerful than the rule of men, *imperia legum potentiora quam hominum* (2.1.1 and 2.3.3–4), the conspiracy of the sons of Brutus prefers a man, *homo*, to

---

[27] Herodotus 6.107. Cf. also the dream of Julius Caesar, Suet., *Caes.* 7.

[28] Brutus' natural mother was in fact a Tarquinia and thus the source of his familial connection with the king (1.56.7).

[29] Thus the *patria iuris* must stand first in our affections because it is a universal bond (*universae civitatis, De leg.* 2.5). So too at *De off.* 1.57 the large *patria* 'embraces all the ties of all men' (*omnes omnium caritates*).

[30] DH *Ant.* 5.7.4 ff. Plut., *Publicola* 4.3–5.2.

laws. 'A man can be entreated, when there is need of justice or injustice, favor and obligation have some scope, a man can get angry and forgive, a man knows the difference between a friend and an enemy.'[31] In other words a man is subject to all sorts of influences which depend upon his personal, as opposed to his public status. He is prone to precisely the same impulses that bind a man to family rather than to state. Similarly, the young conspirators are bound to the conspiracy because of their birth and family connections. Thus the sons of Brutus are admitted into the conspiracy by their maternal uncles, the Vitellii (2.4.1).

In contrast to their conspiracy, the execution of the sons of Brutus represents the final rejection of the social conceptions of the *regnum*, and, through Livy's explicit description of the event as an *exemplum*, establishes a timeless model of the values underlying Roman citizenship. In presiding as a magistrate over the execution of his sons, Brutus adopts the role defined by his position in the state rather than in the family. (It is as magistrate that Brutus acts, there is no question of *patria potestas* here.[32]) Furthermore the execution cannot be understood in isolation, but is complemented by the grant of *libertas* and *civitas* to Vindicius, the slave who revealed the conspiracy (2.5.9). The Republican concept of civic identity, unlike a hierarchy which privileges only birth, allows for the incorporation of new citizens. Hence Vindicius, who was a slave within the *familia*, becomes a citizen in the same ceremony in which Brutus' children are executed (2.5.9–10). The connection of the two actions also provides a final demonstration of the inseparability of individual *libertas*, that of the new *civis* Vindicius, and the collective *libertas* of the state, which the defeat of the conspiracy secures.

The shifts in public forms and individual values encoded in the expulsion of the Tarquins are accompanied by yet another transition, which is signaled most clearly in Livy's narrative of the rape of Lucretia and its aftermath. This transition involves the manner in which public and private, individual and state, are brought into

[31] 2.3.3. The references to *beneficia*, *gratiae*, and *amicitia* recall particularly the language of political competition among the Republican aristocracy and thus give a special relevance to Livy's diagnosis of the threats to *libertas*. Ogilvie (1965: 243) detects a Late Republican patina in the language of the entire episode.
[32] First observed by Mommsen (1889: 22). See below, pp. 429 ff.

contact through media of public display. Not only do the figures within the text manipulate appearances in characteristic ways to control public opinion, but Livy himself associates the monarchy with a distinctive genre of public spectacle, drama. Brutus' expulsion of the Tarquins, on the other hand, depends upon the effective use of spectacles to engender within his audience precisely the sense of civic identity upon which the Republic is predicated.

Under Tarquin the emphasis on the private as opposed to the public and common creates a disjunction between what the king intends and what he allows to be publicly perceived. The king's intentions recede from public view. In war Tarquin relies on deception and guile, as Livy says, the least Roman arts (1.53.4). Hence the strategy for the conquest of Gabii (1.53.4–1.54.10). After Tarquin's son, like Zopyrus at Babylon, has cunningly won the confidence of the Gabines, he sends a messenger to his father. Tarquin, strolling through his garden, makes no response to the messenger but begins to knock off the heads of poppies with his staff. The messenger gets bored and leaves, assuming there is no message, but the son of course understands and has the most important Gabines killed. In this story, father and son alone share a secret language (*tacitis ambagibus*) which is inaccessible to any outside observer.

No event better illustrates the connection between the inversion in social perspective and the inversion of public spectacle under the reign of Tarquin than the overthrow of Servius Tullius. As we have seen, Tarquin's claim to the throne is based upon inheritance. In considering Servius a slave rather than a king, Tarquin defines him by his position within the family rather than his position within the state. The supremacy of the private, family space also appears in the setting of the story. Tarquin must be persuaded to kill the king by his wife, Tullia (1.47.1–6). These exhortations, though they will influence the course of public events, are known only to Tarquin and Tullia. Thus what Tarquin says and does in the Forum when he usurps the royal throne results from motivations that are hidden in two senses. The constitutional justifications that he quotes serve only to conceal his personal ambitions, and these ambitions are kindled in private conversations removed from the gaze of the state (1.47.8–12).

The eruption of family ambitions into public life also manifests itself in a violation of the decorum of public spectacle which occurs just at the moment when Tarquin takes power. At this instant Tullia herself not only appears in her chariot in the middle of the Forum, but actually calls Tarquin forth from the Senate and becomes the first to proclaim him king (1.48.5–6). The impropriety of her appearance in public is emphasized by Livy's comment that she feels no shame at appearing before an assembly of men, and Tarquin himself orders her to leave.

The incongruous prominence of Tullia in the narrative may be connected with another aspect of the historian's presentation of the *regnum*. Livy describes the death of Servius as a tragic crime, produced by the royal palace itself, which also functions almost as a stage set through which Tullia enters and exits (*tulit enim et Romana regia sceleris tragici exemplum*, 1.46.3). Far from simply exemplifying what we might call tragic history, the seamless absorption of tragic techniques to intensify historical narrative, Livy's reference to tragedy actually serves to set his account of this reign apart from the events that surround it. Thus this disruption in the fabric of the narrative corresponds to the improper appearance of Tullia as a sign of the rift that divides this regime from the rest of Roman history.[33]

If the spectacles of the last king concealed private motives from the eyes of the people, then the foundation of the Republic, by which the true center of civic power is restored to the public sphere, is accomplished through an opening outward, a process of revealing what has been concealed. Thus the end of the monarchy depends upon driving Tullia, the symbol of the hidden dynastic machinations of the Tarquinii, out of the palace. The fall of the dynasty is predicted by a serpent gliding out of a wooden column. The motif of revelation appears particularly in Livy's presentation of Brutus himself. Brutus had pretended to be slow-witted and took his name, which means stupid or sluggish, 'in order that under the concealment of that *cognomen*, the spirit that would be the liberator of the Roman people might lie hidden, biding its time' (1.56.8). Brutus represents his character by means of a sign he carries with him, a cornel-wood staff that has been hollowed out to contain a gold wand (1.56.9). This sign operates through riddles, *per ambages*, and it is in the solution of

---

[33] Woodman (1992) has shown that Tacitus similarly excises the tyrannical reign of Nero from his narrative by treating it in an anomalously Herodotean style.

another riddle, that of the Delphic oracle, that Brutus' succession is itself confirmed. This emphasis on riddles is significant because concealed or hidden meaning was one of the characteristics of the Tarquins' communication. Tarquin speaks to his son in *ambages*; Brutus, himself a riddle to be solved, succeeds through his skill at understanding hidden meanings. In fact since the prodigy of the serpent appearing from the wooden column is never actually interpreted, I would suggest that it signifies Brutus himself, whose sign is the gold wand in the wooden staff.

This cluster of images is concentrated two chapters before the central revelation that leads to the overthrow of the monarchy, the revelation of the body of Lucretia. When Tullia pollutes her Penates with the blood of Servius Tullius, their anger is said to insure that this *regnum* will have an end like its beginnings (1.48.7). And indeed the episode which brings about the end of the Tarquins' power is also marked by a transgression of the boundaries of public and private, family and state, which symmetrically answers the disruptions by which the Tarquins gained the throne. Then Tullia, riding out of the *regia*, had not felt shame at appearing before the assembly of men (*nec reverita coetum virorum*, 1.48.5). The Lucretia episode begins when a group of men, leaving the battlefield, enter a *domus* which is inhabited by a truly modest wife. Within the tale, the initial intrusion of Tarquinius is balanced by the exposure of Lucretia's body to an ever expanding circle of spectators. Sextus had threatened that if Lucretia did not consent to his attack, he would put a naked slave next to her corpse to make it seem as though she had been unfaithful (1.58.4). This may be read as the dynasty's final attempt to use appearances to conceal rather than reveal. Lucretia on the other hand kills herself openly, in the presence of her family; her death is combined with a revelation of the secret deeds of the prince. Her body is then carried out of the house and put on display in the forum at Collatia, the ancestral village of the Collatini; next Brutus goes on to narrate her violation in public at Rome itself. Not only does this process generally predict the expansion of individual loyalties described in the preface to the second book, the particular locations where the public revelation takes place even correspond to the levels of communal bond described in Cicero's *De officiis*. The *familia* is succeeded by Collatia, the *patria loci*, or native *patria*, which is followed finally by Rome the center of the *patria civitatis*.

The process of publication in the case of Lucretia also involves a shift in the type of spectacle by which the crime is represented. As a recapitulation of the entire *regnum*, it is appropriate that the rape of Lucretia begin as a drama. Ogilvie and other commentators have invoked both comedy and tragedy to describe the episode. In particular, the idea of a contest of wives has been referred to New Comedy.[34] Here it suffices to observe that Livy both describes the event as a *ludus* and inserts expressions appropriate for stage dialogue, such as *satin salve?* and *age sane*.[35] Yet as the narrative progresses, the dramatic beginning, which corresponds to the motion from battlefield to *domus*, is replaced by the spectacle of the corpse itself on display in the forum. But there is another dimension to this shift, which takes an event of essentially private significance, and invests it with historical consequences for the entire state; here the paradigm of sacrifice is introduced as a new means of portraying Lucretia's death. The reconception of her suicide as a sacrifice is accomplished through the gesture of the oath which Brutus, who chooses this moment to reveal himself, forces the other spectators of the suicide to swear. 'As the others were absorbed in mourning, Brutus snatching the knife from the wound and holding it, still dripping with blood, before him says "By this blood, *castissimum* before the royal injustice, I swear, and I make you gods my witnesses, to drive out with fire, sword and whatever force I might, Tarquinius Superbus together with his criminal wife and children"' (1.59.1). Both gesture and language contribute to the sacralization of the scene. An oath sworn by blood is rare in Roman religion,[36] but where blood is used in ritual, it often derives from sacrificial victims or appears in a sacrificial context.[37] And *coniurationes* were usually

---

[34] Ogilvie (1965: 219 and 222), who cites parallels.

[35] *ludus*, 1.57.11; *age sane*, 1.57.8; *satin salve?*, 1.58.7. The last two are only the most striking examples of dramatic turns of phrase catalogued by Ogilvie.

[36] Ogilvie (1965: 226).

[37] For the ritual use of sacrificial blood see Fowler (1911: 33–4). In Dionysius' narrative after the expulsion of the Tarquins, when the first consuls swear what is virtually the same oath as that proposed by Brutus in Livy, they do so 'standing over the remains of sacrificial victims', DH *Ant.*, 5.1.3.

confirmed through sacrifice.³⁸ The word *castissimum* is also relevant here; though Lucretia as an *univira* was sexually chaste, the adjective *castus* is also used for ritual purity. In fact this is its customary meaning in Livy.³⁹
     But Lucretia's blood is no longer *castus*; her sacrifice is an impure one. The sacrificial interpretation of her death thus becomes another means of representing the impropriety of her violation, but now in a medium that affects not only the *domus* but the entire state. And indeed many Romans may have perceived the expulsion of the kings ritually re-enacted every year in the form of an impure sacrifice on the occasion of the *regifugium*. At this festival, which took place on 24 February, the date that provides the occasion for Ovid's narrative of the rape of Lucretia, a surrogate for the king, the *rex sacrorum*, performs a sacrifice in the Forum and immediately flees the area.⁴⁰

³⁸ Bleicken (1963) has argued that two series of coins, one Roman from the time of the Second Punic War and one minted by the Italian rebels, both of which depict soldiers with swords surrounding a sacrificial victim, are depictions of *coniurationes*. A literary description of such a rite among Italic peoples occurs in Livy's description of the Samnite oath at 10.38; the connection with the coin scenes was made by Instinsky (1964). Alföldi (1971) agrees that the Italian coins show a *coniuratio* but claims that the Roman coins in fact represent a treaty between Aeneas and Latinus.
     The most famous *coniuratio* to be confirmed by blood and/or sacrifice was Catiline's. According to Dio's account a boy is actually brought in, sacrificed, and subsequently eaten by the conspirators, 37.30.3. Sallust's more restrained version has Catiline mix human blood with the wine that was circulated among the conspirators in *paterae*, Sal., *Cat.* 22.1–2. Consciousness of this hideous crime was meant to insure the fidelity of the participants. Sallust connects the ritual element with the gesture of circulating wine, *sicuti in sollemnibus sacris fieri consuevit*. But it is unclear what particular rites are meant; McGushin (1977: 152–3) adduces the wine-oaths of Caucasian tribes, but the words *sollemnibus sacris* ought to refer to official Roman rituals. Latte (1960a: 391) points out that under certain circumstances, such as the festival of the Bona Dea, it was customary for the priests to taste the blood of the sacrificial victim although there is no mention of wine. For the drinking of sacrificial blood in real and imaginary Greek oath rituals, see Herter (1966).
³⁹ The only other occasion where a word related to *castus* is used of sexual purity is earlier in the Lucretia episode (1.57.10). Otherwise cf. 7.20.4; 10.7.5; 10.23.9; 27.37.10, 39.9.4. See also Moore (1989: 121–2).
⁴⁰ Ovid, *Fasti* 2.685–586. Evidence for the 'flight' of the *rex sacrorum* comes from Plutarch, *Quaest. Rom.* 63, who also adduces the expulsion of the Tarquins as a possible explanation for the custom. By contrast, Verrius Flaccus (*apud* Festus, *s.v. regifugium*, p.346L) plainly calls this aetiology false, an insistence which rather suggests that the mistake was a common misconception. See Porte (1985: 368–71), who however presents Ovid as the inventor of the false tradition.

Scullard, using the analogy of the Greek *buphonia*, where the sacrificer is also forced to flee, assumes that the *rex* takes on himself the guilt of an impure sacrifice.[41]

Within the narrative it is precisely at the moment of the oath by blood that the importance of the death of Lucretia is redefined as something greater than a family misfortune. Brutus, one of the two outsiders present, takes the lead, and the other spectators turn from mourning, the act of a father and husband, to anger. Similarly, whenever the body is displayed, the first reaction of the spectators is to weep, out of sympathy for the father, but then Brutus, as a *castigator lacrimarum*, forces them to perceive themselves not so much as members of a family but as members of the state. He urges them to do what befits men and Romans (1.59.4).[42]

Thus the introduction of sacrifice facilitates the moment when the individual spectator establishes his civic identity in the manner highlighted in the preface to Book Two. But how can we understand the meaning of sacrifice in this process? According to René Girard, sacrifice is predominately a social act, in which the concerted violence against one individual, mediated in certain crucial ways, becomes a means of establishing social coherence.[43] Cicero in his descriptions of collective identity also refers to the role of sacred rites, *sacra*. These for him constitute one of the natural bonds that unite both family and by extension *the patria naturae*.[44] And when we look back at Cicero's description of the relationship between the individual and the larger *patria*, there too we find an image of sacrifice. It is the *patria civitatis* 'for which we ought to die and to

[41] Scullard (1981: 81); on the *buphonia* see Burkert (1983: 136–43). For the many explanations modern scholars have provided for the ritual, see the references in Porte (1985) and Rose (1924: 197). For a discussion of other Roman rituals that may have been connected specifically with the expulsion of the Tarquins, see Mastrocinque (1988: 47–8).

[42] Cf. the similar conclusion of Phillips (1979: 90): 'violation of family ties, by outraging a sense of community based in part on such ties, leads directly to the destruction of established political forms.'

[43] Girard (1977). For a fuller description of the socializing function of sacrifice in Roman culture, and its particular importance in Augustan iconography and literature, see the discussions of Gordon (1990), Habinek (1990), Elsner (1991), Hardie (1993), and Feldherr (1998).

[44] Use of the same rites unites the family at *De off.* 1.55, and at *De leg.* 2.3 Cicero identifies Arpinum as the location of his sacred rites, *hic sacra*.

which we ought to dedicate ourselves entirely, and upon which we ought to set out and as it were consecrate all that we have'.[45] This striking series of images suggests that the citizen is both the one who makes the offering and is himself the victim who must die for the Republic. So not only is the role of *sacra* emphasized as a source of collective feeling but the act of joining the *patria* is conceived of in sacrificial terms.

Lucretia's death constitutes a negative image of sacrifice. Rather than participate collectively in the killing, the spectators are bound by sympathy with the victim and revulsion for the society responsible for her death. The beginning of the Republic by contrast offers other examples of collective action where the citizens band together to punish or expel transgressors. The expulsion of Collatinus, while not explicitly described as sacrificial, can be profitably understood according to the logic of sacrifice established in the Lucretia episode. In fact, Livy links Collatinus' banishment directly to Lucretia's death by depicting it as an extension of the oath he swore by Lucretia's blood (2.2.5). The other Tarquins were expelled by violence, but Collatinus is persuaded to go by Brutus. The first words of Brutus' exhortation are *hunc tu tua voluntate* (2.2.7). Collatinus, rather than be subjected to violence, must leave of his own will, in a manner that will absolve the state of any blame, just as the sacrificial victim too must be a willing victim.[46]

Brutus' adoption of sacrifice as a paradigm for representing the death of Lucretia also has implications for Livy's own aims in representing the crimes of the monarchy. First the opposition between sacrifice and drama as forms of spectacle needs an additional qualification because the two phenomena are not exactly comparable. It is only Livy's comment as narrator which depicts the murder of Servius Tullius as tragic. Tarquin and the other characters within

[45] Cic., *De leg.* 2.5.

[46] Other legends too connect the figure of Brutus to transformations in Roman sacrifice, and one in particular presents him as effecting a shift away from the alienating sacrifices instituted by Tarquinius Superbus. Macrobius, *Sat.* 1.7.34–5, tells that Tarquin originally instituted the practice of sacrificing young boys during the festival of the Compitalia in response to the injunction of the Delphic oracle that *pro capitibus capitibus supplicaretur*. Brutus cunningly re-interpreted the oracle by substituting the 'heads' of poppies for those of boys. For an analysis of this and other religious reforms connected with Brutus, see Mastrocinque (1988: 37–65).

the narrative are at pains to conceal the 'dramatic' nature of the event. Thus when Tullia, the inspiring Fury who has actually caused his crime, appears in public, Tarquin must drive her back into hiding. To Livy's audience, Tarquin is a character in a drama but from the perspective of the audience within the text, this dramatic interlude has taken the place of real government. On the other hand the transition to sacrifice is accomplished through the intervention of Brutus, a figure in the narrative. When viewed in this way, the actions of Brutus the revolutionary and Livy the historian both operate towards the same end of exposing what the Tarquins would conceal. The value of the sacrificial paradigm used by Brutus is to reveal the deeds of the Tarquins in a context which makes them emphatically public as opposed to private crimes. Livy, by staging the whole reign as a drama, makes of it a negative example whose ultimate function is to define by contrast the proper conception of the *res publica*.

The essential equation of Livy and Brutus as producers of spectacle receives confirmation when we find Brutus himself acting as an historian. After having displayed the body of Lucretia in the forum at Collatia, Brutus moves on to the Roman Forum where he delivers an oration which not only describes the rape of Lucretia, but also refers to the murder of Servius Tullius, even the digging of the *cloaca maxima* (1.59.7–11). In other words, he recapitulates much of Livy's own narrative. In fact Livy says that Brutus recalled even more horrible deeds which are difficult for the historian to relate (1.59.11). However, this difference in content, even the necessary distancing created by such an authorial aside, is less significant than Livy's implication that at this moment Brutus' action and his own are comparable. Brutus' speech cannot be separated from the historical events it describes; his narrative acts upon its audience as a catalyst in effecting the change in governments and in social structures. As we have seen, this change is not a unique event of purely historical significance, nor does it merely reflect concerns which had a particularly vivid impact on the experiences of Livy's own time, when vast numbers of new citizens, including the historian himself, were coming to think of themselves as Romans. Every citizen, even Cicero, experiences the shift in values that Livy makes responsible for the creation of the Republic. And Livy's narrative, as another representation of that transformation, can have an impact no less vivid nor forceful than the words pronounced by Brutus.

One of the implications of this similarity in function between the historian and the consul is that under the Republic a different relationship obtains between the historian's text and the events it narrates. No longer do the illegitimate spectacles of a Tarquin require exposure; the historian can align his representation of the past with the public displays of the new magistrates in a manner that perpetuates their effect and expands their audience. The first fully described events of the new republic, particularly the execution of the sons of Brutus, reproduce and resolve the tensions between family and civic identity, but now in the form of a public spectacle which Livy's text, rather than exposing or discrediting, strives to recreate for its own audience. In the case of the execution of the sons of Brutus, we shall see that the dynamics of the spectacle described by the historian, where the killing of guilty victims takes place at the command of a presiding magistrate whose presence draws the attention of the crowd away from the execution itself, recall the visual aspect of sacrifice, the very ritual whose successful manipulation by Brutus was crucial for the creation of the republic.

The climactic moment of the execution, when Brutus watches his sons' death with 'a father's spirit shining forth in the execution of public duty', can be read as an epiphany of Ciceronian patriotism. As Yan Thomas interprets the scene, it is not a question of Brutus suppressing the duty of a father in order to do his duty as consul. Rather the two social roles are integrated. Both consular *imperium* and *patria potestas* come together in authorizing the execution.[47] The consequent unity of two levels of social authority both illustrates the civic aspect of the Roman father's power of life and death, and simultaneously establishes a new relationship between the consul

---

[47] 'A connection is established between *uitae necisque potestas* [power of life and death] and *imperium*. A single outward appearance incarnates two powers, the exercise of which, in the eyes of the Roman people, offers the same terrifying spectacle' (trans. edd.), Thomas (1984: 518). Cf. also the argument of Mastrocinque (1988: 121 ff.) that the *regnum* of Tarquinius Superbus was associated with a breakdown of paternal authority over the *iuuentus* and that thus Brutus' restoration of civic order goes hand in hand with his restoration of the proper hierarchical relationship between the generations.

and the *populus* whereby the magistrate becomes the 'father' of the people. This interpretation is explicitly attested by Florus for whom Brutus' execution of his sons indicates that he has 'adopted the people in the place of his sons'.[48] To accept a paternal relationship with the people also implied the rejection of another model of absolute power also present in the *domus*, that of master to slave. The link between the *dominus* and the tyrant, already developed in Greek political theory, perhaps gained a special importance for the Romans who, as Thomas points out, made their unique construction of the father–son relationship a distinguishing characteristic of their own society.[49] Thus in Livy's text Brutus' absorption of the role of *pater* is coupled with a rejection of that of *dominus* implicit in the liberation of his slave Vindicius.

The motif of the consul as a public father shapes the brief remainder of Brutus' life. He dies in battle fighting in single combat with Arruns, one of the sons of Tarquin.[50] After his funeral the married women of Rome mourn for him for an entire year, just as they would a parent, 'because he was such a fierce avenger of outraged chastity' (2.7.4). This claim reveals another link between Brutus' expulsion of the Tarquins and the execution of his sons. To guard the chastity of the women of the household was pre-eminently the responsibility of its male members.[51] In this sense Brutus' transformation of the rape into a national matter, like punishing his sons as a consul, unites family and political authority in a manner directly opposite to that of the Tarquins, who made the public personal.[52] The transition from

[48] Florus 1.3.5, in Thomas (1984: 531–2). Cf. also the crowd's description in Livy of the consulate as 'born from the Junian house', as though in substitution for Brutus' natural offspring (*consulatum ortum ex domo Iunia*, 2.5.7).

[49] For the uniquely Roman aspect of the father's power of life and death, see Thomas (1984: 503 ff.). The link between the tyrant and the master, and correspondingly between the good king and the father, is developed by Aristotle, *Polyb.* 3.8.2, 3.14.15, etc. The comparison also appears in Cicero's treatment of the just king in *De rep.* 1.64. Cf. also *De rep.* 3.37.

[50] In Dionysius' more prolix account of the duel, Arruns calls Brutus a wild beast for putting his sons to death, DH *Ant.* 5.15.1.

[51] Cohen (1991: 117).

[52] Although this part of Livy's work probably appeared a good seven years before 18 BCE, the connection to the issues involved in Augustus' adultery laws seems inescapable.

father to consul is reiterated when Sp. Lucretius Tricipitinus, Lucretia's real father, replaces Brutus as consul (2.8.4).

But Livy's narrative makes it impossible to separate the 'adoption' of the state from the loss of the family. As a sign of this reciprocity, the final battle between Brutus and the 'son' is nothing if not ambiguous. Arruns and Brutus, 'careless of protecting their own body provided they wound the enemy', each die by the other's spear. Both the action itself and the sentence in which Livy describes it are as synchronized as a formal dance (*contrario ictu per parmam uterque transfixus duabus haerentes hastis moribundi ex equis lapsi sunt*, 2.6.9). In his analysis of the execution, Thomas assumes that only the public construction of the father's power over his children, the *vitae necisque potestas*, is involved in Brutus' execution of his children and consequently that the *animus patrius* he revealed has nothing to do with affection but only with discipline.[53] But Livy makes it clear that the fact of Brutus' paternity is a hindrance to the performance of his duty by stating that if he were not consul but only a spectator he would be removed (2.5.5). The consul Manlius Torquatus, who must also execute his own son and compares his situation to Brutus', makes his love for his son explicit: 'Natural affection (*ingenita caritas*) for children moves me' (8.7.18). And this language reminds us that without 'natural affection' the formation of the state would never have been accomplished. Thomas rejects the notion that the subjective response of Brutus as individual should be given too much prominence,[54] but by isolating Brutus within the narrative, by focusing the eyes of the crowd on him alone, it is as an individual that Livy forces his audience to see him.

But the point of this qualification is not to restore sentimentalism *per se*,[55] much less to imply that Livy intentionally undercuts the

[53] Thomas (1984: 518).

[54] 'It is, however, clear that the force of this scene is not limited to the emotional conflict that a *pater* experiences subjectively. Institutions are involved, a law is founded and made manifest, and both paternal and consular functions are engaged: the image of an individual suffering or overcoming suffering is clearly not the best point of departure from which to draw a lesson from this *exemplum*' (trans. edd.), Thomas (1984: 516, n. 36).

[55] Compare, for example, the conclusions of Tränkle (1965: 327–9) that Livy's particular aim in this scene is to render the character of Brutus more sympathetic and human.

patriotic force of the scene; it involves the fundamental techniques of Livy's narrative. The emphasis on perspective, on the perceptions of the onlookers, is not a device for reinforcing a patriotic 'moral' with the greatest possible vividness but a means of allowing his own audience to experience subjectively the shift in values upon which the creation of the Republic is predicated. As in so many of the publicly performed rituals of the Roman state, particularly sacrifice, resolution and harmony can only be achieved through the recreation of tensions and disorder. Thus Livy uses the climax of the revolution to rearticulate the oppositions in social organization and the construction of individual identity that inform the whole narrative, but now in a form that approximates the very ceremonies in which civic leaders presided over similar 'refoundations' of the Roman state.

As a spectacle the episode is focused on Brutus, whose presence makes the execution *conspectius* and whose face at the very moment of death usurps the attention of the crowd, and consequently of Livy's audience. It is in his countenance that the tensions of the scene are represented: *eminente animo patrio inter ministerium publicae poenae*. This moment where civic and familial roles are held in balance and equally accessible to the gaze of the viewer can be read as the true climax of the process of revelation effected by Brutus since his first appearance in the narrative.[56] It must thus be interpreted as a reversal of, for example, Tarquin's deposition of Servius Tullius where the disjunction between the personal and the public is emphasized.

However, Brutus is initially described not as a spectacle but as a hypothetical spectator. In fact Brutus occupies in every sense an intermediate point relative to the execution. Unlike the narratives of Dionysius and Plutarch where Brutus must actually persuade an unwilling crowd to go through with the execution,[57] here his participation is limited to a presiding role: he takes his place as consul and gives the command for the execution although even this moment of active participation is elided by Livy's shift to the passive

---

[56] It is precisely this sense of revelation that distinguishes Livy's version from that of Valerius Maximus. Here the father's spirit 'shines forth', but Valerius reverses the image and has Brutus 'slough off the father to play the consul', *exuit patrem ut consulem ageret*, Val. Max. 5.8.1.

[57] DH *Ant.*, 5.8.3; Plut. *Publicola*, 6.1.

voice (the lictors *were sent* to exact the punishment).[58] This treatment subtly emphasizes the structural resemblance between the execution and public sacrifice, where the killing itself is carried out by subordinates commanded by the presiding priest. It also lends an impersonality and lack of specificity to the proceedings which contrast with the extreme personal involvement of Brutus as *pater*. The description of the execution juxtaposes a simple five-word statement in the historical present emphasizing the ritual instruments of consular power with an adversative *cum* clause describing how the crowd turned their attention to Brutus' reaction. Again at the instant he becomes the object of the crowd's attention, Brutus is also an onlooker.

What is the point of this narrative complexity? As a spectator Brutus occupies the same position relative to the event as the rest of the crowd and perhaps of Livy's own audience as well. Yet at the same time he is distinguished by taking as it were the place of the victim. The effect both highlights the 'subjective' experience of Brutus and, by confusing the distinction between Brutus and the rest of the audience, puts every spectator in his place. The recreation of spectacle through the text thus offers a means for every citizen to experience as a participant the ritualized moment that more than any other provides an aetion of Roman citizenship. Cicero had expressed this transformation as a sacrifice where the individual subject occupies the dual role of presider at a sacrifice and of victim. Thus in Livy's treatment the execution of Brutus' sons balances the impure sacrifice of the death of Lucretia that ended the monarchy. And like Brutus exposing Lucretia's corpse in the Forum, Livy offers a spectacle which modulates sympathy with the father into civic participation.

Livy's use of sacrificial spectacle in these episodes as an instrument for allowing his own audience to experience the transition to full participation in the *res publica* provides a final correspondence between the methods of the historian and those of the *princeps*. A crucial aspect of Augustus' self-representation, and one which possessed a decisive impact for the iconography of all subsequent emperors, was the number of statues, coins, and public monuments which placed the emperor at the center of religious ceremonies,

---

[58] *missique lictores ad sumendum supplicium*, 2.5.8.

particularly as sacrificant.[59] As Elsner has recently demonstrated in
his interpretation of the *Ara Pacis*, such representations, far from
simply denoting the abstract *pietas* of the emperor, served to recreate
and reproduce the sacrificial experience, placing the viewer in the
place of participant and making the emperor the focal point of
the event.[60] Nor was this experience limited to Roman viewers;
the diffusion of these images in Italy and the provinces provided a
prototype for religious activity throughout the empire and helped
create a network of cult practices grounded in the authority of Rome
and of the *princeps* himself.[61] In his own adoption of sacrifice as a
means of 'Romanization' and the use he makes of visual images to
recreate ritual, Livy again anticipates the techniques of empire; but in
place of the emperor stands, in this case, the figure of Brutus,[62] and
the medium through which the image is propagated is no coin,
stamped with the mark of imperial or senatorial power, but the
historian's text.


ADDENDUM


This article illustrates the recent emphasis on the cultural (rather
than constitutional) aspects of Roman political life. On the change

---

[59] Cf. the comments of Zanker (1988: 127): 'Certainly from the time of the Secular
Games in 17 BCE, and probably much earlier, in the 20s, the princeps must have made
it known that henceforth he preferred that statues put up in his honor show him
togate at sacrifice or prayer.'

[60] Elsner (1991: 52): 'In looking at the altar Roman viewers did not simply see
images of a sacrifice that once happened. They saw a cultural process in which they
themselves became involved.'

[61] The thesis of Gordon (1990).

[62] Gordon's description of the sacrificial panel on the arch of Trajan at
Beneventum provides a striking parallel for the visual priorities in Livy's
configuration of Brutus' execution of his sons (1990: 202–3). In this panel, the
sacrifice is presented at one side of the image, while the emperor *capite velato*
dominates the other. Yet none of the spectators in the background observes the
sacrifice: all have their heads turned to face the emperor, who alone directs his gaze
toward the *victimarius* opposite him. In the same way, it is Brutus who attracts the
attention of both the crowd and the reader in Livy's narrative and provides sole access
to the execution itself.

from Republic to Principate and the gulf that opened between the two, see the articles collected in Raaflaub and Toher (1990). Many of the articles reprinted in this volume address related issues: on Livy and religion see the Addendum to Liebeschuetz, with Price (1984) on the ritual 'techniques of empire'; for Livy and Cicero see the Addendum to McDonald; for Livy and drama see the Addendum to Scafuro; for Lucretia and the Lucretia type-scene see the Addendum to Joshel; and on Livian characters see the Addendum to Catin.

Further on the Sabine women and the issues they raise, both thematic and narratological, see Jaeger (1997), chapter 1 (especially interesting on the spatial qualities of the narrative), and Miles 1995, chapter 5. Saller (1986) is fundamental on *patria potestas*; on conspiracies, see Pagán (2004); on civic identity in Italy in the Republic and early empire see Dench (1995) and (2005), and Ando (2000); and on the importance of law in Roman civic life see Crook (1967).

# VI

# Sources and Working Methods

# 16

## Livy and his Sources

### S. P. Oakley

*The editors asked whether pp. 13–20 of* A Commentary on Livy, Books vi–x, *volume I (Oxford, 1997) could be reprinted in this volume. However, I had become dissatisfied with the treatment of Livy's sources found in those pages. What follows is what I should now write were I publishing a second edition of the first volume of my commentary: it certainly contains more information and argument and I hope that it does greater justice to the views of earlier scholars, whom with the confidence of youth I once too much dismissed too easily.*

Much professional modern writing of history is based on primary sources.[1] In the ancient world too those writing contemporary history (such as Thucydides and, on occasions, Xenophon, Polybius, and Sallust) could not write otherwise, but the very different general attitude to research is shown by the tendency among ancient historians to base their accounts of earlier history not on documents but previous narratives: thus Polybius made extensive use of Silenus and Fabius Pictor; Tacitus employed Pliny the Elder, Fabius Rusticus, and Cluvius Rufus; and for Pliny the Younger (*epist.* 5. 18. 12)

---

[1] Livy used virtually the same sources in Books 1–5 as in Books 6–10, and almost all that is said in this chapter applies also to these books. The most important treatment of Livy's sources in the first decade are Nitzsch (1873), Klinger (1884), Unger (1891), Soltau (1896, 1897*a*, 1897*b*, and 1897*c*: 117–39), Klotz (1938*b*, 1939, and 1940–1), Ogilvie (1958 and 1965: 5–17), and Bloch and Guittard (Budé, 1987: pp. ix–xxi). Klinger's study of Book 10 is perhaps the most extensive attempt to ascertain which sources Livy used in any part of Books 6–10. Reading through these works one will find that in the period 1873–1941 the techniques used in investigation were progressively refined; but almost all these scholars were operating with assumptions that will be criticized in what follows.

historical research seems to have consisted in the collation of existing works.[2] This is further testimony to the literary nature of ancient historiography.[3]

Source-criticism ('Quellenforschung') has received a bad name, because in the epoch in which it was most practised (in Livian studies roughly 1870–1945), scholars paid it too much attention at the expense of other interesting questions; they operated in too mechanical a fashion; they reached wide-ranging conclusions that were not always supported by the evidence; they failed to recognize that extant as well as lost writers could innovate; and they treated great works of literature as little more than a quarry for sources that were lost and, if extant, would have been of inferior quality. Yet, if what is said in the previous paragraph is true, source-criticism must be important whatever the vices of some of its practitioners. It follows that properly to evaluate the value of the evidence provided by an ancient writer who based his work on earlier written accounts, one must know something about his sources. For where one can compare the words of a writer with those of his source(s), his historical and literary techniques are revealed with particular clarity. Even if the actual words of a source or sources are not extant, source-criticism may still be profitable if passages can be assigned with confidence to (a) writer(s) whose method of working is well enough understood that the modern scholar is able to take account of his or their general reliability and individual bias. The detailed comparison of passages of Books 30–45 with the relevant surviving portions of Polybius, in which every divergence between the writers reveals something about Livy's techniques and imagination, is a splendid example of what may be achieved in this field and has provided the foundation of the modern study of Livy's literary and historical methods.[4]

---

[2] Polybius: see conveniently Walbank (1957–79: i. 26–35); Tacitus: *ann.* 1. 69. 2,13. 20. 2, 14. 2. 2, 15. 53. 3, and 61. 3 (but note that Tacitus may very well have carried out research in the senatorial records); Pliny: *epist.* 5. 8. 12.

[3] This is not to deny that much modern academic writing of history is based on the work of previous historians and that ancient writers sometimes supplemented their literary sources; note e.g. the personal inquiries of Polybius at Rome.

[4] Nissen (1863) stands at the head of modern scholarship. The best general study is Tränkle (1977); the best detailed studies Briscoe (1973), (1981), and (2008) *passim.*

Livy could perhaps have organized the basic structure of his first decade from his own (doubtless very good) general knowledge of Roman history, without detailed inspection of any source; but for the shaping of smaller portions of the narrative a close working knowledge of earlier writers would have been necessary. Sadly, in sharp contrast to the situation that pertains for Books 30–45, there is virtually no external evidence about his sources: for deducing which authors from the many available he consulted when writing Books 1–10 we are dependent almost entirely on what he himself tells us.[5] For Books 6–10 this may be summarized, book by book, as follows:[6]

## BOOK 6

1. 12 citation of a variant (*quidam... putant* 'some... think'); 2. 8 *dicitur* ('is called'); 4. 3 *constat* ('it is agreed'); 8. 3 *ferunt* ('they say'), 12. 3 *quod cum ab antiquis tacitum praetermissum sit...* ('since this matter is passed over in silence by old writers...'); 12. 6 *ingens certe, quod inter omnes auctores conueniat... Volscorum exercitus fuit* ('certainly, as is agreed by all authorities... the army of the Volscians was huge'); 16. 4 *satis constat* ('it is generally agreed'); 18. 16 *dicitur; sed nec... satis planum traditur* ('is said, but... is not recorded sufficiently clearly'); 20. 4 *apud neminem auctorem inuenio* ('I find in no authority'); 20. 6 *dicitur* ('he is said'); 20. 12 citation of a variant (*sunt qui...* ['there are those who...']); 33. 5 *dicitur* ('is said'); 38. 9 citation of a variant (*seu... ut scripsere quidam, seu...* ['whether... as some have written, or...']); 39. 4 *accipio* ('I understand'), 40. 2 *dicitur* ('is said'); 42. 5–6 Livy records that Quadrigarius placed the duel between Manlius and the Gaul in this year (367), but himself follows *plures auctores* ('more authorities') in preferring 361.

[5] As indeed we are for most of 21–29 and the portions of 31–45 for which Polybius is not extant.
[6] This list includes all the references which Livy makes to his sources in Books 6–10. For a similar list for the whole decade see Forsythe (1999: 22–39).

## BOOK 7

1. 8 *ferunt* ('they say'); 2. 3 *dicuntur* ('are said'); 2. 8 *dicitur* ('is said');
3. 3 *dicitur* ('is said'); 3. 6 *ferunt* ('they say'), 3. 7 *diligens talium
monumentorum auctor Cincius adfirmat* ('Cincius, a studious
authority on such memorials, states'); 6. 1 *dicitur* ('is said'); 6.
6 Livy mentions the difficulties which he has with the story of
M. Curtius; 9. 3–5 citation of variants (*satis constat... Macer
Licinius... scribit... quaesita ea propriae familiae laus leuiorem
auctorem Licinium facit: cum mentionem eius rei in uetustioribus
annalibus nullam inueniam, magis ut belli Gallici causa dictatorem
creatum arbitrer inclinat animus* ['it is generally agreed... Licinius
Macer... writes... the quest for this credit for his own family makes
Licinius an authority of less weight: since in the older annals I find
no reference to this matter, I incline rather to think that the dictator
was created because of the Gallic War']); 10. 5 *quoniam id memoria
dignum antiquis uisum est* ('since to old writers this has seemed
worthy of mention'); 18. 2 *ut scripsere quidam* ('as some have written'), 18. 10 *in quibusdam annalibus... inuenio* ('I find in some
annals'); 21. 6 *meriti aequitate curaque sunt ut per omnium annalium
monumenta celebres nominibus essent* ('they have deserved through
their fairness and concern that they should be celebrated by name
throughout the memorials of all annals') (not certainly a reference
to Livy's sources); 22. 3 *quidam Caesonem, alii Gaium praenomen
Quinctio adiciunt* ('some add to Quinctius the first name Caeso,
others Gaius'); 25. 8 *dicuntur* ('are said'); 26. 15 *cuius populi
ea cuiusque gentis classis fuerit nihil certi est* ('there is no certainty
to which people and to which race that fleet belonged'); 27. 9 citation
of variants (*sunt qui...* ['there are those who...']); 42. 1–7
citation of variants (*inuenio apud quosdam... aliis annalibus proditum est... adeo nihil praeter seditionem fuisse eamque compositam
inter antiquos rerum auctores constat* ['I find in some... it is
handed down in other annals... Indeed, among the old authorities
it is agreed only that there was civil unrest and that this was
calmed']).

## BOOK 8

3. 6 *constat* ('it is agreed'), 6. 1 *proditur memoriae* ('it is handed down to memory'); 6. 3 citation of variant (*exanimatum auctores quoniam non omnes sunt, mihi quoque in incerto relictum sit* ['since not all authorities record that he was killed, I, too, may leave the problem undecided']); 6. 9 *dicitur* ('is said'); 9. 1 *dicitur* ('is said'); 10. 8 ... *ut facile conuenerit inter Romanos Latinosque qui eius pugnae memoriam posteris tradiderunt, utrius partis T. Manlius dux fuisset, eius futuram haud dubie uictoriam* ('with the result that it was easily agreed among those Romans and Latins who passed on to their descendants a record of that battle, that without doubt victory would have belonged to whichever side had been led by Titus Manlius'); 11. 1 *haec... haud ab re duxi uerbis quoque ipsis, ut tradita nuncupataque sunt, referre* ('I have not thought it beside the point to record these things, in the very words, too, with which they were pronounced and recorded'); 11. 2–4 citation of a variant (*apud quosdam auctores inuenio* ['I find in some authorities']); 12. 1 *constat* ('it is agreed'); 24. 1 *proditum* ('it is passed down'), 18. 1 citation of variants (*Flaccum Potitum uarie in annalibus cognomen consulis inuenio* ['I find in the annals that his *cognomen* is recorded variously as either Flaccus or Potitius']); 18. 2 citation of a variant (*nec omnes auctores sunt* ['not all authorities are of this view']); 19. 13 citation of a variant (*prius animaduersum in eos qui capita coniurationis fuerant a consule scribit Claudius* ['Claudius writes that the consul first punished those who were the ring-leaders of the conspiracy']); 20. 4 *dicuntur* ('are said'); 20. 6 citation of a variant (*duplex inde fama est: alii... alii...* ['from then on there are two versions: some...others...']); 23. 17 citation of a variant ( ... *L. Papirium Mugillanum; Cursorem in aliis annalibus inuenio* ['...Lucius Papirius Mugillanus (whom in some annals I find named Lucius Papirius Cursor']); 26. 6 citation of a variant (*haud ignarus opinionis alterius* ['I am not ignorant of the other view']); 30. 4 *uocant* ('they call'); 30. 7 citation of variants (*uiginti milia hostium caesa eo die traduntur. auctores habeo bis cum hoste signa conlata dictatore absente, bis rem egregie gestam; apud antiquissimos auctores una haec pugna inuenitur; in quibusdam annalibus tota res praetermissa est* ['it is recorded that 20,000 of the enemy

were killed on that day. Some writers state that during the dictator's absence twice was pitched battle fought, twice was an outstanding success achieved. However, in the oldest writers just this one battle is found, and in some annals the whole affair is passed over']); 30. 9 citation of variants (*seu ... seu credere libet Fabio auctori* ['whether... or one prefers to trust writer Fabius']); 37. 3 *Q. Aemilio—Aulium quidam annales habent* ['Quintus Aemilius— some annals call him Aulius']), 37. 4 citation of variant (*sunt qui ...* ['there are those who ...']); 40. 1–3 citation of variant (*quidam auctores sunt* ['some writers hold']).

# BOOK 9

3. 9 *dicitur* ('is said'); 5. 2–5 citation of variant (*itaque non, ut uulgo credunt Claudiusque etiam scribit, foedere pax Caudina sed per sponsionem facta est* ['therefore the Caudine peace was not made by treaty, as is commonly believed and as Claudius actually records, but by means of a promise); 7. 2 *dicitur* ('is said'); 12. 5 *satis constat* ('it is generally agreed'); 15. 8 citation of variant (*quod quibusdam in annalibus inuenio* ['as I find in some annals']); 15. 9–11 Livy records major confusion in the *Fasti*; 16. 1 *conuenit iam inde per consules reliqua belli perfecta* ['there is a consensus that thenceforth the rest of the war was finished by the consuls']); 16. 11 citation of a variant (*auctores sunt* ['there are writers']); 16. 19 *quin eum parem destinant animis magno Alexandro ducem* ('they even mark him out as the equal of the great Alexander'); 23. 5 citation of a variant (*inuenio apud quosdam* ['I find in some writers']) (cf. 25. 2); 27. 14 *proditum memoriae est* ('it is handed down to memory'), 29. 10 *traditur* ('it is handed down'); 28. 5–6 complex citation of variants; 36. 2 citation of variants (*Fabium Caesonem alii, C. Claudium quidam ... tradunt* ['some record that he was called Caeso Fabius, others C. Claudius']); 36. 4 *dicitur* ('is said'); 36. 7 *dicuntur* ('are said'); 37. 11 citation of variant (*quidam auctores sunt* ['some writers hold']); 38. 16 citation of variant (*Macer Licinius* ['Licinius Macer']); 40. 16 *dicitur* ('is said'); 42. 3 *in quibusdam annalibus inuenio* ('in some authorities

I find'); 44. 3–4 citation of variant (*hos consules Piso Q. Fabio et P. Decio suggerit biennio exempto* ['Piso, removing two years, attaches these consuls to Quintus Fabius and Publius Decius']); 44. 7–8 *alii... tradunt, alii...* ('some... record, others...'); 44. 15 citation of variant (*quidam auctores sunt* ['some writers hold']); 46. 2–3 citation of variants (*inuenio in quibusdam annalibus... arguit Macer Licinius* ['in some annals I find... Licinius Macer refutes']); 46. 15 *ferunt* ('they say'); 46. 15 *dicitur* (it is said').

## BOOK 10

2. 3 citation of variant (*in quibusdam annalibus inuenio* ['I find in some annals']); 3. 4 citation of variant (*id magis credo quam Q. Fabium ea aetate atque eis honoribus Valerio subiectum; ceterum ex Maximi cognomine ortum errorem haud abnuerim* ['I prefer to believe this rather than that Quintus Fabius, at his age and with his achievements, was made subordinate to Valerius; but I should not deny that the error arose from the *cognomen* Maximus']); 5. 13 citation of variant (*habeo auctores* ['I have authorities']); 5. 14 citation of variant (*tradidere quidam... id unum non ambigitur* ['some have recorded... this one thing is not disputed']); 6. 7–8 Livy did not find the information which he required in his sources; 7. 1 *ferunt* ('they say'); 7. 3 *dicitur* ('is said'); 9. 10–12 complex variants: Livy cites Macer, Tubero and Piso; 11. 9 citation of variant (cf. 9. 10–12) (*ut scripsere quibus...* ['as those have written, for whom...']); 11. 10 *nec traditur causa* ('the reason is not explained'); 17. 11 citation of variants (*huius oppugnatarum urbium decoris pars maior in quibusdam annalibus ad Maximum trahitur; Murgantiam ab Decio, a Fabio Ferentinum Romuleamque oppugnatas tradunt. sunt qui... quidam...* ['in some annals the greater part of the glory for the storming of these towns is transferred to Maximus: they record that Murgantia was stormed by Decius, Ferentinum and Romulea by Fabius. There are those who... some...']); 18. 7 citation of variant (*in trinis annalibus inuenio* [in three annals I find']); 19. 13 *ferunt* ('they say'); 19. 17 *dicitur* ('is said'); 21. 8 *dicitur* ('is said'); 25.

12–13 citation of variants (*nam in utrumque auctores sunt... quidam... uolunt* ['for there are authorities who hold each view... some want']); 25. 17 *ferunt* ('they say'); 26. 5–6 citation of variant (*sunt quibus...* ['there are those for whom...']); 26. 7 *constare res incipit* ('agreement on the affair begins'); 26. 10 citation of variant (*quidam auctores sunt* ['some writers hold']); 26. 12 citation of variant (*sunt qui... tradant* ['there are those who record']); 30. 4–5 citation of variant (*magna eius diei... fama est etiam uero stanti; sed superiecere quidam augendo fidem* ['the repute of that day is great even for someone standing firm in the truth, but some have overshot credibility by exaggerating']); 30. 7 citation of variant (*in pluribus annalibus* ['in more annals']); 37. 13–16 confusion as to who fought where in 294: Livy refers to both Fabius and Claudius; 41. 5 citation of variant (*Sp. Nautius—Octauium Maecium quidam eum tradunt—* ['Spurius Nautius—some record that it was Octavius Maecius—']); 42. 6 *ceterum illud memoriae traditur* ('moreover, it is handed down to memory that...'); 46. 7 citation of variant (*apud neminem ueterem auctorem inuenio* ['I find in no old authority']).[7]

Several conclusions may be drawn from this evidence.

(*a*) Livy frequently cites variants which he found in his sources. Such matters cannot be put on a statistical basis, but he seems to have been conscientious about recording the discrepancies that he found, and this may give us some confidence that he was a fairly reliable witness to the traditions that he was using.[8]

(*b*) There are surprisingly few major variants in these books. This allows the deduction that the tradition which he used was relatively homogeneous.[9]

(*c*) He tells us only very rarely which authority or authorities he has followed: indeed, in the two places where the survival of external

---

[7] For a similar list covering Books 21–22 and Books 23–25, see, respectively, Dorey's Teubner editions pp. 140 and 141.

[8] Note in particular his understanding that old sources were more likely to be reliable; see below, p. 448.

[9] Thus e.g. Cornell (2005: 52). We shall, however, find more signs of divergence when D.S. is compared with Livy (see Oakley [1997–2005: i.106–8]) and should perhaps allow for the fact that it was easier for a historian to take account of minor variations (e.g. on names or figures) than totally inconsistent versions of the events of a year.

evidence suggests strongly that he is following, respectively, Claudius Quadrigarius and Piso, neither is named.[10]

(*d*) The authorities named are, with the exception of Cincius (almost certainly the antiquarian, since he is cited specifically for some antiquarian information at 7. 3. 7), writers of the so-called Roman annalistic tradition: Licinius Macer (cited four times), Claudius Quadrigarius four times), Fabius Pictor (twice), Calpurnius Piso (twice), and Aelius Tubero (once). These are the same writers whom Livy used in his first pentad, except that Quadrigarius, not cited in Books 1–5, began his narrative only with the events of 390, and Livy there cites also Valerius Antias (2. 5. 12, 4. 23. 2 (quoted below)).

(*e*) The one reference to Cincius apart, there is no mention of antiquarian sources.[11] This suggests that Livy drew almost entirely on the annalistic tradition: though some of his material must have derived ultimately from antiquarians, most of it could have been transmitted to him via his normal annalistic sources,[12] and only for the digression on the origin of the *ludi scaenici* ('theatrical games') (7. 2. 4–13 n.) does it seem probable that he consulted directly an unnamed antiquarian (Varro). Moreover, Livy could have found his information even for this discussion in an annalist. Other passages which include material that is likely to have come from outside the annalistic tradition are the digression on Alexander (9. 17–19) and the tale of Cleonymus (10. 2. 1–15).[13]

(*f*) The modern argument that Livy did not directly consult the second-century writers Fabius Pictor and Piso but discovered their views only from discussion of them in the works of Quadrigarius, Antias, Macer, and Tubero is paradoxical,[14] since Livy refers often to

[10] See my commentary on 7. 18. 10, 7. 9. 6–10. 10, and 9. 46. 1–15; the fragments are Quadrigarius fr. 10 *HRR* and Piso fr. 27 *HRR*.

[11] See further Klotz (1940–1: 202–4).

[12] This is in effect the argument of Soltau (1897*a*: 416–17). However, one cannot finally prove that Livy did not consult antiquarians directly.

[13] Klotz added 8. 8. 3–14 (the digression on the history of the legion: see further my note on 8.8.3–14) and 8. 10. 11–11. 1 (on some aspects of *deuotio*). Livy could indeed have consulted (an) antiquarian source(s) for these passages, but their integration into his battle-narrative suggests that the material may have come from his usual annalistic sources.

[14] See e.g. W–M on 8. 30. 7, Soltau (1897*a*: 409, 410–11), who allows that sometimes Livy may have consulted Piso directly, Walsh (1961*a*: 115 and 119),

both in the early books.[15] By contrast, he refers to Antias only twice
in the whole of Books 1–10 and never after Book 4. Furthermore, one
of the few passages for which we can say anything with much
confidence about Livy's use of his sources in this decade is 9. 46
(already mentioned), for which he used Piso. Similarly, it can be
argued convincingly against sceptics that he used Cato as a direct
source in the fourth decade.[16] And that he was well aware of the
greater authority which older narratives might possess is shown by
comments such as 2. 18. 5 *apud ueterrimos tamen auctores... inuenio*
('however, I find in the oldest authorities'), 6. 12. 2 *mihi percensenti
propiores temporibus harum rerum auctores* ('as I scrutinized the
writers closer to the time of these events'), 10. 46. 7 *apud neminem
ueterem auctorem inuenio* ('I find in no old authority'), 25. 11. 20
*ceterum defectio Tarentinorum utrum priore anno an hoc facta sit, in
diuersum auctores trahunt; plures propioresque aetate memoriae rerum
hoc anno factam tradunt* ('however, authorities take different views
on whether the revolt of the Tarentines occurred in this or the
previous year; more of them, and those closer in time to the recording of the events, relate that it occurred in this year'), and 29. 14. 9 *id
quibus uirtutibus inducti ita iudicarint, sicut traditum a proximis
memoriae temporum illorum scriptoribus libens posteris traderem, ita
meas opiniones coniectando rem uetustate obrutam non interponam*
('If it had been handed down by writers nearest to the recording of

Ogilvie (1965: 7 and 14), and Burck (1971: 43 n. 13). Soltau drew attention to 4. 23.
1–3, a well-known passage in which Livy reports that Antias and Tubero recorded
that there was one pair of consuls in 434 BCE, Macer another. Livy then adds that both
Macer and Tubero claimed the authority of the *libri lintei* but *neuter tribunos militum
eo anno fuisse traditum a scriptoribus antiquis dissimulat* ('but neither hides that old
writers had recorded that there were military tribunes in this year'). This does not
prove that Livy did not himself consult Fabius or Piso.

[15] Fabius: 1. 44. 2, 55. 8; 2. 40. 10; 8. 30. 9; 10. 37. 14–15; and 22. 7. 4; Piso: 1. 55.
8–9; 2. 32. 3, 58. 1; 9. 44. 3; 10. 9. 12, and 25. 39. 12–15. There are references also to
*antiquissimi scriptores* ('very old writers') or *ueteres auctores* ('old authorities') or the
like (1. 44. 2; 2. 18. 5, 40. 10; 3. 23. 7; 4. 20. 8; 7. 9. 5 [which shows that Macer was not
amongst these]; 7. 30. 7; 10. 9. 12, 46. 7), by which we must presume that these two
are meant (indeed Piso and Fabius are mentioned explicitly at 1. 44. 2; 2. 40. 10, and
10. 9. 12). See further Steele (1904: 27–8). I therefore side with e.g. Laistner (1947:
84), Luce (1977: 158–69), Forsythe (1999: 59–64), Northwood (2000), and Cornell
(2005: 52). Northwood provides the fullest and best critique of the view that Livy did
not personally consult second-century annalists.

[16] See Tränkle (1971), Astin (1978: 302–7), and Briscoe (1981) on 34. 8. 4–21.

those times, I should gladly pass on to future generations by which of his manly qualities they had been led in forming their judgement in this way; but I shall not interpret a matter obscured by age by making conjectural opinions of my own'). Note too 22. 7. 4 *Fabium, aequa-lem temporibus huiusce belli, potissimum auctorem habui* ('I have regarded Fabius, *a contemporary* of the times of this war, as the most credible authority'), with which contrast 8. 40. 5 *nec quisquam aequalis temporibus illis scriptor exstat quo satis certo auctore stetur* ('nor is there anyone *contemporary* to those times extant on whom one may repose as a sure authority').

(*g*) Livy tends to report discrepancies immediately when they do not much interrupt the flow of his narrative: see e.g. 6. 20. 12, 38. 9; 7. 9. 3–5; 8. 6. 3, 18. 1, 23. 17, 37. 3; 9. 15. 8, 16. 11, 23. 5–6, 36. 2, 38. 16, 44. 3–4, 46. 2–3; 10. 2. 3, 18. 7, 25. 12–13, 41. 5, and 46. 7. On more major matters, where the divergence in his sources was more substantial, he tends to cite variants that are incompatible with his main narrative at its end: see e.g. 7. 42. 1, 42. 3–7; 8. 11. 2, 30. 7, 40. 1–5; 9. 15. 9–11, 37. 11, 44. 15; 10. 5. 13–14, 17. 11–12, 26. 12, 30. 4–7, and 37. 13–16.[17] However, one should not be too schematic in such classification: 6. 1. 12 and 8. 27. 9 fit both lists, and 6. 42. 5–6 fits neither.

(*h*) If one leaves aside vaguer references to sources such as those embodied in *ferunt* ('they say'), *dicitur* ('it is said'), and the like, it is striking how often (and particularly when he names names) Livy refers to sources for versions that he has chosen *not* to follow: into this category fall the first reference to Piso, and the second to Fabius Pictor, all four references to Quadrigarius (that at 8. 19. 13 less clearly than the others); two or three of the four references to Macer,[18] and the reference to Tubero.

(*i*) Klotz (1940–1: 205–8) argued from this evidence that Livy consulted Pictor, Piso, and Quadrigarius only as checks on his main source but never used them for his main narrative.[19] This thesis

---

[17] The best known example of this technique comes at 38. 56. 1–57. 8, where after having given an account of the prosecution of Scipio Africanus based on what he found in Valerius Antias, Livy has to admit at great length that other sources told the story very differently. The most notable instance from the first decade is at 4. 7. 10–12, discussed below.
[18] The clear exception is 9. 46. 3; the reference at 9. 38. 16 is perhaps non-committal. Note that at 10. 9. 10, even though Livy rejects the view of Macer and Tubero, he gives it as much space as the view of Piso that he accepts.
[19] See also Walsh (1961*a*: 117).

accounts for the passages just cited, and certainly Livy's more expansive narrative needed more material than Pictor or Piso could provide. Yet it should not be exalted into a general rule: these citations relate to only a very small proportion of Livy's work in Books 6–10, and it is doubtful that Livy provides us with sufficient evidence to permit such a large generalization. Furthermore, Klotz's view entails two other difficulties: first, it rests on the uncertain assumption that Livy used only one source at a time (see below); second, Livy can be shown to have used Quadrigarius and Piso in the two passages already cited.

(j) All this makes the case of Valerius Antias difficult. That this celebrated *bête noire* is not cited anywhere in Books 5–10 (see above) may be surprising to those who have sampled the abundant modern literature in which numerous falsifications are laid at his door. Given Livy's regular use of him after Book 21, it would be rash to conclude that he did not consult him for our period, and some will take comfort in Klotz's hypothesis that he is not cited because he is often Livy's main source; but one must be alert to the possibility that Livy used him less than, say, Quadrigarius or Macer.[20]

Any discussion of how Livy worked with his sources must inevitably be speculative.[21] However, the passages listed above under (g), in which he immediately registers variants for a disputed matter, prove beyond doubt that before composing his own narrative he read more than one version of events. They refute as well any extreme attempt to argue from the passages where he lists variants at the end of his narrative that he consulted other narratives only after transcribing from one source—which, it must be said, would have been a very stupid method to use.[22]

Nevertheless, from Nissen (1863) through Klotz (1940–1 and various articles) to at least Ogilvie (1958) and Walsh (1961a: 141), scholars have tended to argue that, whatever reading Livy may have done before he started writing, he preferred to work largely from one source at a time. This view is not absurd. Its foundations lie in the

---

[20] Contrast e.g. Soltau (1897a: 410).

[21] For interesting speculation see e.g. Luce (1977: 185–229).

[22] Walsh (1961a: 141) stops just short of imputing to Livy such a method of working.

comparison of Books 31–45 with Polybius, which proves beyond any doubt that for large stretches of narrative Livy based his narrative very closely on one source. Indeed, an unprejudiced comparison reveals that whilst constantly improving the slack sentence structure of Polybius, Livy sometimes follows him even in the detailed organization of his own sentences;[23] and this in turn suggests that as he wrote his own narrative he had a scroll of Polybius open beside him. The best evidence that Livy's practice in Books 1–10 was not much different is provided by comparison of 7. 9–10 and 9. 46 with the fragments of Piso and Quadrigarius just mentioned. This reveals, in addition to numerous artistically induced changes, a wealth of verbal similarities. One may point also to passages where a contradiction in Livy's narrative suggests some kind of change of source.[24] Yet it would be unwise to regard the matter as proved or certain, since (*a*) even in the Polybian sections of Books 30–45 there is evidence that Livy did not entirely ignore what his annalistic predecessors had written and that he made some insertions from them into narratives that basically derived from Polybius,[25] and he could have done the same in Books 1–10; (*b*) it is improbable that Livy thought any of his annalistic sources for Books 1–10 was blessed with authority over rivals similar to that possessed by Polybius for Greek affairs; (*c*) in the African narrative of Book 30 it is possible to see how Livy blended Polybius and Roman annalistic sources, and again he could very easily have operated in this way in Books 1–10; and (*d*) when adapting a writer, Livy may have been reminded of what he had read in other sources, even if he did not feel the need to reread those sources.

Even if Livy did generally employ one main source at a time, his use of the Quadrigarius fr. 10 *HRR* shows that his procedures were not always simple: he rejects (6. 42. 5) Quadrigarius' view that the single combat of Manlius Torquatus was fought in 367, but still makes heavy use of his account when he narrates the single combat in 361.[26]

---

[23] This is revealed by a close comparison of the two authors; about this matter, on which I disagree with Luce (1977: 212–21), I hope to write more fully elsewhere.

[24] On the inconsistency caused by Livy's return to Quadrigarius in 7. 9–10, see Oakley (1997–2005: ii.115); also, on Books 4–5, Ogilvie (1958) (who, however, exaggerates some difficulties).

[25] See esp. Tränkle (1977: 59–72).

[26] See too Oakley (1997–2005: iii.605) on the complexities of 9. 46.

The conclusions that can easily be drawn from evidence just cited are so limited and allow the sources of so few passages to be named that it is hardly surprising that scholars have wished to go further. Before discussion of the techniques that they have used, it must be said at once that their quest involves an element of paradox: even if one could assign passages with confidence to, say, Pictor, Piso, Antias, Macer, or Tubero, the gains would be distinctly limited, since we know so little about the techniques of any of these lost writers.

A favoured technique of source-critics has been to use the evidence of the narrative of Livy (and also of, for example, Dionysius, Plutarch, or Dio) to seek to determine the characteristics of writers such as Antias, Macer, or Tubero. They have then argued on the basis of these alleged characteristics that other passages in these authors were taken from the same source. Quite apart from the possibility that Livy may have blended his sources, this method involves two dangers. The first is the risk of circular argument: characteristics of sources are 'identified' largely on the basis of Livy's text, and then large portions of Livy's text which display these characteristics are said to derive from these sources.[27] A classic instance of this procedure concerns Valerius Antias, to whom it has long been customary to ascribe many passages in which the Valerii are handled favourably:[28] but there is no external evidence for Antias' having proceeded in this way, and the modern view of him is built almost entirely upon inferences from allegedly Antian passages in Livy, Dionysius, Plutarch, and others.[29]

The second danger, to which Klotz (1938*a*: esp. 102; 1938*b*: 42–50; 1940–1: 208–11; 1941: 304–6) devoted much attention (although he himself did not term it a danger) concerns Livy's use of Tubero, the first-century writer of annalistic history. It needs more extended discussion, even though the results of this discussion will be inconclusive. For the certain fact that Livy used Tubero makes it conceivable that information from earlier writers was mediated to Livy via

---

[27] For damning criticism of this procedure see Goodyear (1966: 62 = 1992: 209), Briscoe (1973: 1–12 and 1981: 2–3), and Luce (1977: 139–84).

[28] For examples in earlier scholarship, see e.g. Münzer (1891) and Soltau (1897*c*: 127); for later scholarship see e.g. Wiseman (1979*a*) (via index *s.u.* Valerius Antias).

[29] For further discussion of Antias, see Oakley (1997–2005: i.89–92). Though the evidential basis of the standard modern view of Antias is unsatisfactory, I do not wish to deny that there may be some truth in it.

him: if this did happen, then it becomes still harder to find criteria securely to identify these writers as immediate or ultimate sources of Livy. Even if the characteristics of Livy's annalistic sources have been correctly identified, and even if these characteristics do indeed appear in his narrative, it need not always follow that he was using the writer in question as his source or main source: the material could have come to him via Tubero.[30] Examination of the two passages in which Livy cites Tubero shows that this is more than just an arid possibility. At 4. 23. 1–3 (= Tubero, fr. 6 *HRR*) Livy writes:

> In Licinius Macer I find that the same consuls were reappointed for the following year, Julius for the third time, Verginius for the second time. Valerius Antias and Quintus Tubero state that Marcus Manlius and Quintus Sulpicius were consuls for that year. However, even though their statements differ so much, both Tubero and Macer claim the authority of the linen books, but neither hides that old writers had recorded that there were military tribunes in this year. Licinius does not hesitate to follow the linen books; Tubero is uncertain of the truth. Amongst so many matters that are obscure because of their age, let this too be regarded as uncertain.

This is one of several difficult passages in Livy relating to the consular tribunate that have generated much bibliography. The best solution to the historical problem is that the *scriptores antiqui* ('old writers') (with whom D.S. and probably *Fasti Capitolini* coincided) were right in recording consular tribunes; that one of the names of the consular tribunes has been omitted by Antias and Tubero; and that Macer introduced into the tradition false information taken from the *libri lintei*.[31] Now, if one grants that the *libri lintei* were not a forgery of Macer's, then Tubero too perhaps consulted them and found information in them different from what Macer recorded.

Quite attractive also, however, is the cynical view that Tubero, being either lazy or muddled, took his names from Antias and his reference to the *libri lintei* from Macer.[32] At 10. 9. 10–11 (= Tubero, fr. 7 *HRR*) Livy writes:

[30] What is said here with regard to Livy applies equally to Dionysius.
[31] This is essentially the view of Mommsen (1871: 270–3 = 1864–79: ii.222–4) and Klotz (1937: 217–18, 1940–1: 209). For the *libri lintei*, see Oakley (1997–2005: i.27–8).
[32] Thus Klotz. Unger (1891: 317) argued that the mistake was Livy's: Tubero simply referred to *libri* which he had consulted and Livy assumed that these were the *libri lintei*. This too could be right.

When all the centuries were proclaiming Quintus Fabius consul for this year, even though he was not officially a candidate for election, Macer Licinius and Tubero state that he himself initiated the idea of his consulship being deferred to a year in which there was more warfare. (11) In that year, he said, he would be of more use to the state if he held a magistracy based in the city. Therefore, neither disguising what he would prefer nor officially a candidate, he was elected curule aedile with Lucius Papirius Cursor. (12) That I do not register this view as certain is brought about by Piso, an older writer of annals. He records that Gnaeus Domitius Calvinus, the son of Gnaeus, and Spurius Carvilius Maximus, the son of Quintus, were curule aediles in this year.

Whatever one thinks of the information provided by Piso, there is little doubt that the view of Macer and Tubero is false (see Oakley (1997–2005) iv.139–44). Although they may both be reporting an innovation effected first by an earlier annalist (e.g. Cn. Gellius), it is a strong possibility that Macer himself introduced the change and that Tubero took it from him.

Klotz's own position on Livy's use of Macer, Tubero, and Antias was somewhat ambiguous. He rightly stopped short of arguing that Livy did not himself consult Antias or Macer directly in Books 1–10,[33] and concluded that all three writers were used. Yet he inclined to think that for long stretches Tubero was indeed Livy's primary source.[34] The evidence that he adduced does not allow his case to be proved.[35] Part of it came from various alleged allusions to the period 63–44 BCE that have been detected in Livy: if one accepts both that these allusions are genuine and that Antias wrote in the Sullan period and not later,[36] then they can have originated only in either Tubero (the one source of Livy known to have lived late enough) or himself.[37] Quite apart from the fact that such allusions embrace only a

[33] This would be a variant of the fallacy that Livy found out the views of Pictor and Piso only through later annalists.
[34] He also believed that for long stretches of narrative Tubero was Dionysius' main source: see Klotz (1938*b*).
[35] For sensible discussion of it see Walsh (1961*a*: 115–17).
[36] The date of Antias is controversial. Vell. 2. 9. 6 makes him a contemporary of Sisenna, a dating supported by Asconius (p. 55 Stangl), but there have been several attempts to argue that he wrote in the 50s or 40s BCE. Orthodoxy has been reasserted recently by Walt (1997: 303–7).
[37] Again, what is said with regard to Livy applies equally to Dionysius, in whom these allusions have also been detected.

small part of the narrative, it is a difficulty that few are certain: although the letter with which the Vitellii and Aquilii incriminate themselves is found in both Livy (2. 4. 3–4) and Dionysius (5. 7. 1) (and therefore cannot be the invention of either), it need not necessarily have been modelled on the famous letter of Catiline to the Allobroges.[38] Of the allusions that are more certain, Livy himself could have been responsible for at least some.[39] Klotz further claimed that there are various passages in Livy's first decade where a writer earlier than Livy has combined two narratives so as to effect a doublet, and he devoted an article to a study of Book 9 from this perspective.[40] Although much that he says is exaggerated and over-schematic, some of these doublets do undoubtedly exist;[41] but they need not have been created by a writer as late as Tubero. A certain example of a combination of sources, on which Klotz (1938b: 47–8) placed some emphasis, comes in 444, the year of the first consular tribunate: Livy (4. 7. 10–8. 1) and Dionysius (11. 61. 3–63. 1) both hold that the consular tribunes were forced to abdicate and were replaced by consuls, for whose period of office Macer cited evidence from the *libri lintei*; but other sources know or knew only of consular tribunes. Klotz held that Tubero combined Antias' version in which there were consular tribunes in this year and Macer's in which there were consuls; but we cannot be certain that the combination was not made first by Macer.

Sometimes there is the possibility of a limited escape from circular argument, particularly with regard to Licinius Macer, about whose views something is known from other sources.[42] Livy tells us (7. 9. 5 = fr. 16 *HRR*) that Macer distorted the events surrounding

[38] Ogilvie on 2. 3–5 draws attention to Greek precedents.
[39] One of Klotz's allusions is discussed in Oakley (1997–2005) at 6. 23. 7 (with addendum at Oakley (1996–2005) iv.525). There are certainly Catilinarian allusions in Livy's account of the downfall of Manlius Capitolinus (Oakley (1997–2005: i.481–4, with addenda at Oakley (1997–2005: iv.517 and 522)) but the presence also of allusions to Sallust's *Catiline* makes it virtually certain that they originate with Livy himself.
[40] See Klotz (1938a).
[41] See Oakley (1997–2005: iii.269) (on the events of 318–317) and iii.455 (on the events of 310/309).
[42] For Antias and Quadrigarius external evidence provides nothing. About Tubero, whether he be Lucius or Quintus, we know even more than about Macer, but little of this knowledge seems relevant to his histories.

the nomination of a dictator in 361 to add to the glory of his family, a report that there is no reason to disbelieve. Such behaviour seems not to have been uncharacteristic of ancient historians: whatever one may think of the view that the prominence of the Valerii in our sources for early Roman history owes much to Valerius Antias (see above), Livy himself suppressed information that was to the discredit of prominent Livii, even though he was almost certainly not related to them.[43] The absence of another such remark about Macer makes it difficult to prove conclusively that he behaved in the same way elsewhere, but it would be surprising if his pen does not lie behind at least some of the material in the following Livian episodes, in which the Calvi of the years 400–395 BCE are portrayed notably favourably: the election of P. Licinius Calvus in 400 as (allegedly) the first plebeian consular tribune (5. 12. 8–13);[44] the election of Calvus to a second tribunate for 396 and his resignation in favour of his son (5. 18. 1–6); and the report (5. 20. 4) that in the senate this son asked for the opinion of his father before that of all others.[45] Another possibility concerns the election of the first tribunes of the plebs in 493. Livy (2. 33. 2–3) writes: 'Accordingly, two tribunes of the plebs were created, Gaius Licinius and Lucius Albinius; these created three further colleagues for themselves. Sicinius, the creator of the disturbance, was among these, but there is less agreement about the identity of the other two. There are those who state that only two tribunes were created on the Sacred Hill and that the consecrated law was passed there.' Dionysius (6. 89. 1) mentions L. Junius Brutus and C. Sicinius, who were the current plebeian leaders and then C. and P. Licinius and C. Viscellius Ruga. Plainly at least one of the sources used by Livy and Dionysius must have invented material, and therefore C. Licinius perhaps owes his position in Livy's account to Macer. Note too that C. Licinius Stolo and C. Licinius Calvus were prominent at the time of the passing of the Licinio-Sextian rogations

---

[43] See conveniently Walsh (1961a: 153).

[44] However, in the first passage Livy mentions (but not by name) the views of at least two sources on the reasons for the choice of Calvus. If these sources are Macer and Tubero, then this poses no difficulty for the invention of the whole tale by Macer, since Tubero wrote after Macer. If one of them is Antias, and Antias wrote after Macer, then this remains true; but if one of them is Antias and Antias wrote before Macer, then the notice concerning Calvus' election obviously goes back to writers earlier than Macer.

[45] On which see Mommsen (1864–79: i.266) and Ogilvie (1958: 44).

in 367/6 (see 6. 34–42); although distortion by Macer cannot be proved, their prominence may owe something to him.[46]

Mommsen (1859: 98, 1864–79: i. 315) conjectured that Macer's history reflected his politics in being pro-plebeian in character. Even though it rests on no direct testimony, the thesis has been widely and probably rightly adopted by later scholars:[47] for it passes belief that a *popularis*, who called his own son Calvus after earlier members of his family who had been leading plebeian activists in their day, and to whom Sallust ascribed allusions to the achievements of the early plebeians, should have written a history that was neutral.[48] Furthermore, most extant fragments of Macer refer to internal politics and elections rather than to external affairs, and virtually all references to him in Livy have such a context. It may then be argued that Macer's history specialized in internal affairs and that Livy had particular recourse to it in passages dealing with the Struggle of the Orders.[49] Therefore the general proposition that many of the passages in Livy and Dionysius in which the plebeians are portrayed sympathetically, or at least in which extensive space is devoted to recounting their agitation and grievances, derive ultimately from Macer could be right.[50] Among the passages most plausibly cited are 4. 1–7 (on the Canuleian rogation), 6. 34–42 (on the build-up to the passing of the Licinio-Sextian laws in 367), 7. 18. 3–10 (on nostalgic yearning for the tribunates of Licinius Stolo) and 10. 6–9 (on the Ogulnian rogation).[51] Yet, for the reasons already given, it is

---

[46] On this topic see further e.g. Peter (*HRR*: i.ccclvii–ccclviii, modifying 1870: cccxxxxvi), Ogilvie (1965: 9), and Walt (1997: 184–91); Walt analyses some other episodes in Livy and Dionysius in which Licinii are involved but shows that distortion by Macer is not easily isolated.

[47] See e.g. Oakley (1997–2005: i.29), Scaramella (1897: 20–1), Soltau (1897*a*: 417–23) (with extensive working out of the hypothesis), Walsh (1961*a*: 123), Ogilvie (1965: 10–12), Badian (1966: 22), Briscoe (1971: 9), and Wiseman (2002: 299).

[48] *Contra* Walt (1997: 79, 103–4). The example of Sallust is not necessarily decisive against this argument: although his histories are not obviously biased towards either *optimates* or *populares*, they are politically extremely committed, especially in their treatment of Sulla; and even Sallust does not fit all the criteria just listed.

[49] See e.g. Soltau (1897*a*: 411).

[50] See Scaramella (1897: 21) and Soltau (1897*a*: *passim*).

[51] All cited by Soltau (1897*a*: 418); that from Book 7 also by Wiseman (2000: 82). Soltau (pp. 419–23) cited many others: e.g. most of those in Books 2–3 dealing with agrarian legislation, 3.44–49 on the Decemvirate, 5.29 on discontent after the capture of Veii, and all passages in Book 9 in which Ap. Claudius Caecus is shown in a poor light.

almost impossible to prove this for any particular passage.[52] Even if one grants a possible origin in Macer, these passages have certainly been mediated to us via Livy (who was himself sometimes sympathetic to the plebeians and, being a trained rhetorician, was quite capable of writing speeches that well evoked the nature of their grievances)[53] and perhaps also via Antias (if Antias wrote later than Macer), or Tubero, or both. Tubero's own political views are a further difficulty. The fact that he supported the senate and Pompey against Caesar need not mean that in his narrative of early Rome he had a pronounced bias towards the patricians and against the plebeians: the Aelii were plebeians, first reaching the consulate in 337 (8. 15. 1 n.) and the augurate immediately after the passing of the Ogulnian rogation of 300 (10. 6. 3–9. 2).

Livy's reference to Macer and Tubero at 10. 9. 10 (= Macer, fr. 19 HRR) in the context of the glorification of Fabius Rullianus makes almost irresistible the inference that very similar passages of glorification that follow a few chapters later derive from these same sources (10. 9. 10–13). Yet Livy's very limited naming of sources offers little scope for further deductions of this kind; and even on the topic of Macer and the Fabii there has been unwise speculation. For the notion that Macer had a special interest and knowledge of the history of the Fabii, and even that he had access to Fabian records, lurks in much of what has been written about him.[54] The argument rests upon four main pieces of evidence, none of much cogency. The first is the passage just discussed; but Livy devotes a very great deal of space to the career of Rullianus, and Macer can hardly have been alone in glorifying the most famous Roman between Camillus and Fabius' own great-grandson. At 9. 38. 16 = (fr. 17 HRR) Macer claims to know that the Faucia *curia* held the *principium* in the year of the Cremera, which was the scene of a famous Fabian defeat in 477;

---

[52] The same is true for many of the passages cited by Ogilvie (1965: 10–11), in which he discerns comment on contemporary political issues.

[53] It follows that the verbal and argumentative similarities found by Soltau (1897a: 418–19) in Livy's accounts of the passing of the Canuleian, Licinio-Sextian, and Ogulnian rogation do not prove use of the same source (Macer): Livy himself should be held responsible for his own language and may have used similar language when dealing with similar ideas.

[54] See Soltau (1897a: 422–3, 640–7 [with speculation about use of a family *laudatio* of Fabius Rullianus]), Peter (*HRR*: i.ccclviii), and Ogilvie (1965: 9).

but he says nothing about use of Fabian records, and the claim may be an invention. Livy (6. 34. 5–11) tells us that Licinius Stolo, promulgator of the famous Licinio-Sextian rogations passed in 367—who may not have been an ancestor of Macer but in whom he is likely to have taken a great interest—was married to a Fabia: this provides a motive for goodwill towards the Fabii, but little more. There is no reason to think that Macer glorified the Fabii any more or less than any other annalist, and without other evidence one should not follow Soltau in automatically assigning passages of Fabian glorification in Livy or Dionysius to Macer.

The thesis of a special connection between Macer and the Fabii is not untypical of some of the speculation found in source-criticism. Soltau (1897*a*: 646–50) imagined that Tubero favoured the Decii, Quadrigarius Volumnius Flamma and Livy Scipio. Good evidence is entirely wanting. Even Ogilvie (1965: 10) was not immune: '[o]ne of Licinius' political allies was L. (or Cn.) Sicinius...The Sicinii amply graced the pages of Macer's history', with references to 2. 32. 2, 5. 24. 11, and his notes on those passages. The argument is in some respects attractive, but for the first tribunes of the plebs of 493 some sources had two Licinii, some a Sicinius and a Licinius, and Macer cannot have been responsible for all these inventions.[55] Klinger (1884) made many acute observations about Livy's literary and historical techniques and rightly drew attention to the appearance of various similar or stock motifs in different parts of Livy's narrative.[56] He was, however, too confident in assigning passages in Book 10 to individual authors on the basis of these motifs. Quite apart from the considerations adduced above, his argument that the reappearance of these motifs in different parts of Livy's narrative suggests that Livy used the same source in those different parts is logically flawed: the appearance of similar material in Livy and Dionysius shows that different authors can use the same motifs.

The patrician Claudii provide a cautionary tale. That the portrait of them found in Livy Books 2–10 and the corresponding books of

---

[55] For this evidence see above; for the criticism of Ogilvie's view, see Briscoe (1971: 10).

[56] In this he was ahead of his time and anticipated the approach adopted in this commentary.

Dionysius (where extant) has been the subject of systematic blackening and perversion in which virtually all Claudii are made die-hard patrician reactionaries is not in doubt. Scholars have proposed numerous authors of this portrait: Pictor, Piso, Antias, and Macer have all had their champions, with Tubero too assigned a part; but the truth cannot be recovered.[57]

To conclude. Little can be said with confidence about Livy's use of sources in Books 1–10. It is virtually certain that he used all of Fabius Pictor, Calpurnius Piso, Claudius Quadrigarius (after Book 5), Valerius Antias (at least before Book 5), Licinius Macer, Aelius Tubero; and it is also virtually certain that neither Pictor nor Piso could have provided him with enough material for the more elaborate portions of his narrative. However, the extent of his use of the other four and the methods that he may have used in effecting combinations of their material are obscure.

[57] See Oakley (1997–2005: iii.665–9).

# 17

## Livy's Sources and Methods of Composition in Books 31–33

### J. Briscoe

Since the publication of Heinrich Nissen's *Kritische Untersuchungen über die Quellen der vierten und fünften Dekade des Livius*[1] over 140 years ago it has been clear that it is possible to divide Livy's narrative into those sections which derive from Polybius and those which do not. The surviving fragments of Polybius allow this to be demonstrated for those sections of Livy to which they correspond. The Polybian origin of those sections of Livy to which no surviving fragments of Polybius correspond can be deduced in various ways[2]—they form part of a continuous narrative, other parts of which do correspond to surviving fragments of Polybius; they contain explanations of Greek terms,[3] thus indicating a Greek origin; they have detailed information on military matters or criticism of military tactics, a sphere in which Polybius was particularly interested and qualified;[4] they contain allusions to points of earlier Greek history which would not have been common knowledge in Rome.[5]

In Books 31–3 the following sections correspond to surviving portions of Polybius:

[1] Nissen (1863).

[2] On these criteria cf. especially Nissen (1863: ch. 4).

[3] On the *vocant* formula cf. 31.24.4 n. (References in this form refer to the commentary in Briscoe (1973).)

[4] Cf. 31.38 n.

[5] Cf. e.g. 33.20.2. Omission of *cognomina* in most cases is another sign of Polybian origin.

| Livy | Polybius |
|------|----------|
| 31.14.11–18.8 | 16.25–6, 28–34 |
| 32.32.9–37.5 | 18.1–12 |
| 32.40.8–11 | 18.16–17.5 |
| 33.2.1 | 18.17.6 |
| 33.5.4–13.15 | 18.18–27, 33–4, 36–9 |
| 33.20.2–3 | 18.41a.1 |
| 33.21.1–5 | 18.41 |
| 33.27.5–28 | 18.43, 40.1–4 |
| 33.30–5 | 18.44–8 |
| 33.39–40 | 18.49–51 |

The further criteria allow us to see that Polybius' account of the campaign of Sulpicius by land and Apustius by sea is represented by 31.22.4–47.3, that of the campaign of Villius in 199 by 32.3–6.4, that of the campaign of Flamininus in 198 by 32.9.6–25.12, that of the events of winter 198/7 by 32.32–40, that of the campaign of 197 by 33.1–17, that of other events in the Greek world in 197 by 33.18–21.5, that of the events of winter 197/6 and summer 196 by 33.27.5–35.12, and that of the negotiations with Antiochus by 33.38–41.[6]

There remain the sections for which a Polybian origin cannot be deduced—31.1–13, 19–22.3, 47.4–50, 32.1–2, 7–9.5, 26–31, 33.21.6–27.5, 36–7, 42–45.5. These sections deal with events in Rome and Italy—elections, decisions of the senate on various matters, accounts of prodigies, slave revolts, etc.—and also contain accounts of wars in northern Italy and Spain. These are matters with which Polybius did not concern himself in great detail although he did relate important senatorial decisions. It seems clear, then, that all these sections contain material which Livy found in the works of his predecessors in writing the history of Rome, whom we usually call 'annalists'.[7] That conclusion is made even clearer by consideration of the way in which the Polybian and non-Polybian sections are joined together. Polybius' chronology was based on Olympiad

[6] On 31.14–18 cf. Briscoe (1973: 7, 10, 46–7). On the sources of 32.3 and 33.45.6–49.8 cf. nn. ad locc.

[7] I shall use the term, though really it is misleading. Polybius wrote equally annalistically.

years, running from late summer to late summer.[8] The annalists, on the other hand, used Roman consular years. At the time of the Second Macedonian War the consuls entered office on the Ides of March: but since in fact the Roman calendar was some two and a half months ahead of the corresponding Julian dates, the consular year began in the middle of winter.[9] Livy evidently found difficulty in marrying these two systems together. His account of the consular year 200 runs from 31.5.1 to the end of the book. He makes it clear that Sulpicius arrived late in the campaigning season (31.22.4): it is thus obvious that the campaigns described in chapters 33–47 must in fact belong to the year 199. They had been related by Polybius in his (completely lost) Book 17 under the Olympiad year 200/199. Since the events of the Olympiad year began in the consular year 200, Livy put the whole account under that year. Villius' campaign was very short, and is therefore correctly assigned to the year 199: if he had campaigned in 198, no doubt Livy would equally have put his campaign in 199. But Flamininus, consul in 198, went out much earlier (32.9.6) and, though his initial campaign would have been described by Polybius under the Olympiad year 199/8, the connection with Flamininus' election to the consulship made it possible for Livy to date the campaign correctly. Polybius began his Book 18 with the Olympiad year 198/7. 32.32–40 are placed by Livy in the consular year 197, though they in fact belong to the winter of 198/7. So Livy relates the continuation of Flamininus' command (32.28.3–9) before the events that in fact preceded it. In this case he has made the reverse error to that made in respect of the campaign of 199.[10] The events of summer 197 were continuous with the preceding section in Polybius and hence are correctly dated by Livy. The events of winter 197/6 (33.27–9) are dated in 196, although in this case the events described in fact belong to the latter part of the winter, and so little inaccuracy is involved.[11] The events described in 33.38, however, are again misdated. Livy writes as if the activities of Antiochus in northern Asia Minor belong to 196. In fact they almost certainly

---

[8] Cf. Walbank (1957–79: i. 35–7).

[9] See Addendum.

[10] For cases of both types of dislocation in the third decade cf. De Sanctis (1907–64: iii. 2.327 ff., 440 ff.).

[11] Cf. 33.30.1 n.

took place in autumn and winter 197/6. They were described by Polybius under the Olympiad year 197/6 and placed by Livy in 196.[12] Thus far there is little disagreement among scholars. But the situation is very different when we come to inquire more closely into Livy's sources in the non-Polybian sections. Nissen, with a few exceptions, did not attempt any further sub-divisions of the annalistic sections. But in the years that followed—the peak period of 'Quellenforschung' ('source research')—such attempts were made. Soltau,[13] on the basis of some *a priori* assumptions about the nature of the historical work of Piso, Valerius Antias, and Claudius Quadrigarius, divided the annalistic sections between them. With more attention to detail, Unger,[14] and later Kahrstedt,[15] adduced a number of alleged discrepancies in the annalistic sections and on this basis divided them between Valerius Antias and Claudius Quadrigarius. Reacting against this sort of procedure, Klotz[16] argued that many of the alleged discrepancies did not exist, and that Livy used Antias as his main source for Books 31–8, only using Claudius as a check on him. Antias' treatment of the trials of the Scipios, however, so dismayed Livy that in Book 39 and thereafter Claudius became the main source, with Antias used as the control. Since Klotz there has been little interest in 'Quellenforschung', though Zimmerer in her dissertation on Claudius used methods similar to those of Kahrstedt.[17]

All attempts to divide Livy into his sources on the basis of inconsistencies are doomed to failure. If Livy was capable of including in his history elements which contradicted one another, there is no reason why one of his predecessors should not have done so. Even the first person to write the history of an event may receive conflicting information and, if he is not careful, fail to resolve the conflict. Thus it was as unjustified for Kahrstedt to deduce different

---

[12] Cf. 33.38.1 n.
[13] Soltau (1894*a*) and (1897: ch. 4).
[14] Unger (1878).
[15] Kahrstedt (1913).
[16] Klotz (1915: 481–536) and (1940–1: 1–100).
[17] Zimmerer (1937). Cf. the review by Klotz (1942: 268 ff.). Similar methods are used for Livy's account of Ligurian affairs by G. Mezzar-Zerbi (1958: 5–15), (1959: 152–62), (1960: 329–40), (1965: 66–78, 287–99), and (1966: 211–24).

sources from inconsistencies as it was unnecessary for Klotz to deny the inconsistencies to refute Kahrstedt's view.[18] It is, however, worth considering the alleged discrepancies in more detail.[19] Some are not inconsistencies at all. There is nothing particularly odd about the fact that the appointment of C. Cornelius Cethegus to Spain (31.49.7) had not been previously mentioned. The alleged aedileship of Flamininus in 201 (31.4.5), which would conflict with the statement in 32.7.10, stems only from a manuscript corruption of the *praenomen.* There is no inconsistency between 32.2.4, where the Carthaginian hostages are placed at Signia and Ferentinum, and 32.26.5, where they are being held at Setia. 31.21.10 does not refer to the official number of a legion, and there is thus no inconsistency with 33.22.8 and 33.36.5. There is no problem in the addition of Spanish veterans at 31.49.5 to the African veterans entitled to receive land by the provisions reported at 31.4.1. The colonies planned at 32.29.3 are settled at 34.45.1—the passages are not doublets. The fact that at 31.8.7 and 10.1 trouble in Gaul is not expected does not prove that the war reported at 31.2.5–11 is an invention.[20] 31.10.3 does not imply that Placentia was destroyed and thus conflict with 31.21.18. At 33.22.7 Livy reports the comments of a hostile tribune, and it is not strange that nothing corresponds to it in the account of the Gallic campaign in 32.30–1. The apparent conflict between 32.29.7 and 31.4 on Clastidium can be explained without difficulty.

In other places, however, there are undeniable contradictions. Some are small, and could easily be slips by Livy himself or have stood as such in his source. In this category are the facts that at 32.28.2 M. Sergius Silus is the urban, at 33.21.9 the peregrine praetor, and that the Spanish governor described as Cn. Cornelius Lentulus at 31.50.11 has become Cn. Cornelius Blasio at 33.27.1. The repetition at 32.26.1–2 of the information contained in 32.9.5 may be due only to Livy's carelessness. In other cases it is more likely that the variant

---

[18] On a number of issues Klotz (1940–1) does allow the inconsistency to have stood in the source. Zimmerer (1937: 24) sees the principle correctly, but fails to apply it.

[19] Cf. in particular Kahrstedt (1913: 38 ff.). On all these matters see the notes on the passages concerned.

[20] On this and the following points cf. Zimmerer (1937: 26 ff.).

accounts do stem from different sources. This must be true of the
different versions of the fate of Pleminius at 31.12.2 and 34.44.6,[21]
and is probably the case with the different foundation dates at 31.1.4
and 5.1 (cf. 34.54.6), the apparent confusion between the events of
200 and 197 at 33.23.1–2, and the conflict on the death of Hamilcar
(31.21.18, 32.30.12, 33.23.5).[22]

The titulature of the governors of the Spanish provinces is a more
complex problem. Livy describes them variously as praetors, pro-
praetors, and proconsuls. Kahrstedt believed that this was due to the
use of two sources, one who referred to them as praetors or pro-
praetors, the other who called them proconsuls. Klotz accepted that
the variation between propraetor and proconsul reflected different
sources, and to accommodate the evidence to his view that Livy used
first Antias and later Claudius as his main source, he claimed that
cases of governors being called proconsuls in his 'Claudius section'
were textual errors. His arguments for emendation in these cases,
however, are extremely implausible. When governors appear as praetors in his 'Antias section', Klotz argued, they are still in their year
of office and the usage does not conflict with his thesis. When
C. Sempronius Tuditanus, praetor in 197 (32.27.7, 28.2), appears as
proconsul in 33.25.9, that is because the latter passage in fact refers to
the following year. Klotz's conclusion is unnecessary. The evidence
of the *Fasti* shows that the praetors governed as *praetor pro consule* in
their year of office and as *pro consule* thereafter.[23] In the year of office,
therefore, either *praetor* or *pro consule* is a correct title. But neither
Kahrstedt nor Klotz commented on the fact that at 33.42.5
Sempronius is called *praetor*, and on balance it does seem likely

---

[21] See Addendum.
[22] On the alleged conflicts between 33.43.2 and 44.4 and between 31.49.7 and
33.26.5 see Briscoe (1973: 33.21.6–9 n.).
    It is interesting to note the difficulties into which Kahrstedt's approach could lead
him (1913: 61 ff.). In 31.21.18 Hamilcar is killed in 200, in 32.30.12 his capture in 197
is reported as a variant. Therefore the source of the main account of 32.29–30 is the
same as that of 31.21. But 33.22–3, which has other conflicts with 32.29–30, also has
Hamilcar's death in 197 as a variant. But according to Kahrstedt's scheme, 33.22–3
must come from a source other than that of 32.29–30. Kahrstedt weakly concludes
that the variant in 33.23.5 is only 'apparent'.
[23] Cf. Jashemski (1950: 40 ff.), McDonald (1953: 143–4).

that the different titles in the two passages come from different sources.

It is clear enough that Livy consulted at least two sources for his non-Polybian sections. At 33.36.13 he quotes Antias and Claudius on the numbers of enemy dead and the amount of booty taken in the battle with the Gauls. But are these the only two Roman historians used throughout, and in what way did Livy use his predecessors? It will be easier to answer this question if we first return to the Polybian sections and consider the way in which Livy makes use of the material he found in Polybius.[24]

Livy was far from simply translating Polybius. Sometimes, indeed, he appears to have mistranslated him. Such errors as taking χαταβαλοῦσι τὰς σαρίσας ('lowering their spears') as *hastis positis* ('putting their spears on the ground', 33.8.13) are well known.[25] Other misunderstandings of the Greek in passages where Polybius survives can be seen at 32.36.8, 33.5.9, 7.3, 13.7–12, 30.2, 34.11, 35.8, 40.3: possible cases occur at 31.15.7, 33.6.3, 12.6. Similarly in Polybian sections where Polybius himself does not survive, misunderstanding of the Greek appears to have occurred at 31.22.4, 24.4, 25.2, 28.1, 32.4, 33.6, 39.6, 32.5.4, 40.11, 33.17.6, 18.7, 18.10, 41.5. More doubtful cases occur at 32.14.5, 19.9, 23.9, 40.4, 33.19.9.

But apart from these, which are all matters of detail, it is clear that Livy adapted Polybius to suit his own purposes. He introduces descriptions of emotions, ascribes motives, rearranges the order of points in speeches reported by Polybius, omits passages which seem to him of less importance. Of his additions to Polybius a number can easily be regarded as no more than comments or interpretations by Livy himself. In this category come such passages as 31.15.6, 32.35.1, 33.5.12, 6.7, 9.11, 11.2, 30.4, 31.10, 32.5, 32.6, 33.5–8. Some of these additions make sense, others introduce mistakes. They do not, however, affect matters of substance and there is no difficulty in attributing them to Livy. But there are also a number of places where

[24] Many of the important points about Livy's use of Polybius were noticed by Nissen (1863: ch. 2). Detailed study of Livy's adaptations of Polybius began with Witte (1910: 270–305, 359–419). Cf. also Lambert (1946: 58 ff.), Walsh (1954: 97–114), McDonald (1957: 155–72).

[25] Cf. Walsh (1958*b*). On the points that follow see the relevant notes and Addendum.

there are significant additions, omissions, or alterations in the account of Livy as compared with the corresponding passage of Polybius. In some cases the additions may convey information contained in other passages of Polybius read by Livy but now lost—this is probable for 31.15.5 and possible for 31.15.7, 10, and 33.34.2–3. We are left with a group of passages where more serious changes have occurred. The most striking of these are the suppression of the part played by the Roman ambassadors at Athens and the alterations to the account of the ultimatum delivered by M. Aemilius Lepidus at Abydus (31.14–18), and the series of alterations which have the effect of removing comments in Polybius which appear derogatory to Flamininus—including the possible suppression of the expulsion of the inhabitants of Elatia at 32.24.7.[26] We must also take into account the alterations to 33.10.5–6 to suppress indications of brutality and greed on the part of the Roman army, passages ascribing fear and panic to Philip (33.7.8, 10.6), Livy's explanatory comment on the Isthmian games at 33.33.1–2, and his information on the age of Flamininus at 33.33.2.[27] It would be possible to hold that all these changes are due to Livy himself. Most of the changes would be the result of his desire to avoid criticism of Rome and Roman commanders, and to portray Philip in a bad light. The information on the Isthmian games would result from his reading of a handbook on the subject, that concerning Flamininus' age could be a false recollection of earlier information in Polybius. But it is equally possible that many of these changes reflect the version given by Roman annalists. We know that Livy read both Claudius and Antias for events in the East: he refers to the discrepancies between them and Polybius at 32.6.5–8, 33.10.8–10, 30.8–11. But it is clear that Livy can introduce non-Polybian material without acknowledging it as a variant. That is shown by the false addition of two clauses to the peace-terms with Philip in 33.30.6.[28] It thus seems quite conceivable that some of the other variations also stem from the annalists. This would certainly make excellent sense for the consistent alterations in the account of the prelude to the Second Macedonian War. The

[26] Cf. Briscoe (1973: 32.24.7 n.). On the events at Athens and the Abydos ultimatum, cf. Briscoe (1973: 41–7); on Flamininus, Briscoe (1973: 22–3 n. 4).
[27] Cf. also Briscoe (1973: 31.40.6 n.).
[28] Cf. Briscoe (1973: n. ad loc.).

mission of the Roman ambassadors is misrepresented in the annalistic section, and alterations to accord with this misrepresentation are
made in the Polybian section. The motive for the change is one that
would have been far less likely to have influenced Livy than his
annalistic predecessors.[29] It also seems quite likely that the alterations
in connection with Flamininus stem from the different picture of
him painted by the annalists, and the information on Flamininus' age
may equally come from an annalistic source. If this is accepted, it
becomes possible that some of the passages where I have attributed
the alterations to Livy himself, or to an otherwise lost passage of
Polybius, are also of annalistic origin. Possible candidates are
33.33.5–8 and 34.2–3.[30]

There can be no serious doubt that Livy read Polybius for himself.[31] The stylistic changes and verbal parallels can only be explained
on that hypothesis. If that is not enough the case is proved by the fact
that Livy can quote Claudius and Antias as variants to the Polybian
version. It would pass credibility that the annalists indicated their
own inventions and additions to Polybius. It can, however, be argued
that in cases where the alterations are particularly far-reaching the
contamination of Polybius occurred in the annalists, and was not
produced by Livy combining Polybian and annalistic accounts.[32] The
strongest case for such a possibility would be 31.14–18 which is
consistent with the annalistic account of the sending of the three
ambassadors to Egypt in 31.2.3–4. Yet it is still very difficult to believe
that Livy could have followed Polybius so closely in many details, yet

---

[29] Cf. Briscoe (1973: 47). Similarly, it is very hard to believe that Livy himself
would have been responsible for such recherché alterations to Polybius as are alleged
by Flurl (1969: *passim*) in his claim that Livy rejected Polybius' equation of *deditio*
and *deditio in fidem*.

[30] I doubt if so obscure a detail as the exact relationship of Q. Fabius to Flamininus
(cf. Briscoe 1973: 32.36.10 n.) would have been found in the annalists. Hammond
(1966: 52) argued that the differences between Plutarch and Livy at 32.9 ff. are due to
Livy's use of an annalist. This could be so, but the differences may be alterations by
Plutarch himself, or caused by the use of another source by Plutarch (on Plutarch's
sources cf. Smith (1940: 1 ff.) and (1944: 89 ff.). Petzold (1940: 105) sees 33.39.7 as an
example, but this is probably just Livy's own elaboration. The speeches are a separate
problem (cf. Briscoe 1973: 17–22).

[31] Dahlheim (1968: 166–7) does seem to contemplate the possibility, but he
misrepresents the position of Gelzer (see next note).

[32] Gelzer (1942: 226).

embellished his account in the way he does, if he had only read an annalist who had read Polybius. It is, however, quite likely that the annalists themselves perverted Polybius, and that it was this perverted account which Livy combined with Polybius himself.[33] If there are passages where Polybius has been altered by an annalist, and the annalist alone used by Livy, they must lie in places where there are no such close verbal parallels between Livy and Polybius.

We can now return to the annalistic sections. First, did Livy use only Claudius and Antias, or other Roman writers as well? In the fourth decade, apart from Polybius, Claudius, and Antias, the only specific references are to Cato (34.15.9) and, on an individual point, Rutilius (39.52.1). On occasion Livy refers to sources in a general way as in *ceteri Graeci Latinique auctores quorum quidem ego legi annales* ('other Greek and Latin writers, at least those whose histories I have read', 32.6.8; cf. 39.50.10 *ab scriptoribus rerum Graecis Latinisque* ['by Greek and Latin historians']), or *quidam auctores sunt* ('some report', 32.30.11, 33.23.5). Since Nissen[34] it has generally been held that these phrases are misleading, and that in fact Livy consulted only two sources in annalistic sections, three for eastern events. Now certainly such phrases as *quidam auctores sunt* may only refer to a variant in one source, but the wording at 32.6.8 is a different matter. It seems very hard to take it to mean just Polybius and Claudius. Livy admits that he may not have read all the history books, but he cannot mean that he only read three, two of which differed from the version of Valerius Antias. The absence of specific references to sources other than those mentioned is not significant. Livy quotes sources so rarely that nothing can be deduced from non-quotation. *ceteri Graeci Latinique auctores* may not mean that he has read any Greek historian other than Polybius—though there may have been such Greek writers independent of Polybius, and Livy could have read them.[35]

---

[33] The arguments of Klotz (1951: 243 ff.) only show that it cannot be proved that they did. Badian (1966: 19) argues from the fact that Claudius had only three or four books between the end of the Hannibalic War and the Gracchi that 'the author did not discover Polybius'. Certainly he cannot have used Polybius to anything like the extent that Livy did, but he could still have read him.

[34] Nissen (1863: 47–8).

[35] For the possibility of such a work as the source of Appian's *Macedonica* cf. Meloni (1955), Balsdon (1956: 199–201); *contra* Gelzer (1957: 55 ff.).

But it does mean that he read other Latin historians, and these may have included the second-century writers Cassius Hemina, Piso, Gellius, and Sempronius Tuditanus.[36] That he had read all of these is uncertain, but it is quite possible.

But how did Livy use these earlier historians, and how did he compose his own narrative? In the Polybian sections it is clear enough that he followed Polybius reasonably closely, adding or correcting in matters of substance only rarely. Hence it has been assumed that he must have followed the same procedure in the non-Polybian sections, and that a given passage—whether quite short, as for Soltau and Kahrstedt, or of considerable length, as for Klotz—can be assigned to a single source, the other source or sources being used only for variations and corrections. But it is by no means certain that the procedure was the same in Polybian and non-Polybian sections. Livy knew that for Greek matters Polybius was pre-eminent.[37] But for Roman and Italian affairs no one author had such a pre-eminence. Moreover we must remember the constraints imposed by the difficulties of reading a book in the ancient world. The ancient writer of history could not, like a modern scholar, have a large number of books open on his desk. He could read, or have read to him, just one roll at a time. From it he could make, or have made, notes on what he had read.[38] When Livy came to write his own account he would no doubt refer closely to Polybius for the Greek sections. But for other matters he may not have gone back directly to the books themselves—he may have used his notes or even relied on his memory. Hence in the non-Polybian sections it may be that Livy's narrative often represents his own account based on what he has read, and except for specific citations cannot be assigned to individual sources. Certainly alleged characteristics of the individual annalists cannot enable us to spot their influence in Livy. Even if we decide, for example, that the differing nomenclature of the Spanish provinces

---

[36] *HRR* 1². 98 ff. (Cassius Hemina), 120 ff. (Piso), 143 ff. (Sempronius), 148 ff. (Gellius). Sempronius Asellio (179 ff.) probably did not deal with this period in detail. Similarity of language between 39.6.7 and Piso fr. 34 cannot prove the use of Piso, as Soltau (1897*b*: 30) argued.

[37] Cf. 30.45.5, 33.10.10—deliberate meiosis, not lukewarm praise.

[38] Cf. the younger Pliny's description of his uncle's methods in *epist.* 3.5.

indicates different sources, it does not follow that one source alone has been used for the passage in which the indication occurs.[39]

As we have seen, there are clear breaks between the annalistic and Polybian sections. In most years Livy gives first an annalistic section, then the material from Polybius, and finally another annalistic section (in 200 and 196 there are three annalistic sections, the second one dividing the Polybian section). It is wrong, however, to ask precisely where the divisions between the sections come. The history that Livy gives us is his own and he adapts his material to suit his own purposes. The transitions are his way of linking his material together, and it is futile to seek for the origin of such passages as 31.14.1–5, 33.19.6, 45.5.[40] Again passages concerning elections, assignment of provinces, games, short notices from abroad, and so forth are often, and probably rightly, regarded as basic annalistic material stemming from the *annales maximi*. Yet even here we find such passages as 32.27.3 with moral comments on Cato, or 33.26.5–6 with general remarks on the war in Spain. Whether these are due to Livy or his source, however, is uncertain.

We have seen the presence of annalistic material in the Polybian sections. Are there conversely any Polybian passages in the annalistic sections? Livy presumably read the whole of Polybius, yet in Books 31–33[41] he clearly chose not to follow his account of events at Rome. His omission of Polybius' story of the senatorial decision not to relieve Flamininus of his command (32.37) is part of his suppression of the criticism of Flamininus in Polybius, but the same cannot be true of his use of an annalistic version of Marcellus' opposition to the making of peace in 196 (33.25.4–7) in preference to that of Polybius

[39]  There is no justification for Badian's statement (1966: 19) that Claudius' lack of interest in politics and personalities is phenomenal: he is not even cited for the trials of the Scipios. The non-citation of Claudius does not mean that he did not deal with the trials (cf. Addendum to p. 464). It is true that he described battles at length, but he clearly dealt with political matters also. A random selection of fragments from Livy would contain a great deal of military material.

[40]  It is wrong to assert, as do Nissen (1863: 105) and Klotz (1940–1: 3), that the use of *Macedonia* to mean northern Greece as a whole indicates an annalistic source. Livy naturally described it as *Macedonia*, and it was natural for him to use it in introducing Eastern sections, as at 31.14.2, 32.3.2.

[41]  Sometimes Livy does follow Polybius on Roman matters: cf. e.g. 37.52–6, 42.47 ff.

18.42. It seems that just as he found Polybius superior to the annalists for Eastern events, so for domestic matters he found the detailed history of the annalists preferable to Polybius. In one passage, however, (33.44.8) there are echoes of Polybian language (*haerere et aliud in visceribus Graeciae ingens malu,* 'another huge evil, as well, was stuck in the entrails of Greece') in what is clearly an annalistic passage. But again it is impossible to tell whether this is due to Livy himself or to his annalistic predecessor.

How reliable was the information given by the annalists?[42] In many cases they are clearly guilty of invention. Antias created a victory of Villius in 199 (32.6.5–6) and both he and Claudius made additions to the peace-treaty with Philip (33.30). Antias was often criticized by Livy for his absurd exaggerations of the numbers of enemy dead (33.10.8; cf. 3.5.13, 30.19.11, 36.19.12, 38.6–7, 38.23.8, 39.41.6).[43] The events preceding the Second Macedonian War are violently distorted, and the reports of reinforcements for the army in Greece seem unacceptable (32.1.2 n.). On the other hand a lot of their material is rightly seen as going back to the *annales maximi* or other archival material,[44] and a number of passages which scholars have declared fabrications are probably authentic (e.g. 30.26.2–4, 42.1–10, 31.3.3–6, 32.8.9–16). In some cases the annalistic account

[42] For a long time, following Nissen (1863), 'annalistic' was regarded as almost equivalent to 'false'. Holleaux contributed a lot to this attitude, and it reached its peak in Petzold's wholesale rejection of the annalistic evidence for the beginning of the Second Macedonian War (1940). The main defence of the annalistic tradition came from Klotz (1940–1). In Britain Balsdon challenged the common view (1953: 158 ff.) and (1954: 30 ff.). A good survey of approaches to the problem will be found in Bredehorn (1968: 1 ff.). But Bredehorn's own wholesale defence of almost everything in the annalists is absurd.

[43] Cf. Brunt (1971: 695).

[44] Rawson (1971: 158–69) argued that the *annales maximi* were not used by the annalists to any extent. Her principal arguments are (i) that inconsistencies in the prodigy lists suggest compilation from a number of sources, (ii) that Varro does not refer to the *annales* for prodigies, (iii) that when Cicero wanted to find out the names of the *x legati* of 146 (*ad Att.* 13.4, 5, 6, 30, 32, 33) he did not think of looking in the *annales*. But (i) the sorts of prodigies reported and accepted may in fact have varied from year to year, (ii) Rawson admits that most of Varro's prodigies are from the post-Gracchan period, after the publication of the *annales*, (iii) the fact that certain lists of *legati* were not included does not mean that all were not, or that lists occurring in Livy do not come from the *annales*. (It is noticeable that Livy does not list the names of the *x legati* for the settlements of 201 and 196.)

is preferable to the Polybian (33.45.4 against 34.22.5).[45] For the rest one must decide each case on historical grounds alone, and without general preconceptions about the reliability of the annalists. Thus the danger from Gaul in these years may be exaggerated, though that cannot be proved. As we have seen, some of the inconsistencies that have been detected in Livy's account of the Gallic wars are not such at all. Others remain; but that may indicate only uncertainty about what happened, not that the whole account is an invention. Where there are inventions, there is no need to ascribe them all to the annalists of the Sullan age. Piso was certainly not free from inventions.[46]


## ADDENDUM

In general see Luce (1977: 139–84) and Oakley (1997–2005). On Livy's use of Polybius Tränkle (1977) is of fundamental importance; see my review (Briscoe (1978: 267–9)). Leidig (1994) attempts, without confronting subsequent work in detail, to return to the position of Petzold. Warrior (1996) defends the authenticity of the annalistic parts of Livy's account in Book 31. A new edition, with English translation and commentary, of the writers contained in *HRR* (cf. n. 36) will appear in the forthcoming edition of the fragments of the Roman historians (T. J. Cornell, editor-in-chief).

p. 463 (the calendar). For 'two and a half' read 'between two and a half and three and a half'; see my commentary (Briscoe (1981: 17–26 [table at p. 25])).

p. 464. Klotz's initial view (1915: 528) was that Antias' treatment of the trials of the Scipios led Livy to abandon him as his main source; later (1964: 43) he took the view that Livy's preference for Quadrigarius had grown in the course of Book 38, and he used Antias as his main source for the trials of the Scipios because he provided a unified account—that is, for artistic reasons.

---

[45] The prime example of this is 37.56.1–6, the *S.C.* for the settlement of Apamea. The detail of this is far superior to the general statements of 37.55.4–6 = Polyb. 21.24.7–8. See addendum.

[46] Cf. Latte (1960*b*: nr. 7), Badian (1966: 13). Klotz (1940–1: 99) held that inventions began with the Sullan annalists.

It should be said that it is sometimes possible plausibly to assign to a specific writer a passage of Livy where that writer is not cited. Thus there are good reasons for thinking that Quadrigarius was Livy's source for the version of the trial of the Scipios in which Naevius was the prosecutor of Africanus, his trial and death did not take place in 187, and he died at Rome, and that in which Africanus returned from a mission to Etruria to intervene on behalf of his brother (38.56); finally, that he was Livy's main source for the story of the discovery of Numa's books (40.29).

p. 466 n. 21. 29.22.10, Clodius Licinus' version of the death of Pleminius, should be deleted from the text of Livy; see Oakley (1992: 547–51).

p. 467. On Livy's misunderstandings of Polybius see the different approach of Adams (2003: 4–5).

p. 470. On Livy's use of Cato see my commentary (Briscoe (1981: 63–5)).

It might be argued that Livy could have read the Roman historians who wrote in Greek—the son of Africanus, A. Postumius Albinus (the consul of 151 BCE), and C. Acilius: I doubt, however, if Livy would have referred to them as *Graeci auctores*. It is unlikely that Livy read Cassius Hemina: at 40.29.8 he cites Antias for the statement that Numa's books were Pythagorean in content, when we know from Pliny (*nat.* 13.86 = Hemina fr. 37 *HRR*) that it also stood in Hemina.

p. 473 n. 44. for 'after the publication of the *annales*' read 'when the *annales* were no longer being compiled': cf. Frier (1999: 179 ff.). My point is not affected.

p. 474 n. 45. Cf. Briscoe (1981: 384–5).

*J. B.*

# 18

## Livy and Polybius[1]

### H. Tränkle

A modern historian usually, if at all possible, bases his account on the evidence of records and documents, letters and memoirs, inscriptions, coins, and archaeological discoveries. The surviving Roman historians, by contrast, based themselves above all on the works of historians who wrote closer to the time of the events. Only when these were not available, or when they needed to do occasional checking, did they fall back on the 'primary sources' mentioned above. The esteem the Roman historians soon acquired caused their sources to go virtually unread in late antiquity, a situation which in the end was decisive in bringing about the loss of the writers whose names are so familiar to us in the sometimes heated debates about the sources of Livy and Tacitus. The only exception worth mentioning is a work whose fate did not depend only on its position in the Latin West. I am referring, of course, to a work on which Livy drew freely, Polybius' 'History'.

That the work of the Achaean statesman who had lived many years in Rome and was a close friend of the younger Scipio should meet with esteem amongst the Romans was only to be expected; after all, its purpose was to demonstrate how the Mediterranean area, which had previously been split up into several separate theatres of history, fused together into a unity as a result of Roman rule. Rome and the Romans were, despite criticism in matters of detail, portrayed overall

[1] Lecture delivered on 2 Dec. 1969 at the University of Zurich.

with deep sympathy and admiration. Polybius' history must also have recommended itself by being aimed entirely at the practical instruction of the statesman and the soldier. To what extent other Roman historians before Livy used Polybius is debated, but that some had done so since the end of the second century, and that from then on Polybius was quite often read by the Greek-educated Roman élite, cannot be doubted.[2] Above all, Cicero esteemed him highly: in *De officiis* he calls him an 'especially reliable authority' in historical questions; and his *De re publica* owes Polybius not only its central idea, that the Roman state is a balanced combination of monarchic, aristocratic, and democratic elements, but also the historical overview in Book 2, in which Cicero sets out the stages by which the Roman state had risen to that perfection. Given the significance that Cicero, and in particular the *De re publica*, had for Livy,[3] it is not surprising that he also began to use Polybius' history when he began his account of the years it covered.

In the last chapter of Book 30, at the end of the portrayal of the Second Punic War, Livy first mentions a Polybian variant, after having reported the same event quite differently following the Roman traditional record. Thereafter, on several occasions in Books 31–45 individual reports and whole sections are expressly attributed to the Greek historian. Thus, at the end of his account of the battle of Cynoscephalae (33.10), Livy remarks that he has here followed Polybius, 'a thoroughly reliable authority for Roman history, especially for events in Greece'. The fact that Livy first mentions Polybius only at the end of Book 30 need not mean that he first *used* him only at that point, and most experts have long been inclined to attribute much material in the third Decade to the Greek historian. Although between 1850 and the First World War a seemingly endless number of shorter or longer treatments of this question were published,[4]

---

[2] *Contra* Klotz (1951).

[3] Quint. 10. 1. 39 'so this economical statement, which Livy wrote in his letter to his son, was the safest: "that he should read Demosthenes and Cicero, and then those who were the most like Demosthenes and Cicero"'. Cf. too Liv. 2.1.1–6 with Cic. *Rep.* 2.3 and 21, Liv. 5.54.4 with Cic. *Rep.* 2.5 ff.

[4] Especially important are Hesselbarth (1889) and Kahrstedt 1913*b*. A late example of this branch of scholarship is Klotz (1940–1, repr. Amsterdam, 1964) esp. 101–200.

today there is still no agreement on which sections of Livy's history are at issue. A survey of this not particularly illuminating direction of philological study also shows that its authors paid little attention to whether the agreements that they had noticed between Livy and Polybius in the third Decade necessarily permit one to infer a relationship of direct dependence, or whether we have instead a question of a shared tradition. In my opinion there are good grounds for supposing the latter (although I must refrain from giving them at the moment, since they depend on facts that need to be stated first). But if that was the case, then Livy's direct use of Polybius—which alone concerns us here—would not have begun till Book 30; and furthermore, that direct use would have been (to be precise) on a very limited basis at first. For the Second Punic War abundant Latin sources were available: the wide-ranging later annalists and, above all, Coelius Antipater's seven-book monograph. When, however, Livy began to relate the background and outbreak of the Second Macedonian War, he must very soon have realized that Polybius' account far excelled the native tradition in precision and variety. From Book 31 on he thus narrates the events of the Greek East following Polybius' description without exception; and from Book 34 on he also increasingly follows Polybius for the related proceedings in the Roman Senate. Naturally that included the majority of the important events between 200 and 167 BCE: the Second Macedonian War, with the battle of Cynoscephalae and the liberation of Greece proclaimed at Corinth; the war against the Aetolians and against Antiochus the Great, with the Peace of Apamea; the disputes in the Macedonian royal house that led to the murder of Demetrius; and the war against Perseus, with Aemilius Paullus' victory at Pydna. In total, the sections based on Polybius amount to more than half of the fourth and fifth Decades. To be sure, the portion of Polybius' history that Livy has used here, Books 16–30, survives only in fragments. Yet some of these fragments are very extensive, especially those from Books 16–18, and all told there are some 100 longer or shorter fragments that may be compared with their imitations in Livy.

This is thus the only case in which we can obtain a reliable impression of a Roman historian's way of working not only at isolated moments but over long stretches, and hence can ascertain exactly how he used his sources. Furthermore this involves not just any old mediocrities but two outstanding personalities of distinct individuality. One might have expected that Latinists would fall on the treasure lying at hand, at least from the time when—as was the case in Germany at the turn of the twentieth century—a concern for describing the personal achievements of individual authors had become central to their work. That did not happen. As early as 1863 Heinrich Nissen, in an essay of over 300 pages that may count as a particularly fine example of the patient collection and observation frequently practised in the nineteenth century (*Kritische Untersuchungen über die Quellen der vierten und fünften Dekade des Livius*), had established once and for all (a few exceptions apart) Polybius' share in Books 31–45. Trained as a historian, Nissen endeavoured to attain a well-founded assessment of Livy's credibility. This he thought he could reach soonest by demarcating the portions based on Polybius—that is to say, on a reliable witness—from the annalistic material, which he considered to be falsified. In those places where Livy's text seemed to be based on Polybius, Nissen believed he could possibly settle the question of how Livy had treated his source. In accordance with his purpose Nissen paid close attention only to those divergences that affected the factual content in the strictest sense: those that were due to mistranslations, misunderstandings, or Roman patriotic sentiment on Livy's part. The other changes he classified as rhetorical ornament and paid them little further notice. Operating within the same framework, other historians, in particular Maurice Holleaux, would later add new observations to Nissen's.[5] Only once did a philologist attempt to supplement them and draw especial attention to the rhetorical ornament despised by Nissen: Kurt Witte, in an article in *Rheinisches Museum* for 1910, brought out the particular quality of Livy's narrative. His motto was this: Livy was guided by the intention 'to create individual narratives'. This pointed to a truly fundamental fact: that in Livy, as compared with Polybius, the continuity of historical occurrence is not uncommonly broken up into a loose sequence of individual scenes. Witte, who—like Richard Heinze a few years earlier in his famous book on Vergil—focused exclusively on predetermined narrative technique, strangely considered it in isolation as an application of rhetorical

[5] The relevant studies are collected in Holleaux (1938–68) vols. iv–v.

precepts, a kind of clever artifice. Whether it might rather be the result of a different way of looking at history, or ultimately of a quite different intellectual makeup, was a question it obviously did not occur to him to ask. He thus cheated himself of the true benefit of his discovery—all the more so as his formalistic approach caused him all too often to ignore Livy's more important departures from his source.

After Witte others, in particular Erich Burck,[6] made advances towards a comprehensive characterization of Livy; however, they did not compare Books 31–45 with Polybius, but instead, they compared Livy's first Pentad with Dionysius of Halicarnassus' 'Roman Antiquities'. Conducted with care, this could on occasion be very fruitful, not least because of the especial beauty and importance of this part of the *Ab urbe condita*. But applied continuously, chapter by chapter and book by book, this approach represented a fateful shift. For now, in place of source and dependent narrative, scholars were dealing with two roughly contemporary works that drew on the same or similar sources, but whose relationship could not be determined more precisely. Whether what can be extracted from the comparison is the peculiar quality of Livy's presentation, or techniques that actually belong to a predecessor, we can say with certainty in only a relatively few instances. In the case of Burck's book the result was a sometimes painful indeterminacy in his findings,[7] made worse by the author's concentrating so narrowly on those parts of Livy's history that had a Roman and Augustan significance, as to be in danger of forgetting the historian's everyday drudgery (so to speak), his travails in the thicket of divergent accounts and chronologies.

But just why have classical scholars hitherto made so little use of the unique resource afforded by comparing Livy and Polybius? Why have they not consistently pursued the investigations begun by Witte? One reason must lie in the nature of Polybius' fragments. A very considerable portion of them has reached us only through the collection of excerpts made in the mid-tenth century for the emperor

---

[6] Burck (1934, repr. 1964).
[7] Cf. esp. the reviews by Klingner (1935) and Klotz (1935). Inadequate is Thraede (1970).

Constantine VII Porphyrogenitus. This collection, as is well known, was arranged according to content: thus one section contained reports of embassies, another narratives of military stratagems, a third remarks on human errors and merits, and so on. The editors often had the text copied only as far as was relevant for the given theme; the rest of the original was either omitted or replaced by brief summaries. It follows that when fragments of Polybius and Livy's text differ, we cannot assume *a priori* that the differences are due to Livy. To be sure, this difficulty is not insuperable: given the diverse work already devoted to these fragments, we can now judge the make-up of the excerpts with considerable certainty.

The real reason for scholars' conspicuous reluctance lies elsewhere. For the scholar principally concerned with Livy, the comparison between him and Polybius is at first sight somewhat disappointing—I emphasize at first sight, for I should like to show that on closer examination that is not the case. But certainly no sensational discoveries can be made in this regard. It is not only that there are virtually no immediately visible transformations and revaluations which might afford a striking illustration of the Roman writer's originality. Livy has not even fused his annalistic and Polybian information into a real unity; rather, he has confined himself to inserting Polybius' reports in certain places into his basic annalistic framework. For example, his narrative of the background to the Second Macedonian War begins on the basis of an annalistic source that had gone into unnecessary detail on proceedings in Rome, while offering only the vaguest allusions to the far more significant events in the East. However, having narrated the declaration of war on Philip and the arrival of the Roman army in Epirus, at 31.14 Livy switches to Polybius, adds important details on the background to the war from the Greek historian's narrative, and thereafter follows him as long as the topic is 'events in Greece'. This procedure, once summarily described by Nissen as 'source-compilation', is what makes a clear division possible between the annalistic and Polybian portions of Books 31–45. Simple as it may seem, there were in fact not inconsiderable difficulties attached to Livy's procedure, arising (for example) from the differences in chronological systems. The year used by the Roman annalists—and therefore by Livy as well—was the consular year of office, which until 153 BCE began with the Ides

(15th) of March. It is quite difficult to tell to what date in any given 'natural' year that corresponded, since the Roman calendar before Caesar did not (if one cares to adopt Mommsen's somewhat exaggerated expression[8]) follow either the sun or the moon, but ran wild. Polybius adopted the Olympiad year which, as is well known, ran from autumn to autumn. Within this timespan he treated the individual regions of the Mediterranean basin in a fixed order, beginning with Italy. That must have presented Livy with difficult problems of order. And just what was to happen when the annalists and Polybius, as quite often happened (as indeed in the preliminaries to the Second Macedonian War), offered starkly different accounts of the facts?

It cannot be said that Livy took much trouble to combine reports of different origin into a chronologically coherent and contradiction-free whole. So far as chronology was concerned, he proceeded by equating each Polybian Olympiad year with a Roman consular year— with a few exceptions the one that began during the Polybian year's course. This equation had the considerable advantage that it spared Livy once and for all the difficult decisions concerning which Polybian events should be assigned to the end of one consular year and which to the beginning of the next; it also meant that he hardly even needed to upset the order in which they were narrated. But it necessarily led, in the sections dependent on Polybius, to repeated chronological displacements, sometimes of as much as a whole year. So long as the resulting inconsistencies kept themselves within limits, Livy was not further bothered by them; the reader might think what he will. When they threatened to emerge too blatantly, he adjusted the Polybian portions by means of minor retouching to match the annalistic account; or, more often, he omitted anything that contradicted it. He applied the same 'subtraction procedure' when the contradictions arose not from incorrect ordering but from factual discrepancies in the accounts.

Strange as this may seem to the modern observer, we ought not to forget that Livy, given the gigantic extent of his undertaking, had no time to spend on lengthy critical studies in advance; and above all, that he adhered quite consistently to his procedure. No doubt like every historian (and every human being) he had his good and bad

---

[8] Mommsen (1859: 27).

days, but there is nothing unplanned or chaotic in his dealings with Polybius. Where such problems—chronological displacements that extend beyond *one* year, or stopgaps of any kind—have been attributed to him, it is usually soon clear that the fault lies with his interpreters. As cannot be emphasized too often, in contrast to several of his Roman predecessors Livy was basically concerned with preserving faithfully what had been transmitted. When he had to choose between one piece of transmitted information and another and the discrepancy could not be overcome by a slight change of wording, he would omit material, but always in the sections based on Polybius: for in doubtful cases it was the national tradition with which he and his readers had grown up that provided him with his guiding thread. In those not infrequent cases, moreover, where in his opinion Polybius had misinterpreted and misrepresented the conduct of magistrates or of the Roman Senate, Livy's own exposition is characterized mainly by the omission of the details that he doubted. Other things he modified through his knowledge of Roman political and religious customs, though that does not happen very often. But to all appearances he never added anything of his own invention, either for the sake of national prestige or in order to heighten pathos.

Now, it was quite a substantial task for Livy to select the relevant portions of Polybius, to demarcate them, and to shorten them. Even selection and demarcation were not easy. True, on numerous occasions Livy states it as his principle that he will treat of events in the Greek East only in so far as they are connected with Roman history (39.48.6, cf. also 33.20.13, 35.40.1, 41.25.8.), but from at least the end of the Second Macedonian War the Romans were drawn into everything that happened there, or intervened themselves out of concern for their interests. Where, then, should the line be drawn? Added to this was the absolutely unprecedented extent of Polybius' history. The narrative is notoriously drawn out in every way possible, by reference to even the most trifling circumstances and by the inclusion of all place and personal names available to him. The greatest weight is laid on painfully exact causal connection and on making every action comprehensible. All this is due to the strongly didactic purpose that is one of the chief characteristics of the Polybian work. The rising politician is meant to learn from it everything that must be considered in political and military decision-making. It is consistent with this purpose that Polybius is always intent upon drawing a moral, that he strives to pass from the particular to the general, and again and again, like a pompous schoolmaster, steps out in front of his work with wagging finger. Livy was therefore obliged to abridge if he were not to risk the proportion and artistic coherence of his own books—and that he was definitely not prepared to do. The manner in which he set about this abridgement reveals more about his approach and mindset than one might at first suppose.

Livy relates events; he does not argue about them. He virtually ignores the speculative filler that is so rampant among his predecessors: only very rarely did he admit any of it into incidental remarks, and among Polybius' excursuses, Livy translated only the comparison between Roman and Macedonian camp-building. Having taken over facts, he did not homogenize them into a colourless compendium; rather, he varied the amount of detail. In most cases he abridged them with greater or lesser compression, sometimes even contenting himself with the vaguest of allusions. But certain outstanding and in his eyes especially significant events he relates at no lesser length than his source, some—such as the Liberation Decree at Corinth—at even greater length. As a result, individual portions of his narrative form a perspective in which some parts loom large in the foreground, while others are just barely discernible as shadows with indeterminate contours. Often the background or consequences of an event related in detail are dispatched very briefly. You will recall the well-known encounter between C. Popillius and Antiochus Epiphanes on Egyptian soil, in which the Roman ambassador delivered the Senate's command to break off the struggle against the Ptolemies and leave the land at once. Without returning the king's greeting, Popillius handed him the tablet with the Senate's decree; when Antiochus said he must first discuss the matter with his friends, the Roman drew a circle round him in the sand and demanded an immediate answer. This encounter in 168 BCE is set out by Livy in Book 45 at almost the same length as by Polybius (cf. 45.12.3–8 with Polyb. 29.27.1–13). None of the details in his source is missing. The subsequent events, which were certainly not unimportant, were treated by Polybius as fully as the encounter itself, namely the withdrawal of Seleucid troops from Egypt and Cyprus and Popillius' activity in Alexandria. Livy mentions them only very briefly. Finally,

Polybius' observation that Popillius' disobliging conduct met with success only because the Romans had recently demonstrated their superior power by the victory at Pydna is replaced in Livy by a comment on the great fame of that embassy amongst the peoples of the world. The significance of all this is obvious: for Livy, the meeting between Popillius and Antiochus has ceased to be the link in the chain of historical causation that it was for Polybius. Its preconditions and consequences retreat into the background, while the event itself comes forth to illuminate the world as a manifestation of Rome's power. In addition, Livy fails to consider fully certain strands of action that Polybius follows with great attention. Thus the fate of the cities of Lampsacus and Smyrna was set out in detail in the build-up of the war with King Antiochus, since it demonstrated the grave threat that he posed to the freedom of the Greeks of Asia Minor and how much it was in their interest for the Romans to act against him. However, we hardly hear about them later, with the result that it is not even clear whether they were conquered by Antiochus or not.

With some exaggeration one might say that what in Polybius was a linear presentation is in Livy a discontinuous sequence of points. His reader is not meant to enquire too closely into the whys and wherefores, but to let himself be overwhelmed by the impression of stirring moments as he is shown a sequence of great portraits and impressive scenes. That is entirely consistent with Livy's procedures in the rest of his history; it is also in harmony with his purpose in writing history. Whatever sublime heights his artistry may attain, his work is nevertheless a chronicle of the City and the Empire in the traditional Roman spirit. He is not so much concerned to awaken understanding as to bring the great events of the past before his readers' eyes and thereby to move and uplift them. As he says himself in his *Preface*, 'the most salutary and fruitful feature of history is that one can see examples of every kind commemorated in shining fashion; in it you may find models for you and your state to follow, and shameful undertakings with shameful outcomes that you may avoid' (Preface 10). Even here reference to practical politics is not absent, but in contrast to Polybius it is the strengthening of the will to do what is good and right that is paramount.

It is consistent with this mode of thought that Livy has allocated especially generous space not only to events of central military and political importance, such as decisive battles or peace-treaties (together with the negotiations preceding them), but also to episodes of human significance and power to move, even if they have but little to do with Roman history. The most striking example of this comes in Book 39, when he describes the death of the aged Achaean general Philopoemen followed by that of Hannibal. Having remarked that several historians, including Polybius, put the elder Scipio's death in the same year, Livy appends a 'synkrisis' of the circumstances in which the three men died. Both order and content go back to a passage in Book 23 of Polybius, but there Scipio's death is also related and the synkrisis of the three men is taken much further. Anyone familiar with Polybius' history will hardly be surprised that he placed his Megalopolitan compatriot on the same plane as the two commanders acknowledged to be the greatest of the years around 200: he speaks of him with the greatest respect in numerous places. But Livy? He could have contented himself with portraying Hannibal's suicide, for Philopoemen understandably plays a completely subordinate role in his history; furthermore, Scipio's death, which he dates a few years earlier, he had already (following Valerius Antias) narrated at the end of Book 38. But he was obviously affected by the power of these events to arouse human emotions, and therefore did not wish to leave them out. What still linked the three commanders with each other, even if their deaths did not take place in the same year, was in each case the helpless and lonely end of a great and brilliant life. And here it was precisely Philopoemen who had set a shining example by accepting this bitter fate—in contrast to Hannibal and Scipio—with admirable calm.

Livy's mindset appears in even sharper outline when we see what has become of the passages he abridged more drastically. The historical researcher will miss quite a lot, and will complain of some lack of precision especially in legal and strategic matters, which were so foreign to Livy that compression very easily led him to serious misunderstandings. But for the reader who immerses himself without prior expectations, Livy has done a greater service than Polybius. By eliminating circumstantial detail when it is unimportant or obvious and by avoiding repetitions, he has created the precondition for that manageable and purposeful quality in his narratives that so distinguishes them (to their advantage) from his predecessors', which are weighed down with detail and at times devoid of form. Contributing to this effect is Livy's skill at period-formation, above all his use of a wealth of participial constructions unprecedented in Latin literature, which permitted him to display an abundance of details without unduly inhibiting the speedy advance of the action; contributing as well is the unitary tone bestowed on whole sections by keywords, introductory sentences, or summarizing descriptions.

Even more important, in several regards Livy often offers more by way of content than his predecessor. On the one hand there is the 'enargeia' of his depiction, the effort to substitute for the sober establishment of facts the presentation of vivid details. For example, Polybius relates the state of the Macedonian army on the morning of the battle of Cynoscephalae with the dry words: 'It was in considerable difficulties on the march owing to the fog' (Polyb. 18.20.9). For this we read in Livy: 'But so thick a fog had darkened the day that neither could the standard-bearers see the path nor the soldiers see the standards, and the entire army wandered hither and thither in response to uninformed shouts, as confused as if it were lost at night' (Liv. 33.7.2). Polybius reports facts; Livy portrays them. Very often this portrayal is accompanied by a far more detailed description of thoughts and feelings. Thus whereas Polybius, reporting Philip's conversation in 184 with the Roman envoy Appius Claudius, simply remarks that the king was very deeply shocked by something his guest said and was long embarrassed for an answer (Polyb. 22.14.2), Livy says: 'These words brought the king into such confusion that his colour and expression were altered. When at last he had recovered he said . . .' (Liv. 39.34.7). Not only has he added the external signs of Philip's disturbance, but he has turned the simple description of a state of mind into the representation of a process. Again, of the inhabitants of the Aegean coastal cities expelled by Philip Polybius says only, 'Curses and imprecations were uttered against the king, no longer merely in secret, but quite openly' (Polyb. 23.10.7). Livy represents the scene thus: 'Of those who left their homes with their wives and children, few kept their grievance to themselves; and from the columns of the departing imprecations could be heard against the king as hatred overcame fear' (Liv. 40.3.5). Not only is the image of the masses on the road set before our eyes, we also learn of their conflicting emotions. We have thereby encountered an essential feature of Livy's reworking: the effort to describe the participants' moods as exactly as possible, so that their inner world becomes (as it were) transparent. The psychological side of an action, the emotional driving forces, is moved well into the foreground.

Closely related is another feature: Livy's striking emphasis on the moral situation. Just or reprehensible character dispositions determine human action: *benignitas, clementia, constantia, asperitas, avaritia*, to mention only a few. In general, comments on character are implicit in Polybius and mostly correspond to his judgements, but he was not always thinking of fixed character-traits. The Roman introduces these nouns and a touch of censor-like judgement, of moralizing, which is foreign to his predecessor.

Such is Livy's way of presenting historical events to his readers. Undoubtedly he is inferior to Polybius in critical acumen, insight into political and military contexts—in a word, in rational penetration of his subject; but this loss is compensated by gain on the other side. His presentation is more easily grasped and humanly more rounded; he makes things take on sound and colour; his characters are human beings with real experiences and feelings. It is a world in which readers can make themselves at home, albeit not the world of every day. In it, events point beyond themselves: they manifest a higher meaning and have something of a solemn occasion about them. People move in a measured and dignified manner. Nothing ordinary, nothing frivolous hangs on them—at least according to Livy's wishes. One is almost tempted to say that it is the same tone that dominates the *Aeneid*. Polybius, who was very close to the events he describes and who, moreover, had moved since his youth amongst great men, was more relaxed in this respect. He had spoken quite bluntly about the secret negotiations between Eumenes and Perseus during the Third Macedonian War, comparing Eumenes to a fisherman casting his bait; Perseus (he says) had initially raced up from afar towards the supposed prey, but then been hindered by his greed in snapping it up (29.8.1–4; cf. Liv. 44.24.8, 44.25.12). Livy grants such oddities no place in his work. He does, however, criticize the kings' behaviour in the sharpest terms. At the Conference of Nicaea (197 BCE), if we may believe Polybius, both Philip and T. Quinctius Flamininus had been quite informal; there was no dearth of witty remarks and laughter (18.1.1–10. 11; cf. esp. 4.4, 6.1–5, 7.3–6). Livy reports the fact in Philip's case, but then adds disapprovingly, 'By nature he was more inclined to jokes than is seemly for a king, and not even in serious business could he sufficiently control his laughter' (32.34.2). Livy simply ignores the similar material concerning Flamininus, his overall portrait of whom is levelled out by omissions like no other in the Polybian portion. Significantly, this affects not only passages of Polybius that truly showed Flamininus in a bad light, such as the section on his silent complicity in the murder of the Theban Brachylles (196), but also all references to his ambition, his sanguine temperament, his mental agility, and his much-admired gift for diplomacy. In Livy he is hardly anything other than the radiant champion of Greek freedom and the establishment of law and justice. The essential features rely upon Polybius' account, but all other accretions have, so to speak, melted away.

It was my object to show that the differences between Livy and Polybius do not rest only on a divergent narrative technique, but that the two men have dissimilar ways of looking at history that, despite all their shared material, leads to something imperceptibly—yet also quite perceptibly—divergent. This divergence becomes fully clear when we have the opportunity of comparing not only individual sentences, but whole sections of Livy with their Greek original. I should therefore like to end by translating and commenting on both men's accounts of one of the best-known events in those years, Flamininus' Liberation Decree at the Isthmian Games of 196.

First, Polybius 18.46:

The Isthmian Games were due, and the most eminent men from well-nigh all the world had come in expectation of what would happen. Throughout the whole company that had gathered for the festival many different opinions were being expressed; (2) some said it was impossible that the Romans should withdraw from certain places, others maintaining that they would withdraw from those considered more prestigious, but retain those with less renown but equal utility; (3) to seem better informed, the latter group even devised their own lists of these places in the competition. (4) While everyone was thus in a state of uncertainty, the crowd gathered in the stadium for the Games. The herald advanced, had the trumpeter bid the crowd be silent, and made the following announcement: (5) 'The Roman Senate and the proconsul T. Quinctius now, following the defeat of King Philip and the

Macedonians, grant liberty, freedom from garrisons and tribute, with the right to follow their ancestral laws, to the Corinthians, Phocians, Locrians, Euboeans, Phthiotic Achaeans, Magnesians, Thessalians, and Perrhaiboi.' (6) Such loud applause had greeted the beginning of the announcement some people had not even heard it; others wanted to hear it again; (7) but most of the crowd did not believe it and thought they were only dreaming that they had heard what was being said, so unexpected was this turn of events. (8) Therefore they all for different reasons shouted out for the herald and the trumpeter to return to the middle of the stadium and for the announcement to be repeated; as I imagine, the people wished not merely to hear the speaker but to see him too, since they could not believe what was being proclaimed. (9) When the herald had come forward, silenced the noise by means of the trumpeter, and repeated the announcement in the same words, such great applause broke out that it is hard to give a modern audience a notion of what happened. (10) When at last the applause died down, no one paid any attention at all to the competitors, but all talked to each other or to themselves as if they were out of their minds; (11) even after the Games, their expressions of thanks, through excess of joy, nearly killed Titus. (12) Some wanted to look at him face to face and call him their saviour, others were eager to clasp his right hand, the majority threw garlands and ribbons at him; all in all they nearly tore the poor man to pieces. (13) But however excessive these thanksgivings may seem, one might confidently say that in fact they fell far short of the greatness of his action; (14) for it was astonishing that the Romans and their commander Titus should have adopted the intention to endure every expense and every danger for the sake of the Greeks' freedom. It was a great thing too to have brought with them a force that could carry out their intention, (15) but the greatest thing of all was that nothing on the part of *Tuchē* ('Chance') had counter-acted their plan, but that absolutely everything had worked out towards this moment, so that through a single proclamation all Greeks, both in Asia Minor and in Europe, should be free, without garrisons or tribute, governed by their own laws.

Livy 33.32–3 narrates the same events as follows:

[32] The time had come for the regular celebration of the Isthmian Games. These were always very well attended even at other times, not only because of the people's inborn relish for spectacles at which every manner of contest in the arts, in strength, and in speed is on display, (2) but above all since the place, owing to its favourable situation between two opposite seas, provided for the human race's every need, and hence that market served as the meeting-place for Asia and Greece. (3) On that occasion, however, they

had come from all quarters not merely for the usual purpose, but in the most excited suspense to know what the future status and fortune of Greece would be. They harboured different opinions on what the Romans would do, which they did not keep to themselves but expressed in conversation; but hardly anyone was convinced that they would withdraw from all Greece. (4) They had sat down to watch, when the herald came forward with the trumpeter, as is the custom, to the middle of the stadium, from which it is usual to open the games with a standard formula; and when the trumpet had created silence he proclaimed as follows: (5) 'The Roman Senate and T. Quinctius, commander, following the defeat of King Philip and the Macedonians, bid all the Corinthians, Phocians, and Locrians, and the island of Euboea, the Magnesians, Thessalians, Perrhaiboi, and Phthiotic Achaeans be free, immune from tribute, and autonomous.' (6) He had listed all the peoples who had been subject to King Philip. When they heard the herald's voice the joy was too great for the people to take it in in its entirety: (7) hardly anyone believed he had heard properly and people looked at each other, startled as if by a false apparition in a dream; individually, no one trusted his own ears but asked his neighbours. (8) The herald was called back, for everyone wished not merely to hear but to see the messenger of his freedom, and again proclaimed the same message. (9) Then, now that their joy was sure, there broke out such loud applause and shouting, so often repeated that it could easily be seen that nothing amongst all good things was more pleasing to the multitude than freedom. (10) The games were then celebrated quickly, though no one either cared about the spectacle nor kept his eyes on it, to such an extent had a single cause for joy left them no room for awareness of any other pleasures. [33] When the games were over, almost everyone streamed to the Roman commander, (2) with the result that in the rush of the crowd all to reach the one man, longing to clasp his hand and throwing garlands and ribbons, he was not far removed from danger. However, he was some 33 years old, (3) and both the vigour of youth and enjoyment of so remarkable a reward from his glory gave him strength. (4) The enthusiasm was not confined to that moment, but was repeated over several days with grateful sentiments and speeches, (5) which declared that there was a people on earth that at its own expense, its own trouble and risk, waged war for the freedom of others, (6) and did not perform this service for its neighbours or people of the immediate vicinity or joined by a land route, (7) but crossed the seas, lest there should be any unjust domination in the whole world, and (finally) in which justice, right, and law have the greatest power; by the single voice of the heralds all the cities of Greece and Asia had been freed; (8) to hope for this had been the mark of a bold spirit, to bring it to a conclusion of great courage and great good fortune.

Were we content to stand where Nissen had stood so long ago, we should have to say something like: 'Livy 33.32–3 corresponds exactly to Polybius 18.46. Even the exaggeration that the Romans granted freedom to all the Greek cities was already to be found in the earlier narrative. Livy has simply misunderstood Polybius' remark about the entrance of the herald and added the information about Flamininus' age, apparently from an earlier passage in his source. All remaining deviations are mere rhetorical ornament.' Adopting Witte's approach, we could at most remark that Livy sometimes structures the course of events more purposefully than Polybius and that his report is more self-contained, in that the judgement on the event constitutes the end of the action; he has thus in effect made a complete individual narrative ('Einzelerzählung') of it. This would be to ignore the divergences that constitute the chief reason for the different impression left by Livy's account, which combine to take the narrative in a very definite direction. Of the Isthmian Games Polybius says at the start only that in the relevant year the most eminent men from well-nigh all the world had come to the celebrations, expecting something in the nature of a political demonstration by the Romans. Livy says much the same, but only after emphasizing in a long and powerfully structured period the significance of these games and the place of Corinth in the world. That is more than just one of his not infrequent explanations added for people less familiar with Greek affairs: rather, the reader is primed in advance to suppose that whatever the expected announcement may contain, it will be something of which the world takes notice. The reaction of those present to the herald's announcement is also portrayed differently. According to Polybius, some of the people began clapping loudly even while the herald was speaking—obviously, he means after the words 'grant liberty'. For that reason many listeners could not make everything out, while others wanted to hear the text once again, since they doubted whether they had properly understood. The announcement is repeated, at which point indescribable jubilation breaks out. The herald's words are thus at first almost lost in the noise of a crowd in tumult; then they are fully comprehended, and now joy overwhelms the people. Joy: Livy makes this notion right from the start the keyword of the whole section. In the very first sentence we read,

'When they heard the herald's voice the joy was too great for the people to take it in in its entirety.' Thereafter this same notion returns another four times, including the statement that one could tell from the excess of applause that nothing amongst all good things was more pleasing to the multitude than freedom. That characterizes Livy's outlook: the herald's announcement meets one of the people's inmost needs, whose satisfaction causes the excess of joy that compels the announcement to be repeated. We learn about the happy jubilation at a miracle; of a tumultuously noisy crowd we hear nothing. It is consistent with this that even the danger to Flamininus' life as he is mobbed is portrayed far more mutedly by Livy than Polybius. We hear nothing about killing and tearing to pieces.

Especially important in our context is the end of the account. Polybius expresses his thoughts about the astonishing nature of the event: we must be amazed that the Romans and their commander Flamininus were ready to face so much expense and danger for the sake of Greece's freedom, and also that they had the military strength to do so, but above all that *Tuchē* ('Chance') did not act against them. In Livy all this is presented as the thoughts and words of grateful people; that is how they greet the righteous deed. Nothing at all is said about Flamininus, only about the true hero of Livy's history, the Roman people of former times. They have achieved an astonishing thing, but what they have done for Greece does not stand alone: it is only one example of a far more comprehensive activity directed toward the whole world. What matters for this activity is less the military might of which Polybius had written, but their moral force, *audax animus,*and their *virtus*. If providence also played a part, it did not do so in as striking a fashion as in the Greek original. Without denying the importance of chance in history, Livy wanted nothing to do with the emotively exaggerated emphasis on *Tuchē* which in Polybius counterbalances rational calculation. In addition, the Roman incorporates into his account, like a cornerstone, a thought that has played an absolutely central role since the opening books, namely, that it was the Romans' task to bring about the rule of right and law on the earth. In our passage this notion fits together with the other changes Livy has made to Polybius' account to produce a coherent view of the event portrayed: human beings have a deeply rooted need for freedom and there is a power on earth that satisfies this need by establishing a legal order as well, the *res publica Romana*. That was manifested in the Liberation Decree at Corinth as in a great sign. Almost every detail of Livy's portrayal of this event has developed out of what he found in Polybius. In its tone it is completely different. It has, if I am permitted an expression that does not properly belong in historiography, a proclamatory character. We can understand this essential peculiarity of Livy's history only if we take it together with the painfully pessimistic expressions about the decadence of his own time in the *Preface*. It becomes clear that nothing was further from Livy's thoughts than historical propaganda for the existing power structures. Rather, he attempted intellectually to preserve the heights that he saw deeply threatened in the reality of his own world.

## ADDENDUM

This is a much shorter precursor to Tränkle's book-length study of the same title, *Livius und Polybius* (1977). The exercise of comparing Livy's narrative with Polybius has often been undertaken as a means of understanding both Livy's evaluation of his sources and his working methods (see our Introduction, 2–3). Briscoe's commentaries (1973), (1981), and (2008) include some brief, useful remarks on the subject, as do Walsh's (1990–96), though both tend to emphasize Livy's shortcomings as a historian in contrast with the advantages of Polybius. Gruen (1975) models how Polybius and Livy can be used in tandem to untangle a historical problem. Briscoe's 'Livy and Polybius' (1993) offers another close, comparative reading of the two writers; Levene (2010) looks anew at the two historians, using the techniques of intertextuality and focusing on the third decade.

For Polybius alone, see in particular the works of Walbank: his three-volume commentary (1957–79) and two collections of essays (1985), (2002). Oakley and Rich discuss Livy's use of Roman sources; for a detailed account of the efforts of German scholars to assign a source to each section of Livy, see the Introduction to Luce (1977). For further discussion of Burck, especially his contributions to the course of scholarship on Livy, see the Addendum.

Finally, for the difficulties which arise when writing, or evaluating, narrative history—especially narrative history which uses earlier narratives as a source—see *The History and Narrative Reader* (Roberts (2001)), which anthologizes most of the important theoretical discussions of the problem.

# Major Editions of the Text of Livy

Oxford Classical Texts (OCT):

Books 1–5, ed. R. M. Ogilvie, 1974.
Books 6–10, edd. C. F. Walters and R. S. Conway, 1919.
Books 21–25, edd. C. F. Walters and R. S. Conway, 1929.
Books 26–30, edd. S. K. Johnson and R. S. Conway, 1935.
Books 31–35, ed. A. H. McDonald, 1965.
Books 36–40, ed. P. G. Walsh, 1999.

Teubner Texts:

Books 1–10, 31–45, ed. W. Weissenborn, M. Müller, and
W. Heraeus (Leipzig) 1887–1908.
Books 21–22, ed. T. A. Dorey (Leipzig) 1971.
Books 23–25, ed. T. A. Dorey (Leipzig) 1976.
Books 26–27, ed. P. G. Walsh, 2nd edn. (Leipzig) 1989.
Books 28–30, ed. P. G. Walsh (Leipzig) 1986.
Books 31–40, ed. J. Briscoe (Stuttgart) 1991.
Books 41–45, ed. J. Briscoe (Stuttgart) 1986.

Budé Texts:

Bayet, J. and Bailler, G. *et al.* (eds.) (1940–2001), *Tite-Live Histoire Romaine.* 35
volumes (individual volume editors and translators vary), Paris.

Loeb Classical Library (LCL):

Foster, B. O. *et al.* (eds.) (1922–1959), *Livy with an English Translation.* 14
volumes (vols. 6–8 translated by Frank Gardner Moore; vols. 9–12 by
Evan T. Sage; vols. 13–14 by A. C. Schlesinger), Cambridge, Mass.

Aris & Phillips Texts:

Walsh, P. G. (ed. and trans.) (1990–96), *Livy, Book XXXVI–Book XL.* 5
vols., Warminster.

# Bibliography

This bibliography is intended to help readers find the works cited by the authors anthologized herein; to that end, we have not modernized the references, and we have not tried to make our authors consistent beyond a certain point. (So, for instance, we do not always give both the original and the later version of a paper that appeared in a scholar's *Collected Papers*.)

Adams, J. N. (1974), 'The Vocabulary of the Later Decades of Livy', *Antichthon*, 8: 56–62.

—— (2003), *Bilingualism and the Latin Language* (Cambridge).

Adcock, F. E. (1956), *Caesar as Man of Letters* (Cambridge).

Albrecht, M. von (1983), '*Fides* und Völkerrecht: von Livius bis Hugo Grotius', in Lefèvre and Ohlshausen (1983: 295–9).

Alföldi, A. (1965), *Early Rome and the Latins* (Ann Arbor).

—— (1971), 'Die Penaten, Aeneas und Latinus', *MDAI(R)*, 78: 1–58.

Alfonsi, L. (1962), 'Sul passo Liviano relativo ad Alessandro Magno', *Hermes*, 90: 505–6.

Anderson, W. B. (1908), 'Contributions to the Study of the Ninth Book of Livy', *TAPhA*, 39: 89–103.

—— (1928), *Livy IX* (3rd edn., Cambridge).

Ando, C. (2000), *Imperial Ideology and Provincial Loyalty in the Roman Empire* (Berkeley).

André, J. (1949), *La Vie et l'œuvre d'Asinius Pollion* (Paris).

Astin, A. E. (1978), *Cato the Censor* (Oxford).

Badian, E. (1966), 'The Early Historians', in Dorey (1966: 1–38).

—— (1985), 'A Phantom Marriage Law', *Philologus*, 129: 82–98.

—— (1993), 'Livy and Augustus', in Schuller (1993: 9–38).

Balsdon, J. P. V. D. (1953), 'Some Questions about Historical Writing in the Second Century B.C.', *CQ*, 3: 158–64.

—— (1954), 'Rome and Macedon, 205–200 B.C.', *JRS*, 44: 30–42.

—— (1956), review of Meloni (1955), *JRS*, 46: 199–201.

Bardon, H. (1952–6), *La Littérature latine inconnue*, 2 vols. (Paris).

Barns, J. W. B., Lobel, E., Roberts, C. H., and Turner, E. G. (eds.) (1957), *The Oxyrhynchus Papyri*, Part XXIV, 'Anonymous (Duris?) History of Sicily under Agathocles', (London) 99–106.

Bartsch, S. (1994), *Actors in the Audience: Theatricality and Doublespeak from Nero to Hadrian* (Cambridge, Mass.).

Basanoff, V. (1950), 'M. Caedicius de plebe...et...Q. Caedicius Centurio', *Latomus*, 9: 13–26.

Bauman, R. A. (1969), *The Duumviri in the Roman Criminal Law and in the Horatius Legend, Historia* Einzelschriften 12 (Wiesbaden).

Beard, M. (2007), *The Roman Triumph* (Cambridge, Mass).

——, North, J. and Price, S. (1998), *Religions of Rome*, 2 vols. (Cambridge).

Beck, H. and Walter, U. (2001–4), *Die frühen römischen Historiker*, 2 vols. Vol. 1, 2nd edn. 2005 (Darmstadt).

Begbie, C. M. (1967), 'The Epitome of Livy', *CQ*, 17: 332–8.

Benveniste, E. (1969), *Vocabulaire des institutions indo-européennes*, 2 vols. (Paris).

Berger, A. (1953), *Encyclopedic Dictionary of Roman Law* (Philadelphia).

Bernard, J.-E. (2000), *Le Portrait chez Tite-Live. Essai sur une écriture de l'histoire romaine*, Collection Latomus 253 (Brussels).

Bettini, M. (1991), *Anthropology and Roman Culture: Kinship, Time, Images of the Soul*, trans. J. B. van Sickle (Baltimore).

Bikerman, E. (1946), 'La Lettre de Mithridate dans les Histoires de Salluste', *REL*, 24: 131–51.

Birt, T. (1882), *Das antike Buchwesen* (Berlin).

Bishop, J. D. (1948), 'Augustus and A. Cornelius Cossus', *Latomus*, 7: 187–91.

Bleicken, J. (1963), '*Coniuratio*. Die Schwurszene auf den Münzen und Gemmen der römischen Republik', *JNG*, 13: 51–70.

Bloch, R. (1965), *Tite-Live et les premiers siècles de Rome* (Paris).

Bloom, H. (1973), *The Anxiety of Influence: A Theory of Poetry* (New York).

Bömer, F. (1953), 'Der Commentarius', *Hermes*, 81: 210–50.

——(1969–86), *P. Ovidius Naso: Metamorphosen. Kommentar*, 7 vols. (Heidelberg).

Bonjour, M. (1975*a*), *Terre natale* (Paris).

——(1975*b*), 'Les Personnages féminins et la terre natale dans l'épisode de Coriolan (Liv., 2.40)', *REL*, 53: 157–81.

Bonner, S. F. (1949), *Roman Declamation* (Liverpool).

Bornecque, H. (1933), *Tite-Live* (Paris).

Bowersock, G. W. (1965), *Augustus and the Greek World* (Oxford).

Bredehorn, U. (1968), *Senatsakten in der republikanischen Annalistik* (Marburg).

Brink, C. O. (1971), *Horace on Poetry: The 'Ars Poetica'* (Cambridge).

Briscoe, J. (1971), 'The First Decade', in Dorey (1971: 1–20).

——(1973), *A Commentary on Livy Books xxxi–xxxiii* (Oxford).

——(1978), review of Tränkle (1977), *CR*, 28: 267–9.

——(1981), *A Commentary on Livy Books xxxiv–xxxvii* (Oxford).

——(1990), review of Haehling (1989), *GGA*, 242: 182–97.

——(1993), 'Livy and Polybius', in Schuller (1993: 39–52).

——(2003), 'A. Postumius Albinus, Polybius and Livy's Account of the Bacchanalia', *Latomus* 23, 302–8.

——(2005), 'The Language and Style of the Fragmentary Republican Historians', in Reinhardt *et al.* (2005: 53–72).

——(2008), *A Commentary on Livy Books xxxviii–xl* (Oxford).

Bruckmann, H. (1936), *Die römischen Niederlagen im Geschichtswerk des T. Livius* (Diss. Münster).

Bruère, R. (1950), 'The Scope of Lucan's Historical Epic', *CPh*, 45: 217–35.

Bruhl, A. (1953), *Liber Pater. Origines et expansion du culte dionysiaque à Rome et dans le monde romain* (Paris).

Bruns, I. (1898), *Die Persönlichkeit in der Geschichtsschreibung der Alten* (Berlin).

Brunt, P. A. (1971), *Italian Manpower, 225 B.C. – A.D. 14* (Oxford). Reprinted 1987.

——and Moore, J. M. (1967), *Res gestae divi Augusti: The Achievements of the Divine Augustus* (Oxford). Often reprinted.

Bruwaene, M. van den (1952), 'Approximations sur Tullus Hostilius', *Latomus*, 11: 153–63.

Bryson, N. (1986), 'Two Narratives of Rape in the Visual Arts: Lucretia and the Sabine Women', in S. Tomaselli and R. Porter (eds.), *Rape* (Oxford) 152–73.

Bucher, G. S. (1987 [publ. 1995]), 'The *Annales Maximi* in the Light of Roman Methods of Keeping Records', *AJAH*, 12: 2–61.

Büchner, K. (1974), *Das Theater des Terenz* (Heidelberg).

Burck, E. (1934), *Die Erzählungskunst des T. Livius* (Berlin). Reprinted 1964.

——(1935), 'Livius als augusteischer Historiker', *Die Welt als Geschichte* 1: 446–87 = Burck (1967: 96–143).

——(1950), *Einführung in die dritte Dekade des Livius* (Heidelberg). 2nd edn. 1962.

——(ed.) (1967), *Wege zu Livius* (Darmstadt).

——(1971), 'The Third Decade', in Dorey (1971: 21–46).

——(1992), *Das Geschichtswerk des Titus Livius* (Heidelberg).

Burkert, W. (1983), *Homo Necans: The Anthropology of Ancient Greek Sacrificial Ritual and Myth* (Berkeley).

Calhoon, C. G. (1997), 'Lucretia, Savior and Scapegoat: The Dynamics of Sacrifice in Livy 1.57–59', *Helios*, 24: 151–69.

Cameron, A. (ed.) (1989), *History as Text: The Writing of Ancient History* (London).

Canetti, E. (1960), *Crowds and Power*, trans. C. Stewart (New York).

Canter, H. V. (1917), 'Rhetorical Elements in Livy's Direct Speeches', *AJPh*, 38: 125–51.

Carney, T. F. (1959), 'Formal Elements in Livy', *PACA*, 2: 1–9.

Cavallin, S., and Lambert, A. (1948), 'Nochmals "Avant Zama": Livius 30.29–31', *Eranos*, 46: 54–71.

Chaplin, J. D. (2000), *Livy's Exemplary History* (Oxford).

Chassignet, M. (1996–2004), *L'Annalistique romaine*, 3 vols. (Paris).

Chausserie-Laprée, J.-P. (1969), *L'Expression narrative chez les historiens latins: histoire d'un style* (Paris).

Cichorius, C. (1894), 'Annales', *RE*, 1: 2248–56.

——(1922), 'Ein neuer Historiker und die Anfänge von Livius' schriftstellerischer Tätigkeit', in *Römische Studien* (Leipzig), 261–9.

Cizek, E. (1988), 'La Poétique cicéronienne de l'histoire', *BAGB*: 16–25.

——(1992), 'A propos de la poétique de l'histoire chez Tite-Live', *Latomus*, 51: 355–64.

Clancy, J. P. (trans.) (1960), *Odes and Epodes of Horace* (Chicago).

Clark, E. A. (2004), *History, Theory, Text: Historians and the Linguistic Turn* (Cambridge, Mass.).

Clarke, G. W. (1967), 'The Capitol in 390 B.C.', *CR*, 17: 138.

Clausen, W. V. (1964), 'Callimachus and Roman Poetry', *GRBS*, 5: 181–96.

Cocchia, E. (1922), 'Fonti ed elementi d'imitazione popolare nella leggenda dell'incendio gallico', *Rivista Indo-Greco-Italica*, 6: 17–32.

Cochrane, N. (1940), *Christianity and Classical Culture* (Oxford).

Cohen, D. (1991), 'The Augustan Law on Adultery: The Social and Cultural Context', in D. I. Kertzer and R. P. Saller (eds.), *The Family in Italy from Antiquity to the Present* (New Haven) 109–26.

Coleman, R. G. G. (1999), 'Poetic Discourse, Poetic Diction and the Poetic Register', in Mayer, R. G. and Adams, J. N. (eds.) (1999), *Aspects of the Language of Latin Poetry*, Proceedings of the British Academy 93 (London) 21–96.

Coppola, M. (1983–4), 'Augusto nella praefatio liviano?', *AFLN*, 26: 67–70.

Corbett, P. E. (1930), *The Roman Law of Marriage* (Oxford).

Cornell, T. J. (1986*a*), 'The Value of the Literary Tradition concerning Archaic Rome', in Raaflaub (1986*a*: 52–76 = 2005: 47–74).

——(1986*b*), 'The *Annals* of Quintus Ennius', *JRS*, 76: 244–50.

——(1987), 'Ennius' *Annals* VI: A Reply', *CQ*, 37: 514–16.

——(1995), *The Beginnings of Rome* (London).

Cousin, J. (1951), *Bibliographie de la langue latine* (Paris).

Cova, P. V. (1974), 'Livio e la repressione dei Baccanali', *Athenaeum*, 52: 82–109.

Crake, J. E. A. (1940), 'The Annals of the Pontifex Maximus', *CPh*, 35: 375–86.

Crawford, M. H. (1973), '*Foedus* and *Sponsio*', *PBSR*, 41: 1–7.

Crook, J. A. (1967), *Law and Life of Rome* (Ithaca).

Crosby, T. (1978), 'The Structure of Livy's History', *LCM*, 3: 113–19.

Cumont, F. (1922), *After-Life in Roman Paganism* (New Haven).

Dahlheim, W. (1968), *Struktur und Entwicklung des römischen Völkerrechts im dritten und zweiten Jahrhundert v. Chr.* (Munich).

Damon, C. (1997), 'From Source to *sermo*: Narrative Technique in Livy 34.54.4–8', *AJPh* 118: 251–66.

Davidson, J. (1991), 'The Gaze in Polybius' *Histories*', *JRS*, 81: 10–24.

Davies, J. P. (2004), *Rome's Religious History: Livy, Tacitus and Ammianus on their Gods* (Cambridge).

Degrassi, A. (1937), *Inscriptiones Italiae* XIII.3: *Elogia* (Roma).

——(1947), *Inscriptiones Italiae* XIII.1: *Fasti consulares et triumphales* (Roma).

Deininger, J. (1985), 'Livius und der Prinzipat', *Klio*, 67: 265–72.

De Lauretis, T. (1984), *Alice Doesn't* (Bloomington).

Dench, E. (1995), *From Barbarians to New Men: Greek, Roman, and Modern Perceptions of Peoples from the Central Apennines* (Oxford).

——(2005), *Romulus' Asylum: Roman Identities from the Age of Alexander to the Age of Hadrian* (Oxford).

De Sanctis, G. (1907–23), *Storia dei Romani*, 4 vols. (Turin).

Dessau, H. (1903), 'Die vorrede des Livius', in *Beiträge zur alten Geschichte und griechisch-römischen Alterthumskunde: Festschrift zu Otto Hirschfelds sechzigstem Geburtstage* (Berlin) 461–6.

——(1906), 'Livius und Augustus', *Hermes*, 41: 142–51.

De Ste Croix, G. E. M. (1963), 'Why Were the Early Christians Persecuted?', *Past and Present*, 26: 6–38.

Dixon, S. (1982), 'Women and Rape in Roman Law', *Kønsroller, parforhold og Samlivsformer: Arbejdsnotat nr. 3* (Copenhagen).

——(1988), *The Roman Mother* (Norman, Okla.).

Donaldson, I. (1982), *The Rapes of Lucretia: A Myth and its Transformations* (Oxford).

Dorey, T. A. (ed.) (1966), *Latin Historians* (London).

——(ed.) (1971), *Livy* (London).

Douglas, M. (1984), *Purity and Danger* (London).

Drexler, H. (1938), 'Terentiana', *Hermes*, 73: 39–98.

Drummond, A. (1978), 'The Dictator Years', *Historia* 27: 550–72.

Dumézil, G. (1942), *Horace et les Curiaces*, Paris.

—— (1949), 'Pères et fils dans la légende de Tarquin le Superbe', in *Hommages à Joseph Bidez et à Franz Cumont*: Collection Latomus 2 (Brussels) 77–84.

—— (1956), *Aspects de la fonction guerrière chez les Indo-Européens* (Paris).

—— (1970), *Destiny of the Warrior*, trans. A. Hiltebeitel (Chicago).

Dunkle, J. R. (1971), 'The Rhetorical Tyrant in Roman Historiography: Sallust, Livy and Tacitus', *CW*, 65: 12–20.

Dutoit, E. (1948), 'Silences dans l'œuvre de Tite-Live', in *Mélanges de philologie, de littérature et d'histoire ancienne offerts à J. Marouzeau par ses collègues et élèves étrangers* (Paris) 141–51.

—— (1956), 'Le souci étymologique chez Tite-Live', in *Hommages à Max Niedermann*, Collection Latomus 23 (Brussels) 108–14.

Earl, D. (1961), *The Political Thought of Sallust* (Cambridge).

—— (1967), *The Moral and Political Tradition of Rome* (Ithaca).

Eckert, K. (1970), '*Ferocia*—Untersuchung eines ambivalenten Begriffs', *AU*, 13: 90–106.

Edwards, C. (1993), *The Politics of Immorality in Ancient Rome* (Cambridge).

—— (1996), *Writing Rome: Textual Approaches to the City* (Cambridge).

Elsner, J. (1991), 'Cult and Sculpture: Sacrifice in the Ara Pacis Augustae', *JRS*, 81: 50–61.

Erb, N. (1963), *Kriegsursachen und Kriegsschuld in der ersten Pentade des T. Livius* (Winterthur).

Erkell, H. (1952), *Augustus, Felicitas, Fortuna* (Göteborg).

Ernout, A. (ed. and trans.) (1947), *Salluste* (Paris).

Fantham, E. (1975), 'Sex, Status and Survival in Hellenistic Athens: A Study of Women in New Comedy', *Phoenix*, 29: 44–74.

—— (2004), *The Roman World of Cicero's 'De Oratore'* (Oxford).

Favro, D. (1996), *The Urban Image of Augustan Rome* (Cambridge).

Feeney, D. C. (1998), *Literature and Religion at Rome: Cultures, Contexts and Beliefs* (Cambridge).

—— (2007), *Caesar's Calendar: Ancient Time and the Beginnings of History* (Berkeley).

Feldherr, A. (1991), *Spectacle and Society in Livy's History* (Diss. Berkeley).

—— (1998), *Spectacle and Society in Livy's History* (Berkeley).

Ferguson, J. (1962), 'The Religion of Cicero', in J. Ferguson, L. A. Thompson, A. R. Hands, and W. A. Laidlaw, *Studies in Cicero* (Rome) 83–96.

Ferrero, L. (1949), 'Attualità e tradizione nella Praefatio Liviana', *RFIC*, 27: 1–47.

Flobert, P. (1981), 'La *patavinitas* de Tite-Live d'après les mœurs littéraires du temps', *REL*, 60: 193–206.

Flurl, W. (1969), *Deditio in Fidem* (Munich).

Fornara, C. W. (1983), *The Nature of History in Ancient Greece and Rome* (Berkeley).

Forsythe, G. (1990), 'Some Notes on the History of Cassius Hemina', *Phoenix*, 44: 326–44.

—— (1994), *The Historian L. Calpurnius Piso Frugi and the Roman Annalistic Tradition* (Lanham, Md).

—— (1999), *Livy and Early Rome, a Study in Historical Method and Judgement, Historia* Einzelschiften 132 (Stuttgart).

—— (2000), 'The Roman Historians of the Second Century BC', in C. Bruun (ed.), *The Roman Middle Republic: Politics, Religion and Historiography c.400–133 BC* (Rome) 1–11.

—— (2002), 'Dating and Arranging the Roman History of Valerius Antias', in V. B. Gorman and E. W. Robinson (eds.), *Oikistes: Studies in Constitutions, Colonies and Military Power in the Ancient World Offered in Honour of A. J. Graham* (Leiden) 99–112.

Foucher, A. (2000), *Historia proxima poetis: L'influence de la poésie épique sur le style des historiens latins de Salluste à Ammien Marcellin,* Collection Latomus 255 (Brussels).

Fowler, W. W. (1911), *The Religious Experience of the Roman People* (London).

—— (1914), *Roman Ideas of Deity* (London).

Fox, M. (1996), *Roman Historical Myths: The Regal Period in Augustan Literature* (Oxford).

Fraccaro, P. (1956–7), *Opuscula*, 3 vols. (Pavia).

—— (1957), 'The History of Rome in the Regal Period', *JRS*, 47: 59–65.

Fraenkel, E. (1932), 'Senatus Consultum de Bacchanalibus', *Hermes*, 67: 369–96.

Fredershausen, O. (1912), 'Weitere Studien über das Recht bei Plautus und Terenz', *Hermes*, 47: 199–249.

Frier, B.W. (1979), *Libri annales pontificum maximorum: The Origins of the Annalistic Tradition* (Rome). Revised edn. 1999 (Ann Arbor).

Funaioli, G. (1934), *Studi Liviani* (Rome).

Funari, R. (ed.) (1996), *C. Sallusti Crispi historiarum fragmenta* (Amsterdam).

Fussell, P. (1975), *The Great War and Modern Memory* (Oxford).

Galinsky, K. (1996), *Augustan Culture: An Interpretive Introduction* (Princeton).

Gallagher, C. and Greenblatt, S. (2000), *Practicing New Historicism* (Chicago).

Gantz, T. (1975), 'The Tarquin Dynasty', *Historia*, 24: 539–54.

Gardner, J. (1986), *Women in Roman Law and Society* (London).

Gay, P. (1974), *Style in History* (New York).

Geffcken, K. A. (1973), *Comedy in the 'Pro Caelio'*, Mnemosyne Supplement 30 (Leiden).

Gelzer, M. (1931), 'Nasicas Widerspruch gegen die Zerstörung Carthagos', *Philologus*, 86: 261–99 = (1962–4: ii.39–72).

—— (1933), 'Römische Politik bei Fabius Pictor', *Hermes*, 68: 129–66 = (1962–4: iii.51–92).

—— (1934), 'Der Anfang römischer Geschichtsschreibung', *Hermes*, 69: 46–55.

—— (1935), 'Die Glaubwürdigkeit der bei Livius überlieferten Senatsbeschlüsse über römische Truppenaufgebote', *Hermes* 70: 269–300 = (1962–4: iii.220–55).

—— (1936), 'Die Unterdrückung der Bacchanalien bei Livius', *Hermes*, 71: 275–87.

—— (1942), review of Klotz (1940–1), *Gnomon* 18: 220–30 = (1962–4: iii.270–9).

—— (1954), 'Nochmals über den Anfang der römischen Geschichtsschreibung', *Hermes*, 82: 342–8.

—— (1957), review of Meloni (1955), *BO*, 14: 55–7 = (1962–4: iii.280–5).

—— (1962–4), *Kleine Schriften*, 3 vols. (Weisbaden).

Gilbert, S. M. and Gubar, S. (1979), *The Madwoman in the Attic* (New Haven).

Gill, C. and Wiseman, T. P. (eds.) (1993), *Lies and Fiction in the Ancient World* (Exeter).

Gilmartin, K. (1975), 'A Rhetorical Figure in Latin Historical Style: the Imaginary Second Person Singular', *TAPhA*, 105: 99–121.

Ginsburg, J. (1981), *Tradition and Theme in the* Annals *of Tacitus* (New York).

—— (1993), '*In maiores certamina*: Past and Present in the *Annals*', in T. J. Luce and A. J. Woodman (eds.), *Tacitus and the Tacitean Tradition* (Princeton) 86–103.

Gjerstad, E. (1953–73), *Early Rome*, 6 vols. (Lund).

Giovannini, A. (1983), *Consulare Imperium* (Basle).

Girard, R. (1977), *Violence and the Sacred*, trans. P. Gregory (Baltimore).

Girod, R. (1980), 'Caton l'Ancien et Catilina', in R. Chevallier (ed.), *Colloque histoire et historiographie*, Collection Caesarodunum 15 *bis* (Paris) 61–9.

Goldhill, S. (1991), *The Poet's Voice: Essays on Poetics and Greek Literature* (Cambridge).

Gomme, A. W. and Sandbach, F. H. (1973), *Menander: A Commentary* (Oxford).

Goodyear, F. R. D. (1966), review of Ogilvie (1965), *CR*, 16: 60–3 = *Papers on Latin Literature* (1992) (London) 207–9.

Gordon, R. (1990), 'The Veil of Power: Emperors, Sacrificers and Benefactors', in M. Beard and J. North (eds.), *Pagan Priests: Religion and Power in the Ancient World* (London) 201–31.

Grafton, A. (1997), *The Footnote: A Curious History* (Cambridge, Mass.).

Gries, K. (1949), *Constancy in Livy's Latinity* (Diss. New York).

Griffin, J. (1976), 'Augustan Poetry and the Life of Luxury', *JRS*, 66: 87–105. Revised repr. in (1985) *Latin Poets and Roman Life* (Chapel Hill) 1–31.

Gruen, E. (1975), 'Rome and Rhodes in the Second Century BC: A Historiographical Inquiry', *CQ*, 25: 58–81.

Gschnitzner, F. (1981), 'Das System der römischen Heeresbildung im zweiten Punischen Krieg: Polybios, die Annalisten und die geschichtliche Wirklichkeit', *Hermes*, 109: 59–85.

Gurval, R. (1995), *Actium and Augustus* (Ann Arbor).

Gutberlet, D. (1985), *Die erste Dekade des Livius als Quelle zur gracchischen und sullanischen Zeit*, Beiträge zur Altertumswissenschaft 4 (Hildesheim).

Habinek, T. N. (1990), 'Sacrifice, Society and Vergil's Ox-Born Bees', in M. Griffith and D. J. Mastronarde (eds.), *Cabinet of the Muses: Essays on Classical and Comparative Literature in Honor of Thomas G. Rosenmeyer* (Atlanta) 209–23.

Haehling, R. von (1989), *Zeitbezüge des Livius in der ersten Dekade seines Geschichtswerkes: nec vitia nostra nec remedia pati possumus, Historia* Einzelschriften 61 (Stuttgart).

Hahm, D. E. (1963), 'Roman Nobility and the Three Major Priesthoods, 218–167 BC', *TAPhA* 94: 73–85.

Halkin, L. (1953), *La Supplication d'action de grâces chez les Romains* (Paris).

Hammond, N. G. L. (1966), 'The Opening Campaign and the Battle of Aoi Stena in the Second Macedonian War', *JRS*, 56: 39–54.

Hand, F. (1829–45), *Tursellinus, seu de particulis latinis commentarii* (Leipzig). Reprinted 1969 (Amsterdam).

Hansen, M. H. (1998), 'The Little Grey Horse: Henry V's Speech at Agincourt and the Battle Exhortation in Ancient Historiography', *Histos* 2 (*www.dur. ac.uk/Classics/histos/1998/hansen.html*). Reprinted (2001) *C&M* 52: 95–116.

Hardie, P. R. (1993), *The Epic Successors of Virgil: A Study in the Dynamics of a Tradition* (Cambridge).

Harris, W. V. (1979), *War and Imperialism in Republican Rome, 327–70 B.C.* (Oxford).

Harrison, S. J. (1991), *Virgil: Aeneid 10* (Oxford).

Hartog, F. (1980), *Le Miroir d'Hérodote: essai sur la représentation de l'autre* (Paris) = (1988) *The Mirror of Herodotus: the Representation of the Other in the Writing of History*, trans. J. Lloyd (Berkeley).

Hays, S. (1987), '*Lactea ubertas*: What's Milky about Livy?', *CJ*, 82: 107–16.

Heinze, R. (1928), *Virgils epische Technik* (3rd edn., Leipzig).

—— (1933), *Die Augusteische Kultur* (2nd edn., Leipzig).

Heitland, W. E. (1923), *The Roman Republic*, 3 vols. (2nd edn., Cambridge).

Hellegouarc'h, J. (1963), *Le Vocabulaire des relations et des partis politiques sous la république* (Paris).

—— (1970), 'Le principat de Camille', *REL*, 48: 112–32.

Hellmann, F. (1939), *Livius-Interpretationen* (Berlin).

Henderson, J. (1989), 'Livy and the Invention of History' in Cameron (1989: 64–85). Revised repr. in (1998) *Fighting for Rome* (Cambridge) 301–19.

Herkommer, E. (1968), *Die Topoi in den Proömien der römischen Geschichtswerke* (Stuttgart).

Herter, H. (1966), 'Das Königsritual der Atlantis', *RhM*, 109: 236–59.

Hesselbarth, H. (1889), *Historisch-kritische Untersuchungen zur dritten Dekade des Livius* (Halle).

Heurgon, J. (1964), 'L. Cincius et la loi du *clavus annalis*', *Athenaeum*, 42: 432–7.

—— (1970), *Tite-Live. Histoires: Livre I* (Paris).

—— (1973), *The Rise of Rome*, trans. J. Willis (Berkeley).

Higonnet, M. (1986), 'Speaking Silences: Women's Suicide', in S. R. Suleiman (ed.), *The Female Body in Western Culture* (Cambridge, Mass.) 68–83.

Hinds, S. (1997), *Allusion and Intertext: Dynamics of Appropriation in Roman Poetry* (Cambridge).

Hine, H. (2005), 'Poetic Influence on Prose: The Case of the Younger Seneca', in Reinhardt *et al.* (2005: 211–38).

Hirschfeld, O. (1913), *Kleine Schriften* (Berlin).

Hirst, G. (1926), 'Note on the Date of Livy's Birth, and on the Termination of his History', *CW*, 19: 138–9 = *Collected Classical Papers* (1938) (Oxford) 12–14.

Hoch, H. (1951), *Die Darstellung der politischen Sendung Roms bei Livius* (Frankfurt am Main).

Hoffmann, W. (1942), *Livius und der Zweite punische Krieg, Hermes* Einzelschriften 8. (Berlin).

—— (1954), 'Livius und die römische Geschichtsschreibung', *A&A*, 4: 170–86.

Hofmann, J. B., Szantyr, A., *et al.* (1965), *Lateinische Syntax und Stilistik* (Munich).

Holleaux, M. (1923), 'Les Conférences de Lokride et la politique de T. Quinctius Flamininus (198 av. J.-C.)', *REG*, 36: 115–71.

—— (1938–68), *Études d'épigraphie et d'histoire grecques*, 6 vols. (Paris).

Horsfall, N. (1982), 'The Caudine Forks: Topography and Illusion', *PBSR*, 50: 45–52.

—— (1985), 'Illusion and Reality in Latin Topographical Writing', *G&R* 32: 197–208.

—— (1989), *Cornelius Nepos: A Selection, Including the Lives of Cato and Atticus* (Oxford).

Humphreys, S. (1997), 'Fragments, Fetishes and Philosophies: Towards a History of Greek Historiography after Thucydides', in G. W. Most (ed.), *Collecting Fragments/Fragmente Sammeln* (Gottingen) 207–24.

Instinsky, H. U. (1964), 'Schwurszene und *Coniuratio*', *JNG*, 14: 83–8.

Jaeger, M. K. (1993), '*Custodia fidelis memoriae*: Livy's Story of M. Manlius Capitolinus', *Latomus*, 52: 350–63.

—— (1997), *Livy's Written Rome* (Ann Arbor).

—— (2007), 'Fog on the Mountain: Philip and Mt. Haemus in Livy, 40.21–22', in Marincola (2007*a*: 397–403).

Jal, P. (1975), 'Sur la composition de la V$^e$ décade de Tite-Live', *RPh*, 49: 278–85.

—— (1994), 'L'Organisation du récit livien: quelques remarques', in R. Chevallier and R. Poignault (eds.), *Présence de Tite-Live: Hommage au Professeur P. Jal* (Tours) 35–43.

Janson, T. (1964), *Latin Prose Prefaces: Studies in Literary Conventions* (Stockholm).

Jashemski, W. F. (1950), *The Origins and History of the Proconsular and the Propraetorian Imperium to 27 B.C.* (Chicago).

Jed, S. H. (1989), *Chaste Thinking: The Rape of Lucretia and the Birth of Humanism* (Bloomington).

Johnson, S. K. (1929), 'Oratory and Characterisation in the Later Books of Livy', *PCA*, 25: 36–7.

Joplin, P. K. (1990), 'Ritual Work on Human Flesh: Livy's Lucretia and the Rape of the Body Politic', *Helios*, 17: 51–70.

Jumeau, R. (1936), 'Tite-Live et l'historiographie hellénistique', *REA* 38: 63–8.

—— (1939), 'Remarques sur la structure de l'exposé livien', *RPh*, 65: 21–43.

—— (1966), 'Tite-Live historien', *Latomus*, 25: 555–63.

Kahrstedt, U. (1913*a*), *Die Annalistik von Livius, B. XXXI–XLV* (Berlin).

—— (1913*b*), *Geschichte der Karthager von 218–146* (Berlin).

Kajanto, I. (1957), *God and Fate in Livy* (Turku).

—— (1958), 'Notes on Livy's Conception of History', *Arctos*, 2: 55–63.

Kampen, N. B. (1986), 'Reliefs of the Basilica Aemilia: A Redating', paper delivered at Brown University Conference 'Roman Women: Critical Approaches'. Published as (1991) 'Reliefs of the Basilica Aemilia: A Redating', *Klio* 73: 448–58.

Kappeler, S. (1986), *The Pornography of Representation* (Minneapolis).

Keegan, J. (1976), *The Face of Battle* (New York). Often reprinted.

Keil, J. (1933), 'Das Sogenannte Senatusconsultum De Bacchanalibus', *Hermes*, 68: 306–12.

Kennedy, D. F. (1992), ' "Augustan" and "Anti-Augustan": Reflection on Terms of Reference', in A. Powell (ed.), *Roman Poetry and Propaganda in the Age of Augustus* (London) 26–58.

Kenney, E. J. (1982), 'Books and Readers in the Roman World', in E. J. Kenney and W. V. Clausen (eds.), *The Cambridge History of Classical Literature*. Vol. II: *Latin Literature* (Cambridge) 3–30.

Kern, F. (1960), *Aufbau und Gedankengang der Bücher 36–45 des T. Livius* (Diss. Kiel).

Kissel, W. (1982), 'Livius, 1933–78: Eine Gesamtbibliographie', *ANRW*, II.30.2: 899–977.

Klebs, E. (1896), 'Atilius (51)', *RE*, 2: 2086–92.

Klinger, G. (1884), *De decimi Livii libri fontibus* (Diss. Leipzig).

Klingner, F. (1935), review of Burck (1934), *Gnomon*, 11: 577–88 = (1964), *Studien zur griechischen und römischen Literatur* (Zurich), 594–604.

Klotz, A. (1915), 'Zu den Quellen der vierten und fünften Dekade des Livius', *Hermes*, 50: 481–536.

—— (1926), 'Livius', *RE*, 13: 816–52.

—— (1935), review of Burck (1934), *Philologische Wochenschrift*, 55: 7–13.

—— (1937), 'Diodors römische Annalen', *RhM*, 86: 206–24.

—— (1938*a*), 'Livius' Darstellung des zweiten Samniterkriegs', *Mnemosyne*, 6: 83–102.

—— (1938*b*), 'Zu den Quellen der Archaiologia des Dionysios von Halikarnassos', *RhM*, 87: 32–50.

—— (1939), 'Zur geschichte der römischen Zensur', *RhM*, 88: 27–36.

—— (1940–1), *Livius und seine Vorgänger* (Stuttgart). Reprinted 1964 (Amsterdam).

—— (1941), 'Zu den Quellen der plutarchischen Lebensbeschreibung des Camillus', *RhM*, 90: 282–309.

—— (1942), 'Der Annalist Q. Claudius Quadrigarius', *RhM*, 91: 268–85.

—— (1951), 'Die Benutzung des Polybius bei römischen Schriftstellern', *SIFC*, 25: 243–65.

Koestermann, E. (1963–8), *Cornelius Tacitus Annalen*, 4 vols. (Heidelberg).

Kohl, O. (1872), *Über Zweck und Bedeutung der livianischen Reden* (Programmr. Barmen).

Konstan, D. (1983), *Roman Comedy* (Ithaca).

Korpanty, J. (1983), 'Sallust, Livius und *ambitio*', *Philologus*, 127: 61–71.

Kraus, C. S. (1991), '*Initium turbandi omnia a femina ortum est*: Fabia Minor and the Election of 367 B.C.', *Phoenix*, 45: 314–25.

—— (1994*a*), *Livy: Ab Vrbe Condita Book VI* (Cambridge).

—— (1994*b*), ' "No Second Troy": Topoi and Refoundation in Livy, Book V', *TAPhA*, 24: 267–89.

—— (1997), 'Livy', in C. S. Kraus and A. J. Woodman, *Latin Historians, Greece & Rome* New Surveys in the Classics 27 (Oxford) 51–81.

Krause, W. (1936), 'Zum Aufbau der Bacchanal-Inschrift', *Hermes*, 71: 214–20.

Kroll, W. (1924), *Studien zum Verständnis der römische Literatur* (Stuttgart). 2nd edn. 1964.

Krostenko, B. A. (2001), *Cicero, Catullus, and the Language of Social Performance* (Chicago).

Kühnast, L. (1872), *Die Hauptpunkte der livianischen Syntax* (Berlin).

Laird, A. (1999), *Powers of Expression, Expressions of Power* (Oxford).

Laistner, M. L. W. (1947), *The Greater Roman Historians* (Berkeley).

Lambert, A. (1946), *Die indirekte Rede als künstlerisches Stilmittel des Livius* (diss. Zurich).

Laqueur, R. (1909), 'Über das Wesen des römischen Triumphs', *Hermes*, 44: 215–18.

Latte, K. (1940), 'Livy's Patavinitas', *CPh*, 35: 56–60.

—— (1960*a*), *Römische Religionsgeschichte* (Munich).

—— (1960*b*), 'Der Historiker L. Calpurnius Frugi', *SDAW*, 7: 1–16 = (1964), *Kleine Schriften zu Religion, Recht, Literatur und Sprache der Griechen und Römer* (Munich) 833–48.

Leeman, A. D. (1961), 'Are we Fair to Livy? Some Thoughts on Livy's Prologue', *Helikon*, 1: 28–39 = ('Werden wir Livius gerecht? Einige Gedanken zur der Praefatio des Livius' in Burck (1967: 200–14)).

—— (1963), *Orationis Ratio*, 2 vols. (Amsterdam).

Lefèvre, E. and Ohlshausen, E. (eds.) (1983), *Livius, Werk und Rezeption: Festschrift für Erich Burck zum 80 Geburtstag* (Munich).

Leggewie, O. (1953), 'Die Geisteshaltung der Geschichtsschreiber Sallust und Livius', *Gymnasium*, 60: 343–55.

Leidig, T. (1994), *Valerius Antias und ein annalistischer Bearbeiter des Polybios als Quellen des Livius, vornehmlich für Buch 30 und 31* (Frankfurt am Main).

Lendon, J. E. (1999), 'The Rhetoric of Combat: Greek Theory and Roman Culture in Julius Caesar's Battle Descriptions', *CA*, 18: 273–329.

Leumann, M. (1947), 'Die Lateinische Dichtersprache', *MH*, 4: 116–39.

Levene, D. S. (1993), *Religion in Livy* (Leiden).

Levene, D. S. (1997), 'Pity, Fear and the Historical Audience: Tacitus on the Fall of Vitellius', in S. M. Braund and C. Gill (eds.), *The Passions in Roman Thought and Literature* (Cambridge) 128–49.

—— (2006), 'History, Metahistory, and Audience Response in Livy 45', *CA*, 25:73–108.

—— (2010), *Livy on the Hannibalic War* (Oxford).

—— and Nelis, D. P. (eds.), *Clio and the Poets: Augustan Poetry and the Traditions of Ancient Historiography. Mnemosyne* Supplement 224 (Leiden).

Lévi-Strauss, C. (1966), *The Savage Mind* (Chicago).

—— (1969), *The Elementary Structure of Kinship* (Boston).

Lieberg, G. (1963), 'Die römische religion bei Municius Felix', *RhM*, 106: 62–79.

Liebeschuetz, J. H. W. G. (1979), *Continuity and Change in Roman Religion* (Oxford).

Lintott, A.W. (1999), *The Constitution of the Roman Republic* (Oxford).

Lipovsky, J. (1981), *A Historiographical Study of Livy: Books VI–X* (Salem, NH). Reprinted 1984.

Littleton, S. (1973), *The New Comparative Mythology: An Anthropological Assessment of the Theories of Georges Dumézil*, rev. edn. (Berkeley).

Löfstedt, E. (1933), *Syntactica*. Erster Teil. (Lund).

Lowrie, M. (2007), 'Making an *Exemplum* of Yourself: Cicero and Augustus', in S. J. Heyworth (ed.), *Classical Constructions: Papers in Memory of Don Fowler, Classicist and Epicurean* (Oxford) 91–112.

Luce, T. J. (1965), 'The Dating of Livy's First Decade', *TAPhA*, 96: 209–40.

—— (1977), *Livy: The Composition of His History* (Princeton).

—— (1989), 'Ancient Views on the Causes of Bias in Historical Writing', *CPh*, 84: 16–31.

—— (1990), 'Livy, Augustus and the *Forum Augustum*', in Raaflaub and Toher (1990: 123–38).

—— (1993), 'Structure in Livy's Speeches', in Schuller (1993: 71–87).

Lundström, V. (1915), 'Nya Enniusfragment', *Eranos*, 15: 1–24.

MacBain, B. (1982), *Prodigy and Expiation: A Study in Religion and Politics in Republican Rome* (Brussels).

McClain, T. D. (1998), 'Redeeming Fabia: Sisters and Honor in Livy', *AncW*, 29: 10–18.

MacCormack, G. (1975), 'Wine-Drinking and the Romulan Law of Divorce', *Irish Jurist*, 10: 170–4.

McDonald, A. H. (1938), 'The Literary Art of Livy', summary in *PCA* 35: 25–7.

—— (1944), 'Rome and the Italian Confederation (200–186 B.C.)', *JRS*, 34: 11–33.

—— (1953), review of *MRR*, *JRS*, 43: 142–5.

—— (1954), 'The Roman Historians', in M. Platnauer (ed.), *Fifty Years of Classical Scholarship* (Oxford) 384–412.

—— (1955), review of Treves (1953), *JRS*, 45: 176–8.

—— (1957), 'The Style of Livy', *JRS*, 47: 155–72.

—— (1960), 'On Emending Livy's Fourth Decade', *PCPhS*, 6: 43–8.

McGann, M. J. (1957), 'The Authenticity of Lucan, Fr. 12 (Morel)', *CQ*, 51: 126–8.

McGushin, P. (1977), *Bellum Catilinae: A Commentary*, Mnemosyne Supplement 45 (Leiden).

—— (ed.) (1992–4), *Sallust: The Histories*, 2 vols. (Oxford).

Macleod, C. (1977), 'The Poet, the Critic, and the Moralist: Horace, *Epistles* 1.19', *CQ*, 27: 359–76 = (1983) *Collected Essays* (Oxford) 262–79.

Madvig, J. N. (1875), *Kleine philologische Schriften* (Leipzig).

Magdelain, A. (1964), 'Auspicia ad patres redeunt', in M. Renard and R. Schilling (eds.), *Hommages à Jean Bayet*, Collection Latomus 70 (Brussels) 427–73.

Malcovati, H. (ed.) (1955), *Oratorum Romanorum fragmenta* (2nd edn., Turin).

Marincola, J. (1997), *Authority and Tradition in Ancient Historiography* (Cambridge).

—— (1999), 'Genre, Convention and Innovation in Greco-Roman Historiography', in C. S. Kraus (ed.), *The Limits of Historiography: Genre and Narrative in Ancient Historical Texts* (Leiden) 281–324.

—— (2003), 'Beyond Pity and Fear: The Emotions of History', *AncSoc*, 33: 285–315.

—— (2007*a*) (ed.), *A Companion to Greek and Roman Historiography*, 2 vols. Blackwell Companions to the Ancient World (Oxford).

—— (2007*b*), 'Odysseus and the Historians', *Syllecta Classica*, 18: 1–79.

Marouzeau, J. (1921), 'Pour mieux comprendre les textes latins. Essai sur la distinction des styles', *RPh*, 45: 149–93.

—— (1949), *Quelques aspects de la formation du Latin littéraire* (Paris).

Marti, B. M. (1970), 'La structure de la *Pharsale*', in M. Durry (ed.), *Lucain*, Fondation Hardt Entretiens sur l'antiquité classique 15 (Vandoeuvres) 3–38.

Mastrocinque, A. (1988), *Lucio Giunio Bruto: Ricerche di storia, religione e diritto sulle origini della repubblica romana* (Trento).

Maurenbrecher, B. (1893), *C. Sallustii Crispi historiarum reliquiae* (Stuttgart). Reprinted 1967.

Mayer, R. G. (2005), 'The Impracticability of Latin "Kunstprosa"', in Reinhardt *et al.* (2005: 195–210).

Mazza, M. (1966), *Storia e ideologia in Tito Livio. Per un'analisi storiografica della praefatio ai Libri ab Urbe Condita* (Catania).

Meautis, G. (1940), 'Les Aspects religieux de l'affaire des Bacchanales', *REA*, 42: 476–85.

Mendell, C. W. (1935), 'Dramatic Construction of Tacitus' Annals', *YCS*, 5: 3–53.

Mensching, E. (1966), 'Tullus Hostilius, Alba Longa und Cluilius: Zu Livius I 22 f. und anderen', *Philologus*, 110: 102–18.

Meloni, P. (1955), *Il Valore storico e le fonti del libro macedonico di Appiano* (Rome).

Mette, H. J. (1961), 'Livius und Augustus', *Gymnasium*, 68: 269–85.

Meusel, H. (1988), 'Horatier und Curiatier: Ein Livius-Motiv und seine Rezeption', *AU*, 31: 66–90.

Meyer, E. (1903), *Apophoreton* (Berlin).

Mezzar-Zerbi, G. (1958), 'Le fonti di Livio nelle guerre combattute contro i Liguri', *RSC*, 6: 5–15.

—— (1959), 'Le fonti di Livio nelle guerre combattute contro i Liguri', *RSC*, 7: 152–62.

—— (1960), 'Le fonti di Livio nelle guerre combattute contro i Liguri', *RSC*, 8: 329–40.

—— (1965), 'Le fonti di Livio nelle guerre combattute contro i Liguri', *RSC*, 13: 66–78, 287–99.

—— (1966), 'Le fonti di Livio nelle guerre combattute contro i Liguri', *RSC*, 14: 211–24.

Miles, G. B. (1986), 'The Cycle of Roman History in Livy's First Pentad', *AJP*, 107: 1–33.

—— (1988), '*Maiores, Conditores,* and Livy's Perspective on the Past', *TAPhA*, 118: 185–208.

—— (1995), *Livy: Reconstructing Early Rome* (Ithaca).

Millar, F. (1964), *A Study of Cassius Dio* (Oxford).

Mitchell, J. (1975), *Psychoanalysis and Feminism* (New York).

Modleski, T. (1988), *The Women Who Knew Too Much* (New York).

Moles, J. L. (1986), 'Cynicism in Horace *Epistles* 1', *PLLS*, 5: 33–60 (Liverpool).

—— (1990), 'The Kingship Oratians of Dio Chrysostom', *PLLS*, 6: 297–375 (Leeds).

Momigliano, A. (1942), 'Camillus and Concord', *CQ*, 36: 111–20 = (1960), *Secondo contributo alla storia degli studi classici* (Rome) 89–104.

—— (1981), 'The Rhetoric of History and the History of Rhetoric: On Hayden White's Tropes', *Comparative Criticism* 3: 259–68 = (1984) *Settimo contributo alla storia degli studi classici e del mondo antico* (Rome) 49–59.

—— (1990), *The Classical Foundations of Modern Historiography* (Berkeley).

Mommsen, T. (1859), *Die römische Chronologie bis auf Caesar* (2nd edn., Berlin).

—— (1864–79), *Römische Forschungen*, 2 vols. (Berlin).

—— (1871), 'Fabius und Diodor', *Hermes*, 5 (1871) 271–80 = (1864–79) 2. 221–36.

—— (1879), 'Die gallische Katastrophe', in (1864–79: 2.297–381). Orig. pub. (1878), *Hermes*, 13: 515–55.

—— (1887–8), *Römisches Staatsrecht*, 3 vols. (3rd edn., Leipzig).

—— (1889), *Römisches Strafrecht* (Leipzig).

Moore, T. J. (1989), *Artistry and Ideology: Livy's Vocabulary of Virtue*, Beiträge zur klassischen Philologie 192 (Frankfurt am Main).

—— (1993), 'Morality, History, and Livy's Wronged Women', *Eranos* 91: 38–46.

Morello, R. (2002), 'Livy's Alexander Digression (9.17–19): Counterfactuals and Apologetics', *JRS*, 92: 62–85.

Morgan, J. R. (1993), 'Make-believe and Make Believe: The Fictionality of the Greek Novels', in Gill and Wiseman (1993: 175–229).

Münzer, F. (1891), *De gente Valeria* (Diss. Berlin).

—— (1910), 'Furius (44)', *RE*, 7: 324–48.

—— (1913), 'Horatius (2)', *RE*, 8: 2322–7.

—— (1926), 'Livivs Drusus (12, 13)', *RE*, 25: 853–5.

Nap, J. M. (1935), *Die römische Republik um das J. 225 v. Chr.* (Leiden).

Nicolet, C. (1988), *The World of the Citizen in Republican Rome*, trans. P. S. Falla (Berkeley) = (1976) *Le métier de citoyen dans la Rome républicaine* (Paris).

—— (1991), *Space, Geography, and Politics in the Early Roman Empire* (Ann Arbor).

Nissen, Heinrich (1863), *Kritische Untersuchungen über die Quellen der vierten und fünften Dekade des Livius* (Berlin). Reprinted 1975 (London).

—— (1870), 'Der Caudinische Frieden', *RhM*, 65: 1–65.

Nitzsch, K. W. (1873), *Die römische Annalistik von ihren ersten Anfängen bis auf Valerius Antias: kritische Untersuchungen zur Geschichte der älteren Republik* (Berlin).

Norden, E. (1915–18), *Die antike Kunstprosa*, 2 vols. (3rd edn., Leipzig).

—— (1915), *Ennius und Vergilius* (Leipzig).

—— (1957), *Aeneis: Book VI* (4th edn., Stuttgart). 1st edn. 1903.

—— (1952), *Römischen Literatur* (4th edn., Leipzig).

North, J. A. (1979), 'Religious Tolerance in Republican Rome', *PCPhS*, 25: 85–103.

Northwood, S. J. (2000), 'Livy and the Early Annalists', in C. Deroux (ed.), *Studies in Latin Literature and Roman History 10*, Collection Latomus 254 (Brussels), 45–55.

——(2007), 'Quintus Fabius Pictor: Was He an Annalist?', in N. V. Sekunda (ed.), *Corolla Cosmo Rodewald*, Department of Archaeology, Gdansk University Monograph Series Akanthina 2 (Gdansk).

Oakley, S. P. (1985), 'Single Combat in the Roman Republic', *CQ*, 35: 392–410.

——(1992), 'Livy and Clodius Licinus', *CQ*, 42: 547–51.

——(ed.) (1997–2005), *A Commentary on Livy: Books 6–10*, 4 vols. (Oxford).

Ogilvie, R. M. (1957), 'The Manuscript Tradition of Livy's First Decade', *CQ*, 7: 68–81.

——(1958), 'Livy, Licinius Macer and the libri lintei', *JRS*, 48: 40–6.

——(1965), *A Commentary on Livy: Books 1–5* (Oxford). 2nd edn. 1970.

Oppermann, H. (1934), 'Zur Andria des Terenz', *Hermes*, 69: 262–85.

——(1955), 'Die Einleitung zum Geschichtswerk des Livius', *AU*, 7: 87–98 = Burck (1967: 169–80).

Ortner, S. B. (1978), 'The Virgin and the State', *Feminist Studies*, 4.3: 19–35.

Osgood, J. (2006), *Caesar's Legacy: Civil War and the Emergence of the Roman Empire* (Cambridge).

Packard, D. W. (1968), *A Concordance to Livy*, 4 vols. (Cambridge, Mass.).

Packard, J. (1960), *Official Notices in Livy's Fourth Decade: Style and Treatment* (Diss. North Carolina).

Pagán, V. E. (2004), *Conspiracy narratives in Roman History* (Austin).

Palmer, L. R. (1954), *The Latin Language* (London).

Palmer, R. E. A. (1926), 'Livius Drusus (12, 13)', *RE*, 25: 853–5.

——(1970), *The Archaic Community of the Romans* (Cambridge).

——(1997), *Rome and Carthage at Peace* (Stuttgart).

Paratore, E. (1950), *Storia della letteratura latina* (Florence).

Paschalis, M. (1982), 'Livy's *Praefatio* and Sallust' (Diss. Ohio State).

Peter, H. (ed.) (1870), *Veterum historicorum Romanorum reliquiae* (Leipzig).

Petersen, H. (1961), 'Livy and Augustus', *TAPhA*, 92: 440–52.

Petzold, K.-E. (1940), *Die Eröffnung des zweiten römisch-makedonischen Krieges* (Berlin).

——(1983), 'Die Entwicklung des römischen Weltreiches im Spiegel der Historiographie: Bemerkungen zum *bellum iustum* bei Livius', in Lefèvre and Ohlshausen (1983: 241–66).

——(1999), *Geschichtsdenken und Geschichtschreibung: Kleine Schriften zur griechischen und römischen Geschichte* (Stuttgart).

Peytraud, H. (1939), 'A propos des Horaces et des Curiaces', *Revue universi-taire*, 48, Pt. 2: 32–5.

Pfohl, S. (1990), 'The Terror of the Simulacra: Struggles for Justice and the Postmodern', in M. J. Lerner (ed.), *New Directions in the Study of Justice, Law, and Social Control* (New York) 207–63.

Phillipides, S. N. (1983), 'Narrative Strategies and Ideology in Livy's "Rape of Lucretia"', *Helios*, 10: 113–19.

Phillips, J. E. (1974), 'Verbs Compounded with *Trans-* in Livy's Triumph Notices', *CPh*, 69: 54–5.

——(1979), 'Livy and the Beginning of a New Society', *CB*, 55: 87–92.

——(1982), 'Current Research in Livy's First Decade: 1959–1979', *ANRW*, II.30.2: 998–1057.

Pitcher, L. V. (2007), 'Characterization in Ancient Historiography', in Marincola (2007*a*: 102–17).

Pittenger, M. R. P. (2009), *Contested Triumphs: Politics, Pageantry, and Performance in Livy's Republican Rome* (Berkeley).

Plass, P. (1988), *Wit and the Writing of History* (Madison).

Plathner, H.-G. (1934), *Die Schlachtschilderungen bei Livius* (Diss. Breslau).

Porte, D. (1981), 'Romulus Quirinus, prince et dieu, dieu des princes', *ANRW*, II.17.1: 300–42.

——(1985), *L'Étiologie religeuse dans les Fastes d'Ovide* (Paris).

Price, S. R. F. (1984), *Rituals and Power: The Roman Imperial Cult in Asia Minor* (Cambridge).

Raaflaub, K. A. (ed.) (1986*a*), *Social Struggles in Archaic Rome* (Berkeley). 2nd edn. 2005 (Malden, Mass.).

——(1986*b*), 'The Conflict of the Orders in Archaic Rome: A Comprehensive and Comparative Approach', in Raaflaub (1986*a*: 1–51).

——and Toher, M. (eds.) (1990), *Between Republic and Empire: Interpretations of Augustus and His Principate* (Berkeley).

Raditsa, L. F. (1980), 'Augustus' Legislation concerning Marriage, Procreation, Love Affairs and Adultery', *ANRW*, II.13: 278–339.

Ramage, E. S. (1973), *Urbanitas: Ancient Sophistication and Refinement* (Norman, OK).

Rambaud, M. (1953), *Cicéron et l'histoire romaine* (Paris).

Rawson, E. (1971), 'Prodigy Lists and the Use of the *Annales Maximi*', *CQ*, 21: 158–69.

——(1991), *Studies in Roman Culture and Society* (Oxford).

Reinhardt, T., Lapidge, M., Adams, J. N., and Winterbottom, M. (eds.) (2005), *Aspects of the Language of Latin Prose*, Proceedings of the British Academy 129 (London).

Reitzenstein, G. R. (1927), *Die Hellenistischen Mysterienreligionen* (Leipzig).

Reynolds, L. D. (ed.) (1991), *C. Sallusti Crispi Catilina, Iugurtha, Historiarum fragmenta selecta, Appendix Sallustiana* (Oxford).

Rich, J. W. (1967), *Declaring War in the Roman Republic in the Period of Transmarine Expansion*, Collection Latomus 149 (Brussels).

—— (1984), 'Roman Aims in the First Macedonian War', *PCPhS*, 210: 126–80.

—— (1993), review of McGushin (1992–4) Vol. 1, *CR*, 43: 280–2.

—— (1996), review of McGushin (1992–4) Vol. 2, *CR*, 46: 250–1.

—— (2005), 'Valerius Antias and the Construction of the Roman Past', *BICS*, 48: 137–61.

Richard, J.-C. (1966), 'Énée, Romulus, César et les funérailles impériales', *MEFR*, 78: 67–78.

Richardson, E. (1964), *The Etruscans* (Chicago).

Richlin, A. (1983), *The Garden of Priapus: Sexuality and Aggression in Roman Humor* (New Haven).

—— (1992), 'Reading Ovid's Rapes', in A. Richlin (ed.), *Pornography and Representation in Greece and Rome* (Oxford) 158–79.

Riemann, O. (1885), *Études sur la langue et la grammaire de Tite-Live* (2nd edn., Paris).

Riposati, B. (ed.) (1939), *M. Terenti Varronis De vita populi Romani*, Pubblicazioni dell'Università Cattolica del S. Cuore 33 (Milan).

Roberts, G. (ed.) (2001), *The History and Narrative Reader* (London).

Robinson, O. (2007), *Penal Practice and Penal Policy in Ancient Rome* (London).

Rodgers, B. S. (1986), 'Great Expeditions: Livy on Thucydides', *TAPhA*, 116: 335–52.

Rohde, G. (1942), 'Ovatio', *RE*, 18: 1890–1903.

Roller, M. (2004), 'Exemplarity in Roman Culture: The Cases of Horatius Cocles and Cloelia', *CPh*, 99: 1–56.

Rose, H. J. (1924), *The Roman Questions of Plutarch* (Oxford).

—— (1947), review of G. Dumézil (1940), *Mitra-Varuna: Essai sur deux représentations indo-européennes de la souveraineté*, *JRS*, 37: 183–6.

Rosén, H. (1999), *Latine loqui: Trends and Directions in the Crystallization of Classical Latin* (Munich).

Rosenberg, A. (1921), *Einleitung und Quellenkunde zur römischen Geschichte* (Berlin).

Rossi, A. (2004), *Contexts of War, Manipulation of Genre in Virgilian Battle Narrative* (Ann Arbor).

Rubincam, C. (1991), 'Casualty Figures in Thucydides' Descriptions of Battle', *TAPhA*, 121: 181–98.

Ruch, M. (1967), 'Tite-Live. Histoire Romaine: Points de vue sur la préface', *Didactica Classica Gandensia*, 7: 74–80.

——(1968), 'Le Thème de la croissance organique dans le livre 1 de Tite-Live', *StudClas*, 10: 123–31.

Rüpke, J. (1990), *Domi Militiae: die religiöse Konstruktion des Krieges in Rom* (Stuttgart).

——(2008), *Fasti Sacerdotum: A Prosopography of Pagan, Jewish, and Christian Officials in the City of Rome, 300 BC to AD 499* (Oxford).

Rutgers, J. (1618), *Iani Rutgersii variarum lectionum libri sex* (Lugduni Batavorum [Leiden]).

Sailor, D. (2006), 'Dirty Linen, Fabrication, and the Authorities of Livy and Augustus', *TAPhA*, 136: 329–88.

Saller, R. P. (1986), 'Patria potestas and the Stereotype of the Roman Family', *Continuity and Change*, 1: 7–22.

Sandbach, F. H. (ed.) (1972), *Menandri reliquiae selectae* (Oxford).

Santoro L'Hoir, F. (1992), *The Rhetoric of Gender Terms: Man, 'Woman', and the Portrayal of Character in Latin Prose, Mnemosyne* Supplement 120 (Leiden).

Scafuro, A. C. (1987), 'Pattern, Theme and Historicity in Livy, Books 35 and 36', *CA*, 6: 249–85.

Scaramella, G. (1897), 'Il più antichi Licini e l'annalista C. Licinio Macro', *ANSP*, 12: 5–30.

Schachermeyr, F. (1929), 'Die gallische Katastrophe', *Klio*, 23: 277–305.

Schepens, G. (1980), *L' 'autopsie' dans la méthode des historiens grecs du Vᵉ siècle avant J.-C.* (Brussels).

——(2007), 'History and *Historia*: Inquiry in the Greek Historians', in Marincola (2007*a*: 39–55).

Schibel, W. (1971), *Sprachbehandlung und Darstellungsweise in römischer Prosa: Claudius Quadrigarius, Livius, Aulus Gellius* (Amsterdam).

Schuller, W. (ed.) (1993), *Livius: Aspekte seines Werkes*, Xenia 31 (Konstanz).

Schulz, H. (1886), *De M. Valerii Messallae aetate* (Progr. Stettin).

Schwab, G. (1834), *De Livio et Timagene, historiarum scriptoribus aemulis* (Stuttgart).

Schwartz, E. (1905), 'Duris (3)', *RE*, 5: 1853–6.

Scott, K. (1925), 'Identification of Augustus with Romulus', *TAPhA*, 56: 82–105.

Scullard, H. H. (1951), *Roman Politics, 220–150 B.C.* (Oxford).

——(1981), *Festivals and Ceremonies of the Roman Republic* (London).

Seeley, J. R. (ed.) (1881), *Livy: Book I* (3rd edn., Oxford).

Seibert, J. (1993), *Forschungen zu Hannibal* (Darmstadt).

Serres, M. (1991), *Rome: The Book of Foundations*, trans. F. McCarren (Stanford).

Shackleton Bailey, D. R. (ed. and trans.) (1965–70), *Cicero's letters to Atticus*, 7 vols. (Cambridge).

——(ed.) (1977), *Cicero: Epistulae ad familiares*, 2 vols. (Cambridge).

Sherwin-White, A. N. (1973), *The Roman Citizenship* (2nd edn., Oxford).

Silverman, K. (1980), 'Masochism and Subjectivity', *Frameworks*, 12: 2–9.

Skutsch, O. (1953), 'The Fall of the Capitol', *JRS*, 43: 77–8 = (1968), *Studia Enniana* (London) 138–42 with *postilla*.

——(ed.) (1985), *The Annals of Quintus Ennius* (Oxford).

——(1987), 'Book VI of Ennius' *Annals*', *CQ*, 37: 512–4.

Smith, R. E. (1940), 'Plutarch's Biographical Sources in the Roman Lives', *CQ*, 34: 1–10.

——(1944), 'The Sources of Plutarch's Life of Titus Flamininus', *CQ*, 38: 89–95.

Soltau, W. (1894*a* [1893]), 'Die annalistische Quellen in Livius' IV und V Dekade', *Philologus*, 52: 664–702.

——(1894*b*), 'Einige nachträgliche Einschaltungen in Livius' Geschichts-werk', *Hermes*, 29: 611–17.

——(1896). 'Die Entstehung der annales maximi', *Philologus*, 55: 257–76.

——(1897*a*), 'Macer and Tubero', *NJPhP*, 155: 409–32, 639–52.

——(1897*b*), *Livius' Geschichtswerk: Seine Komposition und seine Quellen* (Leipzig).

——(1897*c*), 'Der Annalist Piso', *Philologus*, 56: 118–29.

——(1908), 'Horatius und Orestes', *BPhW*, 46: 1269–72.

——(1909), *Die Anfänge der römischen Geschichtschreibung* (Leipzig).

Sommer, R. (1926), 'T. Pomponius Atticus und die Verbreitung von Ciceros Werken', *Hermes*, 61: 389–422.

Son, D. W. L. van (1960), *Livius' Behandeling van de Bacchanalia* (Amsterdam).

Sordi, M. (1960), *I rapporti Romano-Ceriti e l'origine della civitas sine suffragio* (Rome).

Spencer, D. (2002), *The Roman Alexander: Reading a Cultural Myth* (Exeter).

Stacey, S. G. (1898), 'Die Entwickelung des livianischen Stiles', *ALL*, 10: 17–82.

Stadter, P. A. (1972), 'The Structure of Livy's History', *Historia*, 21: 286–307.

Starr, R. (1987), 'The Circulation of Literary Texts in the Roman World', *CQ*, 37: 213–23.

Strasburger, H. (1972), *Homer und die Geschichtsschreibung* (Heidelberg) = (1982: ii.1057–97).

—— (1982), 'Komik und Satire in der griechischen Geschichtsschreibung', in *Studien zur alten Geschichte*, 2 vols. (Hildesheim), ii.801–34.

Stübler, G. (1941), *Die Religiosität des Livius* (Stuttgart).

Suerbaum, W. (1995), 'Der Pyrrhos-Krieg in Ennius' Annales VI im Lichte der ersten Ennius-Papyri aus Herculaneum', *ZPE*, 106: 30–52.

—— (2002), *Die archaische Literatur* (Munich).

Suits, T. A. (1974), 'The Structure of Livy's Thirty-Second Book', *Philologus*, 118: 257–65.

Syme, R. (1939), *The Roman Revolution* (Oxford).

—— (1958), *Tacitus*, 2 vols. (Oxford).

—— (1959), 'Livy and Augustus', *HSCPh*, 64: 27–87 = (1979–91) *Roman Papers*, 7 vols. (Oxford) i.400–54.

—— (1964), *Sallust* (Berkeley).

Szemler, G. J. (1972), *The Priests of the Roman Republic* (Brussels).

Taine, H. (1904), *Essai sur Tite-Live* (7th edn., Paris). 1st edn. 1856.

Täubler, E. (1912), 'Camillus und Sulla', *Klio*, 12: 219–33.

Taylor, L. R. (1918), 'Livy and the Name Augustus', *CR*, 32: 158–61.

Theweleit, K. (1987–9), *Male Fantasies*, trans. S. Conway, 2 vols. (Minneapolis).

Thomas, Y. (1984), '*Vitae necisque potestas*: Le père, la cité, la mort', in *Du châtiment dans la cité*, Collection de l'école française de Rome 79 (Rome) 499–548.

Thouret, G. (1880), *Über den gallischen Brand: eine quellenkritische Skizze zur älteren römischen Geschichte*, *JCPh* Supplement 11 (Leipzig).

Thraede, K. (1970), 'Livius im Spiegel der neueren Forschung', in F. Hörmann (ed.), *Dialog Schule—Wissenschaft: Klassische Sprachen und Literaturen*, V. *Neue Einsichten: Beiträge zum altsprachlichen Unterricht* (Munich) 61ff.

Tierney, J. J. (1947), 'The Senatus Consultum de Bacchanalibus', *PRIA*, 51 sect. C, no. 5: 89–117.

Timpe, D. (1972), 'Fabius Pictor und die Anfänge der römischen Historiographie', *ANRW*, I.2.928–69.

—— (1979), 'Erwägungen zur jüngeren Annalistik', *A&A*, 25: 97–119.

Tränkle, H. (1965), 'Der Anfang des römischen Freistaats in der Darstellung des Livius', *Hermes*, 93: 311–37.

—— (1968), 'Beobachtungen zum Wandel der livianischen Sprache', *WS*, 81: 103–52.

—— (1971), *Cato in der vierten und fünften Dekade des Livius* (Mainz).

—— (1977), *Livius und Polybios* (Basle).

Treggiari, S. (1969), *Roman Freedmen During the Late Republic* (Oxford).

Treves, P. (1953), *Il mito di Alessandro e la Roma d'Augusto* (Milan).

Tyrrell, W. B. (1978), *A Legal and Historical Commentary to Cicero's Oratio pro C. Rabirio perduellionis reo* (Amsterdam).

Ullman, B. L. (1942), 'History and Tragedy', *TAPhA*, 73: 25–53.

——(1955), 'The Post-Mortem Adventures of Livy', in *Studies in the Italian Renaissance* (Rome) 55–80.

Ullmann, R. (1927), *La Technique des discours dans Salluste, Tite-Live et Tacite* (Oslo).

——(1929), *Étude sur le style des discours de Tite-Live* (Oslo).

——(1932), 'La Prose métrique de l'ancienne historiographie romaine', *SO*, 11: 72–6.

——(1933), 'La Prose métrique de l'ancienne historiographie romaine', *SO*, 12: 57–69.

Unger, G. F. (1878), *Die römischen Quellen des Livius in der vierten und fünften Dekade*, *Philologus* Supplement 3.2 (Göttingen).

——(1891), 'Die Glaubwürdigkeit der capitolinischen Consulntafel', *NJPhP*, 143: 289–321, 465–96, 625–55.

Usener, H. (1901), 'Italische Volksjustiz', *RhM*, 56: 1–28.

Utard, R. (2004), *Le discours indirect chez les historiens latins, écriture ou oralité? Histoire d'un style* (Louvain).

Vaahtera, J. (2002), 'Livy and the Priestly Records: à propos ILS 9338', *Hermes*, 130: 100–8.

Vahlen, I. (1903), *Ennianae poesis reliquiae* (2nd edn., Leipzig). Reprinted 1963 (Amsterdam).

van Sickle, J. (1980), 'The Book-Roll and Some Conventions of the Poetic Book', *Arethusa*, 13: 5–42.

Vasaly, A. (1987), 'Personality and Power: Livy's Depiction of the Appii Claudii in the First Pentad', *TAPhA*, 117: 203–26.

——(1993), *Representations: Images of the World in Ciceronian Oratory* (Berkeley).

——(2002), 'The Structure of Livy's First Pentad and the Augustan Poetry Book', in Levene and Nelis (2002: 275–90).

Veeser, H. A. (ed.) (1994), *The New Historicism Reader* (New York).

Verbrugghe, G. (1989), 'On the Meaning of *Annales*, on the Meaning of Annalist', *Philologus*, 133: 192–230.

Versnel, H. S. (1970), *Triumphus: An Inquiry into the Origin, Development and Meaning of the Roman Triumph* (Leiden).

Vretska, K. (1954), 'Die Geisteshaltung der Geschichtsschreiber Sallust und Livius', *Gymnasium*, 61: 191–203.

Walbank, F. W. (1938), 'Philippos Τραγοιδούμενος', *JHS*, 58: 55–68.

——(1945), 'Polybius, Philinus, and the First Punic War', *CQ*, 39: 1–18.

——(1955), 'Tragic History: a Reconsideration', *BICS*, 2: 4–14.

—— (1957–79), *A Historical Commentary on Polybius*, 3 vols. (Oxford).

—— (1960), 'History and Tragedy', *Historia*, 9: 216–34.

—— (1965), 'Political Morality and the Friends of Scipio', *JRS*, 55: 1–16.

—— (1985), *Selected Papers: Studies in Greek and Roman History and Historiography* (Cambridge).

—— (2002), *Polybius, Rome and the Hellenistic World: Essays and Reflections* (Cambridge).

Wallace-Hadrill, A. (1981), 'The Emperor and His Virtues', *Historia*, 30: 298–323.

—— (1986), 'Image and Authority in the Coinage of Augustus', *JRS*, 76: 66–87.

—— (1987), 'Time for Augustus: Ovid, Augustus and the *Fasti*', in M. Whitby, P. Hardie, and M. Whitby (eds.), *Homo viator: Classical Essays for John Bramble* (Bristol) 221–30.

—— (1997), '*Mutatio morum*: The Idea of a Cultural Revolution', in T. N. Habinek and A. Schiesaro (eds.), *The Roman Cultural Revolution* (Cambridge) 3–22.

Walsh, P. G. (1954), 'The Literary Techniques of Livy', *RhM*, 97: 97–114.

—— (1955), 'Livy's Preface and the Distortion of History', *AJPh*, 76: 369–83.

—— (1958*a*), 'Livy and Stoicism', *AJPh*, 79: 355–75.

—— (1958*b*), 'The Negligent Historian: Howlers in Livy', *G&R*, 5: 83–8.

—— (1961*a*), *Livy: His Historical Aims and Methods* (Cambridge).

—— (1961*b*), 'Livy and Augustus', *PACA*, 4: 26–37.

—— (1966), 'Livy', in Dorey (1966: 115–42).

—— (1974), *Livy, Greece & Rome* New Surveys in the Classics 8 (Oxford).

—— (1996), 'Making a Drama out of a Crisis: Livy on the Bacchanalia', *G&R*, 43: 188–203.

Walt, S. (1997), *Der Historiker C. Licinius Macer. Einleitung, Fragmente, Kommentar*, Beiträge zur Altertumskunde 103 (Stuttgart).

Walter, U. (2004), *Memoria und res publica. Zur Geschichtskultur im republikanischen Rom* (Frankfurt am Main).

Warrior, V. M. (1988), 'The Chronology of the Movements of M. Fulvius Nobilior (cos. 189) in 189/188 BC', *Chiron*, 18: 325–56.

—— (1996), *The Initiation of the Second Macedonian War* (Stuttgart).

Watson, A. (1967), *The Law of Persons in the Later Roman Republic* (Oxford).

—— (1975), *Rome of the XII Tables* (Princeton).

—— (1979), 'The Death of Horatia', *CQ*, 29: 436–47.

Weinstock, S. (1961), review of Latte (1960*a*), *JRS*, 52: 206–15.

Wheeldon, M. J. (1989), ' "True Stories": The Reception of Historiography in Antiquity', in Cameron (1989: 33–63).

White, H. (1973), *Metahistory: The Historical Imagination in Nineteenth-Century Europe* (Baltimore).

—— (1978), 'The Fictions of Factual Representation', in *Tropics of Discourse: Essays in Cultural Criticism* (Baltimore) 121–34. Orig. pub. in A. Fletcher (ed.) (1976), *The Literature of Fact* (New York) 21–44.

—— (1980), 'The Value of Narrativity in the Representation of Reality', *Critical Inquiry* 7: 5–27. Repr. in (1987) *The Content of the Form: Narrative Discourse and Historical Representation* (Baltimore) 1–25.

Whitehead, D. (1986), *The Demes of Attica 508/7–ca. 250 BC* (Princeton).

Wilkinson, L. P. (1963), *Golden Latin Artistry* (Cambridge).

Wille, G. (1973), *Der Aufbau des livianischen Geschichtswerk* (Amsterdam).

Williams, G. W. (1962), 'Poetry in the Moral Climate of Augustan Rome', *JRS*, 52: 28–46.

—— (1990), 'Did Maecenas "Fall from Favor?": Augustan Literary Patronage', in Raaflaub and Toher (1990: 258–75).

Wirszubski, C. (1950), *Libertas as a Political Ideal at Rome During the Late Republic and Early Principate* (Cambridge).

Wiseman, T. P. (1979*a*), *Clio's Cosmetics: Three Studies in Greco-Roman Literature* (Leicester).

—— (1979*b*), 'Topography and Rhetoric: the Trial of Manlius', *Historia*, 28: 32–50.

—— (1981), 'Practice and Theory in Roman Historiography', *Historia*, 66: 375–93.

—— (1988), 'Roman Legend and Oral Tradition', *JRS*, 79: 129–37.

—— (1993), 'Lying Historians: Seven Types of Mendacity', in Gill and Wiseman (1993: 122–46).

—— (1995), *Remus: A Roman Myth* (Cambridge).

—— (1998), *Roman History and Roman Drama* (Exeter).

—— (2000), review of Oakley (1997–2005), volume ii, *CR*, 50: 81–3.

—— (2002), 'Roman History and the Ideological Vacuum', in T. P. Wiseman (ed.), *Classics in Progress: Essays on Ancient Greece and Rome* (Oxford), 285–310.

—— (2004), *The Myths of Rome* (Exeter).

Witte, K. (1910), 'Über die Form der Darstellung in Livius' Geschichtswerk', *RhM*, 65: 270–305, 359–419. Reprinted in book form, 1969 (Darmstadt).

Wölfflin, E. von (1933), *Ausgewählte Schriften*, ed. G. Meyer (Leipzig).

Wolski, J. (1956), 'La prise de Rome par les Celtes et la formation de l'annalistique romaine', *Historia*, 5: 24–52.

Woodman, A. J. (1983), *Velleius Paterculus: The Caesarian and Augustan Narrative (2.41–93)* (Cambridge).

—— (1988), *Rhetoric in Classical Historiography* (London).

—— (1992), 'Nero's Alien Capital', in T. Woodman and J. Powell (eds.), *Author and Audience in Latin Literature* (Cambridge) 173–88.

—— (1998), *Tacitus Reviewed* (Oxford).

Zancan, P. (1940), *Tito Livio* (Milan).

Zanker, P. (1988), *The Power of Images in the Age of Augustus*, trans. H. A. Shapiro (Ann Arbor).

Ziegler, K. (1951), 'Plutarchos', *RE*, 21.1: 867–706.

—— (1964), *Die Beziehungen zwischen Rom und dem Partherreich* (Wiesbaden).

Zimmerer, M. (1937), *Der Annalist Qu. Claudius Quadrigarius* (Diss. Munich).

# Acknowledgements

Permission to reprint the following articles is gratefully acknowledged.

J. Briscoe, *A Commentary on Livy, Books XXXI–XXXIII* (Oxford: Clarendon Press, 1973), 1–12.

E. Burck, An Introduction to Books 29 and 30 from *Einführung in die Dritte Dekade des Livius* (Heidelberg: F. H. Kerle, 1962²).

L. Catin, 'Le Sens du comique', from *En lisant Tite-Live* (Paris: Les Belles Lettres, 1944), 137–45.

A. M. Feldherr, 'Livy's Revolution: Civic Identity and the Creation of the *Res Publica*', in *The Roman Cultural Revolution*, ed. T. Habinek and A. Schiesaro (Cambridge: Cambridge University Press, 1997), 136–57.

S. R. Joshel, 'The Body Female and the Body Politic: Livy's Lucretia and Verginia', in *Pornography and Representation in Greece and Rome*, ed. A. Richlin (Oxford: Oxford University Press, 1992), 112–30.

W. Liebeschuetz, 'The Religious Position of Livy's History', *Journal of Roman Studies* (1967), 45–55.

T. J. Luce, 'The Dating of Livy's First Decade', *Transactions of the American Philological Association* 96 (1965), 209–40.

T. J. Luce, 'Design and Structure in Livy: 5.32–55', *Transactions of the American Philological Association* 102 (1971), 265–302.

A. H. McDonald, 'The Style of Livy', *Journal of Roman Studies* 47 (1957), 155–72.

J. L. Moles, 'Livy's Preface', *Proceedings of the Cambridge Philological Society* 39 (1993), 141–68.

S. P. Oakley, *A Commentary on Livy, Books VI–X. Volume I: Introduction and Book VI* (Oxford: Oxford University Press, 1997), 13–19.

J. E. Phillips, 'Form and Language in Livy's Triumph Notices', *Classical Philology* 69 (1974), 265–73.

J. Rich, 'Structuring Roman History: The Consular Year and the Roman Historical Tradition', *Histos* 1 (1996).

A. C. Scafuro, 'Livy's Comic Narrative of the Bacchanalia', *Helios* 16 (1989), 119–42.

J. B. Solodow, 'Livy and the Story of Horatius I.24–26', *Transactions of the American Philological Association* 109 (1979), 251–68.

P. Stadter, 'The Structure of Livy's History', *Historia* 21 (1972), 287–307.

H. Tränkle, 'Livius and Polybius', *Gymnasium* 79 (1972), 13–31.

P. G. Walsh, 'The Literary Techniques of Livy', *Rheinisches Museum* (1954), 98–114.